BRITAIN AND
SAUDI ARABIA
1925–1939

BRITAIN AND SAUDI ARABIA
1925–1939

The Imperial Oasis

CLIVE LEATHERDALE

FRANK CASS

First published 1983 in Great Britain by
FRANK CASS AND COMPANY LIMITED
Gainsborough House, 11 Gainsborough Road,
London, E11 1RS, England

and in the United States of America by
FRANK CASS AND COMPANY LIMITED
% Biblio Distribution Centre
81 Adams Drive, P.O. Box 327, Totowa, N.J. 07511

British Library Cataloguing in Publication Data

Leatherdale, Clive
  Britain and Saudi Arabia, 1925-1939.
  1. Great Britain—Foreign relations—Saudi Arabia
  2. Saudi Arabia—Foreign relations—Great Britain
  I. Title
  327.41053'8   DA47.9.S4

  ISBN 0-7146-3220-1

Printed and bound in Great Britain

CONTENTS

ACKNOWLEDGMENTS

It is inevitable that in a work of this scope I should be indebted to many people who, over the course of the past years have given invaluable assistance.

Professor Paul Wilkinson, Mr John Main, O.B.E. and Dr Clive Archer of the Department of Politics (International Relations), University of Aberdeen, and Mr Phil Williams, now of the University of Southampton, have all willingly given their time and advice. Mr Robert Lacey (author of *The Kingdom*) kindly read the manuscript and offered his comments.

In particular, my thanks and appreciation go to Mr David Capitanchik of the Department of Politics, University of Aberdeen, and to Dr Peter Sluglett of the School of Oriental Studies, University of Durham. Without their encouragement and guidance this work would certainly have been the poorer. Their assistance, whilst gratefully acknowledged, in no way implicates them in the views expressed herein. Responsibility for any errors of fact and indiscretion of judgment remain mine, and mine alone.

Clive Leatherdale

A Note on Transliteration and Abbreviations

Transliteration has been kept as simple and consistent as possible. The most commonly used English equivalent is used, save where quotations use variant spellings. Arabic terms or names that are completely unfamiliar to the English language appear in italics. No diacritical marks have been used.

Abbreviations used in this book

CO	Colonial Office
FO	Foreign Office
IO	India Office
WO	War Office
AM	Air Ministry
Adm	Admiralty
GoI	Government of India
SSA	Secretary of State for Air
SSC	Secretary of State for the Colonies
SSI	Secretary of State for India
CAB	Cabinet
CP	Cabinet Papers
CID	Committee of Imperial Defence
ME(O)	Middle East (Official) Sub-Committee
ME(S)	Middle East (Standing) Sub-Committee
L/P&S/	India Office: Letters, Political and Secret
CoS	Chief(s) of Staff
AOC	Air-Officer-Commanding
GOC	General-Officer-Commanding
Ag	Acting
MEC	Middle East Centre, St Antony's College, Oxford
DBFP	Documents on British Foreign Policy
DGFP	Documents on German Foreign Policy
FRUS	Foreign Relations of the United States
TPC	Turkish Petroleum Company
IPC	Iraq Petroleum Company
APOC	Anglo-Persian Oil Company
BAPCO	Bahrain Petroleum Company
SOCAL	Standard Oil Company of California
CASOC	Californian Arabian Standard Oil Company
ARAMCO	Arabian American Oil Company

INTRODUCTION

The development of British interest in the Arab Middle East[1] is one of the major episodes in the history of this country. The attention of scholars has repeatedly been drawn to the variety of British contacts with that part of the world, particularly in the post-World War One mandate period. The British presence in the inter-war years brought a mosaic of arrangements to the Arab world. Iraq, until 1932, and Palestine were mandates – the latter subjected to the provisions of the Balfour Declaration. The area known as Transjordan was partly accountable to the Palestine mandate and partly independent of it. Britain put a king over Iraq but left Transjordan as an emirate. The base at Aden became, in 1937, a Crown Colony, while its extensive hinterland was a formal British Protectorate. The most time-honoured relationship of all was in eastern Arabia where the sheikhs of the Arabian Gulf[2] had signed successive treaties that reduced their sheikhdoms to virtual protectorates. Further south, the independence of the Sultan of Muscat and Oman was compromised by the presence of British 'advisers'. Equally piecemeal arrangements were found in north-east Africa. Egypt witnessed the progression of British occupation, a British Protectorate, and a unilaterally imposed independence before full independence was achieved in 1936. The Sudan provided yet another improvisation: an Anglo-Egyptian condominium. No two territories were exposed to exactly the same form of British influence or control.

The strategic significance of the Middle East lies in its geographical position at the crossroads of three continents – Europe, Asia and Africa. The most geographically central state in the Arab Middle East is Saudi Arabia.[3] States having a formal British connection lay all around Saudi Arabia, yet British relations with the state which embraced the heart of Islam, and which constituted the geographical pivot of the Middle East, have been largely neglected by academic research.

The reasons for this scholarly neglect are various and can only be specu-lated upon. In the first place, it may have been thought that, compared with British relations with the other Arab states – be they mandates, pro-tectorates or colonies – the story of British interest in Saudi Arabia would be peripheral at best, trivial at worst. An inaccessible desert was hardly likely to produce a coherent and vigorous policy response from the British Government. Alternatively, it may have been felt that the only real British interest in Arabia was oil, and that there was little need to search for any deeper, underlying political interest.

Of even greater significance is the fact that Saudi Arabia was an independent state. She may, therefore, have lain outside the historian's interest in the array of devices employed by Britain to maintain her control over, and influence in, the Middle East. Saudi Arabia's independence suggests a different quality of relationship from that which Britain enjoyed with the assorted colonies, mandates and protectorates elsewhere in the region.[4] Indeed, the significance of Saudi Arabia for this study lies in the fact that Ibn Saud was the first Arab ruler to have his complete and absolute independence recognised by Britain.[5] The treaty which Ibn Saud signed with the British Government in 1927 not only acknowledged his independence, but did so on terms of legal equality that enabled him to bring his dominions into the community of nations on an equal footing.

As Ibn Saud was the first fully independent Arab ruler in modern times (at least in the political sense) he has a key role to play in the understanding of a transitional stage in Britain's imperial policy in the Middle East during the mandate period. British policy towards Saudi Arabia illustrates the manner in which Britain responded to the reality of Arab independence in an age of modified imperial practices. The years covered by this book extend over the zenith of what Elizabeth Monroe called 'Britain's Moment in the Middle East'.[6] Never was Britain as secure in that region as in the fifteen-year period examined in this study. Nonetheless, as will be explained, Britain's position with regard to the Middle East in general, and Saudi Arabia in particular, was far less composed in 1939 than it had been in 1925.

This study explores how Britain responded to the existence of Saudi Arabia – the prototype independent Arab state – in the middle of an area of near exclusive British control. With Britain undergoing comparative military, economic and geo-political decline through, for example, the loss of naval superiority, the growth of industrial competitors, and the increasing autonomy of the Dominions, she became particularly fearful for the communication lines with the Empire which passed through the Middle East. Saudi Arabia lay in a geographical, religious and strategic sense at the heart of British interests in that region. The geographical location of the Arabian peninsula endowed it with a special significance for British communications with the Empire. Along its western and southern seaboards lay 2,000 miles of the sea-route to India, the Far East and Australasia. To the north, across the mandates to the Gulf, lay the planned land, air and oil routes. British strategic interests circumvented Saudi Arabia at a time when, according to one scholar, the British Empire represented the greatest example of strategic over-extension known to history: 'The gap between Britain's obligations and her capacity to carry them out had become alarmingly wide'.[7]

Britain was a maritime power. Prior to 1914 her oceanic panorama enabled her to ignore any intervening land-mass unless it presented distinctive reasons for attention of its own, such as was provided by the disintegration of the Ottoman Empire. The Navy was well-suited to some political and strategic situations, less well-suited to others – for example, confronting Saudi Arabia. A navy could not occupy territory. Nor could it engage effectively in even minor land battles that were beyond the range of cannon fire. Naval bombardments or blockades were inappropriate to exercising long-term control over distant political events.[8] Although, by and large, other European states in the inter-war years had their attention held by continental politics and were little disposed to undermine British maritime power, Britain was less reliant on the Navy in the 1920s and '30s than at previous times for protection of the strategic routes to India. She had the Indian Army to call upon to back up aerial, naval or military bases in Egypt, Transjordan, Palestine, Iraq, the Gulf and Aden.[9] These developments, in theory, made central Arabia more accessible to direct penetration.

This is not to say that Britain's interest in Saudi Arabia was solely strategic. The Hejaz contained the birthplace of the Prophet Mohammad, and constituted the religious heartland of Islam. The British Empire embraced about one hundred million Moslems, mostly in India, and the need for good relations with whoever ruled Mecca could never be overlooked. Politically, too, Saudi Arabia was to become, within the period covered by this study, a factor of some consequence, largely through the dominating personality of King Ibn Saud. In addition, there were oil interests although, as will be seen, these were not pressing in the inter-war years and left their mark in political (frontier) questions, rather than commercial ones.

More particularly, Saudi Arabia bordered, or lay in uneasy proximity to, every British connection in the Middle East, and managed, at one time or another, to embarrass Britain at most of those points of contact. The various British-protected territories were of crucial importance to Britain's imperial scheme of things in the Middle East. Those same territories also provided temptation to an ambitious, expansionist-orientated Saudi King. How did Britain come to terms with this implicit, and at times explicit, threat to her Middle Eastern interests?

The independence of Saudi Arabia poses particular questions. Why did Anglo-Saudi relations take the form they did? How, and why, did those relations adapt over the course of the 1920s and '30s? Given that Britain's presence in the Middle East at that time was primarily to protect the imperial needs of empire, what role did Saudi Arabia, an independent state, play in assisting that requirement? Is it meaningful to speak of Britain exercising some form of hegemony over Saudi Arabia, and if so, in what ways was that hegemony manifested? What, in practice, does it mean to speak of Britain having held Saudi Arabia within her 'sphere of influence'? Indeed, in the light of the evidence adduced, is it meaningful to describe Saudi Arabia during this period as within Britain's sphere of influence at all?[10]

This investigation will propose, and try to account for, an attitude of ambiguity behind British policy as it related to Saudi Arabia. This ambiguity operated at several levels. At its most basic level it will be argued that the British Government could never quite make up its collective mind as to whether Saudi Arabia was important or not. At times Ibn Saud presented a remote, inaccessible ruler in a remote, inaccessible kingdom, of interest neither to the British nor to anybody else. At other times, and particularly by the late 1930s, Ibn Saud presented an Arab ruler whose achievements had, in some eyes, already borne comparison with those of the Prophet Mohammad,[11] and who was very much at the heart of Britain's Arab policy. Britain became increasingly drawn into inter- and intra-Arab relations involving Saudi Arabia with her neighbours and outside powers.

Furthermore, the historical importance of the Middle East for the passage of world trade and as a theatre of conquest meant that British dealings with the area comprised, of necessity, a dual aspect. Britain not only had relations with the indigenous rulers – in this study Ibn Saud; she also had to conduct relations with those other states who developed interests in his dominions. Three such states appear in these pages: the United States, Italy and Germany. Of necessity, the course of British relations with certain other powers has a fundamental part to play in understanding Anglo-Saudi relations.

This leads to a further point, one to which this study will need to devote considerable attention. On the one hand, Britain had to deal with an independent Arab state in the middle of an area of near exclusive British control: on the other, Ibn Saud was a ruler with territorial ambitions. This immediately set up a clash of interests between him and the British Government because the mandates and the Gulf sheikhdoms were also the target for Ibn Saud's ambitions. Put another way, Saudi Arabia was in a position to achieve what no outside power could – perhaps even undermine Britain's position across the Arab world.

Paradoxically, it has been a popularly held assumption, not only that Ibn Saud was totally amenable to British pressure, but that he was a staunch Anglophile. Upon his death in 1953 obituaries in the British press extolled his affection for Britain. It will be suggested that the British Government was guilty of taking Ibn Saud at face value. His feelings towards Britain were better described as fear and mistrust. His reaction to Britain is aptly coined in the Arab expression: 'The hand you cannot bite; kiss it'.[12] Britain's misunderstanding of Ibn Saud's basic outlook was to undermine much of her policy towards him in the inter-war years.

A Note on Sources and Methodology

The student of Anglo-Saudi relations in the inter-war years faces particular difficulties as regards source material. As Hourani has remarked, much of the nineteenth and twentieth century history of the Middle East has to be based on British and French diplomatic and consular papers.[13] The introduction of the 'thirty-year rule' has made possible the study of Britain's period of ascendency in the Arab world in some depth. This has enabled what Hourani describes as the 'colonial' relationship to be illuminated – from one side at least.[14]

The very nature of the Anglo-Saudi relationship is partly responsible for the dearth of sources. Unlike the position with, for example, Egypt, Palestine, Iraq, the Gulf and Aden, where scholarship has benefited from a more intense British relationship through an abundance of memoirs, biographies and other secondary accounts of British policy, the existing literature on Anglo-Saudi relations is sparse. Not being dealt with by Britain in the manner of the above territories, Saudi Arabia did not witness the bureaucratic apparatus that could provide a later wealth of information, directly or indirectly, for the scholar. Apart from the handful of accounts by diplomats actually involved with Saudi Arabia between 1925-39 (Clayton, Ryan and Bullard, for example), second-hand information concerning Anglo-Saudi relations can only be gleaned vicariously, from government servants stationed in adjoining states. They, having been officially responsible for territories threatened by tribes from the Arabian interior, provide a collective portrait largely lacking in sympathy with Saudi Arabia, as well as displaying an understandable failure to appreciate Britain's basic policy position with regard to that state.

Such obstacles are exacerbated by the nature of the available literature on the modern history of Saudi Arabia. If, for the moment, we ignore the voluminous publications that have appeared on Saudi Arabia in the wake of the 1973 oil embargo, which brought that state to western attention as never previously and which were themselves largely concerned with oil questions, then the western world has been obliged to turn to two principal sources for an exposition of Saudi history – Philby and ARAMCO.[15] The problem here is contrary to that found in the antipathetic literature emanating from British officials in fringe Arab states. Kelly has forcefully highlighted the repercussions of this dual 'authority' on Saudi Arabia.[16] Philby, undeniably one of the great explorers and Arabists of our time, became Saudi Arabia's principal apologist in the English-speaking world.[17] Philby's links with ARAMCO will be made explicit in a later chapter. The research division of the American oil company, also benefiting from the absence of any rival school of thought, has, according to Kelly, had no difficulty in having its interpretation of modern Arabian history widely accepted. It has even, if he is correct, affected the State Department's relations with Riyadh.[18]

The Philby-ARAMCO domination of modern Arabian history, both, for their own reasons, seeking favour with the Saudi royal family while denegrating the British role, has led to an interpretation which Kelly has criticised as follows:

> All considerations of objectivity, balance and a proper regard for factual evidence were subordinated to the aim of hymning the 'right

praise and true perfection' of the house of Saud. Its dynastic importance was inflated, its virtues extolled, its exploits celebrated, its
excesses concealed and rivals calumniated. To set out a list of the
distortions, suppressions, and falsifications to the historical record for
which the Philby-ARAMCO school of Arabian history are responsible
would require a chapter in itself.[19]

One final handicap to the independent western scholar is the restricted
access available to Saudi Arabia. According to Kelly, the only way a foreign
scholar on Arabia can enter the country is to be sponsored by ARAMCO.[20]
For all these reasons the inadequacy of western literature on modern
Saudi Arabia, while proving a hindrance to this research, has offered an
opportunity to contribute to an area of scholarship of intrinsic importance
in the field of British relations with the Middle East in the first half of the
twentieth century.

The comparative flood of works appearing in the mid- and late-1970s,
where not concerned directly with oil, have been largely rehashes of
previous anecdotal and well-worn material. Gary Troeller's doctoral thesis
and subsequent book, *The Birth of Saudi Arabia: Britain and the Rise of the
House of Saud*,[21] is the sole full-length exposition dealing with the historical
evolution of Britain's relations with Ibn Saud up to the mid-1920s, the point
at which the present study begins. This account is the first systematic analysis
of British policy towards Saudi Arabia in the first decade and a half following
Ibn Saud's unification of the greater part of the peninsula under his rule;
from his conquest of the Hejaz until the outbreak of the Second World War.

To sum up, the prime objectives of this investigation are to try to account
for a whole series of ambiguities which coloured British policy towards Saudi
Arabia in the late 1920s and '30s. These ambiguities stemmed from her
unique position as a politically and legally independent state surrounded by
British interests. Saudi Arabia may not have interested Britain as a colony or
a formal protectorate, but the tradition of empire-building and the keeping
of the Pax Britannica were still habits of British minds.[22] Basically, was
Saudi Arabia seen by Britain as a central or peripheral factor in the Middle
East? Did Britain really respect Saudi Arabia's independence or was that
Kingdom treated as no more independent than the various Arab territories
under overt British control? Did strategic questions, namely Saudi Arabia's
capacity to disrupt neighbouring states and thereby British communication
links with the Empire, dominate British considerations? Or did questions of
a political or economic nature come to demand British attention too? Did
Britain include Saudi Arabia within her sphere of influence over the Middle
East, and if so, by what means, bearing in mind that country's independence? Finally, was British policy eased by dealing with an apparently
well-disposed Ibn Saud, as the popular myth would have us believe? Or was
Britain engaged in a policy flawed by consistent misjudgment of Ibn Saud's
political psychology?

In compiling this book four specific features of British policy recommend themselves for analysis, one or more of which form the basis of each chapter. First, *how* was British policy towards Saudi Arabia made? In other words, what machinery was adopted, and what channels constructed to facilitate relations with the Saudi state? Second, there are the particular problems that stemmed from Saudi Arabia's geographical location. With so many points of contact between Saudi Arabia and British-protected states much of Britain's dealings with Ibn Saud concerned the security and continuing territorial integrity of his neighbours. Third, however inaccessible Saudi Arabia may have been, Britain had, from time to time, to consider external intrusion into the privacy and seclusion of Anglo-Saudi relations. These external factors took several forms: namely, the impact of the United States, Italy, Germany, the League of Nations and Palestine-inspired pan-Arabism. Finally, there is the matter of oil and its economic and territorial ramifications.

REFERENCES FOR INTRODUCTION

1. Various names have been coined for the block of territory at the eastern end of the Mediterranean Sea – notably Asia Minor, the Near East and the Middle East. Each has been fashionable at different times. During the inter-war years the area was commonly referred to as the Near East. This book will, however, adopt the expression currently in vogue – the Middle East. Likewise, the term 'Arab' has referred to different peoples at different times. Today we speak of the Arab world as extending from Morocco on the Atlantic to Muscat on the Indian Ocean. Earlier this century 'Arab' had a narrower meaning. The Arabs were a subject race of the Ottoman Empire and were associated with the Asiatic provinces of that Empire. Consequently, the Arab world, as considered in this book, refers to the territory bordered by the Red Sea and the Mediterranean on the west, and the Arabian Gulf on the east; between Turkey and Persia in the north, and Aden in the south. For a detailed discussion on the geographical limits of the Middle East see: Roderic H. Davison, 'Where is the Middle East?', *Foreign Affairs*, 38 (July 1960), pp. 665-75; G. Etzel Pearcy, 'The Middle East – An Indefinable Region', *Dept. of State Bulletin* (March 1959), pp. 407-16.
2. The Arabian Gulf is also known as the Persian Gulf. Reference in this study will usually be to 'the Gulf'.
3. Although the title of this book refers to the name 'Saudi Arabia' this needs clarification. The name Saudi Arabia was only taken in 1932. Prior to that year the territorial entity under discussion was known through a sequence of names. In 1925 Ibn Saud was only Sultan of Nejd. In 1926 he added the title of King of the Hejaz, and the following year became King of the Hejaz, and of Nejd and its Dependencies. Constant reference to these assorted titles would be unnecessarily burdensome. As the name Saudi Arabia was quite arbitrary, in that it did not attend any extra territorial acquisition, the title of this book refers, for the sake of simplicity and convenience, to the modern familiar name.
4. Other states enjoyed so-called 'independence'. The mandates and the Gulf sheikhdoms were also termed 'independent', despite Britain's ultimate authority.
5. The founder of the state of Saudi Arabia will be referred to in this book as Ibn Saud, in keeping with western tradition. His actual name, by which he is known in the Arab world, was Abd al Aziz ibn Abd al Rahman ibn Faisal al Saud.
6. Elizabeth Monroe, *Britain's Moment in the Middle East*. (Hereafter: *Britain's Moment...*)
7. Paul M. Kennedy, 'Appeasement and British Defence Policy in the Inter-War Years', *British Journal of International Studies*, 4 (1978), p. 161.

8. Roy E. Jones, *The Changing Structure of British Foreign Policy,* p. 72.
9. M. A. Fitzsimons, *Empire by Treaty: Britain and the Middle East in the Twentieth Century,* p. 27.
10. Fisher, for example, speaks without supporting evidence of Ibn Saud being subservient to Britain and to British pressure. S. N. Fisher, *The Middle East: A History,* p. 441.
11. Mohammed Almana, *Arabia Unified: A Portrait of Ibn Saud,* p. 82.
12. Thomas Kiernan, *The Arabs,* p. 303.
13. Albert Hourani, 'The Present State of Islamic and Middle Eastern Historiography' in Hourani, *Europe and the Middle East,* p. 167.
14. ibid., p. 168.
15. Harry St John Bridger Philby. More is said of him in Chapter Eight. ARAMCO – Arabian American Oil Company.
16. J. B. Kelly, *Arabia, the Gulf and the West,* pp. 258-61. (Hereafter: *Arabia ...*)
17. ibid., p. 258.
18. ibid., pp. 260-1.
19. ibid., p. 259.
20. ibid., p. 260. There is an absence of archive material in Saudi Arabia, let alone access to it. The author, who has no connection with ARAMCO, lived and taught in Saudi Arabia prior to commencing research for this book.
21. Frank Cass, 1976. Troeller's study examined British policy towards Ibn Saud up to his becoming King of the Hejaz. A previously remote desert ruler then had the nature of his rule and his dominions transformed by the demands of modern statehood. This is the point at which the present study commences its investigation. Its treatment is not intended as a sequel to that of Dr Troeller. The contrasting subject matter, concerning British responses to an enterprising desert chieftain, and those to an independent sovereign state presents, in itself, quite distinct fields of study. In the era of Troeller's investigation Ibn Saud was seen essentially as an Indian matter, viewed and dealt with as a factor in the defence of the Indian Empire. In the present study the declining influence of the Government of India, and Ibn Saud's greater stature as ruler of the Hejaz as well as of central Arabia, combined to present him increasingly as an object of British, over and above Indian, concern.
22. David Howarth, *The Desert King: A Life of Ibn Saud,* p. 26.

CHAPTER ONE

Historical Background

The Arabian Peninsula in British Imperial Strategy

Arabia, despite the romance with which it is popularly associated, offers one of the bleakest landscapes on earth. Its climate and terrain have, over the centuries, isolated the hinterland of the peninsula from all but the hardiest adventurers. Before the twentieth century there seemed neither need nor desire for Britain to become involved. The Arabian peninsula was claimed as part of the Ottoman Empire. What British contacts there were, beyond the coastal fringes, were largely of an individual, not governmental, nature. Explorers like Richard Burton and Charles Doughty gave the western world its knowledge of Arabia.

The key to British interest was the peninsula's location. Since antiquity traffic between Europe and the Orient had passed through a corridor that ran in a north-west/south-east direction. The corridor was bordered on the south-west by the Sahara, and in the north-east by the mountains of Turkey and Persia. The Arabian peninsula stretched across this corridor. Being impenetrable itself, it obliged traffic to pass around it, either across Syria eastwards to the Euphrates and down to the Arabian Gulf, or through Egypt to the Red Sea. Yet, from the time of Vasco da Gama's discovery of the Cape route in 1498 until the opening of the Suez Canal in 1869, the preference for the only all-sea route, round Africa, reduced, for some four centuries, the significance of the Middle East as an international thoroughfare.

Britain's first interest in the Middle East was commercial.[1] From the days of Tudor England attempts were made to break into Portugal's trade monopoly in southern Asia, and, in 1600, a Royal Charter was granted to the East India Company for this purpose. The success of the Company over the next three centuries had profound consequences: the British replaced the Portuguese; a once commercial enterprise took on governmental responsibilities;[2] and India became the jewel of Empire and principal *raison d'être* for Britain's later presence in the Middle East. In 1858 the Crown took over the functions of the Company; a Viceroyalty was established; and Indian matters, from then on, were dealt with through the India Office in London.[3] India held a special and anomalous position within the Empire. It was not a colony but a separate monarchy ruled by the British King, while at the same time having an Empire in its own right, its own policy-making administration, and control of its own foreign policy.

India depended on trade and was vulnerable to foreign rivals. At the peak of Empire almost every sizable port facing the Indian Ocean was in British hands.[4] To defend that ocean, British Governments sought to command the gateways to it and deny its ports to other powers. In the Arabian Gulf political and naval measures were taken to protect commercial interests.[5] A Company station was established at Bushire, on the Persian shore of the Gulf, which became the home of the British Political Resident in the Gulf. In 1798 a Napoleonic drive into Egypt prompted British fears of further French expansion towards Arabia and the Gulf, and led to an agreement with the strategically placed Sultan of Muscat.[6] Piracy in the Gulf disrupted local trade and led to a series of treaties, culminating in 1853 with the 'Treaty of Peace in Perpetuity', in which the sheikhs of the southern shore of the Gulf, east of Qatar, pledged to use their powers to safeguard maritime trade. The so-called 'pirate coast' became the 'Trucial coast', and the Gulf, in effect, a British lake.[7]

Further treaties, of a political rather than maritime complexion, were signed at the end of the century and during the First World War, by which time the whole Arab littoral of the Gulf was under British protection. Under them, the sheikhs could not make treaties with other powers. Neither could they accept agents or grant concessions without British permission. Slavery and arms traffic were curtailed.[8] In return, the Government of India pledged to protect the sheikhdoms if attacked by sea.

Long-standing threats to British supremacy in the Gulf, whether from France, Russia or Egypt, also threatened the viability of the Ottoman Empire which, rambling and decrepit, extended over much of south-east Europe and the Middle East. Ever since the time of Pitt Britain had feared that, in the event of its disintegration, the Middle East would be exposed to Russia. This prospect, and the measures taken to counter it, became known as the Eastern Question.[9] The objective of sustaining Turkey-in-Asia remained a cornerstone of British foreign policy for a century.[10] By allowing the Turks to administer and police the region, the British Treasury was saved the bother and expense of a more active role. Britain also enjoyed some measure of influence in reforming the more corrupt and inefficient practices of Ottoman rule, not possible with a more abrasive policy.[11] A more efficient Turkey meant more efficient guardianship of the road to India.

During the nineteenth century technological factors began to redirect traffic through the Arabian corridor. The introduction of steamships reduced the many hazards to Red Sea travel: contrary winds, fickle currents, and fanatical Moslems.[12] Steamships, however, brought problems of their own. Although faster,[13] and less vulnerable to pirates and climatic conditions, they were dependent on bases and coaling stations. While Britain acquired these necessary facilities in the Mediterranean, India, in 1839, annexed Aden at the south-western tip of the Arabian peninsula, which henceforth provided an essential naval coaling station and staging post to the Indian sub-continent.[14]

The opening of the Suez Canal, in 1869, together with improvements in steamship technology, offered the attraction of a short, safe, all-sea route to the East. The French construction of the Canal and the fear of increased competition in the Red Sea led to British intervention, and eventual occupation of Egypt.[15] Middle Eastern problems were no longer approached primarily from an Indian perspective, but from bases in Egypt. More crucially, the age-old British dependency on maritime control was abruptly modified by the responsibilities of military occupation.[16]

It is important to emphasise this 'dual' approach to the Middle East. Whereas British involvement in the Gulf stemmed from strategic and regional (i.e. imperial) considerations on the part of India, questions concerning imperial rivals and the European balance of power were the business of the Foreign Office in London. Britain, in other words, approached Middle Eastern affairs from a westerly and northerly perspective: India from an easterly one – although this distinction has less to do with any lack of administrative co-ordination than with the realisation that the 'Middle East' did not as yet constitute an identifiable, homogeneous factor in international strategy.

Concern for the security of the Suez Canal had economic and security aspects. Economically, the shortened route brought with it a tenfold increase in British trade by 1939.[17] Strategically, the possibility of mutual assistance for Britain and the Dominions demanded unhindered communications by sea and air. Britain herself was particularly vulnerable due to her dependence on outside sources of food and raw materials.[18] The Suez route offered the shortest passage for trade and reinforcements for the Empire. Its closure, with more than a quarter of the mercantile marine of the Empire within the Indian Ocean at any one time, would have severely shaken, if indeed it did not shatter, the foundation of imperial defence.[19]

Overall, British aims in the Middle East prior to 1914 comprised several aspects: naval paramountcy; the protection of trade and the communication lanes; and the avoidance of interference in the domestic policies and customs of the indigenous population, or in Islamic practices.[20] India's western approaches were to be safeguarded by denying a foothold in Arabia to any rival power other than Turkey. Britain did not seek to preserve the peninsula for her own exploitation,[21] it being too inhospitable and unprofitable for imperialistic enterprise. She was reluctant to interfere, wanting to ensure only that others did not interfere either. To imperial strategists the land-mass of the peninsula, beyond its coastal fringes, presented a *terra incognita* – a void.[22]

Elsewhere, Britain's strategic position had, by 1914, weakened. Control of the Caribbean had passed to the United States; the Far East to Japan; and the Mediterranean to France.[23] The emergence of air power and the submarine, together with the ailing British alliance with Japan, transformed the British Empire from a source of strength to a source of geo-political weakness, with the increased threat to its lines of communications.[24]

The Rise of the House of Saud

For several centuries the Turks had laid claim to sovereignty over Arabia, but had found that, due to marked variations in the geography and culture of the peninsula, some areas were more amenable to direct control than others. In the west, the Hejaz extends for some six hundred miles down the Red Sea. It contains the two Holiest Cities of Islam, Mecca and Medina, which host the annual Moslem Pilgrimage (*Haj*). Mountainous areas in the south are capable of cultivation, and the attachment to a major international waterway has encouraged a long tradition of trade.

These three factors – religious, agricultural and commercial – had several consequences. First, the Hejaz was the most visited and cosmopolitan region of Arabia. The blood of countless nationalities – Arabs, Indians, Javanese, Africans, Chinese and Russians – is dispersed through its populace. Second, much of the Hejazi population adopted a sedentary lifestyle. A living could be made from the land, or through commerce, or, for which Hejazis were notorious, by exploiting the many thousands of overseas visitors who undertook the Pilgrimage. Third, all three factors made the Hejaz more attractive to the Turks. The link between the Caliph in Constantinople and the spiritual home of Islam provided the religious pretext for the Turks to impose their authority over the Moslem Holy Land. As a consequence, the Hejaz, at least from the nineteenth century, witnessed an active Ottoman presence denied to less holy or less accessible parts of the peninsula. The religious and commercial importance of the Hejaz also encouraged a long tradition of foreign consular posts in Jedda – the port of Mecca.

The vast hinterland plateau of the peninsula, extending to some three-quarters of a million square miles, is known as Nejd. Here lies the source of the great romantic legends of Arabia. Geography has conspired to accentuate the inaccessibility of Nejd. Apart from the extremes of climate, the central populated areas are effectively enclosed by largely uninhabited deserts: the Nafud in the north, the Dahna in the east, and the Rub al Khali (Empty Quarter) in the south. The mountains of the Hejaz complete the isolation of Nejd.

As a result of geography and climate, resources were meagre and the object of fierce competition. Communication was slow, distorted by word of mouth, and that with the outside world almost non-existent. The inhabitants of Nejd were, in practice, more or less autonomous, offering only nominal allegiance to the Turks. They, in turn, paid little attention to the affairs of Nejd, confining the energies of their troops and administrators to the periphery of the peninsula. The absence in Nejd of a peasant class that was bound to the land denied the Turks any social leverage, and its people evolved a culture quite distinct from the urban areas elsewhere in the Arab world where the civil foundation was built on agriculture, commerce and urban structures; where nomads were treated with contempt, and where a greater or lesser familiarity had long been established with the western world.[25]

By contrast, the geography of central Arabia imposed a range of livelihoods, from nomadic pastoralists to settled merchants and agriculturalists.[26] Contrary to the inferior position held by nomads in the more developed parts of the Arab world, in Nejd the bedouin[27] had long thrived on a tradition of independence, pride, nobility and military prowess.[28] It was not uncommon in urban areas for young Nejdis to be sent into the deserts to acquire the bedouin virtues.[29]

Despite the handicaps of nature, Nejd developed a coherent social organisation, producing a wide range of foodstuffs and artifacts.[30] Large oasis settlements acted as agricultural, mercantile and manufacturing centres, and were often located at the intersection of caravan routes. The social structure reflected an acute dependence on water and grazing. It was characterised by an inter-woven, segmentary tribal system which formed economic and military units, and by a complex inter-dependence between the urban and nomadic communities.[31] Competition for scarce resources precipitated fluctuating military alliances between tribes and townspeople that impeded the development of any central authority.[32] The bedouin tribes could, and did, transfer their support at will, as expediency demanded.[33] The lack of foreign influence or any centralised state apparatus encouraged the development of protector-client political, economic and social relationships. The bedouin tribes offered military protection in return for goods and services. These patron-client relationships, leading to the forced payment of tribute, have been described as having legal and ideological implications reminiscent of the mafia, by keeping clients safe and reducing economic competition.[34]

This was the environment into which a dynamic, puritanical, religious doctrine was introduced in the middle of the eighteenth century. It eventually led to the political and social transformation of central Arabia, and culminated in the modern state of Saudi Arabia. A Nejdi theologian, Mohammad ibn Abd al Wahhab, incensed by what he saw as the prevalent superstitions,[35] the laxity and materialism of life in central Arabia, founded a strict unitarian Islamic movement, which became known to its opponents after the name of its founder.[36] Wahhabism urged a return to the simple teachings of the Koran, giving no place to reason in religious matters.[37] It preached monotheism. God was omnipotent, and nothing and no-one could intercede between Him and man. For that reason shrines, tombs and other manifestations of paganism or polytheism were to be destroyed. Traditionally, the *jihad* (Holy War) had been employed by Moslems against non-Moslems. Such was the fanaticism of Wahhabism that non-Wahhabi Moslems were despised as much as non-Moslems.[38] As a result, the instrument of the *jihad* was revived in Wahhabi hands to be directed not only against non-Moslems, but also against decadent, non-Wahhabi Moslems. With Nejd surrounded by other Islamic lands, it followed that the proselytising lust of Wahhabism would be directed, at first, against fellow Moslems.

Wahhabism was dogmatic and fundamentalist. It did not develop any political theory on matters of statecraft or temporal authority.[39] It might not have made any lasting impact on Arabia were it not for one particular disciple. Among its early converts, around 1745, was Mohammad ibn Saud, Emir of Daraiya in central Nejd. He was, at the time, a minor Arabian figure. The Al Saud were not bedouin, though they had proud ancestral links with the prominent Anaiza tribe of northern Arabia. In the hands of Mohammad ibn Saud, Wahhabism became exploited for political ends. The propagation of a common religious faith was aimed at binding the inhabitants of Nejd together. During the rest of the eighteenth century the Saudi-Wahhabi combination embraced Nejd with unbridled fervour. Whom the Koran could not convert, the sword could. In Philby's words:

> Wahhabism became a religio-military ideal under which desert people, stirred by a great idea, embarked upon common action. Common cause was maintained as long as fanaticism was kept at white heat.[40]

Wahhabism accepted Al Saud as a legitimate and hereditary Islamic government.[41] The Saudi ruler was no longer simply a secular authority but, ostensibly, the representative of God and his Divine law on earth. From the time of Mohammad ibn Saud's conversion the Al Saud were no longer referred to as 'sheikhs' or 'emirs', but as 'imams', having religious authority over the populace.[42] The Saudi state was known as an imamate. In the first decade of the nineteenth century Wahhabism was strong enough to break loose from Nejd and come to the attention of the outside world. Shiite shrines at Karbala near the Euphrates were sacked, and Wahhabi hordes ransacked Mecca and Medina, previously considered sacrosanct. By 1811 Saudi-Wahhabi tentacles extended as far north as Aleppo near the present Turkish border, and over the Hejaz, southern Mesopotamia and eastern Arabia as far as Muscat.[43]

Wahhabi desecration of the Holy Cities, as well as in Syria and Mesopotamia, brought about a century of intermittent Saudi reversals.[44] The Turks harnessed the ambitions of Mohammad Ali, the Francophile Albanian Viceroy of Egypt, to combat the Wahhabi surge.[45] Egyptian forces were not finally withdrawn from Arabia, at British insistence, until 1840.[46]

The opening of the Suez Canal not only eased Britain's communications with the East, but also encouraged Turkey to consolidate and expand her position in Arabia. The Turks increased their presence in the Hejaz and the Yemen. They also extended their influence in the Gulf beyond Kuwait by establishing a garrison, in 1871, at Hofuf in Hasa.[47] Turkish influence seemed to be gaining further impetus when, in 1891, a rival Nejdi emir, Ibn

Rashid of Hail, with Turkish encouragement captured Riyadh.[48] The Saudi family, including the eleven year old future King of Saudi Arabia, went into exile, finally taking up residence in Kuwait at the invitation of Sheikh Mubarak.[49] There, the young Ibn Saud was introduced to great-power intrigue amid the proposals for the Berlin-Baghdad Railway, and, through her treaty with Mubarak in 1899, to Britain's paramount position in the Gulf.[50]

In 1902 Ibn Saud recaptured Riyadh for his dynasty in a derring-do fashion [51] which marked the origins of the modern state of Saudi Arabia. For the next twelve years Ibn Saud, in order to reinsure against the Turks and fickle desert loyalties, sought accommodation with the only other power in the area – the British. It became a persistent thread in his search for security to obtain British support to play off against the Turks.[52]

That period was, however, a relatively constructive one for Britain's position in the Middle East. Agreements with France and Russia, in 1904 and 1907 respectively, eliminated them as serious rivals in the Gulf.[53] Only the Turks, with sporadic attempts to assert themselves in Kuwait, proved a nuisance, and even then Ottoman troubles stemming from the Young Turk revolution of 1908, and the consequent upheavals in Bulgaria and Bosnia-Herzegovina, proved ample distraction. The Turks had even been repulsed in an effort to turn the tide of Saudi advances, in Qâsim in 1904, and had grudgingly bestowed upon Ibn Saud the title of District Governor of Nejd, which legitimised his position in central Arabia for the first time.[54]

While the Government of India hoped to harness the ascending Saudi star to the Empire, before Ibn Saud grew strong enough to start disrupting British interests in the Gulf, the Foreign Office, in the delicate pre-war years, wanted to maintain the *status quo*.[55] Besides, with the excesses perpetrated by Wahhabism a century earlier, Britain was reluctant to underwrite the Saudi position in central Arabia. In the balance of international politics at the time, a friendly Turkey outweighed the advantages of a British accord with Ibn Saud.[56] Then, in the spring of 1913, fully aware of Turkish distractions in the Balkans and Italy, Ibn Saud sent a force into Hasa and expelled the Turkish garrison which had been there for over forty years. He took this action without any assistance from the British, and presented himself as a *bona fide* Gulf ruler. Capture of Hasa gave Ibn Saud access to ports and the economic basis upon which to sustain further conquest.[57] British policy had always been to confine attention to the Gulf, into which Ibn Saud had now intruded.

In the feverish diplomatic activity that preceded the First World War, Britain and Turkey embarked upon a series of conventions aimed at resolving outstanding differences between the two Empires, particularly as Turkey was increasingly coming under the gravitational pull of Germany, with the risk of German admission to the Middle East empire lanes.[58] Among the issues concluded in the 1913-14 Conventions was the delineation of British and Ottoman spheres of influence in Arabia.[59] With an eye to the deteriorating situation in Europe, Britain sought an overall settlement not ungenerous to the Turks in the vain hope of winning their support in Europe.[60] Significantly, Hasa, which Ibn Saud had recently taken from the Turks, was not mentioned – presumably an unwritten acknowledgement of Turkish sovereignty.[61]

The dividing line between the spheres of influence stretched from west of Qatar, south and then south-westwards, to the boundary between the Yemen and the Aden Protectorate. The area to the south and east of this line was acknowledged as within the British sphere: the area to the north and west, including the Hejaz, Nejd and Hasa, went to the Turks.[62] In a sense this document was both artificial and short-sighted. The War Office was never going to police the desert frontiers so laboriously agreed upon. Furthermore, with the advent of war with Turkey, Britain found herself committed to a document that was already anachronistic. It was not the Turks who would later challenge these agreements, but Ibn Saud.

Britain and the Arabs During the First World War: Ibn Saud and the Arab Revolt

With Britain's declaration of war on Turkey in October 1914, the maintenance of the Ottoman Empire, hitherto a pillar of British policy, crumbled overnight. Turkey would no longer protect the route to India; she could be expected to impede it. Britain responded with a series of political improvisations geared towards winning control over the Middle East and keeping open the communication lines with the Empire. Britain annexed Cyprus and proclaimed a protectorate over Egypt. In Arabia, Ibn Saud found himself courted for the first time, particularly as he had followed his thrust into Hasa by signing a treaty with the Sublime Porte.

To pre-empt the risk of Ibn Saud taking active steps to assist the Turks, as the Indian campaign in Mesopotamia got under way, the Government of India urged that he be harnessed to the allied cause.[63] Captain Shakespear, the Political Agent in Kuwait,[64] was sent to negotiate a treaty, only to be killed during a Saudi-Rashidi engagement at Jarrab in January 1915. The completion of the treaty was delayed until the following December owing to problems of communication, apathy, and the tangled chain of British responsibilities.[65] British naval power, however, counted for little in Riyadh, or in dealing with undefined frontiers. Nonetheless, the Anglo-Saudi treaty brought about a turning point, not only in Anglo-Saudi relations, but in the British attitude of detachment from the Arabian peninsula.[66]

On the wider front, Britain needed to push the Turks back from their Arab provinces. This task would have been eased by support from the Arabs themselves, particularly after the British defeat at Gallipoli. Britain endeavoured to exploit Ottoman-Arab grievances by promising the Arabs the national identity that had been repressed by the Turks.[67] To lead an 'Arab Revolt' Britain chose Husein ibn Ali – head of the Hashemite family and Grand Sherif of Mecca. Protracted correspondence between Husein and the High Commissioner in Egypt, Sir Henry McMahon, attempted to reach agreement on the political rewards accruing to the Arabs in return for their resurrection against the Turks.

It has often been asked, in the light of Ibn Saud's post-War achievements, and the shortcomings of Britain's subsequent Husein policy, whether Britain might have been better advised to choose Ibn Saud as leader of the Arab Revolt.[68] Certainly, there were those who, at the time, felt that Ibn Saud had the necessary ingredients. Shakespear reported in June 1914, after a meeting with Ibn Saud: 'The Arabs have now found a leader who stands head and shoulders above any other chief, and in whose star all have implicit faith'.[69] One historian has suggested that:

> Had ... not ... at one stroke Ibn Saud been temporarily checked and this trusted officer killed [at Jarrab, in January 1915] the British Government at that early stage would have been bound to recognise Ibn Saud as the principal power in Central and Southern Arabia, and the idea of raising the Sherifians would not have occurred to anyone.[70]

Ibn Saud, moreover, had already demonstrated, by use of arms in Hasa and at Jarrab, that he would fight to be rid of the Turks and their clients. Overall, however, taking account of many factors, Husein's credentials for leadership of an Arab uprising were, at the time, beyond reproach. Britain's position in Egypt enabled better communications with the Hejaz than with remoter parts of Arabia.[71] Strategically, Husein could isolate Turkish garrisons throughout western Arabia, and reduce the threats to British shipping in the Red Sea. Ibn Saud, by contrast, was nowhere in contact with Turkish forces, and could only have attempted to neutralise Ibn Rashid, who had declared for the Turks.[72] Above all, Husein held the position of Grand Sherif of Mecca, and could wield considerable religious influence for the allies.[73] In particular, he was in a position to counter Ottoman demands for a *jihad*.[74] Wahhabism, on the other hand, was feared by Moslems and Christians alike, and had contributed to British reluctance to establish earlier links with Ibn Saud. He had no standing outside central and eastern Arabia, and he regarded the cosmopolitan Arabs of the Hejaz and Syria with contempt; whereas it was hoped that Husein's appeal would span the Arab world, from nationalist urban intellectuals to bedouin. Husein, himself, was in favour of the revolt. If the Turks won the War they would have tightened their control over their Arab provinces, including the Hejaz. Britain, by contrast, was proposing an independent Arab state. Apart from anything else, the alternative – letting the Sherif of Mecca side with the Turks – was unthinkable.

The decision to back Husein also reflected the competing perspectives from within the British Empire. Due to the fragmented system of responsibilities, India was only familiar with the potential of Ibn Saud – and Cairo only with Husein. Equally, the Government of India would not have embarked upon a policy anything like as ambitious as that planned for

Husein from Cairo. This, in part, reflected Cairo's greater experience of the sophisticated intellectual Arabs of Beirut and Damascus – and Cairo. India's direct experience was limited to the poorer, often nomadic populations around the Gulf. Delhi was, consequently, rather more paternalistic than Cairo towards the Arabs of their respective acquaintance. India was understandably slower and more reluctant to appreciate the forces of Arab nationalism let loose by the War, which, in any case, were not expressed in the Gulf.[75]

There were also dangers in an excessive British commitment to Ibn Saud, such as the threat of an alliance between his enemies: the Turks, Ibn Rashid, Husein, and certain disaffected Arabian tribes.[76] Besides, India wanted not a united Arabia, but a weak and disunited Arabia incapable of threatening Indian interests in any way.[77] Perhaps the best summary of the Husein versus Ibn Saud debate was given by Sir Gilbert Clayton:

> I have heard the opinion expressed that we backed the wrong horse, Husein instead of Ibn Saud. To this criticism I would reply that, although the two horses ran at the same meeting, they did not run in the same race ... Ibn Saud could not have influenced the course of operations in Palestine ... It is beside the point that the two horses subsequently ran in the same race when Ibn Saud proved to be the better horse at the distance. We did not bet on that occasion.[78]

The Arab Revolt was supported by a monthly British subsidy of £200,000, while Ibn Saud was also awarded a monthly £5,000, initially to combat the Turks, but then to keep peace with Husein.[79] In the event, the War passed without Ibn Saud taking any active part, other than to send several caravans to break through the British blockade on Ottoman territories.[80] The fact that his two natural adversaries, Husein and Ibn Rashid, had taken opposing sides may have inclined Ibn Saud, out of expediency, towards *de facto* neutrality.[81]

Britain continued to improvise. Husein proclaimed himself King of the Arabs only for Britain to withhold recognition in the face of Arab outrage, and limit her recognition to the title King of the Hejaz. To try and appease Ibn Saud, the Wahhabi emir was awarded the KCIE at a grand durbar (investiture) of local rulers in Kuwait.[82] As for Ibn Rashid, it was eventually decided that his continued existence after the War would provide a valuable makeweight in the Arabian balance of power between Husein and Ibn Saud.[83] By the end of the War British minds once more turned inwards, towards Ireland and demobilisation. At Versailles the focus was on the League of Nations, creating new European frontiers, and settling reparations. At large, Britain was concerned with her global position, and the new threats arising out of her post-War weakness.[84]

The Official Channels of Anglo-Saudi Relations

Before turning to the crucial period at the birth of the mandates it is appropriate to describe the channels of communication and decision-making as they affected Anglo-Saudi relations up to 1925. Communication between states is not simply a matter of personal emissaries or the establishment of diplomatic relations. It also reflects the technology of the day. From the 1830s, with the rapid growth of steamship companies such as Cunard and P & O, a speedier, regular and more dependable mail and passenger service linked Britain with her Empire.[85] Communications were further enhanced by the introduction of the telegraph. In the 1860s a land and submarine telegraph system was linked to India via the Euphrates valley and the Arabian Gulf.[86]

A shrinking world due to improved communications had profound consequences for international relations. Remote centres of power no longer had the same autonomy. One of the chief reasons behind the development of the East India Company's governmental functions was the time taken to confer with the Government in London. Officials in distant parts were endowed with much greater responsibility for decision-making than is the case with diplomatic personnel today. The home government, in the words of one scholar, was chiefly concerned with 'picking up the pieces'.[87] By the end of the nineteenth century the Government of India was beginning to lose much of its autonomy. Many factors accounted for this, not the least of which was the direct voice that these improved communications gave the London Government.

Even so, inaccessible parts of the world could not benefit from active diplomacy. In the case of Ibn Saud, as late as the First World War, a message from him to the British Government had to travel by hand to a Political Agent in the Gulf,[88] then on to the Political Resident, then to India, and finally to London. It would be discussed or otherwise by the India Office, circulated to other interested government departments, and, finally, if a reply was to be sent, the whole process would recommence in reverse. The time taken between the sending of a message from Riyadh and receipt of a reply could, therefore, be months.

Administrative divisions further complicated the problem of communicating with Arab potentates. As already indicated, there was some confusion within the British Empire over who was responsible for what. Prior to 1914, the Government of India, preoccupied with the need to safeguard the interests of the sub-continent, took it upon itself to administer and finance control of the Gulf. The Political Resident at Bushire was a servant of the Indian Government and was answerable to the Foreign Department of that Government. His full title, however, was 'His Britannic Majesty's Political Resident in the Gulf and Consul-General for Fars and Khuzistan'. His duties as Consul-General in Persia meant that he was simultaneously responsible to the British Minister in Teheran, who, being accredited to an independent state, was accountable to the London Foreign Office.[89] The total picture of Britain's Arabian policy at this time was marked, in Busch's words, by conflicting information, incompatible interests, and an elongated and inefficient chain of government communication.[90]

Nevertheless, the various divisions of Arabian responsibilities caused Britain few major problems up to 1914 when Turkey was entrusted with maintaining local stability. It was the abrupt shift of British policy in 1914, from seeking the stabilisation of the Ottoman Empire to seeking its partition or dissolution, that revealed the degree of unpreparedness and disagreement within different parts of the British Empire.

The Government of India viewed the declaration of war on Turkey with alarm, fearing the possible effects on Indian Moslems, and the threat of a political war becoming a religious one.[91] India always feared Islamic militancy. Constitutionally, however, the affairs of India were represented in London through the India Office, which interpreted the views of Delhi to the various departments of the British Government. The effective head of the Government of India was the Secretary of State for India. The relations between the Secretary of State and the Viceroy were nowhere precisely defined, though in any serious disagreement the Viceroy customarily gave way or resigned.[92] Although partly a broker for Indian opinion, the India Office, like the Foreign Office, could not ignore the international aspects of Indian politics. Consequently, there were occasions when the India Office advocated policies agreeable to neither the Government of India nor the Foreign Office.

The First World War also saw the injection of new policy-making bodies into the Middle East. The War Office, for the first time, became involved in the Arab world. In Mesopotamia, the wartime administration set up by the Government of India developed into an autonomous, decision-making body in its own right. Officials in Mesopotamia took over the representation of Indian policy in the Gulf and eastern Arabia, and became directly answerable to London.[93] This left Delhi increasingly remote from the management of the war. Even the financing of Gulf administration passed from India to the Treasury.[94]

The role of Cairo as the base from which Britain approached the Middle East climaxed in 1915 with the creation of the Arab Bureau. This body was a hotchpotch of personnel and functions, being technically under the Foreign Office, funded by the War Office, yet effectively controlled by the Admiralty.[95] It was designed to harmonise British political activity in the Arab world, and also contributed to military intelligence operations.[96] Looked at in retrospect, the Arab Bureau only confused matters relating to overall policy control and was, in any case, of little influence in the Gulf, Mesopotamia and India.[97]

By the end of the War all attempts to develop one central authority for the Middle East, whether for its civil or military aspects, or for the formulation or execution of policy, had failed. There remained only partial successes like the Arab Bureau in Cairo, as well as the Mesopotamian Administration Committee in London, which expanded into the 'Middle East Committee' and the 'Eastern Committee' under the chairmanship of the Foreign Secretary, Lord Curzon. In June 1918 Robert Cecil was appointed Assistant Secretary of State for Eastern Affairs in the Foreign Office, but this only succeeded in causing friction with Curzon's committee and the India Office.[98]

In the melée of contradictory arrangements entered into by the British Government, with regard to the Arabs, the Jews and the French – in large measure a consequence of the divided responsibilities and control during the war years – the need for a single voice after the War became more important than ever. It was no longer just a matter of rival departments, but also of rival promises and commitments. Indian sources had championed Ibn Saud, the Arab Bureau had backed Husein, while the Foreign Office had signed agreements with France and given undertakings to the Jews. The final spur to the complete reorganisation of Britain's policy-making apparatus in the Middle East came with the riots that swept through much of the Arab world in 1920. An alternative to military occupation had to be found which was less wasteful in money, time and manpower, and which would be under the aegis of one government department.[99]

In 1920 it was finally decided that Britain would remain in the Middle East through the medium of mandates for Palestine and Iraq (Mesopotamia). The question was, which government department would administer the mandates. The India Office objected to the very concept of unitary control over the Middle East.[100] With India's vital interests in Mesopotamia and Arabia, it appeared inconceivable that relations with those areas should be put in sole charge of another department, severing the India-Mesopotamia connections forged during the War.[101]

The India Office was particularly opposed to control of the Middle East going to the Foreign Office which, by its very nature, lacked administrative experience. The task of the Foreign Office was to formulate and expound British foreign policy, not administer sizable territories at the same time. Lord Curzon, however, was insistent that control of the Middle East should go to the Foreign Office. He argued that the accountability of the mandates to the League of Nations, and their relations with other states would, in any case, have to remain with the Foreign Office. So, too, would the handling of British relations with the independent Hejaz.[102]

In the event, following the recommendations of the Masterton-Smith report, in 1921, control of the Middle East went to the Colonial Office under the direction of Winston Churchill.[103] The decision was not unanimous. The Colonial Office had no experience of the Middle East, its nearest responsibilities being for Cyprus. Moreover, its function, at least in the public mind, was to rule colonies. Its administration of the mandates would have smacked of annexation, and there were fears of mutinies in some parts of the Middle

East.[104] On the other hand, only the Colonial Office had the requisite experience of handling dependent or semi-dependent territories. Even the Dominions were, at this time, under its wing. Expense and impracticability ruled out the creation of an entirely new department to take responsibility for the Middle East. Cabinet votes decided the issue, the Colonial Office receiving eight votes to the Foreign Office's five.[105]

Originally, the territories earmarked for Colonial Office control were Iraq, Palestine and Aden. Yet these territories were not coterminous. They had no agreed frontiers, and each territory was separated from the others by vast expanses of desert. To ease this complication, and to adhere to the philosophy of unitary control for the whole Middle East, the sphere of Colonial Office responsibility took in the entire land-mass covered by the British mandates and the Arabian peninsula.

Some recognition had to be made, however, of certain existing realities in the Arab world. The Hejaz and the Gulf sheikhdoms were granted special provisions. The Colonial Office, through the Political Resident at Bushire, took over responsibility for the Gulf rulers, including Ibn Saud, but left the Government of India to be responsible for administrative and local matters.[106] On grounds of economy it was considered unnecessary to create a new administrative structure to replace an existing one. India thereby yielded her foreign policy-making, but not her administrative role, in the Arab world. The Colonial Office reserved for itself the deciding voice in all questions of policy affecting the Arabian littoral.[107] In the case of the Hejaz, a wrangle ensued between the Foreign and Colonial Offices for the right to conduct relations with Husein, who had emerged from the War as King of the Hejaz. Churchill pressed for the Colonial Office to be allowed to initiate and regulate policy throughout all Arabia:

> The Arab problem is all one, and any attempt to divide it will only reintroduce the same paralysis and confusion of action ... Feisal or Abdullah, whether in Mesopotamia or Mecca, King Husein at Mecca, Bin Saud at Nejd, Bin Rashid at Hail, the Sheikh of Kuwait, and King Samuel at Jerusalem, are all inextricably interwoven, and no conceivable policy can have any chance which does not pull all the strings affecting them. To exclude Arabian relations would be to disembowel the Middle East Department [of the Colonial Office].[108]

The outcome was that the Hejaz continued to be the initial responsibility of the Foreign Office, subject, when necessary, to the overall sanction of the Colonial Office which would, in any case, deal with purely Arab affairs.[109] To reduce inter-departmental friction the Colonial Secretary was instructed to consult with the Foreign Secretary to reach a working agreement on Arabian policy.[110] The range of responsibilities finally entrusted to the Colonial Office comprised ultimate policy control for the entire Arab world, together with the administration of Mesopotamia, Palestine and Aden.[111]

In 1925, the Colonial Office was divided into eight geographical departments.[112] One of these was the newly created Middle East Department under Sir John Shuckburgh. Where Ibn Saud was concerned, the new arrangements introduced into the Middle East were as confused as ever, inviting not co-ordination, but at best immobilism, and at worst chaos.[113] The Hejaz, when attacked by Ibn Saud in 1924, was, for practical purposes, the responsibility of the Foreign Office; local events in the Gulf continued to be dealt with from Delhi and the India Office; while the Colonial Office took final responsibility for all Arabia.

The Post-War World: Britain, Ibn Saud and the Creation of the Mandates

As Ibn Saud had, in practice, taken no part in the War, the Armistice of Mudros in 1918 had little effect in Arabia, where the friction between the various rulers continued unabated. From the summer of 1918 Ibn Saud began an expansionist drive to the west and north which met with a variety of British attempts to contain him, but which culminated seven years later in the Saudi conquest of the Hejaz. The first campaign centred on the towns of Khurma and Turaba on the Hejaz-Nejd frontier, and began while the war against the Turks was still in progress, depleting the forces of the Hejaz.[114] The immediate threat did not pass until August 1920, when the British Government successfully imposed an armistice on Husein, but the embarrassing prospect of outright war between two of Britain's Arab protégés, both financed by British gold, was a grave portent of things to come.[115]

This Saudi campaign, moreover, introduced a new factor into Arabian warfare – the *Ikhwan* (Brotherhood). Ibn Saud's earlier military successes had been achieved with the aid of urban levies, not bedouin.[116] Yet a durable Saudi regime had to control the proud, yet fickle tribes. More particularly, Ibn Saud feared that Husein, who had dared to call himself King of the Arabs, would, when the War was over, direct his troops into central Arabia. Ibn Saud had already begun a process of 'Islamising' the bedouin. Under his direction Wahhabism affected every aspect of Arabian life, transcending tribal and urban loyalties, and subsuming tribal bonds within a greater loyalty. The story goes that, at Artawiya in 1912, the first of many colonies was established in an attempt to tie the bedouin to the soil by providing them with agricultural implements, weapons for the propagation of the faith, and further instruction in Wahhabism.[117]

The *Ikhwan* became a distinct religio-military movement, the spearhead of Wahhabism, offering Ibn Saud both a police force and an army. By the late 1920s hundreds of *Ikhwan* colonies had been established throughout Nejd, harbouring soldier-saints who were answerable, so it was hoped, not to their sheikhs, but to Ibn Saud alone.[118] The *Ikhwan* gave Ibn Saud access to fanatical fighting men at short notice.[119] Their later successes were due to their high mobility and their attributes as hardened travellers able to survive on little food. Above all, was their religious zeal: they had no fear of death.[120] Nor were they averse to wholesale massacre, women and children occasionally being legitimate victims of their mission.

It was Ibn Saud's blend of religious and political authority that had much to do with his success. Religion and politics became intertwined, each providing justification for the other. Warfare was ostensibly directed to establishing his own hereditary rights, yet was given religious justification.[121] Ibn Saud was nothing if not opportunist. He had to tread a careful path between moderating *Ikhwan* excesses, which began during the Khurma campaign, while simultaneously being dependent on the *Ikhwan* to sustain his authority. Philby described the 'peace and security' brought about by the *Ikhwan* as the *Pax Wahhabica*.[122]

The passing of the immediate threat to the Hejaz served to concentrate British attention upon developments to the north. The collapse of the Ottoman Empire had left a vacuum in the Middle East, with associated risks to the Empire lanes.[123] The task of filling that vacuum was to plague British policy-makers in the years after 1918. Many factors had to be taken into consideration: the Balfour Declaration; the promises of Arab independence (the immediate non-fulfilment of which led to riots in 1920); French suspicion;[124] fear of the Soviet Union; United States' opposition to empire-building; British military and economic exhaustion; public disquiet at increasing overseas commitments alongside domestic poverty; and oil.[125] Much of the Arab world had emerged from the War under British military occupation, and no other power was capable of seriously intervening.[126] Moreover, the strategic sensitivity of the Middle East ruled out any idea of Britain completely abandoning the region,[127] while certain senior statesmen still lived for 'Empire' and could not contemplate its stagnation. Lord Curzon, for example, hoped for an Empire stretching from the Mediterranean to Singapore.[128]

In sum, a compromise had to be found between Britain's need to stay, and the urge to leave. The First World War had spelled the end of the classic age of imperialism. A new age required a new approach, which has been called a 'half-way house' of imperialism.[129] Rather than assume direct control in the strategically sensitive Fertile Crescent,[130] and face the hazards of having to impose, as in India, imperial law and order, Britain adopted a more indirect solution, known as the 'mandate'.[131] At San Remo, in 1920, the Fertile Crescent was carved up and distributed between Britain and France.[132] Ottoman overlordship was substituted by European overlordship. More significantly, authority no longer lay with fellow Moslems, but with Christians. In effect, a new category of empire had been created, with a new breed of imperialists – the Anglo-Arabs – to administer it.[133]

The mandates put the Arabs of the Fertile Crescent under temporary European trusteeship, the intention being to guide the mandated territories to political maturity, by which time the period of tutelage could be brought to an end. Extra respectability was given to the mandate principle by the time-limit which was implied, and by making Britain and France theoretically accountable to the League of Nations for the progress of their respective trustees. From an imperial point of view, the existence of Britain's mandates – Iraq and Palestine (plus Transjordan) – did not fundamentally weaken her position because their foreign relations lay firmly with Britain.[134] Rather than allow Arab national consciousness to develop unchecked, Britain attempted to maintain her influence by co-operating with it, as far as was compatible with the requirements of Empire.

Britain still had to single out the most suitable Arab leaders to rule in her mandates. Her principal protégés, the Hashemites, having seen their promises of an independent Arab world whittled away by British deals with the French and the Jews, appeared out of the running. By 1920 much of the Middle East was aflame at the postponement of Arab independence. Husein's son Feisal, having spearheaded the Arab Revolt and been installed as King of Syria, had found himself unceremoniously dethroned by the French, who were free from commitments to the Hashemites and anxious to shape Syria to their own liking.[135] Husein's exposed position in the Hejaz vis à vis Ibn Saud, and his abject failure to redeem that position through force or diplomacy, further undermined Hashemite prestige. It seemed that the Sherifian family had been removed as a potent factor in the Middle East.

The Cairo Conference of 1921, seeking economies, passed responsibility for defence of Britain's mandates from the War Office to the Air Ministry.[136] Moreover, a certain school of British Arabists, among them Lawrence and the Oriental Secretary in Baghdad, Gertrude Bell, were determined to revive Arab fortunes, if possible, under the Hashemites. Feisal was put back on the throne, not at Damascus, but in Baghdad. He was not the only candidate. Ibn Saud, among others, was fleetingly considered.[137] Yet there were sound reasons for Britain reverting to what became known as the 'Sherifian solution' to the Arab world. On top of Britain's apparent betrayal of Arab independence she had intervened neither on behalf of Husein against Ibn Saud, nor Feisal against the French. Consequently, her prestige in the Arab world was at an all-time low. Renewing British support for the Hashemites went some way to restoring that prestige.[138] This was further evidenced by Feisal's elder brother, Abdullah, being installed as ruler of Transjordan.

Britain planned land and air routes stretching from the Mediterranean to the Gulf. In order that she could watch over these routes it was necessary for the mandated territories through which they passed to be coterminous. This east-west chain, through Iraq, Transjordan and Palestine, could not easily co-exist with the traditional north-south flow of bedouin caravan routes between Nejd and Syria.[139] The significance of these developments for Ibn Saud, and for the future of Anglo-Saudi relations, was manifest. Ibn Saud was no longer confronted only in the Hejaz with a British-backed Hashemite regime. Further Hashemite states had appeared, at British behest and with British financial backing, across his northern frontier, interposing themselves between Nejd and the proclaimed Saudi ancestral domains in Syria. Viewed from Riyadh there could only be one explanation behind Britain installing heretic Moslem rulers in Iraq and Transjordan: to contain Wahhabism in central Arabia, thereby surrounding Nejd with Hashemite states and preventing the forces of Saudi ascendency from expressing themselves. Moreover, the creation of the modern state system in the Middle East, including the introduction of such concepts as 'nation-state' and 'territorial boundary' had an effect on Ibn Saud as profound as that on the Hashemites. Their frontiers were also his.

The revised Sherifian solution did not lead to closer relations between the British Government and King Husein. He refused to sign the Treaty of Versailles, objecting to the establishment of the mandates and the British promises to the Jews, and he also consistently refused to agree terms on an Anglo-Hejazi treaty for the same reasons.[140] Building on the tradition of treaties with coastal sheikhs in eastern and southern Arabia, Britain developed the instrument of signing treaties throughout the Arab Middle East. In the mandates, as in Egypt and Arabia, treaties were to be employed as the means to gain the concessions and bases, or any other favourable conditions, believed to be necessary for Empire defence. More particularly, the treaties would, it was hoped, take some of the sting out of the mandate concept. As for Husein, his sense of betrayal revealed itself in querulousness, corruption, and eventually despotism – he became a downright burden in British eyes. Lord Curzon admitted of Husein: 'I don't think we shall ever have peace until he's gone, but I don't want to administer the final kick'.[141]

In the Arabian peninsula four other sovereign rulers had emerged from the War in addition to King Husein: Ibn Saud; Ibn Rashid of Jabal Shammar; Imam Yahya of the Yemen; and the Idrisi of Asir. The Arabs of the mandated territories were culturally more advanced than those of the peninsula. They had, however, won their limited independence only through British assistance, whereas in Arabia the status of each ruler simply confirmed the position he had made for himself during the War.[142] Whereas the Fertile Crescent had been saddled with mandates, there were no overt restrictions placed upon the sovereignty of the Arabian potentates.[143] Each was left to his own devices. Strategic considerations obliged Britain to impose her presence in the Fertile Crescent, whilst in Arabia she remained outwardly disinterested. Britain did not have to concern herself with European rivalry in the peninsula. At Versailles, the impenetrability of Arabia to foreign colonisation was never seriously questioned, and it was widely assumed that Britain would have a free hand by virtue of her long historical connections with certain parts of the peninsula.[144]

Although the disposal of the Arab provinces of the ex-Ottoman Empire had warranted various British responses, in one important respect the end product was the same: there was no foreign competition. Broadly, Britain had inherited the Ottoman role – subsidies and all. In the peninsula there were simply no rivals to worry about. In the Fertile Crescent, rivals, with the exception of France, were excluded by the introduction of mandates, reinforced by treaties. A form of British 'Monroe Doctrine' had taken shape over the Middle East – from Cairo, to Jerusalem, to Baghdad, to Muscat, and to Aden – with Ibn Saud in the middle.

With British attention firmly focused on king-making in the mandates, the next phase of Saudi expansion began. Balked in the Hejaz, Ibn Saud turned elsewhere. In 1920 his forces occupied the mountainous districts of Asir. A year later Hail was captured, finally putting an end to the lengthy feud with Al Rashid. Ibn Saud was proclaimed Sultan of Nejd, distracting some attention from the crowning of Feisal as King of Iraq. When the town of Jauf, even further north, was taken in 1922 Saudi aggrandisement had brought the territory of the new Sultan up against the southern frontiers of Trans-jordan and Iraq. With this latest acquisition the limits of Saudi rule seemed to have been reached. Ibn Saud was confronted on the west and north by British-supported Hashemite states, and on the east by British-protected Gulf sheikhdoms. The south held only the virtually uninhabitable desert of the Rub al Khali.

From 1922 Britain was forced to counter the developing Wahhabi threat in northern Arabia. *Ikhwan* raids into the mandates, which had no agreed frontiers as yet, were met with reprisals from the Royal Air Force. Yet Britain feared to antagonise Ibn Saud unduly lest he turn his attention back to the Hejaz, which did not have the benefit of British aerial defence.[145]

Britain resorted to negotiation. In the Treaty of Mohammera of May 1922 and the subsequent Uqair Protocol the following December, a frontier was agreed between Iraq and Nejd.[146] Two neutral zones were also established, to the west and south of Kuwait.[147] This frontier constituted the first post-War effort to delineate the Arabian deserts, yet it barely broke the surface of the accumulated grievances between the Saudis and Hashemites. Faced with the constant reminder that both parties were wartime allies still drawing in one way or another on the British Treasury, Britain convened, in December 1923, a conference in Kuwait in an attempt to reach a comprehensive settlement to the Arabian schism. Procrastination occurred on all sides and the Conference was wound up the following spring to save the British Government further embarrassment.[148]

Husein had, by this time, alienated most of those who had previously championed him.[149] Significantly, he contributed to his own downfall. In March 1924 Mustafa Kemal decided to sever the connection between the new Turkish republican state and the Caliphate. Without consulting Islamic organisations the Caliphate was taken up by Husein.[150] In other circumstances his position as King of the Hejaz and Sherif of Mecca would have made him a strong candidate.[151] In view of the mounting grievances against him, however, his action was interpreted as a personal violation of Islam – made worse, it was wrongly thought, by British connivance in hoisting her 'puppet' on top of the Moslem pyramid.[152] By coincidence, in the same month, Britain wound up her subsidy to Ibn Saud, which had hitherto been considered the most straightforward and cheapest way of exerting influence in Arabian affairs.[153]

The events of March 1924 stirred Ibn Saud into action. Husein's abuse of the Caliphate provided Ibn Saud with the pretext to take retribution, and, at the same time, extend his dominions. Support came, it is claimed, from Indian Moslems for a Saudi restoration of the sanctity of the Holy Places.[154] With the withdrawal of his subsidy Ibn Saud no longer feared British economic reprisals.[155] Thus, the conflict which had been threatened since 1918 came about. Ibn Saud invaded the Hejaz. Husein had weakened his own position by years of political misjudgment. Unlike Ibn Saud he had broken with the Turks before securing a firm agreement with Britain. He had never joined the League of Nations and availed himself of the doubtful benefits of collective security. Nor, after several years of negotiations, had he signed a treaty with Britain that might have secured some form of intervention.

Summary

Britain, traditionally, had found nothing inviting at all in Arabia. Economically it was unimportant. It appeared to possess no resources worth the hazards of exploitation. Its religious fanaticism and incomprehensible tribal structure deterred interference. Its people, being isolated, held no threat to the British Empire. Finally, the peninsula was totally inaccessible to political or military enterprise. This unimportance was reflected in the low level of British policy-making: Ibn Saud constituted a departmental matter, not one for the Cabinet. In practice, until his invasion of the Hejaz, he remained the business of India. All the personnel with whom he had any dealings were of the Indian school, and every act of diplomatic intercourse, even those stemming from the mandates, were prompted by the requirements of India and the Empire. Not until he invaded the Hejaz, which enjoyed well-established ties with the outside world, was the Foreign Office obliged to take note of Ibn Saud. Henceforth he became a factor in British, as opposed to Indian or Colonial Office, politics.

The actual solution to the Arabian power struggle between Husein and Ibn Saud would come about, not through remote centres of British policy-making, but through a military victory for one of the combatants. Britain's policy of non-intervention in Arabia invariably worked to the advantage of Ibn Saud, with whom the natural balance of power lay. British policy in Arabia up to 1925 was unsuccessful. She had needed allies in the War and found them, not only in Nejd and the Hejaz, but throughout Arabia. Only Ibn Rashid and the Imam Yahya sided with the Turks. Britain's strategy of an interlocking web of alliances, coupled with minimum financial expenditure and active support of an Arab revolt, succeeded in ousting the Turks from the peninsula and keeping French and Italian ambitions at bay. The Arab world from 1918 was firmly within Britain's control or influence, except that, in designating Iraq's southern frontier she was obliged to police it, and that was to drag Britain even further into desert affairs.

Significantly, Ibn Saud always appeared second best to someone: until 1914 he was subordinate to the policy of good relations with the Turks; from 1915 he was subordinate to an Arab policy that looked no further than to Husein; and from 1920 the needs and requirements of the mandates provided Britain with her principal Middle Eastern commitments. Compared with the Hashemites, Ibn Saud appeared unreliable; at least they had fought loyally for Britain. His religious credentials also made him a risky proposition for a partnership with Britain in the Arab world. Nonetheless, the Turks were removed with the help of Husein, who, in turn, would be removed by Ibn Saud. From then on the lines of conflict would be clear-cut; a line from Aqaba to Kuwait separated Ibn Saud from the surviving Hashemite states.

Ibn Saud's own achievements had been formidable. At the beginning of the First World War he had been surrounded by potential enemies. He had countered these threats by means of a treaty with Britain, he had procured a British subsidy, and managed, in the end, to keep out of the War altogether. His first probings into the Hejaz in 1918-20 produced uncertainty in Britain. Time was on his side and it is hard to find a serious political or strategic misjudgment on his part.

With the invasion of the Hejaz a whole range of new questions presented themselves to the British Government.[156] How should it react to the first political unification of Arabia in over a thousand years? Would a Saudi regime be likely to be stable and enduring? If one of the Hashemite pillars fell, how could Britain reconcile her relations with Ibn Saud with her presence in the mandates and the Gulf? How would Ibn Saud react to those territories? And how well would he administer the Pilgrimage? When Ibn Saud finally invaded the Hejaz, in 1924, Britain was in control of his northern frontiers as well as the entire eastern and southern shorelines of Arabia – with the exception of Hasa. Three of the four corners of the peninsula – Aden, Oman, and Kuwait – were under British possession or control. British acquisition of the fourth, Aqaba, will provide the focus of the next chapter.

REFERENCES FOR CHAPTER ONE

1. See Fisher, p. 296.
2. See John Marlow, *The Persian Gulf in the Twentieth Century*, p. 8. (Hereafter: *The Persian Gulf ...*)
3. ibid., p. 11. A Governor-Generalship had been established in India to supervise British interests in 1784. The Indian Mutiny of 1858 led to direct British intervention.
4. About one half of the British Army, in addition to the Indian Army, was assigned to Indian defence (Monroe, *Britain's Moment ...*, p. 11).
5. Interference in the Gulf came from local peoples (Persians, Arabs and Turks) and from European rivals (Dutch, French and Portuguese) operating with their governments' support.

6. Ravinder Kumar, *India and the Persian Gulf Region*, p. 18.
7. Despite the treaties, piracy remained a problem until the coming of steamships capable of outrunning sail. Much of the piracy during the early nineteenth century was stimulated by religious upheavals in central Arabia.
8. In sum, the four Indian preoccupations before the days of oil were: strategy, piracy, slaves and arms. Control of arms was particularly important because arms smuggled from the Gulf region found their way to the tribes of the north-west frontier of India (Terence Creagh Coen, *The Indian Political Service*, p. 233).
9. At the Congress of Vienna in 1815 Britain joined with other European states in seeking to maintain the territorial integrity of the Ottoman Empire.
10. Palmerston proclaimed, in 1833: 'Turkey is as good an occupier of the road to India as an active Arab sovereign would be' (*The Cambridge History of British Foreign Policy, Vol. II*, p. 162).
11. Troeller, p. 75. Britain at that time did not enthuse at direct Christian involvement in the Arab world. Nor could a European army operate effectively in desert conditions.
12. Sarah Searight, *The British in the Middle East*, p. 117. Efforts were also made to establish a route overland from the Mediterranean to the Euphrates, and then by ship out into the Gulf and the Indian Ocean.
13. The passage round the Cape took between five and eight months by sail, but could still take three months in the early days of steam (Searight, p. 117).
14. In annexing Aden, India had one eye on the search for naval bases and the other on the need to combat Egyptian penetration of Arabia. In 1840, Palmerston secured Egyptian withdrawal under the threat of British intervention.
15. See John Bagot Glubb, *Britain and the Arabs*, p. 27. Disraeli bought the Canal shares off the Egyptian Khedive in 1875, before British occupation occurred seven years later. Egypt remained *de jure* part of the Ottoman Empire, while being *de facto* under British control.
16. Royal Institute of International Affairs, *British Interests in the Mediterranean and Middle East*, pp. 2-3. (Hereafter: *British Interests* …)
17. Royal Institute of International Affairs, *Political and Strategic Interests of the United Kingdom*, p. 105. (Hereafter: *Political and Strategic Interests* …)
18. In terms of distance saved, Australasia benefited less from the new Suez route than did India and the Far East. The Suez route became the gateway for some 29% of Britain's oil supplies by 1939. By the 1930s Britain imported 50,000 tons of foodstuffs and 110,000 tons of merchandise every day (ibid., pp. 125, 243, 245).
19. ibid., pp. 244, 247, 281.
20. Marlowe, op. cit., p. 15. Even the campaign against slavery was directed at the trading of slaves, not their role in Arabian society.
21. See Thomas Marston, *Britain's Imperial Role in the Red Sea Area 1800-1878*, p. 497.
22. Even penetration of Arabia by private explorers was tightly controlled by the British and Indian Governments. Culturally and politically central Arabia was isolated from the outside world by reason of geography; while the eastern and southern seaboards were isolated by British treaty. Even in the Gulf Britain was reluctant to intervene. In 1902, for example, Britain rejected the idea of a formal protectorate over the Trucial sheikhdoms (Donald Hawley, *The Trucial States*, p. 168), but the following year pronounced that the establishment by any other power of a naval base or a fortified port in the Gulf would mean war. When Lord Curzon, Viceroy of India, toured the Gulf, also in 1903, he extolled the independence of the sheikhs while treating them like feudal serfs (Fitzsimons, p. 7).
23. P.A. Reynolds, *British Foreign Policy in the Inter-War Years*, p. 6.
24. Jones, p. 127.
25. Christine Moss Helms, *The Cohesion of Saudi Arabia: Evolution of Political Identity*, pp. 19, 29.
26. ibid., p. 19.
27. Camel-herding nomads, sometimes referred to as bedu (badu).
28. Helms, p. 30.
29. ibid.
30. See Helms, p. 33, for a comprehensive list of domestic trappings.
31. ibid., p. 30.

32. See Louise E. Sweet, 'Camel Raiding of North Arabian Bedouin: A Mechanism of Ecological Adaption', *American Anthropologist*, 67 (1965), p. 1134.
33. At any one time a chief would be on hostile relations with some, and truce relations with other, chiefs (Sweet, p. 1141).
34. Helms, p. 65.
35. This included such activities as tree and stone worship (John S. Habib, *Ibn Saud's Warriors of Islam: The Ikhwan of Najd and their Role in the Creation of the Saudi Kingdom 1910-1930*, p. 3).
36. Sheikh Hafiz Wahba, *Arabian Days*, p. 89. Wahhabis referred to themselves as *muwahhidun*.
37. W. F. Smalley, 'Ibn Saud and the Wahhabis', *Moslem World*, 22 (1932), pp. 227-46.
38. Helms, p. 91.
39. ibid., p. 103. On the other hand, Wahhabism did defer to the secular authority which prosecuted its aims. Few other religions have harnessed the state so effectively to its aims (personal correspondence from Robert Lacey).
40. H. St J. B. Philby, *Arabia*, p. 181.
41. Helms, p. 81.
42. ibid., p. 103. Broadly, an emir rules over a settled population, while a sheikh rules over bedouin tribes. Both are secular, not religious titles. In modern times the distinction between emir and sheikh has become blurred.
43. Troeller, p. 14; Hawley, p. 97.
44. Safeguarding the Holy Places of Islam was one of the main self-appointed tasks of the Ottoman Empire (R. Bayly Winder, *Saudi Arabia in the Nineteenth Century*, p. 6).
45. By the second decade of the century the fire of Wahhabism was temporarily extinguished. Daraiya, the Saudi capital, was razed in 1818. When Wahhabism rose again its capital was nearby Riyadh.
46. Mohammad Ali's early forays into Arabia were under the direction of Constantinople. A concerted Egyptian invasion in the late 1830s was more ambitious, the Viceroy seeking to carve out an Egyptian empire from Turkey's Arab provinces, which, to British disquiet, threatened to undermine the stability of the Ottoman Empire. The only active British move in central Arabia during the nineteenth century was to despatch Colonel Lewis Pelly, Political Resident in the Gulf, to Riyadh in 1865 to investigate claims that Saudi tribesmen were raiding into the Gulf sheikhdoms (Winder, pp. 219-21).
47. Hasa extended from Kuwait to Qatar. Only at its oases in the south was it capable of sustaining a settled population. Nejd remained independent, in practice if not in name, but Turkish control of the Hasa ports enabled them to exert some pressure on the interior (Troeller, pp. 18-19). Turkish successes in the northern half of the Gulf caused Britain to pay closer attention to her position in the Trucial sheikhdoms (Kumar, p. 114).
48. Hail was four hundred miles north-west of Riyadh. The area of Jabal Shammar, of which Hail was the principal town, was strategically situated so as to be able to monopolise the caravan routes passing between Nejd and Syria, and the Gulf and Egypt (Helms, p. 67). Ibn Rashid had been receiving Turkish support as a buffer against any future Saudi expansion northwards, although the Saudi version is that the Rashidi were originally Saudi protégés sent north to administer Hail (personal correspondence from Robert Lacey).
49. H. St J. B. Philby, *Arabian Jubilee*, pp. 5-6.
50. It was proposed to have Kuwait as the eastern terminus of the Berlin-Baghdad Railway. Russia was also contriving to establish a coaling station in the sheikhdom, hence Britain's attempts to counter these possible threats by a treaty with Mubarak.
51. See Troeller, p. 51. Mubarak had, the previous year, also taken on Ibn Rashid but was routed. The Government of India, although aware of arms being passed from Mubarak to Ibn Saud, chose to ignore the fact. Having recently prized Murbarak's goodwill from the Turks, India was unwilling to jeopardise that goodwill. In addition, Curzon admitted that preventing the armsflow to Ibn Saud might increase Turkish dominance in central Arabia to the extent that it undermined Britain's position in the Gulf (Philip Graves, *Life of Sir Percy Cox*, p. 102).
52. The Turks had been responsible for the demise of the earlier Saudi state, and one Saudi ruler had been executed in Constantinople (Helms, pp. 116-17). Britain was a convenient vehicle with which to secure Saudi aspirations in Arabia.

53. Troeller, p. 12. In 1904 a Political Agent was also appointed to Kuwait.
54. ibid., p. 22. With Britain failing to respond to his entreaties, Ibn Saud had threatened to turn to the Russians (Kumar, p. 203).
55. The British Resident in the Gulf, Major (later Sir) Percy Cox, championed the Saudi cause but was unable to sway higher authorities to his thinking (Troeller, pp. 24-5). Ever since the Foreign Office had become involved in the Middle East in its own right by bolstering up the Turks, the Government of India had slowly ceased to provide the definitive voice on Arabian matters. By 1910 the Viceroy had been reduced, on Arabian questions, almost to a cypher of the Foreign Office (H. V. F. Winstone, *Gertrude Bell*, p. 147).
56. Kumar, pp. 203-9.
57. Capture of Hofuf did not give Ibn Saud control of the Hasa bedouin, notably the Ajman tribe, which rebelled against him in 1915-16.
58. Britain's agreement, in 1907, with Turkey's foremost potential enemy, Russia, contributed to Ottoman-German links.
59. These conventions had far-reaching ramifications in the 1930s (see Chapter Nine).
60. Helms, pp. 269, 279.
61. Philby, *Saudi Arabia*, p. 270. Kuwait, despite its treaty with Britain and the presence of a British Political Agent, was reaffirmed as being within the Turkish sphere (J. B. Kelly, *Eastern Arabian Frontiers*, p. 107).
62. Neither party relinquished territory over which it exercised *de facto* control.
63. Briton C. Busch, *Britain, India and the Arabs*, p. 10.
64. Shakespear had been the first Englishman to meet Ibn Saud, back in 1910.
65. The treaty, together with other British treaties with Kuwait (1914) and Qatar (1916) gave Britain complete control of the Arab littoral of the Gulf, control of arms traffic, and the virtual exclusion of all foreign powers from Arabia.
66. No mention was made to Ibn Saud at the time of his treaty that correspondence between Cairo and Sherif Husein of the Hejaz was well advanced in the search for a formula that would lead to a British-Hashemite alliance (Philby, *Arabian Jubilee*, p. 43).
67. The Ottoman policy of *divide et impera* had worked for the maintenance of peace, but militated against wholehearted Arab support in war.
68. Evidence has come to light that the Arab Secret Societies had chosen Ibn Saud to lead an Arab revolt (H. V. F. Winstone, letter to the *Sunday Times*, 10 May 1981).
69. Shakespear to Hirtzel, 26 June 1914, IO L/P & S/10/385.
70. Ernest Main, *Iraq: From Mandate to Independence*, p. 52.
71. Britain, of course, already had consular facilities in Jedda. Lord Kitchener, Secretary of State for War, had previously been British Minister in Cairo, and had discussed the possibility of an Arab uprising with Husein's son Abdullah. Kitchener's exaggerated view of Husein therefore strengthened the Egypt-Hejaz link.
72. Troeller, p. 82. Ibn Rashid's comparative proximity to Constantinople meant that he could not easily flout Turkish pressure.
73. The Hashemite family claimed direct descent from the Prophet's daughter, Fatima, and son-in-law, Ali (Randall Baker, *King Husain and the Kingdom of Hejaz*, p. 1). They had acted as custodians of the Holy Places since the eleventh century, and, since the nineteenth century, had experienced a fluctuating balance of power with the Turkish *Valis*. In theory, the Sherifs had authority over the bedouin and the Pilgrimage, while the *Vali* ruled over urban areas. In view of the Hejaz's religious significance, it paid no taxes, was not liable for conscription, and received direct largesse, salaries and subsidies from Constantinople (Baker, pp. 3, 21, 173). Detractors of Husein, and Britain's attachment to him, point out that, in Arab terms, his position was inferior to that of other rulers, in that Husein was an appointee of the Turks, without the prestige attending the tribal ancestry of hereditary rulers elsewhere (John Marlowe, *Arab Nationalism and British Imperialism*, p. 20. (Hereafter: *Arab Nationalism* ...) As for the supposed lineage from Mohammad, in truth many Moslems resented the Hashemites because, far from being 'Custodians of the Holy Places', all that any Sherif of Mecca had done was to exploit, rob and cheat pilgrims. Husein, at least in the post-War years, was more unpopular than most.
74. Elie Kedourie, 'Cairo and Khartoum on the Arab Question', in Kedourie, *The Chatham House Version and Other Middle Eastern Studies*, Frank Cass, 1970, p. 16.
75. Busch, op. cit., p. 477.

76. Briton C. Busch, *Britain and the Persian Gulf 1894-1914*, p. 264.
77. Busch, *Britain, India and the Arabs*, p. 62.
78. Brig. Gen. Gilbert Clayton, 'Arabia and the Arabs', *Journal of the Royal Institute of International Affairs* (January 1929).
79. Troeller, p. 101. Ibn Saud's subsidy was scheduled to run for six months, but eventually ran until March 1924.
80. Helms, p. 118.
81. Britain's active sponsoring of Husein, and India's reluctance to supply Ibn Saud with arms, led to speculation that the whole purpose of Ibn Saud's treaty and subsidy was to stop him doing anything. India feared that armed Wahhabis would turn not on Ibn Rashid, but on Husein and the Gulf sheikhdoms (Kenneth Williams, *Ibn Saud: Puritan King of Arabia*, p. 162). Ibn Saud, moreover, had serious revolts on his hands, and may have used his British subsidy to buy off his errant tribes rather than take up arms for the British. Of course, he also wanted to guard against weakening himself *vis à vis* Husein by campaigns against Ibn Rashid (personal correspondence from Robert Lacey). In any case, it was nearly three years after Shakespear's death before direct British representation was re-established with Ibn Saud, when Philby made his first appearance in Arabia.
82. Troeller, p. 99. KCIE – Knight Commander of the Most Eminent Order of the Indian Empire.
83. Suggestions that Saudi forces be loosed upon Hail competed with others that Ibn Rashid was not worth bothering about, particularly if it meant handing Ibn Saud a hefty cheque.
84. Reynolds, p. 12.
85. Marston, p. 387.
86. Searight, p. 127.
87. Marston, p. 500.
88. The Political Resident was, of course, stationed at Bushire on the Persian side of the Gulf. His chief subordinates on the Arab side in the inter-war years were a Political Agent at Kuwait and another at Bahrain.
89. Troeller, p. 3.
90. Busch, *Britain and the Persian Gulf 1894-1914*, p. 7.
91. Troeller, p. 74.
92. Sir Charles Petrie, *The Life and Letters of the Rt Hon. Sir Austen Chamberlain, Vol II*, p. 31 (Hereafter: ... *Austen Chamberlain*)
93. Busch, *Britain, India and the Arabs*, p. 477.
94. Troeller, p. 4.
95. Winstone, *Gertrude Bell*, p. 185.
96. Busch, op. cit., p. 101.
97. The various personnel who, at the height of the war, contributed to British policy-making in the Middle East included: The Commander of the Egyptian theatre (General Murray); the High Commissioner in Egypt (Sir Henry McMahon); the Commander-in-Chief East Indies (Vice Admiral Wemyss); the Director of the Arab Bureau (D.G. Hogarth); the Director of Military Intelligence, Egypt (Brig. Gen. Gilbert Clayton); the Sirdar in Khartoum (General Reginald Wingate); the British Representatives in Jedda and Rabigh (Colonels Wilson and Parker); the British Resident in Aden; the Civil Commissioner in Iraq (Percy Cox); the Commander in Mesopotamia (General Maude); the Foreign Secretary of the Government of India (A.H. Grant); the Viceroy of India (Lords Hardinge and Chelmsford); the Secretary of State for India (Lord Crewe, Austen Chamberlain, and Edwin Montagu); and the Foreign Secretary (Sir Edward Grey and Sir Arthur Balfour) (ibid., p. 205).
98. ibid., p. 213.
99. Aaron S. Klieman, *Foundations of British Policy in the Arab World: The Cairo Conference of 1921*, p. 87.
100. Busch, op. cit., p. 432.
101. Klieman, pp. 85ff.
102. ibid., p. 89.
103. Busch, op. cit., p. 442.
104. Stephen Roskill, *Hankey: Man of Secrets Vol II, 1919-1931*, p. 202.
105. ibid. This defeat for the Foreign Office can be seen in the context of a continuing series of reversals that had sapped its prestige since 1914. The Foreign Office's esteem was a

casualty in the case against 'secret diplomacy' which was felt to be largely responsible for the First World War (see Gordon A. Craig, 'The British Foreign Office from Grey to Austen Chamberlain' in Craig and Gilbert (Eds), *The Diplomats 1919-1939*, pp. 16-47). Foreign Office prestige began to reassert itself with the fall of Lloyd George.

106. Troeller, p. 196.
107. CP 2545, CAB 21/186, in J.C. Hurewitz, *The Middle East and North Africa in World Politics: A Documentary Record – Vol II, 1914-1945*, p. 233.
108. Churchill to Lloyd George, in Klieman, pp. 92-3.
109. Hurewitz, p. 234.
110. Klieman, p. 93.
111. Busch, op. cit., p. 460.
112. Sir Charles Jeffries, *The Colonial Office*, p. 105.
113. Hurewitz, p. 231.
114. Territorial disputes between Husein and Ibn Saud can be traced back to 1910. Over Khurma, Britain backed Husein, fearing Moslem outrage for having urged the Arab Revolt upon him, then leaving him weakened in the face of the Saudi threat (Busch, op. cit., p. 323). Husein, who repeatedly threatened abdication, was preventing Nejdis from making the Pilgrimage. Moreover, far from being a localised conflict over one or two frontier towns, the victor would have secured the allegiance of the Utaiba tribal hinterlands. Britain could not put diplomatic pressure on Ibn Saud, because when Philby left Riyadh, in 1918, British representation in central Arabia was abandoned (Elizabeth Monroe, *Philby of Arabia*, p. 98 (hereafter: *Philby* ...)) Britain did, however, threaten unilateral abrogation of Ibn Saud's 1915 treaty (Troeller, p. 142).
115. Although Ibn Saud did not press on to invade the Hejaz, he did not withdraw from the occupied frontier towns.
116. Helms, pp. 113-27. Ibn Saud had concentrated on urban areas because they were militarily easier to capture, and could provide the framework for later economic expansion and political stability.
117. Philby, *Saudi Arabia*, p. 262. The *Ikhwan* (Brotherhood) is not to be confused with the Moslem Brotherhood of Egypt which flourished in Egypt in the 1930s. Ibn Saud's close association with the *Ikhwan* has obscured their origins. Philby, *Arabian Jubilee*, pp. 22-3, and others, maintained that he originated the movement. Others, including H.R.P. Dickson, *Kuwait and her Neighbours*, p. 149, suggest Ibn Saud harnessed a phenomenon that already existed. Habib's definitive verdict, from the available Arab sources, is that Ibn Saud did create the *Ikhwan* (Habib, pp. 6, 22-3).
118. The future *Ikhwan* rebellion provided the test of this split loyalty. *Ikhwan* colonies were often situated in strategic locations. Artawiya was on the route to Iraq; Ghatghat on the route to Mecca.
119. Lebkicher, Rentz and Steineke, *The Arabia of Ibn Saud*, pp. 60-1.
120. Helms, p. 144.
121. ibid., pp. 25, 115. Although the Wahhabi *ulema* (learned men who interpreted the legal and religious requirements of Islam) recognised Al Saud as the holder of a lawful Islamic imamate, Ibn Saud was careful to emphasise his temporal role, his father retaining the religious title of imam (Helms, pp. 105, 130).
122. H. St J.B. Philby, '*Pax Wahhabica*', *The English Review* (March 1933), pp. 313-4. Ibn Saud's control over the remoter and more independent tribes remained tenuous. It is clear that the British Government had no understanding of the role and purpose of the *Ikhwan*. Wingate, for example, saw evidence of Bolshevism in central Arabia, and was encouraged to do so by Husein. Others dismissed the *Ikhwan* as an internal religious phenomenon, not posing a threat to British interests or the international community (see Habib, pp. 21, 27, 105).
123. Turkey relinquished her Arab provinces at the Treaty of Sevres in 1920. The Peace Settlement between Britain and Turkey did not come until the Treaty of Lausanne in 1923.
124. Britain had made pledges to the Arabs, whether or not she intended to keep them. France had not. Her concern with the security of the western Mediterranean had led to her seeking to enhance her position in north Africa. Any British encouragement of Arab political aspirations further east that could serve to undermine that position had to be resisted if possible (Ann Williams, *Britain and France in the Middle East and Nort'*

1914-1967, p. 38).

125. See Reynolds, p. 51. All post-War British Governments acknowledged that they could not assume fresh overseas obligations which they did not have the strength or conviction to sustain (Jones, p. 1).

126. By 1918 British troops were in Damascus and Baghdad, which had never previously experienced Christian conquest. France, Germany, Italy, Turkey and Russia, all for different reasons, were precluded from the area save by British invitation, and the United States lacked official interest (see Klieman, p. 241).

127. After home defence, the maintenance of the lines of communication between Britain and the Empire was the most important objective of the armed forces.

128. Fisher, p. 465.

129. Fitzsimons, p. ix.

130. The Fertile Crescent is the name commonly given to the area between the Arabian peninsula and Turkey; the Mediterranean and the Gulf.

131. Mandates were also established among the territories of the German Colonial Empire. The mandates stemming from the ex-Ottoman provinces were intended to win early independence.

132. France was granted a mandate for Syria and Lebanon, the area of her traditional ties in the Levant. Britain was granted a mandate for Iraq (as Mesopotamia came to be called) and another for Palestine (with the area east of the River Jordan – Transjordan – included within the Palestine mandate). If the mandates are included, the British Empire had now reached its maximum territorial extent.

133. James Morris, *Farewell the Trumpets: An Imperial Retreat*, p. 248.

134. Tories, still hankering after Empire, were appeased by what amounted in practice to British control of an added piece of the globe. Socialists were not averse to Britain undertaking responsibility for the tutelage of 'backward' peoples, and were happy to support almost any scheme that had the blessing of the League of Nations.

135. Klieman, p. 97.

136. £40 million had been spent on suppressing the Iraq riots in 1920, four times the total expenditure on the Arab Revolt (Baker, p. 163).

137. Even while the Cairo Conference was sitting, a government sub-committee was referring to Ibn Saud as the greatest factor in Arabian politics (Klieman, p. 121). The statesmanship of Ibn Saud impressed all who met him, though they remained few. H. R. P. Dickson, the Political Agent in Bahrain, described Ibn Saud as: 'head and shoulders finer than any sheikh I have ever met' (Troeller, p. 146).

138. Klieman, p. 98. Britain fused her obligations to the Hashemites with her mandatory interpretation of empire-building. By having Hashemite rulers across the Arab world Britain hoped to be able to assert pressure from Baghdad to Amman to Mecca.

139. See Troeller, pp. 189-93.

140. The British terms for this treaty might have suggested to Husein the establishment of a Christian protectorate over the Holy Places. Curzon first sent Lawrence to negotiate a treaty with Husein in July 1921. Britain wanted the treaty in order to demonstrate that the wartime relationship was not dictated solely by strategic interests. It was also hoped to reconcile British policy in Palestine with the promises made to Husein. Under the terms of the draft treaty of April 1923, Husein was pledged to maintain friendly relations with Ibn Saud. Britain would use 'its good offices' in any dispute and undertake to restrain 'by all peaceful and practical means' any aggression in the Hejaz, whose frontiers still had to be defined (Hurewitz., pp. 319-20). Moreover, there is some evidence that pressure was put on Husein by Palestinian Arabs not to sign the treaty (see Yeyoshua Porath, 'The Palestinians and the Negotiations for the British-Hejazi Treaty 1920-1925', *Asian and African Studies*, 8 (1972), pp. 20-48).

141. In Troeller, p. 152. Husein's subsidy had been suspended as early as February 1920. This prevented him from subsidising his own tribes, increasing their disaffection which hastened his eventual downfall.

142. George Antonius, *The Arab Awakening*, p. 279.

143. This in itself fuelled resentment about Britain's condescension towards the Arabs. The fact that the inhabitants of Arabia were allowed political independence seemed to confirm the view from the mandates that all that was best in Arab culture was to be suppressed.

144. Prior to the Peace Conference a British Monroe Doctrine over Arabia had been considered, although this did not manifest itself in a mandate. The India Office, in particular, wished to see British influence predominate in Arabia, but deprecated any suggestion of direct administration (Max Beloff, *Imperial Sunset: Vol I, Britain's Liberal Empire 1897-1921*, p. 259).

145. One problem that was to blur British assessments of Ibn Saud for another decade was ascertaining his personal responsibility for the raids and excesses of the *Ikhwan*. If he was a restraining influence on them there were reasons for his receiving British support, not bombs.

146. Much of the territory claimed by Ibn Saud was handed to Feisal in Iraq. Compensation was exacted by taking much of the hinterland of Kuwait and giving it to Ibn Saud, which did little to confirm Britain's support for the rights of small nations. Britain was introducing western notions of government to the Arab world, of which territorial frontiers formed an integral part.

147. The ostensible explanation for the neutral zones was to reduce friction caused by wandering tribes, though Sir Percy Cox, who mediated at the Uqair negotiations as High Commissioner of Iraq, admitted the influence of oil possibilities in the case of the Kuwait-Nejd neutral zone (Troeller, pp. 180-1).

148. ibid., p. 209.

149. India's Moslems resented his revolt against the Caliph, and the manner in which he administered the Pilgrimage. A dispute took place in 1923 between Husein and Egyptian pilgrims bearing the *Mahmal* (litter) destined for Mecca (Arnold Toynbee, *Survey of International Affairs, 1925, Vol I*, pp. 282-92 (Hereafter: *Survey ... year*.).

150. The Caliphate does not depend on descent, but on suitability to fulfil the role as protector of the *Sharia* Islamic law (Baker, p 190).

151. The Husein-McMahon correspondence had spoken of the Caliphate returning to Arabia.

152. Baker, p. 188.

153. Troeller, p. 163. In 1922 Britain had earmarked a total of £150,000 *per annum* for Arabian subsidies. This was cheaper than the cost of maintaining a single battalion of native infantry for one year (see Parliamentary Question, Lambert to Churchill, 2 March 1922, in Ibrahim al Rashid, *Documents on the History of Saudi Arabia, Vol I*, pp. 81-2).

154. Wahba, p. 147.

155. Nejdis had been refused permission to undertake the Pilgrimage since the end of the War.

156. Sir George Rendel, *The Sword and the Olive*, p. 58.

CHAPTER TWO

British Policy During the Hejaz-Nejd War: The Aqaba-Maan Affair 1925

The Hejaz-Nejd War

The timing of the Saudi invasion of the Hejaz was prompted by the withdrawal of Britain's subsidy to Ibn Saud and the assumption by King Husein of the Caliphate, which in turn contributed to the breakdown of the Kuwait Conference.[1] In August 1924, after diversionary raids into the mandates, the *Ikhwan* swept into the Hejaz. In October, the notables of Mecca and Jedda successfully demanded Husein's abdication. His eldest son, Ali, assumed the throne but not the Caliphate. Britain prudently withheld recognition of Ali's sovereignty.[2] Almost immediately Mecca fell to the Wahhabis and Ali retreated to Jedda. Husein tried to seek refuge with Abdullah in Amman, but was prevented from doing so by the British Government in case his presence in Transjordan invited a Saudi assault on the emirate. Husein's yacht anchored off Aqaba pending a British decision on his future.[3] By the turn of 1924-25 Ali's rule was confined to the towns of Jedda, Medina and Yanbo. The rest of the Hejaz was in the hands of Saudi forces.

In the first months of the conflict Britain faced a simple power struggle in Arabia between its two most prominent rulers. There were no external, complicating factors for Britain to take into consideration. She announced a policy of neutrality along with other European powers. The reason given was that the conflict was of a religious, not political, nature and was, therefore, no place for a Christian power. This response was both practical and traditional. Husein, as has already been emphasised, was not universally popular in the Moslem world, many elements of which could not think of the wartime Anglo-Hashemite alliance as other than a direct threat to the Caliphate. Husein was widely viewed as a British puppet, further supported by his sons' later connivance with Britain. Without his British subsidy with which to buy the allegiance of Hejazi tribes, Husein had weakened his power base.[4] Shorn of British finance he resorted to extracting massive taxes from pilgrims.[5] One Islamic interpretation of the Hejaz-Nejd war is that of a quasi-nationalist cause attempting to rid the Arabs and Islam of the corrupt and heretic Hashemites.[6] Whatever the case, Britain feared the reaction of India's Moslems if she made any move to assist Husein.[7] Nor would military intervention have been an easy matter. Once before, over Khurma and Turaba between 1918-20, Ibn Saud had stood poised to invade the Hejaz and had found Britain reluctant to take firm measures to assist Husein.

Britain turned her back on Hashemite pleas for assistance. She did, however, face two particular anxieties. One was the risk to the coming Pilgrimage in June 1925, even though it was unlikely that Ibn Saud had any desire to inflame Moslem opinion or the British Government by making difficulties for pilgrims. The other was the safety of the small European diplomatic and consular community in Jedda.[8] Mindful of the need not to endanger the lives of Europeans, which might have induced outside intervention, Ibn Saud followed up his sweeping military successes by the employment of siege tactics on Jedda. This had the inevitable effect of prolonging the war.

The British Government's attitude to Husein had hardened over the years. By 1924 he had become both a despot and a figure of fun. The British Consul in Jedda described him thus:

> Imagine a cunning, lying, credulous, suspicious, obstinate, vain, conceited, ignorant, greedy, cruel Arab sheikh suddenly thrust into a position where he has to deal with all sorts of questions he doesn't understand, and where there is no human power to restrain him, and you have a picture of King Husein ... Lying, robbing, and other crimes no more come amiss to him than they did to the founder of his religion.[9]

Husein's frequent telegrams requesting Britain to honour her promises became a standing joke as they found their way through the various government departments. In retrospect, the breakdown of treaty negotiations, which might have required some form of British intervention, and perpetuated Britain's commitment to Hashemite rule in the Hejaz, was cause for some relief in London.

British pragmatism, too, was evident. In the light of Ibn Saud's rapid victories it would have been a short-sighted policy to back Husein and antagonise the man seemingly about to unite Arabia. Against this, the notorious fickleness of the Arabian tribes meant that the final outcome of the war could not be predicted with certainty. For all these reasons it was sound policy for Britain to sit back and reach out the hand of congratulations to the victor when his moment of triumph arrived. At the same time, Britain had to take account of her comprehensive Sherifian policy. In particular, because the Hejaz bordered Transjordan, there was the risk of Abdullah taking active steps to assist the Hejaz. Britain also had to consider the effect that her neutrality would have on Iraq and Transjordan. Abdullah freely admitted to being first a Hashemite, and only secondly a ruler of a British mandated territory.[10]

For as long as the war confined itself to the Hejaz, Britain could remain neutral. Unfortunately, it threatened to spill over into Transjordan. Husein's refuge in Aqaba was likely to bring Saudi forces in pursuit. The prospect of *Ikhwan* armies descending upon Transjordan highlighted the problem that the emirate had no defined frontiers with Arabia.

Husein's sanctuary in Aqaba, from October 1924, acted as a provocation to Ibn Saud. Sir Herbert Samuel, High Commissioner for Palestine (and Transjordan) was concerned that the entire Hejaz Government might follow Husein's example, and bring in its wake an influx of undisciplined Saudi tribesmen and war material.[11] It was feared that a focal point for any disturbances might be the town of Maan, sixty miles north-east of Aqaba. Maan was a principal town on the Hejaz Railway which traversed Transjordan from north to south, and which provided the easiest means of communication between Syria and the Hejaz.

Britain's initial response was to warn Ibn Saud away from the area. No sooner did Husein arrive in Aqaba than notes were sent to Ali and Abdullah informing them that Britain regarded Maan as being within Transjordan.[12] A further note was despatched to Ibn Saud via the Political Agent in Bahrain, warning that any unprovoked aggression on his part towards Aqaba and Maan would be regarded as an attack upon territory for which Britain was responsible. In such an eventuality the British Government reserved for itself full liberty of action.[13]

Following this warning to Ibn Saud there were no reports of Wahhabi movements in northern Hejaz, although the siege of Jedda continued. It soon became apparent, however, that Husein's real motive for remaining in Aqaba was to use the town as a base from which to recover his Kingdom. Husein was exploiting his position in order to liaise between Ali and Abdullah.[14] Recruits for Ali's forces, together with war materials from the mandates, were finding their way southwards into Ali's hands.[15] All this the British Government was happy to ignore so long as Ibn Saud kept his distance. Samuel, though, demanded that the Aqaba-Maan region be annexed to Transjordan.[16] More than that, he wanted the annexation undertaken with the full pomp that would accompany the visit of a high-ranking British official to Maan.

Samuel's proposals met with firm opposition from the British Government. Flying the British flag over Maan meant policing and administering the area, which would be both troublesome and expensive, particularly while the chaotic situation in the Hejaz persisted. Economy of administration had been one of Churchill's guiding principles in assuming control of the Arab world for the Colonial Office. Samuel's ideas would have required an increase in the British grant-in-aid to Transjordan.[17] A number of Colonial Office officials hoped to avoid extending formal Transjordanian authority over Maan because increasing the size of the emirate would have increased the share of the Ottoman debt which fell upon its resources.[18]

The Colonial Office was only prepared to sanction measures whose cost would fall elsewhere. To appease Samuel, and make some gesture towards safeguarding the southern part of Transjordan, the Colonial Office sought to extend the control of the Palestine Railway Administration to cover the

Amman-Maan stretch of the Hejaz Railway. Ostensibly, this was designed to benefit future Pilgrimages. Its main purpose, however, was to assert Transjordanian authority over its undefined frontier with the Hejaz.[19]

The Colonial Office planned to finance the policing and security of the Railway at Maan by drawing on the central funds of the Hejaz Railway, which had been frozen by the Treaty of Lausanne. These funds, if secured, would have provided some two thirds of the extra grant-in-aid necessary to extend the administration and policing to the Maan area.[20] This proposal led to a sharp interchange of views with the Foreign Office, who argued that to tamper with the Hejaz Railway for the obvious benefit of British and Christian interests would provide much capital for Arab extremists.[21] The Railway was a pious foundation – a *waqf*. Since the break-up of the Ottoman Empire, Britain had held part of the Railway in trust until the various parties concerned – Britain, France and the Hejaz – could come to some arrangement for operating the Railway over its entire length. To have drawn from the Railway's central funds and used them for the policing of Maan would, felt the Foreign Office, be a departure from the spirit and wording of the Treaty of Lausanne.[22]

The Colonial Office did not have to face these wider responsibilities. If Transjordan hoped to achieve any measure of control over Maan, it would have to be paid for, in part, by local funds.[23] Hitherto it had been established practice for local policing functions to be offset against the central funds of the Hejaz Railway. The Colonial Office argued that policing Maan with Transjordanian officials did not constitute a violation of the terms or the spirit of Lausanne. The tasks of the police would not have been of a 'political' nature.[24] Nonetheless, Foreign Office pressure succeeded in halting the Colonial Office proposal.[25]

It was, nevertheless, difficult to leave matters in their existing unsatisfactory state as regards Transjordan's frontiers. Outside bodies were taking a close interest. The Permanent Mandates Commission of the League of Nations would closely examine dubious methods employed by the mandatory in establishing its authority over ill-defined areas.[26] Moreover, the International Quarantine Organisation was concerned with trying to improve the standards of health and general welfare of Moslem pilgrims. This body was engaged in setting up quarantine stations at all points of entry into the Hejaz. Maan was one such place. The International Quarantine Organisation was embarrassing the British Government by insisting on a quarantine station at Maan, necessitating a swift, public announcement on the whereabouts of the frontier.[27]

Even in the face of a possible Saudi threat to Aqaba and Maan, British complacency impeded common action to forestall that threat. The spur to a more urgent British response came from Ibn Saud. In May 1925, having seen Husein exploit his position in Aqaba for seven months, with the war being drawn out as a result, Ibn Saud announced that a force of *Ikhwan* was marching on Aqaba.[28]

The Birth of Transjordan and the History of Aqaba and Maan

Before proceeding, it is necessary to examine the history of Transjordan and, in addition, of Aqaba and Maan. The area around Aqaba forms the southernmost land crossroads between Arabia and Africa. Disputes over its sovereignty can be traced back to 1841 when, at the Conference of London, Egypt was awarded possession of Sinai and several Red Sea garrison towns, including Aqaba.[29] From the 1890s until 1905 a resurgent Turkey administered Aqaba as part of the *Vilayet* of the Hejaz,[30] whereupon an excessive Turkish presence in Aqaba and Sinai led to unrest in Egypt, a British ultimatum, and a strain in Anglo-Ottoman relations.[31] From that time, the Turks looked after Aqaba through the independent *sanjak* (district) of Medina, before transferring the administration of the town to the *Vilayet* of Damascus in 1910.[32] In contrast, Maan had, since the 1890s, enjoyed uninterrupted administration as part of the *Vilayet* of Damascus.[33] In other words, when the forces of the Arab Revolt occupied Aqaba and Maan in 1917, both places were regarded by the Turks as outside the Hejaz.

The First World War provided the seeds of the later frontier dispute. Hejazis claimed the territorial limits of the Moslem Holy Land as extending northwards beyond Aqaba.[34] From 1917 Husein laid claim to the region on the additional, secular grounds of conquest, and asserted that Medina would be cut off and isolated were it not for access to Aqaba.[35] Yet even in 1917 Britain had no intention of permitting Aqaba to remain in Husein's hands indefinitely. A small fishing port had been turned into a major British base. Clayton warned:

> The occupation of Akaba by an Arab force is open to various objections ... It might result in Arabs claiming that place hereafter ... It is essential that Akaba should remain in British hands after the War.[36]

General Allenby had been given supreme authority over an area liberated from the Turks extending, according to Antonius, to one hundred miles south of Aqaba.[37] The interior of Turkish Syria, from Aleppo to Aqaba, was administered as 'Occupied Enemy Territory Administration (East)', and was governed initially by Feisal from Damascus.[38] It was from OETA (East) that the Emirate of Transjordan was later carved, although throughout the centuries of Ottoman presence in the Fertile Crescent the desert area east of the River Jordan had been largely neglected as a *terra incognita*.

By 1919 British forces had withdrawn from this easterly area leaving the local administrative arrangements confused. In Aqaba, a *qaimmaqam* (district governor) had been appointed who disregarded both Husein in Mecca and Feisal in Damascus with impunity.[39] Another *qaimmaqam* had been appointed by Feisal at Maan, despite Husein having instructed the official at Aqaba to extend his jurisdiction over Maan.[40] Britain, at the same time, decided to develop a joint Arab-Palestine free port in the Aqaba area, though there existed strong doubts over Aqaba's suitability as a future port.[41]

In withdrawing the military Britain was not abandoning her interest east of the River Jordan. In August 1920 Samuel proclaimed that the whole area east and west of the river was under the control of the Palestinian mandate.[42] An excessive British presence was not intended for Transjordan both for financial considerations and because of the risk of increasing local Anglophobia. Instead, Britain resorted to establishing local administrations operating with the assistance of British political officers.[43] Conditions in Transjordan, nevertheless, continued to deteriorate, witnessing frequent bedouin raids into Palestine and Syria.

In the spring of 1921 Britain attempted to retrieve the situation by making use of Abdullah in the development of the mandate policy. There were several reasons for this. Feisal had been ousted from Syria and was destined for the throne of Iraq. In the smaller backwater area of Transjordan, which was too small and politically insignificant to constitute a kingdom,[44] Abdullah could fill the vacuum.[45] He was on the spot, having gathered a force in Amman ready to march against the French in defence of his family's interests.[46] Having Abdullah as ruler of Transjordan would, it was hoped, further fulfil Britain's wartime pledges to his father, but this necessitated a re-examination of the terms of the Palestine mandate. Transjordan was no longer considered as a part of Palestine, but remained within the area administered under the Palestine mandate.[47] The Balfour Declaration, for example, was not to be extended to the Transjordan section of the mandate.[48] In any event, Britain, having withdrawn from Transjordan in a military capacity in 1919, re-established herself in a civil capacity through Abdullah two years later. The economic backwardness of the emirate, and its dependence on British grant-in-aids, served to consolidate British control.

Initially, Transjordan had been of no particular military importance to Britain, although it did form a land link between the Red Sea, Palestine and Iraq, and could assist in protecting the Suez Canal and the proposed over-land route to the Gulf. But with the decision to create air routes to Iraq and India from the Mediterranean, which would change the whole shape of imperial defence, Transjordan became a key unit in the strategy of empire.[49] An airforce base was constructed at Amman, and native recruits organised into the Arab Legion to act as an internal police force.[50]

Ikhwan raids in the summer of 1922 through the ancient caravan route between Nejd and Syria (the Wadi Sirhan) bestowed yet another role upon Transjordan, that of buffer zone for Palestine and Egypt against bedouin raids from Arabia. An effective buffer had to secure the remote area around the Gulf of Aqaba and protect the Hejaz Railway. Philby maintained that when Britain considered sending troops to Maan as an outpost against these Wahhabi attacks, Husein successfully refused permission on the grounds that Maan was part of the Hejaz.[51] Philby also asserted that Lawrence, whom he succeeded as Chief British Representative in Transjordan, wanted Maan within the emirate: Abdullah was to be asked to seek from Husein its transfer to Transjordan.[52] As for Aqaba, it was vested with immense strategic significance. In 1939 the Royal Institute of International Affairs noted:

> Aqaba is of great strategic importance. It is the only town on the east coast of the Red Sea where a harbour could be constructed. Moreover, the route from Palestine to Aqaba is an overland alternative to the sea route by the Suez Canal; for Aqaba could be connected by motor road through Maan to Amman whence there is a road to Jerusalem crossing the Jordan ..., and the connection with Maan also gives railway communications with Syria, Palestine (via Damascus) and the Mediterranean. The construction of a railway down the Wadi Araba from the Dead Sea has also been contemplated. These routes would be of extreme importance for troop transport in the event of the obstruction of the Suez Canal, or in the case of conflict between Transjordan and Saudi Arabia. The importance of Aqaba is enhanced by the possibility that there may be oil in the neighbourhood.[53]

Without access to the sea in the region of Aqaba, Transjordan would have become the only Arab state without access to a port, with the economic and general disadvantages which that entailed. Despite suggestions from British officials in the mandate that Aqaba should become a southern port for Palestine, the Palestine Order-in-Council, in September 1922, defined the western frontier of Transjordan as starting from a point two miles west of Aqaba.[54] To compensate Palestine, a small stretch of coast to the west of Aqaba, around the future port of Eilat, was granted to it.[55]

Two years after the initial British decision to extend the Sherifian solution to Transjordan, Abdullah, in May 1923, proclaimed the independence of the emirate, subject to the restrictions of mandatory control.[56] The need for established frontiers became more important than ever. The abortive Kuwait Conference, which assembled in December of the same year, had on its agenda the recognition of Transjordanian authority over Aqaba and Maan. If Husein objected to this arrangement he was to be offered, as compensation, the towns of Khurma and Turaba on the Hejaz-Nejd frontier which had been under Saudi occupation since 1918.[57] The dissolution of the Conference deferred a settlement of the Aqaba-Maan issue. In any case, even while the Kuwait Conference was in session, early in 1924, Husein had reorganised the administration of Maan, which had effectively been governed from Mecca since Feisal's expulsion from Damascus. Britain offered no objections.[58] Other, non-confirmed reports spoke of Husein on more than one occasion supposedly transferring the area to Abdullah.[59] It was Husein's personal presence in Aqaba from October 1924 and, more particularly, the specific Saudi threat to the area that materialised the following May, that induced the British Government to demonstrate greater resolve in settling the disputed frontier. With the imminent fall of the Hejaz, Britain realised that the notion of leisurely and amicable arrangements with Husein or Ali was no longer viable.[60]

It is important to consider why Husein was allowed to continue thinking that the sovereignty of the Hejaz extended over Aqaba and Maan from 1917 when the British Government all along was determined to exclude the area from the Hejaz. Firstly, the strategic significance of Aqaba must be appreciated. Whoever controlled Aqaba possessed considerable leverage over that part of the Middle East. Effective control of Aqaba required control of its hinterland around Maan. The loss of Maan would cut Aqaba off from Transjordan and invite Wahhabi access to Palestine and Egypt. In addition, it was considered impolitic to inform the instigator of the Arab Revolt that his occupation of Aqaba was to be temporary.[61] Hashemite support for the various stages in Britain's reconstruction of the Middle East had to be secured if possible, and there was little sense in inviting trouble with Husein over Aqaba. There was also the sheer scale of the territories that had fallen before the Arab advance. Prior to the creation of Transjordan it would have been difficult to make out an urgent case for Husein to relinquish control over Aqaba at a time when Hashemites were ruling up to the frontier with Turkey.

After the creation of Transjordan, complacency continued because Aqaba was secure whether it was under the sovereignty of Abdullah or Husein. Furthermore, Husein had turned seventy. If the British Government exercised patience his successor might be more amenable to a satisfactory solution to the Aqaba-Maan problem.[62] Ibn Saud's threat put an end to this complacency.

Husein's Removal: the Annexation of Aqaba and Maan

Britain's reaction to Ibn Saud's threat to Aqaba prompted a rush of interdepartmental correspondence. The seriousness of the threat brought the Cabinet, for the first time, into the handling of Anglo-Saudi relations. Arguments were adduced between and within government departments. The legal position of the undefined frontier was examined, and the possibility of British military intervention also canvassed. The British Government was faced with three pressing questions. What was to be done about Husein? How, and by what means, could Britain use force, if necessary, against marauding Wahhabis in the Aqaba region? And what political measures had to be introduced to clear the confusion surrounding the sovereignty of Aqaba and Maan?

The Foreign Office found itself sorely troubled by the news of Ibn Saud's intent. While acknowledging that the Aqaba-Maan question was primarily the concern of the Colonial Office and the Air Ministry – in their administrative and defensive capacities for Transjordan – the Foreign Office deprecated any arrangement that could lead to trouble with Ibn Saud. The

Foreign Office outlook had undergone something of a metamorphosis since 1915 when it had looked no further than the Hashemites in its Arabian policy. Ibn Saud had not so much been rejected as ignored. By the spring of 1925, however, it was perfectly evident that neither Husein nor his successor Ali could prevent the complete Saudi assimilation of the Hejaz. A Wahhabi regime on the Red Sea was inevitable. The Foreign Office preferred a constructive and conciliatory policy to meet the new regime in the Moslem Holy Land. It was more than just a question of Arabia or the mandates. Empire considerations, namely its one hundred million Moslems, necessitated good relations with the new ruler of Mecca, as they had with the Turks and Husein in earlier days. It was no longer a matter of whether a Saudi Hejaz was preferable to a Hashemite one. The Hashemite regime was about to fall and the Foreign Office wanted to come to terms with that fact. Faced with the inevitable Saudi triumph, and the need to embark upon a fresh policy towards Ibn Saud, the Foreign Office was not averse to a speedy conclusion to the war. If Saudi forces reached Aqaba, thereby cutting the Hejaz Railway, a swift end to the war could be effected, and the need to prolong the siege of Jedda obviated. In these circumstances the Foreign Office saw no overriding reason to obstruct Ibn Saud,[63] particularly when it was conceded that Aqaba belonged to the Hejaz.[64]

The Colonial Office took a narrower and more defensive view. That department had only been dealing with the Middle East for four years, and was responsible for the welfare and security of the mandates. Almost from the moment that the Colonial Office had assumed control of them it had been forced to deal with the Saudi threat from the south, and had sought the incorporation of Aqaba into Transjordan to reduce that threat. From 1922 Saudi menaces had been confined to sporadic raids into Iraq and Transjordan, but by May 1925 the Colonial Office was confronted by the prospect of bitter adversaries of the Hashemites ruling from the Gulf to the Red Sea, and, in addition, occupying territory that ate deep into the underbelly of the Palestine mandate.

Leopold Amery, the Colonial Secretary, demanded immediate military precautions, and an ultimatum to be delivered to Ibn Saud.[65] Amery requested that the Admiralty despatch a sloop to Aqaba forthwith. He was not concerned about the letter of Britain's neutral obligations; about whether Aqaba was or was not part of the Hejaz; or about its abuse by Husein.[66] Amery was a 'staunch and pugnacious imperialist'.[67] He described Aqaba as 'lent' to the Hejaz and insisted that the British Government concentrate upon the central fact that a warning with regard to Aqaba had been delivered to Ibn Saud the previous October. That warning had been disregarded.[68] Amery's assessment invited sharp criticism from the Foreign Office:

> I cannot ease my mind of the conviction that the CO have been gambling with luck and have never taken seriously enough the position of Akaba ... Men have been drafted from the area for the service of

Ali, and Bin Saud has a good deal to be said for his action ... The warning conveyed to him in October 1924 should have rendered it impossible to see that nothing against Bin Saud was done at Akaba or Maan ... We should have been prepared to discuss with him earlier, voluntarily, not now that his threat has wrung it from us.[69]

This raised the problem of communication with Ibn Saud. He had, in 1924, asked for a British representative to be stationed in Nejd. The Colonial Office took the opportunity provided by his threat to Aqaba to come down firmly against this proposal until such time as relations between Nejd and the mandates were more satisfactory.[70] The Foreign Office had been more favourably disposed to the idea. Ibn Saud was simply too powerful to exclude from some form of diplomatic channel, but the Foreign Office concurred in deferring the question until the Aqaba problem was settled.[71] The Foreign Secretary, Sir Austen Chamberlain, took the view that the direct cause of that problem was the inflammatory presence of Husein in Aqaba:

It is monstrous that we should allow Maan and Amman to be used as foci of intrigue and as a recruiting ground for Ali, and at the same time cry 'hands off' to Bin Saud. We have been placed in a thoroughly false position.[72]

Chamberlain's suggestion that Husein be removed was received disapprovingly by Amery, who expressed reluctance in 'hustling' Husein out of Aqaba for fear of its effect on Abdullah. Chamberlain retorted:

Amery objects to hustling Husein unduly, but not to hustling Bin Saud with warships and landing parties. If we don't hustle him he will stay where he is. Amery asks my concurrence in an ultimatum which may lead to war. I will not give it unless Husein is removed without delay – by 'invitation' if possible, but otherwise if necessary. Why should we be involved in war by or for Husein?[73]

These sentiments indicate the final and complete reversal of Foreign Office attitudes in the ten years that had elapsed since the McMahon proposals. By the spring of 1925 Husein was an unmitigated burden on Britain's position in the Arab world. It had been the Foreign Office which had been early associated with Britain's Hashemite policy from 1915. In 1921 control of that policy had passed to the Colonial Office, and by 1925 the Foreign Office was ready to shed its last vestige of commitment to a Hashemite presence in Arabia. Expediency demanded the transfer of Britain's commitment to Ibn Saud. It was not considered how Britain's betrayal of a wartime ally would be interpreted by the watching Arab world. Nor was it anticipated that, in the future, Arabs, including Ibn Saud, could question Britain's sincerity in the light of her treatment of Husein.

Austen Chamberlain had brought a fresh perspective to bear on the office of Foreign Secretary. From 1915-17 he had been Secretary of State for

India, and so was in a position rare in recent Foreign Secretaries – being familiar with the arguments by the advocates of both Husein and Ibn Saud. He was probably the first Foreign Secretary to appreciate the full significance of Ibn Saud, and felt justified in giving himself a pat on the back. 'I have always thought that Bin Saud is the most live man in Arabia ... A general agreement with him would be all to the good'.[74]

The mid-'20s was a relatively quiescent period for European politics. Chamberlain's own commitment to French security, and the need to involve Germany and Italy in the comity of nations, was to lead to the crowning achievement of his tenure as Foreign Secretary – the Locarno Treaty of November 1925. The achievement belonged all the more to Chamberlain in the light of the free hand offered him in foreign affairs, and the loyalty shown him by Prime Minister Baldwin.[75] Chamberlain was even to be accused of forsaking the imperialist traditions of his family in favour of closer British links with Europe.[76]

Chamberlain's association with the Middle East was less tranquil. Shortly after he took office, in November 1924, the assassination occurred, in Cairo, or Sir Lee Stack, Governor-General of the Sudan and Commander-in-Chief of the Egyptian Army. The Foreign Secretary promptly ordered British troops into Cairo and Alexandria.[77] Faced with disorder in the strategically vital Egypt, Chamberlain did not relish continuing chaos and uncertainty on the opposite shore of the Red Sea. Neither did he welcome the prospect of, and implications for, any active British intervention in or around Aqaba. On general matters of policy, however, the relationship between Chamberlain and Amery was cordial. Amery admired Chamberlain as Foreign Secretary.[78] Both men, for example, shared the goal of strengthening the ties between Britain and the self-governing Dominions.[79]

Strategic questions concerning the Hejaz-Transjordan frontier were related to recent political developments in Egypt. If Ibn Saud ever seized Aqaba he would have been able to threaten Sinai. The antipathy between the Egyptians and the Saudis had its roots in the campaigns of Mohammad Ali in the nineteenth century. In 1925, following the unilateral withdrawal of the British Protectorate three years earlier, Egypt was less openly susceptible to British pressure than she had previously been.

Moreover, questions surrounded, and would continue to surround, the extent of Ibn Saud's ultimate territorial ambitions and his control over the more fanatical of his followers. If some of the *Ikhwan* wanted to follow up the conquest of the Hejaz by moving against Transjordan, Palestine or Egypt, Ibn Saud might be powerless to prevent them. In this respect, Ibn Saud was likely to be even less receptive to British diplomatic pressure than the Turks and Husein had been. And, of course, force was impractical for a Christian power to employ in the sacred Hejaz, even in the event of a Saudi assault on the mandates or Egypt. Use of Moslem troops from India would have been equally provocative.

Long before the lifting of the Protectorate over Egypt in 1922 there had been fears that Aqaba might be used as a gateway for arms and ammunition into Egypt.[80] With the creation of the mandates on Egypt's Asian frontier her protective shield had, in effect, been pushed eastwards from Sinai to Transjordan. This safeguard would have been removed if Aqaba fell to the Wahhabis. During the First World War the Germans had hoped to use Aqaba as a submarine base.[81] Those plans had been thwarted by the Arab advance. Nonetheless, officials in Egypt, mindful of that possibility, were uneasy at the prospect of Aqaba falling into dubious foreign hands.[82]

To meet the threat of a Saudi controlled Aqaba, Sinai would have to be strengthened militarily. Such action would, however, conflict with the progress towards Egyptian independence. Britain was pledged to relaxing her military control over Egypt, not tightening it. In addition, maintaining some kind of buffer between the Hejaz and Egypt accorded with the latter's preference, at that time, for retarding any sign of Islamic solidarity.[83] Refusing Ibn Saud access to territory he had never held would, according to this analysis, save Britain much future trouble, as well as avoid the possible effects of appearing to lack imperial muscle.

The above argument was a cogent one in the Colonial Office armoury. Further support came from the Admiralty and, to a lesser extent, the Air Ministry. To the Admiralty, the principal value of the Middle East lay, as it traditionally had done, in its geographical position on the route to the Empire. The Admiralty had always been sensitive about the Red Sea, and urged a firm policy for dealing with all the Arab rulers adjacent to it, whether at Suez, the Bab al Mandab, or in the Gulf of Aqaba. As far as possible, the Admiralty wanted these places, including Aqaba, to be under British control.

The brief of the Air Ministry was less global. The Royal Air Force was still in its infancy, having been constituted as a separate service only in 1918. It had been assigned to the Middle East, along with the Colonial Office, since 1921, when defence of the mandates and the imperial routes designed to pass across them was transferred from the War Offfice to the Air Ministry. The debate over the inclusion of Aqaba in Transjordan had to acknowledge that the defence of the town would fall upon the Air Ministry. The governing factor in fixing the southern and eastern frontiers of Transjordan was, according to this perspective, the extent to which British forces were able to protect those frontiers.

By 1925 the only permanent RAF base in Transjordan was at Amman, which was too far from Aqaba to provide effective aerial defence.[84] The Transjordan contingent of the RAF presence in the Palestine mandate amounted to only four planes.[85] To meet these weaknesses, which were reinforced by the difficulty of ground forces being supplied quickly and easily from Egypt, the Air Ministry preferred that any extension of Transjordanian authority be implemented by political, not military means.

Logistic difficulties for both the RAF and ground forces, coupled with the desire of the Colonial Office and the Air Ministry to minimise the cost of Transjordan's defence,[86] meant that the task of countering the Saudi threat fell to the Admiralty. A sloop was despatched to Aqaba as Amery had requested. A Cabinet sub-committee acknowledged that the political repercussions of this move would be interpreted by Ibn Saud as a further sign of support for the Hashemites.[87] Denying Aqaba to Ibn Saud, but not to Husein, was not consistent with a policy of neutrality, and was admitted as such.[88] Husein's presence in Aqaba had previously passed without British intervention: Ibn Saud's was to warrant a British gunboat.

The British Government decided not to occupy Aqaba by force. Naval action alone was felt to be sufficient to repel any Saudi troops entering the town.[89] The sub-committee also decided that, in the face of Ibn Saud's threatening posture, Transjordanian authority should, after all, be extended over Maan. Husein's claim to the area had been based on its occupation during and after the War. The Hejaz's claim to Aqaba and Maan would, it was decided, extinguish with the demise of Hashemite rule in the Hejaz. The exercise of Transjordanian authority over Maan would pre-empt claims by Ibn Saud to similar rights to the area stemming from conquest.

As for Aqaba, it was decided to administer the town from Maan.[90] The exact date of the incorporation of Aqaba-Maan into Transjordan was to be left to the discretion of local officials. In the event of a prolonged Saudi campaign around Aqaba, in which Transjordanian forces proved inadequate, Britain was to resort to measures agreed upon by the Air-Officer-Commanding Palestine and the General-Officer-Commanding Egypt.[91] Sir Samuel Hoare, Secretary of State for Air, informed the Cabinet that the active assertion of authority by the Palestine mandate over the southern part of Transjordan would require additional manpower and aerial facilities.[92]

The Cabinet sub-committee agreed to Chamberlain's demands that Husein be removed from Aqaba. After several days of delay due to the conflicting perspectives of the Foreign and Colonial Offices, ultimatums were sent to both Husein and Ibn Saud. The latter was warned, once again, not to approach Aqaba or Maan.[93] Husein was 'invited' to leave Aqaba within three weeks.[94] The officer commanding the sloop HMS Cornflower was instructed to remove Husein by force if a Wahhabi threat materialised.[95] The Colonial Office, for all its commitment to the Hashemite presence in Transjordan and Iraq, shared some of the Foreign Office's contempt for Husein. When discussing alternatives for his removal, Husein, himself, had put forward one option – 'the grave'. Vernon, in the Middle Eastern Department, agreed: 'This was Husein's first suggestion and it is no doubt the right one, but the first requisite for a funeral is a willing corpse, and that we have not at present got'.[96]

Despite the ultimatums and the decision to extend Transjordanian authority over the Aqaba-Maan area, the Foreign Office continued to be critical of the Colonial Office, and sought the establishment of an organised policy with regard to the Saudis and Hashemites. Chamberlain's view was quite emphatic:

Either we govern the district and discharge the duties of government, including the preservation of neutrality, or we ought to adandon it to whomever has the power to take and hold it. The policy of the CO is no policy and the CID and the Cabinet must lay down clear lines for our guidance.[97]

Husein was understandably reluctant to yield to the British request for him to vacate Aqaba. His departure would spell the inevitable collapse of Jedda and the end, whether temporarily or otherwise, of his dynasty in the Hejaz. Perhaps for the first time, several voices within the British Government were raised in sympathy for him. It was certainly an ignoble blow to a distinguished family and a staunch ally in the War. His expulsion brought little credit upon the British Government. Instructions were issued to those entrusted with his removal that Husein be treated with as much dignity as the situation would permit. He was even offered some choice as to his place of exile, though his preferences for Baghdad or Amman, or else London, were rejected as constituting too great an embarrassment and political risk to Britain.[98]

Cyprus was eventually settled upon as the most convenient and least politically sensitive place of exile. Husein left Aqaba on 18 June 1925, only to suffer one final humiliation. Cyprus officials, in accordance with their domestic regulations, refused to permit Husein's retainers to bring their personal arms ashore, thus depriving Husein of any bodyguard. This provoked a sharp retort from London and the regulation was put aside. On 6 July Amery announced the annexation of Aqaba and Maan by Transjordan.[99]

Aftermath: The Hadda and the Bahra Agreements

With the incorporation of Aqaba and Maan into Transjordan, the British Government reverted to its policy of neutrality between Ibn Saud and King Ali. Britain declined to intervene unless it was requested by both parties. While Ali welcomed any intervention, Ibn Saud, his victory assured, did not.[100] British interests, however, had to consider Saudi control of Arabia. There were many issues which could be settled by a frank interchange of views with Ibn Saud – notably the troublesome frontiers between his dominions and the British mandates. If Britain delayed in this initiative, Ibn Saud might complete his conquest of the Hejaz and once more turn his attention to the north. Ibn Saud, too, had every incentive to win British goodwill. It was in his interests to force Britain to come to terms with Feisal and Abdullah, and settle the frontier question with Iraq and Transjordan. It was Ibn Saud who first requested discussions on these matters.[101] The British Government chose, as its negotiator, Sir Gilbert Clayton, recently retired as Chief Secretary to the Government of Palestine.

Clayton met with Ibn Saud on the road to Mecca, with Jedda still under siege, in October/November 1925.[102] The outcome was two documents that were to regulate Nejdi relations with Iraq and Transjordan until the 1930s. The Bahra Agreement tightened the administrative and tribal loopholes that had come to light in the Uqair Protocol, which had defined the Iraq-Nejd frontier in 1922. The Hadda Agreement succeeded in the more difficult task of settling the Nejd frontier with Transjordan.[103] These documents finally established the northern frontiers of Nejd. The frontier between the Hejaz and Transjordan remained outstanding. The Hejaz was still in a state of war, and was therefore outside the scope of the discussions. The Hadda and Bahra Agreements covered many of the points intended for discussion at the Kuwait Conference almost two years previously and, between them, provided legal machinery for separating and organising the tribes along the frontiers.[104]

Clayton also took the opportunity to raise the subject of British mediation in the closing stages of the Hejaz-Nejd war. Ibn Saud responded. First of all he attempted to reassure Hejazis that his aims were only to purify the *Kaaba* (the Holy Shrine at Mecca) and to see not annexation, but self-determination for Hejazis.[105] This was followed by Stanley R. Jordan (the Acting British Consul in Jedda, following the departure of Bullard) acting as intermediary for Ali's surrender on 22 December 1925.[106] Ali's lack of popular support could sustain the war no longer. The drawn-out conflict was interfering with the pilgrimage and its exploitation, which provided the basic livelihood of many Hejazis.[107] Jordan was as impressed by Ibn Saud as were others beforehand:

> During this, my first meeting with the Sultan Abdul Aziz, I could hardly withhold my admiration for his charm of manner and the generosity of his nature in his hour of victory. Many of the conditions are pure acts of generosity, and greatly helped to assure the success of the efforts for peace and the prevention of bloodshed.[108]

Ali had won his life but not his throne. He followed his father into exile but went, not to Cyprus, but to his brother Feisal's court in Baghdad. Ibn Saud gave further notice of his intentions through the Mecca newspaper *Umm al Qura*:

> I do not intend to extend my sovereignty over the Hejaz..., our plan is that the Hejaz belongs to Hejazis in regard to its domestic affairs and to the Moslem world by virtue of its possession of the two holy cities..., it will be independent and will follow a neutralist policy. It will not conclude any political or commercial treaty with non-Moslem countries. The Moslem delegates to the Moslem world conference will fix the Hejaz border and organise its financial and administrative systems.[109]

To reassure the anxious Moslem world and emphasise the temporal rather than religious nature of his rule, Ibn Saud convened an International Islamic Conference in Mecca in June 1926. He emphasised his secular title, for he had been proclaimed King of the Hejaz. Ibn Saud was never referred to as Imam.[110] The Conference, when it considered the Hejaz's frontiers, passed a resolution demanding the return of Aqaba and Maan. Whatever Ibn Saud's personal inclination, he had, through the Moslem Conference, become publicly committed to the restoration of Aqaba and Maan to the Hejaz.

Another factor had, by this time, been introduced into the Aqaba-Maan question. Clayton had brought back from his mission to Ibn Saud a formal request for revision of his 1915 treaty with the British Government. As Clayton pointed out, such a request was inappropriate while the Hejaz was in a state of war and the general Arabian situation so uncertain. But with the fall of Jedda and the other besieged towns, and with the encouraging signs emerging from the first months of Saudi administration, a comprehensive British accord with Ibn Saud became a matter of some importance.

In the context of a fresh treaty with the ruler of a united Arabia, Aqaba and Maan took on a different hue. Lack of an immediate breakthrough in the treaty negotiations led to rumours in Palestine and Transjordan that the Aqaba-Maan region was to be returned to the Hejaz in an attempt to smooth the passage of those negotiations. Lord Plumer, the new High Commissioner of Palestine, felt such a prospect to be catastrophic, both for the development of Transjordan and for Empire defence. Cession of the region would have provided evidence of Britain's military weakness, and acted as a fresh stimulus to Arab agitation against European influence.[111] Plumer declined to be held responsible for public security in Transjordan with the limited forces at his disposal if Aqaba and Maan were returned to the Hejaz.[112] The High Commissioner's veiled threat of resignation contrasted sharply with the attitude of the Foreign Secretary:

> I cannot see that these two places are worth the bones of a British Grenadier. Transjordan seems to me to be an ill-controlled country ruled by an inefficient and untrustworthy prince, and a source of nothing but trouble to us.[113]

Chamberlain, it seemed, had quite lost his patience with the Hashemites *per se*.

There was more to Foreign Office unease than just an unwillingness to upset Ibn Saud. With time to stand back and assess the situation free from an atmosphere of war, the legal basis of Transjordan's annexation of Aqaba and Maan appeared thin, as the following quotations illustrate:

> The Akaba question is rather an unpleasant one and I am not satisfied that our claim is watertight.[114]

> I cannot convince myself that our case would appeal to any court or arbitrator.[115]

> I cannot convince myself that this [Ibn Saud's rightful territory] does not include, at any rate in Bin Saud's opinion, all territory that King Husein at any time held.[116]

Such divergences of opinion between the Foreign Office and the Colonial Office, together with Ibn Saud's refusal to agree to the British disposal of the problem, meant that the Aqaba-Maan question would feature prominently in Anglo-Saudi relations in later years. In 1937, for example, the Peel Report on the future of Palestine recommended that Aqaba be retained under mandatory administration.[117] Only in 1965 did the then Saudi King agree to the existing frontiers.[118]

Summary and Conclusions

The acquisition of Aqaba and Maan by Transjordan has been described as one of the most confusing chapters in that country's history.[119] Similarly, Britain's policy of neutrality in the face of the Saudi assault on the Hejaz was, at the very least, contrary to the spirit of the Sherifian solution to British interests in the Arab world. The Foreign Office and the Colonial Office, whatever their other disagreements, were at one in considering Husein a hindrance to those interests. Had Ali succeeded his father earlier, and before the Saudi invasion materialised, a successful Anglo-Hejazi treaty might have pulled British policy in a different direction. Indeed, evidence has already been put forward to suggest that the British Government was waiting for the death of Husein in order to reach an agreement with his successor over the transfer of the Aqaba area to Transjordan.[120] Certainly, Ibn Saud was the prime beneficiary of British disaffection with Husein, and the policy of neutrality that ensued from it.

Britain's neutrality also reaffirmed her traditional non-involvement in Arabian affairs at the expense of the more recently acquired Sherifian solution to the Arab world. From 1925 that 'solution' would be restricted to the mandates themselves. This accorded with a narrower definition of British strategic and imperial interests, divested of fading wartime sentiments. This was not because of the attractiveness of Ibn Saud, who must have posed, in modern parlance, an 'Ayatollah-like' figure to Britain, but because of frustration with Husein. In effect, Husein was sacrificed by Britain for the strategic advantage of seeking stable frontiers for the mandates.[121]

An important question concerns the extent of British surprise at Ibn Saud's attack on the Hejaz. The British general public, it seemed, was not surprised. A letter to *The Times* in 1922 had warned:

> It is a fact that since the British Cabinet set up Abdulla beyond the Jordan and Feisal in Iraq nothing much stands between the ravaging of Mecca and Medina by Bin Saud's Wahabite followers except the £60,000 *per annum* which the British taxpayer pays Bin Saud to avert this calamity. That the charm will work permanently is improbable.[122]

It has been argued that when Husein assumed the Caliphate, thereby provoking the wrath of the Moslem world:

> The British realised that they had backed the wrong horse all the time. The very basis of the sherifian policy completely disappeared. Husein was not the Moslem rallying point ... Why then should they continue to subsidize Ibn Saud in order to prevent him from attacking Husein? ... The British stopped the £5,000 monthly subsidy to Ibn Saud thus giving clear notice to Husein's rival that he was free to deal with his enemy as he saw fit.[123]

This extreme view, suggesting that it was almost a British objective for Ibn Saud to oust Husein, is untenable. None of the documentary evidence suggests that the British Government was seeking Saudi hegemony at the expense of Hashemite hegemony in the Hejaz. Disenchantment with Husein was more likely aimed at replacing him by an alternative Hashemite ruler; not turning the Hejaz over to Ibn Saud, who was a proven enemy of the Hashemites. British policy-makers, in the main, still operated in 1924-25 in considerable ignorance of Ibn Saud. This was reinforced by the reduction of Indian influence in British foreign policy. If the British Government held any discernible attitude towards Ibn Saud it was apprehension at the excesses of Wahhabism and the effects of fanatical Islamic fundamentalism on Britain's interests in the Moslem world. There was no conscious question asked about whether to choose between Hashemite or Saudi rule in the Hejaz.

Ever since Ibn Saud had halted his advance into the Hejaz following the First World War, the British Government had doubted his capacity, or will, to conquer the Hejaz, particularly if that meant invoking the displeasure of London. Lord Curzon, for example, when Foreign Secretary, had tried to reassure Feisal that the Saudi threat to the Hejaz was exaggerated.[124] Early in 1924, as the Kuwait Conference began to disintegrate, reports from Iraq warned of Ibn Saud 'blazing out' against the Hashemites.[125] After Husein's assumption of the Caliphate, war preparations were reported from Nejd.[126] It seems, though, that Iraq and Transjordan were expected to bear the brunt of Saudi aggression. Indeed, major *Ikhwan* raids into the mandates did precede the actual invasion of the Hejaz.

Furthermore, the decision to wind up the Arabian subsidies was taken in March 1923, a year before the precise date of expiry.[127] British policy in Arabia was never sufficiently co-ordinated as to conspire for Husein's removal, let alone by a Wahhabi. The decision to conclude the policy of subsidies to rulers in eastern and southern Arabia, including that to Ibn Saud, was taken quite independently of any ideas to further his ambitions. If Ibn Saud was expected to become Lord of Arabia then the British Government might have wanted to increase its favour with him, not sever it at such an inopportune moment by withdrawing the subsidy. It was economic arguments alone that dictated the cessation of the Arab subsidies.

As long as Hashemites governed from both Amman and Mecca, the British Government showed little enthusiasm for the cost and bother of extending Transjordanian authority over its remote southern regions. Britain's argument for denying Aqaba and Maan to Ibn Saud was that Husein's claim to the area was taken to be political, not religious: based on wartime conquest and subsequent administration, not on what Husein professed constituted the inviolable jurisdiction of the Moslem Holy Land. Yet this argument lay uneasily alongside Britain's wider perspective on the Hejaz-Nejd war, for her neutrality had stemmed precisely from the war being considered as a religious, not political, conflict.

Aqaba and Maan were crucial to the Colonial Office, but only distractions to the Foreign Office who considered that to appease Ibn Saud on the vexed question of the Hejaz-Transjordan frontier carried greater political dividends than antagonising him by insisting on a conspicuous Hashemite presence in Aqaba, which appeared to be rightfully part of the Hejaz. The provision of only nominal defences in southern Transjordan would not, in any case, have kept out a determined force of *Ikhwan*.

It is possible that Ibn Saud had 'put one over' on the British Government. His forces did not attack Aqaba. Nor are there any recorded movements of hostile Wahhabis congregating around the area. Ibn Saud may well have calculated that Britain would remove Husein for him without involving bloodshed and strained relations with London.

The pattern of territorial disputes involving the British Government with Ibn Saud had begun over the Hejaz in 1918, then turned to the mandates, and culminated back in the Hejaz in 1925. The territorial limits of modern Saudi Arabia had almost been reached. At the same time, Britain had strengthened her control over the Arab world. The acquisition of Aqaba gave Britain control of the fourth and final corner of Arabia. Yet the annexation of Aqaba-Maan by Transjordan did not close that particular episode in Anglo-Saudi relations. The repercussions persisted throughout the inter-war years and provided a foretaste of more protracted territorial disputes in the 1930s. Nonetheless, the culmination of the Hejaz-Nejd war, and the various efforts to settle Ibn Saud's northern frontiers through a combination of British annexation and Clayton's diplomacy, paved the way for a complete re-examination of British relations with Ibn Saud.

REFERENCES FOR CHAPTER TWO

1. See p. 51.
2. Baker, p. 209.
3. CID Sub-Committee on Situation in Akaba, 3 June 1925, Secret 613-B, CAB 16/60. (Hereafter: CAB 16/60.)
4. Husein had quarrelled with Britain over Palestine, France over Syria, India over the

Pilgrimage, his sons over their betrayal in accepting British mandates, Egypt over the pretensions of King Fuad, and Ibn Saud (Baker, p. 173).

5. Baker, p. 174.
6. Helms, p. 119.
7. Troeller, p. 219.
8. The religious sensitivity of Mecca meant that foreign representatives were confined to Jedda – the port of Mecca and commercial centre of the Hejaz.
9. Bullard to Ryan, 23 December 1923, Ryan Papers, Box 6, File 5, MEC.
10. See FO E/389/68/91: 371/10815.
11. Morgan (FO) memorandum, 22 May 1925, FO E/2990/10/91: 371/10808.
12. CAB 16/60.
13. CO to Ibn Saud, 15 October 1924, in FO E/2990/10/91: 371/10808.
14. FO memorandum, 6 January 1925, FO E/37/10/91: 371/10808.
15. Bullard to FO, No 79, 20 May 1925, FO E/2958/10/91: 371/10808.
16. Samuel to CO, 19 December 1924, in FO E/96/68/91: 371/10814.
17. CAB 16/60.
18. Mallet (FO) minute, 16 January 1925, FO E/96/68/91: 371/10814. With the dismemberment of the Ottoman Empire its long-established public debt was divided among the detached territories.
19. Mallet (FO) minute, 13 March 1925, see FO E/1495/68/91: 371/10815.
20. CAB 16/60.
21. Mallet minute, op. cit.
22. Shearman (FO) minute, 14 March 1925, FO E/1495/68/91: 371/10805.
23. Samuel to CO, 7 March 1925, ibid.
24. Shuckburgh to FO, ibid.
25. CAB 16/60.
26. Benjamin Shwadran, *Jordan: A State of Tension*, p. 157. (Hereafter: *Jordan* ...).
27. Mallet minute, 26 January 1925, see FO E/389/68/91: 371/10815.
28. Bullard to FO, No 76, 17 May 1925, FO E/2858/10/91: 371/10808.
29. H. H. Frischwasser-Ra'anan, *Frontiers of a Nation: A Re-evaluation of the Forces which Created the Palestine Mandate and Determined its Territorial Shape*, p. 35. This settlement followed Mohammad Ali's withdrawal from Arabia.
30. Mallet memorandum, 'Transjordan's Claim to Akaba and Maan', 22 October 1926, FO E/5967/572/91: 371/11444. (Hereafter: FO memo 1926.).
31. Lord Lloyd (Cairo) to Chamberlain, No 821, 31 December 1926, FO E/156/156/91: 371/12247. Britain feared the Turks building an extension to the Hejaz Railway in 1906 from Maan to Aqaba. This would have linked the Mediterranean and the Red Sea, by-passing British control of the existing access between the two seas via the Suez Canal (Frischwasser Ra'anan, p. 38).
32. British Embassy Istanbul to FO, 23 September 1935, FO E/5944/341/25: 371/19011.
33. ibid.
34. FO memo 1926. This claim is questionable. Although the Ottoman *Vilayet* of the Hejaz extended northwards to around Aqaba, the emirate, under the authority of the Grand Sherif, extended, according to Baker, only to the ruins of Medain Saleh, between Aqaba and Medina (Baker, p. 31).
35. See FO E/3143/10/91: 371/10808.
36. Brig. Gen. Clayton, FO memo 1926.
37. FO memo 1926. This is a matter of some confusion. According to Frischwasser Ra'anan, Occupied Enemy Territory Administrations stopped well north of Aqaba, which was cleary marked within the independent Hejaz (Frischwasser-Ra'anan, p. 153).
38. Antonius, p. 281.
39. Shwadran, op. cit., p. 123. It is not clear who appointed the *qaimmaqam*.
40. ibid.
41. Frischwasser-Ra'anan, pp. 105–6. For a detailed survey of the question of Palestine's southern frontier, see pp. 97–141.
42. Shwadran, op. cit., p. 125.
43. ibid.
44. The population of Transjordan by 1938 was estimated at only 300,000.
45. A.H.H. Abidi, *Jordan: A Political Study 1948-1957*, p. 6.

46. Abdullah was offered Transjordan on condition that he refrain from attacking Syria (Frischwasser-Ra'anan, p. 139).
47. Shwadran, op. cit., p. 138..
48. The setting-up of an independent Transjordan deprived Palestine of two-thirds of its area.
49. Shwadran, op. cit., p. 144.
50. RIIA, *Political and Strategic Interests* ..., p. 154.
51. H. St J.B. Philby, *The Observer*, 15 August 1926.
52. H. St J.B. Philby, *Forty Years in the Wilderness*, pp. 99-100. (Hereafter: *Forty Years* ...)
53. RIIA, op. cit., p. 153.
54. Abidi, p. 7.
55. Frischwasser-Ra'anan, p. 140.
56. Abdullah's proclamation necessitated a comprehensive agreement with Britain. This document was not completed until February 1928.
57. FO memo 1926.
58. CAB 16/60.
59. See Troeller, p. 222; Shwadran, op. cit., p. 155; Philby, *The Observer*, 15 August 1926.
60. FO memo 1926.
61. ibid.
62. ibid.
63. Morgan (FO) minute, 18 May 1925, FO E/2858/10/91: 371/10808.
64. Bullard to FO, No 79, 20 May 1925, FO E/2958/10/91: 371/10808; CAB 16/60.
65. Amery to Chamberlain, 21 May 1925, FO E/2966/165/91: 371/10817.
66. Osborne (FO) minute, 23 May 1925, FO E/2990/10/91: 371/10808.
67. Troeller, p. 225.
68. Osborne minute, op. cit.
69. Oliphant (FO) minute, 23 May 1925, FO E/2990/10/91: 371/10808.
70. CO to FO, 23 May 1925, FO E/2997/165/91: 371/10817.
71. Morgan minute, 25 May 1925, ibid.
72. Chamberlain minute, 23 May 1925, FO E/2990/10/91: 371/10808.
73. Chamberlain minute, 25 May 1925, ibid.
74. Chamberlain minute, 17 June 1925, FO E/3515/10/91: 371/10808. Curzon's experience of India as Viceroy at the turn of the century had concluded before the Saudi grip on Nejd had consolidated. Chamberlain had also been offered the Viceroyalty, in 1920, but had declined it (Petrie, ... *Austen Chamberlain, Vol II*, p. 153).
75. ibid., p. 246.
76. Sir Charles Petrie, *The Chamberlain Tradition*, p. 175.
77. ibid., p. 190.
78. Rt Hon. L.S. Amery, *My Political Life: Vol II – War and Peace*, p. 298.
79. Roskill, p. 401.
80. Lloyd to Chamberlain, 31 December 1926, FO E/156/156/91: 371/12247.
81. ibid.
82. ibid.
83. ibid. (see Chapter Ten).
84. Vernon (CO) to FO, 23 May 1925, FO E/2990/10/91: 371/10808.
85. Hoare to CID sub-committee, 22 June 1925, (315/25) CAB 24/174.
86. Amery to CID sub-committee, ibid.
87. CAB 16/60.
88. ibid.
89. ibid.
90. ibid. There were no permanent officials in Aqaba.
91. CID sub-committee, op. cit.
92. CID sub-committee, 1 July 1925, 32(25)5, CAB 23/50.
93. FO memorandum, 1 May 1925, FO E/2247/2247/91: 371/10820.
94. Telegram to *HMS Cornflower*, 27 May 1925, FO E/2990/10/91: 371/10808.
95. ibid.
96. Vernon minute, 4 June 1925, CO/25235/25: 727/10.
97. Chamberlain minute, 2 June 1925, FO E/3149/10/91: 371/10808.
98. See FO E/3515/10/91: 371/10808.

99. Amery in House of Commons, 6 July 1925, Parl. Debates. Commons, Vol 186, Cols: 44-45. Husein died in Amman in June 1931.
100. The Egyptian Government made a futile attempt at mediation.
101. Ibn Saud to HMG, 30 June 1925, IO L/P&S/10/1144.
102. See Clayton's Diary of his Mission to Ibn Saud 1925, Clayton Papers, Box 1, File 4, MEC.
103. See CO/55640/25 in FO E/7696/165/25: 371/10808.
104. Helms, p. 222. This scholar has suggested that the two agreements were substantial triumphs for Ibn Saud. The Transjordan-Nejd frontier was drawn in such a way as to give Ibn Saud the strategic advantage of possessing the Wadi Sirhan. He also seemed to have won benign British neutrality towards his actions. It should be added that the Hadda and Bahra Agreements were equally to the advantage of Britain. Stability in northern Arabia had been encouraged, and formal acknowledgement received of the mandate corridor to the Gulf. The Clayton mission was hailed in Britain as a considerable success.
105. *Umm al Qura*, 6 November 1925, in FO E/7385/10/91: 371/10810.
106. See FO E/33/11/91: 371/11432. The towns of Medina and Yanbo surrendered during the same month.
107. Sir Reader Bullard, *The Camels Must Go*, p. 140.
108. Jordan (Jedda) to FO, 28 December 1925, FO E/363/11/91: 371/11432.
109. *Umm al Qura*, 27 December 1925, in M. Al Jazairi, *Saudi Arabia: A Diplomatic History* (Unpublished Ph. D.), p. 40.
110. Helms, p. 110.
111. Plumer to Amery, 27 January 1927, CO/44130/27: 733/134.
112. ibid.
113. Chamberlain minute, 19 November 1926, FO E/5967/572/91: 371/11444.
114. Mallet (FO) minute, 23 August 1926, FO E/4913/572/91: 371/11444.
115. Oliphant minute, 16 December 1926, FO E/6874/572/91: 371/11444.
116. Oliphant minute, 11 January 1927, FO E/156/156/91: 371/12247.
117. RIIA, *Political and Strategic Interests* ..., p. 154 (see Chapter Ten).
118. Kelly, *Arabia* ..., p. 236.
119. Shwadran, *Jordan* ..., p. 154.
120. FO memo 1926 (see page 44).
121. Helms, p. 251.
122. Arthur Moore to *The Times*, 10 July 1922.
123. Shwadran, op. cit., pp. 153-4.
124. Klieman, p. 100.
125. Troeller, p. 209.
126. ibid.
127. ibid., p. 193.

CHAPTER THREE

The Anglo-Saudi Treaty of 1927
(The Treaty of Jedda)

The external impact of the Saudi conquest of the Hejaz was considerable. For the first time in many centuries Hashemites had been expelled from the Moslem Holy Land. Now that Britain had secured her position in southern Transjordan by annexing Aqaba and Maan, and settled the shape of the corridor across to the Gulf, she had to think in terms of formal relations with Ibn Saud. Her first task was to acknowledge the complete shift in Arabian politics and put Anglo-Saudi relations on a new upgraded footing through a fresh treaty that reflected the new stature of Ibn Saud.

British Recognition of Ibn Saud

On 8 January 1926 the leading civic figures in Mecca, Medina and Jedda proclaimed Ibn Saud King of the Hejaz. This was the first time Ibn Saud had ever been referred to as King (he remained for the time being Sultan of Nejd and its Dependencies).[1] Despite his earlier reassurances regarding the independence of the Hejaz, Ibn Saud was acclaimed King in natural succession to the Hashemites.[2] Through conquest the nature of Ibn Saud's dominions had changed. Previously he had ruled over small towns, tribes and oasis dwellers where few outsiders had penetrated. Capture of the Hejaz brought Ibn Saud to the attention of the outside world. The Hejaz had diplomatic and consular connections with European and Moslem countries. Ibn Saud's rule, and the legacy of Wahhabi propagation of Islam, came under the gaze of the world.

All this prompted a crisp debate within the British Government. How should it respond to Ibn Saud's assumption of the Hejaz throne? Should it recognise his new status, and if so, when and how? Should Britain bestow recognition upon Ibn Saud immediately, or pause to assess the aftermath of his victory? Should she recognise his legal, *de jure* authority over the Hejaz, or restrict herself to a more cautious acknowledgement of his *de facto* position?

Even before the respective arguments had had time to be aired, a minor incident created some embarrassment in London. *HMS Cornflower*, the sloop which had been despatched to Aqaba the previous spring, was scheduled to put into Jedda on 19 January. Her captain properly enquired after the correct naval gun salute for Ibn Saud.[3] Husein had customarily been treated to the traditional twenty-one gun salute for an independent monarch. Gulf sheikhs, such as the Sheikh of Mohammera, received thirteen guns.[4] Ibn Saud was, on the one hand, a Gulf ruler. On the other, he was King of the Hejaz, though as yet unrecognised as such by Britain. Rather than confront the issue the ship was initially instructed not to stop at Jedda at all,[5] though the captain was later authorised to put in and give a full, twenty-one gun salute, not in recognition of Ibn Saud's legitimate rule, but as a personal honour pending recognition.[6]

Over the Aqaba-Maan dispute the principal protagonists within the British Government had been the Foreign Office and the Colonial Office, in their respective capacities towards the Hejaz and Transjordan. The Colonial Office had no stake in the question of the recognition of Ibn Saud, which was a purely Hejazi affair. Its place as co-formulator with the Foreign Office in considering recognition and Ibn Saud's subsequent treaty revision was taken by the India Office. Any British recognition of a Wahhabi regime controlling Mecca had to take account of the susceptibilities of Indian Moslems.

Although Ibn Saud had won widespread Moslem sanction for purification of its Holy Places, the Islamic world watched anxiously in case Wahhabi malpractices exceeded those of the Hashemites. Shiite Moslems from Persia, and some from India, had never recognised any Caliph. Nor were they necessarily well-disposed towards Wahhabism.[7] India might interpret Ibn Saud as a British stooge if his rule was immediately endorsed from London. Many Indian Moslems, it was believed, would have preferred the ruler of the Hejaz to be nominated by the united voice of Islam – not by a Saudi *fait accompli* sanctioned by the British Government.[8] Indeed, the likelihood that Ibn Saud would not be the unanimous choice of the Moslem world may have been an additional factor behind his securing the throne for himself so quickly.

The India Office wanted to avoid any accusation that Britain had encouraged Ibn Saud's offensive and meddled in the affairs of Islam. It wanted to defer recognition until such time as a Moslem state or responsible institution had set an example, particularly as Ibn Saud had not specifically requested British recognition.[9] Doubts about British disinterest in Arabia might be raised if, having shown no sign of favour during the course of the Hejaz-Nejd war, Ibn Saud's victory was immediately endorsed. The title 'King of the Hejaz' had been introduced in 1916 for Husein by the allied governments because it carried the least pan-Arab implications. But that title could not easily be disassociated from the religious links with Mecca.[10] Lord Birkenhead, Secretary of State for India, had his own solution: to address Ibn Saud orally and in correspondence as King of the Hejaz, yet refrain from any action which could be interpreted as a formal declaration recognising his independence.[11]

The India Office was not alone in wanting to delay recognition of

Ibn Saud. In the mandates, too, Feisal and Abdullah were angered by the prospect of Britain's acquiescence in Ibn Saud's success.[12] He had, they argued, already gone back on his public pledges not to extend Saudi sovereignty over the Hejaz. The Acting High Commissioner in Iraq feared that Feisal's response would be to delay ratification of the Bahra Agreement recently negotiated on Iraq's behalf by Sir Gilbert Clayton.[13]

The anxieties of the India Office stemmed primarily from religious considerations. The Foreign Office, aware of this, had no intention of recognising Ibn Saud as Caliph. The Caliphate was the depository of all religious, political and military power in the Moslem community, and was the only legitimate political institution in Islam.[14] If it was a matter of Ibn Saud becoming Caliph, Britain would indeed have sought to delay recognition, at least to follow that of another Moslem country. As it was, Ibn Saud had taken the secular title of King, not Caliph.

Sir Austen Chamberlain wanted to accord *de jure* recognition of Ibn Saud's position in the Hejaz from the moment he had been pronounced King.[15] This implied neither moral approval of the new order, nor condemnation of its predecessor. Alienating Ibn Saud at such a time might, reasoned Chamberlain, lead to unforeseen repercussions for the Moslem parts of the Empire. The Foreign Office was ill-inclined to subordinate its policy to the religious sentiments of Indian Moslems who seemed to disagree upon everything except opposition to British imperialism. To delay recognition, as the India Office was proposing, would have meant, in practice, delaying it until after the Pilgrimage in May. By then Ibn Saud would have been too distracted by domestic matters to give much thought to British recognition, and long before then he would have wanted to know why he was not being addressed correctly.[16] France, too, eager to pursue her own interests in the Arab world, was likely to lose no opportunity in extending full recognition upon Ibn Saud, and, in so doing, perhaps assuming the predominant European influence with him.[17]

The Colonial Office, similarly, saw no pressing political reasons to delay *de jure* recognition.[18] Withholding it would, if anything, make Ibn Saud more of a threat to British interests. Nonetheless, swift recognition, as proposed by the Foreign Office, was viewed with some distaste:

> FO alacrity to help Bin Saud is almost indecent. They consistently refused to help poor old Husein for fear of ... making it appear that HMG were trying to interfere. But as soon as the Hejaz falls into strong hands, the FO falls all over them.[19]

The Foreign Office was unimpressed by arguments that Britain should wait for some Moslem state to recognise the Wahhabi regime. If Britain, which in Ibn Saud's eyes was a powerful state, hung back and took her cue from the likes of Egypt, Persia, or even Afghanistan, then 'our position is parlous'.[20] In any case, the only Moslem country in 1926 with consular representation in the Hejaz was Egypt. The historical animosity between

Nejd and Egypt was unlikely to lead to early Egyptian recognition. King Fuad entertained ideas of establishing an Egyptian Governorship or Vice-royalty over the Hejaz, as in the Sudan, and had canvassed the strength of Moslem support for his own claims to the Caliphate.[21] The rise of Saudi power hindered his ambitions.

As the weeks passed and Ibn Saud's hold on the Hejaz consolidated, the Foreign Office continued to urge recognition, 'acquiring such kudos as is to be gained therefrom'.[22] Contrary to India Office apprehension that hasty recognition would imply British favour with Ibn Saud, delaying that recognition, according to the Foreign Office, implied regret at the expulsion of the Hashemites.[23] But should that recognition, when it came, be de facto or de jure? There were those, even within the Foreign Office, who acquiesced in the idea of de facto recognition of the new King, but who hesitated in the face of de jure recognition because of the greater implication of interference in Moslem affairs.[24]

The very suggestion of such legalistic niceties as de facto versus de jure recognition in the context of a raw desert chief, as if he was head of state of a rival European power, seems curiously self-defeating. Having to explain the difference between the two to an Arab chief untutored in western law could have been interpreted as hair-splitting, or else raised Ibn Saud's suspicions that Britain did not really want to recognise him at all.[25] Explaining the distinction, and then offering the less prestigious alternative, would have caused more problems than if the distinction was overlooked.

To meet Indian objections, the Foreign Office agreed to recognise Ibn Saud only as temporal ruler of the Hejaz, insisting that all religious questions were solely for Moslem concern.[26] He was recognised as 'King of the Hejaz, and Sultan of Nejd and its Dependencies' on 25 February 1926, some seven weeks after his assumption of the throne. Britain decided upon de jure recognition,[27] but was not the first state to recognise him. That honour fell to the Soviet Union, who had Moslem interests of her own and who wanted to embarrass Britain in the Middle East.[28] The Soviet representative in the Hejaz, Kerim Hakimov, technically became the doyen of the diplomatic community in Jedda.[29] Within ten weeks of being crowned King of the Hejaz, Ibn Saud had been recognised by the Soviet Union, Britain, France and the Netherlands,[30] but not by a single Islamic state.[31]

British recognition was a considerable coup for Ibn Saud. In August of the same year he displayed his gratitude by suggesting that his son Faisal[32] visit Britain and also those other European states, together with the Soviet Union, which had accorded recognition.[33] This gesture would bring further international attention to his regime, but was considered embarrassing for the British Government. Recognising Ibn Saud was one thing: flaunting it quite another. If Faisal's visit was made official it might be viewed in India as a further sign of Britain's support for her Saudi puppet.[34] Rather than involve the Bolshevik Government even deeper in Saudi affairs, Ibn Saud was dissuaded from including the Soviet Union in Faisal's itinerary; it being suggested that Moscow was too cold for someone used to the deserts of Arabia![35] Attempts were also made, unsuccessfully, to get the French and Dutch Governments to discourage Faisal's visit to their countries.[36] Visits of this kind were awkward for their 'attendant bother and expense',[37] and might compromise the renegotiation of the 1915 treaty.[38] It was considered whether to fob Ibn Saud off with the excuse that King George V and most of his Ministers would be on holiday and unable to entertain Faisal.[39]

At the same time, the visit provided an opportunity for Britain to demonstrate her warm sentiments to Ibn Saud in view of the coming treaty revision. The warmth of Faisal's welcome would be compared with that of his earlier visit in 1919, and that of Abdullah in 1922.[40] As Faisal's itinerary included France and the Netherlands, Britain felt duty bound to make hers the more lavish and impressive stay, particularly in view of the importance attached by Arabs to matters of hospitality. All three states insisted upon the visits remaining unofficial. Faisal, whose trip to Britain lasted from September to October 1926, was granted an audience with King George and also decorated with the KCMG – Honorary Knight Commander of the Most Distinguished Order of St Michael and St George.[41]

British Arms and Finance

The treaty that had emerged from the ill-fated journey of Captain Shakespear in 1915 was patently inappropriate to the circumstances of 1926. That document had come about through the exigencies of war. It had dealt with Ibn Saud in the manner of a Gulf sheikh and been confined to essentials. The wartime situation that gave rise to the treaty no longer existed. In 1915 Ibn Saud had held only Nejd and Hasa. By 1926 his territory had expanded to include not only Jabal Shammar and Jauf to the north, but the sacred Hejaz to the west. Unless the existing treaty was revised Ibn Saud could have stood accused in Arab eyes of admitting a Christian power to an exclusive or protectorate position in the Hejaz.[42] In reality, the 1915 treaty only applied to territories then under Ibn Saud's control, though its general vagueness may have encouraged confusion on that point.[43]

Besides wanting a revision of his treaty, Ibn Saud had an eye on more practical favours, such as financial assistance and the importation of British arms.[44] The question of financial assistance was a delicate matter for an independent Arab king. No Arab could openly take aid and assistance from a western nation without it being considered as 'colonial assistance'.[45] Nor was there any question of British subsidies being reintroduced into Arabia.[46] Moreover, as Ibn Saud could count on the Pilgrimage as a future source of revenue, his financial position might have improved, although those revenues had to cater for the whole breadth of his dominions. An inter-departmental conference agreed to dispense with any specific aid programme to Ibn Saud for fear that it would be misinterpreted in Moslem quarters as an attempt to gain control over the Holy Places.[47]

The arms question proved more complex. Britain, France, Belgium, Italy and Japan had subscribed to Arms Traffic Conventions in 1919 and 1925 which banned licences for the export of munitions to, among other areas, Arabia.[48] British neutrality in the Hejaz-Nejd war provided a further reason for withholding arms shipments to either combatant. Ibn Saud would only become eligible for arms when he could demonstrate his complete control over the Hejaz. There again, arms shipped to Arabia might easily be employed against the surviving Hashemites, in the mandates, and provide further evidence to Indian Moslems of Britain's commitment to Ibn Saud.[49] Furthermore, British arms supplies to Ibn Saud might lead to the Italian Government supplying arms to the Yemen, where they would doubtless be used against the Aden Protectorate.[50]

The Foreign Office and the Colonial Office agreed that the case for allowing arms supplies was stronger than that for continuing the embargo. Arms supplies could secure goodwill and, hopefully, a predominant British influence in Arabia.[51] By supplying British arms it also became easier to control the supply of ammunition were they to be directed at British interests. The surrender of Jedda and Medina would already have yielded caches of Hashemite arms to Ibn Saud, and, if Britain declined to supply him with any more, he could simply get them elsewhere.[52] Expediency conflicted with principle. The Foreign Office considered that:

> It is necessary to weigh the cogent arguments of expediency against the not altogether unconvincing arguments of principle ... It is not good to arm all the Arabs, especially when that involves commercial advantage ..., we could satisfy our qualms of conscience by blaming the Italians.[53]

The British embargo on arms to Arabia was lifted, with the exception of the Yemen, which was creating difficulties on the frontier of the Aden Protectorate, in June 1926.[54] As Ibn Saud was in contact with so many vital British interests the decision to allow him British arms can be seen to thrust Britain even deeper into the role of policeman of Arabia. To Britain, earning Ibn Saud's gratitude by supplying him with arms carried greater logic than the risk of those arms being used either against the mandates, or by a handful of *Ikhwan* fanatics against Ibn Saud himself. Rival European influence had to be excluded from the peninsula. Rather than Italy or France arming Ibn Saud, Britain preferred to retain her pre-eminence in all matters affecting him. The decision to grant Ibn Saud arms, yet deny him purely financial assistance, accorded with the economising principle behind Britain's Middle Eastern policy. Selling arms to Ibn Saud made business sense: giving him financial aid did not.

The Treaty of Jedda, May 1927

By the spring of 1926 the British Government had agreed to renegotiate the 1915 Saudi treaty. In taking this step Britain was obliged, from the outset, to offer Ibn Saud a treaty with fewer restrictions on his complete independence than that with any previous Arab ruler. Not only would the new treaty have to dispense with all the restrictive clauses of the 1915 treaty, but, with captured Hashemite documents in his possession, Ibn Saud would be able to compare the terms offered to him with those offered to Husein in the draft Anglo-Hejazi treaty of April 1923.[55] Moreover, Clayton had just made an abortive attempt to win a treaty with the other independent Arabian ruler, the Imam Yahya of the Yemen.[56] As Clayton observed, if Britain sought to make a treaty with the Imam, who had been an enemy during the War, she could hardly refuse revision of Ibn Saud's treaty, nor give him less favourable terms, when he had been an ally.[57]

The mistakes learned from the failure of Husein's treaty ensured the better prospects of Ibn Saud's. Husein's proposed treaty was a document of inordinate complexity, running into some twenty Articles. That with Ibn Saud would have to be more straightforward. No attempt could be made to compel him to recognise Britain's obligations to the Zionists, as had happened with Husein. Not only would Ibn Saud have refused, as had Husein before him, but the attempt would have brought universal Moslem criticism upon Britain. Clayton's opinion was that Britain's predominant position in Arabia could best be served by a simple gesture of mutual confidence with Ibn Saud. For that reason, there was no necessity for the treaty, any more than its 1915 predecessor, to be too detailed.[58]

Clayton, with the successful Hadda and Bahra Agreements behind him, and the rapport established with Ibn Saud, was the obvious choice to lead the negotiations. He was, however, unavailable, and the task fell initially to the inexperienced Acting Consul in Jedda, Stanley Jordan.[59] Both Ibn Saud and the British Government preferred that the treaty be hastily concluded. Ibn Saud wanted to display it to the coming Islamic Conference and Pilgrimage. Friction with the Imam over the tiny sandwiched principality of Asir provided another explanation for Ibn Saud's urgency: he might try to invoke his treaty against Yemeni aggression.[60] Britain, too, saw reasons for haste, preferring the treaty to be completed before the influx of 'every anti-British pilgrim, Indian seditionist and Bolshevik' during the Pilgrimage pressed Ibn Saud to raise his demands.[61] Delay could find the Arabian situation changing once again. Other powers might have become involved. Quick completion of the treaty might also have a salutory effect on the Imam, and encouraged him to be more amenable to the terms of an Anglo-Yemeni treaty.

It soon became apparent that the treaty revision would be a long and complex business. This was not so much because of disagreement between Ibn Saud and the British Government: the treaty could not proceed quickly for fear of establishing a faulty precedent. Dissenting voices, mainly from the Government of India and the India Office, were uneasy at the very concept of such a treaty, and endeavoured to make its composition substantially different from that proposed by the Foreign Office. Bearing in mind the legacy of Wahhabi sacking of the Holy Places in the nineteenth century, India wanted the treaty negotiations deferred in order to gauge the opinion of Indian Pilgrims returning from the Hejaz.[62]

There was conflicting evidence during 1926 about the success of Ibn Saud's first months in control of the Hejaz. He had certainly achieved some stability and discipline, and reduced the corrupt practices of his pre-decessors, all of which endeared him to the Foreign Office. Yet the religious fervour of some of his followers had led to accusations of shrines and tombs being destroyed in Medina and other towns, which, whether exaggerated or otherwise, fuelled resentment in Persia and India. Sir Percy Loraine, from Teheran, and the India Office demanded the curbing of Wahhabi excesses in order to gain the gratitude of Moslems elsewhere.[63]

These suggestions the Foreign Office refused to entertain. Whatever the popular beliefs held in other parts of the world, the Foreign Office knew the limits of British influence with Ibn Saud. Britain would reap more trouble from misplaced and futile intervention than by taking no action at all.[64] The Foreign Office wanted the Government of India and the India Office to accept its policy of treating the Hejaz and Nejd as completely independent countries.[65] Britain would abstain from all religious disputes in the Hejaz except those involving actual British subjects undertaking the Pilgrimage.[66]

Another problem was that of guaranteeing Ibn Saud against foreign aggression. The principle of keeping the peace between Arabian rulers could only succeed by protecting them all. Since Ibn Saud was surrounded by states enjoying British protection, any guarantees would be directed explicitly at rulers dependent on Britain, with the risk of dragging Britain into future Arabian conflicts. If a clause was inserted to restrict the guarantee to an extra-Arabian attack, Ibn Saud would not comprehend its logic. It would also cause offence to France and Italy to whom it would, by implication, be directed.[67]

Between the years 1919-26 none of Britain's international engagements had contained military commitments.[68] Apart from the desire of seeking stability in the Arab world, this policy accorded with Britain's views on international security as linked with the League of Nations.[69] An inter-departmental conference in May 1926 agreed not to guarantee Ibn Saud against foreign aggression. This avoided possible accusations of restricting Ibn Saud's independence. Giving various degrees of protection to different Arab rulers complicated Britain's relations with Arabia, particularly when the Moslem world was demanding a fully independent Hejaz.[70]

Moreover, the Hadda and Bahra Agreements had, hopefully, stabilised Saudi relations with Transjordan and Iraq. The Gulf states, by contrast, had no protection other than that implied in the 1915 Anglo-Saudi treaty. The Government of India feared that if this protection was withdrawn in the new treaty Ibn Saud would think that Britain was no longer committed to their territorial integrity.[71] There was, nevertheless, some doubt about the effi-cacy of a treaty clause safeguarding the sheikhdoms. No mere treaty would, it was admitted, deter Ibn Saud from annexing one or more of the Trucial sheikhdoms if he was determined to do so.[72] This risk could only have been countered through Britain binding herself even closer to the Gulf rulers. Yet, even in the 1920s, there were those who saw Britain's relations with the Trucial states as anachronistic. Her treaty commitments with them were so vague as to encourage, rather than deter Saudi aggression.[73] In the event of Ibn Saud overrunning any of the sheikhdoms Britain wanted to retain flexibility of response,[74] and refused to commit herself to their physical protection. More significantly, in the light of later developments in Anglo-Saudi relations, Britain declined to consider the precise frontier between Ibn Saud's dominions and the Trucial states.

The Government of India was sceptical about the stability of the Wahhabi regime. Ibn Saud's successor might be less able to control *Ikhwan* fanaticism. Consequently, the Government of India preferred Britain to think twice about a hasty and ill-conceived treaty with the Wahhabi King. At the very least, it ought not to be a perpetual treaty of friendship, with its implied dynastic guarantees upon which Ibn Saud was insisting. Preferably the treaty should be personal to Ibn Saud, expire automatically upon his death and, in any case, be limited to a maximum period of six years.[75] This would allow for future modification in the light of events. The Government of India, it should be remembered, no longer had a voice in the framing of British policy in Arabia, though its paternalistic attitude, even to a ruler of Ibn Saud's standing, was still evident. At the same time, the very existence of an Arabian policy was to safeguard access to India. Her susceptibilities could not, therefore, easily be overlooked by London.

Nonetheless, the suggestion of a 'personal' treaty with Ibn Saud was rejected by the Foreign Office on the grounds that such a treaty was almost without precedent. On one issue, however, the positions of the Foreign Office and India Office were so polarised as to threaten the entire future of the proposed treaty. This was the question of the Capitulations. The Capitulations were extra-territorial arrangements whereby unilateral concessions of a juridical or fiscal nature were granted to foreign governments.[76] Subjects of specified states, in this case Britain, were considered immune from the jurisdiction of local courts. Charges against British subjects were withdrawn from those courts and dealt with by British consular courts. Long before the First World War the Capitulations invited scandal throughout the world and were seen as a provocation to nationalist sentiment.[77]

In keeping with her view that the Hejaz be recognised as a totally independent state – to allay Moslem criticism – India argued that a new Anglo-Saudi treaty should not contain any Capitulations. The rights of British subjects could be protected by the normal consular powers of intervention on their behalf. At the same time, India sought the inclusion of a clause which would guarantee freedom of religious observance for Indian pilgrims in the face of rigid Wahhabi practices.[78] For example, Hejazi barbers had been instructed not to shave completely the faces of pilgrims or residents as this was, apparently, against the teaching of the Prophet. At least fifteen hairs had to be left on the face.[79] The conflicting pressures on the Government of India, to provide protection for its subjects as well as insist on the 'independence' of the Hejaz, irritated the Foreign Office:

> As usual India wants it both ways. We are to protect the pilgrims and save the tombs, but in no way are we to exercise influence or interference in the internal affairs of the Hejaz or Holy Places.[80]

To the Foreign Office, the Government of India was trying to hunt with Ibn Saud and run with the Moslems of India.[81]

Unlike the India Office, the Foreign Office did want Capitulatory rights in force in the Hejaz. It felt uneasy at exposing the small British community, plus the large numbers of pilgrims, to the unfamiliar Koranic-based *Sharia* courts.[82] More significantly, to give way on the question of the Hejaz Capitulations would weaken the status of similar claims being exacted in Egypt, Persia and China.[83] Other countries, such as Italy, were at that time seeking British co-operation in reasserting the Capitulations in the Hejaz.[84]

The basic postures of the India Office and the Foreign Office were confused by the legal position. Britain had enjoyed Capitulations with the Ottoman Empire. Those rights had been waived with respect to Turkey in 1923, and were also nullified in the mandates. Technically Britain had never admitted the abolition of the Capitulations in the Ottoman province of the Hejaz,[85] nor had she ever had occasion to claim those rights for British residents or pilgrims.[86] Moreover, as Jordan pointed out, Ibn Saud was unlikely to accept extra-territorial rights in his new treaty.[87] He would not have risked including in a published document anything that could be interpreted as interfering with *Sharia* law. Husein had never acknowledged Capitulations, nor had Ibn Saud in his 1915 treaty. Introducing them in 1926 would have been an anachronism.

Faced with this weight of argument the Foreign Office agreed to exclude any Capitulations clause from the new Saudi treaty, but not to formally renounce any such rights in the Hejaz. This in itself raises certain questions. Over the Capitulations the respective positions of the Foreign Office and the India Office seem contrary to what might have been expected. By 1926 the Foreign Office felt the greatest sympathy with Ibn Saud, while the India Office and the Government of India harboured the greatest suspicions. The turnaround in the attitude of the Foreign Office towards Ibn Saud was considered in the previous chapter. Here it can be noted that the position of India, too, had shifted. From being Ibn Saud's foremost advocate up to and during the First World War, the Government of India had adopted a more guarded attitude towards the Wahhabi regime. This was, of course, because Ibn Saud was no longer the minor desert chieftain unable to inflict telling damage on Indian interests. India could favour Ibn Saud with her paternalism in the local affairs of the Gulf, but Saudi control of Mecca could radically affect Moslem attitudes world-wide. This necessitated circum-spection on the part of Indian authorities.

Accordingly, the Foreign Office had favoured recognition of Ibn Saud while the India Office urged caution. On the matter of the Capitulations, then, it might have been expected that the Foreign Office would try to sweep away all possible hindrances to a healthy Anglo-Saudi treaty; while the India Office, with both eyes fixed firmly on Indian susceptibilities, would try to obstruct it. In reality, the positions were reversed. It was the Foreign Office which sought Capitulatory privileges, while the India Office calculated that the interests of Indian Moslems could best be served by the complete removal of all obstructions to Ibn Saud's absolute and unequivocal independence.

Why, then, did the Foreign Office, so anxious to please Ibn Saud in almost all other respects, take the hardest line over the Capitulations? And why did Indian pressure succeed in having them withdrawn? It must be appreciated that the Foreign Office did not have regional interests to defend in quite the same way as did the India Office. The responsibilities of the Foreign Office were global, and it is in the context of these world-wide concerns that matters of precedent raised their head. The Foreign Office could not deal with the Hejaz Capitulations in a vacuum. They were inextricably associated with imperial designs and they invoked controversy in all parts of the world. Egypt, for example, in 1922, had been offered independence by the British Government – subject to certain restrictions, one of which was the maintenance of Capitulations. The Foreign Office, like the India Office, had to look beyond the Hejaz when debating the Capitulations, but in a different direction. Egyptian unrest might have been exacerbated if the comparatively primitive Hejaz was excused extra-territorial rights. This reveals a certain opportunism and pragmatism on the part of the Foreign Office; trying to acknowledge Ibn Saud's complete independence with one hand, while trying to reconcile competing international considerations by imposing restrictions upon it with the other.

By contrast, the India Office and the Government of India looked to no outside sources of reference. Their concerns were with abating the seemingly permanent antagonisms of certain Indian Moslem organisations, such as the Khilafat Committee. The India Office thought this pressure could best be alleviated not by slipping a loose rein over Ibn Saud in the form of extra-territorial restrictions on the sovereignty of the Hejaz, but by giving the new King free rein, in the sense of unrestricted independence – provided he would agree to freedom of religious practices! India, that is to say, was prepared to surrender any powers of formal intervention on behalf of Indian pilgrims apprehended in the Hejaz for the wider benefits of appeasing anti-British agitation in India. Pilgrims who were foolish or unfortunate enough to fall foul of the Hejazi authorities would have to take their chances.

It remains to be considered why the Foreign Office gave way over the Capitulations. In the first place, it will be remembered that policies for Arabia were formulated through inter-departmental consultation. This had the effect, at times, of emasculating the Foreign Office even within its traditional areas of authority:

> It is really very difficult to conduct affairs properly with Bin Saud when we have to consult IO or CO. Such delay must diminish the good effect of our attitude on an Arabian chieftain with no experience of a multitude of government offices.[88]

Furthermore, Delhi's single-minded determination to avoid the risk of inflammatory measures such as the Capitulations contrasted with the less partisan, and therefore less immediate or pressing concerns of the Foreign Office. In addition, the Foreign Office was divided within itself on the question. One Foreign Office suggestion was to compromise, restricting the jurisdiction of the Capitulations to the port of Jedda where the small western community lived.[89] This was rebuffed by others within the Foreign Office who considered that this skeletal claim to Capitulations would be more likely to prejudice similar rights in Egypt and Persia than would its complete omission.[90]

Finally, and perhaps decisively, the Capitulations clause was abandoned because the overriding need was to get some form of treaty with Ibn Saud, even if its actual provisions amounted to little more than affirmations of friendship and goodwill.[91] If the proposed treaty was loaded with doubtful clauses then Britain could anticipate a lengthy wrangle with probably nothing to show for it in the end.[92] The Foreign Office agreed to settle such cases as might arise outside the *Sharia* courts. Ibn Saud was also to be induced, if possible, in lieu of the Capitulations, to accept the general principles of international law in force between independent governments. [93]

Delay in formulating an agreed British draft of the treaty, allied to Ibn Saud standing firm on a number of points, caused the negotiations to drag on into 1927. Clayton was called upon to take over the negotiations in place of Jordan. The basic points of disagreement concerned the mandates and Gulf sheikhdoms. Ibn Saud rejected any written acknowledgement of Britain's special position in the mandates, and raised the question of his frontiers both with Transjordan and the Trucial states.[94]

A further inter-departmental conference considered the breakdown in a pessimistic light. Shuckburgh, on behalf of the Colonial Office, considered that if Ibn Saud refused to recognise Britain's special relations with the mandates then there was no advantage in accepting what would be a truncated treaty.[95] The India Office, confronted with the similar question of Britain's responsibilities to the Gulf states, followed Shuckburgh's line. Lord Birkenhead proposed that the treaty negotiations be dropped, or at least temporarily discontinued.[96]

Faced with the risk of Britain forfeiting any formal influence with Ibn Saud by his turning to another power to cement his independence, Clayton returned to sign the treaty on 20 May 1927. The previous January a tribal delegation in Riyadh had transformed the Sultanate of Nejd into a King-dom. Ibn Saud thereupon became King of the Hejaz and of Nejd and its Dependencies. At the time this constituted the only dual monarchy in the world, and was the first occasion that central Arabia had ever had a king.[97] Feisal was the only other King in adjacent territories but that had been a British-inspired development.[98]

As with all previous treaties Ibn Saud made sure that it referred to the legality of his secular and historical rights, ensuring his right to choose his successor.[99] The stumbling blocks which had caused the earlier break-down were settled in various ways. Rather than repeat the deadlock reached in Husein's treaty, the issue of Britain's special position in the mandates was completely omitted. Her special interest in the Gulf states was acknow-ledged in diluted form, Ibn Saud merely undertaking to maintain friendly and peaceful relations with the sheikhs, without expressly acknowledging Britain's commitments. As for Aqaba and Maan, it was considered inappro-priate to fix a disputed frontier in a general treaty of amity. The two parties set out their positions and agreed to differ in an exchange of notes appended to the treaty. Ibn Saud agreed to accept the *status quo* until circumstances permitted a solution. Further regulations regarding slavery and the formal removal of the embargo on Britain's export of war materials to Ibn Saud were also included in an exchange of notes.[100]

It can be suggested that the greater concessions in finalising the treaty were made by Britain. Despite this, the Foreign Office was not displeased with the final outcome. Only the phraseology pertaining to one of the slavery paragraphs was felt to tarnish Clayton's otherwise considerable diplomatic achievement.[101] Ibn Saud had become the first Arab ruler to secure a treaty whereby the British Government recognised his complete and absolute independence.[102] It was referred to as the Treaty of Jedda.

Postscript

The Anglo-Saudi treaty was scheduled to run for a period of seven years, to be renewed or renegotiated at the end of that time. Continuing disagree-ment, particularly over Aqaba and Maan, and the suppression of slavery in Arabia, induced Ibn Saud to threaten to denounce the treaty in the spring of 1934.[103] The 1927 treaty had specified that, in the event of divergent interpretations of the English and Arabic texts, the English one was to prevail. Ibn Saud would insist on the equal rights of the Arabic language, whilst absolving himself of all responsibility for the restriction of slavery, in all future treaties with European powers.[104] On the other hand, the British, unlike subsequent French and Italian treaties, did not include most-favoured-nation treatment, nor did it provide for a commercial treaty with Ibn Saud's dominions.[105]

In 1935 Ibn Saud proposed an extension of the treaty for a further ten years if the British Government would agree to two amendments: the equality of the Arabic and English texts, and Britain's renunciation of her right to manumit slaves.[106] Britain had already privately informed Ibn Saud that he could have no satisfaction for his claim to Aqaba and Maan.[107] Further negotiations culminated in October 1936 with a renewal of the Treaty of Jedda. Britain agreed to the equal validity of the two texts, although there had been no quarrel over any particular interpretation.[108] She also renounced her right to manumit slaves. Philby had described the original slavery clause as no more than a little harmless balm for sentimental consciences.[109] In return, Ibn Saud gave a vague undertaking to terminate the slave trade in Arabia.[110] Each party agreed to retain its previously stated position over Aqaba and Maan.

Summary and Conclusions

The 1927 treaty was more consonant with the realities existing in Arabia after Ibn Saud's conquest of the Hejaz. The British Government, and in particular the Foreign Office, felt that Ibn Saud was the only authority who could bring order out of chaos in Arabia.[111] The desire for a new treaty with Ibn Saud stemmed from two principal incentives. The first was the self-contained motive of improving Anglo-Saudi relations; of coming to terms with the new strongman in Arabia, and securing the best interests of the mandates and Gulf sheikhdoms. The second motive reflected Britain's post-First World War policy of securing her position throughout the Middle East by the use of treaties. Almost the whole Arab world was tied to Britain by treaty as part of the philosophy of protecting British interests without a direct or, in places, indirect imperial presence. The nature of the treaties varied with the country in question. Those with Egypt and the mandates retained extensive British powers. That with Ibn Saud did not. It should also be remembered that Britain had sought a treaty with the independent Yemen in 1925-26. British policy desired to treat Ibn Saud and the Imam, as far as possible, on similar lines in accordance with the principles of one general Arabian policy.[112]

The significance of the Treaty of Jedda lay not so much in that it dispensed with the restrictive clauses pressed upon Husein, particularly *vis à vis* the mandates, as in the fact that Ibn Saud presented a far greater threat to the mandates than ever Husein did. Britain had, after all, tried to impress upon Husein her special position in territories ruled by his sons. Yet, given the animosity between the Saudis and Hashemites, and the history of friction over the mandates' southern frontiers, it is noteworthy that Britain was still prepared to relax similar demands on Ibn Saud.

That Britain did so was due to two factors. Firstly, Ibn Saud had put his relations with Transjordan and Iraq on a firmer footing through the Hadda and Bahra Agreements of 1925. It was hoped that those documents would ease the tension along the Nejd-mandate frontiers. Secondly, Ibn Saud had already shown himself to be the outstanding Arab of his day, a fact not lessened by Britain seeking to treat with him through an Acting Consul. The mid-20s was, in relative terms, a quiescent period in the Arab world. Not for another ten years would Britain have to portray any urgency in her Arab policy. Ibn Saud's achievements, unlike those of Husein or Feisal, had been attributable to his own efforts alone. His greater stature meant that it was all the more important for him to be brought into treaty relations with Britain. The motives behind the proposed treaty with Husein had, by contrast, been more cosmetic; to demonstrate to a world audience that a British ally would not be left isolated from Britain's post-War rearrangement of the Arab world.

The Treaty of Jedda highlighted the inter-dependence of the British Empire. No major decision, it seemed, could be taken with regard to Ibn Saud without it affecting, perhaps vitally so, some part of that Empire. The post-1925 perspectives on Ibn Saud of both the Foreign Office, on the one hand, and the India Office and the Government of India, on the other, changed from those of earlier times. Both the Foreign and India Offices proclaimed their desire for the total independence of the Hejaz. Yet it is apparent that Ibn Saud's 'independence' was viewed differently. The Foreign Office, for example, wanted to acknowledge his complete independence, but, in the climate of the time, failed to perceive that the imposition of Capitulations was a substantial smear on Ibn Saud's, or anybody else's, independence. In advocating Ibn Saud's treaty of independence, the Foreign Office was looking less at Jedda than at Cairo and Teheran.

Similarly, the India Office, while less enamoured with a proselytising Islamic regime guarding the Holy Places, also sought the complete independence of the Hejaz. This, it was felt, would relieve accusations that Britain was seeking a muted form of colonialism over the Islamic Holy Land. Even so, the position of the India Office and the Government of India was compromised by their seeking to impose conditions that would grant freedom of religious expression for Indian Moslems who undertook the Pilgrimage. In formulating its policy, the India Office looked towards Lucknow in much the same way that the Foreign Office looked towards Cairo.

The British Government sought no formal hold or influence over Ibn Saud's territories, although he had shown himself to be a ruler sufficiently powerful as to demand British attention. Britain's treaty with Ibn Saud, acknowledging his full and absolute independence, was almost unique in that it was not aimed at a state, such as Egypt or Iraq, but at a man. Indeed, the Government of India had tried to ensure that this personal quality of the treaty was written into it, by limiting its validity to the reign of Ibn Saud. Where the taint of imperialism left its trace was in the few attempts to impose some form of restraint on his sovereignty. The Capitulations provided the most obvious example. Two other limiting factors actually found their way into the treaty. These were the insistence of the British Government that Ibn Saud take steps to curb slavery in his dominions, and the superiority granted to the English version of the treaty in the event of any dispute over its interpretation. This gave Britain advantages that were denied to France and Italy in their subsequent treaties, and which were withdrawn in the amended treaty of 1936.

The Treaty of Jedda regulated Anglo-Saudi relations at a formal level, but said nothing about the practical management of those relations. The only British official accredited to Ibn Saud's dominions was an Agent and Consul in Jedda, an inadequate channel for Anglo-Saudi communications.

REFERENCES FOR CHAPTER THREE

1. The expression 'Nejd and its Dependencies' was a reference to the territories that had fallen to Ibn Saud beyond Nejd. Hasa, for example, was taken as one such dependency. In future, when reference is made to Nejd, as opposed to the Hejaz, it will be taken to imply Nejd and its Dependencies, including Hasa.

2. No fully satisfactory explanation has been offered as to why Ibn Saud became King of the Hejaz after insisting upon its independence earlier through *Umm al Qura*. Perhaps it was opportunism. Perhaps Hejazis did urge the throne upon him. Perhaps Ibn Saud was referring to the spiritual, not temporal independence of the Hejaz. As will be seen, no effort was made for six years to merge the Hejaz and Nejd into a single state. A Saudi Viceroy would be responsible for the Hejaz. Philby noted how Indian Moslems were shocked at Ibn Saud's assumption of the throne. They wanted his authority limited to foreign, defence and economic policy, leaving the internal administration of the state to be conducted by a democratic body composed of all Islamic states. Indian Moslems feared Ibn Saud's susceptibility to the British no less than Husein's. Had he not negotiated the Hadda and Bahra Agreements and lost Aqaba to the infidel? Ibn Saud, in reply, stressed his own religious orthodoxy, and that the independence of the Hejaz was guaranteed against foreign influence or control (Philby, *Arabian Jubilee*, pp. 84-5).

3. See FO to Jordan (Jedda), No 7, 15 January 1926, FO E/350/350/91: 371/11441.

4. Mallet (FO) minute, 18 January 1926, ibid. For a comprehensive list of naval gun salutes, from 21 guns down to 9 guns, for Indian ruling princes, see Coen, pp. 262-4.

5. FO to Jordan, No 4, ibid.

6. FO to Jordan, No 6, ibid.

7. V.B. Metta, 'Ibn Saud, Aspirant for Leadership of the Moslem World', *Current History*, 24 (April 1926).

8. GoI to IO, 27 January 1926, see FO E/734/7/91: 371/11431.

9. IO to FO, 2 February 1926, FO E/801/7/91: 371/11431.

10. ibid.

11. IO to FO, 23 February 1926, FO E/1282/7/91: 371/11431.

12. CO to FO, 27 January 1926, FO E/654/7/91: 371/11431.

13. Ag. High Commissioner Iraq to SSC, 27 January 1926, in FO E/654/7/91: 371/11431.

14. Elie Kedourie, *England and the Middle East: The Destruction of the Ottoman Empire 1914-1921*, pp. 52-3. (Hereafter: *England* ...)

15. FO to CO & IO, 15 January 1926, FO E/245/7/91: 371/11431.

16. Mallet minute, 2 February 1926, FO E/801/7/91: 371/11431.

17. Oliphant minute, 23 February 1926, FO E/1282/7/91: 371/11431. The French, suspicious of Abdullah in Transjordan and of the Hashemites in general, had earlier been rumoured to be intriguing with Ibn Saud (Habib, p. 106).

18. CO to FO, 27 January 1926, CO/2244/26: 727/12.

19. Young (CO) minute, 29 January 1926, ibid.

20. Oliphant (FO) minute, 2 February 1926, FO E/801/7/91: 371/11431.

21. Henderson (Cairo) to FO, 10 July 1926, FO E/4312/7/91; FO E/5065/7/91: 371/11432.

22. Tyrrell (FO) to Jordan, see FO E/801/7/91: 371/11431.
23. FO to IO, 16 February 1926, FO E/1052/7/91: 371/11431.
24. Osborne (FO) minute, 2 February 1926, FO E/801/7/91: 371/11431.
25. Tyrrell minute, 2 February 1926, ibid.
26. Chamberlain to Jordan, 25 February 1926, FO E/1282/7/91: 371/11431.
27. Hurewitz, p. 417.
28. Jordan to Chamberlain, 29 March 1926, FO E/2069/7/91: 371/11431: Soviet *de jure* recognition was extended on 11 February.
29. Bullard, *The Camels Must Go*, p. 210.
30. The Dutch interest in the Hejaz was second only to that of Britain, owing to large numbers of Moslem pilgrims coming from the Dutch East Indies and elsewhere.
31. *Survey ... 1925*, p. 311.
32. This book follows the western tradition of spelling Ibn Saud's son 'Faisal', and Husein's son 'Feisal', as a means of distinguishing between them.
33. Jordan to FO, 11 August 1926, FO E/4735/7/91: 371/11431.
34. Mallet minute, ibid.
35. ibid.
36. FO to French and Dutch Embassies, 2 September 1926, FO E/4972/7/91: 371/11432.
37. Tyrrell to French Ambassador, 15 September 1926, FO E/5302/7/91: 371/11432.
38. Mallet minute, op. cit.
39. ibid.
40. FO minute, 9 September 1926, FO E/5180/7/91: 371/11432.
41. See FO E/5689/7/91: 371/11432.
42. IO to FO, 5 January 1926, FO E/180/180/91: 371/11437.
43. Mallet minute, ibid.
44. Clayton to FO, 16 December 1925, FO E/322/180/91: 371/11437.
45. RIIA, *British Interests ...*, p. 58.
46. Mallet minute, 16 December 1925, FO E/322/180/91: 371/11437.
47. Inter-departmental conference, 20 May 1926, in FO E/3843/180/91: 371/11438.
48. See FO E/710/710/91: 371/11444.
49. ibid.
50. ibid. The Italians had a considerable presence in the Red Sea due to their colony in Eritrea (see Chapter Six).
51. Shuckburgh to Chamberlain, 27 May 1926, FO E/3265/710/91: 371/11444.
52. ibid.
53. Osborne (FO) minute, 4 June 1926, ibid.
54. See CO/4031/26: 725/9.
55. For draft of this treaty, see Hurewitz, p. 321.
56. See Chapter Six.
57. Clayton to CO, 6 January 1926, in FO E/735/28/91: 371/11433.
58. Clayton to Shuckburgh, 26 April 1926, in FO E/2580/180/91: 371/11437.
59. See Jordan to FO, No 51, 4 May 1926, FO E/2815/180/91: 371/11437.
60. Mallet minute, 5 May 1926, ibid.
61. ibid.
62. IO to FO, 28 May 1926, FO E/3314/180/91: 371/11438.
63. Loraine (Teheran) to FO, 5 June 1926, FO E/3439/20/91; IO to FO, 12 June 1926, FO E/3631/20/91: 371/11433.
64. Rendel (FO) minute, 5 June 1926, FO E/3439/20/91: 371/11433.
65. FO memorandum, 1 September 1926, FO E/5100/7/91: 371/11432.
66. ibid.
67. See inter-departmental conference, 20 May 1926, in FO E/3843/180/91: 371/11438.
68. Anne Orde, *Great Britain and International Security 1920-1926*, p. 155.
69. ibid.
70. GoI to FO, 12 July 1926, FO E/4218/180/91: 371/11438.
71. See inter-departmental conference, 6 October 1926, CO/19237/26: 725/9.
72. See inter-departmental conference, 20 May 1926, FO E/3843/180/91: 371/11438.
73. IO to FO, 10 August 1926, FO E/4708/180/91: 371/11438.
74. See inter-departmental conference, 11 August 1926, FO E/4920/180/91: 371/11438. (see Chapter Nine.)

75. GoI to FO, 12 July 1926, FO E/4218/180/91: 371/11438.
76. Laurence Grafftey-Smith, *Bright Levant*, p. 10.
77. ibid.
78. Inter-departmental conference, 6 October 1926, CO/19237/26: 725/9.
79. Jordan to FO, No 35, 31 March 1926, FO E/2627/367/91: 371/11442.
80. FO minute, 26 August 1926, FO E/4992/20/91: 371/11433.
81. Osborne minute, 15 July 1926, FO E/4218/180/91: 371/11438.
82. ibid. Ibn Saud had not interfered with the existing legal structure of the Hejaz.
83. ibid.
84. ibid.
85. Memorandum on preliminary draft treaty, 19 July 1926, FO E/4266/180/91: 371/11438. The draft Anglo-Hejazi treaty of 1923 had included three Articles attempting to get round the problem of the Capitulations (see Hurewitz, p. 321).
86. Memorandum, ibid.
87. Inter-departmental conference, 6 October 1926, FO E/5794/180/91: 371/11438.
88. Oliphant minute, 10 February 1926, FO E/902/180/91: 371/11437.
89. Something similar had been intended for Husein, see Hurewitz, p. 321.
90. Osborne minute, 19 October 1926, FO E/5794/180/91: 371/11438.
91. Inter-departmental conference, 6 October 1926, CO/19237/26: 725/9.
92. ibid.
93. Oliphant to Jakins (Jedda), No 114, 3 October 1927, FO E/4168/3642/91: 371/12252.
94. Jordan to Chamberlain, 26 January 1927, FO E/477/119/91: 371/12244.
95. Shuckburgh to inter-departmental meeting, 19 January 1927, CO/49008/27: 732/23.
96. Wakely (IO) to inter-departmental conference, 4 February 1927, ibid.
97. K. Williams, p. 209. The Hejaz-Nejd flag, too, was unique: green (the colour of paradise); plus a sword (for the *jihad* to spread Islam); plus the words from the Koran 'There is no God but Allah and Mohammad is his Prophet'. This constituted the only national flag to include writing on it (George A. Lipsky, *Saudi Arabia: its People, its Society, its Culture*, p. 309).
98. France, unlike Britain, in having dispensed with her own monarchy, did not engage in king-making in her mandate (Helms, p. 110).
99. Helms, p. 110.
100. *Survey ... 1928*, p. 287.
101. FO minute, 23 June 1927, FO E/2582/119/91: 371/12245.
102. The first Arab to have his 'complete and absolute independence' acknowledged by any European power had been the Imam Yahya of the Yemen. In September 1926 Italy had signed such a treaty with the Imam, even allowing, in the absence of anybody in the Yemen who spoke Italian, the supremacy of the Arabic text. Secretly, however, a supplementary agreement promised Italy Capitulatory rights. Nor did the Italo-Yemeni treaty pave the way for diplomatic relations (Hurewitz, pp. 380-1).
103. Ryan (Jedda) to FO, 8 May 1934, FO E/2838/2838/25: 371/17940. (See Chapter Nine.)
104. Ryan to FO, 11 April 1935, FO E/2704/318/25: 371/19008.
105. Ryan memorandum, 17 October 1933, FO E/6284/6284/25: 371/16874.
106. Ryan to FO, No 82, 5 April 1935, FO E/2246/318/25: 371/19008.
107. Ryan memorandum, op. cit.
108. Ryan to FO, 11 April 1935, FO E/2704/318/25: 371/19008.
109. H. St J. B. Philby, 'Britain and Arabia', *Nineteenth Century and After*, 117 (1935), p. 574.
110. Bullard (Jedda) to Eden, 28 February 1937, FO E/1637/1637/25: 371/20843.
111. Rendel, p. 57.
112. Clayton to Shuckburgh, 21 April 1926, FO E/2580/180/91: 371/11437.

CHAPTER FOUR

The Channels of Anglo-Saudi Relations

Victory in the Hejaz extended Ibn Saud's authority to two separate states. This unusual situation was interpreted, from Britain, as the 'personal union' of Hejaz-Nejd. They were distinct political entities sharing a common sovereign. In addition to the social, economic and geographical differences between them, Ibn Saud took no immediate steps to impose political unification. This, doubtless, owed something to his need to reassure the people of the Hejaz. To this end, Ibn Saud, after the fall of Jedda, proclaimed the continuing independence of the Moslem Holy Land. While Nejd continued to be governed as a sheikhdom, or congeries of sheikhdoms, the Hejaz enjoyed a written constitution, promulgated by Ibn Saud in 1926. The two states even had separate treasuries until 1930, whereupon successive measures were taken to unify Hejaz-Nejd as a single state.[1]

Ibn Saud quickly made provision for orderly government to be brought to his enlarged dominions. His eldest son, Saud, was appointed Viceroy of Nejd, and his second son, Faisal, more widely travelled, became Viceroy of the Hejaz. The sheer size of the territory under his control compelled Ibn Saud to seek advisers and administrators. Yet he faced obvious difficulties in this respect. Nejd was so inaccessible that few of its people had any knowledge of the outside world. Hostility to Christians and Hashemites alike meant that Ibn Saud had to search afar for competent officials. Four of those that he found remained in his service throughout the late 1920s and '30s. These were Sheikh Hafiz Wahba – an Egyptian; Fuad Bey Hamza – a Lebanese Druze, who became Deputy Minister for Foreign Affairs; Yusuf Yasin – a Syrian, who eventually became Political Secretary to Ibn Saud; and Abdullah Sulaiman – a Nejdi, who was Minister of Finance.[2] By the late '30s Sulaiman had responsibility for Finance, Defence and the Pilgrimage, and was the most powerful of Ibn Saud's inner circle. This small group of officials, by 1930, constituted the core of the Hejaz-Nejd Government. Its composition said something about Ibn Saud's pragmatism. Having a Druze within his entourage was scarcely commensurate with the tenets of Wahhabism. Moreover, despite constructing a centralised bureaucracy, Ibn Saud maintained a roving court (*majlis*) to dispense justice and impose his authority over the more distant regions of his dominions.

The Treaty of Jedda provided a formal, public document regulating the relationship between Ibn Saud and the British Government. How that relationship was to be put into practice, particularly in the absence of diplomatic relations, remained unclear. Arabia was still remote from the centres of British power. The problem of easing that remoteness and facilitating relations between London, Jedda and Riyadh involved two distinct aspects. The first of these was the question of physical communication. How could the conduct of Anglo-Saudi relations overcome the obstacles presented by a desert kingdom practically devoid of technological innovations such as the telephone and wireless telegraphy, and even roads for mechanised transport? Secondly, in 1927, the only existing diplomatic bridge between Britain and Hejaz-Nejd was the British Consulate in Jedda, which had been given the added status of diplomatic Agency as an improvisation during the First World War.[3] Nejd had no direct contact with Britain at all, communications with central Arabia having to pass through the Indian political network in the Gulf. All these handicaps to the swift and efficient interchange of communication between Britain and Ibn Saud became the more glaring after the 1927 treaty, and it became important to update communications, both physical and diplomatic.

The Role of Technology in Anglo-Saudi Relations

In the modern world of telex, satellites and supersonic air travel, the difficulties of effective communication with remote parts of the globe in earlier times are apt to be overlooked. Arabia, beyond its coastlines, lay at the frontiers of European experience. Nejd possessed no press. The Hejaz availed itself of a weekly newspaper, *Umm al Qura* (Mother of the Villages – Mecca), control of which was assumed by Yusuf Yasin. Another, *Saut al Hejaz* (Voice of the Hejaz), was established in 1932.[4] Both were carefully controlled by the Saudi Government. There were no foreign press correspondents, even on the Red Sea coast. Europeans had neither permission nor facilities for travel beyond Jedda; the sacred Hejaz being denied to non-Moslems. The lack of a free press and the confinement of Europeans to Jedda prevented the Consulate from acquiring knowledge of conditions beyond the city walls, and made it heavily dependent for information on rumour percolating through the bazaars.[5] Poor intelligence was especially irritating for Britain because the Hejaz, due to the annual influx of pilgrims from all parts of the world, was an obvious focus for anti-European agitation.[6]

By 1930 there was no internal telegraph system for Hejaz-Nejd, merely a few scattered wireless sets. Only Jedda could take advantage of telegraphy. Among other obstacles to its introduction throughout Arabia was the claim by certain Wahhabis that such devices as the wireless were the work of the infidel.[7] Between 1930 and 1932 Marconi supplied and installed a network of wireless telegraphy stations throughout Hejaz-Nejd.[8] By 1932 Riyadh even possessed a rudimentary telephone service to link up with a similar service which had existed in Mecca, Medina and Jedda since Turkish times.[9]

A one-way journey from Jedda to Riyadh by camel took about four weeks.[10] Yet before the Riyadh link was installed, in 1932, a return telegraphic message to the Nejdi capital still took some three weeks, the message having to pass from Jedda to Riyadh via Bahrain, and back again.[11] Furthermore, the cost of each word telegraphed was then three shillings, which compelled messages to be brief, often to the point of unintelligibility.[12]

The introduction of telegrams did not necessarily expedite British communications, particularly in times of tension in Anglo-Saudi relations. Due to the 'exorbitant rate which the Eastern Telegraph Company charge', details of Arabian developments were transmitted by telegraph to certain specific destinations, by sea mail to others.[13] Consequently, different parts of the Empire were apprised of those developments at different times. This frequently caused delay in formulating a joint response. Moreover, even after the acquisition of wireless telegraphy, when Ibn Saud was in the desert with his *majlis*, communication still had to be undertaken by hand, although this task was increasingly transferred from the camel to the motor car. In 1925 there was a total of four cars in the Hejaz.[14] By 1929 the number had risen to fifteen hundred.[15] By that date around half the pilgrims were using cars in preference to camels, with much disruption to the traditional Hejazi way of life.[16] Roads, however, were in short supply, so that, by 1930, it could still take a week for a letter from Jedda to reach Riyadh.[17] Frequent breakdowns due to non-existent roads and poor drivers made motoring in Arabia in the inter-war years a hazardous and unreliable form of communication.

The influx of mechanised transport into Arabia was partly due to Philby, who had set up in Jedda a branch of a British trading company known as Sharqieh (Eastern) Ltd. Among other things Philby used to import Ford motor cars.[18] The innovation was not all American: 'The first Austin Seven has appeared in the Hejaz. It has not yet struggled through to Mecca, but there is every hope that with a following wind it will one day do so'.[19]

Inter-departmental Communications with Arabia

Throughout 1926 government departments pondered the new situation in Arabia. It was apparent that the system set up in 1921, whereby the Colonial Office oversaw policy for the Arab world but was obliged to consult with the Foreign Office over the independent Hejaz, was rendered anachronistic by Ibn Saud's unification of Arabia. In 1926 the Colonial Office found itself dealing with Ibn Saud as Sultan of Nejd, while the Foreign Office dealt with him as King of the Hejaz.[20]

Both the Colonial Office and the Foreign Office wanted exclusive jurisdiction over Ibn Saud's dominions. The Colonial Office suggested that Shuckburgh's Middle Eastern Department be extended to include the

Hejaz, which ought, it was argued, to be dealt with by the same department as its neighbours. With Nejd already under the umbrella of the Colonial Office, Ibn Saud's new territory should be under it too.[21] Moreover, in view of the tension between Saudis and Hashemites, there were obvious benefits if the department responsible for the mandates also handled the Hejaz. The unsettled situation on the Hejaz-Transjordan frontier could be eased if the same department dealt with both states. This was preferable to the delay, inefficiency and conflicting interests characterised by the existing Colonial Office/Foreign Office dichotomy. If the Foreign Office continued to deal with Ibn Saud, so the Colonial Office argued, then there existed the possibility of partisanship damaging British interests, much as had been threatened over Aqaba and Maan. That particular dispute had reaffirmed in Colonial Office eyes the popular grievance against the Foreign Office – that it could act in a manner inimical to fundamental British interests by seeking to avoid, at all costs, serious disagreements with other countries.[22]

The Colonial Office was still pressing towards consideration of the 'Arab problem' as an organic whole.[23] Despite the Hejaz's links with the outside world the Colonial Office was inclined to think that Ibn Saud would adopt, at least initially, an inward-looking policy of isolation and consolidation. This would make it less apparent that an independent monarch was the recipient of Colonial Office attention.[24] In any case, the Colonial Office was happy to allow the Foreign Office to continue as the visible channel of communication with Ibn Saud,[25] and deal with any Parliamentary Questions concerning him.[26]

The Foreign Office viewed things differently. Ibn Saud's new impact on the world, together with his impending treaty with Britain which would acknowledge his 'complete and absolute independence', meant that the handling of relations with Ibn Saud would increasingly fall under the auspices of the Foreign Office.[27] The objections against Colonial Office ties with the Hejaz, which had been put forward in 1920-21, were even stronger in 1926, for the Hejaz had been formally recognised as an independent state. Ibn Saud, himself, strongly objected to any suggestion of Colonial Office interference in his affairs, particularly when Husein had dealt with the Foreign Office.[28]

Further afield, racial questions at that time causing unrest in Kenya and South Africa were being attributed in some quarters to the policies and methods being pursued by the Colonial Office.[29] Both to avoid the risk of similar unrest appearing in Arabia, and thereby affecting Indian Moslems, and because the very existence of an Arabian policy was to safeguard the communications with the Empire, the Foreign Office proposed that all countries bordering the Red Sea should come within its ambit.[30] It wanted relations with Ibn Saud brought within its Eastern Department, headed by Lancelot Oliphant, which covered relations with Turkey, Syria and Persia in addition to existing Arabian responsibilities.[31]

A series of inter-departmental conferences decided that the Foreign

Office and the Colonial Office should liaise even more closely in the light of the unification of Hejaz-Nejd. On the matter of the pathways of communication, it was agreed that they hinge on wherever Ibn Saud happened to be at the time. When in Mecca he would be reached through the Jedda Consulate, and when in Riyadh he would be accessible via the Political Resident at Bushire and the Political Agent in Kuwait.[32] These decisions were taken in defiance of Foreign Office protests that communication with Ibn Saud through the Gulf hindered the task of the British Agent/Consul at Jedda. The Foreign Office preferred that Bushire be eliminated as a channel of information with Ibn Saud, and that all his dealings should pass through Jedda.[33] The general view of the conference, however, was that, owing to the vastness of Arabia and the poor communications therein, it was impractical for any one British representative to take full responsibility for Ibn Saud.[34] A further conference confirmed the decision to continue the existing arrangements. The Foreign Office would handle all communication between Britain and the Hejaz, monitor Ibn Saud's relations with foreign powers, and continue to minister to the needs of pilgrims.[35] All purely Arab affairs relating to either the Hejaz or Nejd would pass to the Colonial Office.

Stand-in arrangements like these were no substitute for a clearly defined policy towards Arabia. In view of the great shift in Britain's involvement in the Middle East since 1915 the Colonial Office, in November 1926, prepared a detailed memorandum on British interests in Arabia. It noted that, as a general proposition, British policy remained to seek to interfere in Arabian affairs as little as possible, except within the narrowest limits imposed by British interests.[36] These interests encompassed three basic areas. First, there was the strategic significance of the Red Sea. By constituting the principal sea-route to the Empire, this was the factor of chief concern to the Foreign Office. The Admiralty, too, stressed that the tiny Kamaran and Farasan Islands at the southern end of the Red Sea were vital imperial interests that required a firm Red Sea policy to safeguard them.[37] This contradicted the inclination of the Colonial Office which was to have as little as possible to do with any of the territories adjoining the Red Sea.[38]

The second major concern was the mandates. This was the particular prerogative of the Colonial Office. The main external threat to Feisal and Abdullah came from the south.[39] The memorandum noted that there was no reason to suppose that Ibn Saud had reached the limit of his territorial ambitions. On the other hand, provided he did not violate the Hadda and Bahra Agreements, or encroach upon any areas for which Britain was responsible, British policy would strive to keep on good terms with him.[40] This conclusion seems curiously inappropriate to the premiss which preceded it. As it was conceded that Ibn Saud had not reached the limit of his territorial ambitions, then he was bound to encroach upon British interests sooner or later.

The third interest was Aden, stressed by the India Office as well as the Colonial Office, but as Aden and its Protectorate were separated from

Hejaz-Nejd by the Yemen and the Rub al Khali, it lay outside policy discussions on relations with Ibn Saud. Taken as a whole, the memorandum refuted any case for framing an all-embracing Arabian policy.[41] It was felt that, even if such an approach was desirable in itself, the politics of the peninsula were habitually too fluid to sustain one.[42] The fact that, in 1926, Saudi rule was ascendent gave no guarantee of its longevity. The memorandum concluded that individual questions pertaining to Arabia should be dealt with on their merits, and that 'the only safe attitude towards Arabian affairs was to meddle with them as little as possible'.[43] The Committee of Imperial Defence (CID) recommended similar conclusions to the Cabinet.[44]

These recommendations are of significance for several reasons. Individual departments, such as the Colonial Office and the Admiralty, had been urging some kind of cohesive response to the 'Arab problem'. Yet it was apparent that various departments viewed that 'problem' differently. The fluidity of Arabian politics, coupled with the low profile adopted to the peninsula as a whole, accounted for the decision to interfere in the politics of the peninsula only when necessary, and then on an *ad hoc* basis.[45]

Nevertheless, events in Arabia continued to invite reassessment of Britain's channels of communication with Ibn Saud. For some two years after his latest triumph Ibn Saud's presence was required for stabilising the Hejaz. From the winter of 1927-28 disturbances along the Iraq-Nejd frontier necessitated his personal intervention, so much so, that he became quite out of touch with Jedda. Ibn Saud was, by this time, reluctant to deal with minor British personages like a British Consul in Jedda or a Political Agent in Kuwait. Nor did he welcome making use of senior officials such as the British High Commissioners in Jerusalem and Baghdad because of their responsibility for defending the interests of his Hashemite rivals.[46] As a result, Ibn Saud had taken to sending one of his advisers, Sheikh Hafiz Wahba, to Cairo in order to communicate with London through the High Commissioner, Lord Lloyd.[47] This practice was not welcome in London. Lloyd was hardly acquainted with Anglo-Saudi relations, regardless of the added complications caused by a further channel of communication.

In view of the gravity of the situation on the Iraq-Nejd frontier, the High Commissioners at Jerusalem and Baghdad, in their communications with Ibn Saud, began to by-pass Jedda and use the more direct channel via Kuwait. The Foreign Office and the Colonial Office agreed that this should only be done in the case of a genuine emergency, when there was no time for direct communications through Jedda. All normal correspondence between the mandates and the Hejaz-Nejd should continue to pass through Jedda, where the Consul would have discretion for toning down 'asperities of style'.[48]

In 1930 the Cabinet invited a further rearrangement of the policy-making machinery towards the Middle East as part of the new Labour Government's search for administrative economies of all kinds.[49] In July a body was set up known as the Middle East (Official) Sub-Committee of the Committee of Imperial Defence. It was to deal with all Middle Eastern questions that concerned two or more government departments.[50] The Official Sub-Committee would be summoned as required and would comprise representation from the Colonial Office, Foreign Office, India Office, War Office, Admiralty, Air Ministry and the Treasury. In the event of the Official Sub-Committee failing to dispose of a problem, a Ministerial Sub-Committee would be convened.[51] The Foreign Office was normally represented on the Official Sub-Committee by George Rendel, head of its Eastern Department from 1930-38. The India Office was represented by Gilbert Laithwaite, and the Sub-Committee chaired by Sir John Shuckburgh of the Colonial Office.

This new apparatus brought a considerable degree of satisfaction to the departments concerned. For example, when a complaint was received from Jedda about the length of time elapsing in getting responses from London, the Foreign Office admitted that any delays were no longer due to lack of departmental co-operation. The delays were caused by 'the peculiar nature of relations with the Iraqi and Transjordanian Governments, and the fact that the interests of the Government of India were not necessarily identical wth those of HMG in the United Kingdom'.[52] Furthermore, co-operation between the various interested departments was, by 1930, so much more efficient that the British Government was usually able to deal with any urgent Arabian question, after convening the Official Sub-Committee, within a matter of hours.[53] The Foreign Office conceded that no more time was lost than if it was in sole control of the Middle East.[54]

The Colonial Office's Arabian 'empire' was finally terminated at its own request in July 1933.[55] Iraq had won independence the previous year, leaving the Colonial Office's central concern, Palestine, remote from the affairs of the Gulf. The India Office resumed responsibility for the political as well as internal affairs of the Gulf except where Ibn Saud was concerned. He, henceforth, came under the effective control of the Foreign Office. The Colonial Office also withdrew from the Middle East Sub-Committee, the chairing of which passed to the India Office.[56]

The Establishment of Diplomatic Relations with Hejaz-Nejd

The British Consulate in Jedda suffered its frustrations. In the last years of Hashemite rule, the then British Consul, Reader Bullard, remarked on the stimulus of working directly with the Foreign Office without the mediating influence of a legation or embassy.[57] By the late 1920s, however, the greatly enhanced status of Ibn Saud, and the seemingly multifarious channels of communication with him, produced uncertainty and confusion in Jedda. The incumbent Agent/Consul, Hugh Stonehewer-Bird, requested clarification of his position.[58] Was he primarily a diplomatic Agent or a Consul? Consular work is practical and ephemeral, more concerned with people than politics, with little business carrying over from one day to the next.[59] In Jedda, the Consul's task was almost exclusively taken up with caring for the interests of the annual influx of pilgrims from India. Apart from the Jedda Consulate, only one British company was represented in the town; the firm of Gellatly, Hankey and Co.[60] Whereas the head of a consular post was no more than an agent of his country, the head of a British diplomatic mission was the direct representative of his sovereign, entitled to negotiate directly with the host Ministry of Foreign Affairs.[61]

The Foreign Office admitted that it was difficult to know whether the Jedda Agent/Consul should have primarily diplomatic or consular rank. He was, under the existing governmental arrangements, only allowed to deal with consular matters. Any diplomatic status would imply that he would take a more important part in questions under Colonial Office supervision.[62] The Foreign Office acknowledged the anomalous situation of having a consular officer as the only British representative to Ibn Saud,[63] yet feared that raising his status to make him accountable to the Colonial Office would possibly weaken its own role in the Hejaz.

Repeated pressure from Ibn Saud spurred a further British innovation. In August 1928 he requested that all British communications pass through Jedda.[64] Ten months later, in June 1929, he suggested the complete transformation of the existing minimal British representation in his dominions. Ibn Saud proposed an exchange of diplomatic representation, with a Hejaz-Nejd Embassy to be established in London and the Jedda Consulate elevated to a comparable position.[65]

The Foreign Office had no intention of setting up a full embassy in Jedda. The volume of work did not seem to require one. The title of an ambassador in diplomatic parlance had already been debased by the world-wide trend of unnecessarily raising to embassy status many minor diplomatic missions.[66] The British Government had no wish to further contribute to the trend, particularly as the title of ambassador was no longer necessarily regarded as superior to that of minister plenipotentiary. Moreover, there was something undignified about the idea of a British Embassy in Jedda, 'the Hejaz not being entirely civilised or used to the customary niceties of diplomacy'.[67] The Hashemites, too, would have been angered by such a prestigious coup on the part of Ibn Saud. For that reason the proposal could expect to receive little support either from the Colonial Office or the India Office. On the other hand, the existing arrangements were causing so many difficulties that the Foreign Office agreed to press the Colonial Office and India Office to converting the Jedda Consulate into a diplomatic mission below the status of an embassy – a legation.[68]

Lord Monteagle, head of the Foreign Office's Eastern Department at the time, enumerated a list of points in favour of setting up a legation. Ibn Saud was far and away the strongest power in Arabia and was, therefore, a factor of prime importance from the point of view of India and the entire

Middle East. Second, Ibn Saud's goodwill was imperative when the strategic position of Hejaz-Nejd was appreciated, and when the air routes to India were in operation. Third, the thousand mile stretch of frontier which Ibn Saud shared with the mandates and the Gulf states demanded close and efficient relations with him. Fourth, the interests of the Pilgrimage could only be enhanced by more efficient channels of communication with Ibn Saud. Finally, by the time Ibn Saud made his suggestion, he had ruled over the Hejaz for more than three years. The Foreign Office, if not the other departments of government, saw no reason to doubt the stability of his regime. His enforcement of public security in the Hejaz, and the standard of its administration, compared favourably with anything under the Hashemites.[69]

The India Office concurred immediately, welcoming this further demonstration of Saudi independence.[70] The Colonial Office was more circumspect. The new Colonial Secretary, Lord Passfield (Sidney Webb), feared the consequences of establishing full diplomatic relations with Hejaz-Nejd which, as the following chapter will demonstrate, was believed at the time to be close to anarchy.[71] The Colonial Office was, furthermore, uneasy at the prospect of allowing Arab spokesmen to operate freely in Britain, which a Hejaz-Nejd mission would entail.[72] Again, the introduction of diplomatic relations would possibly involve further adjustment of the Colonial Office/ Foreign Office condominium in Hejaz-Nejd. Ibn Saud's Foreign Minister was styled 'Minister of Foreign Affairs of the Hejaz, and of Nejd and its Dependencies'. The British Consul, however, was authorised to deal only with the Hejaz. A future British Minister would, therefore, have to be accredited to both the Hejaz and Nejd.[73]

Arabia threw up a host of practical problems for the establishment of a British Legation. For one thing, Jedda's humidity and stifling heat, not to mention its lack of basic amenities, made it quite unsuitable for a senior man with a family.[74] This may have led to a shortage of suitable candidates, and required a change in the staffing of the post every two or three years in order to spare the strains on the incumbent's health.

A further difficulty concerned the selection of the appropriate Minister. Should he come from the Diplomatic Service, or the specialised Levant Consular Service? At that time there existed a General Consular Service alongside several specialised services for China, Japan, Siam and the Levant, although they all merged into the General Consular Service in 1936.[75] The responsibilities of the Levant Consular Service extended from Morocco to Egypt, from the Yemen to the Balkans, and from western Turkey to eastern Persia.[76] The Levant Service had staffed the Jedda post in the past, and had a long and distinguished record of dealing with the Orient and the Arab world. Senior diplomatic representation throughout the world was, however, traditionally reserved for the Diplomatic Service. Yet the Levant Service, with its past record, would have felt slighted if it lost the post at the moment that its status and immoluments were raised.[77] Opportunities for promotion within the Levant Service had, unlike the General Consular Service, always been limited, there being few vacancies for the rank of Consul-General.[78] It was decided to make the Jedda Legation a 'plum' for the Levant Service by giving ministerial rank to one of its officers.[79]

Opting for the Levant Consular Service solved the problem of who was to staff the new Legation, yet the difficulty remained of choosing a suitable candidate to fill it. The existing Agent/Consul, William Bond, was, at 36, considered to be too junior for the post. Conversely, he had only recently taken up his duties, and it would have been wasteful to move him so soon when he was gaining valuable experience.[80] Ibn Saud was not likely to object to Bond's appointment. He had requested a change in the status of the Consulate, not its personnel.[81] Full diplomatic relations were established in December 1929, and by way of compromise Bond was appointed *Chargé d'Affaires* until such time as a more appropriate Minister could be found.[82]

To circumvent the problems presented by the climate of Jedda, it was decided to stipulate not a special two-year tenure of appointment, but the standard five-year period, with extra facilities for leave amounting to four or five months *per annum* on full salary.[83] Not only was this a more economical arrangement, it also avoided the problem of flooding the Levant Consular Service with ex-Jedda Ministers who were bound to be demoted.[84] Moreover, a short-term appointment would involve inefficiencies. Little valuable work was normally done in the first few months of a foreign posting when the diplomat was finding his feet. Similarly, his usefulness diminished in the closing months of duty when much of his time was spent winding up old business.[85] Nor would the British Government seek any precedence for its Minister, such as the High Commissioners enjoyed in the mandates. This was a reflection both of Ibn Saud's complete independence, and of the fact that any attempt at securing such precedence would have been vilified by the Moslem world.[86] Britain was beaten, both in recognition of Ibn Saud and in establishing diplomatic relations with him, by the Soviet Union.[87]

The first British Envoy Extraordinary and Minister Plenipotentiary to Hejaz-Nejd was Sir Andrew Ryan, an Irishman, who arrived, with considerable experience of Oriental affairs, from the post of Consul-General in Rabat, Morocco, which he had held since 1924. Ryan's *forte* was Turkish law; he had done important work at the Lausanne Conference. Despite reservations about moving from a salaried consular career to a diplomatic posting, which still expected its servants to rely on private income, Ryan eventually presented his credentials to Ibn Saud in May 1930. Significantly, Ryan, though he spoke Turkish, did not speak Arabic.[88] The *Evening Standard* remarked on the inefficiency of separating the Diplomatic and Consular Services, together with the effective barrier to consular promotion, and suggested that Ryan's appointment was a notable breakthrough.[89]

His opposite number, in London, was Sheikh Hafiz Wahba, who was to remain as Minister, later Ambassador, for over thirty years. Wahba was a pan-Islamic Egyptian who had displayed Anglophobic tendencies during the First World War. He had moved to India where he had come into contact with the anti-British Khilafat Movement.[90] Moving to Kuwait he found favour with Ibn Saud. Wahba became the first Saudi administrator of Mecca, and later Assistant Viceroy of the Hejaz. Around 1927 his personal relations with Ibn Saud deteriorated. It was not immediately apparent, therefore, whether posting Wahba to London showed further disfavour with Ibn Saud, or a reinstatement of his earlier prominence. In any case, by 1930, Wahba was considered to have modified his earlier Anglophobic tendencies.[91]

Notwithstanding the exchange of Ministers, Ryan found innumerable obstacles in the way of efficient diplomatic relations with the Hejaz-Nejd Government. One problem was Ibn Saud's inaccessibility for much of the year when resident in Nejd, and the fact that his subordinates, widely believed to be in the grip of Anglophobia, could take no major decisions without consulting him. Moreover, the Hejaz Ministry of Foreign Affairs was situated in Mecca, which led Ryan to remark that the only relevant power not represented in Jedda was Hejaz-Nejd itself.[92] Personal links between Jedda and Mecca were infrequent, and the telephone of only 'moderate efficiency'.[93] Consequently, there existed few opportunities for Ryan to discuss serious questions with either Ibn Saud or his Foreign Minister. The normal social exchanges, as a means of gathering information, were not possible for Ryan and his small staff. Nor was he in a position to acquaint himself with the Mecca Foreign Ministry.[94] Ryan's incarceration in Jedda contrasted with Wahba's freedom to travel as he pleased in Britain. Yet apart from climatic hardships the British Legation rarely suffered from overwork, except at periods of particular tension or during the annual Pilgrimage. In 1937 Ryan's successor, Reader Bullard, confided: 'I feel that I do little enough to earn my living in normal times'.[95]

Partly in response to British requests Ibn Saud, in December 1930, reorganised his Foreign Ministry. The Emir Faisal added the title of Minister of Foreign Affairs to his existing title of Viceroy of the Hejaz.[96] This reorganisation allowed, in theory, closer contact between Ibn Saud and his foreign representatives, by having Faisal in Mecca in his titular capacity, with his Deputy Foreign Minister, Fuad Bey Hamza, able to spend more time in Jedda.[97]

The establishment of a British Legation together with normal diplomatic relations required further revision of the communication channels operating with Hejaz-Nejd. The High Commissioners in Jerusalem and Baghdad were still permitted to approach Ibn Saud directly on matters of extreme urgency, if he was in the interior, but a copy of the correspondence and a covering explanation had to be sent to Jedda.[98] The arrival of a British Minister and the apparatus of the Official Sub-Committee on the Middle East enabled governmental decisions to be reached quicker and with less special pleading. All this provided for the more efficient management of Anglo-Saudi relations throughout the 1930s.

Diplomatic Representation in Ibn Saud's Dominions

By the end of 1930 five countries had established legations in Jedda. Those of Britain and the Soviet Union contained Ministers; while those of the Netherlands, Iran and Turkey had a permanent *Chargé d'Affaires*.[99] France was in the anomalous position of having retained a Consulate, but maintaining a *Chargé d'Affaires* at its head.[100] A further burst of diplomatic activity occurred in the middle of the decade. By 1936 Belgium and Czechoslovakia were represented by Honorary Consuls. France upgraded her Consulate to a Legation, and her *Chargé d'Affaires* to a Minister. The Governments of Italy, the Netherlands, Turkey and Iraq had appointed *Chargé d'Affaires*, while those of Egypt, Afghanistan and Iran had Ministers.[101] During 1939 Germany and the United States also established diplomatic relations with Saudi Arabia.

Summary and Conclusions

Both diplomatic innovations of 1930 – the exchange of Ministers and the setting-up of the Official Sub-Committee on the Middle East – paved the way for easier and more effective communications between Britain and Hejaz-Nejd. These developments inevitably increased the role of the Foreign Office in Saudi affairs at the expense of the Colonial Office, despite earlier suggestions that the opposite might occur. A British Legation could not remain indefinitely under the aegis of the Colonial Office. Nor could the creation of the Official Sub-Committee but dilute the Colonial Office's paramount position in Arabian affairs.

Internal developments in the Arab world further reduced the links between the Colonial Office and Ibn Saud. His ever-increasing stature through the 1930s, and the consequent desire of the British Government to stand well by him, thrust the Foreign Office deeper into its accustomed role of dealing directly with independent governments. Elsewhere in the Arab world the role of the Colonial Office was further reduced, both by the ending of the mandate in Iraq in 1932 (with her admission into the League of Nations and transfer of responsibility to the Foreign Office) and by the general expressions of independence being generated during that decade throughout the Middle East. For all these reasons, the theatre of Colonial Office operations steadily diminished until, by 1939, only Palestine and Aden at opposite ends of the Arab world were accountable to it.[102] It will be noticed that, whereas in 1925 the Colonial Office wielded greatest influence in Britain's Arabian policy, as evidenced during the Aqaba-Maan dispute, by the late 1930s the bulk of that influence lay with the Foreign Office.

The exchange of diplomatic legations with the British Government was a considerable boost to Ibn Saud's international standing. In this respect, the establishment of diplomatic relations can be seen as the second of Ibn Saud's three objectives aimed at bringing his dominions, as equal members, into the world fraternity of nations.[103] The first objective, already accomplished, was recognition by Britain of his legitimate sovereignty over the Hejaz. The third, bringing his dominions into the League of Nations, will be the focus of a later chapter.

All things considered, it can be seen that, notwithstanding British tardiness in establishing diplomatic relations with Hejaz-Nejd, and the solution to staff the Jedda Legation with a non-Arabic speaking member of the Levant Consular Service, the eventual establishment of the legation reflected that, under Ibn Saud, Hejaz-Nejd commanded greater international attention than the sum of its constituent parts. The anomalous position of the Colonial Office in Anglo-Saudi relations illustrated not so much the desire to impose controls on Saudi independence, as the need to take the susceptibilities of all branches of Government into account in framing British policy.

Up to 1929 the evidence of this and previous chapters would suggest that the British Government, while taking heed of the exploits of Ibn Saud and the need to adapt relations with him, still had not come round to viewing him as a critical factor in Britain's position in the Arab world. Ibn Saud was still some seven or eight years from achieving that kind of prominence. Nonetheless, even while Britain was engaged in upgrading her various channels of communication with him, developments on the Iraq-Nejd frontier had deteriorated to the extent that, briefly, Britain was at war with Nejd.

REFERENCES FOR CHAPTER FOUR

1. See Ryan to FO, Annual Report for 1930, No 149, 18 April 1931, (hereafter: Annual Report 1930), FO E/2485/2485/91: 371/15300.
2. See Bullard to FO, January 1937, FO E/585/585/25: 371/20842.
3. Grafftey-Smith, p. 145.
4. Ryan to FO, Annual Report for 1932, 26 February 1933: 371/16876. (hereafter: Annual Report 1932.)
5. Mayers (Jedda) to FO, No 26, 5 April 1927, FO E/1606/323/91: 371/12248.
6. ibid.
7. Philby, *Arabian Jubilee*, p. 91.
8. Annual Report 1932.
9. FO Trade Report, 26 June 1936, FO E/5458/1041/25: 371/20063.
10. Grafftey-Smith, p. 151.
11. Stonehewer-Bird (Jedda) to FO, 10 January 1928, FO E/485/1/91: 371/12988.
12. Dobbs (Baghdad) to Shuckburgh, 3 November 1928, CO/59129/28: 732/35.
13. Bond (Jedda) to Rendel, 18 July 1929, FO E/3948/63/91: 371/13725.
14. Butler (FO) memorandum, 23 July 1929, FO E/3755/200/91: 371/13729.
15. ibid.
16. ibid.
17. Warner (FO) minute, 12 August 1930, FO E/4309/4309/91: 371/14483.
18. Monroe, *Philby* ..., p. 148.
19. Jakins (Jedda) to FO, No 78, 1 April 1929, FO E/2171/94/91: 371/13728.

20. The position in the Gulf was giving rise to particular confusion. The Political Resident was accountable to the Colonial Office for political matters, to the India Office for recruitment and administration, and to the Foreign Office on Iranian questions.
21. CO memorandum, 12 March 1926, CO/2244/26: 727/12.
22. For a discussion on attitudes to the Foreign Office, see William Wallace, *The Foreign Policy Making Process in Britain*, p. 50.
23. CO memorandum, op. cit.
24. ibid.
25. ibid.
26. Inter-departmental conference, 12 March 1926, FO E/2026/180/91: 371/11437.
27. Rendel, p. 60.
28. Inter-departmental conference, op. cit.
29. Clayton to Shuckburgh, 21 April 1926, in FO E/2580/180/91: 371/11437.
30. ibid.
31. Rendel, p. 48.
32. Inter-departmental conference, 8 March 1926, FO E/1738/180/91: 371/11437.
33. Oliphant minute, 9 March 1926, FO E/1738/180/91: 371/11437.
34. See Monteagle (FO) minute, 27 November 1929, FO E/6109/2322/91: 371/13738.
35. CO memorandum, op. cit.
36. CO memorandum on British Interests in Arabia, 27 November 1926 (hereafter: CO memorandum 1926), in FO E/6578/870/91: 371/11445.
37. ibid.
38. Osborne (FO) minute, 22 November 1926, FO E/5967/572/91: 371/11444.
39. Iraq's northern frontier with Turkey had been settled earlier the same year.
40. CO memorandum 1926.
41. ibid.
42. ibid.
43. ibid.
44. ibid.
45. From 1921 the Colonial Office had kept a separate 'Arabia' file. This file was wound up as from 1926.
46. Osborne minute, 11 January 1928, FO E/165/1/91: 371/12988 (See Chapter Five on the *Ikhwan* rebellion).
47. ibid.
48. CO to FO, 18 January 1928, CO/59208/28: 732/36.
49. Franklyn A. Johnson, *Defence by Committee: The British Committee of Imperial Defence 1885-1959*, p. 222.
50. See CAB 44(30)7, 23 July 1930, CAB 23.
51. ibid. The Ministerial Sub-Committee was composed of the appropriate Secretaries of State.
52. See FO E/5789/5789/91: 371/14484.
53. ibid.
54. ibid. Not everybody was so impressed with such sub-committees. Lloyd-George, for example, who had been involved in many, described them as 'useful for exploration: but futile for action' (Johnson, pp. 222-3).
55. British Interests in the Persian Gulf: Report of the Political Department of British India, 25 June 1935, L/P&S/18B 450.
56. ibid.
57. Bullard, *The Camels Must Go*, p. 123.
58. Stonehewer-Bird to Rendel, 6 April 1928, FO E/2271/317/91: 371/13008.
59. Grafftey-Smith, p. 13.
60. ibid., p. 169.
61. Lord Strang, *The Foreign Office*, p. 123. An Agent was somewhere between a Minister and a Consul in status, but, unlike Consuls, he was empowered to deal directly with sovereign governments (Baker, p. 120).
62. Rendel minute, 14 May 1928, FO E/2771/317/91: 371/13008.
63. ibid.
64. CO to FO, 30 August 1928, CO/59176/28: 732/36.
65. Hafiz Wahba to FO, 24 June 1929, FO E/3252/821/91: 371/13734.

66. Strang, p.77. The traditional tasks of an Ambassador/Minister had included those of communicating the wishes of his government and seeking to fulfil them, as well as sending objective reports on the political, economic and social conditions of the country to which he was accredited. The advent of the telephone and the telegraph had reduced his role as negotiator (though this was less evident in the case of Jedda) and less emphasis was given to Ambassadorial reports under the sheer weight of foreign correspondence (Gordon A. Craig, 'The Professional Diplomat and his Problems 1919-1939', *World Politics*, 4 (1952), p. 150). In 1913 the number of overseas despatches received at the Foreign Office was 68,000. By 1938 the number was 224,000. Consequently, the reading of 'situation reports' tended to be deferred in favour of 'urgent' despatches (DBFP, 1st series, 1. p. iii).
67. Oliphant minute, 27 June 1929, FO E/3252/821/91: 371/13734.
68. ibid.
69. Monteagle to Treasury, 29 November 1929, FO E/6131/821/91: 371/13734.
70. IO to FO, 19 July 1929, FO E/3643/821/91: 371/13734.
71. CO to FO, 1 August 1929, CO/69146/29: 732/41.
72. Monteagle minute, 14 August 1929, FO E/3857/821/91: 371/13734.
73. See Rendel minute, 7 May 1929, FO E/2404/821/91: 371/13734.
74. Butler (FO) minute, 13 August 1929, FO E/3857/821/91: 371/13734.
75. Strang, p. 67.
76. Grafftey-Smith, p. 1. Much of the work of the Levant Consular Service was concerned with extra-territorial issues. This made it, in effect, a semi-imperial institution in character. It had been badly affected by Turkey's entry into the War and the closure of many of its posts. Moreover, with the widespread abolition of extra-territorial rights after 1918, one major function of the consular services disappeared (Peter Byrd, 'Regional and Functional Specialisation in the British Consular Service', *Journal of Contemporary History*, 7 (Jan–Apr 1972), pp. 135, 137).
77. Monteagle minute, 21 August 1929, FO E/3857/821/91: 371/13734.
78. Grafftey-Smith, p. 9.
79. Monteagle minute, op. cit.
80. ibid.
81. ibid.
82. The first unofficial British representation in Jedda occurred in the 1830s. For much of the nineteenth century the post was filled on a makeshift, unpaid basis, with Consuls of various nationalities. During the First World War the military mission to the Hejaz became a branch of the Arab Bureau. Reconstitution of the Agency under the formal control of the Foreign Office began after the War.
83. Treasury to FO, 5 December 1929, FO E/6349/821/91: 371/13734; Sir Andrew Ryan, *Last of the Dragomans*, p. 261.
84. FO minute, FO E/3857/821/91: 371/13734.
85. Rendel minute, 26 August 1929, ibid.
86. Rendel minute, 7 November 1929, FO E/5693/821/91: 371/13734. The India Office would have obstructed any move to establish a Legation based on the British Minister holding perpetual precedence.
87. See FO minute, FO E/6349/821/91: 371/13734.
88. See FO E/6074/3094/91: 371/14481. The wide differences of language and politics within the Levant area prevented officials from achieving complete inter-service availability (Byrd, p. 142).
89. *Evening Standard*, 31 January 1930. From a career point of view Ryan was indeed fortunate. In the same month as his appointment was announced nine fellow Levant Consul-Generals demanded a committee of enquiry to look into the demoralisation and slow promotion within the service (Byrd, p. 141).
90. See FO memorandum, April 1928, FO E/2137/2137/91: 371/13015.
91. ibid., FO E/4713/334/91: 371/14468.
92. Philby, *Saudi Arabia*, p. 314.
93. Ryan to FO, No 187, 22 July 1930, FO E/4309/4309/91: 371/14483.
94. ibid.
95. Bullard to Ryan, 13 June 1937, Ryan Papers, Box 6, File 5, MEC. Consular work, it seemed, was not heavy throughout the Gulf region (Coen, p. 227).
96. Annual Report 1930.

97. Ryan to Rendel, 2 February 1931, FO E/543/282/25: 371/15292.
98. CO to FO, 7 November 1930, CO/79137/30: 732/44.
99. Annual Report 1930.
100. ibid.
101. Trott (Jedda) to FO, 1 August 1937, FO E/4918/580/25: 371/20841.
102. Aden was, in fact, only transferred to Colonial Office administration in 1937. (See Chapter Ten).
103. Annual Report 1930.

CHAPTER FIVE

The Nejd-Mandate Frontiers: The *Ikhwan* Rebellion

Frontiers are the chief anxiety of nearly every Foreign Office in the civilised world and are the subject of four out of every five political treaties. Frontier policy ... has a more profound effect upon the peace or warfare of nations than any other factor, political or economic. (Lord Curzon, *Frontiers*, pp. 3-4)

This chapter deals principally with frontier issues.[1] Only months after the signing of the Treaty of Jedda, tribal unrest spilled into Iraq from her southern frontier. For more than two years the security of the mandate was under threat, and even the viability of Ibn Saud's regime brought into question. The significance of this protracted episode for this study is twofold. Firstly, it gives further consideration to the relationship between British policy towards the Hashemites and that towards Ibn Saud. The unrest spot-lighted the fragile stability caused by the exposed southern reaches of the mandates and the northward momentum of Wahhabi proselytisation. Many of the issues raised in the Aqaba-Maan affair find fuller expression in the unfolding of the *Ikhwan* rebellion; one of the most prominent episodes to emerge from the uncomfortable juxtaposition of Ibn Saud's dominions with British interests. Secondly, these hostilities broadly coincided with, and indeed facilitated, political developments aimed at strengthening the channels of Anglo-Saudi relations as described in the previous chapter. Problems of communication, both diplomatic and physical, feature prominently in the coming pages.

The needs of the Hejaz demanded Ibn Saud's presence in Mecca in the months that followed its conquest. The contrasting nature of his dominions (Hejaz and Nejd) required contrasting policies. To win the confidence of the Hejazis, to attract pilgrims and to appease the watching outside world, Ibn Saud had to appear to relax the excesses of Wahhabism.[2] Like Husein before him, Ibn Saud now depended on the Pilgrimage for his principal source of income. That necessitated securing the Hejaz from the plunder of the *Ikhwan*, as well as enticing the world's Moslem community by restraining the more extreme Wahhabi practices, such as the destruction of tombs and other sacred places.[3]

Nejd, in contrast, remained an isolated mediaeval theocracy. Many of Ibn Saud's activities as King of the Hejaz deeply offended his one-time closest and most fanatical supporters. The very title 'King of the Hejaz' smacked of worldly indulgence, and had been besmirched by the heresies of his Hashemite predecessors.[4] Ibn Saud had put an end to the warring and looting upon which the *Ikhwan* thrived. Many of the new tribes to fall under his sway were long and bitter enemies of the *Ikhwan*, who found their accustomed position as Ibn Saud's trusted militia being eroded.[5] Ibn Saud was flirting with instruments of the infidel – motor cars, telephones and wirelesses. Indeed, when the Persian Government hesitated to allow Imperial Airways landing facilities for its newly planned route to India, Ibn Saud was reportedly considering a British request to grant facilities for infidel flying machines in Hasa.[6] His apparent new policy of conciliation and progressiveness infuriated the *Ikhwan*, as did his insistence that he saw himself foremost as the political, not religious, leader of the Hejaz. For his part, *Ikhwan* attacks on the Egyptian *Mahmal* in 1926 angered Ibn Saud by affronting established Islamic practices.[7]

During the *Ikhwan* campaigns of the 1920s, victims had been obliged to pay *zakat. Zakat* was originally an Islamic alms tax, payment of which gradually evolved into a symbol of political allegiance. The act of giving was more important than the alms.[8] Most of the income of tribal chiefs came in the form of *zakat* and other tribute. *Ikhwan* raids brought Ibn Saud considerable revenues. Not only did he receive direct taxation, but the allegiance that stemmed from it entitled him to all the economic rewards of the victims' territories. Part of this income went, in turn, to buy tribal support. In 1927 Ibn Saud, perhaps for financial reasons stemming from the vastly increased responsibilities incurred in administering the Hejaz, withheld certain allowances due to the *Ikhwan*.[9] Worst of all, preoccupied in the Hejaz, Ibn Saud disbanded the *Ikhwan* and sent them back, redundant, into the interior. They had, in any case, found the transition from their traditional economic, political and religious lifestyle difficult to sustain,[10] and had antagonised other members of Nejdi society – merchants, farmers and the *ulema*. They began to abandon their colonies (*hijras*), reverting to their original tribal alliances and means of livelihood. While Ibn Saud established a Saudi bureaucracy in the Hejaz, and dared to negotiate a treaty with Clayton, the *Ikhwan's* grievances multiplied. As Philby summarised it:

> No sooner had the Wahhabis done what was required of them in war then they were packed off home to brood on the iniquity of the world at large and to await their next summons to do such work as God might require them. Some of their leaders may already have begun to wonder whether their chief, whom they had served so faithfully, was not slackening in his zeal for the service of God, while they themselves were burning to teach in Iraq and Syria the lessons that they had taught among the people of the Hejaz.[11]

On 5 November 1927, less than two years after Ibn Saud had been proclaimed King of the Hejaz, and only weeks after the ratification of the Treaty of Jedda, a party of *Ikhwan* attacked and killed a score of coolies and policemen engaged in constructing a fortified police-post at Busaiya, in the southern desert of Iraq. This act was the first incident of what later became known as the *Ikhwan* rebellion.[12]

A History of Iraq and of Desert Raiding prior to 1927

The mandated territory of Iraq, approximating to the historic area known as Mesopotamia, emerged out of the post-First World War reconstruction of the Arab provinces of the Ottoman Empire.[13] Largely as a result of Feisal's intransigence and pressure from Iraqi nationalist sentiment, Iraq was not administered under the terms of the mandate, but, more acceptably under the terms of a series of bilateral treaties.[14] These treaties provided Iraq with a parliament and a constitution. Any disputes arising out of the treaties were referred not to Geneva, but to the Permanent Court of International Justice at The Hague.[15]

In the early 1920s the principal value of Iraq to Britain was strategic.[16] It lay on the overland route to India, and, together with Palestine and Transjordan, provided a continuous belt of British-backed territory from the Mediterranean to the Gulf. This 'bridge' was implicit in the creation of the mandates, and was made explicit in the 1925 Hadda Agreement which extended Transjordan's frontiers to join those of Iraq.

The strategic value of Iraq steadily increased during the 1920s as plans for road, rail and air links with the East, which would traverse the mandate, matured.[17] With the growth of air travel, particularly as a means of moving troops, the strategic routes to India increasingly turned over the mandates at the expense of Suez. Iraq's deserts became studded with dumps and landing grounds. Oil further enhanced Iraq's importance. The oilfields of western Iran lay near the Iraqi frontier. In 1927 a massive oil strike at Kirkuk, in northern Iraq, ensured the mandates's economic, as well as strategic importance to Britain. A pipeline, eventually completed in 1934, was earmarked to carry the oil to Haifa on the Mediterranean.[18]

Iraq was an artificial construction: geographically, ethnologically and constitutionally. It comprised both Sunni and Shiite Moslems. It had various racial minority groups, notably Kurds and Assyrians, which periodically sparked political tension.[19] It had a King imported from the other side of Arabia. Under the terms of the mandate and the Anglo-Iraqi treaty of 1922, King Feisal and his Government enjoyed juridical sovereignty, but undertook to 'be guided by the advice of His Britannic Majesty tendered through the High Commissioner on all important matters affecting the international and financial obligations and interests of His Britannic Majesty'.[20]

Territorially, Iraq embraced marshland, plains, mountains and desert.

It was the desert, particularly the 'southern desert' south of the River Euphrates, which led to difficulties with Nejd. Britain's strategic and economic interests in Iraq concentrated attention on the populous urban areas, which offered most benefits for transport and communications.[21] To the British it made more sense to draw frontiers through the deserts, where there were no settled populations, than make use of any natural frontiers, such as the Euphrates and Tigris river systems.[22] The deserts, it was wrongly assumed, were of comparatively little significance to the population, yet artificially imposed frontier lines cut through tribal grazing homelands (*diras*) and centuries-old commercial and political links.[23] Furthermore, Britain needed a defensive perimeter for Iraq which would protect the urban areas flanking the great rivers – particularly with the Wahhabi sacking of Shiite shrines at Karbala near the Euphrates in 1801 not forgotten.[24] It was important to keep Nejdi tribes away from the planned communication lines. And, not insignificantly, deserts were cheaper to defend than were urban centres.[25]

In 1922 Iraq's first High Commissioner, Sir Percy Cox, in settling the Iraq-Nejd frontier on arbitrary, mathematical principles rather than geographical or tribal ones, imposed it some 150 miles south of the Euphrates.[26] In doing so, Cox, in the words of one writer: 'gave a strip of desert to Iraq, and the Government of Iraq, a country which was settled, agricultural and even urban in its outlook, did not really want a desert and was poorly equipped to rule it'.[27] Besides, the frontier was not demarcated on the ground.[28] The maps of the day operated with a scale of 1 : 1 million. They contained a dearth of identifiable place names. Only Arabs with access to and the ability to read those maps had the remotest idea of where the frontier lay.[29] For the ordinary bedouin the frontier was both unidentifiable and incomprehensible.

Inter-tribal camel-raiding (*ghazzu*) was an endemic feature of Arabian life. As portrayed by British observers at the time, raiding was viewed somewhat patronisingly as a sport. Dickson, for example, was more condescending than admiring when he wrote:

> Raiding is the breath of life to the Badawin ... Just as in the civilised West man must have his various sports, football, cricket, ... etc., to keep him happy, so in Arabia the primitive Badawin must have his raids. They denote to him everything that is manly and sporting [and] do not, as a rule, entail much bloodshed.[30]

More objective accounts of bedouin camel-raiding castigate the ideal of the romanticised warrior-nomads.[31] In northern Arabia, status, power and prestige were measured in terms of camel herds.[32] The camel was a multi-purpose beast in the bedouin economy, being the primary source of nutrients, wool, leather, transport and freight, not to mention its military value.[33] As camels were never bought and sold, the only method of circulation among the tribes was through raiding.[34] The dispossessed would make up their losses on another tribe. The natural equilibrium of the desert ensured that tribes neither prospered nor suffered for very long.[35]

Camel-raiding, moreover, was a year-round institutionalised activity, not a direct response to camel losses, and was closely related to tribal hierarchies.[36] Raids often witnessed minimal violence, but rather than this being due to 'sporting' considerations, it has been suggested that raids were non-lethal because of the lack of any bedouin loyalties. They had no home, country, honour or religion to fight for.[37] Economically, peace tended to diminish wealth, so that plunder became necessary in order to survive. In view of the sharp contrast in the geographical conditions in neighbouring *diras* raiding was the only means of restoring camel strength. Paradoxically, raiding contributed to desert stability and, through reciprocal raids, encouraged continuous communication and negotiation among the desert tribes.[38]

In contrast to camel-raiding, there were various other types of conflict in Arabian society, such as attacks on weaker tribes for tribute, or the simple extension of hegemony.[39] In such instances, where one or more of the combatants was not considered a 'noble' tribe, raiding etiquette was less sharply defined.[40] Certain tribes, such as the Ajman of Hasa, and the Mutair of northern Nejd, were regarded as 'noble' Arabs.[41] This gave them an elite position in the desert among tribal genealogies. Any tribal chieftain who was obliged to pay tribute to another could lose his hold over his people.[42]

Two factors introduced a new dimension into desert raiding in the early 1920s, one internal, the other external. The internal factor was the emergence of the *Ikhwan*. By 1927 the number of active *Ikhwan* males was estimated at around 150,000.[43] They traditionally fought under the immediate orders of their respective sheikhs who, in turn, paid allegiance to Ibn Saud.[44] Religious zeal, allied to the greater size of an *Ikhwan* raiding party, invariably transformed a raid into a massacre.[45]

The external factor was the creation of the mandates and the use of the Royal Air Force to defend them. Given the economic aspect of bedouin raids, and the network of tribal relationships criss-crossed throughout Arabia, the imposition of boundary lines bisecting the desert had a disruptive effect on desert life. Climatic factors had for centuries determined that Nejdi tribes would seasonally migrate northwards in search of fresh grazing, as well as plunder. In sum, the very existence of British-defended mandates threatened the traditional bedouin way of life in northern Arabia. Moreover, the introduction of western technology, such as weaponry, tools and transport, affected the demand for camels and the distribution of water resources.[46]

In the 1920s raids across the Iraq-Nejd frontier began to have political connotations. Despite the arbitrary division of territory, the tribes continued to pay allegiance not to a remote government but to their effective overlord. Frontier lines drawn through the desert gave legal sanctuary to tribes which crossed them, enabling them to avoid paying *zakat*. After Ibn Saud's conquest of Hail in 1921 certain Shammar tribes, rather than pay homage to Ibn Saud, moved across the Iraq frontier, from where they repeatedly raided back into Nejd before fleeing to the sanctuary of Iraq.[47] Similarly, *Ikhwan* raids into the mandates were followed by swift withdrawal back into Nejd to avoid aerial reprisals.

The tribal balance of southern Iraq was courting trouble with the *Ikhwan*. The majority of tribes south of the Euphrates were not camel-herding bedouin, but relatively defenceless shepherds, who were also Shiites and fundamentally opposed to the tenets of Wahhabism.[48] In an earlier age the shepherds would have exchanged tribute for protection from a powerful local sheikh. By the 1920s their only recourse was to appeal to the Government at Baghdad, which could do nothing without fortifying the frontier. Besides, the signing of the Bahra Agreement had not fully satisfied Ibn Saud. He had hoped to break desert custom by having extradition rights included which would prevent tribes escaping his authority. Nor did that document reassure all British officials in the Middle East:

> Frontier lines drawn on maps across desert regions will not prevail … against the logic of tribal relations and interdependence. Without any formal infringement of his treaties with Clayton, Bin Saud's influence could spread north of the accepted frontier and Bin Saud would be astride the motor and air communications, as well as the possible railway and pipeline between Iraq and the Mediterranean.[49]

With the *Ikhwan* occupied by the Hejaz campaign, the Iraq frontier enjoyed a period of calm. Signs of future disturbances were in the air, however. Reports from the Gulf, late in 1926, warned of *Ikhwan* agitation directed towards Iraq and Kuwait.[50] The chiefs of the Mutair, Utaiba and Ajman tribes had allegedly pledged an oath of mutual support against Ibn Saud.[51] Moreover, the effectiveness of the Hadda and Bahra Agreements had been compromised by abortive attempts to set up the tribunal machinery for which they provided as a method of settling responsibility for past raids. Disagreement with Ibn Saud over the presidency and location of the tribunal, together with his professed scepticism at such a dilatory process, led to months of inconsequential wrangling and the eventual abandonment of the tribunal.[52] Such was the background to the attack at Busaiya.

The British Reaction to Busaiya: from London, Baghdad and Bushire

The Busaiya raid constituted an attack upon territory for whose defence the British Government was responsible. Two years previously a Saudi threat to Aqaba had resulted in urgent inter-departmental consultation and Cabinet intervention. The situation in Iraq in 1927 was both more grave and more complex. The danger to Aqaba had been hypothetical: that to Busaiya had materialised without warning. Aqaba was considered by Ibn Saud to be part of the Hejaz, whereas Busaiya, although of little significance in itself, lay deep in Iraq. Finally, the menace posed to Aqaba was Ibn Saud himself. It was not certain whether he was similarly behind the attack on Busaiya or whether the British Government was dealing with genuine renegade Nejdis. Ibn Saud had disavowed direct responsibility for the raid.[53]

Despite the gravity of the Busaiya incident the facts were slow to emerge. It was not until late December that a clear picture of events reached London. In formulating a policy response in the early weeks of 1928, conflicting interpretations were voiced. Three major sets of interests were at stake. First, there was the position from Iraq itself. Second, there were the anxieties stemming from nearby Kuwait, which affected the India Office. Third, there was the international context as perceived by the Foreign Office in London.

The reaction of Sir Henry Dobbs, High Commissioner of Iraq, was unequivocal. Busaiya had been followed by further raids. Dobbs pressed for all possible punitive measures to be adopted against Nejd.[54] The savagery of the raids, the fear that Ibn Saud would be unwilling or unable to march against an alliance of *Ikhwan* chiefs, and the need to safeguard British prestige, combined to make Dobbs demand military intervention.[55] Iraq held a permanent fear of Wahhabism since the sacking of Karbala. Following that incident the Ottoman Empire had endeavoured to suppress Wahhabism: now, Dobbs argued, Britain should do the same.[56]

Dobbs was aware that to plead for the vulnerability of Iraq would carry little weight when the British Government had to take so many factors into consideration, not all of them local ones. Accordingly, Dobbs played on the wider strategic implications affecting Iraq as a stepping stone to the East. It was only a month before the Busaiya incident that oil had been struck at Kirkuk – establishing Iraq, along with Iran, as the major Middle Eastern oil producers of the time.[57] An unsettled Iraq-Nejd frontier bore the risk of having to re-route the proposed pipeline and railway further north through Syria. This would mean a Mediterranean terminus not, as hoped for, at Haifa in Palestine, but in French mandated territory. Such a prospect would deprive Britain of exclusive control over the whole length of the communications chain. Britain's trade with the region would suffer, as would the development of Haifa, and Palestine in general.[58] In the event of a wider conflict breaking out in the Middle East, in which France remained neutral, the British Mediterranean fleet would be unable to use the Syrian oil terminal.[59] Strategically, too, the line of communications for military reinforcements from Egypt would be broken by a successful Wahhabi thrust into southern Iraq.[60]

As for Ibn Saud, Dobbs pronounced him guilty by association, suggesting that he enjoyed only nominal suzerainty over the affairs of Nejd, much as the Turks had done in earlier times. Even so, Dobbs considered him a 'complacent ally' of the raiders.[61]

Broad support for Dobbs' position came from the Air Ministry. The presence of the Royal Air Force as guarantor of the mandates' security had established an international precedent.[62] The substitution of the RAF for the War Office's army of occupation in Iraq in 1922 had been justified on several grounds, notably that of expense.[63] A few planes could, hopefully, do the job of an army. The Egyptians in the nineteenth century, and the Turks early in the twentieth, had demonstrated that troops were not effective in the Arabian deserts. Lack of roads made marching difficult and raised problems of supply. Poor communications, heat, and Iraq's varied terrain added to an army's difficulties. Aircraft were immune from these handicaps and those of the time could land almost anywhere. They had the additional advantage of speed. Engaging a desert enemy with troops took weeks or months to prepare and execute. Aircraft could be airborne, engage the enemy, and return to base within a matter of hours.[64]

In practice, the RAF found matters rather more difficult. It had to contend with prolonged scepticism from the other, more senior service departments.[65] As had been demonstrated during the Aqaba affair, Air Force bases were so few and far between, and the range of aircraft so limited, that the RAF had been unable to give assurances of adequate protection. Similarly, as the Iraq-Nejd frontier was at least one hundred miles from the nearest RAF base in the mandate, the Air Ministry could not undertake to police it.[66] Moreover, from the sky, it was impossible to tell friend from foe. Without any intelligence system directing the planes to specific locations, there was every risk of bombing mistaken targets. Bombs were indiscriminate, killing women and children, sheep and camels, as easily as *Ikhwan* – yet because raiders tended to scatter at the sight or sound of an aeroplane, casualties were relatively light. Desert conditions, too, such as sandstorms, frequently ruled out RAF operations.[67] In the two years of stability on the Iraq-Nejd frontier which followed the signing of the Bahra Agreement, RAF pilots had been given no opportunity to gain experience of *Ikhwan* tactics.[68]

Nonetheless, the impression is gained through examining Air Ministry correspondence that the *Ikhwan* rebellion provided an opportunity to vindicate the decision to entrust mandate defence to the Royal Air Force. The Air Ministry's case benefited from the uncompromising attitude of Sir Hugh Trenchard, Chief of the Air Staff. The key to control in a vast country like Iraq, argued Trenchard, was instant retaliation by air against raiders crossing the frontier.[69] He admitted that aircraft could not prevent raids, but insisted that retaliatory air strikes could deter them.[70] Trenchard's solution was to hit hard at the villages in northern Nejd from which the raiders came.[71] This would serve several functions: it would punish and deter the *Ikhwan*; it would make them more submissive to Ibn Saud's authority – if he had not sanctioned the raids; and also discourage other tribes from similar attacks.[72]

It was during this period, in April 1928, that Trenchard prepared his major contribution to global strategic thinking. A paper entitled 'The War

Object of an Air Force' outlined proposals by which air power could, in effect, win a future war on its own, without the assistance of the Army or Navy.[73] This involved the use of bombing campaigns against enemy populations, which one critic suggested might 'cross the borderline of humanity'.[74] Trenchard's thesis was, of course, directed at Europe, not Nejd, yet the commitment to the significance of air power was apparent even over the Iraq-Nejd frontier disturbances. Indeed, at the end of 1929, Trenchard advocated that the RAF should replace military and naval forces in many parts of the world, including the Red Sea.[75]

Air Ministry attempts at what amounted to initiating policy questions in the Middle East caused irritation among the political departments. An inter-departmental meeting reaffirmed the need for the Colonial Office and the Foreign Office to liaise more closely on Arabian questions, leaving the Air Ministry to be consulted only as regards implementation of their decisions.[76]

The Colonial Office, like Dobbs, doubted Ibn Saud's innocence over Busaiya.[77] Ibn Saud may not have wanted to quarrel with Britain so soon after the prestigious coup secured by the Treaty of Jedda, but he may have wondered at the lengths to which she would go to defend Iraq. Britain had left Husein to his fate, and Ibn Saud may have reasoned similar indifference to the future of Feisal.[78] Shuckburgh was convinced that Ibn Saud was attempting to detach Iraqi tribes from their allegiance, and would continue until the British Government intervened.[79]

Shuckburgh felt that if Britain was unable or unwilling to defend Feisal's Kingdom against an attack from a predatory Arab neighbour then the whole fabric of the mandate policy would fall apart, and any claim to have super-vised and controlled Iraq in the name of the League of Nations would become an idle pretence. He wanted Busaiya to be a test case upon which Britain's whole Middle Eastern policy stood or fell.[80] Amery added: 'Bin Saud must accept responsibility for the action of Nejdis, and HMG must accept respon-sibility for the defence of Iraq. They [air strikes] are police measures against criminals, not military measures against Nejd'.[81]

It comes as no surprise to find the Colonial Office, the High Commissioner and the Air Ministry, with their direct commitment to Iraq, in favour of firm measures against Nejd. Other voices, with competing responsibilities, pressed for caution. The Foreign Office was reluctant to believe that Ibn Saud had authorised the Busaiya and subsequent raids. After all, a policy designed to support his regime could not easily co-exist alongside firm evidence of his culpability. Irrespective of the menace to Iraq, the Foreign Office was loath to endorse any policy that would strain Anglo-Saudi relations, especially if, as hoped, Ibn Saud was already engaged in bringing his recalcitrant tribes to order.[82]

Ibn Saud was, in the view of the Foreign Office, in an invidious position. He could not, without grave loss of face, publicly admit that he was no longer in control of the *Ikhwan*. Nor could he seek British intervention without openly betraying the very tribes to which he owed his position.[83] Ibn Saud was faced with risking either the open and unrestrained insurrection of the *Ikhwan*, or, possibly, limitless reprisals from Britain and Iraq.[84] If the *Ikhwan* were to be brought to heel, his standing demanded that it be achieved without the intervention of a foreign power. Nonetheless, Chamberlain minuted: 'We have put our money on Bin Saud and now we seem to be in grave danger of a serious row with him'.[85]

Although the British Consulate at Jedda was poorly placed to keep up with developments on the other side of the peninsula, and had to rely to a great extent on Hejazi-biased rumour and out-of-date information, the indications were that, for the first time since Ibn Saud had come to the notice of the British Government over twenty years previously, he was not demonstrably in control of his own circumstances.[86] The Hejaz was seething with gossip that Ibn Saud, conqueror of Hasa, Hail and the Hejaz, was unable to control his fellow Nejdis.[87]

The proximity of Kuwait to the frontier raids had led to Air Ministry demands for the RAF to attack raiders passing through the sheikdom[88] – which witnessed its first direct assault from the *Ikhwan* early in 1928. The Political Resident, Colonel Haworth, wanted Kuwait kept out of the frontier troubles. Otherwise, not only would the sheikhdom become embroiled in the disturbances, but the tensions which had existed between Ibn Saud and Kuwait since the death of Sheikh Mubarak would be exacerbated. Haworth supported the Foreign Office in warning that RAF activity over Nejd could only add to Ibn Saud's difficulties.[89]

Like the Foreign Office, the Government of India had come to view the stability of the peninsula as bound up in the continuing authority of Ibn Saud. Delhi feared that British bombs dropped on the dominions of the King of the Hejaz would have repercussions for the 1928 Pilgrimage.[90] Whereas officials in Iraq argued that Ibn Saud's authority would benefit from a display of force from the RAF, whether or not he was involved in the frontier raids, Bushire reasoned that such action would provoke Ibn Saud into joining the *Ikhwan* in order to confront a common enemy. Haworth explained:

> That I should view matters from a different standpoint from Iraq is inevitable, if not indeed necessary ..., all that matters is Bin Saud, not local tribes who are a side issue and who affect local not imperial policy ... If HMG disgruntle Bin Saud, it will affect us throughout Arabia, and all because of a raiding tribe. HMG should wait to see what action Bin Saud takes. Only if he doesn't punish the raiders should Britain adopt aggressive measures.[91]

The assessments of the Foreign Office and the Political Resident coincided – except on one point. If there was going to be any bombing, then the Foreign Office preferred that it be done over Kuwait rather than Nejd.[92]

British Diplomatic and Military Options

From examining the reactions of various individuals and departments it is apparent that there was no consensus regarding the action to be taken against the *Ikhwan*. Basically, there were two problems. First, was Ibn Saud behind the attacks? In other words, could measures be taken against the state of Nejd, or did Ibn Saud and the British Government share a common interest in suppressing the *Ikhwan*? Second, was force, in either case, the appropriate response? Britain's first initiative was to try to persuade Ibn Saud to meet the Political Resident. This was unsuccessful,[93] possibly because Ibn Saud did not think it fit for a King to stoop to negotiations with a lowly representative of the Indian Empire. As the raids continued, military measures became inevitable. There were three possible courses of action, each with distinct political overtones according to its 'offensive' or 'defensive' intent. These were a policy of naval blockade, aerial reconnaissance and bombing, and a system of desert fortifications similar to the construction at Busaiya.[94]

A naval blockade was, and is, an act of war. It was urged by Dobbs as a way of threatening the *Ikhwan* with starvation by cutting off the vital food supplies that reached Arabia through the Gulf.[95] Dobbs drew on his own experiences when, as Foreign Secretary to the Government of India, a blockade had been imposed on the Hasa coast during the First World War.[96]

The Colonial Office and the Foreign Office agreed that running a naval blockade was fraught with political and practical obstacles.[97] It would have been too provocative to Ibn Saud, its consequences indiscriminately affecting all of Arabia – including loyal Nejdi subjects – and Bahrain, through which most of the trade with Nedj passed.[98] The effects of a blockade would take many weeks to produce results, and could be offset by smuggling.[99] To be effective it would have to be extended beyond Hasa, round the whole Arab shore of the Gulf from Kuwait to Dubai.[100] Many of the inhabitants of the sheikhdoms might be driven into the arms of Ibn Saud for survival. In addition, Indian trade, which also passed largely through Kuwait, Bahrain and Dubai, would suffer.[101]

Undeterred, Dobbs urged the imposition of a blockade throughout 1928. He spoke of dealing with the Wahhabis as had the Egyptians in the nineteenth century.[102] He advocated extending the blockade to the Red Sea, imposing it upon the Hejaz. The High Commissioner suggested that Indian Moslems would not object to a blockade of the Hejaz ports if the alternative was the threatened stability of the Pilgrimage.[103]

The blockade option was not pursued, nor was it seriously proposed outside the High Commission in Baghdad. Naval blockades and/or bombardments had always been regarded as futile weapons against central Arabia.[104] An alternative was to utilise the resources of the Royal Air Force. This comprised both 'offensive' and 'defensive' elements. The RAF had been in the habit of pursuing raiders since the first *Ikhwan* raids of 1922. Action beyond that of 'hot pursuit', namely reconnaissance and bombing expeditions over the frontier, raised difficulties when Britain herself had drawn the frontier and been anxious for all parties to respect it. Initially, Foreign Office pressure restricted RAF activity to machine-gunning in hot pursuit, coupled with reassurances to Ibn Saud.[105] But escalating *Ikhwan* activity in Iraq and Kuwait at the end of January led the Air Ministry to demand retaliation.[106] Permission was finally given for the RAF to cross Kuwait and bomb retreating raiders in Nejd.[107] Chamberlain withdrew his objection to a bombing campaign, although he feared possible *Ikhwan* reprisals against Kuwait, which did not have RAF protection.[108]

By this time the frontier was the scene of *de facto*, if not *de jure*, war between Britain and Nejd, a matter of weeks after ratification of the Treaty of Jedda. At least one plane was shot down and its pilot killed.[109] Rumours began to circulate that Nejd was about to declare a *jihad* on Iraq.[110] A British warship, *HMS Emerald*, was despatched to stand off Kuwait, and naval forces landed on the sheikhdom.[111] It was suggested that infantry brigades and accompanying artillery be held in readiness in India ready to embark for Kuwait if necessary.[112] Sir Samuel Hoare, Secretary of State for Air, remonstrated against the delay in getting governmental permission for full-scale RAF operations over the frontier. Hoare felt that the role of air power as an instrument for controlling 'semi-civilised countries' was poorly understood. 'The air arm is a delicate weapon which is easily blunted if misused, either by wielding it too early, or too late.'[113] He reminded the Cabinet that 'the generally accepted axiom of air power was that it achieves its results through its morale effect on the enemy, and the fact that the enemy has no aircraft to counter'.[114] Without RAF bases nearer the Nejd frontier, aerial activity was hampered by the distances involved. The Air Ministry sought permission to operate from Kuwait, and make use of improvised bases across the Nejd frontier from which to bomb the major *Ikhwan* colony at Artawiya.[115] This was the home of Faisal al Dawish, Paramount Chief of the Mutair tribe.

Kuwait-Nejd relations had never recovered the close links of Mubarak's day, when Ibn Saud had used Kuwait as a springboard for recapturing Riyadh. Kuwait was a natural trading entrepôt in north-east Arabia. From 1916 Ibn Saud demanded part of the customs dues from Kuwait.[116] He also tried, with little success, to divert trade from Kuwait and Bahrain to the Hasa ports of Uqair, Jubail and Qatif.[117] By 1920 Ibn Saud had imposed a blockade on trade between Nejd and Kuwait which would persist until the late 1930s. Yet, despite Kuwaiti antipathy to Nejd, the Sheikh could not afford to be seen siding with Britain against fellow Arabs.[118]

Haworth watched the escalation of the conflict with alarm. The Political Resident supported his view by reference to legal argument, objecting that the sending of aircraft over the Nejd frontier was 'contrary to law'.[119] By this he was referring to Article Six of the Bahra Agreement which read:

'The forces of Iraq and Nejd may not cross the common frontier in the pursuit of offenders, except with the consent of both governments'. By international convention aerial reconnaissance, let alone bombing, over an agreed frontier was 'offensive' action.[120] Technically, there was no distinction between crossing an international frontier with an aeroplane or with a troop of cavalry.[121] Similar aerial activity over, say, a European power, might have led to rather more severe consequences. Supposing Ibn Saud acquired aircraft of his own. How would Britain react to their deployment over the Iraq frontier?

By the end of February Britain pulled back from the bombing campaign. Ibn Saud had requested a conference aimed at settling the disturbances by negotiation.[122] An inter-departmental meeting refused permission for temporary air bases to be constructed in Nejd, and agreed to suspend all military operations pending the conference.[123] The British Government did not wish to drive Ibn Saud into having to choose between further antagonising his people or risking open warfare with Iraq.[124] Neither did it wish to assume responsibility for the maintenance of public security in Nejd.

With 'offensive' air action suspended, attention turned to the third military option open to the British and Iraqi Governments. This was the issue that had provided the first flash-point of the rebellion, the question of frontier posts, which the RAF were constructing as part of the Iraq 'Desert Defence Organisation'. Unlike the blockade and aerial bombing options, desert fortifications were intended solely as a defensive measure. Being situated in Iraq, they could not directly bring pressure to bear on events in Nejd.

Iraqi frontier posts were not new. They had previously been erected in north and north-east Iraq against the Turks and the Kurds.[125] The decision to build the Busaiya post had been taken in February 1927, partially in response to Ibn Saud's complaints about Iraqi raiding into Nejd, and work on it began in September, two months before it was attacked.[126] It was not intended as a solitary post but as one of a string of similar fortifications designed to extend the length of Iraq's southern frontier, from Transjordan to Kuwait, at varying distances from the frontier with Nejd.[127] They were described as 'police posts' – having internal, not external, functions. It was hoped they would provide intelligence about desert movements, supplying early warning of impending raids which could lead to their interception. The posts would, therefore, protect local tribes, prevent the paying of tribute to the *Ikhwan*, and guard against Iraqi reprisals.[128]

While they were nominally intended to control tribal movements, the desert posts were really a tactical ploy, aimed at establishing a buffer zone to protect Iraq's cities and strategic routes.[129] Their effect, moreover, in interrupting the traditional payment of tribute, was to invite retribution upon the sheltering tribes.[130] The RAF and the Iraq authorities had affected the traditional equilibrium of the desert.

Ibn Saud had protested as soon as construction work on Busaiya began.[131]

The posts were to be sited near wells or oases, inevitably near tribal encampments – implying that even water was being brought under the control of the Iraq Government. At the same time, prior to wireless installations being fitted to the posts, the only means of communication with the Iraq authorities was to assign military personnel to specific posts. This encroached upon desert habits even more. Besides, it was unlikely that the police could rely on the loyalty of the tribes for whose protection the posts had been constructed.[132]

In making his request for a conference, Ibn Saud had enumerated a number of complaints. Feisal was, he claimed, inciting Nejdi tribes.[133] Britain had violated both the Bahra Agreement and the Uqair Protocol. Ibn Saud disassociated himself from the 1922 Treaty of Mohammera, to which the Uqair Protocol was appended, by insisting that the whole point of the treaties had been to prohibit fortified posts in the desert.[134]

The Jedda Conferences of May and August 1928

In the absence of diplomatic relations with Nejd, the call for a negotiated settlement meant that recourse had to be taken, once again, to the personal emissary. Sir Gilbert Clayton was the obvious candidate. He was selected for his third major mission to Ibn Saud, in the hope of repeating his successes with the Hadda and Bahra Agreements of 1925, and the Treaty of Jedda of 1927.

The idea of a conference was not universally popular within the British Government. The Colonial Office backed Dobbs' opinion that the purpose of Clayton's visit was ill-founded. All Clayton could do, argued Dobbs, was explain the position of the British Government over the desert posts and ascertain Ibn Saud's reply. He could not bargain with Ibn Saud over the terms of the Bahra Agreement because the Iraq Government was quite content with the existing terms, and did not admit to having infringed them in any way.[135] Accordingly, the Colonial Office tried to obstruct the conference, and attacked the whole conciliatory approach of the Foreign Office and its desire to send Clayton immediately.[136]

> How can we hope for any permanent peace in Arabia, or any sort of decent relations with a barbarous chief if we now treat this outrage [Busaiya] as justified? FO arguments are based on (i) Bin Saud being a lamb whom the Air Force wolves have wantonly attacked, (ii) a formidable power with whom we must have peace at any price.[137]

The Colonial Office offered some imaginative excuses for delaying the conference, such as the fear that Clayton might be seized by the *Ikhwan*. Large-scale raiding could not, in any case, recommence until the autumn/ winter rains could sustain them.[138] That gave Ibn Saud half a year in which to reassert his authority.[139] In the event, neither the Cabinet nor the Foreign Office were persuaded by Colonial Office logic, preferring personal contact with Ibn Saud as soon as possible.[140]

Nevertheless, Dobbs felt sufficiently angered to threaten his resignation should the Busaiya post be dismantled.[141] He was not prepared to be responsible for Iraq's security without desert fortifications.[142] Only a few years previously, Lord Plumer had offered a similar threat of resignation over the question of Saudi control of Aqaba. British High Commissioners in the mandates, it seemed, would brook no nonsense where the menace from Nejd was concerned. Dobbs' threat was not well received. Chamberlain told Amery: 'Dobbs' resignation is not an impressive threat. Worse things can happen and I could at once suggest a better man to you'.[143] Chamberlain probably had in mind Clayton himself, as will be explained.

Chamberlain, supported by Haworth, was anxious to be conciliatory. So was Lord Lloyd in Cairo, through whom Ibn Saud, in the absence of any regular diplomatic channels, had temporarily chosen to communicate.[144] Desert posts seemed to be creating more problems than they solved. Chamberlain warned Amery that the paramount consideration from the Foreign Office's point of view was peace with Ibn Saud, and that Clayton might have to give way over Busaiya: 'If Clayton reports that it [Busaiya] is the only outstanding point, I reserve my right to appeal to the Cabinet'.[145] The Political Resident agreed:

> If HMG concede the Busaiya claim, his [Ibn Saud's] Oriental mind must realise that this is a gift from strength ..., not a concession through weakness or a desire to placate his tribes ... As long as it is our wish to hold him responsible for Arabia it is necessary to strengthen him, not weaken him.[146]

The conference was held in Jedda in May. Clayton acted in a dual capacity, as he had during the Bahra negotiations, representing the governments of Britain and Iraq.[147] Just as Clayton started out on his mission, in late April, the British Government was informed that bombs had been dropped over the Nejd frontier. In response to urgent demands for an explanation Dobbs admitted to RAF reconnaissance across the frontier, because neither he nor the Air-Officer-Commanding (AOC) Iraq were convinced that Ibn Saud could, or would, restrain his tribes.[148] Dobbs denied the dropping of bombs.[149] Nonetheless, the Foreign Office considered Dobbs' actions 'dreadful', feeling that any such disturbances, and the inevitably exaggerated versions that would reach Ibn Saud, would be bound to compromise the conference.[150]

Although Clayton's brief was to discuss a wide range of issues, including Italian activities in the Red Sea and reports of Bolshevik subversion in the Hejaz, it was the question of the desert posts that became the *sine qua non* of the conference. The very existence of the frontier posts was used by Ibn Saud as a useful ploy through which blame for the frontier incidents could be laid with the British Government. Ibn Saud directed his attack at what he considered to be Britain's violation of Article Three of the Uqair Protocol, which read:

> The two governments mutually agree not to use the watering places and wells situated in the *vicinity* of the border for any *military purposes* such as building forts on them, and not to concentrate troops in their *vicinity*. (author's italics)

Clayton found Ibn Saud unbending in his attitude towards the desert posts. Disagreement centred on the word 'vicinity'. Ibn Saud maintained that the Busaiya fort was in the vicinity of the frontier, even though it was fifty miles north of the nearest point of the Iraq-Nejd neutral zone, and seventy five miles from Nejd proper.[151] The decision to commence building the fort had been taken before the signing of the Treaty of Jedda, and Ibn Saud had been warned in advance of the intention to build it.[152] This, at the very least, suggested that Britain had not intended to violate her undertaking.

It transpired that the Arabic translation of 'the vicinity of the border' was more like 'on either side of the border'.[153] Although Busaiya was seventy five miles from Nejd, another post in the process of construction, at Shabicha, was only twenty seven miles from the frontier, which, the Foreign Office conceded, probably came within even the English interpretation of 'vicinity'.[154] Sir Percy Cox, however, Dobbs' predecessor as High Commissioner, who had attended the Uqair Protocol negotiations, recalled the meaning of vicinity as within sight or rifle shot of the frontier.[155]

A second linguistic confusion concerned the expression 'for military purposes'. The distinction between policing and military activities may have been clear to Britain – the police for internal defence; the military for external defence. The distinction was hard to enforce in the context of Arabia, as any kind of post was intended to prevent the free movement of tribes through the desert.[156] If they were not dismantled, Ibn Saud absolved himself of responsibility for his tribes.[157]

International law seemed to support Iraq's policy of frontier posts. A state was, as Dobbs repeatedly stressed, at liberty to do whatever it chose within its own territory without reference to the wishes of other states, so long as its acts were not directly injurious to them.[158] Accordingly, there was nothing to prevent a state from fortifying or policing its frontiers – unless prohibited from doing so by the terms of a treaty. The Treaty of Versailles, for example, had expressly prohibited the German Government from fortifying its frontier within fifty kilometres – thirty two miles.[159]

One can question the application of international law to the Arabian deserts. It is possible to have a certain sympathy with Ibn Saud about western hairsplitting over 'vicinity' and 'military purposes'. British frontier practices could not, at a stroke, erase centuries of desert habits. Moreover, the Bahra Agreement, by being ostensibly an inter-Arab document between

Iraq and Nejd, was officially drawn up in Arabic. This rendered the English interpretation irrelevant. Against this, Ibn Saud had already agreed, however reluctantly and however much he tried to disown the fact, to the frontier being drawn where it was. Ibn Saud was opportunistically making use of the frontier when it suited him, and criticising it when it did not.

Clayton adopted several tactics to win Ibn Saud's concurrence for the posts. He offered to substitute a specific distance – twenty five miles – for the expression 'in the vicinity'.[160] Seeing that the nearest Iraqi post was planned to be twenty seven miles from the frontier, Clayton's offer would not have resulted in any posts being sacrificed. Ibn Saud was also encouraged to build reciprocal forts on his own side of the frontier, which he declined.[161] With no apparent way out of the deadlock, Clayton requested suspension of the Conference as the 1928 Pilgrimage approached. He was recalled for consultations with the Colonial Office after agreeing with Ibn Saud that, during the period of suspension, neither side would undertake any offensive action, or permit their tribes to do likewise.[162] This was a worthless guarantee, considering that it was Ibn Saud's influence over the *Ikhwan* which was partially at issue.

With the mounting threat of open war, the responsibility for handling the crisis passed to the Cabinet. To reduce the inefficiencies and delays in communicating between the various departments, a special sub-committee of the Committee of Imperial Defence was set up, known as the Sub-Committee on Akhwan Defence. This body even commanded the attention of the Prime Minister, Stanley Baldwin.[163]

The Cabinet took the view that it was not possible to give way to Ibn Saud on the principle of desert posts inside Iraq, as that was an immutably held axiom of desert defence.[164] At the same time, as a gesture towards Ibn Saud, the Cabinet was prepared to be flexible about the number of posts. This apparent concession was taken in the face of continuous objections from the Colonial Office and the Air Ministry against abandoning any posts.[165] Hoare insisted that the whole principle of Iraq's defence was at stake. Without desert posts it would be impossible to hold so big a country with such a small garrison.[166]

The Air Staff eventually agreed to reduce the number of proposed posts from eight to six.[167] Ibn Saud was reassured that Britain would scrupulously observe the existing agreements regarding the Iraq-Nejd frontier, and would not cross the frontier in pursuit of offenders – except in extreme circumstances.[168] The Air Ministry had accepted responsibility for the defence of Iraq in full knowledge of the restrictions imposed on that defence by Article Six of the Bahra Agreement. Future operations would be planned accordingly.

The Colonial Office considered reviving Indian methods to reorganise the tribes of southern Iraq, such as enhancing the authority of specific sheikhs through the use of subsidies.[169] Dobbs was not enthusiastic, there being, in his experience, too few sheikhs of sufficient stature. Besides, governmental control over them depended on the capacity to defend their tribes and flocks – in which case desert posts were needed.[170]

Clayton's second attempt to reach agreement with Ibn Saud took place at the beginning of August. The emissary found him polite but immovable on the question of the posts, and had to withdraw without a solution.[171] The one positive outcome of the second meeting was a mutual desire to simplify and speed up the channels of communication between Ibn Saud and the British Government. Jedda was agreed upon as the single pigeon-hole for Anglo-Saudi relations, and Ibn Saud would introduce a motor car service between Jedda and Riyadh to accelerate communications with London.[172]

The Iraq Factor: The Influence of Captain Glubb and King Feisal

John Bagot Glubb (Glubb Pasha) was to become one of the foremost authorities on the Arabs. He became Commander of the Arab Legion until 1956, having acquired his early experiences of Arabia in the Iraq desert in the 1920s. His significance for the understanding of Anglo-Saudi relations is immense, even though his loyalty to the Hashemite governments must never be overlooked. With the problems of unreliable information with which the British Government had to contend in assessing the *Ikhwan* revolt, Glubb's position among the desert tribes made him an indispensable source of information. Moreover, it will be suggested that Glubb's was the most accurate diagnosis of the *Ikhwan* rebellion, and Ibn Saud's role within it.

Glubb served, initially, as a British military intelligence officer in Iraq, and, early in 1925, became a Special Service Officer 'Ikhwan Defence'.[173] In October 1926 he resigned his British Army commission for the post of Adminstrative Inspector with the Iraq Government.[174] Early in 1928 he was despatched to the southern desert where he could make most use of his knowledge of Arabic.[175] The detailed reports about the frontier situation, which Glubb began to submit from that time, caused the British Government some discomfort – for the remedies which Glubb proposed would have needed Anglo-Saudi relations to be recast in a very different mould. Glubb had formed part of Clayton's team that travelled to Jedda. Before setting off he noted the:

> wide impression that Bin Saud is a devoted ally of the British, but he is inspired only by not provoking it [sic] too far ... He is a completely unscrupulous Oriental monarch ... He only associates himself with 'unauthorised raids' when they work ... Past history shows that Bin Saud is not actuated by any feelings of friendship or fidelity to Great Britain, or to anyone else ... In most raids Great Britain had not punished him, so he sees no reason to suppress Dawish because he is always bringing him more subjects.[176]

If the *Ikhwan* were severely dealt with by Iraq, however:

> they would not trouble him [Ibn Saud] again. Bin Saud holds the

money, the supplies, guns and ammunition, and the power to deny supplies from the Hasa ports if he wanted to ..., but this would destroy the moral unity of the Wahhabi brethren on which Bin Saud's successes resulted ... When Britain used planes in 1924, raiding stopped on the orders of Bin Saud. He is probably repeating the 1924 policy of letting the Ikhwan have their fling ..., brings him more tribes and taxes, but stopping them when Great Britain gets angry.[177]

If it was not for the fact that the *Ikhwan* were veterans of desert campaigns, Glubb would have been in favour of Iraqi tribes competing with the *Ikhwan* in open warfare, using *Ikhwan* tactics of surprise, organisation, weight of numbers, and wholesale massacre.[178] Glubb expounded his 'Provocation Theory' to counter what he saw as British reluctance to provoke Ibn Saud or the *Ikhwan*:

> The basis of the provocation theory, which is the cornerstone of HMG policy, depends purely on the word of Bin Saud. Bin Saud no longer trusts Iraq and Britain ... Arabs always join the side that is winning, so if Iraq Government forces appear, who are strong, tribes will defect – hence the provocation theory that the British Government in reality seeks strength, but in theory wants to appear weak. The Arab does not understand moderation. If he is stronger then no end to violence ..., once he is losing he changes over because to surrender to the strong is no disgrace.
>
> British policy is diametrically opposed to the requirements of peace. Only a display of overwhelming force will cease raiding. It is only the action of a weak enemy which is regarded as a provocation by Arabs. The theory that strong government forces will 'provoke' the Ikhwan is rubbish.[179]

Glubb's proposal was as follows:

> We should not approach him with an infinity of ceremonial and argue about the 'vicinity' of the frontier. We should shake him by the arm and say, 'Look here Abdul Aziz, if the Ikhwan raid again there will be the devil of a row and no excuses will be accepted'.[180]

The force of Glubb's argument, backed by the absence of alternative expertise, made an impression even on the Foreign Office. 'Excellent, but does Glubb understand the wider issues?'[181] Bombing across the frontier, as Glubb was advocating, might have turned the whole of Nejd upon Ibn Saud, and it was not in the interests of the Foreign Office, nor the British Government, that he should fall and central Arabia and the Hejaz relapse into chaos.[182] The scope of British relations with Ibn Saud went far beyond the issue of the Iraq-Nejd frontier. Glubb followed up with a glimpse into the Arab mind:

> The building [Busaiya], cars and wireless have proved the one effective way of controlling vast desert spaces. Ikhwan want the forts

removed to give them a free hand to raid to the sand belt as before ...
Bin Saud, when he signed Uqair, thought no civilised government
could ever function in the desert. The Turks tried and failed because
internal wars carried on just the same. The mediaeval mind of Arabia
is to enlarge dominions à la Machiavelli, not to ensure universal peace
à la Geneva. Any prince who sits still and does nothing is regarded
as a very poor prince. Except at Jarab, which was Shakespear's fault,
the Ikhwan and Bin Saud never fought a pitched battle ... Bin
Saud's success is by unauthorised raids, attrition of enemy tribes and
treachery. There is no hope of Ikhwan permanently ceasing to raid
until HMG prevent them.[183]

Glubb did not remark on the fact that the Arab practice *vis à vis* enlarging
dominions is probably the natural inclination of any ruler, irrespective of
whether or not he was an Arab, and that it was the League of Nations
that was historically out of step with man's political instinct to acquire
territory. As if to recognise this, Glubb did not suggest extinguishing the
Ikhwan flame through collective security, but through *force majeure*. The
only workable approach, he argued, was one that frightened Ibn Saud more
than could the *Ikhwan*.[184] By the summer of 1929 Glubb calculated that, by
one means or another, about half the Iraq bedouin had transferred their
allegiance to Nejdi sources.[185] Ibn Saud, not surprisingly, detected Glubb as
his immediate adversary, and complained on several occasions about his
provocations.[186]

Glubb commenced reorganising the intelligence and security system of
southern Iraq. He wanted the Iraq tribes to defend themselves, using
the RAF as a supporting arm.[187] The Air Staff preferred to evacuate the
southern desert of its tribes, leaving the RAF a clear field for its activities.
This meant that Glubb had to embark upon his schemes without the full
co-operation of the RAF.[188] His methods culminated, in September 1928,
with the formation of the Southern Desert Camel Corps, supplemented by
armoured cars of the RAF, under Glubb's command.[189]

One of the difficulties confronting Glubb was that Britain was viewed by
both Iraq and Nejd as sympathetic to the other side.[190] Iraqis were aware
that Ibn Saud had been a British protégé since 1915, and that he had
continued to enjoy a British subsidy long after Husein's had been withdrawn. Further evidence of Britain's apparently pro-Saudi attitudes had
been demonstrated with the terms of the Treaty of Jedda, which had recognised Ibn Saud's 'complete and absolute independence' while Iraq still
laboured under the mandate. Having seen Britain stand aside while Ibn
Saud overthrew one Hashemite regime, in the Hejaz, Iraqis were convinced
that she had secretly sanctioned the *Ikhwan* attacks upon them.[191]

On this point it is important to distinguish the Iraq Government from King
Feisal. The Government of Iraq considered itself presiding over a modernis-
ing state. It had little time either for the nomads of central Arabia, or,

indeed, its own bedouin desert dwellers.[192] The very idea of raiding was viewed with distaste by the Iraq Government, which regarded the frontier disturbances as a sideshow – a 'trifling little war'.[193] Reflecting this, as recently as 1925, the Iraq Government had not employed a single civil official or policeman in the desert.[194] The signing of the Bahra Agreement, in that year, had further encouraged Iraqi complacency.[195] Ever since the granting of the mandate the inclination of the Iraq Government had been to avoid interference with inter-bedouin raiding, and to keep clear of the desert generally to avoid unnecessary commitments and expenditure.[196]

Furthermore, in the late 1920s, the attention of the Government of Iraq was elsewhere, notably on oil, the Kurds, and the recently settled frontier with Turkey.[197] The demand for removal of the mandate and admission to the League of Nations strained Anglo-Iraqi relations.[198]

King Feisal, on the other hand, had a rather more personal stake in developments on Iraq's southern frontier. Wahhabi raids stirred up a nationalistic and religious response against both Britain and Ibn Saud, all of which Feisal hoped would work to his advantage.[199] He had taken Britain's recognition of Ibn Saud's complete independence as a personal slight, to be rectified by similar recognition of Iraq as soon as possible.[200] The *Ikhwan* raids provided an opportunity for Feisal to demand a strong national army for Iraq, and for conscription to provide it.[201] Britain, however, with her many commitments in the Middle East, had no intention of immediately relinquishing control of the Iraq military.[202]

It was to Feisal's advantage to inflame the frontier disturbances. In 1928 he wrote: 'One remedy for this situation is to raid them in their own country. We must lure them on and compel them to seek combat with forces prepared to give them battle at the lance's point'.[203] To the Foreign Office this was a 'shocking document', vindicating Ibn Saud's worst suspicions that Feisal was provoking retaliatory raids into Nejd and harbouring *Ikhwan* fugitives.[204] Rendel noted: 'The Iraqis are most tiresome to deal with and are quite capable of giving the Ikhwan much gratuitous provocation'.[205] Similar Foreign Office remarks had been directed towards Transjordan during the Aqaba-Maan affair.

Evidence of Feisal's intrigues increased as the months passed. By the autumn of 1929 news reached London that Feisal was sending paid envoys to encourage the *Ikhwan*, suggesting that Britain would aid them in their fight against Ibn Saud.[206] The High Commission in Baghdad became embarrassed by Feisal's activities:

> There is no doubt in my mind that he [Feisal] has been sending agents to the rebels with messages of encouragement and, in some cases, with material assistance ... Moreover ..., one of the reasons for the visit of the Amir Abdullah to Baghdad was ... to discuss how the fall of Bin Saud might be hastened, and how it might be subsequently used to the best advantage.[207]

The Foreign Office was angered at these developments. Under the 1922 Anglo-Iraqi treaty Feisal was bound to be guided by the advice of the British Government, through the High Commissioner, on important matters affecting Britain's international obligations. Feisal was pressured into agreeing to withdraw his agents.[208]

Ibn Saud, like Feisal, had reasons to think that Britain was conspiring with his enemies against him. Far from seeing himself as a British protégé, Ibn Saud saw Britain setting up Hashemite obstacles at every turn. The present infringement of the desert with police posts was only the latest example. Talk of mandates could hardly have clarified things for Ibn Saud. Where did ultimate responsibility for the actions of Iraq lie, in Baghdad or London? If Iraq was independent, why could Ibn Saud not act towards it as he chose? And why were the British bound to defend an independent Iraq with their own forces? If, however, Iraq was not independent, how could it have a king? What could British motives be in denying Feisal's independence, except an excuse for preventing a resurgence of Saudi rule? What else could be the purpose of forts in the desert, except to contain Ibn Saud in Nejd while promoting the rule of Feisal to the north? Ibn Saud wanted Britain either to take responsibility for everything Feisal did, or else to stand aside and not interfere.[209]

Elsewhere, Anglo-Saudi relations were not enhanced by the failure, in August 1928, of a conference at Haifa on the future of the Hejaz Railway. Delegates from Britain, France and Hejaz-Nejd could not agree on a formula for settling ownership of the Railway along its entire length.[210] At the same time, Britain knew that Ibn Saud would be reluctant to antagonise her while the situation in south-west Arabia, involving Asir, the Yemen, and the Italians, was cause for uncertainty. Ibn Saud wanted British reassurances to offset any possible increase in Italian ambitions in the Red Sea.[211]

The Nejd Civil War

On 5 November 1928, by coincidence the first anniversary of the Busaiya raid, Ibn Saud (who had inherited the title Imam of Wahhabism upon the death of his father some months previously[212]) convened a huge assembly of Nejdis at Riyadh and offered to abdicate.[213] Whether meant seriously or otherwise, the offer was rejected by the congregation. The main instigators of the revolt, however, including Faisal al Dawish, declined to attend, and that act of insubordination transformed the frontier disturbances into civil war. With the sanction of the Nejdi *ulema* for his introduction of modern devices,[214] such as the motor car and the wireless, Ibn Saud became pledged to reassert his authority over the *Ikhwan*.[215]

For the British Government the autumn rains which heralded the start of a five or six month raiding season brought further complications. Raids had occurred to the west, within Transjordan, although they did not appear to be part of a concerted *Ikhwan* campaign. In fact, first reports suggested it was

Transjordanian tribes raiding Nejd, and not the other way around.[216] The tribes of Transjordan, having frequently suffered raids from Nejd in the past, had been dissuaded from counter-raids pending the result of Clayton's talks with Ibn Saud. The failure of those negotiations, and the absence of any prospect of agreed reparations, led to certain tribes endeavouring to recover their camels and other possessions by force.[217]

The situation in Transjordan presented difficulties over and above those in Iraq. Although Britain had a general reponsibility for Transjordan, there had been, since the Aqaba business, no significant improvements in the security of the eastern part of the emirate. The area east of the Hejaz Railway (the greater part of Transjordan) was neither administered nor controlled from Amman.[218] Transjordan's tribes roamed free, raided into Nejd and, when threatened with reprisals, relied upon the protection of the RAF.[219] Under the terms of the February 1928 Anglo-Transjordanian Agreement the Arab Legion was to be responsible for internal security, and constituted the armed force of the Transjordanian Government. A Transjordan Frontier Force, whose personnel were technically British imperial troops, was established for the purposes of external security.[220] The two forces owed allegiance, therefore, to different governments.[221]

Transjordan was poorly placed in comparison with Iraq to act effectively to prevent raiding. Its financial resources, together with its imperial grant-in-aid from London, could not support adequate control over its eastern regions.[222] Its High Commissioners – Lord Plumer, and his successor from the autumn of 1928, Sir John Chancellor – were not of the same opinion as Sir Henry Dobbs that the best method of desert defence was a string of police posts,[223] despite there being no equivalent for Transjordan of the troublesome 'vicinity' expression. Nor was the RAF, with its rapid turnover of personnel in the mandates, necessarily the foremost expert on desert defence.[224] For Transjordan, frontier posts were expensive, ineffective if sited at permanent water sources because they would disturb local tribes, and politically inexpedient through provoking Ibn Saud.[225]

The Nejd frontier with Iraq was considerably longer than that with Transjordan, and nearer the main *Ikhwan* colonies of north-eastern Arabia. Consequently, the Iraq section of the strategic routes was more vulnerable.[226] Furthermore, the tribal groups in Iraq were larger and generally more difficult to manage than those in Transjordan. The emirate did, however, make one concession to the need for increased vigilance. It replaced its single officer employed in desert intelligence by one who could speak Arabic![227] Amery told Chancellor:

> Even if you don't think it desirable or practical to establish police posts, some arrangement similar to Iraq, where comprehensive responsibility is entrusted to a single British officer for maintaining touch with the tribes and organising a system of tribal intelligence would help the present difficulties.[228]

Substantive improvements in the defence of Transjordan had to be post-poned when, in the summer of 1929, violent disturbances shook Palestine. At that time there were two companies of armoured cars, plus one RAF squadron, with the task of policing all of Palestine and Transjordan.[229] When the riots in Palestine broke out all the cars were in Transjordan and had to be diverted to Palestine.[230] Eventually, a Tribal Control Board was established in Transjordan by mechanising part of the frontier forces.[231]

One possibility of dealing with the vexed question of frontier disturbances was through arbitration. In November 1928 Britain agreed to Ibn Saud's request to put into motion arbitration machinery on past claims and counter-claims arising from the frontier disputes.[232] Arbitration was, of necessity, a lengthy process, and neither Ibn Saud nor the British Government were fully convinced that their best interests could be served by this procedure.[233] Ibn Saud, for example, showed signs of wanting the entire Iraq-Nejd frontier question reopened.[234] For all these reasons, and because frontier conditions were never stable enough to support arbitration, by the time the *Ikhwan* revolt had been finally suppressed no arbitration tribunals had been estab-lished.

The first months of 1929 saw a repeat of the concentrated *Ikhwan* activity that had plagued north-east Arabia in the corresponding period of the previous year. The increased presence of air and ground forces of the RAF, together with the Iraq Army, desert posts, and Glubb's intelligence-gathering, gradually strengthened Iraq's capacity to resist the *Ikhwan*. Kuwait, by contrast, became all the more vulnerable. In January 1929 an *Ikhwan* raid into the sheikhdom killed an American missionary, Dr Bilkert, who was travelling by car with another American – the philanthropist Charles Crane.[235] With no sign of Ibn Saud mobilising counter-measures, the resources of the RAF were extended to Kuwait.[236]

Two events in March 1929 marked the turning point in Ibn Saud's fortunes. The first was a diplomatic move. Sir Gilbert Clayton succeeded Dobbs as British High Commissioner of Iraq. His appointment had been mooted the previous summer, and had even been confided to Ibn Saud at his August meeting with Clayton.[237] Of the first three High Commissioners in Baghdad – Cox, Dobbs and Clayton – Cox and Clayton had been seminal figures in the improvement of Anglo-Saudi relations over a period of some twenty years. Dobbs' undisguised hostility to Ibn Saud put him out of step with his colleagues and, as earlier recorded, had earned him the sharp dis-pleasure of the Foreign Office. In the event, Clayton's death in September, just six months after taking up his post, threatened implications for British relations with Ibn Saud as grave as those that had followed Shakespear's death in 1915 – the more so since, at the same time, the Colonial Secre-tary, Lord Passfield, announced Britain's unconditional support for Iraq's membership of the League of Nations.[238]

The second event was on the battlefield. After a winter of organisation and minor skirmishes with the *Ikhwan*, Ibn Saud moved against them with a large force at Sibila, reinforcing Glubb's view that, in the end, *force majeure* would be the decisive factor. The rebels were routed, Dawish wounded, believed fatally, and Ibn Saud returned to the Hejaz for the coming Pilgrimage believing the rebellion to be over.[239] Dawish, however, did not die, and returned to spearhead the final stages of the revolt. Furthermore, shortly after Sibila, another tribe, the Ajman of Hasa, whose chief, Ibn Hithlain, had been murdered, joined the rebellion.[240]

Ibn Saud was, by this time, aware of the need to crush the revolt by any means, including that of British assistance. In May he requested a troopship in order to transport a thousand troops from Jedda round to Hasa to put down the Ajman rising.[241] To this end, Ibn Saud also requested three thousand Lee Enfield rifles and accompanying ammunition.[242] An interdepartmental conference declined to supply the troopship, but acquiesced in the request for arms, which were willingly supplied by the Government of India.[243] Ibn Saud also demanded, and received, assurances from Britain that *Ikhwan* fugitives would not be given asylum if they crossed the Iraq or Kuwait frontiers.[244] Aware of the advantages of aerial power, Ibn Saud negotiated the purchase from Britain of four aircraft, plus the hire of British pilots and mechanics.[245] The planes were to operate from bases in Hasa. As Ibn Saud journeyed back from the Pilgrimage with a fleet of motor cars, he requested the RAF to bomb the *Ikhwan* in Nejd.[246] Clayton was authorised to continue to bomb raiders caught red-handed and to permit planes to pursue fugitives across the frontier in hot pursuit, but not to search for rebels or initiate operations in Nejd.[247]

At this juncture, developments elsewhere affected Colonial Office perceptions. In June 1929 Ramsay MacDonald formed his second Labour administration. Amery was succeeded as Colonial Secretary by Lord Passfield. The disturbances in Palestine and the decision to relinquish the mandate in Iraq meant that the conclusion of the *Ikhwan* revolt was played out to a distracted Middle East division of the Colonial Office.

The north-east corner of Nejd became the scene for the impending climax. Motorised columns of Saudi militia approached from the southwest.[248] Tightened frontier security in Iraq pressurised the *Ikhwan* from the north-west. Kuwait lay exposed, presenting the only available grazing in the area capable of supporting concentrated rebel encampments.[249] Britain realised that the gravity of the threat to Kuwait had serious political ramifications for her position in the Gulf. 'If Bin Saud knew he could invade Kuwait because Britain was too weak to protect it, it would have a terrible effect throughout the Gulf.'[250] Kuwait was quite defenceless, and had no regular police force capable of ejecting invading *Ikhwan*.[251] Iraqi forces were too stretched themselves to provide assistance and, in any case, there were overriding political objections to Hashemite forces intervening in a dispute involving Ibn Saud and the Sheikh of Kuwait.[252] The India Office was opposed to anything that appeared to question Kuwait's independence, such as its 'protection' by either Iraqi or British forces.[253]

An inter-departmental meeting decided that the political objections to Ibn Saud's penetration of Kuwait in pursuit of the *Ikhwan* were insuperable.[254] Britain, it seemed, was not averse to the RAF crossing the Nejd frontier, but Ibn Saud was not allowed to do likewise. Like Feisal, the Sheikh was sympathetic to the rebels. He hoped that, with Ibn Saud's downfall, he could recover control of the tribes and territory stripped from Kuwait by the Uqair Protocol, and, to this end, had been passing on supplies to the *Ikhwan*. To hasten their defeat Britain secured a pledge of neutrality from the Sheikh and a cessation of the supplies of food and ammunition.[255]

Dawish tried to extricate himself from his sandwiched position between the forces of Ibn Saud and Iraq by approaches to the Sheikh of Kuwait and the British Government. First, he tried to win the Sheikh's protection, promising that the Mutair tribe would once again pay allegiance to Kuwait as they had in Mubarak's time.[256] Were it not for British attentions this would have been an ideal arrangement for the Sheikh. Second, as tension increased on the Kuwait frontier, Dawish made a number of approaches to the British Government through the new Political Agent, H. R. P. Dickson. At first his questions were tactical: what would Britain's reaction be towards the women and children of his tribes if he left them on the frontier unprotected while he marched the Mutair south against Ibn Saud? And would the *Ikhwan* be held responsible for shooting down British-piloted Saudi planes that might attack them?[257] Britain refused to give Dawish the assurances he needed, thereby giving clear indication of her preferred outcome.[258] The prospect of Ibn Saud instructing his British pilots to fly over Kuwait or Iraq, to be met by other British pilots in the service of Iraq, was not one upon which the British Government liked to dwell. In the event, his planes and their pilots did not reach Hasa until December, and were not needed in the final stages of the revolt.[259]

Dawish's final gesture was for a direct agreement with the British Government. He offered to remain on good terms with Iraq and Kuwait, provided that the *Ikhwan* were allowed to defend themselves by buying munitions and supplies from Kuwait.[260] Dickson pointed out that Dawish was in revolt against his King, who enjoyed treaty relations with the British Government. Britain had promised Ibn Saud that she would deny supplies to the *Ikhwan* and refuse them entry into Kuwait or Iraq. The penalty for entering either territory was to be bombed.[261] It was noted with some irony that the *Ikhwan*, who had rebelled against their King because, among other reasons, of his flirtation with Britain, were now themselves offering to treat with her.[262]

The End of the Rebellion

This concerted British political and military pressure accelerated the end of the rebellion. It will be recalled that Britain had agreed, by late 1929, to establish full diplomatic relations with Hejaz-Nejd, and had taken firm action to restrict Hashemite intrigue. The need to act speedily when the climax arrived, without being burdened by delay in referring matters for inter-departmental consultation, had already seen the Gulf officials given a free hand to take appropriate measures without reference to a higher authority.[263] Bombing, however, was to be used only as a last, desperate resort.[264]

Fears that Ibn Saud might seek a final showdown with the *Ikhwan* led, in late November, to the AOC Iraq and Dickson co-operating in preparing military measures to prevent either the rebels trying to merge with Kuwaiti tribes, or Saudi forces entering Kuwait in pursuit of them.[265] It was impossible to communicate with Ibn Saud. All that was known was that he was somewhere 'north of Riyadh'. Dickson could not approach him personally because of the large concentration of rebel tribes interposed between them.[266] If the *Ikhwan* fled into Kuwait, then on what grounds could Ibn Saud be prohibited from following them? It would not be possible to hand over the rebels unconditionally because of the possible retribution that might befall the women and children. To try and forestall unfavourable developments British forces were posted near the Iraq frontier, and a fifteen mile-deep zone along the Kuwait frontier was cleared of local tribes to avoid problems of identification.[267]

At the turn of the year the *Ikhwan* tribes began to flee over the Kuwait frontier. Reports spoke of panic-stricken people rushing in terror from both the RAF and Ibn Saud.[268] Early in January 1930 the rebels began surrendering to the ground forces of the RAF on condition that they would not be handed over to Ibn Saud against their will.[269] Dawish himself surrendered on 10 January.

Britain then faced the difficulty of what to do with the *Ikhwan*. According to the Arab custom of *dakhala* an Arab could seek refuge in the house of a neighbour, or even an enemy.[270] For that reason Ibn Saud had tried to outlaw the tradition as a way of reducing the authority of tribal sheikhs and expediting the return of offenders.[271] The Sheikh of Kuwait, however antipathetic to Ibn Saud, did not want to be seen handing the rebels back to him, because to do so would have stood him dishonoured in the eyes of all Arabs.[272] The new Political Resident, Colonel Hugh Biscoe, supported the Sheikh, insisting that any responsibility for handing over the rebels must lie publicly with the British Government, to whom the *Ikhwan* had surrendered.[273]

Despite Ibn Saud's complaints against the delay in returning the *Ikhwan*,[274] Britain was reluctant to hand them over without conditions, fearing either summary execution of large numbers, possibly including women and children, or alternatively, a free pardon, enabling them to raid again in the future.[275] Deportation of the *Ikhwan* leaders to Cyprus was one possibility, except that the Treasury refused to foot the bill,[276] and, in any case, the *Ikhwan* were political refugees, not prisoners.[277] Extradition was not possible, not only because there was no appropriate agreement, but also because of the general principle that rendered political offenders immune from extradition.[278] Against this, the *Ikhwan* could easily be deported as 'undesirables', especially as they had entered Kuwait in defiance of instructions to the contrary.[279] That still left the problem of humanitarian considerations, although these must be seen in the context of a government that attempted to impose its authority in that part of the world by aerial bombing. It was not the fate of the *Ikhwan* that concerned Britain, so much as the international condemnation that might come her way for passing whole tribes over to Ibn Saud unconditionally.

Later in January Biscoe met Ibn Saud to negotiate the transfer of the rebels. Ibn Saud promised to spare their lives and pledged that there would be no further raids into Iraq or Kuwait. If there were, he would take full responsibility for them.[280] The Bahra Agreement would be exhumed to deal with grievances resulting from past and future raids.[281] Despite objections from Sir Francis Humphrys (Clayton's successor) and the Air Ministry, Biscoe declined to press for more detailed conditions, feeling that they would be unnecessary if Ibn Saud showed good faith and worthless if he did not.[282]

At the end of January 1930 the principal instigators of the revolt were flown to Ibn Saud from their internment aboard *HMS Lupin*.[283] Barring lingering disagreements over the fate of one or two chiefs who surrendered in Iraq, and who claimed not to be Nejdi subjects and hence not liable for return to Ibn Saud, the *Ikhwan* rebellion was over.[284] With Ibn Saud placated, the British Government took the opportunity to engineer a peace settlement between Ibn Saud and Feisal. The two Kings met, for the first time, on *HMS Lupin* on 22 February. A *Bon Voisinage* agreement was drafted, and provision made for settlement of the frontier posts question by arbitration. Extradition procedures and permanent diplomatic relations between Iraq and Nejd were to be established.[285]

Postscript: The Transjordan Troubles

Despite the conclusion to the *Ikhwan* rebellion, troubles across the Transjordan frontier continued for some years longer. Various factors made these disturbances assume a different complexion from those recently ceased. The *Ikhwan* were no longer a factor. They had served their purpose and were gradually disbanded by Ibn Saud. Many of the bedouin tribes eventually formed the core of the Saudi National Guard, and even the name '*Ikhwan*' began to slip from the Arabian vocabulary.[286] An era of Arabian history had passed. Sibila was the last major desert campaign of its type in Arabia; thereafter the advent of the motor car and the aeroplane transformed desert combat, making the ubiquitous camel redundant as an artifact of war.[287] Ibn Saud faced the troubles from Transjordan not with camels and the *Ikhwan*, but with cars and soldiers.[288]

Notwithstanding his triumph over the *Ikhwan*, Ibn Saud's was not necessarily a popular victory in his dominions. Rumours of discontent filtered through to the British Legation. His harnessing of the *Ikhwan* around 1918, and his abandonment of them in the early 1930s, suggested that he had exploited them not as an instrument of religion, but of politics.[289] Nor could Ibn Saud disguise the fact that he had drawn upon the assistance of an infidel power to deal with his own subjects. Husein had committed a similar heresy in 1916 by attacking the Caliphate with British help. Nejd had seen the loss of several of its most powerful sheikhs who had led the rebellion, and without whose assistance Ibn Saud would never had achieved his earlier conquests. Dawish himself died in a Saudi dungeon in 1931.[290] Nonetheless, Philby's verdict is that 'the Frankenstein of his own creation would surely have destroyed him if he had not taken the initiative of destroying it himself'.[291]

Improvement in physical and diplomatic communication also marked 1930 as a transitional year in the development of the Saudi State. Aside from the influx of the motor car, Ibn Saud embarked on his programme of installing wireless telegraphy throughout his dominions. Never again would remote tribes be able to take advantage of their remoteness. In May Sir Andrew Ryan took up his appointment as first British Minister to Hejaz-Nejd. For all these reasons Britain would be better informed about Arabian affairs than previously. In October 1930 Glubb was transferred to the service of Transjordan where he was appointed Intelligence Officer to the Arab Legion.[292] Ibn Saud objected strongly to his appointment.[293] Arbitration procedures began sorting out responsibility for past raids across the Transjordanian-Nejd frontier, the MacDonnell tribunal recommending that the claims of the two sides be cancelled out.[294]

From the time of his arrival in May until January 1931 Ryan was successful in urging a low-key British response to the raids, avoiding, if possible, recriminations against Ibn Saud.[295] Then, in Ryan's words, Britain was 'stampeded' by Glubb and Sir John Chancellor into a 'violent' response.[296] The British Government drew up, in February 1931, what amounted to a quasi-ultimatum to Ibn Saud which he was bound to interpret as a threat of British invasion to control the Wadi Sirhan.[297] This, coupled with Ryan's own blunt, formal style of diplomacy,[298] inevitably led Ibn Saud to associate Ryan with the ultimatum,[299] even though the British Minister had managed to have it toned down to avoid any personal accusation against Ibn Saud.[300]

Ryan had not been in Jedda for a year before he admitted to becoming something of a *persona ingrata* in the Hejaz.[301] He, himself, proposed that he be replaced as Minister, perhaps by an Arabic-speaking 'bull in a China-shop'.[302] 'If my methods led to the failure of my efforts I should not shrink from being relieved of a post which had its disadvantages.'[303] The implications of such a step, whether or not Ryan was replaced by another minister, would have provided Ibn Saud's first diplomatic setback in thirty years, less than a year after Ryan's arrival had crowned his international standing.[304] The Air Ministry favoured both force and the withdrawal of the British Minister.[305] The India Office decried both steps as leading to unfavourable repercussions in India, particularly in the wake of recent British policy statements on Palestine.[306] The Middle East (Official) Sub-Committee finally endorsed the Foreign Office view that force ought to be deployed only as a last resort – when the British Government was more sure of the facts than it was at present.[307]

Moreover, the precise nature of the relationship between Britain and Transjordan was called into question over the frontier disturbances. The British Government, in this instance, preferred direct communication between Abdullah and Ibn Saud as a way of easing Hashemite-Saudi tension.[308] Abdullah, however, refused to contemplate any act that would imply recognition of Ibn Saud.[309] As a consequence, the anomaly persisted whereby Transjordan maintained a hostile attitude towards Hejaz-Nejd, although Britain was responsible for the emirate's foreign relations.

Further major frontier incidents in late 1931 led to Ryan being despatched to Jerusalem to discuss the situation with the Palestine and Transjordan authorities. Ryan complained that the British Government was removing his discretion, leaving the initiative increasingly with the High Commissioner in Transjordan.[310] In February 1932 Ibn Saud's disenchantment with Ryan led to a virtual request for his withdrawal:

> Since his arrival Ryan has been placing obstacles in the way of good relations. He has exceeded the limits on several occasions when dealing with Ibn Saud, and has been speaking to him in an unaccustomed manner. He has accused Ibn Saud of personally disturbing the peace on the frontier with Transjordan, and the Hejaz-Nejd Government wonders whether he is acting on instructions.[311]

Ryan was immediately summoned to London. It was clear that Ibn Saud was holding Glubb and Ryan as principally responsible for the deterioration in Anglo-Saudi relations.[312] Among other things, Ryan had told Ibn Saud that he lived 'in a world of fantasy'.[313] The Saudi Minister in London, Sheikh Hafiz Wahba, was informed that if the note was not withdrawn Ryan would not return to Jedda, but neither would another British Minister.[314] A fortnight later Wahba presented a second letter which semi-retracted the previous complaints,[315] and, upon Foreign Secretary Simon's instructions, Ryan returned to Jedda.

In May 1932 a group of Hejazi exiles, led by Ibn Rifada who had been living in Egypt, moved into the Hejaz through Transjordan, leading to fears of escalating unrest and a second rebellion.[316] These incursions were widely attributed to the intrigues of Ibn Saud's neighbours: Abdullah, Feisal, the Imam Yahya, and King Fuad – who was renewing his claims to the Caliphate.[317] The Foreign Office noted that the Transjordanian frontier was now posing the greatest threat to the continuing stability of Anglo-Saudi relations.[318] At one stage there were genuine fears that Ibn Saud was about to attack Transjordan.[319] Britain found herself being torn by competing obligations. When Ibn Saud suggested a treaty with Abdullah, an act which would involve the latter's recognition of the legitimacy of Ibn Saud's regime, the British Government found itself unable to put pressure on Abdullah to comply. His expressed goodwill over the precarious situation in Palestine, and the fear of an anti-Jewish movement springing up in Transjordan, meant that Britain was loath to antagonise Abdullah.[320] In the event, Ibn Rifada's force, which had been estimated at some six thousand men, was defeated by a mechanised, mobile Saudi army.[321] This was followed, partly through an initiative of Sir Andrew Ryan, by Abdullah and Ibn Saud recognising each other in April 1933, and signing a treaty in the summer.[322] Saudi-Hashemite animosity never again threatened the stability of Arabia.

Summary: British Policy During the Ikhwan Rebellion

The *Ikhwan* rebellion stemmed from a combination of factors: religious tensions in Arabia, internal dissension within Nejd, bedouin anarchy, modern statehood, British defence policy in southern Iraq, and Saudi-Hashemite rivalry.[323] Perhaps the rebellion was the inevitable consequence of Britain's bisection of the Arabian deserts with invisible lines. In retrospect, it can be seen that it posed the greatest threat to Ibn Saud's rule in Arabia at any time from his capture of Riyadh in 1902 until his death in 1953. The gravity of the threat was precisely because it was internal. In consequence, Britain's policy of support for Ibn Saud as a figure of stability in Arabia had its greatest challenge in 1928-29. The Colonial Office and the Air Ministry claimed that Britain's imperial and mandatory commitments to Iraq outweighed any considerations towards Ibn Saud. In contrast, the Foreign Office and the India Office were quite prepared to sacrifice certain principles relating to Iraq's defence for what amounted to the appeasement of Ibn Saud.

On the matter of Ibn Saud's role in the Iraq-Nejd frontier raids of 1927-29, which invited so much disagreement within the British Government, the most convincing explanations are those already put forward by Glubb. Tribal raiding into the mandates was not lawlessness but, on the contrary, a deliberate policy designed to extend Ibn Saud's authority. He was pursuing a policy of northerly expansion through the indirect use of *Ikhwan* raids, confident of the futility of external retribution.[324] Two instances of contemporary evidence can be adduced in support of this view. First, in March 1928, a Major Fink of the Iraq Army stationed on the Euphrates reported:

> A man from Shammar, recently arrived from Nejd territory, had heard that about a fortnight ago Bin Saud had issued orders to the sheikhs in northern Nejd territory to collect all available men for a raid against Iraq ... Bin Saud is stated to have said in his orders that the boundary of Iraq was the railway and the Euphrates, and that all the territory south and westward of that was Nejd territory. Posts erected in this zone constituted a direct infringement of the authority of the Akhwan.

It was necessary to attack Iraq as early as possible before the fortified posts, which it would be extremely difficult to capture, could be established, and that tribes camping in the area must pay taxes to Nejd: otherwise they would be treated as unbelievers and exterminated.[325]

Further evidence was supplied to Dickson. During a meeting with Faisal al Dawish, the *Ikhwan* leader told him that Ibn Saud had, many times in the past, ordered raids into Iraq and Kuwait.[326] When Britain had complained, as after Busaiya, Ibn Saud had replied that his tribes were out of control, yet he continued to order them to raid. In the face of British bombs, however, he told the *Ikhwan* to stop raiding and to return stolen loot to Iraq. Ibn Saud had then treacherously attacked them at Sibila.[327]

One might expect evidence from Iraqi and *Ikhwan* sources to implicate Ibn Saud. Nevertheless, the similarity of the accounts lends credibility to their content. As Ibn Saud could not allow the *Ikhwan* to plunder the Hejaz, how better to further the momentum gathered in the Hejaz campaign than by permitting their energies to be turned on the Hashemites to the north? This, in passing, suggests one reason why Ibn Saud directed his grievances towards the desert posts in Iraq. Not only were they preventing *Ikhwan* successes in Iraq, but their existence was turning the *Ikhwan* against him because of his inability to get them removed.

There is, furthermore, an economic argument to explain the frontier raids. In the late 1920s Hejaz-Nejd was virtually bankrupt. For some thirteen centuries the Hejaz had taken gold from pilgrims, as well as from the Turks or the British. In 1926 Arabia's treasuries and subsidies had dried up. Only the proceeds of the Pilgrimage, upon which Ibn Saud was forced to capitalise, provided a regular if modest income to serve both the Hejaz and Nejd. In these circumstances, it has been argued, more force was needed beyond Ibn Saud's frontiers.[328]

Notwithstanding Ibn Saud's sanction of earlier raids, it became clear that, by 1928, the choice confronting him was either to break the *Ikhwan* or risk the intervention of the might of the British Empire. Unable to contemplate an outright breach with Britain, Ibn Saud turned on the *Ikhwan*. His requests for British assistance in the spring and summer of 1929 reinforce this point. Indeed, it is possible to distinguish religion from political expediency on the part of Ibn Saud. He threatened the *Ikhwan* not with religion, but with physical force.

As to the value of British assistance, both Glubb[329] and Dickson[330] agreed that, but for British political and military intervention, Ibn Saud would have fallen. Britain kept Iraq and Kuwait neutral although the natural inclination of their rulers had been to give all possible assistance to the rebels.[331] For accepting a neutral stance, and for ceasing to pass supplies to the rebels, Sheikh Ahmad of Kuwait was awarded the KCIE.[332] Moreover, it is significant that Ibn Saud, an intractable opponent of linear frontiers ever since Britain first applied them to his dominions in 1921, made full use of them, and the associated concept of 'nation-state', to defeat the *Ikhwan*. Perhaps western-style frontiers sparked off the rebellion: they certainly expedited its conclusion by hemming the *Ikhwan* against the Iraq-Kuwait frontier. This shift in Ibn Saud's attitude would culminate during the south-east Arabian frontier dispute to be considered later.

Throughout 1929 Britain sought to assist Ibn Saud to regain his authority. This raises questions about the nature and purport of British policy. Some decisions, such as the increased aerial and military activity along the Iraq and Kuwait frontiers, can be explained as simply defending states for which Britain held responsibility. Others are not so easily accounted for. Whilst Britain was successful in keeping King Feisal and Sheikh Ahmad neutral, for fear of a major confrontation between Arabian rulers all of whom enjoyed treaty relations with Britain, she herself did not pursue a policy of neutrality over the civil war, but one aimed at assisting Ibn Saud to restore his authority. This flew in the face of centuries of British preference for non-intervention in the affairs of central Arabia. Given the religious ingredient to the rebellion, Britain's reaction is all the more noteworthy. Even in the absence of extradition arrangements Britain undertook to try and prevent *Ikhwan* ingress into Iraq and Kuwait, and deny asylum to those who achieved it. On the military side, Britain supplied Ibn Saud with arms, and, even more significantly, with four brand new aeroplanes on favourable terms with pilots and technicians, with no restrictions on their use. Moreover, the decision to supply them was taken without consulting the Iraq Government. It was never considered whether Britain would ever be in the position of having her planes and pilots confronting each other over the Iraq-Nejd frontier.

The desire to conciliate Ibn Saud was also evident on the question of the frontier posts. Militarily they were proving of some value against the raiders; politically they were causing a good deal of trouble with Ibn Saud. The Cabinet took the decision, against Colonial Office and Air Ministry advice, to reduce the number of posts in the southern desert in deference to him. The implementation of similar structures in Transjordan was also delayed.

The significance of all this is that, contrary to the evidence of previous chapters, there are signs that from around 1929 such was Ibn Saud's stature that he was becoming a critical factor in Britain's overview of the Arab world, not just to the Foreign Office. It was during the second half of that year that Britain agreed to establish full diplomatic relations with him. Glubb noted that Britain, throughout the frontier raids into Iraq, was only interested in 'high international politics' and conciliating Ibn Saud.[333] There seems some evidence for the validity of Amery's assertion that the Foreign Office considered Ibn Saud to be a 'formidable power with whom peace had to be secured at any price'.[334]

Britain had always been disposed to support any ruler likely to bring stability to any particular region of the world. That, indeed, was how Britain, in previous years, had seen Ibn Saud. By 1929-30 it is possible to detect a greater commitment to him. In previous campaigns Ibn Saud had benefited from Britain standing aside and allowing natural Arabian forces to take their course. In 1929 Ibn Saud was too important to risk the outcome. For the first time, Britain took an active, as opposed to a passive, line to support him. This can be best accounted for as further modification of the Sherifian solution to the Arab world. Initially, Arabia was to become a Hashemite kingdom under Husein. Later this was redefined as a series of small Hashemite states, only one of which was to be immediately independent. In 1929 it is possible to detect yet another variation: Arabia was to be tacitly divided along a line from Aqaba to Kuwait, approximating to the 30th parallel. Britain entrusted Hashemite rulers to govern north of that line, while being no less committed to Ibn Saud's position to the south. Without Ibn Saud's authority the five hundred-odd mile Iraq-Nejd frontier lay open to anarchic disruption from the south, with all that that implied for Britain's oil and strategic interests in Iraq.

Glubb maintained that British policy during the *Ikhwan* rebellion was 'diametrically opposed to the requirements of peace'.[335] In support of this view, it can be seen that Ibn Saud did, in time, take up arms against the *Ikhwan*. In the years leading up to the First World War, the Foreign Office had declined to meet Indian demands for a constructive policy towards Ibn Saud on the simple grounds that, whatever Britain did, he could not afford a breach with the British Government. This maxim was as true for 1929 as for 1912. A more resilient British response to the raids on Iraq would not have permanently damaged Anglo-Saudi relations for the reason that Ibn Saud had nowhere else to turn, as the events of 1929 confirmed. Whether, as the Foreign Office feared, increased RAF activity would have led to the *Ikhwan* turning on Ibn Saud, with unknown results, must remain a matter for speculation.

Another outcome of the *Ikhwan* rebellion was a crystallisation of the view that Ibn Saud and the British Government shared certain interests in the Arabian peninsula. Each needed the other in retaining stability in Arabia and encouraging the conditions in the Hejaz that would benefit pilgrims worldwide. This harmony of interests, however, operated only within certain definable limits. Britain may have desired and encouraged the stability of Saudi rule, but only within frontiers of her choosing and which were non-negotiable. This arrangement was likely to be less than satisfactory to Ibn Saud because of his aims to re-unite the desert up to Syria and the River Euphrates under Saudi rule. In terms of Ibn Saud's territorial aspirations, as opposed to his territorial *status quo*, Britain was an object of his resentment and suspicion. Britain's simultaneous furthering of the interests of Feisal and Abdullah north of a British-imposed line, and of Ibn Saud south of it, could have won neither his comprehension nor his sympathy.

This dichotomy between Ibn Saud and the British Government sharing certain fundamental interests in Arabia while, at the same time, fearing the territorial policies of the other, constituted a dual framework within which Anglo-Saudi relations operated throughout the 1930s. Britain did not want to quarrel with too many Arab rulers simultaneously. Moreover, there was the fear that, had Ibn Saud fallen, the wider Arab and Moslem world would have held Britain responsible, with unforeseeable consequences throughout the Middle East and India.

The Iraq-Nejd frontier disturbances took on many of the characteristics of a secret war. Despite, or perhaps because of, their gravity the raids were given little public attention in Britain. This was partly because there were no press correspondents to report the fighting. In part, too, it was a reflection of the British Government's desire to play down anything which could be interpreted as a colonial war.[336] In the latter stages of the rebellion attention was also diverted by events in Palestine. Few questions were asked in Parliament about the state of affairs on the Iraq-Nejd frontier.

The *Ikhwan* rebellion provided further justification for the need to update the machinery of British policy-making towards Arabia. It is worth bearing in mind the number of treaties which bound Britain, Nejd, Iraq and Kuwait together:

> The British Treaty with Iraq – 1922
> The British Treaties with Kuwait – 1899 and 1914
> The British Treaty with Hejaz-Nejd – 1927
> The Treaty of Mohammera, and the Uqair Protocol – 1922
> The Bahra Agreement – 1925

In addition, that small area of north-east Arabia saw the Foreign Office, the Colonial Office and the India Office adopting such incompatible standpoints that the Cabinet had to intervene. Against this background it is not surprising to see the creation in 1928 of the CID Sub-Committee on the Akhwan Situation, and the frequent summoning of inter-departmental meetings. In 1930 the CID Official Sub-Committee on the Middle East was the natural outcome of the need to reduce inter-departmental inefficiencies.

To combat the problem of scarce and often unreliable information emanating from Arabia, Britain adopted a position of bluff. Britain had to display to Ibn Saud an air of firmness and resolve where, in reality, there was neither – for example, her admission that she could not adequately protect Kuwait. Ibn Saud was not to know that the British Government had invested him with such significance in Arabia, otherwise he might have embarked upon an expansionist programme with greater confidence. Britain knew, if Ibn Saud did not, that she was largely helpless when it came to imposing her wishes in Arabia against determined resistance.

Britain had contravened her own agreements with Ibn Saud not to violate the Iraq-Nejd frontier. Arrangements for settling frontier disturbances, already provided for in the Bahra Agreement, had not been put into effect. Nonetheless, the meeting between Feisal and Ibn Saud was a considerable coup for British policy, easing the way for closer Saudi-Hashemite relations. By 1930 Ibn Saud stood in control of Arabia as never before. Correspondingly, Britain's commitment to his regime was more apparent than ever.

REFERENCES FOR CHAPTER FIVE

1. Use of the term 'frontier' leads to the wide geo-political issue of 'frontiers' and 'boundaries'. In modern usage, a frontier is a zone rather than a line; a tract of territory dividing two sovereignties. A boundary is a line; a clear divide capable of being put on a map (Alastair Lamb, *Asian Frontiers: Studies in a Continuing Problem*, pp. 4-6). Technically, when speaking of the line between Nejd and the mandates we are referring to a boundary, not a frontier. Following the example set by Lord Curzon (*Frontiers*), the terms 'frontiers' and 'boundaries' were used more or less interchangably. This study will adopt the term 'frontier' when speaking of 'boundaries', in accordance with the popular terminology of the time.
2. Howarth, p. 140.
3. George Rentz, 'The Iraq-Nejd Frontier', *Journal of the Central Asian Society*, 17 (1930), p. 85.
4. Kelly, *Arabia* ..., p. 237.
5. Rentz, p. 86.
6. Dickson, p. 286.
7. Philby, *Arabian Jubilee*, p. 89.
8. Helms, p. 152.
9. ibid., p. 163. Alternatively, he may have withheld their allowances as a sign of disapproval, having dispensed with their services (personal correspondence from Robert Lacey).
10. Helms, pp. 260-1. For a comprehensive list of *Ikhwan* grievances, see Habib, p. 122.
11. Philby, *Arabian Jubilee*, p. 90.
12. Political geographers would call this the 'trigger action' which sparked off the frontier dispute (see J.R.V. Prescott, *The Geography of Frontiers and Boundaries*, p. 110). Certain aspects of the tribal revolt against Ibn Saud have already been thoroughly explored. In particular, the reader is directed to J.B. Glubb, *War in the Desert* (hereafter: *War* ....); Helms; and Dickson, for detailed accounts of the rebellion's logistics, psychology, and much else of interest from the perspectives of the combatants. What is missing is an account of the pressures operating in London, within the British Government, in response to the unfolding of the revolt, and how those pressures conflicted with those experienced in Baghdad, Bushire and elsewhere. This chapter is concerned less with the rebellion than with the British reaction to it.
13. Iraq comprised the Ottoman provinces of Mosul, Baghdad and Basra, plus large areas of desert.
14. Arab antipathy to the term 'mandate' led Britain to ban it from circulation, except at Geneva, and to substitute the euphemism 'bilateral treaty' (Monroe, *Britain's Moment* ..., p. 77).
15. See Main, p. 82.
16. M. V. Seton-Williams, *Britain and the Arab States*, p. 18.
17. The rail link was never built, on grounds of expense.
18. Stephen Longrigg, *Oil in the Middle East*, pp. 76-7 (hereafter: *Oil* ...).
19. Seton-Williams, pp. 26-32; Peter Sluglett, *Britain in Iraq 1914-1932*, pp. 116-25.
20. Hurewitz, pp. 310-11.
21. Helms, p. 192.

22. Strictly speaking, there is no such thing as a 'natural' boundary or frontier since they are all artificial, political constructs (see Prescott, p. 13).
23. Helms, p. 192. This problem was not confined to Arabia. In arriving at frontier settle-ments colonial powers often overlooked local factors. Frequently the sources of tension created only became apparent after the passing of the imperial government (Lamb, p. 9).
24. It was common colonial policy to locate a linear boundary beyond the limits of actual administration, thereby creating a frontier tract which, if difficulties arose, could operate as a buffer (Lamb, p. 9).
25. Curzon believed deserts to be the best type of defensive frontier, despite their often providing the habitat for mobile and warring tribes plundering in order to obtain the necessities of life (C. C. Davies, *The Problem of the North-West Frontier 1890-1908*, p. 179).
26. Curzon had defined three types of boundary: (i) astronomical – following the lines of latitude or longitude; (ii) mathematical – connecting two or more specific points; (iii) referential – the frontier being defined with regard to some specific location, involving arcs of circles and straight lines. Geometric frontiers usually implied little information about topography and drainage. Curzon distinguished between frontiers of contact and frontiers of separation, depending on the ease with which they could be crossed by virtue of trade, migration or armed conflict (see Prescott, pp. 13, 42). By this distinction the Iraq-Nejd frontier was a 'contact' frontier. Moreover, the frontier meant different things to each side. To Nejd it constituted the cell wall of a sovereign state. From the perspective of Iraq, as with most colonial or semi-colonial territories, the frontier was shaped by the needs, strategic or economic, of the imperial power.
27. Howarth, p. 145.
28. A 'delimited' boundary is one that has been defined and is capable of being set down on a map. When the boundary is marked out on the landscape, with accompanying frontier posts, it is termed 'demarcated' (Lamb, pp. 4-5; Prescott, p. 30).
29. Glubb, *War* ..., p. 87.
30. Dickson, pp. 285-6 (see Rentz, pp. 80ff for similar accounts).
31. See Sweet, pp. 1132-50.
32. ibid., p. 1134.
33. ibid., pp. 1136-8. This is to overlook its value for economic and social security, or as an article of exchange through '*zakat*', inheritance, bridal gifts, compensation, etc. (ibid., p. 1137). Nor did the camel compete with the bedouin for scarce resources, being able to drink unpotable water.
34. ibid., p. 1137.
35. Rentz, p. 80.
36. Sweet, p. 1142.
37. ibid., p. 1133.
38. ibid., p. 1147.
39. ibid., pp. 1139-40.
40. ibid., p. 1145.
41. ibid., p. 1133.
42. Alois Musil, 'Northern Negd', *American Geographical Society* (1928).
43. Helms, p. 138.
44. ibid., p. 143.
45. Rentz, p. 82.
46. Sweet, p. 1148.
47. Dickson, p. 266.
48. Rentz, pp. 79-82.
49. Smart (Damascus) to FO, No 112, 8 April 1926, FO E/2260/180/91: 371/11437.
50. More (Kuwait) to Bushire, 23 October 1926, CO/21900/26: 727/8.
51. Dobbs (Baghdad) to Amery, 1 January 1928, CO/58117/28: 730/130. These tribes were based in the north, west, and east of Nejd respectively, and strategically could hem loyal Saudi forces in central Arabia. The chiefs of the Mutair (Faisal al Dawish) and the Utaiba (Sultan ibn Bijad) had hoped for the governorships of Medina and Mecca (Almana, p. 74).
52. See FO minute, 1 July 1927, FO E/2908/56/91: 371/12240.
53. Inter-departmental meeting, 30 December 1927, in FO E/5616/56/91: 371/12242.

54. Dobbs to Amery, No 39, 10 January 1928, CO/58117/28: 730/130.
55. ibid.
56. Dobbs to Amery, 25 February 1928, CO/59068/28: 732/32.
57. Longrigg, *Oil* ..., p. 69.
58. Dobbs to Amery, No 104, 22 February 1928, in FO E/941/1/91: 371/12989.
59. ibid.
60. Trenchard minute, 30 December 1927, in FO E/5615/56/91: 371/12241.
61. Dobbs to Amery, 13 March 1928, CO/59068/28: 732/32.
62. Glubb, op. cit., p. 69.
63. Klieman, pp. 111-12. Eight squadrons, at one time, had been assigned to Iraq – about one third of the entire RAF (Thornton, p. 181). (See also, Sluglett, pp. 259-70.)
64. Glubb, op. cit., p. 69.
65. Roskill, pp. 446-9.
66. Hoare to FO, 27 February 1928, FO E/1047/1/91: 371/12989.
67. Dobbs to Amery, 25 February 1928, CO/59068/28: 732/32. The planes were De Haviland DH.9. biplanes – 'ninaks'.
68. Glubb, op. cit., p. 194.
69. Trenchard minute, 30 December 1927, in FO E/5615/56/91: 371/12241.
70. ibid.
71. ibid.
72. ibid.
73. Roskill, pp. 446-7.
74. Hankey to Trenchard, 28 April 1928, in Roskill, p. 447.
75. Roskill, p. 448.
76. Wilson (CO) minute, 20 January 1928, in FO E/533/159/91: 371/13008.
77. Inter-departmental meeting, 30 December 1927, FO E/5615/56/91: 371/12241.
78. ibid.
79. Shuckburgh to Oliphant, 29 December 1927, ibid.
80. ibid.
81. Amery to Dobbs, No 40, 21 January 1928, CO/58117/28: 730/130.
82. Osborne (FO) minute on inter-departmental meeting, op. cit.
83. Gladwyn Jebb (FO) minute, 8 February 1928, FO E/573/1/91: 371/12988.
84. Stonehewer-Bird (Jedda) to FO, No 4, 7 February 1928, FO E/629/1/91: 371/12988.
85. Chamberlain minute, 29 December 1927, FO E/5615/56/91: 371/12241.
86. This is to overlook Ibn Saud's difficulties with the Ajman tribe in Hasa in 1915-16.
87. See FO E/5326/56/91: 371/12241.
88. See CO/49198/27: 732/28.
89. Haworth (Bushire) to CO, 9 February 1928, CO/58117/28: 730/130.
90. Viceroy to SSI, No 876, 27 February 1928, FO E/1034/1/91: 371/12989.
91. Haworth to Amery, No 27, 18 February 1928, CO/59022/28: 732/31.
92. Gladwyn Jebb minute, 17 December 1927, FO E/5400/56/91: 371/12241.
93. Stephen Longrigg, *Iraq: 1900-1950*, p. 219 (hereafter: *Iraq* ...); *Survey ...1928*, p. 301.
94. Frontier questions of this kind plagued the British throughout the Empire and the routes to it. For comparisons with the situation in Uganda in 1911, note the following: 'The north-east had to be controlled, not because it afforded a source of revenue or offered prospects of development, but because tribal fighting had to be stopped' (James Barber, *Imperial Frontier: A Study of Relations between the British and the Pastoral Tribes of North-East Uganda*, p. 118).
95. Dobbs to Amery, 29 March 1928, CO/59068/28: 732/32.
96. ibid. In 1918 Kuwait began smuggling supplies to the Turks, whereupon Britain clamped a blockade upon the sheikhdom (Kelly, *Arabia* ..., p. 170).
97. FO minute, 30 December 1927, FO E/5615/56/91: 371/12241.
98. Haworth to Amery, No 38, 6 December 1928, CO/69006/29: 732/37.
99. FO minute, op. cit.; Helms, p. 238.
100. Haworth to Amery, op. cit.
101. ibid.
102. Dobbs to Amery, 25 February 1928, CO/59068/28: 732/32.
103. ibid.
104. Helms, p. 30.

105. Jt. memorandum SSC & SSA, March 1928, CP 70, CAB 24/193.
106. ibid.
107. ibid.
108. AM to FO, 5 January 1928, FO E/89/1/91: 371/12988.
109. Howarth, p. 149.
110. IO to FO, 9 March 1928, FO E/1260/1/91: 371/12990.
111. See Biscoe (Bushire) to Passfield, No 7, 5 January 1930, in FO E/110/1/91: 371/14449; *Survey ... 1928*, p. 302.
112. Jt. memorandum SSC & SSA, op. cit.
113. Hoare memorandum, 8 May 1928, CP 160(28), CAB 24/195.
114. ibid.
115. Dobbs to Amery, No 93, 17 February 1928, CO/58117/28: 730/130.
116. Helms, p. 166. Ibn Saud was also angered by the Sheikh of Kuwait giving asylum to dissident tribes.
117. ibid., p. 167; Kelly, *Arabia* ..., p. 236.
118. Gladwyn Jebb minute, 14 June 1929, FO E/2986/2322/91: 371/13736. Kuwait's trading interests meant that the sheikhdom disapproved of any single ruler controlling the whole peninsula (Habib, p. 107).
119. Haworth to Amery, 1 February 1928, CO/58117/28: 730/130.
120. FO minute, 9 June 1928, FO E/2982/1/91: 371/12994.
121. ibid.
122. Philby, *Saudi Arabia*, p. 307.
123. Amery to Dobbs and Haworth, 22 February 1928, CO/58117/28: 730/130.
124. ibid.
125. Hoare to CID, 22 May 1928, CP 163(28), CAB 24/195.
126. Rendel minute, 3 April 1928, FO E/1749/1/91: 371/12992; Glubb, *War* ..., pp. 192-3.
127. Seymour (FO) minute, 16 May 1928, FO E/2568/2068/91: 371/13013.
128. Dobbs to Amery, 28 January 1928, CO/58117/28: 730/130. FO minute, 15 September 1928, FO E/4485/3261/91: 371/13017.
129. Helms, p. 228.
130. Osborne minute, 1 March 1928, FO E/1042/1/91: 371/12989.
131. CO memorandum, 3 May 1928, CO/59361/28: 725/17.
132. Luke to Amery, 29 September 1928, CO/59493/28: 831/3.
133. Stonehewer-Bird to FO, No 7, 26 February 1928, FO E/992/1/91: 371/12989.
134. See FO E/995/1/91: 371/12989; FO E/5184/3261/91: 371/13018.
135. Dobbs to Amery, 9 March 1928, in FO E/1320/1/91: 371/12990.
136. Oliphant memorandum, 30 May 1928, FO E/2914/1/91: 371/12994.
137. Amery to Chamberlain, 26 April 1928, FO E/2217/1/91: 371/12993.
138. Normally in summer the climate obliged tribes and herds to congregate near permanent water sources. In autumn the tribes moved out to their *diras* to await the winter rains (Sweet, p. 1135).
139. See FO E/1079/1/91: 371/12989.
140. Oliphant memorandum, 30 May 1928, FO E/2914/1/91: 371/12994.
141. Dobbs to Amery, 11 March 1928, in FO E/1322/1/91: 371/12990.
142. ibid.
143. Chamberlain to Amery, 11 April 1928, FO E/1820/1/91: 371/12992.
144. Lloyd (Cairo) to FO, 10 January 1928, FO E/165/1/91: 371/12988.
145. Chamberlain to Amery, 11 April 1928, FO E/1820/1/91: 371/12992.
146. Haworth to Amery, 11 April 1928, FO E/1919/1/91: 371/12992.
147. See CO/59092/28: 732/33.
148. Dobbs to Amery, No 299, 26 May 1928, CO/59129/28: 732/35. The AOC Iraq was responsible to the High Commissioner, not to the Air Ministry (Sluglett, p. 263).
149. Dobbs to Amery, op. cit.
150. Rendel minute, 31 May 1928, FO E/2814/1/91: 371/12994.
151. See FO E/1042/1/91: 371/12989; CO/58117/28: 730/130.
152. Seymour (FO) minute, 14 September 1928, FO E/4485/3261/91: 371/13017.
153. Minute of Sub-Committee on Akhwan Situation, 26 June 1928, CAB 16/88.
154. Seymour minute, 14 September 1928, op. cit.
155. Beckett (FO) minute, 15 September 1928, ibid.

156. Clayton report, in FO E/2568/2068/91: 371/13013.
157. ibid.
158. Orchard (FO) memorandum, 3 September 1929, FO E/4479/3/91: 371/13716.
159. ibid.
160. Stonehewer-Bird to FO, No 34, 15 May 1928, FO E/2568/2068/91: 371/13013.
161. ibid.
162. Stonehewer-Bird to FO, No 37, 21 May 1928, FO E/2688/2068/91: 371/13013.
163. Minute of Sub-Committee on Akhwan Situation, op. cit.
164. Amery to Dobbs, No 232, 25 May 1928, CO/59016/28: 732/29.
165. Amery memorandum, 16 June 1928, see CP 187(28), CAB 16/88.
166. Hoare to CID, 22 May 1928, CP 163(28), CAB 24/195.
167. See CP 180(28), CAB 16/88.
168. ibid.
169. Dobbs to Amery, 15 July 1928, CO/59106/28: 732/34.
170. ibid.
171. Clayton to Amery, 3 September 1928, CO/59176/28: 732/36. See draft of proposed Green Book on Clayton's 1928 negotiations, in Clayton, Box 16, File 3, MEC.
172. Clayton to Amery, op. cit.
173. Glubb, *War* ..., p. 140.
174. ibid., p. 191.
175. ibid., p. 201.
176. Glubb to Cornwallis (Adviser to Iraq Ministry of Interior), 17 March 1928, CO/59068/28: 732/32.
177. ibid.
178. See CO/59022/28: 732/31. It is apparent that by the time Glubb came to write his books on his experiences, he had mellowed considerably from his early years in the desert.
179. Glubb memorandum, CO/59197/28: 732/36.
180. ibid.
181. Gladwyn Jebb minute, 12 November 1928, FO E/5302/1/91: 371/12996.
182. ibid.
183. Glubb to Cornwallis, No 54, 17 January 1929, CO/69006/29: 732/37.
184. Cornwallis to Dobbs, 22 March 1928, CO/59068/28: 732/32.
185. See CO/69006/116/29: 732/37.
186. Annual Report 1930.
187. Glubb, *War* ..., p. 202.
188. ibid., pp. 202, 249.
189. ibid., p. 225.
190. John Bagot Glubb, *Arabian Adventures: Ten Years of Loyal Service*, pp. 132-4, (hereafter: ... *Ten Years* ...)
191. ibid.
192. Glubb, *War* ..., pp. 62, 142.
193. ibid., pp. 233, 263.
194. ibid., p. 82.
195. ibid., p. 191.
196. Rentz, p. 83. For composition of Iraq Government, see Sluglett, p. 5.
197. Seton-Williams, pp. 18, 32.
198. ibid., pp. 26, 34.
199. Khadim Niama, 'Anglo-Iraqi Relations During the Mandate' (unpublished Ph. D.), p. 118.
200. ibid., p. 241.
201. ibid., p. 265.
202. ibid.
203. Feisal memorandum, CO/59129/50/28: 732/35.
204. FO minute, FO E/4661/1/91: 371/12995.
205. Rendel minute, 28 February 1929, FO E/1033/3/91: 371/13714.
206. Bond (Jedda) to FO, No 255, 30 September 1929, FO E/5418/2322/91: 371/13738.
207. Young (Baghdad) to Passfield, 21 October 1929, IO L/P&S/10/1246.
208. Butler (FO) minute, 24 October 1929, FO E/5422/2322/91: 371/13738.
209. See FO E/5945/3261/91: 371/13018.

210. RIIA, *Political and Strategic Interests* ..., pp. 163-4; *Survey ... 1928*, p. 305.
211. See Chapter Six.
212. Kelly, *Arabia* ..., p. 237.
213. K. Williams, p. 224.
214. The *ulema* could authorise changes within Wahhabi tradition.
215. Dickson, pp. 297-8. For a full account of Ibn Saud's meeting with the Nejd *ulema*, see Habib, pp. 134-5.
216. CO to FO, 20 October 1928, CO/59421/28: 831/2.
217. Plumer to Amery, No 47, 16 October 1928, ibid.
218. AM to CO, 13 December 1928, FO E/5925/3182/91: 371/13017; CO/69421/29: 831/5.
219. ibid.
220. John Bagot Glubb, *The Story of the Arab Legion*, p. 64.
221. ibid.
222. Luke (Amman) to Amery, 20 September 1928, CO/59493/28: 831/3.
223. CO to AM, 19 October 1928, ibid.
224. Luke to Amery, op. cit. The RAF term of service in Iraq was only two years, as against five years in India and Egypt.
225. AM to FO, 18 March 1930, FO E/1408/89/91: 371/14458.
226. Rendel minute, 25 October 1928, FO E/5089/3261/91: 371/13017.
227. Amery to Ag. High Commissioner Baghdad, 20 August 1928, CO/59129/28: 732/35.
228. Amery to Chancellor, 5 February .1929, CO/69421/29: 831/5.
229. Monroe, *Britain's Moment* ..., p. 81.
230. ibid.
231. AM to FO, op. cit.
232. See FO E/4943/3261/91: 371/13018; CO/59176/28: 732/36. Dickson, p. 298.
233. Inter-departmental meeting, 12 April 1929, CO/68080/29: 730/140.
234. Stonehewer-Bird to FO, 6 February 1929, FO E/676/3/91: 371/13713.
235. Dickson, p. 300. See Chapter Eight for more on Crane.
236. CO to Baghdad, No 76, 23 February 1929, CO/69056/29: 732/40. Glubb, *War* ..., p. 272. In March 1929 the RAF assumed defence of the Gulf, see page 222 below.
237. See FO E/2568/2068/91: 371/13013.
238. Main, p. 94.
239. Dickson, pp. 302-4.
240. The Ajman had deserted Ibn Saud at Jarrab in 1915 and been given sanctuary in Kuwait. Habib points out that the tribal leaders who revolted against Ibn Saud each had distinct grievances (Habib, p. 137). Hasa, moreover, being more exposed to outside influences than Nejd, was less willing to adopt Wahhabism. Indeed, more than half of its population was Shia (Kelly, op. cit., p. 237).
241. Jakins to FO, Nos 53-54, 7 May 1929, FO E/2327/2322/91: 371/13736.
242. ibid.
243. ibid. An arms deal was also secured with Poland (Philby, *Arabian Jubilee*, p. 108).
244. Glubb, *War* ..., p. 300.
245. See FO E/5254/66/91: 371/13727. The bases were later transferred to the Hejaz.
246. Bond to FO, No 91, 19 June 1929, FO E/3146/2322/91: 371/13736.
247. CO to Clayton, No 200, 14 June 1929, in FO E/3007/2322/91: 371/13736. Ibn Saud's request brought to the surface the whole policy of aerial bombing in the Middle East. The question had previously been comprehensively considered at the instigation of J. R. Thomas, Labour Colonial Secretary, in 1924. He had concluded that there was no viable alternative to the existing RAF strategy. By 1929 RAF bombing on the Iraq-Nejd frontier was considered to be of so minor and limited a character, that it was decided not to reopen the issue at inter-departmental level (Rendel memorandum, 21 June 1929, FO E/3191/2322/91: 371/13736). For more on the 1924 survey on aerial strategy in Iraq, see Sluglett, pp. 264-5.
248. A large percentage of Ibn Saud's forces were townspeople, a reversion to the methods of his earlier military successes.
249. The *Ikhwan* were with their tribes, and so had their families and animals with them.
250. Bushire to CO, No 13, 11 June 1929, in FO E/2986/2322/91: 371/13736; see also FO E/2426/2322/91: 371/13736.
251. Biscoe (Bushire) to Passfield, No 7, 5 January 1930, in FO E/110/91: 371/14449.

252. Clayton to Amery, 9 June 1929, in FO E/2954/2322/91: 371/13736.
253. Rendel minute, 29 August 1929, FO E/4095/2322/91: 371/13737; see also FO E/2986/ 2322/91: 371/13736.
254. Inter-departmental meeting, 14 June 1929, FO E/3007/2322/91: 371/13736.
255. Bushire to CO, No 34, 12 July 1929, in FO E/4330/2322/91: 371/13737.
256. Zahra Freeth and Victor Winstone, *Kuwait: Prospect and Reality*, p. 56.
257. Dickson, p. 316.
258. ibid.
259. Annual Report 1930.
260. Dickson to Bushire, No 433, 18 July 1929 in FO E/4651/2322/91: 371/13737.
261. ibid.
262. Rendel minute, 17 September 1929, FO E/4651/2322/91: 371/13737.
263. FO to Bond, 26 June 1929, FO E/3241/2322/91: 371/13736.
264. ibid.
265. Passfield to Bushire, 29 November 1929, in FO E/6188/2322/91: 371/13739.
266. Rendel minute, 30 November 1929, FO E/6205/2322/91: 371/13739.
267. Laithwaite (IO) minute, 2 January 1930, IO L/P&S/10/1246.
268. Biscoe to Passfield, No 11, 8 January 1930, in FO E/18/1/91: 371/14449.
269. Passfield to Humphrys (Baghdad), No 6, 4 January 1930, ibid.
270. Dickson, pp. 318, 322.
271. Helms, p. 146.
272. Biscoe to Passfield, No 31, 9 January 1930, in FO E/159/1/91: 371/14449.
273. The Sheikh was appeased by Britain undertaking to find a settlement to the Kuwait blockade question in return for his co-operation against the *Ikhwan*.
274. Bond to FO, 13 January 1930, FO E/234/1/91: 371/14449.
275. Passfield to Humphrys and Biscoe, 10 January 1930, in FO E/236/1/91: 371/14449.
276. Inter-departmental meeting, 15 January 1930, ibid.
277. Passfield to Humphrys and Biscoe, op. cit.
278. Warner (FO) memorandum, 10 January 1930, FO E/259/1/91: 371/14449.
279. ibid.
280. Biscoe to Passfield, 28 January 1930, in FO E/480/1/91: 371/14450.
281. ibid.
282. ibid.
283. ibid.
284. Annual Report 1930.
285. K. Williams, p. 238; Longrigg, *Iraq* ..., p. 220.
286. Philby, *Saudi Arabia*, p. 313.
287. Glubb, ... *Ten Years* ..., p. 149.
288. Dickson, p. 329.
289. Glubb, *War* ..., pp. 57-8.
290. Dickson, p. 326.
291. Philby, *Saudi Arabia*, p. 313. Presumably Philby had overlooked that Frankenstein was the creator, not the monster.
292. Glubb, ... *Ten Years* ..., p. 209.
293. Annual Report 1930.
294. ibid. The MacDonnell findings were held to be a failure by the British Government.
295. Ryan to Oliphant, 21 April 1931, Ryan Papers, Box 6, File 8, MEC.
296. ibid.
297. ibid.
298. Ryan once complained to the Saudi Government after Ibn Saud had failed to enquire after the British Minister's health.
299. Ryan to Oliphant, op. cit.
300. Ryan to Oliphant, 22 January 1932, op. cit.
301. Ryan to Oliphant, 21 April 1931, op. cit.
302. Ryan to Oliphant, 22 January 1932, op. cit.
303. Ryan to FO, No 126, 2 April 1931, FO E/2225/387/25: 371/15294.
304. Ryan to FO, No 54, 5 March 1931, FO E/1137/387/25: 371/15294.
305. Rendel memorandum, ME(O), 7 March 1931, FO E/1149/387/25: 371/15294.
306. ibid.

307. ibid.
308. FO memorandum on inter-departmental meeting, 29 September 1931, FO E/4934/387/ 25: 371/15294.
309. ibid.
310. Ryan to Oliphant, 22 January 1931, op. cit.
311. Hejaz-Nejd Government to FO, 8 February 1932, FO E/657/640/25: 371/16021.
312. Rendel minute, 11 May 1931, FO E/2526/387/25: 371/15294.
313. Ryan memorandum, Ryan Papers, Box 6, File 8, MEC.
314. Simon to Sheikh Hafiz Wahba, 21 March 1932, FO E/1038/640/25: 371/16022.
315. Wahba to FO, 5 April 1932, FO E/1686/640/25: 371/16022.
316. Dickson, p. 329.
317. ME(O), 9 June 1932, FO E/2859/76/25: 371/16014.
318. Warner (FO) memorandum, 6 May 1932, FO E/2276/76/25: 371/16013.
319. Annual Report 1932.
320. Rendel minute, 6 May 1932, FO E/2276/76/25: 371/16013.
321. Dickson, p. 329.
322. K. Williams, p. 270.
323. If the *Ikhwan* had successfully overthrown Ibn Saud, they would, more than likely, have been defeated sometime later by whoever could obtain modern weapons, aeroplanes and British support (personal correspondence from Robert Lacey).
324. Not every scholar takes this view. Helms, for example, doubts Ibn Saud's complicity over Busaiya because of what she sees as his policy of appeasement which he was pursuing towards the Moslem world as a whole. (Helms, pp. 227-8).
325. CP 180(28), CAB 16/88.
326. Dickson to Bushire, No 433, 18 July 1929, in FO E/4651/2322/91: 371/13717.
327. ibid.
328. *Survey ... 1925*, p. 325.
329. Glubb, *War* ..., preface, pp. 307ff.
330. Dickson, p. 328.
331. Britain not only kept Iraq and Kuwait neutral. She also protected them from the *Ikhwan*, who would possibly have succeeded in conquest up to the Euphrates but for Britain, and in so doing, of course, have enjoyed Ibn Saud's support, not his wrath (personal correspondence from Robert Lacey).
332. Dickson, p. 326.
333. Glubb, ... *Ten Years* ..., p. 192.
334. See page 106.
335. See page 111.
336. Glubb, *War* ..., preface.

CHAPTER SIX

South-West Arabia: Anglo-Italian Rivalry in the Red Sea and Saudi-Yemeni Confrontation 1925-1934

Conflicts on the western side of Arabia, on the Red Sea, had a different complexion from those near the Gulf. The Red Sea was an international waterway: the Gulf a British lake. The populations of western Arabia were both more numerous and more cosmopolitan than those in the east. It was, therefore, less likely that Britain could deal with frontier questions on the Red Sea in the seclusion and freedom from great power rivalry that she enjoyed on the other side of Arabia. Consequently, British policy had to contend with the attention of the outside world. In this instance that attention is provided by Italy, the first time that an international factor is introduced into this study. Anglo-Italian relations are central to this chapter. Moreover, by introducing the affairs of the Yemen, the only other independent Arab state until 1932, yet another dimension is introduced into Britain's policy towards Ibn Saud.

Background to Asir, the Yemen and Aden

Until the nineteenth century Asir, the strip of Arabian littoral and mountainous hinterland between the Hejaz and the Yemen, was under the sovereignty of the Imams of Yemen.[1] The respective histories of Asir and the Yemen began to diverge in the early 1870s when the Turks, taking advantage of the newly-opened Suez Canal, reasserted their authority along both the eastern and western littorals of the Arabian peninsula. The Turks had enjoyed a chequered career in the Yemen, gaining control and losing it several times since the sixteenth century.[2] In 1872 the Ottoman Government constituted the *Vilayet* of the Yemen, with Asir as one of its constituent *sanjaks*.[3] This arrangement was a reflection of Turkish administrative control, not a confirmation of the extent of the *de facto* authority of the Imam.[4] In effect, as elsewhere in the Ottoman Empire, Turkish control in south-west Arabia was never absolute, although the Porte was recognised internationally as the sovereign power in the region.[5] Increasingly, the Turks were challenged by two separate rebellious chiefs with distinct histories and grievances – the Shiite Imam of the Yemen and the Sunni Idrisi of Asir. Acknowledging the separate causes of the unrest, the Turks imposed political distinctions between Asir and the Yemen. In 1910 Asir was detached from Yemeni administration and reconstituted as a completely separate administrative unit, without the status of a *vilayet*, but directly under the central government at Constantinople.[6] Due to successful local resistance, the Imam was offered a large measure of autonomy in 1911, though this included neither the withdrawal of the Turkish *vali*, nor recognition of the Imam's claims to authority over Asir.[7] The coming of the First World War brought further complications. The Imam continued his fealty to the Turks throughout the conflict because of the Christian, British presence to the north, in the Hejaz, and the south, in Aden. He, and Ibn Rashid at Hail, were the only notable Arab potentates to resist British overtures. Upon the collapse of the Ottoman Empire in 1918, the Yemen became a successor state.

The passage of events in Asir was more complex. In April 1915 the Idrisi signed a treaty with the British Government, backed by a supplementary agreement two years later.[8] He was the first Arab ruler to join the allies, and was prompted by his fears of the Turks and the Imam. Under the treaty Britain undertook to safeguard the Idrisi's territories from all attacks on his seaboard. He was also guaranteed independence in his own domain and was promised that, at the conclusion of the War, Britain would use every diplomatic means in her power to adjudicate between the rival claims of the Idrisi and the Imam, or any other ruler.[9]

The pressure of war exacerbated Britain's strategic vulnerability in the Red Sea, particularly with regard to certain islands at its southern end. The Kamaran Island, just off the coast of the Yemen, with its vital deep water anchorage, was occupied by British forces who remained there after the War in *de facto* occupation.[10] The second group of islands, the Farasan Islands, were larger and lay about one hundred miles to the north of Kamaran, off Asir. They, too, provided a serviceable harbour and offered the bonus of possible oil reserves.[11] At the beginning of 1915 the Idrisi assumed control of these islands from the Turks. Britain's supplementary agreement with him, in January 1917, sought to safeguard the Farasan Islands through diplomatic means rather than through occupation. Britain recognised the islands as under the sovereignty of the Idrisi, promising to protect them from any hostile action and to preclude the intervention of any foreign power.[12] She promised the Idrisi assistance with arms and ammunition both during the War and afterwards.[13] Due to successive Arms Traffic Conventions covering the Red Sea in 1919 and 1925, those arms were not forthcoming.

With the return of peace and the dismemberment of the Ottoman Empire, two distinct sovereignties had emerged in south-west Arabia. Britain, in 1921, evacuated the occupied Yemeni port of Hodeida and allowed it, as a reward, to be annexed by the Idrisi, despite its geographical links with the Yemen.[14] At this juncture, Ibn Saud made his first introduction into the affairs of Asir. He had commenced his initial westward thrust into the Hejaz in 1918, while Husein had already encroached upon part of northern Asir. In 1920 an agreement was reached with the Idrisi which gave Ibn Saud control of the mountainous eastern hinterland of Asir, known as Asir Surat.[15] Some of this area had allegedly formed part of the earlier, nineteenth century Wahhabi state.[16]

Later developments in the Hejaz were to underline the precarious existence of Asir. Already, the death in 1923 of the Idrisi with whom Britain had treated had resulted in a family feud for the succession. The Imam took advantage of this and the distraction of the Hejaz-Nejd war, by retaking some of the coastal areas, including Hodeida.[17] At the turn of 1925-26, as Ibn Saud consummated his conquest of the Hejaz, the remnants of the Idrisi's territory found themselves sandwiched between the predatory aspirations of an enlarged Saudi state to the north and the Yemen to the south.

The turbulent events sweeping Arabia in the mid-1920s precipitated British diplomatic intervention to seek accommodation with the man primarily responsible for them – Ibn Saud. This led to the series of missions to the Hejaz led by Sir Gilbert Clayton between 1925 and 1928. Two other factors necessitated Britain extending her initiative beyond Ibn Saud to the Imam Yahya of the Yemen. These were, first, the problem of Yemeni encroachment into the Aden Protectorate, and second, the growing threat of Italian activity in the Red Sea, accompanied by Mussolini's wooing of the Imam. It fell to Clayton to follow up his successful negotiations of the Hadda and Bahra Agreements with Ibn Saud in November 1925 with a visit, the following January, to the Imam at his capital, Sanaa.[18]

The port of Aden, near the south-western tip of the Arabian peninsula, had become, since its occupation by the British in 1839, a vital naval base, coaling station, submarine cable centre and trading entrepôt. It was a link in the imperial chain of bases – Gibraltar, Malta, Cyprus, Suez, and on to Singapore and Hong Kong – from which the Navy could operate.[19] Aden provided the only fortified British port between Malta and Bombay, and helped to ensure Britain's naval command of the Indian Ocean.[20] Britain needed to secure Aden against an Arab attack from the hinterland. Yet the desire to secure the hinterland ran counter to Britain's long-standing reluctance to become involved in Arabian affairs. Consequently, because Britain's visible authority did not extend beyond a ten mile radius of Aden,[21] the tribes of the hinterland and the Hadramaut were subjected to the traditional Indian policy of treaties prohibiting relations with other powers.[22] Individual chiefs were left virtually autonomous and in the areas furthest from Aden there was no effective British influence at all.[23]

The hinterland of Aden (the Aden Protectorate) was ill-defined except for the disputed frontier with the Yemen, and was treated as a condominium between the Colonial Office and the India Office.[24] In one sense, Aden had temporarily lost some of its strategic sensitivity due to the demise of

Ottoman authority in nearby Yemen, and was regarded as something of an imperial outpost.[25] In any case, the pre-1914 objective of trying to police the hinterland in order to protect Aden had been completely abandoned by 1926.[26]

Tension over Asir 1925-1926

Unlike the inhabitants of central Arabia, those of the Yemen were Shiite and mostly mountain people, engaged in sedentary cultivation.[27] The Yemen had ruled Aden during the seventeenth and eighteenth centuries,[28] and it was known as 'the eye of the Yemen'.[29] Between 1903 and 1905 the boundary between the *Vilayet* of the Yemen and the Aden Protectorate had been agreed between the British and Ottoman Governments.[30] This boundary was included as part of the 'violet line' of the Anglo-Turkish Conventions of 1913-14.[31] Upon the collapse of the Ottoman Empire its Arab provinces, previously having no need of frontier delineation, were transformed into succession states without any recognised, let alone agreed, frontiers. The Imam and the British authorities in Aden faced each other for the first time without Ottoman intermediaries.

The Imam Yahya ruled over the Yemen from 1904 until 1949. He emerged from the First World War as an independent ruler and repudiated the Anglo-Ottoman boundary agreement concerning the Yemen and the Aden Protectorate, arguing that it was a document contrived by two foreign powers which had no legal application to the Yemen.[32] By 1918 many of the chiefs in the Aden Protectorate, having suffered from the economic priva-tions of the war, had transferred their allegiance to the Imam.[33] In 1919 Yemeni forces occupied parts of the Aden Protectorate, possibly in order to bargain for the return of Hodeida.[34] British officials in Aden considered that the removal of the Turks rendered the Yemeni-Aden Protectorate boundary redundant, and were prepared to relinquish control of many of the remoter hinterland protectorates to the Imam.[35] To those officials, a con-tinued British position in the Protectorate was pointless, expensive and illogical.[36] Britain had not established even minimal security there in almost a century. The British Government, however, took a contrary position, feeling that to pull out would imply illegal British occupation of the areas in the first place, which could create unfortunate precedents throughout the Empire.[37] It was argued that the Yemen was an Ottoman successor state, and the Imam should recognise the Anglo-Ottoman boundary agreement and Britain's legitimate position in southern Arabia[38] – although this was doubtless a rationalisation to explain a refusal to give up parts of the Empire.

British negotiations aimed at the withdrawal of Yemeni forces proved fruitless, and in 1925 Yemeni positions were bombed.[39] Available British air strength proved inadequate, and Clayton's mission early in 1926 attempted, once more, to secure the evacuation of Yemeni troops through diplomacy.

At the same time, Britain was concerned to counter Italian penetration of the peninsula. Italian interest in the Red Sea extended back to the nine-teenth century when Italy occupied Eritrea, where the Civil Commissioners offered work to Yemenis.[40] In February 1924 Mussolini had proclaimed that the lines of Italian expansion lay towards the east.[41] This expansionist programme began in earnest in 1926 with the Italian drive into Albania, a move which had the tacit support of the British Government.[42] Italian adventures in the Red Sea were, however, another matter. Italy saw herself as a Mussalman power, and showed signs of seeking to establish herself on the Arabian mainland, that is, on both sides of the Red Sea. She was attempting to use the Yemen as a gateway to Arabia, to extend the economic hinterland of Eritrea, and was seeking a potential pincer-grip upon the southern end of the Red Sea comparable to Britain's control of its northern end.[43] There was even speculation that Italy was striving for an empire spanning the southern areas of the Red Sea and the Arabian peninsula. Britain feared that any Italian control of the eastern shore of the Red Sea would threaten Egypt and the Sudan, and endanger the entire Red Sea route.[44] It was natural in these circumstances for Britain to seek to neutralise these threats by means of an Anglo-Yemeni treaty.

For his part, the Imam's foreign policy took on distinctive features. He feared that his independent Yemen might suffer administration or occupa-tion by European powers, as had happened to the Arab lands to the north. Consequently, he adopted a policy of almost absolute isolationism.[45] Yet this policy was compromised by his dynastic aspirations. Like Ibn Saud, the Imam Yahya was motivated by the need to recapture the lands of his ancestors.[46] The Imam dreamt of a Greater Yemen, extending from Asir on the Red Sea to Dhofar on the southern coast of the peninsula.[47] These schemes inevitably brought the Imam into conflict with the *de facto* rulers in the territories claimed, namely the Idrisi, Ibn Saud, and the British Govern-ment.[48] Because of Britain's links with Aden it was natural for the Imam to turn to Italy, the only possible counter-weight in the Red Sea.

A feature of Britain's Arabian policy at this time was still the indis-criminate signing of treaties with Arab rulers. Britain already had a treaty with the Idrisi, and was about to re-negotiate her treaty with Ibn Saud. A similar treaty with the Imam would have meant British treaties with all the principal rulers of south-western Arabia. The Imam, like Husein some years previously, could not agree to Britain's terms. Britain would not recognise his independence unless his forces vacated the Aden hinterland.[49] The Imam, again like other Arab rulers, wondered how Britain could offer him friendship when she was actively supporting his neighbours – in his case, Ibn Saud, the Idrisi, and the chiefs of the Aden Protectorate.

Asir, sandwiched between the newly independent Yemen and the Hejaz, was being squeezed out of existence, particularly as there were no agreed frontiers with its neighbours. While Clayton was in Sanaa, the Idrisi appealed to Britain to honour her wartime pledges.[50] Britain's defensive commitments to him, with the promise of arms which had not been forthcoming, invited the admission: 'Unfortunately the Idrisi's complaint is not without some justification. The danger is that the Idrisi may turn to Italy if we let him down'.[51] Britain had expected to wind up her commitments to the Idrisi at the Paris Peace Conference, but had been distracted by graver matters from doing so.[52] It was hoped that if Clayton's visit to the Imam was successful, leading to a reduction in tension in south-west Arabia, Britain could avoid facing her obligations to the Idrisi.[53] Instead, she had to seek other grounds upon which to avoid intervention on his behalf. Asir was, as it happened, ruled traditionally by two families, the most northerly of which once supposedly paid allegiance to Al Saud.[54] Moreover, the death of the wartime Idrisi and the struggle over the succession was now taken to invalidate the treaty, as was the fresh interpretation that the British guarantee was only intended to cover attack from a European source, not a neighbouring Arab one.[55] This latter argument was admitted to be flimsy. One such European power, Italy, was pouring in arms to the Yemen despite the embargo, so was clearly connected with the threat to Asir.[56] Nonetheless, the Idrisi was informed that Britain would adopt a neutral stance in the event of war within his territory.[57] Expediency demanded that Britain did not jeopardise her relations with the ascendant Ibn Saud and the Imam for the sake of the Idrisi, whose time was clearly up.

Throughout the spring of 1926 reports reached London of accelerating arms supplies arriving from Italy to the Yemen.[58] The Italian Government had been claiming the Farasan Islands since the Paris Peace Conference in 1919, as part of its War compensation in Asia and Africa.[59] The British delegation had rejected Italian claims on the grounds of Britain's strategic requirements and the fact that the islands had already been awarded to the Idrisi.[60] Rather than deliver an ineffectual protest to Rome about the arms supplies, the British Government, taking account of many factors – the desire to meet Ibn Saud's own requests for arms, the absolvement of responsibility for the Idrisi, and the obvious commercial advantages – decided to waive its own embargo.[61] This was done in June 1926; the Imam was excluded owing to his continued encroachment upon the Aden Protectorate. The effect with regard to the Idrisi was no more than cosmetic. He received too little too late to be able to defer his fate,[62] and was, in any case, told he would not receive arms if he intended using them against the Imam, with whom Britain was at peace.[63]

In the meantime Rome was taking full advantage of Clayton's rebuff at the hands of the Imam, and the Imam's blatant playing off of Britain against Italy. In September 1926 the Italian Government concluded a Treaty of Amity and Commerce with the Yemen.[64] The Imam had needed outside support for his dispute with Britain. He seems to have been unwilling to approach the Italians because his first, unsuccessful, overtures were to the Turks.[65] Italy, during the First World War, had calculated that her Red Sea interests were best served by supporting the Idrisi,[66] and her consequent shift in policy in later years did not entirely erase the Imam's suspicions.

Italy was the first European state either to recognise the full and absolute independence of the Yemen, or to enter into treaty relations with an
Arabian ruler since the collapse of the Ottoman Empire. She was inspired by
the need to check British influence in south-west Arabia and extend her
own. The Imam was referred to as 'King of the Yemen' and given valuable
political support to add to his material supplies in a way which did not
compromise his independence.[67] The terms of the Treaty avoided mention
of the territorial limits of the Imam's authority,[68] and also failed to provide
for the establishment of diplomatic relations.

The Italian treaty with the Imam was a setback to the British Government,
which had hoped to keep others out of the Yemen so as not to have to
increase British influence. The continuing isolation of the Imam had been
preferable to a British treaty which would bind him to exclude external
influences.[69] No active encouragement had been given to British concession-
hunting companies, either in the Yemen or Asir, the resources of the region
being considered insufficient to warrant political intervention.[70] No political
gains had been sought either from the Idrisi or the Imam, other than for the
latter to withdraw from the Aden Protectorate. Whatever the outcome of
the Ibn Saud/Idrisi/Imam struggle, Britain was not concerned to intervene,
except in the defence of Aden.[71] Now that Italy had achieved her foothold in
Arabia, it was hoped that Ibn Saud would not be equally amenable to Italian
advances.

The Italo-Yemeni treaty, coupled with the change in Britain's armaments
policy and the fear of further Italian diplomatic success, this time with Ibn
Saud, precipitated a more robust British policy towards Rome. Hitherto,
Britain had tried to restrain Italian activity in the southern reaches of the
Red Sea by pointing to her defensive commitment to the Idrisi.[72] With
military and naval assistance ruled out, both because of unwillingness to
become involved in local disputes and because of the risk of such action
aggravating relations with Italy, explicit warnings were passed to the Italian
Government that further penetration of Arabia or the Farasan Islands
would be considered a threat to Britain's imperial defence.[73] In effect, a Red
Sea 'Monroe Doctrine' had been declared, Britain warning that she would
not tolerate the intrusion of alien naval power on the Arabian shore of the
Red Sea.[74] More accurately Britain was operating a dual Monroe Doctrine:
first, a loose concept which had extended over the whole of Arabia since the
fall of the Turks, and second, a specific doctrine covering the Red Sea aimed
at a specific power in a specific place.

In the last months of 1926 the fate of Asir appeared to hang in the balance,
as Saudi and Yemeni pressure intensified. The British Consul in Jedda felt
that the last thing Ibn Saud wanted, when he was preoccupied with ordering
the affairs of the Hejaz, was a major campaign against the Imam. The 1927
Pilgrimage needed to be successful to refurbish the coffers of the Hejaz after
the war, in which case Ibn Saud needed to demonstrate to the Moslem world
his good relations with all its rulers, including the Shiite Imam.[75]

The British Government speculated about the fate of Asir. Ibn Saud, like the Idrisi, was a British ally. He was, moreover, a strong ally, better able to protect the Farasan Islands from the Imam than could the moribund Idrisi.[76] Whether Asir remained an independent principality or not would have been unimportant were it not for the strategically sensitive Farasan Islands.[77] Italian arming of the Imam and possible encouragement of Yemeni aggression towards Asir might result in Italian bases on the islands.[78] It was, therefore, cause for some British satisfaction and Italian suspicion when, in September 1926, the Idrisi, still clinging to hopes of British assistance, granted an oil concession for the Farasan Islands to the Shell Group.[79]

The British Government was further encouraged in January 1927 when news was released of the Treaty of Mecca, signed three months previously by the Idrisi and Ibn Saud.[80] The Idrisi, fearful of the threat posed by the Italo-Yemeni treaty, agreed that Asir become a Saudi protectorate. He was to retain his own position and internal powers, but hand over control of his external relations, defence and finance (including economic concessions) to Ibn Saud.[81] The Saudi-Idrisi pact had the effect of making the territories under Ibn Saud and the Imam coterminous, and of making the Zeidi sect of Shiite Islam march with the strict Wahhabi Sunni puritanism. The pact also forestalled any Italian hopes of winning access to the Farasan Islands through a quick Yemeni invasion and, for practical purposes, obscured Britain's obligations to the Idrisi.[82]

The Treaty of Mecca temporarily stabilised the situation in south-west Arabia.[83] The state of Anglo-Italian relations, by contrast, took another turn for the worse. The treaty was viewed with some satisfaction from Britain, particularly by the Admiralty, because the Farasan Islands had become more secure against Italian penetration.[84] For the Italian Government, however, the Treaty of Mecca hindered its aspirations in the Red Sea, and was viewed as a success for Britain, even though she had no part to play in it.[85]

The Rome Conversations

Italian sensitivity to the poverty of Eritrea, together with Britain's desire to reduce political friction in the Red Sea led, briefly, to consideration of Britain sharing the Farasan oil concession with Italy.[86] Britain did not fear genuine Italian economic and commercial competition in the Red Sea. The deteriorating political situation, however, and the need for clarification of the two countries' respective positions led, in January 1927, to the despatch to Rome of Sir Gilbert Clayton.

News of the Treaty of Mecca was received as the Rome conversations got under way. Italy attempted to persuade Britain not to recognise the treaty as it implied British support for Ibn Saud against the Imam.[87] Italy had no intention of recognising the treaty, out of deference to the Imam.[88] Nor had she yet recognised Ibn Saud as King of the Hejaz. The Foreign Office was reluctant to withhold recognition of a treaty between two rulers friendly to Britain in order to promote the claims of a third, hostile ruler.[89] Nor did the Italian Government demonstrate on what grounds – ethnographical, geographical, historical or religious – the Imam could lay claim to the Farasan Islands.[90]

The overriding need to reach an understanding with Italy led Britain to temporise. She hedged over recognition of the Saudi-Idrisi treaty on the grounds of her disinterest in internal Arabian affairs.[91] Ibn Saud was privately reassured by a reminder that British non-intervention and neutrality with regard to Husein had worked to Saudi advantage.[92]

The Rome Agreement was signed early in March 1927, despite objections from the Admiralty, which wanted to guard against conceding any Italian rights on Kamaran.[93] The main provisions of the Agreement allowed for mutual recognition of the sensitivity of the Red Sea, and that it was against the interests of both signatories for any European power to establish itself on the Arabian shore. Neither government was to intervene in any dispute involving Ibn Saud, the Idrisi or the Imam. Britain and Italy agreed, in future, to maintain close contact on all questions affecting the Red Sea and southern Arabia. Although the Agreement may have diminished the risk of direct European involvement in a Saudi-Yemeni dispute, it also diminished Britain's potential usefulness to the Imam:[94] Britain could not act freely without bringing in Italy.

Despite the Agreement, the Italian Government continued to act in mischievous fashion. Reports from Aden and Jedda suggested active Italian propaganda in Asir.[95] Italy attempted to persuade the Idrisi to abrogate his treaty with Ibn Saud, and enter into a fresh pact with the Imam to safeguard his interests.[96] He was also offered financial incentives to cancel the Shell concession on the Farasan Islands.[97] The British Government was unable to intervene on the company's behalf without both disregarding the Rome Agreement and implicitly recognising the Treaty of Mecca.[98] In the event, the Red Sea Petroleum Company (of the Shell Group) stayed to work the Farasan concession until 1929, when lack of success caused the abandonment of the enterprise.[99]

A Saudi-Yemeni war had been averted for the time being. Possibly the Imam could not afford to be on bad terms with Ibn Saud and the British simultaneously. Neither ruler was prepared to risk war for such small stakes as fragments of Asir.[100] By the summer of 1927 the southern coastal area of Asir (Asir Tihama), opposite the Farasan Islands, was effectively under a Saudi-appointed governor.[101]

Britain, still trying to counter the possible effects of the Italo-Yemeni treaty, switched responsibility for the defence of Aden, in 1928, to the RAF. A single bomber squadron replaced a battalion of troops. The impact of the aeroplane on the hitherto impenetrable Yemeni mountains was spectacular. The ensuing bombing campaign, directed at occupied districts and Yemeni towns, was partially successful in evacuating Yemenis from the Aden Pro-tectorate,[102] although the Imam countered by signing a Treaty of Commerce and Friendship with the Soviet Union.[103] By this time the British Government was engaging in some critical self-analysis. It was clearly embarrassing for Britain to be in a state of semi-belligerency with one of Arabia's major powers, particularly over territory whose complete retrieval was doubtful.[104] The way had been paved for Italy and the Soviet Union to break Britain's monopoly on Arabia's foreign relations.

Lord Lloyd, from Cairo, reflecting Egypt's particular interest in the Red Sea, questioned British policy, pointing out the consequences of the Arabs seeing a second-rate power like Italy undermining British prestige. Indeed, during 1927 Ibn Saud had anxiously enquired about Britain's role in the event of an increased Italian presence in the Red Sea.[105] Lloyd appreciated that British policy towards Italy and the Red Sea rulers was governed by wider considerations than those imposed by the Arabian horizon, and that those considerations had served to prevent a determined British response against Italian intrigue.[106] Despite this, Lloyd suggested that the future of Anglo-Italian relations, and Britain's position in Arabia, was best served by firm demands that Italy cease encouraging the Imam. Not only was he usurping parts of the Aden Protectorate, but he was also, thanks to Italian support and arms, contemplating aggression against Ibn Saud, the principal Arab ruler to whom Britain had entrusted Arabian peace and stability.[107] According to Lloyd, Britain's policy towards Italy bore the risk of threatening the stability of the Saudi regime, with all that that entailed.

The Foreign Office did not disagree with Lloyd's assessment. Various departments were struggling to co-ordinate British policy in south-west Arabia. The Colonial Office, the India Office, the Air Ministry from 1928, and the Resident were all responsible for the affairs of Aden. The Foreign Office was responsible for handling relations with Italy, and the Admiralty was preoccupied with the whole strategic question of the Red Sea. Sir William Tyrrell complained: 'We seem to be drifting in a dangerously haphazard manner and losing such control as we ever had over developments in the Red Sea area'.[108]

By the time British attention returned once more to the inter-Arab affairs of south-west Arabia, in 1930, the problem of inefficient inter-departmental consultation had been somewhat remedied. The recently concluded *Ikhwan* rebellion to the north had been partly responsible for the creation of the Middle East (Official) Sub-Committee, which could be convened as and when necessary to assist inter-departmental decision-making. A Foreign Office memorandum in August of that year proposed a certain revision of Britain's post-1927 Red Sea policy. If possible, Britain's interests would be best served, not by a successful Saudi assault on the Imam, but by the continuance of the existing balance-of-power between the two rulers.[109] This modified interpretation owed something to the views of the newly-arrived British Minister in Jedda, Sir Andrew Ryan, and the spirit engendered by the Rome Agreement. It was also a tacit reflection of Ibn Saud's still greater stature by 1930. Saudi control of the Yemen would simply substitute one expansionist-orientated regime on the frontier of the Aden Protectorate with another. An Arabian balance-of-power was seen as the best protection for British interests.

This shift of policy had several corollaries. Rather than regard Britain's wartime undertakings about the Farasan Islands to the Idrisi as defunct, it was preferred to keep them in abeyance, in case Ibn Saud should lose control of Asir. In that eventuality Britain might want to invoke the 1917 treaty in order to prevent the Idrisi attempting to cede his seaboard or the Farasan Islands to the Italians.[110] Britain was prepared to remain disinterested only for as long as Ibn Saud retained ultimate sovereignty over Asir. On the other hand, Britain's preference for a balance-of-power in south-west Arabia constituted yet another departure from her traditional dissociation from internal Arabian politics.[111]

No sooner had the Foreign Office considered these matters than Ibn Saud, in November 1930, announced the annexation of Asir,[112] which henceforth became a Saudi dominion alongside the Hejaz, Nejd and Hasa. The Idrisi was permitted to remain only as nominal head of the province. A Saudi governor would administer Asir and give effect to the Wahhabi-based *Sharia* law.[113] Ryan attributed Ibn Saud's motives to be, first, the attraction of Asir's agricultural fecundity compared with the general barrenness of his other dominions, and second, a real or imagined religious sympathy with the tribes of Asir, who were Sunni, and opposed to the Imam's Zeidi sect of Shiism.[114]

1930 had been a significant year in the internal development of the Saudi state, commencing with the suppression of the *Ikhwan* rebellion in January. Ibn Saud had followed that triumph by accelerating his programme of wireless communication to all corners of his Kingdom. The treasuries of the Hejaz and Nejd were also merged. The annexation of Asir is, perhaps, best seen in the context of a general drawing together of Ibn Saud's dominions. It provided the final territorial acquisition of the modern Saudi state.

News of Asir's annexation was well received in London. Britain had benefited by having her treaty with the Idrisi formally lapse owing to his disappearance as an international factor.[115] On the other hand the continued existence of Asir as a buffer between the Hejaz and the Yemen could have retained advantages by reducing tension in the area. Britain did not want Ibn Saud to invade the Yemen, completing the circular network of contacts between British interests and Saudi territory.[116] In contrast, Asir's annexation was received as another setback to Italian ambitions.[117] Rome sought to recoup her losses by diplomatic means and in February 1932 signed a Treaty of Friendship with Hejaz-Nejd.[118] Asir, which formed Italy's only real interest in Ibn Saud's affairs, was not mentioned. Ibn Saud, failing to win satisfactory British assurances against the Italians, would, for the rest of the 1930s, attempt to secure his interests by playing Britain off against them.

'Hejaz-Nejd' becomes 'Saudi Arabia'

Quite unexpectedly, in September 1932, Ibn Saud announced that he was changing the name of his dominions. As from the autumnal equinox, 22 September, the Kingdom of the Hejaz, and of Nejd and its Dependencies became the Kingdom of Saudi Arabia. George Rendel, head of the Foreign Office's Eastern Department, felt that the new name was something for which he personally could take some credit.[119] Sheikh Hafiz Wahba had informed Rendel that Ibn Saud wished to call the new state after his own name, and suggested 'Saudiyah'. Rendel advised that the outside world would fail to appreciate the significance of that title, and came up with 'Saudi Arabia', a suggestion which was adopted.[120]

The Mecca press announced that the change of name was a response to an Arabia-wide appeal that Hejazis and Nejdis were brothers. 'Saudi Arabia', it was explained, had been ordained by Allah as the centre of an Arab union.[121] A more cogent explanation for the timing of the change of name, if not for the change itself, was to distract attention from events in Iraq. Baghdad was preparing for a conference of pan-Arab states to be held in the winter.[122] In October Iraq was due to take her place in the League of Nations as an independent state. Ibn Saud's initiative was a timely reassertion of Saudi prominence.

As to the broader justification for the change, Ibn Saud had, for some months, been emphasising the unity of his dominions.[123] The Foreign Office doubted the popularity of the change among Hejazis, who would not have liked the loss of their identity, not to mention their resources, to the lesser order Nejdis and an alien monarchy.[124] In 1926 Ibn Saud had pledged his intention of keeping the Hejaz separate under its own constitution. He had represented himself as conquering the Hejaz only in order to purge it of its unworthy rulers, and proclaimed his intention to hold it in trust for the benefit of Hejazis and the Moslem world as a whole. The change in name consummated the reversal of that declaration. It can, moreover, be seen as a further advance in the Saudi interpretation of 'nation-state', a concept brought to Arabia by western-type frontiers, and exploited by Ibn Saud in the concluding stages of the *Ikhwan* rebellion.

The Jedda Legation proposed four basic reasons behind the change – dynastic, financial, imperial and constitutional.[125] The dynastic reason was to consolidate the Hejaz as a Saudi possession, and for this to act as an ultimate discouragement of Hashemite revanchism – the Hashemite claim to the Hejaz was made more difficult by its disappearance as a distinct state. The change also forestalled any separatist moves by Hejazis themselves.[126] The resources of the Hejaz were absorbed into Nejd to facilitate the management of a single Saudi budget. Asir was assimilated more closely under Saudi rule, and constitutional confusion surrounding the dual King-dom of Hejaz-Nejd was cleared away.[127] The new name doubtless aimed at emphasising the essentially Arab character of the state and its inhabitants, as well as commemorating Ibn Saud's part in creating a unified state under his authority. The memory of the *Ikhwan* rebellion would have provided yet another reason for Ibn Saud taking measures to centralise his domains. In 1933 he took a further step in formalising the structure of his Kingdom by proclaiming his eldest son Saud as heir to the throne of Saudi Arabia.[128]

Anglo-Italian Relations Since World War One

It is necessary at this stage to say something more about the nature of Anglo-Italian relations in the 1920s and early '30s. The Mediterranean was vital to British imperial strategy, both for communications with the Empire and for influencing events in Europe. Consequently, good Anglo-Italian relations were vital to imperial defence. Those relations in the inter-war years were largely shaped by the First World War and, in particular, by the outcome of the Paris Peace Conference which succeeded it. The Italian Government and people suffered from an acute sense of grievance.[129] Italy had achieved national unity in the nineteenth century and had hoped to join in the imperial games of the other European powers. Her heritage and level of civilisation were felt to be no less worthy of export than those of her European neighbours,[130] and she considered she had a strong case for overseas possessions on account of her poverty of natural resources and expanding population.[131]

Prior to the First World War Italian relations with Britain had traditionally been cordial. The intervention of the British fleet had assisted Garibaldi's expedition which eventually led to the union of Italy in 1870.[132] Besides, Italy's inability to adequately defend her long coastline necessitated good relations with the dominant Mediterranean naval power.[133]

The Paris Peace Conference ignored Italy's claims to a slice of the imperial cake. It had been considered undesirable to award any of the ex-German colonies to Italy, fearing that she had not the means to administer them effectively. Nor was she offered a mandate that she desired, least of all Palestine.[134] Twentieth century Italy has always seemed a matter of some ambivalence. She seemed to be at one and the same time too weak to be considered as one of the great powers, yet too strong to be put among the second rank states. It was the French who were particularly hostile to the granting of overseas territories to Italy, but it was Britain who was held by Rome to be mainly responsible for allied policy.[135] Italy resented Britain's attitude that her belated attempts to acquire overseas possessions were ill-judged and reprehensible.[136] She was not going to be accommodating to the overseas interests of her European rivals so long as her resentment persisted. With hindsight, Britain had some sympathy for Italian grievances:

> It is probably the greatest condemnation of our [British] policy towards Italy after the First World War that it could have eventually

become possible for Mussolini to obtain the support of even a proportion of the Italian people for his policy of alliance with Germany
and of aggressive adventure.[137]

This 'alliance' with Germany still lay in the future. The actual coming to
power of Mussolini, in 1922, brought, at least initially, a coming together of
Anglo-Italian relations.[138] The Duce knew that Britain was virtually Italy's
only disinterested friend of any consequence, and that only through Anglo-
Italian co-operation could he best secure added weight for his country in the
councils of Europe.[139] This is not to say that Mussolini was an Anglophile:
British imperialism was something resented, envied, and, if possible, to be
emulated.[140]

Britain's own control of the Mediterranean was being threatened, first by
the submarine, then by the bomber. Not unaware of this, Britain moved,
belatedly, to settle the question of colonial compensation with Italy. In July
1924 Britain ceded to Italy the region of Trans-Jubaland adjoining Italian
Somaliland, and within two years sponsored a treaty between Italy and
Egypt that finally delimited the Libyan-Egyptian frontier.[141] Britain's desire
to appease Mussolini in the mid-1920s was also apparent in other ways,
such as by Austen Chamberlain's acquiescence in the Italian occupation
of Albania, and by an agreement reached in December 1924 which pro-
visionally recognised an Italian sphere of influence in eastern Abyssinia.[142]

Despite Mussolini's proclamation in 1924 that the lines of Italian expansion lay towards the east, on many issues Anglo-Italian relations proceeded
amicably, with Tory and Labour Governments alike.[143] In the mid-1920s,
for example, the Soviet-Turkish Treaty of Alliance which followed the
League's granting of Mosul to Iraq, led to a brief intensification of relations
between London and Rome.[144] Italy's possession of Rhodes and the Dode-
canese in the eastern Mediterranean made her an obvious British partner in
the region against any Turkish or Soviet southward advance.[145] On the
disarmament issue, too, Italy was found to be, at first, a co-operative
partner.[146] On European questions generally, Anglo-Italian relations until
the early '30s were amicable enough, a trend assisted by most of the Italian
diplomats still being of the old-school aristocratic type, few of whom were
committed to the philosophy of fascism.[147]

Friction did exist over the League of Nations, of which Italy had a
profound mistrust. Fascism as a doctrine was not impressed by the principle
of self-determination for peoples and their theoretical equality.[148] The very
idea of an international forum of world states savoured of the parliamentary
system of government overthrown by Mussolini.

From 1930 revisionism increasingly began to colour Italian foreign
policy, and Mussolini embarked upon the path that would eventually lead
to the Axis pact. The collapse of the London Naval Conference and the
Geneva Conference on Disarmament precipitated the dismissal of Grandi,
the Italian Foreign Minister, in July 1932 and heralded a further Italian

lurch towards Germany.[149] Grandi became Italian Ambassador in London. Anglo-Italian disagreements in this period centred largely on the Arab world and Africa, with the southern end of the Red Sea being the most contentious area of all.[150] But there was friction over Malta, the Somaliland and Libyan-Egypt frontiers, and the Palestine and Iraq mandates.[151] Italy endeavoured to emphasise the international character of the mandates and prevent any tendency by Britain to treat them as colonies, or otherwise restrict Italian commercial enterprise.[152] Generally, Mussolini worked on a policy of improvisation in Europe, while in north Africa and the Arab world he proclaimed himself as the protector of Islam.[153]

A combination of all these grievances and Eritrea's dependence on external resources led to increased Italian economic and political activity in the Red Sea. The Italian Government in Rome may have felt ill-inclined, out of expediency, to provoke a strain in Anglo-Italian relations, but the Italian Governor and authorities in Eritrea took a much stronger line in seeking advantages for the colony. Yemen was the first Arab territory to receive Italian attention, both because it lay opposite Eritrea, and because the Imam was the only Arabian ruler entirely free from British or other foreign influence.[154] Consequently, Italy's chief Arabian obstacle was Ibn Saud, who wanted no outside support for his southern rival.

Furthermore, British relations with Ibn Saud were often embarrassed by Italy's intemperate advocacy of the Imam's cause and Ibn Saud's repeated requests for British reassurance. The 1927 Rome Agreement temporarily eased Anglo-Italian relations in the Red Sea, although the Italian Government continued to urge modification of the Agreement on the grounds that Ibn Saud's absorption of Asir in 1930 had altered the whole position.[155] This, the British Government resolutely refused to contemplate. It regarded Asir as an integral *de facto* and *de jure* part of Saudi Arabia, despite continuing to defer formal recognition of the fact.[156] Besides, the mutual undertakings to refrain from interference in the internal affairs of Arabia restrained the advance of Italian influence.

The Approach to War

The ignition of the 1934 Saudi-Yemeni war was the Saudi absorption of Asir four years previously. Throughout the late 1920s evidence had been accumulating of Hashemite-Yemeni intrigue aimed at curtailing the rule of their common enemy, Ibn Saud. In 1932 a plot involving simultaneous attacks on the Hejaz from the south, and from the north, which involved Ibn Rifada's revolt described in the previous chapter, was unsuccessful, partly due to poor co-ordination.[157] Ibn Rifada's rising was put down in May. The Idrisi, with Yemeni support, rebelled against the Saudi Governor in October.[158] The uprising was put down early in 1933, but not before an Italian warship had angered Ibn Saud by patrolling the Farasan Islands and the Asir coast.[159] The Idrisi fled into the Yemen, and by the summer of 1933

Yemeni troops had entered the inland frontier town of Najran and other parts of Asir, and were demanding the return of all the Idrisi's dominions.[160]

Ibn Saud turned to Britain for arms.[161] This request was declined, partly because payment was still outstanding on arms supplied during the *Ikhwan* rebellion, but mainly to try and dissuade him from any hostile enterprise.[162] Britain still had no intention of becoming involved in, or precipitating, an inter-Arabian conflict.[163] The only conceivable British gain from hostilities in south-west Arabia was the possibility of expelling the remaining Yemenis from the Aden Protectorate, and in securing the release of some Aden hostages seized by the Imam in 1928.[164] The Cabinet had already issued ultimatums on these questions in 1928 and 1931. Rendel considered whether a further ultimatum, followed by aerial bombing, might not only secure these objectives but, at the same time, work to Ibn Saud's advantage by providing an unwelcome distraction to the Imam.[165] The Foreign Office found no support from the Colonial Office, India Office or Air Ministry for encouraging fresh hostilities with the Imam. Such adventures might incur British casualties, largely for the purpose of supporting Ibn Saud's regime in Asir.[166] The Foreign Office's consideration of tactical aerial activity on Ibn Saud's behalf is, however, yet another indication of its commitment to his rule.

The last months of 1933 passed with Saudi and Yemeni envoys trying to reach an internal settlement, accompanied by intermittent hostilities. The British Government was convinced that Rome was largely responsible for the Imam's warlike stance. Rendel suggested: 'It is difficult to believe that the Imam who is old and ill and impoverished would attack Saudi Arabia' but for continued arms sales to him.[167] Similarly, the Foreign Office doubted Ibn Saud's willingness to undergo the financial and political strain of another war.[168] If Ibn Saud was bent on force, Britain had no intention of using counter-force to restrain him. Nor was she prepared to 'fritter away' whatever influence she possessed by ineffectual offers of advice.[169]

The Italian outlook, despite the Italo-Saudi treaty of February 1932, was that Ibn Saud's aggression in annexing Asir constituted the root of the problem.[170] Perhaps his tribes, who had not enjoyed any serious fighting since the suppression of the *Ikhwan* rebellion, were straining at the leash. Perhaps, too, Ibn Saud was well aware that the Yemen, unlike Iraq, was not a British ally, and therefore unlikely to invite British interference. Both Britain and Italy preferred buffers of one kind or another in south-west Arabia. Italy still wanted that buffer to be Asir to keep open the possibility of an Italian foothold on the Farasan Islands.[171] Britain had accepted Asir's incorporation into Saudi Arabia and had come to view the existence of the Yemen itself as a useful buffer to check further Saudi expansion towards the Aden Protectorate.

At the turn of 1933-34 the Italian Government began to press Britain to accept a further conference.[172] It was clear that Italy regarded the future status of Asir as the centrepiece of any negotiations. The Italian thesis seemed to be that it was desirable, quite regardless of the *de facto* position, for Asir to become a buffer state.[173] Britain began to find her earlier declarations on Asir rebounding against her. By having agreed to Italy's request for withholding recognition, as well as specifically mentioning three Arab rulers (Ibn Saud, the Imam, and the Idrisi) in the Rome Agreement, the Italian Government regarded Britain as committed to the maintenance of Asir as a distinct political entity. Rome had to be reminded that this was not the British position at all, merely deference to Italian sensibilities. Britain regarded Asir as part of Saudi Arabia, and the exact location of the Saudi-Yemeni frontier was an internal matter to be settled by Ibn Saud and the Imam.[174]

Furthermore, Italy hoped that fresh negotiations would modify the 1927 Rome Agreement to reflect the circumstances of 1934. Britain was not enthusiastic for a conference for several reasons: Asir was not seen as an issue; Britain was content with the terms of the Rome Agreement as they stood; and she was also fearful that the holding of a conference would be misunderstood in south-west Arabia as a sign of Anglo-Italian intervention.[175] Britain took the view that: 'Satisfaction is not an Italian habit of mind and, in Fascism, is almost synonymous with stagnation'.[176] Giving concessions to Rome was felt more likely to whet Italy's appetite than extinguish it.

Britain, meanwhile, was giving further evidence of her piecemeal and pragmatic approach to policy in Arabia by signing, in February 1934, a Treaty of Friendship and Mutual Co-operation with the Yemen.[177] Negotiations for such a treaty had been proceeding, intermittently, since 1919. During the intervening years Italy, the Soviet Union and, most recently, the Netherlands had successfully concluded treaties with the Imam. The latest rounds of talks had commenced in October 1931, with Britain insisting upon the final evacuation of the Aden Protectorate and the release of the hostages held by the Imam.[178] In return for his signature Britain lifted the embargo on arms to the Yemen.[179]

This treaty may have helped precipitate the war that followed. In previous years Ibn Saud and the Imam had faced potential conflicts on two fronts. Apart from their own mutual antagonism, Ibn Saud was preoccupied with the mandates, and the Imam had his grievances over the Aden Protectorate. Both these latter sources of distraction had dimmed by 1934, leaving both rulers free to concentrate on each other. This, too, was doubtless in the mind of the Imam. He could only realistically take on Ibn Saud by placating Britain and putting his claims to the Aden Protectorate in cold storage.[180]

The treaty acknowledged the complete and absolute independence of the Imam (styled King) Yahya in all affairs of whatever kind, but made no reference to Asir, nor to British aid in the event of a threat to the Yemen, nor to the continuing disagreement over the Yemeni-Aden Protectorate frontier.[181] As the treaty did not pave the way for diplomatic relations to be established with the Yemen, all local information continued to reach Britain via Jedda and Aden. Britain, although aware of the implications of undertaking a friendly gesture towards the Imam at a time of particular tension in south-west Arabia, tried to reassure Ibn Saud. The previous November he had been informed of the likelihood of an imminent Anglo-Yemeni treaty and that, far from implying any weakening of Britain's ties with Saudi Arabia, formal British links with the Imam would enable Britain to exercise a moderating influence in the area.[182] In any event, Britain, like Italy, now had a treaty with both Saudi Arabia and the Yemen.

By the spring of 1934, the major conflict that had threatened to break out for a decade became inevitable. In February Saudi-Yemeni negotiations took place in Abha, the Asir capital, the supposedly favourable outcome of which prompted *The Times* to declare 'Arabia still fortunate'. Prudent diplomacy, thought *The Times*, had averted war.[183] In March, however, the Emir Faisal, the Saudi Foreign Minister, informed Ryan that all attempts at negotiations had failed.[184] Ibn Saud had made certain demands of the Imam, including: i) that Saudi rights be recognised in Najran, and that the area be partitioned, ii) the mountainous area recently encroached upon by Yemenis was to be evacuated, and iii) the Idrisi was to be returned to Saudi custody.[185] A satisfactory reply to these demands had not been forthcoming. In 1934 the Pilgrimage was held in March. Yemeni forces were the first to mobilise. Once most of the overseas pilgrims had safely arrived, Saudi forces launched a counter-attack, on 20 March.[186]

The Saudi-Yemeni War: March-May 1934

Ryan proposed that an appeal be made to Ibn Saud, who had adhered to the Kellogg Pact for the renunciation of war in 1932, to explore the possibility of a settlement by arbitration or mediation. This would enable the two rulers to extricate themselves from war without loss of face. The Kellogg Pact, however, had no enforcement mechanism. Nor was the Imam a party to it.[187]

As Britain could not intervene without Italy doing likewise, Ryan suggested utilising the United States for the purposes of mediation.[188] Only a year previously American oil interests had won a concession in Saudi Arabia.[189] This proposal was similarly rejected by the Foreign Office for both strategic and diplomatic reasons. Hearing of an approach to the US Government, Ibn Saud might hesitate, allowing the Imam to take advantage.[190] Besides, no direct American interest was threatened by the conflict. Washington would have interpreted a British request for a diplomatic initiative within an acknowledged British sphere of influence with considerable suspicion.[191] In a futile attempt at mediation Colonel Reilly, Chief Commissioner in Aden, undertook a mission to Sanaa. The Colonial Office considered that further personal approaches from Aden would more likely injure British relations with the Imam than improve his relations with Ibn Saud.[192] The moment for successful British intervention, if one ever existed, had passed, and the British Government duly allowed matters to take their own course.

Only on the coast (the Asir Tihama), where the Emir Faisal was directing Saudi operations,[193] could an accurate picture be gathered of the fighting. There it was apparent that Yemeni forces were being routed. Rumours reached Britain of further anti-Saudi agitation by the Hashemite rulers. They were, apparently, organising a fund to contribute to the Imam's cause.[194]

As Ibn Saud's armies, no longer composed of *Ikhwan* units, swept south-wards, Britain began to fear for the fate of some three hundred British Indians resident in the port of Hodeida, who were seen to be at risk either from Wahhabi blood lust or local rioting.[195] The Foreign Office, Colonial Office and the Admiralty agreed that a sloop be sent to the port – reluctantly, because the British Government did not wish to be seen imitating the Italians.[196] *HMS Penzance*, having already patrolled the ports of Loheia and Midi, reached Hodeida on 1 May, four days ahead of the Saudi forces. Her Captain reported a breakdown of law and order in the port, and, despite British reluctance to antagonise Ibn Saud, the RAF from Aden made a demonstration flight over the town.[197]

Various factors combined to make Ibn Saud question Britain's attitude to him.[198] He interpreted the Anglo-Yemeni treaty as implying British opposition to a Saudi assault on the Yemen. The British Government, in spite of its earlier assurances, had declined to offer him any advice prior to the outbreak of hostilities, and, since then, it had sent a mission to Sanaa and deployed warships along the Asir coast, insulting his ability to manage affairs in the captured ports.[199] It is not clear whether Ibn Saud knew of the removal of the embargo on British arms to the Imam, who received a con-signment of 35 armoured lorries after the Saudi occupation of Hodeida.[200] Moreover, Ibn Saud had just been informed that, on the other side of his Kingdom, Britain was attempting to hold him within an old Turkish frontier with which he was unfamiliar and which was known as the 'blue line'.[201]

British policy, unlike that towards the *Ikhwan* rebellion, was one of com-plete neutrality, although no formal declaration to that effect was made.[202] It was preferred not to give the conflict an unwarranted importance in the eyes of the world, or in Parliament, where awkward Questions would have been asked.[203] Britain had not given any proclamation of neutrality concerning an international conflict since she had joined the League of Nations.[204] All interested parties – Saudi Arabia, the Yemen, and Italy – knew that Britain was pledged to non-intervention and that she enjoyed treaty relations with both belligerents.[205] Furthermore, the British Government had taken no steps to prevent private manufacturers from exporting arms to either side.[206]

To British concern, the impending defeat of the Imam, in the first days of May, brought reports of an Italian warship, the *Ostia*, embarking Italian native troops from Massawa in Eritrea ready to sail to Hodeida.[207] The ship was small and would, therefore, have had to land troops on the Arabian mainland.[208] Yemeni requests for mediation had, apparently, gone out to fellow Arab countries, as well as the Soviet Union.[209] All were rejected by Saudi Arabia.[210]

It became apparent that the different interpretations put upon the Rome Agreement were threatening a serious rift in Anglo-Italian relations. Drummond, from Rome, informed the Foreign Office that Italy regarded Britain as not adequately observing the spirit of the Agreement, which demanded some form of diplomatic initiative on the part of the signatories to try and halt the fighting.[211] He warned that, without close Anglo-Italian co-operation in the present conflict, future difficulties which might arise with Italy in the Red Sea or Europe might be more difficult to handle.[212]

Nonetheless, Britain held to her preferred interpretation of the Rome Agreement. The Italian Government was informed that Britain was not committed by it to prevent the defeat of one Arabian ruler by another.[213] Nor did that document intend to seek to maintain the then existing balance-of-power in Arabia.[214] This interpretation was upheld mindful of the risk that, by refusing to mediate with Italy, she might be spurred to act independently, thereby achieving a stronger footing in Arabia.

By the second week in May Britain, Italy and even France had warships at Hodeida.[215] This response seems to have been prompted, on the part of Britain, by the desire to protect the interests of nationals and counter any Italian initiatives, rather than attempt to affect the course of the war in one direction or another. In response to further Saudi fears of Italian intervention, Ryan warned that the deeper Saudi forces penetrated into the Yemen, the greater the danger that Italy would intervene.[216] It was not known how much, if anything, Ibn Saud knew about the Rome Agreement. Ryan's suggestion that he be supplied with a copy was turned down, rather than put Ibn Saud in a position to appeal to Britain on the grounds of Italian violation of the Agreement.[217] There were already two competing interpretations: there was no need to invite a third.

The Italian Government justified its alarm on the grounds that Saudi armies were still advancing despite the Imam's acceptance of peace terms. There were Italian doctors and commercial interests in the Yemen which had to be protected.[218] The Saudi advance, according to Italy, might upset the political equilibrium in the Red Sea, which was a totally separate matter from the Rome Agreement.[219] To the British Government, Italian actions were more straightforward: Italy had backed the wrong horse and was now trying to retrieve her position.[220] On balance, the Foreign Office doubted whether Italy would severely provoke Britain by a serious attempt at intervention.[221]

Aftermath of the War: The Treaty of Taif

On 12 May Ibn Saud announced a ceasefire on all fronts.[222] The war had lasted seven weeks. Although there was no longer any need for foreign warships to be stationed at Hodeida and off the Yemeni coast, Britain was reluctant to pull her ships away before the Italians because, on grounds of prestige, it was considered bad for the British flag to be outnumbered or outgunned by Italian vessels.[223] By the end of June Ibn Saud and the Imam had signed and ratified a Treaty of Islamic Friendship and Brotherhood: the Treaty of Taif. The Imam agreed to Ibn Saud's demands for the release of Saudi hostages, the settlement of disputed regions, and the surrender of the Idrisi and his entourage.[224]

The moderate terms imposed by Ibn Saud created a favourable impression not only with the British Government but throughout the Arab world.[225] Apart from Saudi Arabia being given a secure title to Najran, which Ibn Saud had earlier demanded be partitioned, it appeared that he had kept to his pre-war demands.[226] Hodeida was evacuated, whereupon Italian warships withdrew, and Saudi forces also retired from the rest of occupied Yemeni territory. The wider Arab world hailed the treaty as one of the greatest strides ever taken towards Arab unity.[227] This was apparent not so much in its provisions, as in its affirmations of Islamic and Arab Brotherhood, and the guiding principle that the two warring states had formed one nation.[228] In the treaty Ibn Saud referred to the Imam as 'King' of the Yemen, the first time he had been referred to as such by Saudi Arabia.[229] In view of Ibn Saud's jealously regarded kingship in the Arab world, this was a conciliatory move of some import. Provisions were also made for fixing the Saudi-Yemeni frontier.

Dissenting voices from the Gulf contradicted the general British and Arab approval heaped upon Ibn Saud's statesmanship and moderation. Fowle, the Political Resident, considered that, despite Saudi Arabia's ostensible victory in the war, Ibn Saud's standing had probably fallen in the eyes of Gulf Arabs, as well as with his own tribes.[230] Fowle expressed the average Arab's idea of statesmanship as: 'the good old rule, the ancient plan, that he shall take who has the power, and he shall hold who can'.[231] It had been anticipated that Ibn Saud would follow up his successes by the capture of Sanaa itself, exacting a vast indemnity from the Imam and, perhaps, even installing the Emir Faisal as Viceroy of the Yemen.[232] Instead, none of these expectations had materialised.

There were various reasons put forward to account for Ibn Saud's moderation. Fowle's view, given after consultation with the Sheikh of Kuwait, was that Ibn Saud would never have given such generous terms to the Imam had he been strong enough to impose tougher ones.[233] Ibn Saud had paused after taking Hodeida, probably fearing his armies being surrounded. Consequently, British officials in the Gulf regarded the outcome as a moral victory for the Imam, who had succeeded in winning a Saudi withdrawal without surrendering any Yemeni territory or paying an indemnity.[234]

The general interpretation from London was more generous to Ibn Saud. Rendel considered the view from the Gulf to be vitiated by an intense anti-Saudi prejudice.[235] Even before the war the reports from Dickson (the Political Agent in Kuwait) and Fowle had carried marked anti-Saudi bias and the expectation that Saudi Arabia was bound to be heavily defeated.[236]

The Gulf's constant fear of Saudi encroachment accounted for much of this attitude. A truer picture was felt to be that Ibn Saud was reluctant to risk stability in the rest of his dominions by attempting to annex the Yemen.[237] Any dissatisfaction expressed by Saudi tribes was more likely to be accounted for by their enjoying little plunder from their first major campaign for some years.[238]

The third perspective, proffered by Ryan from Jedda when he came to write his annual report for 1934, was more speculative. He admitted that Ibn Saud had gone against many of his entourage, who had expected him to conquer all of the Yemen and/or exact a massive war indemnity.[239] Ryan adduced several factors to account for Ibn Saud's pull-back. It was possible that the war had imposed a considerable strain on Saudi Arabia's financial resources and that, contrary to Wahhabi mythology, many of his tribesmen had shown little appetite for a war on such a distant front.[240] Desert warriors were not familiar with mountain campaigns, and Ibn Saud may have feared renewed insurrections in central Arabia if he over-stretched himself in the south.[241]

International considerations could also have played a part in Ibn Saud's moderation. He may have exaggerated the risk of Italian intervention should he completely undermine the balance-of-power in south-west Arabia, particularly as Britain had constantly counselled him to the effect that she would not intervene in such an eventuality.[242] The presence of European warships off Hodeida may, in itself, have had a deterrent effect, as may the recent British treaty with the Imam. Again, the presence of a European community in Hodeida may have provided a further deterrent, as that in Jedda had done during the 1924-25 Hejaz-Nejd war. Moreover, while Ibn Saud may not have had broader Arab considerations foremost in his mind when he offered his peace terms, he may not have been unaware of the advantages of playing to an Arab gallery.[243] His concern over Italian enterprise in the Red Sea area did not disappear with his victory or the terms of the Treaty of Taif. Although Italo-Saudi relations were to be temporarily smoothed, from late 1935 Italian involvement in the Red Sea would intensify, but that is the concern of a later chapter.[244]

Summary and Conclusions

An examination of British policy towards Saudi Arabia over events in the Red Sea highlights certain aspects of the general framework of Anglo-Saudi relations. For example, leaving aside Aden, where British interests were crucial, it is apparent that the Foreign Office was the one political department to take a close watch on the Saudi-Yemeni situation. All three interested parties – Italy, Saudi Arabia and the Yemen – were independent states. As the Saudi-Yemeni war did not directly threaten British responsibilities in the Middle East, it was the Foreign Office which paid greatest attention to it.

Another point is that in observing a decade of Saudi-Yemeni tension from 1925-34, it can be seen that British policy was shaped almost exclusively by external considerations. The need to consider Italy outrode any of the internal developments in Arabia. Hence, this chapter has said as much about Anglo-Italian relations as about Anglo-Saudi relations.

The reason for this paramount concern with Italy is straightforward. The Red Sea constituted one of the world's most sensitive waterways through which the flow of imperial traffic was obliged to pass. In 1930, for example, of the 370-odd ships that entered the port of Jedda, 224 were British owned.[245] British strategy demanded that no alien power should control the islands within that waterway, or both its coastlines. The independence of the Hejaz posed no threat to that strategy while Egypt and the Sudan on the opposite shore were effectively under British control. The southern half of the Red Sea was more vulnerable. Eritrea, on the African side, was an Italian colony. The Yemen, opposite Eritrea, was independent, but without the international sanction that diplomatic relations with the outside world would have conferred, and which made Hejaz-Nejd unique in the Arab world until 1932. To further emphasise British vulnerability, certain islands in the southern parts of the Red Sea offered tempting targets, whether through oil or harbour facilities.

The need to keep Italy away from those islands and block the political gateway to them through the Arabian mainland provided Britain with her foremost anxieties in south-west Arabia. Ibn Saud played a part in relieving those anxieties by the degree of his control over Asir. The formal aspect of British policy towards Italy in the Red Sea had been set down in the Rome Agreement of 1927, which gave Britain virtually all she required locally. Yet it became apparent that the two signatories enjoyed different interpretations of the Rome provisions. To Italy the spirit of the Agreement was to forestall the outbreak of war in south-west Arabia – or rather to do so if the Imam showed signs of losing. To Britain, the non-interventionist aspects of the Agreement were inviolable, no matter what course a war in south-west Arabia was taking. This interpretation was in line with centuries of British policy towards the Arabian mainland. Furthermore, at the close of the First World War Britain had taken on Arab and Moslem responsibilities that would not tolerate British interference in the affairs of the Hejaz. British intervention, for or against Ibn Saud, would have been political tinder to Moslem areas of the Empire.

Britain was not averse to putting different shades of meaning upon the Rome Agreement to meet changing developments in south-west Arabia as expediency demanded. Indeed, with the gradual disappearance of Asir as an independent entity, she was pretty well compelled to adjust her perspective to keep the relevance and significance of the Rome Agreement, from her point of view, intact. Britain clung tenaciously to Paragraph Three of the Agreement:

Paragraph Three

While continuing to exert their influence in the cause of peace, the two governments should not intervene in any conflict which may break out between those chiefs.

She could, moreover, adhere to this paragraph with equanimity seeing that it was Yemeni and Italian interests which were being retarded. At the same time, Britain paid less heed to Paragraphs One and Two, which were, perhaps, rather more fundamental to the spirit and whole purpose of the Agreement:

Paragraph One

It is the common interest of the two governments to pursue a policy of pacification in order to avoid, as far as possible, conflicts between various Arab chiefs.

Paragraph Two

Such influence as the two governments may be in a position to exercise wth Ibn Saud, the Imam and the Idrisi, shall be directed towards eliminating the causes of conflict in order to arrive, if possible, at pacific and friendly settlements between those chiefs.

Britain, it must be said, did little to exercise any influence aimed at prevention of the 1934 war. To have done so would have invited parallel Italian influence. While it is a matter of argument whether, by naming the Idrisi in the Rome Agreement, she was obliged to seek to maintain his sovereignty, Britain, in the end, stretched the non-interventionist feature of the Agreement to its extreme.

On the question of Italian ambitions, the interests of Britain and Ibn Saud coincided at one point: diverged at another. Neither wanted to see Italy gain any kind of a foothold in Arabia. Fortunately, neither did the Imam, beyond the necessary minimum. At the same time, Italy was beginning to prove a useful counter-weight to Britain in the eyes of Ibn Saud, although this trend would be more noticeable later in the 1930s. Italy was becoming a useful lever for Ibn Saud to employ against the omnipresent British. Whilst from Britain's point of view the Rome Agreement signalled her determination to stand clear of Arabia, and, in the process, keep Italy back too, from the standpoint of Ibn Saud, it would have appeared as the machinations of two imperial powers imposing their protectorate umbrella over the Red Sea area and over certain named rulers, of whom he was one.

The two sources of Saudi conflict between 1927-34, the *Ikhwan* rebellion and the war with the Yemen, had totally different complexions. Internally, the religious aspect of Ibn Saud's rule, so prominent in the late 1920s, however much he tried to underplay it, had all but disappeared by 1934. The Saudi-Yemeni war was a battle between two rival kingdoms for disputed territory, uninflamed by the kind of religious antagonisms that had spurred previous Saudi campaigns. The Imam was accused of bad faith and aggression, but not heresy.[246] Furthermore, in the history of Saudi conflicts since 1902, that with the Yemen was the only instance of Ibn Saud not being overtly the aggressor.

The response of the British Government was also markedly different to each conflict. Its involvement in the defence of Iraq was predictable: first, as the mandate looked to Britain for its defence; second, because the imperial communication channels with the East had to be protected. Yet, even when raids into Iraq had virtually ceased, Britain contrived to intervene both militarily and politically on behalf of Ibn Saud to quell the rebellion. Similar intervention did not take place during the Saudi-Yemeni war. The Yemen was not Iraq: Britain having no comparable interest at stake.

One general, if unwritten, article of policy towards Arabia was the maintenance, wherever possible, of Ibn Saud as its principal source of political authority. His continued stability formed the core of Britain's Arabia policy. This policy had been most in evidence during the latter stages of the *Ikhwan* rebellion. Over the war with the Yemen there were fewer outward manifestations of this policy. It was not that Britain no longer desired Ibn Saud's continuing rule in Arabia, but that this general principle was compromised by two other considerations. These were, first, Anglo-Italian relations which, as had already been emphasised, took precedence over other British considerations in the Red Sea, and second, the realisation that the Imam was unlikely to pose a threat to the future of Ibn Saud. The Imam did not number among his ambitions the conquest of Saudi Arabia. Consequently, the outcome of any Saudi-Yemeni war was seen in terms of an enhanced or diminished Yemen, not in terms of an extinguished Saudi state. The conflict was strictly a local one, not between rival dynasties for the mastery of Arabia, but over the disputed buffer territory of Asir. A defeat for Ibn Saud in that corner of Arabia would not necessarily have weakened his hold elsewhere.

These factors enabled Britain to assume a certain air of moral and physical detachment from the Saudi-Yemeni war, more so, for example, than towards the Hejaz-Nejd war and the *Ikhwan* rebellion. This detachment was checked only by the extent of the Italian threat. Ultimately, however, it was in British interests for the Yemen to continue as a buffer and counter-weight to total Saudi hegemony in south-west Arabia provided, of course, that the Yemen did not prove to be the gateway for Italian penetration of the peninsula – hence the need for good relations with the Imam as well as with Ibn Saud, as manifested by the Anglo-Yemeni treaty of 1934 and the lifting of the arms embargo. The effect of the Italian presence in the Red Sea on Anglo-Saudi relations from 1936 will be considered in a later chapter.

REFERENCES FOR CHAPTER SIX

1. Ryan to Simon, Annual Report for 1933, 28 April 1934, FO E/3126/3126/25: 371/17941. (Hereafter: Annual Report 1933.)
2. Hurewitz, p. 380.
3. Annual Report 1933.
4. ibid.
5. ibid.
6. ibid.; Ryan memorandum, 22 November 1933, FO E/7186/759/25: 371/16874.
7. Annual Report 1933. Yemeni semi-autonomy was finally granted by the Treaty of Daan, ratified in 1913.
8. See CO/19017/26: 725/9; FO E/5762/2660/91: 371/11448.
9. ibid.
10. FO minute, 21 February 1927, FO E/843/22/91: 371/12236; CO/48023/27: 725/12.
11. See Chapter Eight.
12. See CO/19017/26: 725/9; FO E/5762/2660/91: 371/11448.
13. ibid.
14. Hurewitz, p. 382.
15. Annual Report 1933.
16. ibid.
17. Hurewitz, p. 382.
18. See FO E/735/28/91: 371/11433.
19. Gillian King, *Imperial Outpost – Aden: Its Place in British Strategic Policy,* p. 6.
20. RIIA, *Political and Strategic Interests ...,* p. 161.
21. *Survey ... 1928,* p. 309.
22. ibid.
23. ibid., p. 310.
24. Rendel, pp. 60, 84. In 1917 the Government of India transferred military control of Aden to the War Office and control of the Protectorate to the Foreign Office.
25. R J Gavin, *Aden Under British Rule 1839-1967,* p. 252.
26. Shuckburgh memorandum, 27 November 1926, in FO E/6578/870/91: 371/11445.
27. *Survey ... 1934,* p. 310.
28. Fisher, p. 580; 9th Aden Newsletter, 30 September 1926, in FO E/6031/97/91: 371/11435.
29. Manfred W Wenner, *Modern Yemen 1918-1966,* p. 148.
30. FO circular despatch 1933, FO E/7161/759/25: 371/16874.
31. ibid. (see Chapter Nine).
32. Wenner, p. 45.
33. ibid., p. 49.
34. ibid., p. 150.
35. ibid., p. 149.
36. ibid., p. 157.
37. ibid., p. 149.
38. ibid.
39. FO circular despatch, op. cit.
40. Wenner, p. 153.
41. H Stuart Hughes, 'The Early Diplomacy of Italian Fascism 1922-1932', in Craig and Gilbert, p. 224.
42. ibid., pp. 222-3.
43. RIIA, *Political and Strategic Interests ...,* p. 160.
44. ibid.
45. Wenner, p. 141.
46. ibid.
47. ibid.
48. ibid.
49. *Survey ... 1928,* p. 310.

50. Henderson (Cairo) to FO, 7 February 1926, FO E/427/4/91: 371/11431; FO E/979/4/91: 371/11431.
51. FO minute, FO E/979/4/91: 371/11431.
52. FO minute, FO E/733/22/91: 371/12236.
53. ibid.
54. Wenner, p. 142.
55. Note on appeal of Idrisi, 26 June 1926, FO E/5239/29/91: 371/11434.
56. ibid.
57. See FO E/1038/4/91; 371/11431.
58. Aeroplanes, ammunition, fuel and cartridge-making machinery were being landed at Hodeida (4th Aden Newsletter, 30 April 1926, FO E/3247/97/91: 371/11435). Although the embargo did not technically apply to the export of war munitions for 'lawful purposes', that is, use by the government of a country for whom the arms were intended, the Italian Government had given specific assurances that it would not furnish either the Imam or the Idrisi with arms (Graham (Rome) to FO, No 450, 25 May 1925, FO E/3179/176/91: 371/10818; FO minute, 12 February 1926, FO E/710/710/91: 371/11444).
59. Field (FO) memorandum, 7 July 1926, FO E/4679/2660/91: 371/11448.
60. ibid.
61. Shuckburgh to Chamberlain, 27 May 1926, FO E/3265/710/91: 371/11444. This embargo referred to the granting of export licenses for the private supply of arms. Removing it did not mean the British Government would supply arms itself.
62. Shuckburgh memorandum, 27 November 1926, in FO E/6578/870/91: 371/11445.
63. 8th Aden Newsletter, 31 August 1926, in FO E/5348/97/91: 371/11435.
64. Hurewitz, pp. 380-1. The agreed language of the treaty was Arabic; there being no-one in the Yemen who spoke Italian.
65. Wenner, p. 152.
66. ibid., p. 153. The Italians had been helping the Idrisi rebel against the Turks since 1909. This served as a distraction for Italian moves against Tripoli, the Turks' last possession in Africa (Baker, pp. 26-7).
67. 9th Aden Newsletter, 30 September 1926, in FO E/6031/97/91: 371/11435.
68. ibid. The treaty was signed while the Colonial office was contemplating further action against Yemeni forces entrenched in the Aden Protectorate.
69. Gavin, p. 295.
70. Shuckburgh memorandum, op. cit.
71. ibid.
72. Osborne, (FO) minute, 19 November 1926, FO E/6648/4/91: 371/11431.
73. ibid.
74. ibid.
75. Mayers (Jedda) to FO, No 133, 3 November 1926, FO E/6655/367/91: 371/11442.
76. The British Government hoped that the Idrisi would become a sort of viceroy under Ibn Saud (FO minute, 3 September 1926, FO E/5409/367/91: 371/11442).
77. Shuckburgh memorandum, op. cit.
78. ibid.
79. Reilly (Aden) to SSC, 10 November 1926, & 30 November 1926. The Red Sea Petroleum Co. was set up in 1927 to operate the concession.
80. Hurewitz, pp. 382-5.
81. ibid.
82. Osborne minute, 10 January 1927, FO E/135/22/91: 371/12235.
83. Later in 1927 visits by Saudi and Yemeni delegations to Sanaa and Mecca further reduced tension (*Survey ... 1928,* p. 320).
84. Osborne minute, op. cit.
85. ibid.
86. See Chapter Eight.
87. Clayton to Oliphant, 14 January 1927, FO E/266/22/91: 371/12235.
88. ibid.
89. Osborne minute, 17 January 1927, ibid.
90. Jordan minute, ibid.
91. Instructions to Clayton in Rome, 21 January 1927, FO E/376/22/91: 371/12235. As the

treaty involved certain territorial adjustments this was all the more reason for Britain to withhold recognition. (Rendel minute, 16 February 1927, FO E/1242/22/91: 371/12236.)

92. Rendel minute, 16 February 1927, FO E/1242/22/91: 371/12236.
93. One effect of the Agreement was to preclude Britain from establishing naval or air bases on the Farasan Islands. Another concerned the assurances given to the Italian Government regarding economic and commercial freedom on the Arabian coast and islands of the Red Sea. Accordingly, the arms supply from Aden and the Shell Oil Company to the Idrisi was suspended, and support withheld from British oil interests in Kamaran. (See Amery to FO, 14 March 1927, CO/48023/27: 725/12.)
94. Gavin, p. 295.
95. Stonehewer-Bird to FO, No 31, 25 July 1927, FO E/3285/22/91: 371/12237. The Italian Government replied that it was difficult to restrain the Imam in the face of Ibn Saud's 'provocation' (FO minute, 26 August 1927, FO E/3664/22/91: 371/12238).
96. Reilly to Amery, No 147, 6 July 1927, CO/48004/54/27: 725/11.
97. ibid. The Idrisi also announced a desire to grant the concession to Italian interests (CO to FO, 8 August 1927, CO/48007/27: 725/11).
98. Dashwood (FO) minute, 10 August 1927, FO E/3461/22/91: 371/12237.
99. Longrigg, Oil ... p. 101.
100. Survey ... 1928, p. 320.
101. Reilly to Amery, No 59, 4 August 1927, CO/48004/27: 725/11.
102. FO circular despatch 1933, FO E/7161/759/25: 371/16874.
103. Wenner, p. 155. For a comprehensive analysis of the British-Yemeni-Aden triangle in the inter-war years, see Gavin, pp. 250-306.
104. Gavin, p. 263.
105. See Mayers to FO, No 17, 23 February 1927, FO E/1242/22/91: 371/12236; see FO E/384/80/91: 371/13003.
106. Lloyd to Chamberlain, No 682, 29 November 1927, FO E/5081/22/91: 371/12239.
107. ibid.
108. Tyrrell (FO) to Wilson (CO), 14 December 1927, FO E/5343/22/91: 371/12239.
109. Warner (FO) memorandum, 12 August 1930; Ryan minute, 4 October 1930, FO E/4522/4522/91: 371/14483.
110. Warner minute, 12 October 1930, ibid.
111. ibid.
112. Hope Gill (Jedda) to FO, No 231, 25 November 1930, FO E/6382/4522/91: 371/14483.
113. Annual Report 1930.
114. ibid.
115. Beckett (FO legal adviser) minute, 9 January 1931, FO E/6943/4522/25: 371/14483.
116. Warner minute, 12 October 1930, FO E/4522/4522/91: 371/14483.
117. Graham (Rome) to Henderson, No 375, 29 May 1931, FO E/2869/1098/25: 371/15298.
118. Annual Report 1932.
119. Rendel, p. 60.
120. ibid. In 1931 the Foreign Office had given administrative confirmation of its confidence in the Saudi state. Previously its 'Arabia' file embraced Ibn Saud's dominions – No 91. In 1931 Hejaz-Nejd was given a separate file – No 25, which was renamed the Saudi Arabia file in 1934.
121. Hope Gill to Simon, No 443, 7 November 1932, FO E/6396/1197/25: 371/16024.
122. ibid.
123. Annual Report 1931.
124. ibid.
125. Hope Gill to Simon, No 401, 25 September 1932, FO E/5269/1484/25: 371/16025.
126. Rendel minute, 23 September 1932, FO E/4845/1484/25: 371/16025.
127. Hope Gill to Simon, op. cit.
128. Paradoxically, the naming of Saud as Crown Prince did not contribute to stability but led to a power struggle for the succession in the 1950s and '60s.
129. Rendel, p. 129.
130. ibid.
131. FO memorandum, 'Italian Policy towards the UK', 27 March 1934, R/1885/395/22: 371/17918. (Hereafter: 'Italian Policy ...'.) Prior to 1914 Italy had embarked on

imperialistic adventures with mixed success in Libya, Corsica, Tunis, Abyssinia and Greece.

132. RIIA, *Political and Strategic Interests* ..., p. 107.
133. ibid.
134. Rendel, p. 131.
135. ibid.; 'Italian Policy ...'.
136. Rendel, p. 130.
137. ibid., p. 131.
138. Culturally there remained a strong affinity between the upper echelons of both nations. Anglo-Italian marriages among the aristocracies were still common. Mussolini enjoyed good relations with Britain's Foreign Secretary Austen Chamberlain. (Maxwell HH Macartney and Paul Cremona, *Italy's Foreign and Colonial Policy 1914-1937*, pp. 170-4).
139. 'Italian Policy ...'.
140. Alan Cassels, *Mussolini's Early Diplomacy*, p. 310.
141. Hughes, p. 221.
142. ibid., p. 227.
143. ibid., p. 229.
144. Hans Kohn, *A History of Nationalism in the East*, pp. 124, 313.
145. ibid., pp. 313-4.
146. 'Italian Policy ...'.
147. Hughes, p. 226.
148. 'Italian Policy ...'.
149. Hughes, pp. 232-3.
150. By 1931 Italy's expatriate population in her Arab and African colonies was as follows:–
Libya – 49,400; Eritrea – 4,600; Italian Somaliland – 1,700; there were also sizable Italian minorities in other Mediterranean countries: Algeria and Morocco – 150,000; Tunisia – 100,000; Egypt – 65,000 (RIIA, *Political and Strategic Interests* ..., p. 133).
151. 'Italian Policy ...'.
152. ibid.
153. Hughes, p. 225; RIIA, op. cit., p. 133. Fascist imperialism has been described as different from that practised by Italy's European rivals, who were tending towards neo-colonialism. Italian imperialism was more like neo-mercantilism, as part of a new international struggle (CJ Lowe and F Marzari, *Italian Foreign Policy 1870-1940*, p. 240).
154. 'Italian Policy ...'.
155. ibid.
156. Johnstone (FO) minute, 28 September 1933, FO E/5694/759/25: 371/16872.
157. Wenner, pp. 144-5.
158. Ryan memorandum, 21 November 1933, FO E/7186/759/25: 371/16874.
159. ibid.
160. Calvert (Jedda) to FO, No 140, 20 July 1933, FO E/4010/759/25: 371/16872.
161. Annual Report 1933.
162. ibid.
163. Rendel memorandum, 24 July 1933, FO E/4064/759/25: 371/16872.
164. ibid. (& Hurewitz, p. 455).
165. ibid.
166. ibid.
167. Rendel minute, 21 July 1933, FO E/4010/759/25: 371/16872.
168. Johnstone minute, 10 October 1933, FO E/5990/759/25: 371/16873.
169. Johnstone minute, 27 October 1933, FO E/6447/759/25: 371/16873.
170. Graham to FO, 5 October 1933, FO E/5990/759/25: 371/16873.
171. Johnstone minute, 10 October 1933, ibid. More particularly the only part of Asir over which Italy expressed any interest was the coastal Tihama which faced the Red Sea.
172. Rendel memorandum, 30 November 1933, FO E/7330/759/25: 371/16874.
173. Rendel memorandum, 17 April 1934, FO E/2405/2/25: 371/17918.
174. ibid.
175. FO to Drummond (Rome), 15 January 1934 FO E/50/2/25: 371/17918.
176. 'Italian Policy ...'.
177. Hurewitz, pp. 454-6.

178. ibid.
179. Gavin, p.297.
180. Tom Hickinbotham, *Aden*, p.69.
181. Hurewitz, pp.455-6.
182. Annual Report 1933.
183. *The Times*, 9 February 1934.
184. Ryan to Simon, Annual Report for 12934, 18 May 1935, FO E/3607/3607/25: 371/19017; (Hereafter: Annual Report 1934).
185. ibid.
186. ibid.; FO memorandum, 7 May 1934, FO E/2861/79/25: 371/17925. Philby says Saudi forces crossed the Yemeni frontier early in April. (Philby, *Arabian Jubilee*, p. 185).
187. Ryan to FO, No 44, 23 March 1934, FO E/1862/79/25: 371/17923.
188. ibid.
189. See Chapter Eight.
190. Warner (FO) minute, 24 March 1934, FO E/1862/79/25: 371/17923.
191. FO minute, 26 March 1934, ibid.
192. Rendel minute, 26 March 1934, ibid.
193. Annual Report 1934.
194. ibid.
195. See FO E/2648/79/25: 371/17924.
196. Johnstone (FO) minute, 30 April 1934, ibid.
197. Eric Macro, *Yemen and the Western World Since 1571*, p. 59. Britain did not want to land naval forces at Hodeida. It was felt that some forty British sailors had little chance of protecting the 300-odd Indians against marauding Saudi tribesmen. Moreover, as Arabian warriors did not wear easily recognised uniforms, it would have been difficult to distinguish Saudi from Yemeni forces.
198. Ryan to FO, No 85, 1 May 1934, FO E/2734/79/25: 371/17924.
199. ibid.
200. Gavin, p.297.
201. Ryan to FO, op. cit. (see Chapter Nine).
202. Beckett minute, 7 May 1934, ibid.
203. ibid.
204. ibid.
205. Rendel minute, 5 May 1934, ibid.
206. ibid.
207. *HMS Penzance* to Aden, 5 May 1934, in FO E/2853/79/25: 371/17925.
208. ibid.
209. FO memorandum, 7 May 1934, FO E/2861/79/25: 371/17925.
210. Annual Report 1934. With Saudi forces poised to take the town there were fears of a major incident. Indeed, it was feared that the Italian troops had been instructed to engineer such an incident in order to gain an excuse for further intervention.
211. Drummond to FO, No 124, 3 May 1934, FO E/2812/79/25: 371/17925.
212. ibid.
213. FO to Drummond, No 134, 6 May 1934, ibid.
214. ibid.
215. FO minute, 9 May 1934, FO E/2947/79/25: 371/17926. Small Italian and British signalling parties had gone ashore. The Saudis refused the landing of a larger Italian contingent.
216. Ryan to FO, No 101, 7 May 1934, FO E/2928/79/25: 371/17926.
217. Ryan to FO, No 113, 13 May 1934, FO E/3084/79/25: 371/17926.
218. Drummond to FO, 12 May 1934, FO E/3091/79/25: 371/17926.
219. Drummond to Simon, No 394, 8 May 1934, FO E/2933/79/25: 371/17926.
220. FO memorandum, 8 May 1934, FO E/2948/79/25: 371/17926.
221. ibid.
222. Annual Report 1934.
223. Rendel minute, 14 May 1934, FO E/3077/79/25: 371/17926.
224. Ryan to FO, No 163, 29 May 1934, FO E/3998/79/25: 371/17928.
225. Annual Report 1934.
226. Warner minute, 26 June 1934, FO E/4125/79/25: 371/17928.

227. Annual Report 1934.
228. ibid.
229. Ryan to FO, No 202, 27 June 1934, FO E/4452/79/25: 371/17929.
230. Fowle to Laithwaite (IO), 7 November 1934, in FO E/7352/79/25: 371/17930.
231. ibid.
232. ibid.
233. ibid.
234. ibid.
235. Rendel minute, 17 December 1934, ibid.
236. ibid.
237. ibid.
238. Johnstone minute, 11 December 1934, ibid.
239. Annual Report 1934.
240. ibid.
241. ibid. It later transpired that Saudi forces had made little headway in the mountainous interior of the Yemen (Almana, p. 210-11). Ibn Saud would also have appreciated that Shia Yemeni troops would have fought devotedly for the Imam against Wahhabis (personal correspondence from Robert Lacey).
242. Annual Report 1934.
243. ibid.
244. See Chapter Eleven.
245. Annual Report 1930.
246. Annual Report 1934.

CHAPTER SEVEN

Ibn Saud and the League of Nations

Italy affected the security of Saudi Arabia in a number of ways in the late 1920s and early '30s. She also could, and did, affect British attitudes towards Ibn Saud on a number of issues. One such example concerns the League of Nations. The League was an organisation with which Britain was heavily involved, and which a newly independent state like Hejaz-Nejd could not entirely ignore. Italian enterprise in the Red Sea was one of the threats which prompted several Saudi enquiries about membership between 1929-36.

The League of Nations was closely associated with Britain's imperialistic presence in the Middle East. Britain's mandates, Iraq and Palestine, had been given international respectability by having their administrations accountable to the League.[1] The issue of Saudi membership, therefore, raises certain questions about Britain's attitude towards promoting the internationalism of Ibn Saud's dominions: whether to make his affairs public before the world, or continue to take advantage of the remoteness of his Kingdom by encouraging his reliance on British guidance in his international affairs.

The question of bringing the Saudi state into the League was first raised privately by the League Secretariat in 1929.[2] The proposal elicited little attention in London.[3] In the spring of 1930, however, with the *Ikhwan* rebellion finally suppressed, and with Sir Andrew Ryan's arrival in Jedda, the subject came in for deeper discussion. Questions were even asked in the House of Commons about the advisability of admitting Ibn Saud's Kingdom into the League; but before turning attention to Ibn Saud's enquiries, and Britain's responses to them, it is necessary to examine the place of the League of Nations in British foreign policy in the 1920s.

British Foreign Policy and the League of Nations 1919-1930

Schemes for a world organisation which could assist the preservation of peace through some form of collective security can be dated back to the fourteenth century.[4] In the years up to 1914 it was the British labour organisations which were most prominent in fostering an international spirit opposed to any future European war.[5] The Great War, when it came, provided the impetus for an international body aimed at banishing armed conflict and facilitating the peaceful settlement of international disputes. The old world order associated with the 'Concert of Europe' – compulsory conscription, the balance-of-power alliance system, and secret diplomacy – were all felt to be largely responsible for the horrors of the War.[6] Wartime proposals for future international supervision of inter-state disputes ranged from a Fabian Society proposal for an international High Court to which nations should agree to submit their disputes, to plans for an international army and parliament which would not be accountable to individual states.[7] These proposals, it was hoped, would encourage world disarmament and give international authority for the maintenance of international law and order.[8]

Such debate was not strictly within party lines, although the Labour and Liberal Parties were the more energetic in canvassing support for a body which could settle international disputes and control the spread of instruments of war.[9] The bulk of the Conservative Party and its press lacked enthusiasm for such schemes, regarding them as Utopian or worse.[10] Lloyd George's Government of 1919 was committed to promoting the League, less from ideological reasons than out of the need to co-operate with President Wilson, who was a leading champion of it.[11]

The actual League of Nations which emerged at Versailles was neither a super-state nor an alliance. It resembled a multilateral treaty, except that the purposes for which the League existed were nowhere precisely defined.[12] Its essential character fluctuated between a multilateral treaty and an alliance, depending on the degree of co-operation between the powers.[13] At heart, Britain did not see the League as recasting the fundamentals of international relations.[14] Even such an advocate as Lord Cecil stressed the conservative nature of the new institution, its purpose being: 'to devise some really effective means of preserving the peace of the world consistently with the least possible interference with international sovereignty'.[15]

As the 1920s progressed, it became apparent that the League was marred by differing interpretations placed upon it by Britain and her continental partners, and by the apathy or latent hostility of certain British statesmen. Britain (unlike France who was preoccupied with the need to prevent German aggression – and membership) saw the League as a loose co-operative association of independent states.[16] Not having witnessed a war on home soil, Britain was concerned less with the League's security aspect than with its possibilities as a philanthropic and humanitarian agency.[17] Many British politicians believed in the League, and supported it, without placing undue emphasis on the obligations embodied in the Covenant.[18] The ideals of the League (the pacific settlement of all disputes, the rule of law superseding the rule of force, a realisation of the dangers of excessive patriotism, and a belief in the sanctity and efficacy of international public opinion which could deter aggressors by moral suasion)[19] found more adherents in theory than in practice. British conceptions of the League became strongly attached to the logic of appeasement, that is, an acknowledgement of Britain's weakening international position, fear for her global responsibilities and foreign entanglements, and an overwhelming desire to avoid wars.[20]

Furthermore, the absence since the League's inception of the United States (and of Germany until 1926, and the Soviet Union until 1934) meant that the forum to which Britain had been committed in theory was rather different from the one she actually joined. Britain found herself with the burden of peacekeeping falling largely on her shoulders.[21] This burden became the heavier with the changes in the constitution of the British Empire. The Dominions, with their separate membership of the League, were no longer inclined to permit their own foreign policies to be dictated from London – let alone Geneva.[22] Taken together, all the factors which contributed to Britain's international decline restricted her participation in the League.[23] As the pre-eminent member, Britain was faced with being a 'producer' of security rather than 'consumer' of it.[24]

Of course, the very notion of self-determination was largely incompatible with the principle of Empire. The conception of a world order as embodied in the League ran counter to Britain's imperial privileges.[25] These difficulties were exacerbated by the varying degrees of commitment shown to the League by British Governments in the 1920s and '30s. Conservatives provided, in the main, the League's greatest detractors.[26] Of the senior Conservative politicians of the 1920s, few were ardent supporters of the League. Stanley Baldwin was disinclined to allow it to exert too much influence on Britain's foreign policy and in 1928 his Government attempted to reduce the proportion of the League's budget which fell upon Britain.[27] Curzon, too, doubted 'whether the League of Nations is going to be the great and potent and world-pacifying instrument that its creators desire'.[28] Churchill declared: 'A League of Nations is no substitute for the British fleet'.[29] Only about a third of Baldwin's Cabinet in 1925 were considered adherents of the League.[30] Austen Chamberlain, however, after initial scepticism as Foreign Secretary, emerged as a firm advocate.[31]

Labour was temperamentally more attuned to the principles of the League, though the Party leader, Ramsay MacDonald, had no great enthusiasm for it. He was a politician of the old school, preferring the principles of traditional diplomacy whereby a few selected persons sitting in private could settle the affairs of Europe.[32] He viewed the League with aloof suspicion.[33] His short-lived Government of 1924 rejected the League's draft Treaty of Mutual Assistance which was intended to oblige member states to come to the assistance in the event of aggression against any member.[34] Neither did his Government ratify the Geneva Protocol which aimed to provide for automatic and compulsory recourse to arbitration.[35] Of course, MacDonald knew that in 1924 a minority government could not sustain a radical commitment to the League. Nonetheless, he was determined to expand its membership, and was the first British Prime Minister or Foreign Secretary to go to Geneva.[36]

The second Labour Government, of 1929-31, was notably more enthusiastic towards the League. This was, in part, due to the post of Foreign
Secretary going to Arthur Henderson, a committed advocate of it and,
incidentally, widely regarded as one of the most successful Foreign Secretaries of the inter-war years.[37] It was also partly a reflection of the League's
prestige being at its peak – the successive disappointments of the 1930s yet
to come.[38] Henderson had acted quickly in the Middle East upon taking
office, removing Lord Lloyd, the High Commissioner of Egypt and one of
the pillars of conservatism, for being obstructive to the harmony of Anglo-
Egyptian relations.[39] Henderson saw British policy moving towards minimal
intervention in Egyptian affairs, and worked for a satisfactory treaty which
would grant Egypt complete independence.[40]

Although the League as it existed fell short of the 'internationalism' for
which many in the Labour Party had striven, Henderson hoped to make it
the first principle in the foreign affairs of the Labour Government.[41] He was,
however, hindered in his commitment both by Ramsay MacDonald and the
extreme left of his Party, which, as with the right wing of the Conservative
Party, was never reconciled to the League. Peaceful co-operation, the left
argued, was impossible through an alliance of capitalist governments.[42]
Henderson's foreign policy was further hampered by the onset of the Great
Depression and the consequent growth of militarism in Europe. He, was,
nevertheless, awarded the Nobel Peace Prize shortly before he died, in
1935.[43]

Another significant member of the second Labour Government, in the
context of the League of Nations and the Middle East, was Sidney Webb,
Secretary of State for the Colonies. Webb, seventy years of age and a
founding father of British socialism, had been President of the Board of
Trade in 1924.[44] He was persuaded by MacDonald in 1929 to enter the
Upper House as Lord Passfield.[45] As Colonial Secretary, he had to deal with
the disturbances in Palestine, and was responsible for the final decision to
terminate the mandate and admit Iraq to the League of Nations. This did not
make him an anti-imperialist: he still believed in the potential of social
reform through a well-administered 'colonial' system.[46]

Overall, Parliaments in the 1920s were reduced to a basic cleavage
between those who wanted British foreign policy wholly based on the
League, irrespective of its lack of enforcement machinery, and those who
felt that the British Empire and its allies were a surer foundation upon which
to build world peace.[47] While no British Government could ignore the
League, there was, by and large, little understanding of its workings or the
obligations of the Covenant upon which it rested.[48] Largely as a result of
this, all Governments of the 1920s followed, to some extent, a dual policy,
paying lip-service to the League in principle, while resisting all attempts to
strengthen it.[49] This, then, is the context of the League and Britain's role
therein, within which Ibn Saud's feelers for membership have to be gauged.

The First Saudi Approach: Arthur Henderson

In the spring of 1930 reports from Jedda spoke of Ibn Saud contemplating the benefits of League membership. This invited a wide-ranging discussion within the Foreign Office. As Britain was both the leading influence in the League, and the Saudi Government's major source of advice on international affairs, it was natural for suggestions of Saudi membership to pass initially through Britain. It was a working principle of British Governments that membership of the League should be as extensive as was commensurate with furthering its aims.[50] One Arab state, Iraq, was already preparing for membership, although her admission to the League had been implicit from the inception of the mandate. The question was, would Britain, and the League, stand to gain from the admission of the Saudi Kingdom?

Much of the debate within the Foreign Office centred on juridical and technical problems, for example the role of the Saudi Hejaz as a successor state to the Hashemite Hejaz. The Kingdom of the Hejaz had been among the list of states described as original members of the League, as listed in the annex to the Covenant.[51] In practice, states were obliged to undertake some act adhering to the obligations of the League, such as ratifying the Treaty of Versailles, before membership was consummated. This was something that King Husein had not fulfilled.[52] In this respect, the position of the Hejaz was analogous to that of the United States, who likewise declined to accept the responsibilities which membership entailed, shunning the pioneering work of President Wilson.[53]

The analogy was only partial. There was an additional complication regarding the identity of the Hejaz. Was it, in 1930, the same international entity as it had been in 1919? The Foreign Office worked on the principle that a change in dynasty did not constitute a change in the identity of a state.[54] Consequently, there seemed no legal objection to Ibn Saud ratifying the Treaty of Versailles over a decade after the original signatories, thereby taking the Hejaz directly into the League without applying afresh.[55] On the other hand, Ibn Saud had repudiated all acts of his Hashemite predecessors and had for practical purposes created a new Hejaz state. This raised doubts about whether the Saudi Hejaz could effectively become a party to a treaty signed but not ratified by the Hashemites.[56]

The issue was further muddled by Ibn Saud simultaneously being King of the Hejaz and of Nejd. Hitherto, the British Government had, since 1926, regarded Hejaz-Nejd as two distinct states under one common King. This was termed a 'personal union'.[57] The two states had separate administrations and the Hejaz, unlike Nejd, enjoyed a constitution. Moreover, Britain had recognised Ibn Saud as King of the Hejaz without any mention of Nejd. Although Britain regarded the Hejaz as persisting as the same international unit under both Husein and Ibn Saud, Nejd was a separate Kingdom, and was peremptorily dismissed as a serious candidate for the League, irrespective of the fate of the Hejaz, on account of its backwardness.[58] Shortly after his arrival Ryan reported, in July 1930, a deepening Saudi awareness of the League.[59] Accordingly, the Foreign Office began to consider the question in greater depth, including whether it was really in Britain's interest to regard Hejaz-Nejd as two states rather than one.

It was possible, both in theory and in practice, for two states with democratic, parliamentary institutions, and with a king as a constitutional monarch, to retain their separate status under a common king. This was, indeed, the case in the former union of Britain and Hanover.[60] The Foreign Office admitted that such a stand was less easy to uphold when the said king was an autocrat and sole source of government for both states. A common king, in this instance, was in effect a common government, notwithstanding separate administrations.[61]

On reflection, the Foreign Office preferred to consider the international position of Hejaz-Nejd as more like the 'real union' as found, for instance, in the former Austria-Hungary monarchy, than the 'personal union' previously favoured.[62] This view was reinforced by the manner in which the foreign affairs of Hejaz-Nejd were conducted. There was just one Foreign Office, in Mecca, and one Foreign Minister. No known international treaties with Ibn Saud had been duplicated – with one for the Hejaz and another for Nejd. Nor had they been with the old monarchy of Austria-Hungary. Although the precise nature of the relationship between the Hejaz and Nejd was known only to Ibn Saud, the legal department of the Foreign Office now took the view that both states had ceased to exist as separate international entities, and had been replaced by a new single unit in the form of the union of Hejaz-Nejd.[63] Consequently, the path into the League by Ibn Saud ratifying the Treaty of Versailles was closed owing to the Hejaz no longer existing as a separate state.[64] In any case, a ten-year delay in ratification of the treaty by a state commonly thought to be within a British sphere of influence might produce considerable international resentment.[65]

This interpretation saved the British Government some embarrassing consequences from persevering with the concept of 'personal union'. Hitherto, not only had it been open for Ibn Saud to secure the admission of the Hejaz via the Treaty of Versailles, but he could also have taken out a fresh application for Nejd which, if successful, would have entitled him to two votes at Geneva. Britain henceforth treated Hejaz-Nejd as a single state for international purposes, if for no other reason than to guard against precipitate attempts by Ibn Saud to take the Hejaz into the League of Nations.[66]

Other, wider considerations also pointed to British reluctance to have Ibn Saud represented in the League. One of the requirements of membership was the prohibition of slavery. Despite a loose undertaking in the Treaty of Jedda to curtail the Arabian slave trade, Ibn Saud was rejecting any anti-slavery provisions in his proposed treaties with Italy and France.[67] Although the League stood in open condemnation of slavery, its stand on this cause had been somewhat weakened by the admission of certain slave-practising states – notably Abyssinia.[68] The inclusion of Hejaz-Nejd might, therefore, further hinder the aim of abolishing slavery.

The attitude of the League towards slavery had, moreover, been recently tightened, extending condemnation to include domestic slavery as well as slave-trading.[69] There was no realistic possibility of domestic Arabian slavery, which was at the root of the economic and social fabric of Arabian life, being abolished within the foreseeable future.[70] Having too many 'primitive' countries in the League would, consequently, serve to act against progressive measures and prove a source of weakness, not strength, to it.

Another of the League's requirements was that member-states possess agreed and stable frontiers. In 1930 Hejaz-Nejd was hardly so endowed, although Ibn Saud no longer opposed the principle of linear boundaries. Most of Hejaz-Nejd's inland frontiers were the subject of actual or potential dispute with Britain, with the exception of south-west Arabia where the frontier dispute lay with the Yemen. The most sensitive area of territorial friction between Britain and Hejaz-Nejd remained Aqaba and Maan. Ibn Saud had not raised that particular issue since acknowledging the territorial *status quo* in an exchange of notes appended to the Treaty of Jedda. Nor had the matter been raised at Geneva in connection with Britain's mandatory responsibilities for Transjordan. The British Government had no desire to see the Aqaba-Maan question raised in connection with a Saudi application for League membership, particularly as it was not prepared to give way on the matter.[71] Accordingly, it was felt safest to deny Ibn Saud an opportunity to embarrass Britain by dissuading any approach by him to the League. Rendel, less convinced, considered that territorial questions by themselves were insufficient to determine Britain's response.[72] More significant considerations, he felt, were those concerning Britain's imperial interests, and how they were likely to be affected by putting Britain's monopoly over such questions as the Middle Eastern air-route through the Gulf and health control for the Pilgrimage under League scrutiny.[73]

Ryan, in the second half of 1930, undertook a comprehensive assessment of the advantages and disadvantages of Saudi membership. He was less sceptical than the Foreign Office about the possible benefits of having the Saudi Kingdom within the League, both from the standpoint of Britain and of Hejaz-Nejd. What objections did exist were, felt Ryan, those from the standpoint of the League itself.[74] At first he considered Ibn Saud to be suspicious of the League, regarding it as a Christian European wolf disguised in harmless, international, sheep's clothing.[75] Ibn Saud knew nothing of the purposes of the League, the circumstances which had given rise to its creation, the moral ingredient that sustained it, or the intricacies of international affairs beyond the Arab world. He appeared to regard war as the natural concomitant of human existence. Perhaps he was prompted by questions of prestige, for no other Arab state had yet been admitted to the League, and also by the wish to advance the Saudi state in international terms, a process begun with British recognition and the exchange of diplomatic representation.

Ryan reckoned Ibn Saud's motives to be psychological rather than political. He wished, thought the British Minister, not so much to collaborate with other states through the medium of a world forum, as to escape from an international stigma of real or imagined inferiority.[76] Ibn Saud had shown little inclination to adopt basic European principles concerning the international responsibilities of succession states. Nor was there any evidence to suggest that he was anxious to increase the international connections of his Kingdom at that time. Hejaz-Nejd was not, for example, a party to the International Telegraph Convention, though Ibn Saud had sent a representative to, and later ratified, the Postal Union Congress held in London in 1929.[77] If Ibn Saud had ratified any other international agreements Ryan, in the absence of any reliable local official publications, did not know about them.[78]

Notwithstanding doubts over Saudi motivation for wanting to join the League, the British Minister outlined several advantages to be gained from Hejaz-Nejd membership. Britain's principal policy considerations *vis à vis* the League, namely disarmament and collective security, would not be affected either way,[79] although membership would expose Hejaz-Nejd to international standards on such questions as international aviation regulations.[80] Britain was attempting to establish an air route to the East which would take advantage of landing facilities not only across the mandates, but along the Arab littoral of the Gulf. An arrangement through the League's auspices whereby Britain could obtain facilities in Hasa was not one to be lightly overlooked, particularly with Ibn Saud's reticence on the matter when approached directly.[81] Similar assistance could have been won through the League on the delicate matter of international health control for the Pilgrimage, upon which the Hejaz-Nejd Government was not always cooperative.[82]

Ryan even found advantages in having Nejd within the League. The machinery at Geneva could be used to reduce tension along the Iraq-Nejd frontier, particularly if both states joined at the same time – Iraq being scheduled for admission in 1932. The Iraq-Nejd frontier question, taken with the matter of aerial bases in Hasa, led Ryan to suggest that, whereas the Hejaz was generally the less problematic part of Ibn Saud's dominions as regards membership, it was from the point of view of having Nejd within the League that Britain could reap the greater advantages.[83]

Then again, there was a further problem for a Labour Government to consider. Was it to the advantage of the League itself, despite vague ideals about embracing as many states as possible, to include Hejaz-Nejd within its ranks? The nature of modern state intercourse seemed totally inappropriate to Ibn Saud's bureaucratic structure, and the rigid enforcement of Koranic law.[84] The promotion of European 'civilisation' would hardly be furthered by Saudi membership.

Ryan's judgment, given at the end of October 1930, was to shelve the question and not refer to it unless specifically requested to do so by the Hejaz-Nejd Government.[85] To cater for present contingencies Ryan suggested informing the Saudi Government that Britain's basic attitude was in favour of Hejaz-Nejd membership of the League, while at the same time stressing the obstacles in the way of a successful application.[86] Prophetically, in the light of what was to happen two years later, Ryan mused that Ibn Saud might consider forming a single state for international purposes, rather than persist with the constitutionally confusing dual Kingdom of Hejaz-Nejd.[87]

The Foreign Office broadly concurred. Arthur Henderson, however, and his Under-Secretary, Hugh Dalton, preferred a less discouraging reply.[88] Other Middle Eastern states were enjoying British approval for their membership. Apart from Iraq, the candidatures of both Turkey and Afghanistan were being supported, in the case of the latter on no more substantial grounds than the desirability to expand membership of the League.[89] Ryan was instructed, in the spring of 1931, to adopt an attitude of guarded neutrality towards any firm overtures from the Hejaz-Nejd Government.[90]

In the event, circumstances combined to postpone further discussion of Hejaz-Nejd's candidature. The onset of the Depression in Europe brought about the fall of the Labour Government in the summer of 1931, and the arrival of the National Government. Although Ramsay MacDonald continued as Prime Minister, the arch-champion of the League, Arthur Henderson, and the bulk of Labour went into Opposition. Henderson was replaced as Foreign Secretary briefly by Lord Reading and then by Sir John Simon. Also in 1931, the Japanese invasion of Manchuria provided the League with the first of the eventually fatal threats to its international credibility.

In retrospect, never were conditions so favourable for the admission of the Saudi Kingdom into the League than in its halcyon days of 1929-30. Internationally, the prestige of the League was at its highest and, domestically, Britain witnessed her most pro-League Government and Foreign Secretary of the inter-war years. It is worth asking why the Labour Government did not do more to assist in bringing Hejaz-Nejd into the League, when its record in the Middle East had been a far-sighted one: the decision had been taken to end the mandate in Iraq, the League applications of Turkey and Afghanistan were being supported, and fresh initiatives pursued to find a new treaty with Egypt.

Part of the explanation lies with the complexities surrounding Hejaz-Nejd's constitutional identity as one state or two. In addition, a Government and Foreign Secretary so committed to the League would have faced competing obligations: what was good for Britain versus what was good for Geneva. The universal membership principle of the League competed with the need to strengthen its humanitarian goals, such as the abolition of slavery. Nejd appeared to be too backward to benefit either the League or itself by membership. There was also the technical problem of whether Ibn Saud could find sufficient educated bureaucrats to serve the interests of both Hejaz-Nejd and the League. Moreover, the views of the Foreign Secretary, on the one hand, and the British Minister and the Foreign Office, on the other, while not exactly out of step, probably delayed reaching agreement on promoting the candidature of Hejaz-Nejd. Finally, and perhaps decisively, Ibn Saud himself had still done no more than raise the question in general terms. He had made no firm move towards entry, and the British Government was hardly likely to raise his suspicions by attempting to foist entry upon his Kingdom.

Then again, there were British interests to be considered. Arguments in favour of membership, such as the increased likelihood of aerial facilities being constructed along the Gulf, competed with arguments against, notably the opening up of Arabia to European interest. The religious significance of the Hejaz meant that Saudi membership of a Christian-dominated League might have unforeseen ramifications throughout the Moslem parts of the Empire. Moreover, outright support of Hejaz-Nejd's candidature was, in itself, no guarantee of its success. Should the League reject it, on any of the various issues discussed above, then that decision would have been a snub to the British Government as much as to Ibn Saud. In such an eventuality he, being unfamiliar with the League's mechanisms, might have blamed Britain for his rejection, with consequent damage to Anglo-Saudi relations.

The Second Saudi Approach: Sir John Simon

Ibn Saud was too preoccupied with internal affairs to make further earnest representations about the League of Nations until 1933. Troubles across the Transjordanian frontier continued. The Depression had also reached Arabia in 1931 with the number of pilgrims falling by more than half in a single year.[91] This was a prominent period for Ibn Saud's involvement on the international plane. In 1931 Hejaz-Nejd had been invited to attend the League Conference at Geneva on narcotics, and had signed the resultant agreement.[92] In January 1932 Ibn Saud acceded to the Rome Convention on Health (1907) at Britain's suggestion.[93] In April he acceded to the Kellogg Pact of 1928 for the international renunciation of war.[94] In that same year, Ibn Saud was represented at the League Disarmament Conference, adhering to the proposed one-year armaments truce.[95] All this culminated in September, with the announcement that 'Hejaz-Nejd' was to become 'Saudi Arabia'. This act removed forthwith any debate about whether Ibn Saud ruled one state or two.

The Foreign Office's legal department was consulted to see if the new name raised any legalistic problems concerning Britain's commitments to Ibn Saud. It was established that the new name did not affect any existing treaties, obligations or contracts.[96] Nor was there felt to be any need for formal recognition of the new name. The most recent example of a similar occurrence had been in 1929, when the Serb-Croat-Slovene Kingdom had become Yugoslavia. On that occasion the British Government had not offered any further recognition in Belgrade.[97] The same applied to Saudi Arabia, personal congratulations to Ibn Saud from the British Minister being considered sufficient.[98]

1933 continued Ibn Saud's policy of gradually opening up his Kingdom to the wider world. The United States won an oil concession in May. In June/July he was represented by Sheikh Hafiz Wahba at the World Economic Conference in London. The Saudi Minister had already reopened the question of Saudi membership of the League of Nations, in March, with the Foreign Office.[99] This prompted a fresh examination of the whole question, against a background of Ibn Saud's concern over Italian warships then patrolling off Asir.

Britain's assessment of the merits of Saudi membership was different in 1933 from what it had been in 1930-31. On the one hand, the transformation of Hejaz-Nejd into Saudi Arabia had dispensed with the legalistic objections. The Hejaz in international terms had ceased to exist. If Saudi Arabia wanted to join the League a fresh application was needed. On the other hand, international developments had already begun to tarnish the League's image. Moreover, the Foreign Secretary, Sir John Simon, did not possess the dedication to the League that had been the hallmark of Arthur Henderson.

Simon was to remain as Foreign Secretary until June 1935. During the years 1931-35, which Baldwin and Churchill later described as 'years that the locust hath eaten'[100] – an admission of tragic lost opportunities – Britain's commitment to the League of Nations began to wane. Amid economic and political unrest in Europe, Britain adopted a deliberate, if cautious, tendency to minimise the obligations of League membership.[101] In 1933 Simon even raised doubts as to whether the British Government intended to fulfil its obligations both to the Covenant and to the Locarno Treaty.[102] Simon's contribution to the success of the League has been described as follows:

> The British Foreign Secretary [Simon] had ceased to be a guide or a leader, and had even become a source of discouragement and weakness. His predecessors had, generally speaking, identified the interests of their country with those of the League: to uphold the principles of the Covenant and to support the institutions of the League was for them to follow the central lines of British policy. Simon's view was, as it seemed, exactly opposite to this. To his mind it was dangerous to strengthen the League since this meant that his country would be tied all the more closely to the general commitments of membership. He preferred to consider each question in isolation and to determine what the particular British interest in regard to it might be. ... It was possible for him even in regard to questions of vital importance ... to separate the action of Britain as a Member of the League from her action as an

individual state. She might be compelled to take certain measures in virtue of the Covenant: if those measures failed, the failure would be that, not of Britain, but of the League, and its consequences would fall upon the League, and not on Britain.[103]

Of course, the reasons for Simon's disenchantment with the League lay not in the Middle East, but with a combination of events – the Japanese invasion of Manchuria, and the various political and military activities of France, Germany and Italy. Nonetheless, without the *esprit de corps* which Austen Chamberlain and Arthur Henderson fostered with regard to the League, it was clear that Simon's less developed sympathies could not but discourage an application for membership by a state possessing the international and domestic liabilities of Saudi Arabia.

Moreover, the difficulties connected with Saudi Arabia's tradition of slavery, together with hundreds of miles of undelimited or disputed frontiers, remained. Wahba insisted that the frontier with the Yemen was no longer in dispute, having been agreed with the Imam.[104] The area was so remote, however, that Britain had no independent source of confirmation, and events later that year showed that the frontier situation in south-west Arabia was far from settled.[105] The Italian Government, too, might have posed problems for Saudi admission by refusing to recognise the annexation of Asir. Iraq's admission, as it happened, had not been dependent upon actual delimitation of her frontiers.[106] Only France had raised the matter during Iraq's application, out of concern for the north-west frontier facing Syria.[107]

The Saudi-Transjordan frontier had become particularly contentious. The religious aspect of the Saudi claim to Aqaba, as constituting part of the Moslem Holy Land, meant that Ibn Saud could not publicly renounce his claims to the area. To make matters worse, disagreement was no longer confined to the Aqaba-Maan region. Mistakes had been discovered in the map co-ordinates specifying the frontier in the Hadda Agreement of 1925.[108] Britain feared that Ibn Saud might deliberately and publicly attempt to obtain a new demarcation of the frontier, thereby accusing Britain of maintaining an obstacle to Saudi Arabia's eligibility for League membership.[109]

On the equally sensitive problem of slavery, Wahba raised the precedent established by Abyssinia. He suggested that the suppression of slavery might be more easily tackled within the League than outside it.[110] Indeed, the precedent set by Abyssinia could not be ignored, for it had demonstrated that domestic slavery was not an insuperable obstacle to membership. All that had been necessary in order to procure Abyssinian membership was an expressed desire to proceed towards abolition with, if necessary, the League's assistance towards that end.[111] Abyssinia had been admitted to the League in the heady, optimistic days of 1923, largely as a result of French intrigue and in an atmosphere of sentimentality which characterised the League in its early years.[112] Since her admission, Abyssinia had signed but not ratified the Slavery Convention of 1926. Nor had any pressure been put upon Emperor Haile Selassie to do so.[113]

Nonetheless, it was felt that the League was likely to be less complacent about admitting a slave-practising state in 1933 than it had been ten years previously, particularly in the light of the religious sensitivities attending any Saudi application.[114] Saudi Arabia, in other words, was unlikely to get the support in Geneva in 1933 that Abyssinia had received in 1923, especially when it was inconceivable that Ibn Saud could, or would want to, abolish domestic Arabian slavery.[115] International scepticism of the League, following Abyssinia's successful application, had worked to undermine something of its moral standing, and the subsequent inability to induce Abyssinia to abolish slavery had lowered its stature still further.[116] In any case, Saudi Arabia would also have to contend with the planned creation, in 1934, of a new Permanent Commission on Slavery designed to avoid previous laxity in that respect.[117]

Once again the Foreign Office was concerned not so much with technical aspects of Saudi membership as with whether her entry was in Britain's interest. Saudi Arabia's admission would bring with it exposure to all manner of commissions of enquiry on various subjects.[118] Italy might have been particularly prone to embarrass Saudi Arabia in order to demonstrate her loyalty to the Imam.[119]

It remained doubtful whether in 1933 the international attention which would befall Saudi Arabia in the wake of League membership would be politically advantageous to Britain. The more that the outside world and its institutions were kept out of Saudi Arabia's affairs the easier it was for Britain to retain her paramount influence with Ibn Saud, and overcome the numerous possible sources of friction along his frontiers. In sum, anything that threatened to intrude upon the British special relationship with Ibn Saud, including the League of Nations, was best avoided.[120]

Furthermore, although the Foreign Office was relatively assured of the durability of the Saudi regime, the Colonial Office and India Office remained of the opinion that what stability Saudi Arabia then enjoyed was unlikely to survive the death of the present king.[121] All departments were agreed that Saudi membership might turn out useful in the event, likely or otherwise, of an imminent end to Ibn Saud's rule. The League could then be called upon to prevent other powers encroaching upon Saudi Arabia and undermining Britain's pre-eminence in the peninsula.[122]

There were signs, too, that a successful Saudi application might lead to resentment elsewhere. Discontent in Egypt might multiply. There was not any popular movement in Egypt towards the League at the time, yet Egyptian sensibilities would be further aggravated if the comparatively uncultured Saudi state could take a seat at Geneva while a country with Egypt's heritage was denied a voice in world affairs. There were, therefore, grounds for Britain avoiding anything which might further hinder her delicate relations with King Fuad and the Wafd Party.[123]

The Egyptian argument was somewhat neutralised by the experiences of two other Middle Eastern states, Iraq and Persia. Both countries had considerably strengthened their international position by joining the League – Persia at its inception, Iraq in 1932.[124] Saudi Arabia had potential sources of dispute with both states which could disrupt British imperial interests. Any such conflicts would be more manageable and less damaging to Britain's position in the Middle East if all parties to them were under the aegis of the League of Nations.[125]

The outcome of this second comprehensive investigation into the desirability of Saudi Arabia's admission to the League was a flat rejection, much less equivocal than during 1930-31. The general case against influencing Ibn Saud to apply in 1933 was considered 'extremely strong'.[126] When issues of a technical nature, such as slavery and problematical frontiers, were set aside and the question posed solely in political terms, the balance of argument seemed clearly in favour of keeping Saudi Arabia out of the League, or at least doing nothing to help her to get in. In the last resort Britain felt that she could get a better deal from Saudi Arabia through bilateral relations than through the cumbrous machinery at Geneva.[127]

The principle of previous British Governments, and of the League, of seeking to make membership as universal as possible had, in the face of the Depression, disarmament, and the militarisation of Europe in the early 1930s, rather less impact than in earlier, more idealistic, periods. The League no longer stood as the panacea of international ills. The British Government was disinclined to run after states to induce them to join.[128] Mexico, in 1931, had become the first new state to enter the League for five years.[129] That, in itself, was something of a snub for Britain who, together with the United States, had managed to exclude Mexico from the list of original members, disapproving of the Mexican Government of the day.[130] Her admission had opened the flood-gates, and five further states had been admitted within the following three years, three of them (Turkey, Iraq and Afghanistan) from the Middle East.[131] Britain, having been badly bitten by the Mexico experience, was therefore less inclined to strongly influence the League one way or another in regard to future admissions.[132]

In the light of the arguments as they appeared in 1933, the Foreign Office felt that it should adopt an attitude of rigid neutrality, giving the Saudi Government such information as it requested, but offering no definite lead in either direction. Britain hoped to refrain from anything that could be interpreted as a snub, but would not minimise the obstacles impeding Saudi admission, nor do anything to force the pace of her candidature.[133] The British Government, it is true, was not in the habit of promising states support in advance but, in May 1933, Wahba asked directly whether a Saudi application would be viewed favourably by Britain.[134] He received a stalling answer; that it was better to await developments on Saudi Arabia's frontiers.[135] This reply would, it was half hoped, make Ibn Saud more amenable to a final settlement of the Saudi-Transjordan frontier.[136]

The Foreign Office decision not to encourage Saudi candidature in any way was conveyed in May 1933.[137] It was vindicated by events across the Arabian peninsula over the succeeding months. Also in May, an American oil company won a major concession in eastern Saudi Arabia. Although it was not appreciated at the time, hindsight showed there to be a considerable discrepancy between discouraging League of Nations access to Saudi Arabia, while acquiescing in American economic access. In addition, major disturbances in the newly independent Iraq involving the Assyrian minority had led to mass killings which provoked accusations from League quarters that Britain had abandoned her mandate before it was fully mature.[138] The League had given Iraq's admission a cool reception, harbouring doubts for the well-being of minorities, and being sceptical about the political administration and social progress of the country prior to 1932.[139] The Council of the League compelled Iraq to sign a declaration guaranteeing minority rights and her adherence to international law.[140]

Furthermore, tension between Saudi Arabia and the Yemen broke out into open war early in 1934, and the entire basis of Saudi Arabia's eastern frontiers with the Trucial states was thrown into question at the same time.[141] These developments would inevitably have made the British Government even more reluctant to sanction Saudi admission to the League. Fortunately, they also served to concentrate Ibn Saud's attention firmly on Arabian affairs so that until 1935 there were no more serious questions asked about the League.

The Third Saudi Approach: Hoare and Eden

In the latter half of 1935 further enquiries were put out by the Saudi Government, and Nuri al Said, the Iraqi Foreign Minister, let it be known that his Government was prepared to support Saudi Arabia's candidature.[142] The motive behind Iraq's interest in Saudi membership of the League had its roots in pan-Arabism.[143] The Saudi Government pointed to anti-slavery measures being introduced as part of the revision of the Treaty of Jedda, stating that it would invoke the precedent established by Abyssinia and Afghanistan.[144]

Before the end of the year developments in the Red Sea ensured that Saudi Arabia's renewed interest in the League was less pan-Arab and increasingly European in emphasis. As Ibn Saud watched Mussolini's threats to Abyssinia turn into invasion in the autumn of 1935, he sought further reassurances from Britain that, should Italy menace Saudi Arabia, Ibn Saud could count on material assistance. He also enquired whether the League would give him the support which, at that time, Abyssinia seemed to be enjoying.[145]

Partly to assuage Saudi anxieties Ryan was authorised to reveal confidentially to the Saudi Government Paragraphs 2-4 of the 1927 Rome Agreement, which dealt with the relevant aspects of Ibn Saud's fears.[146]

Doubtless this revelation unwittingly did more to convince Ibn Saud of Anglo-Italian machinations than reassure him of British goodwill. Otherwise, Ryan gently reminded the Saudi Government that, although the new domestic slavery regulations were sufficient to justify Britain renouncing her right to manumit Arabian slaves, they would not satisfy the League.[147]

In November, the Co-ordination Committee at Geneva requested that Saudi Arabia adhere to the policy of sanctions just adopted against Italy in response to the invasion of Abyssinia.[148] After some delay the Saudi Government, having consulted Ryan, replied that it could not assist the League without sacrificing its desire to be on equally good terms with both Italy and Abyssinia.[149] Saudi Arabia declared herself bound by two paramount considerations. First, because of her unique religious responsibilities, she was obliged to maintain friendly and stable relations with all neighbouring countries.[150] Second, she was anxious to support any measures designed to promote world peace. As, however, Saudi Arabia was not a member of the League, she considered that her participation in economic sanctions would involve heavy responsibilities without the privileges and advantages conferred on members.[151] All things considered, Saudi Arabia would observe a policy of strict neutrality in the conflict unless specific measures were adopted to grant non-member states the same rights and privileges as those accorded to member states.[152] Ryan anticipated that Ibn Saud would demand the recompense of financial losses incurred if he did impose sanctions, and possibly a pledge of League support should Italy retaliate against Saudi Arabia in any way.[153] The British Government was quite content with this outcome. It had already decided against coercing the Gulf states into applying sanctions, and felt that little could be gained and much lost by trying to bring Saudi Arabia into the sanctions policy.[154]

By early 1936 League circles were hinting at rumours of Saudi Arabia's impending application.[155] The Saudi Government showed signs of being prepared to contribute to the work of the Disarmament Conference.[156] Unfortunately, by having the attention of the League focussed on Abyssinia, that attention was also focussed, indirectly, on slavery. Ryan, as he had done six years previously, saw arguments for Britain to support Saudi Arabia's candidature. He suggested that, in view of the crisis of confidence which the League was experiencing, it could conceivably reap much needed prestige from a fresh application, from whatever source.[157]

The Foreign Office was disinclined to revise its earlier judgment. It was feared that once the Abyssinian crisis passed and Saudi Arabia lost her fear of Italian aggression she would, if a member, be tempted to use the League to obtain favourable settlement of her territorial difficulties with Britain.[158] More generally, the Foreign Office thought that Ryan underestimated the League's embarrassment in having backward and under-developed countries within its ranks.[159] Nor did the Foreign Office consider it advisable to make British support dependent on prior settlement of slavery and frontier questions, as had happened with Iraq. Such a policy would have committed Britain to endorsing Saudi Arabia's application, which might even then be rejected – to the detriment of Anglo-Saudi relations.[160] The new Foreign Secretary, Anthony Eden, informed Ryan that British policy remained unchanged, the Italo-Abyssinian war having emphasised the folly of including backward states within the League.[161]

Eden's flat rejection marked the last occasion on which the issue of Saudi membership of the League was raised. The fate of Abyssinia, annexed by Italy in May 1936, may well have caused Ibn Saud to ponder the worth of joining an organisation which appeared powerless against the very state he feared most. In his eyes Britain and the League had probably abandoned Abyssinia to her fate.[162] Moreover, he would have seen in this not a failure of Britain's or the League's ability to support Abyssinia, but of their will to do so.[163] Ryan felt that Ibn Saud interpreted events not so much as a war between Italy and Abyssinia, but as a wider struggle between Italy and Britain for supremacy in the Red Sea. This struggle Italy appeared to be winning, shaking the prestige of both Britain and the League in the process.[164] Both had shown themselves incapable of resisting Italian aggression in the Red Sea, first with regard to the Yemen, and now Abyssinia.

As Ibn Saud dared not turn openly against either Britain or Italy he began to expound the new policy of Saudi Arabia's 'neutrality'.[165] During the course of 1936 Saudi interest turned from the League of Nations to a series of bilateral treaties with neighbouring states. By 1937 Sir Reader Bullard, Ryan's successor as Minister in Jedda, reported that, if Ibn Saud ever held any desire to join the League of Nations, that desire had disappeared.[166] At the birth of the League the only Moslem state represented was Persia: by 1939 the only independent Middle Eastern state not represented was Saudi Arabia.[167]

Summary and Conclusions

The issue of Saudi membership of the League of Nations revealed perceptible differences in the attitudes of the Labour Government through its Foreign Secretary, Arthur Henderson, and the National Governments of the 1930s. Those differences were blurred by the contrasting international circumstances attending the League over the period of Saudi interest. The pro-League Labour Government of 1930 had the extra advantage of handling Ibn Saud's enquiries at a time when the prestige of the League was at its height. Later Foreign Secretaries, with less personal commitment to the League, had to consider Saudi Arabia's expressed interest against the background of international circumstances which saw the League decline from its highest standing in 1929-30 to its lowest ebb in 1936. From that year the League no longer counted in European affairs.[168]

Britain held the key where Saudi membership was concerned. Ibn Saud's ignorance of the League's functions meant that he was bound to consult the outside power with which he was most familiar. Not surprisingly, perhaps,

Britain considered the merits of Saudi membership more from the perspective of her own benefits than those of Saudi Arabia or the League itself. It was admitted that there were several benefits to be gained from the standpoint of Saudi Arabia, the Arab world as a whole, and the universal membership principle of the League. It was the political risks to Britain which carried most weight.

As the candidature of Iraq, Turkey and even Afghanistan had met with British approval it ought to be asked why it was preferred that Saudi Arabia remain outside the League. A provisional answer must suggest that the League was threatening to intrude upon Britain's sphere of influence over Arabia. Certain territorial disputes, notably over Aqaba and Maan, and later in south-east Arabia, found Britain admitting a weakness in her position according to international law. These problems, it was felt, were best kept away from the scrutiny of the League which, after all, was specially designed to settle frontier disputes.

Critics of Britain's policy could point to an almost nineteenth-century attitude of trying to exclude all outside influences from a declared sphere of influence, in this case Arabia, and protecting what prestige she felt she possessed by enforcing and exploiting a political vacuum into which no outside power or institution could intrude. Similarly, few of the internationalist ideals which Britain had invested in the League were evident during the period of Saudi enquiry. Whether or not Britain, in the last analysis, was primarily responsible for keeping Saudi Arabia out of the League, cannot be answered. Ibn Saud's interest died of its own accord. Nonetheless, this particular episode provides the firmest indication so far of Britain's 'Monroe Doctrine' as it applied to Saudi Arabia.

REFERENCES FOR CHAPTER SEVEN

1. Note the anomalies in the case of Iraq on page 95.
2. See Warner (FO) minute, 16 August 1930, FO E/4310/1409/91: 371/14478; FO/4920/4920/91: 371/13741.
3. ibid.
4. H.R. Winkler, 'The Development of the League of Nations Idea in Great Britain 1914-1919', *Journal of Modern History*, June 1948, p.95.
5. ibid.
6. ibid.
7. ibid., p.97.
8. Reynolds, pp.8-9.
9. Winkler, op. cit., pp.106, 108-9.
10. ibid., p.105.
11. ibid., p.111.
12. Alfred Zimmern, *The League of Nations and the Rule of Law 1918-1935*; pp.280-1.
13. ibid., p.282.

14. F.S. Northedge, *The Troubled Giant*, p. 119.
15. Viscount Cecil, *A Great Experiment*, p. 97.
16. Zimmern, p. 339.
17. ibid., p. 323.
18. ibid., pp. 327-8.
19. Paul M. Kennedy, 'The Tradition of Appeasement in British Foreign Policy' in *British Journal of International Studies*, 2 (1976), p. 204.
20. ibid., p. 207.
21. Northedge, op. cit., p. 231.
22. ibid., pp. 231-2.
23. ibid.
24. Zimmern, p. 328.
25. See James Morris: *Farewell the Trumpets*, p. 211.
26. The bulk of the post-war Tory MPs came from the commercial classes, replacing the old land-owning generation of Conservatives. The extreme right of the Party, in particular, was violently hostile to the League, refusing to endorse any move to assist in banning war. (Cecil, pp. 102, 189).
27. ibid., pp. 146, 196.
28. Curzon to Hankey, April 1919, in Roskill, pp. 65-6. Neither Baldwin nor Curzon ever visited the League at Geneva.
29. Northedge, op. cit., p. 118.
30. Cecil, p. 163.
31. ibid., pp. 163, 293.
32. ibid., pp. 156, 161.
33. Mary Agnes Hamilton, *Arthur Henderson*, p. 209.
34. Roskill, p. 363.
35. The Geneva Protocol was finally rejected by the Baldwin Government.
36. He held both positions in 1924.
37. Henry R. Winkler, 'Arthur Henderson' in Craig and Gilbert, p. 311.
38. Cecil, p. 206.
39. Hamilton, op. cit., pp. 295-304.
40. ibid.
41. ibid., pp. 312-3.
42. Winkler, op. cit., p. 312. Henderson's uneasy relationship with Ramsay MacDonald meant that, in effect, Britain had two foreign policies between 1929-31, with MacDonald keeping firm control of Anglo-American relations in his own hands.
43. ibid., p. 342.
44. Mary Agnes Hamilton, *Beatrice and Sidney Webb*, p. 269.
45. ibid., p. 274.
46. George Woodcock, *Who Killed the British Empire?*, p. 243.
47. Roskill, p. 195.
48. Gordon A. Craig, 'The British Foreign Office from Grey to Austen Chamberlain', in Craig and Gilbert, p. 40.
49. ibid.
50. Henderson to Ryan, No 137, 8 April 1931, FO E/584/584/25: 371/15297.
51. Henderson to House of Commons, 17 March 1930, FO E/1409/1409/91: 371/14478.
52. ibid.
53. Beckett (FO legal adviser) minute, 4 November 1930, FO E/4310/1409/91: 371/14478.
54. ibid.
55. Rendel minute, 15 March 1930, FO E/1409/1409/91: 371/14478.
56. ibid.
57. Beckett minute, 4 November 1930, FO E/4310/1409/91: 371/14478.
58. Warner (FO) minute, 1 April 1930, FO E/1762/1409/91: 371/14478.
59. See FO E/4310/1409/91: 371/14478.
60. Beckett minute, 4 November 1930, FO E/4310/1409/91: 371/14478.
61. ibid.
62. ibid.
63. ibid.
64. ibid.

65. Malkins (FO) minute, 4 November 1930, ibid. The British Government feared to antagonise other member states at that time in view of its hopes of ending German reparations.
66. ibid.
67. Rendel minute, 29 October 1930, FO E/4310/1409/91: 371/14478.
68. ibid.
69. ibid.
70. ibid.
71. Malkins minute, 4 November 1930, ibid.
72. Rendel minute, 28 January 1931, FO E/584/584/25: 371/15297.
73. ibid.
74. ibid.
75. Ryan minute, 30 October 1930, FO E/4310/1409/91: 371/14478.
76. Annual Report 1930.
77. ibid.
78. ibid.
79. Rendel minute, 29 October 1930, FO E/4310/1409/91: 371/14478.
80. ibid.
81. ibid. For more on the air route, see Chapter Nine.
82. ibid.
83. ibid.
84. Rendel minute, 15 March 1930, FO E/1409/1409/91: 371/14478.
85. Ryan minute, 30 October 1930, FO E/4310/1409/91: 371/14478.
86. ibid.
87. ibid.
88. Henderson to Ryan, No 137, 8 April 1931, FO E/584/584/25: 371/15297; Rendel minute, 10 March 1933, FO E/1210/840/25: 371/16875.
89. ibid.
90. ibid.
91. Annual Report 1932.
92. M. Al Jazairi, 'Saudi Arabia: A Diplomatic History' (Unpublished Ph.D.), p. 185.
93. Annual Report 1932.
94. ibid.
95. Al Jazairi, p. 185.
96. FO minute, 26 September 1932, FO E/4847/1484/25: 371/16025.
97. ibid.
98. Oliphant to Hope Gill (Jedda), 26 September 1932, ibid.
99. Wahba conversation Oliphant, 3 March 1933, FO E/1210/840/25: 371/16875.
100. David Thomson, *England in the Twentieth Century*, p. 151.
101. F.P. Walters, *A History of the League of Nations, Vol II*, p. 543. Nonetheless, as late as April 1936 a secret FO memorandum acknowledged that the Covenant of the League of Nations constituted Britain's principal foreign commitment (DBFP, Series 1A, Vol 1, pp. 846-81).
102. Walters, op. cit., p. 543.
103. ibid., pp. 612-13.
104. Wahba conversation Oliphant, 3 March 1933, FO E/1210/840/25: 371/16875.
105. See Chapter Six.
106. Warner minute, 9 March 1933, FO E/1210/840/25: 371/16875.
107. Rendel minute, 10 March 1933, ibid.
108. Warner minute, op. cit.
109. ibid.
110. Wahba conversation Oliphant, op. cit.
111. Warner minute, 9 March 1933, FO E/1210/840/25: 371/16875.
112. Peterson (FO) minute, 11 March 1933, ibid.
113. ibid. It had been left to the Anti-Slavery Society at a later date, to elicit from him the undertaking that slavery would be abolished – but only within fifteen to twenty years.
114. ibid.
115. ibid.
116. Peterson minute, 11 March 1933, ibid.
117. ibid.

118. Warner minute, 9 March 1933, ibid.
119. ibid.
120. ibid.
121. Rendel minute, 10 March 1933, ibid.
122. ibid.
123. Peterson minute, 11 March 1933, ibid.
124. Rendel minute, 13 March 1933, ibid.
125. ibid.
126. ibid.
127. Howard-Smith (FO) minute, 13 March 1933, ibid.
128. ibid.
129. Walters, Vol I, p. 462.
130. ibid., pp. 37-8, 462.
131. ibid., Vol II, pp. 562-3.
132. Howard-Smith minute, 13 March 1933, FO E/1210/840/25: 371/16875.
133. Rendel minute, 13 March 1933, ibid. Should Saudi Arabia have decided to press ahead for entry, the British Government did not consider itself justified in actually discouraging her candidature.
134. Wahba conversation Oliphant, 11 May 1933, FO E/2491/840/25: 371/16875.
135. ibid.
136. Rendel minute, 14 May 1933, ibid.
137. FO to Ryan, No 124, 12 May 1933, ibid.
138. Walters, Vol II, p. 563.
139. Sir Reader Bullard, *Britain and the Middle East – From the Earliest Times to 1950*, p. 111. (Hereafter: *Britain ...*)
140. ibid.
141. See Chapter Nine.
142. FO memorandum, 30 July 1935, FO E/4666/4666/25: 371/19019.
143. See Chapter Ten.
144. Ryan to Eden, Annual Report for 1935, 29 February 1936, FO E/1538/1538/25: 371/20064. (Hereafter: Annual Report 1935).
145. ibid.; Calvert to FO, No 210, 11 November 1935, FO E/6674/5599/25: 371/19020.
146. Annual Report 1935.
147. ibid. These regulations prohibited the importation of slaves by sea, and also by land unless proof could be produced that the victim had also been a slave in the country of his origin at the time of the introduction of the regulations. No free person could be enslaved in Saudi Arabia. (Annual Report 1936).
148. Calvert to FO, No 210, 11 November 1935, FO E/6674/5599/25: 371/19020.
149. Ryan to FO, No 24, 18 February 1936, FO E/894/56/25: 371/20056.
150. ibid.
151. ibid.
152. ibid.
153. ibid.
154. FO minute, 12 November 1935, FO E/6674/5599/25: 371/19020.
155. FO minute, 18 November 1936, FO E/894/56/25: 371/20056.
156. ibid.
157. Ryan to FO, 3 January 1936, FO E/81/57/25: 371/20057.
158. Ward (FO) minute, 7 January 1936, ibid.
159. Rendel minute, 9 January 1936, FO E/81/57/25: 371/20057.
160. ibid.
161. Eden to Ryan, 6 February 1936, ibid.
162. Bullard to Eden, Annual Report for 1936, 28 February 1937, FO E/1637/1637/25: 371/20843. (Hereafter: Annual Report 1936).
163. ibid.
164. ibid.
165. Ryan to FO, 17 May 1936, FO E/3322/56/25: 371/20056.
166. Bullard to Halifax, Annual Report for 1937, 26 March 1938, FO E/2338/2338/25: 371/21908. (Hereafter: Annual Report 1937).
167. RIIA, *Political and Strategic Interests ...*, p. 172.
168. Northedge, *The Troubled Giant*, p. 408.

CHAPTER EIGHT

British Foreign Policy and Arabian Oil

The tasks of this chapter are twofold: first, to introduce for the first time in this study the oil factor in British policy towards Saudi Arabia; second, to continue the examination of Britain's response to external stimuli intruding into her Arabian 'Monroe Doctrine'. It had been widely presumed that Saudi Arabia's only plentiful resource was sand. There had seemed little incentive to tempt foreign commerce in economic speculation in such an unwelcoming territory. That this assumption should prove to have been, with hindsight, perhaps the most significant oversight in the history of British involvement in the Middle East provides the necessity for this chapter. Today, Saudi Arabia is synonymous with oil. That oil was discovered and exploited not by Britain, the one outside power with whom Ibn Saud had any degree of contact or familiarity, but by the United States, whose prior involvement in the affairs of the Middle East had been negligible.[1]

The History of Middle Eastern Oil prior to 1933

Oil is, in essence, a twentieth century resource. Before 1900 oil was exploited in only a handful of places, such as Russia and the Dutch East Indies. The United States was the early leader of the petroleum industry.[2] Furthermore, hyper-sensitivity relating to oil is a post-World War Two phenomenon. In the modern world oil has taken on political dimensions quite out of keeping with its influence earlier this century. The popular association of the Middle East with oil is also largely a post-1945 development. The period under investigation is free from the political and economic pressures operating in the current climate of OPEC diplomacy. A few statistics will illustrate the point (see next page):[3]

Oil companies have traditionally operated as private ventures in the capitalist-orientated world. Oil was, at least in the 1920s and '30s, of little concern to governments except in certain circumstances, such as in times of political uncertainty or upheaval when they felt they could no longer leave oil supplies to the vagaries of purely market forces or possible dislocation from foreign companies or governments. Sensitive strategic interests in a

WORLD OIL PRODUCTION
(million tonnes)

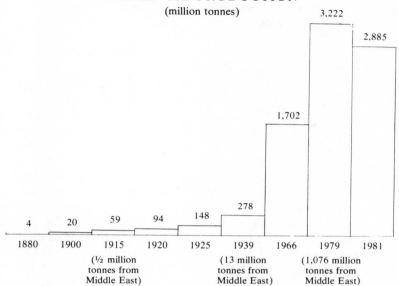

4	20	59	94	148	278	1,702	3,222		2,885
1880	1900	1915	1920	1925	1939	1966	1979	1981	

(½ million tonnes from Middle East)   (13 million tonnes from Middle East)   (1,076 million tonnes from Middle East)

SAUDI OIL PRODUCTION
(million tonnes)

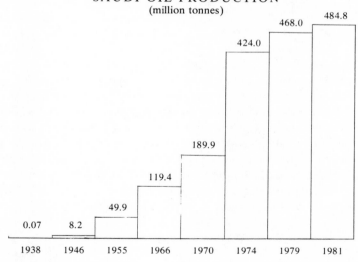

0.07	8.2	49.9	119.4	189.9	424.0	468.0	484.8
1938	1946	1955	1966	1970	1974	1979	1981

Sources: Longrigg, *Oil ...,* p. 48
   Christopher Tugendhat, *Oil: the Biggest Business,* p. 308
   BP Statistical Review of the World Oil Industry 1979
   Council for the Advancement of Arab-British Understanding, Teacher's Notes,
      'Saudi Arabia'
   Petroleum Economist April 1982

particular area, for instance along Britain's route to India, could also lead to governmental pressure on behalf of its private oil interests.[4] By and large, while governments appreciated the importance of oil, they were reluctant, under normal circumstances, to play an active role in its development.

The British Government was the first to intervene in the business of government oil shareholding. Oil possesses many advantages over coal, such as ease of handling, cleanliness, thermal efficiency and versatility.[5] In the years before 1914 the Royal Navy gradually changed the primary fuel of its ships from coal to oil.[6] This innovation had obvious political implications. At the time, the world oil market was effectively monopolised by American and Dutch concerns, yet the switch in naval fuel could only operate effectively if the Admiralty could guarantee its own oil supplies. There was, however, no appreciable oil anywhere in the British Empire.[7]

The Middle East had long been recognised as a potentially lucrative yielder of oil. Persia was the first country to repay that optimism. In 1912, when the recently formed Anglo-Persian Oil Company (APOC) was under full production with a completed pipeline and refinery,[8] a Royal Commission decreed that the supply of Persian oil to the Admiralty could best be guaranteed through direct British representation in the company.[9] Early in 1914 the Treasury duly acquired 51 per cent of APOC's shares.[10] This link between government and private enterprise would not be overlooked during the quest for the Saudi concession almost twenty years later.

The threat of war stimulated further governmental initiatives over Middle Eastern oil. In the Arabian Gulf, for example, fears about the Berlin-Baghdad railway proposals encouraged the Government of India to prohibit the Sheikhs of Kuwait and Bahrain from granting oil concessions without prior British consent.[11] The treaty with Ibn Saud, in 1915, contained no specific mention of oil. He pledged in general terms not to grant concessions of any kind to foreign nationals except with British concurrence.[12] The War emphasised to all governments the importance of oil. Developments in the internal combustion engine and the expansion of industry and mechanised transport ensured the intensification of the post-War search for commercially viable petroleum deposits in the Middle East.[13] With the dissolution of the Ottoman and German Empires, together with the internal distractions in Russia, the exploitation of potential Middle Eastern oilfields lay largely with Britain, whose oil companies began to enter the industry on a scale which seriously challenged American leadership.[14]

Previously, the United States had taken little interest in oil exploration in the Middle East, far away from her immediate strategic concerns. Pre-War optimism about domestic supplies was replaced by alarm that her wartime generosity had depleted her own reserves. The United States may not have harboured political ambitions in the Middle East but as regards oil hers became a persistent pressure. Renewed emphasis was placed on the principle of the 'Open Door', through which the United States Government, under considerable pressure from American oil companies,[15] insisted upon

equal rights for American overseas enterprises, even in dependent territories such as the mandates.[16]

The years 1927-28 were significant ones in the history of Middle Eastern
oil. In 1927 a massive strike was made in Mosul. Such was its size that the
Turkish Petroleum Company, in which 50 per cent of the shares were
British, abandoned for some years all its operations elsewhere.[17] British oil
interests now owned the major stake in the oil reserves of both Persia and
Iraq. At the same time, American pressure had been reduced owing to
substantial domestic finds in Oklahoma, Texas, Louisiana and California.[18]
Nonetheless, now that British supplies were secure, United States participation was invited in Turkish Petroleum. In July 1928 the management of Iraqi
oil passed to a new consortium, which was renamed the following year as the
Iraq Petroleum Company (IPC). The ownership of this consortium was as
follows:[19]

23¾% D'Arcy Exploration Co. (APOC Group)	British owned
23¾% Anglo-Saxon Petroleum Co.	
(Royal Dutch Shell group)	60% Dutch: 40% British
23¾% Compagnie Française des Pétroles	French owned
23¾% Near East Development Co.	American owned
5% Participation and Investment Co.	Calouste Gulbenkian
	(Armenian entrepreneur)

Although the international composition of the company had been
widened, British interests still predominated. APOC held 23¾% of the
company's shares. Royal Dutch Shell held another 23¾%, of which British
shares amounted to 40%. The total British shareholding in Iraq Petroleum
was, therefore, over 33%. Furthermore, the company was technically
British. Its convention stipulated that it must be registered in Britain, and its
chairman must be a British subject.[20]

The real significance of this new consortium lay not so much in its international character as in the restrictive practice operated by the company and
to which the American companies now adhered. This became known as the
Red Line agreement.[21] The 'Red Line' encircled the Arabian Peninsula, the
Fertile Crescent and Turkey. Egypt, Kuwait and the Farasan Islands lay
outside the line, but the Kuwait-Nejd neutral zone and Bahrain lay within it.
The purpose of the agreement was to prevent all participating companies in
the consortium from seeking consessions within the Red Line independently. Such concessions would have to be won either for the consortium or else
by non-participating companies. The motive was to eliminate competition
among the owners of Iraq Petroleum in the development of Middle Eastern
oil resources, and by so doing collectively brush aside the Open Door
philosophy. As the United States was now inside, there was no longer any
need for an Open Door. As Elizabeth Monroe put it: 'A door that is open
always feels more open to those inside than those outside it'.[22]

There followed a lull in the interest taken in Middle Eastern oil. World oil supplies, by the end of the decade, outstripped demand. The onset of the Depression added to the general inactivity. The oil question did not come alive again until 1932-33 when it did so on three fronts: Iran (Persia), Bahrain and Saudi Arabia. As far as British attention was concerned, it was with Iran that developments were of most importance. The rich benefits accruing to APOC after the First World War had led to the concession being renegotiated in Persia's favour in 1920. But the changed circumstances of the following decade, and the arrival of Reza Khan, produced friction between host government and company. By 1930 Iran had become the fourth largest world oil producer, after the United States, the Soviet Union and Venezuela.[23] Further negotiation proved unsuccessful and in December 1932 the Iranian Government cancelled the concession. The matter was referred to the League of Nations, although in April 1933 APOC signed a fresh agreement with the Iranian Government.[24]

Developments of a different kind were taking place some four hundred miles south of the Iranian oilfields, in Bahrain. A central figure in these developments was Major Frank Holmes. A New Zealander, Holmes represented the Eastern and General Syndicate, which sought Middle Eastern oil concessions in order to sell them to major oil companies. In 1922 Holmes had been in attendance upon Sir Percy Cox and Ibn Saud during the Kuwait-Nejd frontier negotiations. The following year he secured a concession from Ibn Saud for some 30,000 square miles of Hasa in return for an annual rental of £2,000 for the prospecting rights.[25] Before his conquest of the Hejaz Ibn Saud did not have to concern himself with Moslem opinion regarding concessions to infidels. Holmes attempted, unsuccessfully, to sell the concession to various oil companies.[26] He defaulted on the third and subsequent annual payments and, in 1928, Ibn Saud cancelled the concession.

Holmes was to have better luck elsewhere. In 1924 he won concession rights for the Kuwait-Nejd neutral zone, which also in time lapsed, but the following year received from the Sheikh of Bahrain an exclusive exploration permit for the archipelago, plus an option on any further concession. It will be recalled that, in 1914, the Sheikh of Bahrain had agreed not to award concessions to foreign concerns without the concurrence of the British Government. In accordance with this stipulation Holmes tried to interest both APOC and Shell in his Bahrain concession. In 1926 APOC geologists, after exploring Bahrain, advised the company that neither it nor the Hasa mainland was likely to contain oil-bearing strata.[27] British interest in Bahrain oil evaporated henceforth.

Finally, by a tortuous route, the Bahrain concession passed to Standard Oil of California (SOCAL) in December 1928. In order to circumvent the restrictions placed on the nationality clause, agreement was reached between the Colonial Office and the American State Department for a specially designated, Canadian-registered company, the Bahrain Petroleum Company (BAPCO), which was established in 1930.[28] BAPCO was simply a wholly-owned subsidiary of SOCAL. The discovery of large quantities of oil in Bahrain in May 1932, only twenty miles from Hasa, provided the touch-paper for interest in Saudi oil.

Philby

At this juncture it is necessary to introduce a new factor, both in the quest for the Saudi oil concession and in Anglo-Saudi relations generally – Harry St John Bridger Philby. His impact on Britain's understanding of Arabia is immense. Much of our knowledge of the peninsula's history, geography, and animal and plant life is due to the efforts and enterprise of Philby. When he died, in 1960, he had known Arabia for over forty years. Scholarship in many fields is indebted to Philby, but it is important to assess his impact on British policy towards Saudi Arabia.[29]

Philby was an adventurer. He was, for example, determined to become the first westerner to cross the Rub al Khali, and to gain a foothold in Arabia he set up in Jedda, in 1926, a branch of a British trading company known as Sharqieh (Eastern) Ltd.[30] He obtained a contract from Standard Oil for marketing kerosene and petroleum in the Hejaz, sold a few Ford cars, and dabbled in cranes, cables, and iron piping. For some years Philby, confined to Jedda, saw Ibn Saud only infrequently. The King had problems placating his Moslem critics and suppressing the *Ikhwan* rebellion. Besides, Philby had the religious barrier to overcome. As a non-Moslem he was not only confined to Jedda; he could not be truly integrated into Arab ways. Realising that his business and personal opportunities were hindered by his confinement to Jedda, in 1930 he took the unusual step for a westerner at that time of becoming a Moslem.[31] From that date he was admitted to Ibn Saud's private *majlis*.

Philby's burning ambition remained to cross the Rub al Khali, but Ibn Saud balked at offending Moslem opinion by granting permission. Few Arabs took Philby's conversion seriously.[32] In January 1932, how-ever, Philby set out on the desert crossing that would bring him inter-national acclaim. Returning to London, he was approached in July by Francis B. Loomis, a former American Under Secretary of State, who was then an executive of SOCAL. Loomis wanted to discuss Saudi oil in view of the find in Bahrain.[33] This meeting was to lead, a year later, to the disposal of the Saudi concession.

For some years the British Government had suspected Philby of influenc-ing Ibn Saud in favour of a strong line against Britain on a variety of issues. Over the Aqaba and Maan affair and the *Ikhwan* rebellion, Philby had penned numerous articles campaigning against British policy towards Ibn Saud. Various government departments were embarrassed by Philby's activities, particularly as he was still drawing an Indian pension.[34] Of the departments dealing with Arabia, the Foreign Office was the least con-cerned by Philby's antics.[35] The Colonial Office and the India Office for example, were more anxious about his potentially disruptive influences.[36]

This was partly because the Foreign Office benefited, through its Jedda mission, from direct links with British servants best able to assess the effects of Philby.

At first the Agency/Consulate was alarmed at Philby's ability to cause friction in Anglo-Saudi relations. In the aftermath of Ibn Saud's victory in the Hejaz, Stanley Jordan, the Acting British Consul, sought a method of securing Philby's removal from Arabia. He felt that Philby was trying to instil ideas of non-co-operation with the British Government, and he was also known to frequent the Soviet Agency.[37] The Consul was not averse to Philby being permitted to cross the Rub al Khali, 'where in all probability he will meet an untimely end'.[38] When Philby went so far as to publish an article on the Husein-McMahon correspondence, the Colonial Office suggested that he be charged under the Official Secrets Act and his pension suspended. Reluctantly, it was admitted that Philby might have won in court and, in any case, would have enjoyed the glare of publicity.[39]

As the Hejaz gradually stabilised, reports from Jedda suggested that Philby was having little influence on Ibn Saud. The Consulate reported in 1928 that 'he [Philby] is a nuisance rather than a power of evil. The King, I am convinced, though he likes and admires him, rarely takes him seriously'.[40] Hugh Stonehewer-Bird, then British Agent/Consul, could confirm that outside Ibn Saud's inner circle no one believed Philby because they thought he was working for British interests.[41] In the light of these reports the Colonial Office and the India Office eased off their campaign to suspend Philby's pension, realising that the whole business was being given spurious importance.[42]

In 1931 Ryan wrote, 'His [Philby's] influence and ability have been exaggerated both by those who see in him the power behind the throne and those guileless or anti-British enough to think him a British Agent. Philby is supposed to use his influence in an anti-British sense. This view is exaggerated'.[43] By 1933, as interest in Saudi oil developed, Ryan felt confident enough to say that:

> Philby is still a minor factor in Arabian politics. His political role in Saudi Arabia is not really great despite legends to the contrary. ... It was smaller in 1932 than before ..., [he] has come to detest certain aspects of the [Saudi] administration and has become a little doubtful of Ibn Saud's ability to control the situation.[44]

Ryan's successor, Reader Bullard, was no more impressed by Philby, commenting in 1936: 'I admire Philby as an arch-humbug'.[45]

The significance of this discussion of Philby is not to ascertain the extent of his influence with Ibn Saud. What is of relevance is that, rightly or wrongly, the British Government worked on the supposition that he had little influence, and therefore did not consider him an important factor in British policy. His 'fame' stemmed from a combination of popular romanticism, his almost unequalled knowledge of Arabia, and his public devotion to Ibn Saud. How could Philby possibly think so much of Ibn Saud if Ibn Saud did not think equally of Philby? Rather than being privy to the confidences of both the British Government and Ibn Saud, he was excluded from each. It cannot be stressed sufficiently that whatever Philby's position in Arabia, he was not a factor in British policy-making towards Ibn Saud, either before his conversion to Islam or afterwards. This is not to remark upon the accuracy or otherwise of Philby's interpretation of British policy. The nearest that he came to having a significant impact on Anglo-Saudi relations was during the lead-up to the Saudi oil concessions.

The Granting of the Saudi Concession – May 1933

The commencement of American interest in Saudi oil can be put down as February 1931, with a visit to Ibn Saud in Jedda from the American philanthropist Charles Crane. According to Philby, Crane's visit was a result of his suggestion.[46] Crane was 73 years old and had made his fortune from the manufacture of sanitary utensils.[47] He had held several political appointments, including that of United States Minister to China. He had attended the Paris Peace Conference with President Wilson, and had jointly headed the King-Crane Commission to the Fertile Crescent in 1919 to gauge the political aspirations of its peoples.[48] A further, unofficial visit to Syria in 1922 attracted the attention of the British and French Governments. Crane's anti-French sentiment was believed to be partly responsible for the unrest in Syria which required the imposition of martial law.[49] The French Government accused him of inciting rebellion and sentenced him in his absence to twenty years imprisonment.[50]

Crane had already visited the Yemen, and become involved in road and harbour development projects.[51] In 1926 he went to Jedda but had not met Ibn Saud. In 1928 the British Government granted him a visa to visit Iraq, although he was warned to exercise diplomatic care and not to use the mandate as a base for political disaffection.[52] His meeting with Ibn Saud, in February 1931, resulted two months later in the first of many visits to Arabia by Karl Twitchell, an American mining engineer. Twitchell's brief was to explore the possibilities for Arabian development; covering agriculture, irrigation, minerals, water, gold, oil, and roads.[53]

The Foreign Office, watching disinterestedly, was unperturbed by Crane's visit. Neither did it share Twitchell's enthusiasm over Arabia's mineral potential. 'It seems fairly clear that nothing of much importance will result from Mr. Twitchell's investigations. He appears to be something of a busybody.'[54] The Foreign Office's disdain was sometimes expressed more colourfully:

> Everybody knows that Arabs are incompetent, improvident, conceited, penurious and generally difficult to deal with. Everybody also knows that American prospectors in unpromising and unexplored regions are apt to be interested adventurers.[55]

As for the ability of Ibn Saud and his people to develop such resources as Arabia may possess there is no power and no might save in God alone.[56]

Ibn Saud's chief requirement, as befitted a desert society, was the supply of water.[57] Twitchell, moreover, in an age of world over-production of oil, advocated caution in the development of possible oil reserves in Arabia.[58] He noted that the low oil prices being fetched at that time meant that Ibn Saud would not get as favourable a concession as could possibly be negotiated at a future date. Twitchell recommended that Ibn Saud construct a new port at Ras Tanura on the Arabian Gulf, but that nothing should be done with respect to Saudi oil before the borings in Bahrain had been proved or disproved.[59] Within a few weeks oil was struck in Bahrain.

Whereas US diplomatic assistance was necessary in order to counter British opposition to American entry into Bahrain and Kuwait, none was needed in order to win Saudi oil concessions. Accordingly, Twitchell hunted for interested American companies, but only one, Standard Oil of California (SOCAL), which had taken the Bahrain concession off Holmes, expressed interest in taking a full concession – which Ibn Saud was insisting upon before allowing any geological exploration. Having struck lucky once they were happy to try again. There was no great rush to compete. With world oil supplies in surplus there seemed little incentive in risking the ardours of eastern Arabia in search of more oilfields. The pace of oil exploration was determined by the price that the oil could obtain, not the likelihood of finding it. In October 1932, according to Philby, he was asked by SOCAL to approach Ibn Saud about the company working a concession in Hasa and the Kuwait-Saudi neutral zone.[60]

Interest from British sources was never wholehearted. The Red Line arrangements had 'queered the pitch' for concession hunters in the Arab world, while the quarrel between APOC and the Iranian Government further discouraged oil speculation in the Middle East.[61] APOC, under the terms of the Red Line, could not contest the Saudi concession directly. If any company with British representation was to do so it had to be Iraq Petroleum. When IPC did, belatedly, take an interest, in March 1933, the Foreign Office noted: 'It looks as if IPC may be letting the American oil group steal a march on them.'[62] The British Government was waking up very late in the day to the fact that an American oil company was poised to take sole ownership of a Saudi Arabian oil concession. Rendel minuted: 'If the Americans succeed in getting a firm footing there [Hasa] the whole political situation in the Persian Gulf may be drastically affected.'[63] There were few other indications of British concern.

Of course, the British Government was not strait-jacketed. It was under no obligation to leave the United States a clear field in Hasa.[64] Saudi Arabia, unlike Bahrain or Kuwait, was an independent state without any restrictive agreements with Britain. Britain was, therefore, free to back her own interests in Saudi Arabia should she so desire. Nonetheless, official British interest in the destiny of the Saudi concession was minimal.

A third contestant briefly entered the race. This was Holmes' Eastern and General Syndicate. Holmes' defaulting on the payments for his earlier Hasa concession excluded him as a serious candidate. Ibn Saud might have demanded the full back-payment of £6,000 rental arrears before even considering Holmes' offer.[65] Yet, even with just two contenders it was apparent that Iraq Petroleum was not in the running. SOCAL's offer was many times greater, and the American company was prepared to pay in gold whereas Iraq Petroleum would only offer rupees.[66] When, on 29 May 1933, Ibn Saud finally awarded the concession to SOCAL, the Foreign Office casually noted its feelings: 'It is a pity that it [the concession] has gone to entirely non-British interests, but no help for it. ... This may make a big difference in Hasa which ... [has been] hitherto strictly preserved.'[67] What was 'strictly preserved' about Hasa was, of course, that it fell within the loose British sphere of influence. The fear was whether American commercial interests would weaken that preserve.

Why British Interests lost the Saudi Oil Concession

The foregoing has set the background for the granting of the Saudi oil concession to an American company in 1933. As for the reasons for Britain losing the concession various factors need to be taken into account, and these will be considered in turn.

(i) *The Association of the British Government with Iraq Petroleum*   Perhaps the first question that needs to be asked is whether the association of the British Government in Middle Eastern oil ventures acted as a deterrent against Ibn Saud granting the Hasa concession to Iraq Petroleum. After the purchasing of a majority of APOC's shares in 1913 the world's oil interests could not dissociate the motives of the British Government from those of any other self-interested shareholders.[68] Any financial advantages accruing from the company's use of public funds were offset by the liability, as in this case, of foreign governments' suspicions about granting concessions to a government, rather than a private company.[69]

Ibn Saud had already revealed his fears in this respect during the granting of the first Hasa concession back in 1923 to Holmes' Eastern and General Syndicate. Although it appeared to have little significance at the time, APOC was also interested in that concession. Sir Percy Cox had attempted to induce Ibn Saud to negotiate with APOC in preference to the Eastern and General. Ibn Saud's refusal was largely attributed to his apprehensions about dealing with a semi-governmental concern.[70]

Ibn Saud's circumstances in 1933 were very different from what they had been ten years previously. From being a comparatively minor, remote Arab chief, he had become almost an international figure. His own sense of grievance at the hands of the British Government, as evidenced in previous chapters, may well have prompted him to turn to a country that could counteract the weight of British influence in Arabia. As regards oil, it is submitted, this is not a cogent argument. No one was really confident of finding oil in Saudi Arabia, least of all Ibn Saud. Indeed, Philby relates how Ibn Saud dozed off with tedium when the draft SOCAL contract was being read to him.[71] Nor must it be overlooked that in 1933, the competitor for the Hasa concession was not APOC, as it had been in 1923, but Iraq Petroleum which unlike APOC was not owned by the British Government. APOC was, however, a participant in Iraq Petroleum and so, therefore, was the British Government.

(ii) *The British Oil Dispute with Iran*   A related point concerns developments elsewhere attracting the attention of Ibn Saud and the British Government during the negotiations for the Hasa concession. In particular, the dispute between the Shah of Iran and APOC, which reached a peak in the early months of 1933, was put in front of Ibn Saud at an unfortunate time from the British point of view. One of the Shah's grievances had been that the world economic slump had led to a lower demand for oil and, therefore, less oil revenues for himself.[72] At the same time, Ibn Saud would have observed that Britain elected not to use force to reach a settlement, but to allow the whole business to go before the League of Nations.

(iii) *Ibn Saud's Preference for a non-British Company*   There were, perhaps, other grounds for Ibn Saud choosing a non-British company. Cordell Hull, for example, the United States Secretary of State, asserted that Ibn Saud granted the concession to American interests because of his fears of Britain.[73] A powerful anti-colonial counterpoise to Britain in the form of the United States was, it has been suggested, a long range objective of Ibn Saud.[74]

Such an interpretation has almost no credence. In its grossest form, suggesting a major policy upheaval on the part of Ibn Saud away from dependence on Britain, the notion rests on oil being as important in the context of 1933 as in the present day. But for an accident of geology, Saudi Arabia sitting on immeasurable oil wealth, there would be little justification for the existence of this chapter. The events of 1933 were of barely superficial interest at the time, either to the British or American Governments – or, for that matter, to Ibn Saud.

The more abstract assertion, that Ibn Saud for purely personal reasons was disinclined to favour a British concessionaire, can be refuted on two counts. Firstly, there is the evidence of Philby himself. Ibn Saud would, Philby claimed, all things being equal, have preferred to grant the concession to the British. 'Ibn Saud, like a bird mesmerised by a snake, was known to be personally desirous of giving this very Hasa concession to a British company if only he could get something in return.'[75] That something was money, a sufficient quantity of which Iraq Petroleum would not put on the table. Philby described Ibn Saud's policy at this time as being based on two pillars: the defence of his sovereign independence; and the maintenance of good relations with Britain.[76]

Secondly, there is the evidence of Ibn Saud's subsequent dispensing of oil concessions within his Kingdom. In June 1933, just a month after SOCAL won the Hasa concession, Ibn Saud approached the British Government over another oil concession covering Asir and the Farasan Islands.[77] As a previous concession covering part of this area had already expired without oil being found, there was little response – except from an Italian group.[78] Eventually, in July 1936, Petroleum Concessions Ltd., a company formed under identical ownership to Iraq Petroleum, won a concession for the whole of the Red Sea coast of Saudi Arabia (including the Farasan Islands), apart from a stretch either side of Jedda.[79] The Saudi Government approached the American company with news of the British bid, but it declined to compete.[80] The mere approach suggests not preference for the Americans, but for the highest bidder. Moreover, it should be added that in 1935 Ibn Saud agreed to the formation of a Saudi Arabian Mining Syndicate – a British corporation having some American capital and employees, including the promoter and general manager, Karl Twitchell.[81]

These moves on the part of Ibn Saud demonstrate his preparedness to grant concessions to British interests. There is a tendency, because of the huge oil reserves found in eastern Saudi Arabia, to limit discussion of Anglo-Saudi oil relations to the Hasa concession. It may be tempting to suggest that Ibn Saud consciously gave his most promising concession to the United States and a worthless one to Britain.[82] Yet this is to overlook that oil exploration was (and is) an imprecise science. Philby reports Ibn Saud as never being confident of finding oil in his Kingdom.[83] Certainly, by 1936, oil was no nearer being found. The fact that the Hasa concession yielded oil, whereas the Hejaz concession did not, is a matter for geology, not international relations. It may suggest better American geological and business practice, and doubtless Arab rulers would have been impressed by American efficiency after oil was struck in Bahrain. Ultimately, however, Ibn Saud would have given his concession to the highest bidder.[84] This was fully understood by the British Government. Rendel explained to Sir John Cadman, the Chairman of Iraq Petroleum: 'The whole policy of the Saudi Government is to get what cash it can at the outset for uncertain prospects and hope for more if they materialise'.[85]

Iraq Petroleum may have thought its terms reasonable in 1933, but for the 1936 Hejaz concession Petroleum Development (Western Arabia), an affiliate of Petroleum Concessions, began to offer terms more appropriate to the empty coffers of Ibn Saud.[86] £32,000 in gold was paid upon signing the concession, and £7,500 *per annum* rental agreed for four exploration years, after which the subsequent annual rental would rise to £10,000.[87] If oil was found in commercial quantities the company would loan the Saudi Arabian

Government £50,000 free of interest over the following two years.[88] When it is remembered that three years earlier Iraq Petroleum had offered Ibn Saud a mere £200 monthly rental, or £10,000 for the full concession, the change in attitude can be appreciated. Furthermore, in 1936 there was no greater probability of finding Saudi oil – yet the concession was strongly supported by the British Government.[89]

(iv) *The Motives of the Iraq Petroleum Company*   It is pertinent to consider why Iraq Petroleum contested the Hasa concession in such half-hearted fashion. Iraq Petroleum's interest, such as it was, was not prompted by the urge to discover oil. The company was also involved in Qatar, where it agreed to prospect for a specified period in return for a modest outlay. Iraq Petroleum was not prepared to pay 'big' money for the right of extracting hypothetical oil reserves in Qatar, any more than in Hasa.[90] Stephen Longrigg, IPC's negotiator, had only asked Ibn Saud for an exploring license.[91] Only if and when the company found a promising source of oil would a proper concession have been negotiated, based on the realistic chances of finding oil (exactly as was happening in the case of Qatar). Longrigg preferred that payments to Saudi Arabia be graded according to the results of the initial exploration. Accordingly, Iraq Petroleum was hesitant about either offering a lump sum settlement for the concession or agreeing to a guaranteed rate of actual exploration.[92]

At the same time, the Iraq Petroleum Company was, apparently, doubtful whether SOCAL would part with a sizable outlay, together with a loan, in order to win the Hasa concession, and hoped that when Ibn Saud realised this he would be glad to settle for IPC's more modest (and realistic) terms.[93] The terms of the SOCAL concession were: a preliminary 'loan' of £50,000 gold, of which £30,000 was payable at once;[94] an annual rental of £5,000 pending discovery of oil in commercial quantities; two further advances of £50,000 each, at an interval of one year when commercial deposits of oil were discovered; and a royalty of four shillings gold per ton of oil produced.[95] This amount seems a pittance by today's standards, but was still many times greater than that offered by Longrigg.

Iraq Petroleum, as a large oil concern, unlike SOCAL, was motivated by different factors. It was clearly not determined to win the Hasa concession. Longrigg had admitted to Philby that his company did not need any more oil.[96] Even looking into the future, IPC had all the oil it could possibly market for years to come.[97] The company was more concerned about forestalling competition throughout the Middle East.[98] After the discovery of oil in Bahrain, Iraq Petroleum could not be indifferent to the possible flooding of oil markets. Although the discovery of oil in Bahrain had been a great boost to SOCAL it had been received with less enthusiasm by Iraq Petroleum. So keen was SOCAL to break into the Middle Eastern oil network that, despite not being pushed by IPC, the American company still won the Hasa concession for less than the maximum it might have paid had

competition been more vigorous.[99] The main oil companies operating in the
Middle East – Iraq Petroleum and APOC – were more interested in preserving their existing monopolies than in searching for competitive fields. The
attitude of the British-backed companies is well summed up in the following
quotation about APOC's Middle Eastern oil policy:

> Although the geological information we possess at present does not
> indicate that there is much hope of finding oil in Bahrain or Kuwait we
> are, I take it, all agreed that even if the chance be 100:1 we should
> pursue it rather than let others come into the Persian Gulf and cause
> difficulties of one kind or another for us.[100]

Perhaps Iraq Petroleum counted too heavily on the supposed friendship
of Ibn Saud towards Britain, and relied on the good offices and energetic
support of the British Legation to back its claim.[101] It was, however, in Ibn
Saud's economic interests to award the concession to a company which
would actually search for oil. SOCAL was obliged to commence geological
exploration by September 1933 – within four months of signing the contract,[102] a condition with which Iraq Petroleum would have been reluctant to
comply.

(v) *The Role of Philby*   Philby's role in the triumph of American over
British oil interests in Saudi Arabia was not negligible. Unbeknown to
anybody else at the time, be they Ibn Saud, Ryan, Twitchell or Longrigg,
SOCAL had in February 1933 secretly won Philby's services as mediator
on the company's behalf.[103] Longrigg confided in Philby throughout the
negotiations, even revealing Iraq Petroleum's terms, in the belief that Philby
was either sympathetic or else completely neutral.[104] Philby had, in other
words, a personal, material reason for wanting SOCAL to win the concession. Beyond this he sought the best possible terms for Ibn Saud, even if
that meant procuring a bigger price from SOCAL.[105]

There was also a political element in Philby's thinking. He preferred that
the concession go to SOCAL not only because he stood to gain financially,
but because to Philby the record of American oil ventures was free of
imperialistic connotations.[106] Ryan, unaware, was of the opinion that Philby
was uncommitted either to SOCAL or to Iraq Petroleum.[107] Privately, the
British Minister backed Longrigg, and according to Philby seemed quietly
confident that the British company would win the concession.[108] Ryan
knew, perhaps more clearly than anybody else, how American concessions
might affect future relations between Britain and Saudi Arabia. Philby
reported Ryan as being 'thunderstruck' when he heard the news of SOCAL's
success.[109]

Philby's influence on the outcome was, therefore, considerable. He was in
a unique position to counter Ibn Saud's professed preferences for the British
company. Being the confidant of Longrigg, Ryan and Ibn Saud, Philby was
well placed to direct the concessionary negotiations along paths of his

choosing. For reasons of personal profit, mistrust of British intentions, and the desire to secure the best possible deal for Ibn Saud, Philby acted to SOCAL's advantage.[110]

(vi) *The Background of Anglo-Saudi Relations During 1932-1933*   Anglo-Saudi relations at the time of the Hasa concession were amicable enough and provide no suggestion of Ibn Saud wanting to slight Britain. Indeed, relations in 1933 were somewhat smoother than they had been the previous year. Ibn Saud's disenchantment with Ryan[111] seemed to have been pushed into the background, although a minor incident did occur early in 1932 when a Royal slave took refuge in the British Legation and, to Ibn Saud's chagrin, was smuggled by Ryan aboard *HMS Penzance*.[112] On the diplomatic front Ibn Saud and the Emir Abdullah had recognised each other's regime in April 1933. Tension was increasing, however, in south-western Arabia where hostilities would commence within a few months. This was, though, the one part of Arabia where the British Government was not directly answerable for the activities of Ibn Saud's neighbours. Even so, Ibn Saud feared friction with Britain in case he needed her support against Italian backing for the Imam.[113]

In addition, Saudi Arabia had early in 1933 made an enquiry to Britain about possible membership of the League of Nations. In May, she received a polite but firm reply which, while not dismissing the idea out of hand, spelled out the difficulties confronting Saudi Arabia should she decide to apply.[114] There is no reason to suppose that the question was of sufficient importance for Ibn Saud to feel aggrieved at the reply.

(vii) *The World Economic Factor*   There were economic reasons why the British Government would not become excited at the prospect of hypothetical Saudi oil. The world-wide Depression affected Britain and Saudi Arabia alike. The boom period for Britain's manufacturing industry which followed the restoration of peace in 1918 gradually lost its impetus in the 1920s as other countries experienced rapid industrial growth.[115] In August 1931 the Labour Government was replaced by a National Government. One month later Britain went off the Gold Standard, an event which led to a 'chaotic period' in the Hejaz.[116] In Britain, the slump led to rising unemployment, a boost for protectionist ideals, contraction of invisible earnings, and, from 1933, a balance of payments problem. The Treasury responded with economic orthodoxy, reducing public expenditure and overseas financial commitments.[117]

The world oil industry suffered not only from restricted demand, but also from a surplus of oil-producing capacity that had been developed during the 1920s.[118] The leading American companies had been trying to restrict output within the United States. The main international companies were doing likewise on a world scale.[119] SOCAL was not so handicapped. Prior to winning the Bahrain concession SOCAL had been a purely domestic oil producer and marketer of oil products.[120] Its success in Bahrain made the company ambitious to establish itself in world markets.

The economic situation pertaining in Saudi Arabia was equally worrisome. Historically the fluctuation in the world economy made little impact upon Nejd. But upon its union with the Hejaz, Ibn Saud effectively linked the prosperity of Saudi Arabia to the economic barometer of the outside world.[121] The Pilgrimage was a sensitive meter of world trade.[122] As the Depression spread, the number of pilgrims from all ends of the Moslem world able to undertake the journey to Mecca began to fall.

Numbers of Overseas Pilgrims Arriving at Jedda.[123]

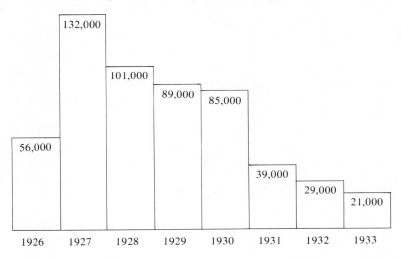

During his relatively more prosperous years in the late 1920s Ibn Saud had spent freely on the devices of statehood, such as arms, wirelesses, roads, cars and aeroplanes – not to mention dispensation to his tribes – the bills for which, when the slump in the Pilgrimage arrived, he could no longer meet.[124]

Two other factors contributed to Saudi Arabia's increasing economic problems. First, there was the increase in mechanised transport. The ubiquitous role of the camel in Arabian society was rapidly being supplanted by motor cars, which were bought from abroad and fed on fuel from abroad, thereby causing impoverishment and dislocation of the Arabian economic system.[125] The second factor was the religious hostility to non-believers taking any active part in the economic life of Ibn Saud's Kingdom.[126] At the Hejaz National Conference in 1931, after the *Ikhwan* rebellion had been suppressed, Ibn Saud reaffirmed that concessions would only be given to Moslems, a proclamation that did nothing to reassure the non-Wahhabi Hejazis who stood to benefit from foreign investment.[127] It was, according to Philby, he who persuaded Ibn Saud that the only escape from his poverty was to find more reliable sources of revenue than the precarious Pilgrimage, and to open up his Kingdom to western capital and technology.[128] Such was Ibn Saud's despair at the time that Philby noted: 'He talks of nothing but women and camels'.[129] Ibn Saud is reputed to have said to Philby: 'If anyone would offer me a million pounds now, I would give him all the concessions he wants'.[130] It was shortly afterwards that Crane was introduced to Ibn Saud.

With the British economy in disarray the question of financial aid to Ibn Saud was peremptorily rejected. The matter of direct aid had previously been fully debated, and rejected, in 1929 during the *Ikhwan* rebellion. He had only been offered a standard form of commercial treaty through the Board of Trade which, in any case, failed to materialise.[131] Ibn Saud could offer no security of any kind in return for financial assistance. Nor were Saudi debts, such as for the arms bought from India during the *Ikhwan* rebellion, being repaid. By 1932, these total debts amounted to some £120,000 in gold:[132] tiny in the context of Britain; immense to Saudi Arabia.

The Foreign Office would have liked to help: 'It is important that we leave no stone unturned to try to help Ibn Saud re-establish his position'.[133] As regards encouraging British concession-hunters in Arabia, however, the Foreign Office received a firm reminder from the Department of Overseas Trade of the unofficial embargo on the export of capital from Britain, which was to operate through the duration of the economic crisis.[134] All these factors played a part in Iraq Petroleum's losing out. Such was Ibn Saud's need for money that he insisted on a substantial advance to precede any concession.[135] Even SOCAL initially hesitated over this prerequisite.[136]

(viii) *The United States, Oil and Arabia*   Successive United States administrations were concerned to stabilise the domestic American oil industry. General over-production of oil and falling prices were aggravated in 1931 by spectacular new finds in Texas, together with new fields in Rumania, the Soviet Union and Venezuela.[137] The policy of President Hoover and the initial policy of President Franklin Roosevelt, who succeeded Hoover in March 1933 (two months before SOCAL secured the Hasa concession), were based on similar principles.[138] Hoover denied any federal responsibility for maintaining stability in the American oil industry.[139] His Government's emphasis was on voluntary attempts at co-operation, stabilisation and conservation, together with curtailment of oil imports.[140] It was against this atmosphere that American oil companies interested in the Middle East had to contend in the early 1930s. The American economy feared more oil on world markets. If SOCAL went ahead with the Hasa concession it would be in a political and economic climate far removed from that of the 1920s.

On the other hand, the United States and her oil companies were well placed when it came to securing favours in Arabia. America had no record of any kind of political interference in the Arab world.[141] Before 1939 not even the Zionist issue in Palestine could provoke State Department intervention.[142]. As a working rule the United States had been happy to regard

Palestine and all of Arabia as a British sphere of influence.[143] There was only one American consular post in the whole peninsula, at Aden, and the only Arabian ruler to have been recognised by 1929 was the Sultan of Oman – as early as 1833.[144] America had never recognised the Hashemite regime in the Hejaz, a point strongly in her favour in the mind of Ibn Saud.[145] He, in turn, must have presented a pleasing figure in American eyes, being a self-made man in consonance with American ideology.[146]

It was the Anglo-Saudi treaty of 1927 that brought Ibn Saud and his Kingdom to the attention of the United States and the outside world. At that time there were no American commercial interests in Arabia. In 1930 the United States Government had recognised Iraq, still a mandated territory, an act which may have affronted Ibn Saud.[147] In that same year an American report revealed that some three per cent of the total imports to Hejaz-Nejd were then coming from the United States, mainly in the form of cars and trucks, some of which were handled by Philby.[148] The report was optimistic for the future. It was calculated that some $40,000 worth of exports had gone to Fiat when Ibn Saud stopped the purchase of American cars pending official US recognition of his regime.[149]

Due to its remoteness from American official interest, Hejaz-Nejd was one of the few sovereign states not to have received American diplomatic recognition. This anachronism was remedied in May 1931, shortly after Crane's visit.[150] The British Government was duly informed of American intentions in this respect, and the British Legation in Jedda saw no grounds upon which to object.[151] United States recognition was prompted on general economic and commercial grounds at the peak of the Depression, not by specific oil interests or a reconsideration of American foreign policy in the Middle East. Nor was it intended that recognition be followed by the appointment of a US diplomatic or consular representative in Jedda. The American action was, it seemed, geared only to paving the way for easier commercial arrangements with Hejaz-Nejd.[152] The British Government was at first totally dismissive of any kind of economic lure from the Arabian deserts. When, for example, Crane first met Ibn Saud it was assumed from London that the meeting owed less to business or philanthropic motives than to diplomatic ones concerning imminent American recognition of Ibn Saud.[153]

(ix) *Anglo-American Relations in the Early 1930s*   The 1920s were comparatively lean years for Anglo-American relations.[154] The retreat of the United States from the League of Nations and her resumption of isolationism contrasted with Britain's unsought role as major power at Geneva. Friction between the British and American Governments occurred at several points. Ireland presented one problem; commercial rivalry, as in the Middle East, another. More serious was American suspicion of the 1902 Anglo-Japanese alliance, and strained American relations with both states.[155] An associated area of tension was naval competition between

Britain and the United States. This, and the Japanese issue, were partially settled in 1922 when the Anglo-Japanese alliance was terminated, and the Washington Naval Conference temporarily established the relative strengths of British, American and Japanese fleets.[156] Britain was aware that she could not afford a war with the United States and was eventually reconciled to the surrender of her historic naval supremacy.[157] Anglo-American naval disagreements continued, however, particularly after the failure of the Geneva Naval Conference of 1927.[158] It took a further conference in London, in 1930, 'to end forever British mistrust of American naval equality'.[159]

Another protracted problem was that of British War debts to the United States. By 1920 Britain had borrowed some $4 billion, while lending, in turn, $8 billion to other allies.[160] Although the British Government was prepared to dispense with both debts, at a net loss, Washington continued to demand full repayment of her debt.[161] It occurred to the India Office that if America agreed to a moratorium on outstanding War debts, then Ibn Saud might press for similar consideration regarding his own debt to Britain.[162] In the event, Hoover's all-round moratorium on international debts was only a temporary, stop-gap measure.[163]

Japan's invasion of Manchuria from the autumn of 1931 produced yet more tension between London and Washington. The invasion provided a major crisis for the cohesion of the League. Any action which sought to exert pressure on Japan required the active participation of the United States.[164] Britain felt America to be largely responsible for the termination of the Anglo-Japanese alliance, which had previously served as a valuable channel of western influence on Japanese policy.[165] The United States, however, was anxious not to offend Japan for fear of weakening the liberal Japanese Government then in office.[166] Against this background, the British Government was reluctant to further strain Anglo-American relations, particularly over something as marginal as Saudi oil concessions. Indeed, with the United States presenting no perceptible threat of imperial rivalry over Arabia, unlike, for example, Italy, she was seen as a preferred commercial competitor.[167]

(x) *British Oil Policy* A variety of instances have been adduced to illustrate the largely peripheral role of oil in British foreign policy in the Middle East up to the Second World War.[168]

The case of Italy provides a notable example of Britain being prepared to surrender oil concessions for political advantage. In 1926 the British-represented Red Sea Petroleum Company, of the Shell Group, won a concession from the Idrisi of Asir for oil exploration on the Farasan Islands. Having won the concession the company attempted to obtain official British recognition, to act as guarantee against any malpractice on the part of an unreliable Arab ruler who could not have been brought before any international court.[169]

This guarantee the British Government was not prepared to give. The significance of the Farasan Islands was considered to lie not with oil, but with their strategic location. It was felt to be important that Italy should not secure a naval base on the islands, or otherwise use them to assist in economic and political penetration of the Arabian peninsula.[170] In fact, so small a part did Farasan oil play in British policy calculations at that time that, were it not for Italian unpopularity throughout the area, the Foreign Office would have considered sharing the concession with an Italian company.[171] This might have brought political rewards by allaying Italian suspicions of British motives in the Red Sea. The Foreign Office considered there to be little economic profit to the Italians from sharing the Farasan concession. It was estimated that the total value of Farasan oil was no more than £100,000.[172] Of course, it might have been the unattractiveness of the oil prospects, as seen from London, which prompted the Foreign Office to contemplate Italian participation.

It was felt that by not making room for Italian commercial enterprise on Farasan trouble might be provoked elsewhere, particularly in view of the poverty of the Italian colony of Eritrea, and the need for Italian economic development in the area.[173] The main apprehension of the Foreign Office was the risk of Italian commercial interest turning into political interest, 'otherwise we care nothing about the concession'.[174] The whole idea was dropped only after intractable resistance from the Admiralty, which would not consider assisting the Italians in any way in the Red Sea.[175]

Similarly, the tiny Kamaran Island to the south was the subject of an attempt by the Colonial Secretary, Leopold Amery, to encourage a British company to operate a concession. He feared that to refuse could increase political uncertainty in the Red Sea.[176] The island was of dubious international status, having been occupied by British forces during the First World War.[177] The Foreign Office continued to view the whole question in terms of its likely effects on Anglo-Italian relations. At that time, detailed discussions were taking place with the Italian Government in Rome regarding the Red Sea, during the course of which the British Government promised not to exert political influence to support commercial interests. The Foreign Office was determined, for political reasons, not to become associated with commercial developments on Kamaran.[178]

Overall, oil questions were given low priority by the British Government in the 1920s and '30s. Generally speaking, compromise was at the very heart of British Governments' attitudes towards oil,[179] which was used as a bait to smooth possible sources of political friction. When oil is in surfeit it does not constitute much of a political weapon; hence the policy of sacrificing it to secure political ends.

(xi) *British Strategic Considerations*   One final element which can be brought forward to suggest why Britain was unsuccessful in winning the Hasa concession was the strategic overview of the British Government that operated in the early 1930s. In 1919 the Admiralty had produced a document arguing that Britain was unlikely to have to fight a major war for at least another ten years.[180] This '10-year' principle was extended until its cancellation, due to events in the Far East, in 1932. During the 1920s only the Soviet Union and Japan constituted the slightest threat to the British Empire. With war seeming so remote, there was less urgency for the British Government to associate itself with the search for fresh oil reserves,[181] at least until the declining international circumstances of the mid-1930s.

In conclusion, it can be stated that, having considered a whole host of possible explanations – personal, religious, economic, political and strategic – Ibn Saud's decision to award the Hasa concession to an American company was the result, above all, of his quest for revenue, unalloyed by other considerations. Ibn Saud would have turned anywhere for income. SOCAL's offer was many times larger than that of Iraq Petroleum. For its part, the British Government did not contest the matter. It had no need for oil; international considerations being its primary concern. Nonetheless, an economic competitor had now installed itself in Saudi Arabia.

Aftermath of the Hasa Concession: British Policy and Arabian Oil 1934-1939

The loss of the Hasa concession to an American company in May 1933, while not considered a great reversal for British policy in the Middle East at the time, did constitute something of a watershed as regards the significance of oil concessions in the Gulf sheikhdoms. Twitchell suggested that Saudi Arabia was probably the only country in the world where development of oil and mining resulted from purely philanthropic sentiment.[182] Neither SOCAL nor Iraq Petroleum received direct assistance from any government quarter. Proponents of the Open Door would argue that the Hasa concession was practically the only example in Middle Eastern oil history in which Open Door conditions were allowed to operate.[183]

From May 1933 a new feeling of urgency characterised the British Government's outlook on Arabian oil. All departments admitted in retrospect that a mistake had been made in letting the Americans into Bahrain in 1932.[184] Over Kuwait, the United States Embassy in London was still bringing considerable pressure to bear in the name of the Open Door.[185] The risk of United States access to Kuwait, a key sheikhdom in the security of the Gulf, particularly now that Iraq had won her independence, elicited some dissension within the British Government. As Kuwait lay outside the Red Line any company could compete for the concession, including APOC. The possibility of Kuwaiti oil concessions going to non-British interests produced a major clash between the Admiralty and the India Office on the one hand, and the Foreign Office on the other. The Admiralty protested:

A concession in the Persian Gulf by arrangement or neglect of local commercial interests which now underlie political and military control, will imperil GB's naval situation in the further East; her political position in India; her commercial interests in both; and the imperial ties between herself and Australasia.[186]

The Foreign Office took a contrary view:

It is essential, so far as possible, not to be obstructive to American interests. The CO, Petroleum Dept. of the Board of Trade, and the FO would all be willing to abandon the British nationality clause, but the IO is extremely sticky.[187]

Other factors were also important: APOC was unpopular in the region (a result of the dispute with the Iranian Government and the British Government's majority shareholding in the company); Ibn Saud may have influenced the Sheikh against favouring a British company – for otherwise his own aspirations for eventual absorption of Kuwait would have been hindered; and Britain had bound herself to the United States not to use her special position in the sheikhdom to affect the outcome of the concession.[188] The Foreign Office won the grudging consent of the Admiralty for adopting an attitude of impartiality over the disposition of Kuwaiti oil concessions. In these circumstances it was, therefore, a triumph for international co-operation when APOC and the American Gulf Oil Company secured a joint concession in 1934 to operate what became the Kuwait Oil Company.[189] By that time the question had involved the British Cabinet and all the principal departments of state. Oil had not been at stake: the issues were British imperial prestige and the United States Open Door policy.[190]

The Kuwait-Saudi neutral zone proved troublesome.[191] Prior to 1933 Saudi Arabia's frontier problems had been of a political and tribal nature. After 1933 they were increasingly motivated by the oil factor. The Kuwait-Saudi neutral zone provided the first example of this. After the loss of the Hasa concession, Britain tried to stimulate her oil interests along the Arab littoral of the Gulf. The neutral zone, estabished in 1922 as part of the Kuwait-Nejd frontier settlement, lay within the Red Line. It therefore enjoyed the same restrictions on concession-hunters as did Saudi Arabia. Moreover, Ibn Saud, in granting the Hasa concession to SOCAL, had given the company an option on the Saudi share of the rights in the neutral zone.[192]

It was generally agreed that it was not in British interests to allow SOCAL another concession in the Gulf.[193] Such were the complications, both political and administrative, of oil concessions in the neutral zone, that the first inclincation of the Foreign Office was to 'sterilise' the zone in order to keep out all concessionary ventures.[194] This accorded with the traditional British view of Arabia that it was not its resources that were important, so much as denying them, and access to them, to any other power. The Foreign Office suggested that the keeping of basic law and order in concession areas would present difficulties when Ibn Saud and the Sheikh of Kuwait possessed equal rights.[195] Britain could not offer effective safeguards in respect of the neutral zone, but nor could she divest herself of all political responsibility in the event of a concession materialising. The question of economic benefits being derived from those concessions was barely considered. The Foreign Office was concerned solely with political matters; with preventing political inconvenience rather than economic loss.

The India Office did not share the Foreign Office's interpretation. From the point of view of Indian interests, the sensitivity of the Gulf and the fear of foreign intervention made 'sterilisation' seem impracticable, and would have exposed Britain to international criticism.[196] Furthermore, no matter who won the concession in the neutral zone, it could have led to political instability in the region. If the concession went to the Americans, Ibn Saud's political ambitions towards Kuwait would intensify. Similarly, success for a British company might have whetted the Sheikh of Kuwait's appetite for the whole zone.[197] Again, if American oilmen were caught up in frontier disturbances, Britain would be compelled to take action, or else, which was worse, allow the United States to do so.[198] Accordingly, the India Office, following an inter-departmental meeting, made an 'informal' approach to Iraq Petroleum to contest any concession which became available.[199]

It is, of course, commonplace for Oriental rulers to indulge in telling their listener what he wants to hear. Through all the oil negotiations which affected his Kingdom, Ibn Saud persisted in telling both the British and the Americans that they were his most favoured clients. Over the neutral zone concession Ibn Saud 'confided' to Ryan his unwillingness to grant another concession to the United States.[200] Yet if Ibn Saud had reneged on his undertaking to SOCAL, and favoured a British company, Washington would have suspected the Sheikh of Kuwait, and hence the British Government, of operating unfairly against American interests.[201] In addition, it would have been difficult for Britain to prohibit the Sheikh from granting the neutral zone concession to the Americans, if that particular concession was wanted by both himself and Ibn Saud and there were no other competitors.[202] In that case, Britain could hardly stall, for to do so could lead to difficulties with Ibn Saud, especially if he stood to lose revenue as a result of delaying the concession.[203] All things considered, from the Foreign Office point of view, deadlock held most attractions.

The Admiralty demanded a stronger line, urging the British Government to exercise physical protection within the neutral zone on behalf of both rulers.[204] This proposal was rejected by the other departments. It was not felt to be in Britain's interests to undertake such direct involvement in the neutral zone. Nor would Anglo-Saudi relations have been improved through such an advertisement of British control at the expense of Ibn Saud's.[205]

The Saudi Government suggested that the neutral zone be bisected, either for the specific purpose of dealing with oil concessions, or else by partition, with a new Saudi-Kuwaiti frontier running through the middle of the zone.[206] The British Political Agent in Kuwait, H.R.P. Dickson, strongly opposed the suggestion.[207] The welfare of Kuwait depended on maintaining the zone. It offered the best grazing on the whole eastern seaboard of the Gulf, and the Sheikh nurtured hopes of its eventual re-assimilation into Kuwait.[208] The most likely oil-bearing areas were in the southern half of the zone, namely, the part that would go to Saudi Arabia. Partition was also bound to precipitate a Saudi-Kuwaiti clash across the new frontier (which had been one of the reasons behind the zone in the first place), the likely outcome of which would be bad for Kuwait and therefore for Britain. Moreover, the zone was not fortified. The memory of the *Ikhwan* rebellion was too fresh to invite an extension of fortifications in the Arabian deserts. Finally, Dickson, in keeping with Indian governmental opinion, harped on the impermanence of Ibn Saud's rule.[209]

The weight of Dickson's argument caused the British Government to accept the retention of the neutral zone for the foreseeable future.[210] Britain wanted no quarrel with Kuwait, and her veto on foreign concessions remained to be cast if necessary. In any case, British companies in the late 1930s won oil concessions or prospecting rights in south and south-eastern Arabia – in Qatar, Abu Dhabi, Muscat, Dhofar, and the Aden Protectorate.

Although there were no further developments in neutral zone oil concessions by the outbreak of the Second World War, the general attitude towards the whole peninsula had changed. British, German, Italian and Japanese concession hunters flocked to Arabia.[211] In 1939 the British Minister, Reader Bullard, noted how 'oil is inseparable from politics in Saudi Arabia'.[212] Even six years earlier such a statement was inconceivable. Oil was only discovered in 1938, yet the whole political climate had altered. In May 1939 a pipeline from the new oilfield to the port of Ras Tanura was opened. The royalties paid by the American company constituted, even in the first year of production, the main portion of Saudi Arabia's income.[213] By July 1939 oil was arriving at Ras Tanura at 1,500 barrels a day. Amid the excitement a new concession was negotiated which extended the area at the company's disposal in return for £140,000 gold, with an annual rental of £20,000.[214] The balance of British and American oil concessions in the Middle East in 1939 was as follows: America had control of Saudi and Bahrain oil; one half of Kuwait oil; and almost a quarter stake of Iraq Petroleum. British companies controlled Iranian oil; half of Kuwait oil; and about one third of Iraq Petroleum.[215]

Summary and Conclusions

Saudi Arabia was among the first states outside the traditional sphere of American interest in which a significant political and strategic interest came to be vested. She was also the first independent Arab state to develop important relations with the United States. Moreover, Saudi Arabia was the first area outside the western hemisphere where American political and strategic influence substituted that of Britain.[216] Although this take-over did not occur within the period under examination in this study its roots went back to 1933: American political influence grew directly out of a commercial oil concession.

British policy in the Middle East in the inter-war years had never been dictated by oil interests. In Iraq, for example, in the mid-1920s, despite the operations of the Turkish Petroleum Company, more excitement was generated by the prospect of wheat than oil.[217] It is important to remain detached from the modern world's preoccupation with oil. In the early 1930s, in particular, the world was in economic depression. Oil flowed in surfeit, with no indication that within half a century its shortage could threaten the economic collapse of the western industrialised world.

There is no suggestion among government records of the time of undue concern at the destiny of Saudi Arabian, as opposed to Iraqi or Kuwaiti, oil concessions. In the Annual Reports being submitted from the Jedda Legation from 1930, oil merited little mention. Writing in 1957, Sir George Rendel outlined in his memoirs the Iranian oil dispute of 1932-33, but gave the Hasa concession not a word.[218] Little in Britain's reaction to the Saudi oil concession of 1933 substantiated the Foreign Office wartime remark of 1918 that oil 'cannot be treated as a purely commercial venture but must be envisaged as a national responsibility, which admits of no half-measures or ill-considered action'.[219]

Saudi Arabia did not become a major oil producing state until after the Second World War, although the concession was granted before any of this was forseeable. The vast capital to be outlayed, from which no return was guaranteed, made unnecessary ventures like those in Saudi Arabia seem impracticable, especially when oil supplies elsewhere were ensured. In the 1930s British enterprise did not possess much capital so that, providing Britain's political influence over Arabia was not threatened, there were no great objections to American capital being injected into Saudi Arabia. With a boosted income from the concession Ibn Saud might even have honoured some of his debts to Britain.[220] At the same time, so confident were the British Government and oil companies of the absence of oil in Saudi Arabia that there was little need to protest against American oil activities. Once SOCAL realised its misjudgment it was expected that the company would pack up and withdraw. As it happened, events took a different turn.

The Admiralty expressed the importance of Britain's oil policy as follows:

> From a strategic point of view the essential point is that Great Britain should control the territories in which the oilfields are situated ... provided this can be secured, the composition of the company or companies which work the oilfields is a matter of less importance.[221]

True to this assessment Britain, despite the SOCAL concession, retained Saudi Arabia within her area of influence, a position which the United States never sought to challenge until the latter stages of the Second World War. In

1939 the American oil population in Nejd and Hasa amounted to only about three hundred drillers and technicians.[222] No doubt the British Government felt comforted by the comparative predominance of its political relations with Ibn Saud and the knowledge that, in the event of any untoward happenings in world affairs, it could still reassert its political control to wrest the oil from less favourably placed competitors. Indeed, something like this actually occurred from 1943 when British and American oil interests collided over Saudi oil.

Nor must it be overlooked that by 1933 Britain had secured all the oil she was likely to need from the Middle East – in Persia and Iraq. Only thus shielded was she prepared to invite the United States into the management of Iraqi oil, permit American ingress into Bahrain, and stand completely aside during the developments in Saudi Arabia. In the inter-war years commercial adventures by foreign nations, without an accompanying political or imperialistic motive, were, in general terms, not so much feared as encouraged by Britain in the days of the Open Door, when appearances of exclusive economic British control led to friction with her industrial competitors. The examples of the United States and Italy, in their different ways, lend credence to this general principle.

As long as the United States did not seek political influence to accompany her oil concession, the British Government was not too concerned. It took the particular circumstances of a world war and the changed international situation to concentrate attention on Saudi Arabia's oil resources. A slightly harsher view is offered by Klieman: America, under British protection, was able to establish and broaden contacts in Arabia, deriving benefits without commensurate responsiblities.[223]

The quest for oil in those states for which Britain had a mandatory or protectorate responsibility, notably Iraq and Kuwait, precipitated a certain strain in Anglo-American relations. Saudi Arabia, by virtue of her independence, led to no such conflicting interests. As for Ibn Saud, in the final analysis he would have turned almost anywhere for money. Britain conveyed no displeasure at his granting an oil concession to non-British interests. Nor do the records of the British Government reveal any suggestion of the SOCAL concession being regarded as an unfriendly act by Ibn Saud.

In conclusion, it can be suggested that the broad attitude of compromise and international co-operation which characterised Britain's Middle Eastern oil policy in the inter-war years was evident in the case of Saudi oil. That policy witnessed a conflict between the perceived strategic needs of the Admiralty, and the financial and political constraints within which other departments operated.[224] Saudi oil concessions must be seen in the context of a vague, overall British oil policy which operated not within a grand design or global context but on an *ad hoc* basis, fluctuating according to the economic, strategic and political conditions of the time.

REFERENCES FOR CHAPTER EIGHT

1. Some preliminary remarks are necessary at the start of this chapter. 'Oil' is the one issue examined in this study which has been exhaustively covered in recent literature. It has not been thought necessary to repeat well-known expositions. The affairs of private oil companies are not pursued. This account is concerned only with the role of the British Government in Saudi Arabia which, as will be made clear, was not unduly concerned with the 1933 Saudi oil concession upon which this chapter is based. Similarly, the United States State Department, while active in support of American companies elsewhere in the Middle East, had no cause for intervention in the case of the 1933 concession. As a consequence, this chapter limits itself to two principal issues: firstly, why did the 1933 concession go to American rather than British interests; and secondly, how did the British Government react to Arabian oil questions in the light of that concession?

2. Longrigg, *Oil* ..., p. 11.

3. In 1938, when Saudi Arabia yielded her first commercial quantities of oil, the Middle East, as a whole offered only 4–5% of the total world output. Britain, at that time, imported 57% of her oil from the Americas, and only 22% from the Middle East – most of which came from Persia. The detailed figures for Britain's oil imports are: Dutch West Indies & Venezuela – 35%; USA – 12%; Trinidad and other British territories – 5%; Mexico – 5%; Rumania – 4%; Iraq – 4%; Peru – 3%; USSR – 3%. (Monroe: *Britain's Moment* ..., p. 95; RIIA, *Political and Strategic Interests* ..., p. 129).

4. Monroe, op. cit., p. 96.

5. C. Davies, 'British Oil Diplomacy in the Middle East 1919-1932' (unpublished Ph.D), p. 1.

6. This culminated in 1911 with Winston Churchill, the First Lord of the Admiralty, introducing a three-year programme of naval expansion, the new ships to be fuelled by oil (Winston Churchill, *The World Crisis*, p. 134). As far back as 1882 it was remarked that 'the general adoption of oil instead of coal as the fuel for ships would immediately increase the fighting capacity of every fleet by at least 50%' (Captain John Fisher, later First Lord of the Admiralty, in Anton Mohr, *The Oil War*, p. 3).

7. George Stocking, *Middle East Oil*, p. 17.

8. An English entrepreneur, William Knox D'Arcy, won a concession in Persia in 1901. (Longrigg, op. cit., p. 17). Seven years later oil was struck in marketable quantities, and in 1909 D'Arcy became a director of the Anglo-Persian Oil Company (APOC). These developments made Persia the obvious place to assuage the Admiralty's anxieties.

9. Monroe, op. cit., p. 96. The alternative was for APOC to amalgamate with other companies, the Navy having to face inflated oil prices and uncertain supplies. The House of Commons approved the measure, but not before Ramsay MacDonald had warned that 'all commercial concessions, especially with government money in them, have a very unhappy knack in the course of time of becoming territorial concessions' (Stocking, p. 18).

10. Longrigg, op. cit., p. 12. The timing of this transaction, so near to the outbreak of war, has prompted the view that the two events were related: acquiring oil to fight the war. Monroe argues that the motives of the British Government were broader, seeking to protect the country both in peace and war against the vicissitudes of private oil companies (Monroe, op. cit., p. 98).

11. Longrigg, op. cit., p. 26.

12. The Foreign Office also sponsored, in March 1914, an agreement between British (50%), Dutch (25%) and German (25%) interests in a reorganised Turkish Petroleum Company (TPC) to develop oil deposits in Mosul (Monroe, op. cit., p. 101). After the War the British Government expropriated the German shareholding and transferred it to French interests (Stocking, p. 54).

13. H. St J.B. Philby, *Arabian Oil Ventures*, p. 3. Early interest in oil was in kerosene (paraffin). The development of the internal combustion engine made possible the harnessing of the more explosive gasoline (petrol) (J. E. Hartshorn, *Oil Companies and Governments*, p. 33).

14. France was appeased by her stake in Turkish Petroleum, while the United States became Britain's main rival in the search for Middle Eastern oil.
15. John DeNovo, *American Interests and Policies in the Middle East 1900-1939*, p. 168.
16. Gerald D. Nash, *United States Oil Policy 1890-1964*, pp. 47-9. The United States argument was based on 'co-belligerency'. The United States and its companies could not be deprived of the rights and privileges won after their contribution to victory over the central powers. The United States threatened that, if the Open Door was not observed, she would retaliate by closing all the areas under her influence to British oil operations (DeNovo, pp. 167-202, 389). On political grounds the United States did not seek a mandate for herself, but she did fear exclusion from oil exploration in Mosul, particularly when responsibility for the mandates passed to the Colonial Office (Niama, p. 64). In March 1921 Senator Henry Cabot Lodge protested at Britain's violation of the Open Door in Mesopotamia and proclaimed that 'England is taking possession of the oil supplies of the world' (Monroe, op. cit., p. 102). At that time Britain controlled only 5% of the world's oil production as against 80% under American ownership. The United States interpreted the figures differently. She was producing 68% of the world's oil while possessing only 16% of its known resources (J. Walt, 'Saudi Arabia and the Americans 1928-1951' (unpublished Ph.D.), pp. 59-61).

    It is worth stressing that during the early 1920s the lure of Middle Eastern oil lay only in is potential. Only Persia was producing oil at this time, apart from an erratic trickle from Egypt (Longrigg, op. cit., pp. 39-41). As communications and security improved, interest in Middle Eastern oil increased.
17. Longrigg, op. cit., p. 71.
18. Nash, p. 49. This quietened American fears about her domestic supplies and somewhat reduced her need for foreign oil until the Second World War (Walt, p. 92).
19. Stocking, p. 62.
20. Petroleum Dept. to FO, 22 June 1933, FO E/3361/487/91: 371/16871.
21. Stocking, p. 58.
22. Monroe, *Britain's Moment* ..., p. 102.
23. Stocking, p. 21.
24. Longrigg, *Oil* ..., p. 58.
25. Almana, p. 217.
26. Walt, pp. 70-1. Holmes also attempted to sell the concession to British oil interests (Benjamin Shwadran, *The Middle East, Oil, and the Great Powers*, p. 308).
27. Walt, p. 72.
28. ibid., pp. 77-8.
29. Philby's life has been well documented, not only by himself, but also in a biography by Elizabeth Monroe, *Philby of Arabia* (Hereafter: *Philby* ...,).
30. Monroe, *Philby* ..., p. 148. Philby was born in 1885, and was five years the junior of Ibn Saud. Upon leaving university he went, in 1908, into the service of the Government of India as a civil servant. In November 1915 the need for competent linguists and political officers provided him with his first taste of the Arab world, in Mesopotamia. One of Philby's duties was to prepare a detailed memorandum on conditions in central Arabia, thereby familiarising himself with the accomplishments of Ibn Saud. Philby was later chosen to lead a mission to Ibn Saud whom he met for the first time in November 1917.

    The troubles in Iraq, following the deposition of Feisal in Damascus in the summer of 1920, led to Philby being appointed Adviser to the Iraq Ministry of the Interior. He urged a republic for Iraq. When Feisal was put on the Iraq throne in 1921 Philby was transferred to Transjordan where, although still a British servant, he hoped to fulfil the aspirations of 'true' Arab independence. He took up the post of Chief British Representative in Amman but fell foul of the British High Commissioner, Sir Herbert Samuel, and the Emir Abdullah. He left the service of Transjordan in April 1924, although he continued to receive a pension from the Government of India (ibid., pp. 57, 66, 113, 132).
31. ibid., pp. 155, 164.
32. ibid., p. 164.
33. ibid., p. 203.
34. See FO E/1597/5/91: 371/11431.
35. This contradicts Monroe's contention (Monroe, *Philby* ..., p. 149).
36. See Monteagle minute, FO E/6109/2322/91: 371/13738.
37. Jordan (Jedda) to FO, 15 February 1926, FO E/1597/5/91: 371/11431.

38. ibid.
39. Wilson (CO) to Tyrrell (FO), 2 December 1926, FO E/6697/5/91: 371/11431.
40. Jedda Report for December 1928, FO E/484/484/91: 371/13010.
41. Stonehewer-Bird to Oliphant, 10 March 1928, FO E/1620/491/91: 371/13010.
42. Shuckburgh to Oliphant, 26 April 1928, CO/59057/28: 732/31.
43. Annual Report 1930.
44. Annual Report 1932.
45. Bullard to Ryan, 9 December 1936, Ryan Papers, Box 6, File 5, MEC.
46. Philby, *Saudi Arabia*, p.163; *Arabian Oil Ventures*, pp.74-5.
47. FO memorandum, 20 March 1931, FO E/1316/569/25: 371/15297.
48. Antonius, p.296. The Commission favoured the United States taking a mandate for the whole of historical Syria – that is, including Palestine and Lebanon (ibid., p .297).
49. FO memorandum, op. cit.
50. ibid.
51. Philby, *Saudi Arabia*, p.330.
52. See FO E/555/30/93: 371/15297.
53. FO minute on Twitchell's report, March 1932, FO E/1701/412/25: 371/16021.
54. Helm (FO) minute, 20 April 1932, FO E/1896/412/25: 371/16021.
55. FO minute, ibid.
56. Hope Gill to FO, No 160, 31 March 1932, ibid.
57. Tugendhat, p.89.
58. Hope Gill to FO, No 214, 18 May 1932, FO E/2818/412/25: 371/16021.
59. ibid.
60. Philby, *Arabian Oil Ventures*, p.79. It has been claimed that SOCAL made earlier efforts for the Saudi concession, in 1930, but had been rebuffed by Ibn Saud (Roy Lebkicher, *Aramco and World Oil*, pp.25-6).
61. Philby, op. cit., p.83.
62. Warner (FO) minute, 27 March 1933, FO E/1498/487/25: 371/16870.
63. Rendel minute, 28 March 1933, ibid.
64. Rendel minute, 28 March 1933, FO E/1558/487/25: 371/16870.
65. Philby, op. cit., pp.98-9.
66. Longrigg, *Oil* ..., p.107. Iraq Petroleum's directors pulled out of the Hasa negotiations on 5 May, on the negative advice of its geologists (Shwadran, op. cit., p.304).
67. Warner (FO) minute, 31 May 1933, FO E/2844/487/25: 371/16871.
68. Monroe, *Britain's Moment* ..., p.99.
69. ibid.
70. ibid., p.100.
71. Philby, op. cit., p.124.
72. Monroe, op. cit., p.107.
73. Cordell Hull, *Memoirs – Vol II*, p.1511. See also *New York Times*, 15 July 1933. As DeNovo has pointed out, the popular British view of the disposal of the concession is that SOCAL offered more money. The prevalent opinion from across the Atlantic is that Ibn Saud was anxious to be free from British economic restraints (DeNovo, p.207).
74. Ameen Rihani reports how some years previously Ibn Saud often spoke favourably about the United States (Rihani, *Ibn Saoud of Arabia: His People and his Land*, p.223). Rihani was, however, a Lebanese-American, having a connection with the US State Dept.
75. Philby, op. cit., p.126. Saudi sources also suggest that Ibn Saud kept delaying the SOCAL deal in the hope that Iraq Petroleum would offer more (personal correspondence from Robert Lacey).
76. Philby, op. cit., p.87.
77. Annual Report 1933.
78. ibid.; Annual Report 1936.
79. Annual Report 1936. This area was withheld from the concession out of deference to Moslem opinion. The concession was won against Italian pressure to gain the oil rights on the Farasan Islands.
80. Walt, p.133.
81. Ryan to Eden, Annual Report for 1935, 29 February 1936, FO E/1538/1538/25: 371/20064. (Hereafter: Annual Report 1935).
82. The Hejaz Concession was wound up in 1940.

83. Philby, *Arabian Oil Ventures*, p. 133.
84. This conclusion is also forcefully maintained by Shwadran, based on the testimony of Philby and Iraq Petroleum records (Shwadran, op. cit., p. 310).
85. Rendel to Cadman, 12 July 1933, FO E/3804/487/25: 371/16871.
86. Shwadran states that in 1935, only two years after losing the Hasa concession, the Anglo-Iranian Oil Company (AIOC), as APOC became known that year, offered £6 million to try and gain the Hasa concession (Shwadran, op. cit., pp. 312-3).
87. Calvert (Jedda) to FO, 10 July 1936, FO E/4348/1283/25: 371/20064.
88. ibid.
89. Annual Report 1936. World demand for oil was beginning to increase, in part as the Depression receded, in part because of the deteriorating international situation: Italy had annexed Abyssinia, Spain was on the verge of civil war, Germany had reoccupied the Rhineland, and Britain was commencing to rearm.
90. Ryan to FO, 15 March 1933, FO E/1750/487/25: 371/16870.
91. ibid. (& Philby, op. cit., p. 108).
92. ibid.
93. Philby, op. cit., pp. 110, 119-20.
94. These loans were, in fact, non-recoverable, but deductable from future royalties (Shwadran, op. cit., p. 312).
95. Annual Report 1933.
96. Philby, op. cit., p. 106.
97. ibid.
98. ibid.
99. Karl Twitchell, *Saudi Arabia*, p. 84.
100. Minute by Sir Charles Greenway (Chairman) to APOC Management Committee, 9 September 1924, in Tugendhat, p. 89.
101. Philby, op. cit., p. 121.
102. Twitchell, p. 81.
103. Philby, op. cit., p. 87.
104. ibid., pp. 119-20.
105. ibid., pp. 86-7.
106. ibid., p. 86.
107. Ryan to FO, 16 May 1933, FO E/2995/487/25: 371/16871.
108. Philby, op. cit., p. 88.
109. ibid., p. 125.
110. It should be noted that Twitchell does not mention Philby's role in helping SOCAL to win the concession (Twitchell, pp. 147-50). Nor does Crane. An early ARAMCO publication, by contrast, not only affirms Philby's role but minimises the freelance activities of Twitchell (Lebkicher, op. cit., pp. 25-6). See Shwadran for detailed discussion on this (Shwadran, op. cit., p. 310). Critics of the Philby-ARAMCO school of Arabian history point to this episode as an early indication of their partnership.
111. See pages 121-2.
112. Hejaz Memorandum, 8 February 1932, by Ryan, Ryan Papers, Box 6, File 8, MEC.
113. See Chapter Six.
114. See Chapter Seven.
115. Davies, p. 54.
116. Annual Report 1931.
117. Kennedy, 'Appeasement ...', p. 204.
118. Twitchell, p. 83.
119. ibid.
120. ibid., p. 88.
121. Howarth, p. 165.
122. ibid.
123. Annual Reports 1930 and 1933.
124. Howarth, p. 165. Ibn Saud was fortunate that when the slump arrived his internal position was relatively secure.
125. Annual Report 1933.
126. Philby, op. cit., pp. 73-4.
127. ibid.

128. ibid.
129. Hope Gill (Jedda) to Lord Reading, No 375, 30 September 1931, FO E/5141/1600/25: 371/15298.
130. Philby, op. cit., p.74.
131. Annual Report 1930.
132. Hope Gill to Simon, No 428, 19 October 1932, FO E/6086/165/25: 371/16019.
133. Rendel minute, 19 August 1931, FO E/4298/2064/25: 371/15299.
134. Dept. of Overseas Trade to FO, 14 October 1932, FO E/5370/412/25: 371/16021.
135. Philby, op. cit., p.99.
136. ibid., p.87.
137. Nash, p.99.
138. ibid., p.128.
139. ibid., p.127.
140. ibid., pp.105-9. Large integrated companies which were importing oil from the Middle East and Venezuela were warned that state legislatures might prohibit the operation of such corporations within their boundaries.
141. American links with the Middle East, apart from oil, before the Second World War were principally religious, educational and medical. These activities, particularly medical works, left a favourable impression in Arabia, as did Wilson's views on self-determination (DeNovo, pp.321, 355-6).
142. DeNovo, pp.334-5. The State Department did not appear to give much weight to the arguments of oil companies, that putative pro-Zionism might adversely affect American oil interests.
143. Walt, p.40. Official US policy throughout the inter-war years was characterised by deference to British political hegemony in the Middle East (DeNovo, pp.321, 346).
144. ibid., pp.40-4. There were American mission stations in Bahrain, Kuwait and Muscat.
145. Malcolm Peck, 'American Foreign Policy Towards Saudi Arabia' (unpublished Ph.D.), p.60.
146. ibid.
147. Walt, p.50.
148. ibid., p.46.
149. ibid., pp.47-8.
150. Peck, pp.53-4.
151. US Vice-Consul Aden to Sec. State, 6 May 1931, in Walt, p.44.
152. B. Thaw (US Embassy, London) verbally to FO, 7 May 1931, FO E/2421/1110/25: 371/15298.
153. Rendel minute, 3 April 1931, FO E/1601/569/25: 371/15297.
154. See Bruce M. Russett, Community and Contention: Britain and America in the Twentieth Century, p.13.
155. Northedge, The Troubled Giant, p.278.
156. Russett, p.10; Northedge, op. cit., pp.278-90.
157. H.C. Allen, Great Britain and the United States, pp.700-5, 735-44.
158. Russett, p.12.
159. Allen, p.750.
160. Russett, p.12.
161. ibid.
162. IO to FO, 19 July 1933, FO E/3990/234/25: 371/16868.
163. Russett, p.13.
164. Northedge, op. cit., p.359.
165. ibid., p.360.
166. ibid., p.359.
167. This view is shared by Finnie, who argues that Britain allowed American economic interests into the Gulf region because the United States was seen as the best possible partner in view of Britain's declining political and economic power (David Finnie, Desert Enterprise: The Middle East Oil Industry and its Local Environment, p.36).
168. For example, during the British quarrel with Turkey in 1923-4 over possession of the Mosul province, Monroe claims it was with strategic issues, to provide Iraq with a defendable mountainous northern frontier against Turkey, not the promise of oil, that Britain was primarily concerned (Monroe, Britain's Moment ..., p.103. A contrary view is proposed by Sluglett, pp.103-4, 114).

169. Reilly (Aden) to CO, 8 December 1926, CO/23448/26: 725/9.
170. Osborne (FO) minute, 15 January 1927, FO E/229/22/91: 371/12233.
171. Oliphant memorandum, 6 January 1927, FO E/175/22/91: 371/12233.
172. ibid.
173. Graham (Rome) to Chamberlain, No 11, 13 January 1927, FO E/229/22/91: 371/12233.
174. Osborne minute, op. cit.
175. See FO E/376/22/91: 371/12235.
176. Shuckburgh to FO, 18 February 1927, CO/48023/27: 725/12.
177. Dashwood (FO) minute, 21 February 1927, FO E/843/22/91: 371/12236.
178. Osborne minute, 24 August 1927, FO E/3621/22/91: 371/12238.
179. Davies, p.xiii.
180. ibid., p.62.
181. ibid., pp.62-3, 71, 84-5.
182. Twitchell, p.211.
183. Walt, p.105.
184. FO to Ryan, 13 April 1933, FO E/1750/487/25: 371/16870.
185. See FO E/1825/487/25: 371/16870.
186. See Freeth and Winstone, pp.137-8.
187. Oliphant to Vansittart, January 1932, ibid., p.135.
188. FO to Ryan, op. cit.
189. See Longrigg, *Oil* ..., p.111.
190. See Freeth and Winstone, p.162.
191. To strategic planners, neutral zones served the same function as other types of buffer zones, except that they were not constituted into separate political units, but were administered, usually, by both flanking states (Prescott, p.47).
192. Annual Report 1934.
193. Inter-departmental meeting at IO, 15 February 1934, FO E/1166/4/25: 371/17918.
194. ibid.
195. ibid.
196. ibid.
197. ibid.
198. Rendel minute, ibid.
199. Rendel minute, 17 February 1934, ibid.
200. Ryan to FO, 9 February 1934, FO E/1427/4/25: 371/17918.
201. Johnstone (FO) minute, 8 March 1934, ibid.
202. Ryan to FO, 20 March 1934, ibid.
203. Warner (FO) minute, 11 April 1934, FO E/2065/4/25: 371/17919.
204. Warner minute, 9 April 1934, ibid.
205. ibid.
206. FO memorandum 8 November 1934, FO E/6809/4/25: 371/17919.
207. Dickson has already been featured in connection with the *Ikhwan* rebellion (see pages 118-19). He had developed opinions sufficiently anti-Saudi to register considerable disquiet in Foreign Office minutes (see Rendel minute, 14 October 1934, FO E/6189/4/25: 371/17919).
208. FO memorandum, op. cit.
209. ibid.
210. ibid. The Saudi Government did not press its desire for bisection of the neutral zone.
211. Shwadran, op. cit., p.307.
212. Bullard to Halifax, No 62, Political Review 1939, FO E/2720/1194/25: 371/24589.
213. ibid.
214. Bullard to FO, Jedda Monthly Report, July 1939, FO E/588/588/25: 371/23271/588. The area covered by the enlarged concession was 440,000 square miles (Shwadran, op. cit., p.312).
215. The Second World War, and particularly the entry of the United States, hindered the development of Saudi oil. Nearer sources were at hand. After the war, production and exploration mushroomed, leading to the resulting oil giant that dominates the oil world today. To operate the Saudi concession SOCAL had set up the Californian Arabian Standard Oil Company (CASOC) which, in 1944, took on the modern name of the Arabian American Oil Company (ARAMCO). ARAMCO became the largest single overseas American investment with $2 billion being invested by 1970 (Sheikh Rustum Ali,

Saudi Arabia and Oil Diplomacy, p.76).

216. Peck, p.ii.
217. Monroe, *Britain's Moment* ..., p.96 (see also Sluglett, pp.2-3).
218. Rendel, *The Sword and the Olive*.
219. FO memorandum, 14 March 1918, in L/P&S/10/2249/1915/1918/1/996, in Sluglett, p.107.
220. By 1939 little impression had been made on those debts. Saudi Arabia still owed substantial amounts for the purchase of arms from the Government of India in 1929, as well as more than £100,000 to Sharqieh, Gellatly Hankey Ltd., and the Eastern Telegraph Co.
221. Adm to FO, 6 December 1922, in Sluglett, p.110.
222. Bullard to Halifax, No 62, Political Review 1939, FO E/2720/1194/25: 371/24589.
223. Klieman, p.252.
224. Davies, p.86.

CHAPTER NINE

South-East Arabia: The Anglo-Saudi Frontier Dispute from 1934

Immediately following the award of a Saudi concession to the Standard Oil Company of California (SOCAL) in 1933, problems arose over the precise geographical limits of that concession and possible future ones. The problem escalated until it became apparent that the entire issue of the frontiers between Saudi Arabia and the British-protected coastal territories of eastern and southern Arabia was at stake.

This dispute is, therefore, in addition to its dependence on the oil factor, another example of the significance of territorial issues in Anglo-Saudi relations. Furthermore, as Sir Andrew Ryan admitted, this was to constitute the most serious disagreement between the two countries in the 1930s.[1] The frontier dispute in south-east Arabia, like the *Ikhwan* rebellion, was partially precipitated by a clash between Arab (tribal) and western (territorial) concepts of 'frontier'.[2] Unlike the position in northern Arabia, however, Britain had not, by 1933, agreed an eastern and southern frontier for Ibn Saud's Kingdom, so that while the boundary between Saudi Arabia and the mandates had been settled, that with the Gulf sheikhdoms (with the exception of Kuwait) had not. As suggested in the previous chapter, any frontiers imposed on Arabia after 1933 had to take account, to a greater or lesser extent, of the oil factor.[3]

Background to the Dispute

The series of Gulf treaties with Britain, mostly extending back to the nineteenth century, concentrated on four basic points. The rulers agreed firstly, not to cede, sell or mortgage territory, except with British consent; to suppress the slave trade; and prohibit arms traffic. Secondly, with the exception of the Sultan of Muscat, they agreed not to enter negotiations with, or receive representatives from, other powers. Similarly, with the exception of Muscat, the sheikhs were promised British protection from aggression by sea. Finally, all the rulers, apart from the Sheikh of Kuwait, promised peace in perpetuity with the British Government.[4]

The strategic significance of the Gulf to Britain after the War, what with the establishment of the mandates and the quest for oil concessions, was greater than ever. As from 1914 India reactivated her practice, abandoned back in 1897, of maintaining a permanent naval presence in the Gulf.[5] The advent of long-distance aircraft then transformed the Gulf from a maritime cul-de-sac and a British lake into an aerial through-route for both military and commercial purposes. From 1925 the Gulf was flanked by two national-istic, independent rulers: Ibn Saud and Reza Khan. Persia posed an ineffec-tive buffer against the Soviet Union who, with the development of air power and cross-country vehicles, could overcome the technical obstacles to reach-ing the Gulf.[6]

The Air Ministry was trying to establish a line of bases from Cairo to the Cape, and from Cairo to Singapore.[7] From 1929 British Imperial Airways commenced their services to the East, via Persia. Biscoe described the air route as 'one of the romances of the British Empire',[8] and Trenchard proclaimed that 'a rupture of the Persian Gulf link would be just as grave a disaster to the Air Force as the closing of the Suez Canal would be to the Navy'.[9] In March 1929 the RAF's existing responsibilities in Iraq were extended throughout the Gulf.[10] Because the RAF was assigned to assist in the establishment of the imperial route, it inevitably became more and more involved in Gulf politics and administration. The age-old axiom of non-intervention in internal Gulf affairs was largely eroded by 1939.

The Persian aerial rights were precarious and short-term, and in the face of deteriorating Anglo-Persian relations (such as the operations of APOC) the Foreign Office, from October 1932, switched the route to the opposite, Arab shore of the Gulf – via Basra, Bahrain, Sharjah and Gwadar in Baluchistan.[11]

The British Government had entered into protracted negotiations with Ibn Saud about the establishment of emergency landing strips in Hasa, in return for an agreed rent. The supply of planes to Ibn Saud in 1929, the negotiations for which had been proceeding since 1926, were, in part, intended to encourage his compliance in an Arabian air route.[12] Despite his need for revenue, the rental demanded was far above that which Britain was prepared to offer,[13] and in any case Ibn Saud was acutely conscious of the opposition from within and without his country to granting any such facilities to the British infidel. Moreover, Ibn Saud must have feared the prospect of foreign planes in his Kingdom after observing their effect during the *Ikhwan* rebellion. By 1932, however, developments in aerial technology enabled aircraft, with their greater range, to need fewer landing grounds or refuelling stops,[14] and pressure on Ibn Saud to provide bases gradually abated.

By 1939 BOAC (as Imperial Airways was renamed in 1938), together with Dutch and French airlines, were all running regular services to the Far East via the Gulf, and the Arabian staging posts had all been developed into amphibious international landing grounds.[15] The new strategic significance of the Gulf states, as air bases and facilities were extended during the course of the 1930s, coupled with the coincident interest in oil in eastern Arabia, provided a brace of compelling reasons for fixing the frontiers between Saudi Arabia and Britain's protégés.[16]

Conflict between the House of Saud and the Gulf sheikhs can be traced back to the early years of Wahhabi expansion in the eighteenth century. In the summer of 1925, during the Hejaz-Nejd war, the sheikhs of various tribes in the Abu Dhabi and Muscat hinterland banded together out of fear of the Saudi Governor of Hasa, Abdullah ibn Jiluwi.[17] Within two months of Ibn Saud being proclaimed King of the Hejaz, Ibn Jiluwi sent officials to collect *zakat* (the tax was paid to any ruler capable of extracting it) from the tribes of the Dhafrah desert south of Abu Dhabi, and as far eastwards as the Buraimi oasis on the Abu Dhabi-Muscat frontier.[18] Buraimi had not been in Saudi hands since 1869.[19] Some of the tribes, it was believed, paid the tax, an acknowledgment in Saudi eyes of Ibn Saud's sovereignty. The Political Resident, Colonel Prideaux, considered that Ibn Saud was seeking to subjugate the Trucial states and Oman by exploiting inter-tribal rivalry.[20]

The British Government had yet to give serious consideration to the frontiers separating Ibn Saud's dominions from the Gulf states. The Political Resident's advice was disquieting. He urged that if Britain wanted to preserve the sheikhdoms from Saudi aggrandisement then the strongest possible warning had to be delivered to Ibn Saud. Prideaux enquired whether the British Government was ready to concur in the Saudi annexation of Buraimi. He half anticipated that the Gulf sheikhs would ask to come under Ibn Saud's protection, mollifying Britain by agreeing not to repudiate their maritime truce. Prideaux expected the whole hinterland of south-east Arabia to be eventually absorbed by Nejd – if it was not already.[21]

In August 1926 an inter-departmental conference considered the problem of Ibn Saud's expansionist aims in south-east Arabia. Britain was, at that time, in the first stages of negotiating a new treaty with Ibn Saud. He would be furnished with copies of all Britain's treaties with the Gulf rulers, but not, significantly, with the Anglo-Turkish Conventions which before the First World War had marked off British and Ottoman spheres of influence in the region. The India Office feared that the Gulf treaties were so vague as regards Britain's defensive obligations that divulging them was more likely to encourage than deter Saudi aggression.[22]

The general opinion of the conference was that it was undesirable for Britain to be committed *vis à vis* Ibn Saud to the protection of the Trucial sheikhdoms.[23] It was admitted that 'this is a weak but ... a wise policy'.[24] As for establishing a recognised eastern frontier for Ibn Saud's dominions, it was considered whether to fall back on the 'blue line', which had formed part of the Anglo-Turkish Conventions of 1913-14.[25] These documents had bisected the map of Arabia with blue and violet lines. The blue line presented a convenient eastern frontier for Ibn Saud's Kingdom, even though he was later to disclaim any knowledge of it. The blue line ran roughly through the centre of the Jafurah desert, which constituted a natural geographical division between Nejd and Hasa on the one hand, and eastern Arabia on the other.

The India Office suggested, rather self-defeatingly, that if Ibn Saud would agree to this frontier he could, as a reward, still collect *zakat* from Wahhabis east of the blue line.[26] This notion, of imposing a linear frontier while condoning the exercise of Ibn Saud's tribal and religious authority beyond it, raised doubts about the whole object of the frontier. The Foreign Office appreciated, in this context, that Britain's engagements with the Trucial states were both anachronistic and dangerous, and hoped that they would be reviewed at an early date.[27] No further action was taken regarding *zakat*-collecting expeditions pending the conclusion of the new treaty.[28]

From 1926 the problem temporarily subsided. Although occasional reports of *zakat*-collecting missions continued to reach British officials until 1929, they warranted no response. Ibn Saud had problems enough, first of all in the Hejaz, and then with the *Ikhwan* rebellion to be concerned about aggrandisement in south-east Arabia. The British Government had no desire to invite a quarrel with Ibn Saud over an area that was largely uninhabited and unexplored. Besides, there was at the time little liaison between the Foreign Office, which tended to concentrate on pre-World War One international agreements such as the Anglo-Turkish Conventions, and the India Office, which reflected pragmatic, local Gulf considerations.[29]

Nonetheless, Prideaux's successor as Political Resident, Colonel Haworth, was so alarmed at Ibn Saud's potentially disruptive effect on the Trucial sheikhdoms that he advocated a change in Britain's whole policy in the Gulf. Rather than abstain from all but naval commitments, Haworth felt the necessity for Britain to assume a wide range of measures to protect the sheikhdoms from Ibn Saud, such as offering protection by land as well as by sea, and making provision for orderly succession among the Trucial rulers.[30] When the Treaty of Jedda dispensed with any undertaking on the part of Ibn Saud to refrain from aggression in the Gulf, Haworth went so far as to advocate a string of 'Gibraltars' around the Gulf to be occupied by the Admiralty.[31] This amounted to a call for a formal protectorate to be established over the Trucial coast. It was rejected (as a similar suggestion in 1902 had been) on the grounds that it would incense all parties – the sheikhs, Ibn Saud, and Arab opinion in general – not to mention encourage provocation on the part of the sheikhs.[32]

An incident at the end of 1931 provided the only other occasion for British concern at Ibn Saud's interest in eastern Arabia prior to the granting of the Hasa oil concession. Philby, seeking permission to cross the Rub al Khali, told the Mecca newspaper *Umm al Qura* that:

> I undertake to furnish Your Majesty's Government [of Hejaz-Nejd] with all the information I may collect during that journey ... such information would be the property of Your Majesty's Government ... I declare that my Government [Britain] have no right to claim any-

thing as a result of the discoveries I may make. All the territories I may discover and information I may obtain are the property of Your Majesty and no-one has the right to claim any of them. I undertake to place your flags of victory over every high place we may pass by.[33]

Ibn Saud, referring to Philby's journey, spoke of the Rub al Khali as his own country.[34] Hope Gill, in Ryan's absence from Jedda, passed this information to the Foreign Office, adding that 'this seems to have no practical importance at the moment. The north and north-west, at any rate, of the Rub al Khali, so far as they belong to anyone, do, I suppose, belong to him [Ibn Saud]'.[35] Rendel was less sympathetic. The blue line idea, mooted in 1926, had apparently taken root:

> We regard the south-eastern boundary of Ibn Saud's territories as the line laid down in the unratified Anglo-Turkish Conventions of 1914 [sic] ... All of the Rub al Khali is regarded in south-east Arabia as no-man's land under nobody's sovereignty. We don't want Ibn Saud, or Philby on his behalf, putting out claims to the hinterland of the Trucial Coast or the Hadramaut.[36]

These remarks are of significance for two reasons. First, they show that even before the introduction of oil in Saudi affairs, the Foreign Office was not prepared to permit excessive Saudi expansionism eastwards. Second, the Foreign Office had tacitly decided upon the blue line as marking the eastern limit of Ibn Saud's territories.

In 1933 the Sheikh of Qatar visited Ibn Saud at Riyadh. The Sheikh had been trying for some time to win a British guarantee against attack by land (from Ibn Saud), not just by sea as his treaty stipulated.[37] Ryan suspected him of reinsuring with Ibn Saud. At the time, APOC was winding up its prospecting in Qatar under a licence granted the previous year.[38] The SOCAL concession in Hasa had been worded as extending up to the eastern frontier of Saudi Arabia[39] – whatever and wherever that was. Before the end of 1933 the United States Government requested from Turkey and then from Britain the exact location of that frontier.[40]

The Sheikh of Qatar had previously been resisting British pressure to grant a full oil concession to APOC – presumably under direction from Ibn Saud. It was feared that Ibn Saud might demand a favourable Saudi-Qatar frontier, and that he would encourage SOCAL to move for a concession in Qatar.[41] Laithwaite, of the India Office, suggested that while the blue line should be upheld as Saudi Arabia's eastern frontier, the southern limits of Qatar should be a line put forward by the Iraq Petroleum Company, which left a void between it and the blue line.[42] Because of this discrepancy Laithwaite hoped to avoid raising the whole question.

Ryan warned that Ibn Saud would resist the blue line, because it implied that he was restricted as successor to the Turks. If any attempt was made to settle Qatar's land frontier, Ibn Saud would assume he ruled up to it.[43]

Fowle, the latest Political Resident, admitted that because the Anglo-Turkish Conventions treated Nejd and Qatar as coterminous when settling British and Turkish spheres of influence, Ibn Saud would regard any frontier proposed by Iraq Petroleum for Qatar as superseding the blue line.[44] The Middle East (Official) Sub-Committee decided to make a stand on the blue line, declaring that the territory between it and the base of Qatar should be considered as within Britain's sphere of influence, and appertaining to Qatar.[45] In the absence of any specific reference to south-east Arabian frontiers in any of Ibn Saud's treaties with Britain, the Anglo-Turkish Conventions constituted the only internationally recognised sanction for division of spheres of influence between Ibn Saud and the British Government. Without adherence to the blue line, the British Government felt that it would be deprived of any legal grounds for contesting future Saudi expansion over the whole south-eastern mass of the peninsula.[46]

In the spring of 1934 war broke out between Saudi Arabia and the Yemen. Were it not for the embarrassment of America's request for clarification of the frontier, and the fear that Ibn Saud might hear of Britain's reply through American channels, Britain would have preferred to delay conveying the blue line decision to Ibn Saud indefinitely.[47] Ibn Saud was already aggrieved at the lack of British advice or assistance over his confrontation with the Yemen.[48] Unable to stall any longer, on 28 April 1934, with Saudi forces in the Yemen apparently on the ascendent, and shortly after the British decision on the blue line was communicated to the United States, Ryan passed a similar message on to the Saudi Arabian Government, plus copies of the relevant Anglo-Turkish Conventions.[49]

The Development of the Dispute

(i) *Ibn Saud's Reaction to, and Ryan's Assessment of, the Blue Line*   The reaction of the Saudi Government to the blue line frontier was unequivocal, as Ryan had warned. The circumstances pertaining to 1914, it was maintained, had no standing twenty years later. The applicability of the Anglo-Turkish Conventions was refuted on several counts.[50] First, the Turkish Government had no *locus standi* in the matter of Saudi frontiers following the expulsion of Turkish forces from Hasa in April 1913.[51] Second, the Anglo-Saudi treaty of 1915 undertook to recognise Saudi sovereignty on the basis of ancestral territories, which, it was claimed, extended way beyond the blue line. The supposedly independent territories of Qatar, Muscat and Oman were not true sovereignties at all, but part of Saudi dominions. All the tribes living between the coastal towns of Qatar and the coast of Oman and Hadramaut belonged, it was insisted, to Saudi Arabia. They were entirely submissive to the laws of that state, paid *zakat*, and were obedient to the calls of the Saudi Government in time of war.[52]

Whether or not by coincidence, the Saudi Government also brought up the question of the Treaty of Jedda which was due for renegotiation, should either party desire it, seven years after its signature in May 1927. One of the Articles in contention was Article Six, which related to Britain's special position with the Gulf states.[53] The Foreign Office was confident that the Saudi Government would not, out of its own interests, revoke the treaty, particularly with the continuing uncertainty in the Red Sea. Saudi protestations were considered to be cosmetic rather than substantial.

The British Government duly replied to Ibn Saud that Saudi expansion since 1913 had no bearing on the validity of the blue line or the Anglo-Turkish Conventions.[54] Nonetheless, the force of the Saudi reaction necessitated a closer look at the commitment to the blue line. It was Ryan himself who was largely responsible for this reappraisal. In July 1934 Ibn Saud took the unprecedented step of inviting Ryan, who was about to journey to London on leave, to the mountain resort at Taif, outside Mecca, to discuss a range of problems – but particularly the blue line.[55] Ryan later confided to the Foreign Office that he had found the meeting difficult and embarrassing. With regard to the blue line, Ryan considered Ibn Saud to have a strong case.[56] Ryan's arguments are significant because they cast so much doubt on the integrity of Britain's blue line policy:

> I cannot personally believe in the undoubted validity of the blue line. It appears to me that, in 1915 and 1927, HMG were content to treat Qatar, the Trucial sheikhdoms, and Muscat and Oman as coterminous with Bin Saud's dominions, whatever the boundaries. ... I do not think that it can seriously be maintained that GB has a sphere of influence in eastern Arabia except in the sense that her influence extends to the coastal principalities up to their territorial limits, whatever these may be. ... Moreover, the treaty of 1915 destroyed the validity of the blue line by substituting a new criterion for determination of Bin Saud's boundaries. He was to be recognised as independent up to his ancestral limits, probably well east of the blue line. Nor can we say that the 1927 treaty re-entitled Britain to rely on the blue line because Bin Saud was no longer a rebel against the Turks but the ruler of a succession state. In which case Britain should have made this clear, but they made no reference to the blue line and treated, by implication, the coastal rulers as though they were Bin Saud's neighbours. Whatever the legal position the political position is equally important. Hatred of the Turks is in his blood and he won't accept any position which rests on *ex post facto* recognition of their rights.
>
> Certain tribes have been within his influence for years. He won't accept a compromise of a British sphere of influence in the interior of Arabia as distinct from a sphere of quasi-protectors of the coastal states. If he did recognise such a British sphere he would go down in history as one of the lost leaders.[57]

On the magnitude of the dispute before Britain Ryan was quite emphatic:

> I do not think I exaggerate when I say that the future relations of HMG

with Bin Saud depends very largely on their attitude in regard to this question. I have regretted the unwillingness of HMG to admit frankly to Bin Saud that their interest in the area in dispute is due largely to its oil possibilities. Bin Saud knows this but is too canny to say so himself.[58]

Back in 1932 Ryan had considered the best all-round British policy towards Ibn Saud. He had on that occasion advocated a middle course, adopting a friendly *laissez-faire* position rather than one of either positive support or, at the other extreme, a rigid attitude to British interests.[59] Even at that time, Ryan had hinted at future problems over the Gulf sheikhs, at least some of whom were known to be paying tribute to Ibn Saud.[60]

As Ryan learned at Taif, through taking advantage of a rare face-to-face meeting with Ibn Saud, the looming frontier difficulties in south-east Arabia were symptomatic of a potentially exacting period for Anglo-Saudi relations. Not only had Ibn Saud just emerged from a war with the Imam, with whom Britain had recently signed a treaty which had possibly encouraged Yemeni aggression, but the independence of Iraq in 1932, and the sudden death of King Feisal the following year, heralded years of uncertainty in Iraq's affairs. Ibn Saud expressed fears of foreign intervention in his Kingdom, not only from Italy, but also from Turkish or Persian menaces that threatened to engulf Iraq under a tide of nationalist sentiment.[61] The blue line, on top of everything else, had 'thrown Ibn Saud into one of his periodic fits of anxiety over his position with Britain'.[62] Ibn Saud sought Ryan's views on a possible defensive arrangement between Saudi Arabia and Iraq under British auspices.[63] This was the first in a series of approaches by Ibn Saud aimed at a defensive alliance involving Britain, one which was peremptorily rejected. Having just freed Iraq from the mandate, Britain was not enthusiastic to enter further Middle Eastern pacts. Under the 1930 Anglo-Iraqi Treaty of Alliance, Britain was bound to aid Iraq in any war. An Iraqi-Saudi pact would, therefore, involve Britain in any military commitments that Iraq undertook with Saudi Arabia.[64]

Ryan was aware that there were other contentious issues in Anglo-Saudi relations. These included the still unresolved question of possible landing facilities in Hasa, unpaid Saudi debts, and concern over various parts of the Saudi-Transjordan frontier.[65] In addition, there was Saudi Arabia's strained relations with Kuwait and Bahrain. Ibn Saud's trade blockade on Kuwait, imposed in 1920,[66] had become even more sensitive by 1934 owing to the political disturbances in Iraq and the increased pivotal position of Kuwait as a strategic focal point in the Middle East. Bahrain had also witnessed a protracted dispute over the transit dues imposed on Nejdi trade passing through the sheikhdom.[67]

These various difficulties prompted Ryan to reassess his broad policy proposals made in 1932. He now advocated a more constructive policy towards Ibn Saud, even an Anglo-Saudi entente, the cornerstone of which would be a generous settlement of the eastern frontier question.[68] The expiration of the initial period of the Treaty of Jedda, Ryan felt, provided a good opportunity for a comprehensive understanding with Ibn Saud of all desiderata.[69]

1934 was a notable year for face-to-face contact in Anglo-Saudi relations. Not only was Ryan invited to Taif to meet Ibn Saud, but in the autumn he persuaded the Saudi King to send Fuad Bey Hamza, the Deputy Saudi Foreign Minister, to London.[70] Fuad Hamza's presence, together with that of Ryan and Sheikh Hafiz Wahba, would lead to several audiences with the Foreign Office. These meetings enabled both parties to state their positions clearly with less risk of misunderstanding. In view of the depth of Ibn Saud's feelings, coupled with the British Minister's sympathy with them and his arguments for a new policy to deal with the matter, the weeks before Ryan's and Fuad Hamza's arrival saw a thorough re-examination of Britain's position on the blue line.

(ii) *The Legal Position*   The first approach was to consider the strength of the blue line according to international law.[71] The Western yardstick in such cases has turned on 'sovereignty' and 'undisturbed possession'.[72] The legal minds of the Foreign Office soon came up with the verdict that Britain had no case at all.[73] In the first place, Ibn Saud's presumed territorial claims extended over the whole hinterland of south-east Arabia where no pretence could be made that effective rule was maintained by Britain's protégés. The Gulf sheikhs ruled over limited stretches of coast with little and ill-defined influence inland. So, when the United States had been informed that the blue line divided Saudi Arabia from a British sphere of influence, it was not a realistic picture. It was truer to say that the blue line divided Ibn Saud's Kingdom from a vast political vacuum, where the only infiltration was from the direction of Saudi Arabia.

The legal position seemed to be as follows. One of the principal Saudi arguments was that the Turks were not sovereign in Hasa at the time of the Anglo-Turkish Conventions. Ibn Saud had captured the province weeks before the signing of the 1913 Convention.[74] Yet his subsequent treaty with the Turks in May 1914 reaffirmed the continuity of Turkish sovereignty and earmarked Nejd as a succession state.[75] Yet this only meant that Ibn Saud could not claim territory beyond the blue line as an agent of the Turks. It was admitted that since 1914 he had acquired sovereignty beyond the blue line in his own name, not that of the Turks. By contrast, the sovereignty of Britain's Gulf protégés extended nowhere near it.[76]

The legal advisers of the Foreign Office accepted that the whole sparsely populated hinterland of south-east Arabia was a political void, open to acquistion by Ibn Saud or anybody else.[77] Under international law if a territory was not under the sovereignty of a particular state it was open to occupation by another state. As was conceded by the Foreign Office, 'spheres of influence' in international law meant nothing at all. If Britain or any other state claimed a sphere of influence, yet exercised no *de facto* sovereignty within it, then, in the absence of specific international treaties banning encroachment, other powers were perfectly entitled to assert themselves.[78] Spheres of influence may have had currency in political terms, but legally they had none.

Similarly, a mere claim to 'sovereignty' over a territory, without physical backing to the claim, could not exclude other states. Rendel felt that Britain's legal case might have been unassailable had the territory on the immediate eastern side of the blue line been under effective British sovereignty.[79] As it was, the Sheikh of Qatar, in whose name the British Government wanted to claim much of the area, had never exercised sovereignty as far westwards as the blue line – nor was he aware of Britain's desires to enlarge his sheikhdom on his behalf.[80] Even if, in his 1914 treaty with the Turks, Ibn Saud had implied that the area immediately east of the blue line near the Gulf belonged to Qatar, this could not prevent either Turkey or, later, Saudi Arabia occupying empty and unclaimed desert.[81] No credibility would have been attached to any claim that the disputed area belonged to the Sheikh of Qatar.

Further weaknesses in Britain's position stemmed from her treaties with Ibn Saud, which had not only avoided mention of the blue line, but had implied that Nejd and Qatar were coterminous. The 1915 treaty had laid down that future negotiations on Ibn Saud's frontiers would be based on ancestral factors although, to be precise, the treaty had listed certain specific territories as constituting Ibn Saud's ancestral rights. The 1927 treaty specifically abrogated the earlier treaty stipulation that Ibn Saud was not to disturb the *status quo* in eastern Arabia, and had substituted no comparable undertaking. Furthermore, the 1922 frontier negotiations mediated by Sir Percy Cox had adopted, in the case of Kuwait, frontiers which bore little resemblance to those agreed upon with Turkey in the 1913 Convention.[82] This, in itself, implied that the boundaries of the old Ottoman Empire, as well as the Anglo-Turkish agreements, were hardly sacrosanct or held to be immutable by the British Government. The conclusion of the legal examination left no doubt over the strengths of Britain's position:

> There is no doubt that the attempt to impose on Bin Saud the 'blue and violet' lines after twenty years of silence regarding them can only strike Bin Saud as an attempt to trick him by legal subtleties today out of what we led him to expect when we wished to enlist his support in downing the Turks.[83]
>
> Legally, the sphere of influence argument is hopeless, and substantial use of it seems to be an admission of weakness on our part and a virtual giving away of any legal case we may have. I do not think that we should win before a tribunal operating on legal principles.[84]
>
> Whether our case with regard to the blue line is sound or not it is all we have. We shall have to take our stand on it and make the best use of

it with the knowledge that we shall not be able to maintain the line but will have to accept something less favourable.[85]

The legal position had been re-examined and it now seemed clear that it would be most difficult for HMG to establish an unassailable legal case.[86]

In summary, whether or not Ibn Saud had a strong legal claim to an area east of the blue line, the British Government had not. Consequently, if Ibn Saud did grant further oil concessions to the Americans in that area, Britain had no legal grounds upon which to object. She had no *de jure* or *de facto* authority in the eastern Arabian hinterland and, whatever Ibn Saud's present influence there, he was perfectly free to extend it at will into what was simply a political vacuum.[87]

Britain was not technically in a position to offer a fresh frontier, even one favouring Saudi Arabia, because she was not legally in a position to offer anything.[88] It was apparent that Britain had no legal right of interference except where the established authority of the Trucial chiefs was being compromised, and even then Britain was only pledged to safeguard them from a seaward attack. Consequently, whatever case Britain salvaged, it was clear that it would have to be constructed around political considerations rather than legal ones. It was hoped that Ibn Saud would not contest the blue line according to international law, and in that case Britain was quite prepared to make minor territorial adjustments, irrespective of her right to do so, in his favour.[89] Rendel's overview of the British position was thoroughly bleak:

> We have from the first recognised that the blue line is a bad frontier: our rights are very doubtful and Bin Saud's prestige is so deeply involved that he is unlikely to give way, except over compulsion, which HMG are not prepared to undertake. We could, of course, attempt to bluff, and we must to some extent do so, or we may find ourselves with no means of opposing possible claims by Bin Saud to practically the whole of south-east Arabia.[90]

Rendel's admission that force was not to be contemplated reaffirmed the traditional British view of detachment and non-involvement where Arabia was concerned, save where vital imperial interests were affected. Such interests had been raised in the case of Iraq during the *Ikhwan* rebellion; those interests being protected by a defensive treaty and the presence of imperial forces. The Trucial sheikhdoms, in 1934, lacked this importance. Britain was clearly not going to risk conflict with Saudi Arabia for the sake of the Sheikh of Qatar who, in any case, was not a party to the quarrel.[91]

It was also conceded that, in a sense, Britain had created a problem where none had previously existed. Whilst it was acknowledged that the rights and interests of Britain's Gulf protégés should be protected, none of the sheikhdoms claimed more than a small strip of coastline. In the Treaty of Jedda Ibn

Saud had agreed to maintain that obligation, and by 1934 Saudi agents were causing rather less nuisance than at certain times in the past.[92]

At this stage it becomes apparent that there was more to British thinking than oil and the need to protect the Trucial sheikhdoms. There was also the matter of British prestige in Arabia. The British Government did not want to be seen to back down to Ibn Saud for fear of the effect it would have throughout Arabia.[93] It is probable that a rather insignificant frontier disagreement over sparsely inhabited desert escalated into a major crisis, not because of the issues at stake, but because Britain, having prematurely adopted one position, feared for future developments if she appeared to back down.

The Foreign Office agreed to Ryan's suggestion of making concessions on the blue line with a *quid pro quo*. A comprehensive new settlement was to be sought with Ibn Saud which would replace and supersede the Treaty of Jedda. Substantial territorial concessions would be made to Saudi Arabia, but would be camouflaged within a general settlement of Anglo-Saudi desiderata. That Britain had found herself involved in an unnecessary quarrel from which she was unable to retreat was given further credence when Rendel admitted: 'I am convinced that the proposed concession would not, in fact, be any real sacrifice to us'.[94] The new strategy was endorsed by Sir Robert Vansittart, Permanent Under-Secretary of State at the Foreign Office, who was 'convinced that we had better have a new deal if we can get one. There is no trick-taking power in our hand at all'.[95]

To prepare the way for the London conversations with Fuad Hamza the Middle East (Official) Sub-Committee of the CID was convened on 13 September 1934. Representatives from the Foreign Office, Colonial Office, India Office, War Office, Treasury, Admiralty and Air Ministry – together with Ryan and Fowle (the Political Resident) – reflected the conflicting departmental perspectives on eastern Arabian frontiers. The sub-committee had to contend with two basic facts: first, Ryan's warning of Ibn Saud's depth of feeling on the matter, and that the future harmony of Anglo-Saudi relations was at stake; and second, the Foreign Office's admission that Britain could not legally hold the Anglo-Turkish Conventions as binding on Saudi Arabia.[96]

To Rendel's proposal of making the maximum possible concessions to Saudi Arabia in return for concessions elsewhere, Fowle stressed that Britain was, as things stood, under no obligation to protect the Gulf sheikhdoms by land. Any fixed frontiers would involve Britain in policing them – as they had in Iraq and Kuwait during the *Ikhwan* rebellion. This would involve modification of the whole complexion of the British guarantee. From the point of view of Indian interests, the existing flexible situation as regards frontiers tended to work to Britain's advantage, and as such should not be hastily thrown away to appease Ibn Saud.[97]

The Air Ministry sided with the India Office. Having had to bear the brunt of defending Iraq against the *Ikhwan*, the Air Ministry had gained valuable experience in desert campaigns. The technical limitations of aeroplanes meant that the existing defensive air strategy in the Trucial sheikhdoms required pilots to operate up to the blue line.[98] If aerial activities were restricted to the base of the Qatar peninsula it would have been simple for Saudi raiders to reach the Qatar oil installations and retreat under cover of darkness across any new frontier. To counter this risk the Air Ministry sought either the creation of a neutral zone between Saudi Arabia and Qatar, or, failing that, a fixed frontier as far as possible west of the oil establishments in Qatar.[99] The idea of another neutral zone was unwelcome to the sub-committee. Similar zones in Iraq and Kuwait had proved of little value. It was preferable, argued Rendel, to draw a new frontier which left whole stretches of territory unprotected against Saudi mischief than create another neutral zone.[100]

The sub-committee failed to reach a solution, though all parties agreed not to risk a major quarrel with Ibn Saud on the issue before them. It was decided to redouble efforts for a breakthrough on the Kuwait blockade and the Bahrain transit dues as part of a comprehensive new settlement. Fuad Hamza would be informed that Britain still regarded the blue line as constituting the legal eastern frontier of Saudi Arabia, but that Britain was prepared to treat the matter generously in consideration with these other matters, without prejudicing her legal rights.[101]

This strategy was soon shown to be unworkable. Fuad Hamza declined the bait. The Saudi Government would, he said, prefer to treat each question separately on its merits, just as the British Government had always insisted upon in the past![102] In answer to his enquiry as to why the Saudi Government had not been informed of the Anglo-Turkish Conventions over a period of twenty years, when they supposedly dealt with Saudi frontiers, Rendel could only tamely reply that Ibn Saud had not asked for them.[103]

Unwilling to operate on strictly legal principles, and unable to secure its ends by a process of give and take, the British Government was forced to reassess its approach. Ibn Saud had, as yet, put forward no concrete counter-proposals for the eastern and southern frontiers of his Kingdom, although he had intimated that his claims were extensive and would extend over the Empty Quarter.[104] It was clear that a new British strategy was needed, and it proved to be one of both innovation and disguised capitulation.

(iii) *Innovation and Capitulation*   By the time the Middle East Sub-Committee convened again to consider the frontier problem, on 8 November 1934, it did so with considerably more anxiety, even though Ibn Saud had still not submitted a precise territorial claim. Several alternative courses of action lay before the British Government: holding fast to the blue and violet lines would invite a major quarrel with Ibn Saud and probable defeat before any international tribunal; a 'package' solution had already been ruled out by Fuad Hamza; capitulation would injure British prestige both with Ibn Saud and the Gulf sheikhs, and lead to an unstable territorial situation in south-east Arabia, particularly if the regional balance of tribal power shifted against British interests; procrastination would encourage Ibn Saud to extend his authority; while the increased emphasis on oil concessions provided a firm reason for an early British initiative.[105]

A number of ideas were mooted, such as imposing arbitrary and utterly fanciful limits to the sovereignty of the coastal potentates at distances of one or two hundred miles inland from the Gulf and the Indian Ocean.[106] The department most troubled by talk of territorial compromise with Ibn Saud was the India Office, which drew up a detailed *Historical Memorandum on the Relations of the Wahhabi Amirs and Bin Saud with Eastern Arabia and the British Government 1800-1934.*[107] The purpose of this memorandum was to forestall the spread of Saudi sovereignty in the proximity of the Trucial sheikhdoms, and it reassessed Ibn Saud's *de facto* sovereignty east of the blue line. Although in 1926 the Governor of Hasa had indeed sent officials to collect *zakat* as far east as Buraimi, the memorandum questioned the success of this and subsequent missions. The role of *zakat*-collecting in Arabian society, furthermore, has been described thus:

> It is an insurance premium, and by no means signifies a voluntary or lasting acknowledgement of sovereignty, though lip service may be paid at the moment.[108]

By 1934 the India Office had established that Ibn Saud no longer had an agent at, or near, Buraimi, though his *zakat* gatherers went there occasionally to collect what they could.[109] The acid test of an Arabian potentate's influence was the extraction of *zakat*, which was no longer being paid. Moreover, in the past, Buraimi constituted the only significant Wahhabi outpost in Trucial Arabia. The oasis was, by the 1930s, held by a tribe hostile to Wahhabism. Consequently, the India Office concluded that there were no grounds for accepting any Saudi sovereignty east of the blue line.[110]

In a sense this memorandum missed the point. It was not a question of whether or not Ibn Saud at that moment enjoyed rights in south-east Arabia. In the nature of Arabian politics the extent of his influence would have fluctuated and been difficult to ascertain. The point was that he was quite free to pursue his expansionist goals in that direction, for the British government had no legal grounds upon which to restrain him.

Fowle could see little wrong with the existing state of affairs. The great advantage in having no firm frontiers was that there could be no encroachment of them, or need to police them.[111] Frontiers may have been indispensable between the Hashemite states and Saudi Arabia, for strategic, dynastic and tribal reasons. They were not, argued Fowle, necessary in the south-east, where Ibn Saud would soon discover that they could be violated with impunity. The only alternative was for Britain to agree to some sort of tribal, as opposed to territorial frontier, even though this did not erase the risk of Ibn Saud claiming the allegiance of tribes in proximity to the Gulf.[112]

To the India Office oil was, at that stage, but a superfluity. It was with the Trucial sheikhdoms that the India Office was preoccupied. Yet it is difficult to resist the suspicion that the India Office was playing it all ways. The arguments against any firm frontiers overlooked the fact that Britain was ostensibly operating such a frontier: the blue line. On the one hand, the India Office tried to restrict Ibn Saud to it by virtue of outdated documents of dubious applicability; on the other, it was maintained that, not only had he no *de jure* interest east of the blue line, he had no *de facto* interest either.

The War Office, broadly supported by the service departments, saw Britain's requirements as twofold: strategically, to prevent Ibn Saud piercing the ring of sheikhdoms to reach the southern shore of the Gulf; and also, to prevent future oil concessions from falling into entirely non-British hands. The only way to satisfy both these requirements, it was argued, was for a firm frontier to be drawn somewhere (the precise co-ordinates were less important) and for Ibn Saud to be unable to plead ignorance as to its whereabouts.[113] The north-west frontier of India offered illuminating comparisons, being, in effect, a double frontier. An outer line constituted the political boundary, while a second, inner line marked the limits of effective administrative control. The War Office considered this a sensible model for south-east Arabia.[114]

Out of these contrasting interpretations and conflicting interests George Rendel proposed a novel and unprecedented solution to a territorial problem of this nature. He adapted the neutral zone concept by proposing a 'desert zone' in south-east Arabia enclosed by a 'ring fence'. The desert zone would create a political and territorial enclave in south-east Arabia. The northern, eastern and southern boundaries of the enclave would specify the inland limits of the coastal chieftains' jurisdiction, from Qatar round to the Aden Protectorate, and, as a corollary, the limits of Britain's responsibilities as suzerain of those chiefs. Ibn Saud would be sovereign up to the western boundary of the enclave, beyond which he would renounce any territorial claims. Within the desert zone he would enjoy 'personal' and 'tribal' authority over the tribes therein, but not territorial authority.[115]

It was hoped that the desert zone would enable future British oil concessions in the Gulf to increase the territory at their disposal, all the way from the littoral to the limits of the ring fence.[116] No concessions would be granted, from any source, within the zone for a period of twenty years. Overall, the plan was hoped to safeguard British oil interests, keep Ibn Saud away from the Trucial sheikhdoms, make a gesture towards a 'tribal' interpretation of sovereignty, and salvage British prestige.

Such a novel approach to an international problem raised a host of difficulties, not least the risk of penetration of the desert zone by third parties, and the political status of tribes inhabiting the zone. Rendel saw his concept as a *res nullius*, a complete territorial vacuum as regards traditional notions of territorial sovereignty. It was not a neutral zone, where the adjoining states shared equal rights; nor a no-man's-land where there were no rights at all. It was more akin to the concept of the 'high seas' than to any kind of existing territorial entity.[117] One particular problem concerned the exact relationship between the Gulf rulers and the British Crown. Britain shunned any publicity given to her sovereignty over the sheikhdoms.[118] The India Office did not welcome formal extension of British sovereignty up to the northern, eastern and southern boundaries of the ring fence. Another problem was the lack of reliable maps upon which to base the frontier. Although the ring fence was a linear frontier, it was sufficiently vague in its exact implications to eventually reassure the India Office that Ibn Saud was not going to be appeased at the expense of the Trucial sheikhdoms.

Moreover, the Sultan of Muscat and Oman was in a different position from the Gulf sheikhs. His own sovereignty did not surrender control of foreign affairs to the British Government. In 1862 there had been an Anglo-French declaration to support his independence.[119] Accordingly, his co-operation would be needed, otherwise he might join the scramble for territory and claim part of the desert zone for himself.[120]

Despite further reservations from the Admiralty that Rendel's proposal might encourage Ibn Saud's influence in eastern Arabia to expand unchecked, and would have the effect of 'sterilising' oil developments within the desert zone,[121] the sub-committee generally agreed that no British interest would be seriously injured if some concession was made to Ibn Saud. It was unanimously agreed to proceed along the lines of Rendel's ring fence.[122]

By January 1935 this idea had matured. Ryan was given instructions to advance towards a solution by offering Ibn Saud step-by-step territorial concessions east of the blue line, with the special desert zone to be offered if all else failed.[123] These concessions would be of a vague semi-circular nature, conceding territory deep in the desert hinterland of south-east Arabia, but not near the Gulf or the Indian Ocean. They were partly based on tribal considerations as preferred by Fowle and Dickson, and partly based on surrendering the western part of the envisaged desert zone.[124]

Barely had this new approach been agreed upon when Fuad Hamza presented Ryan with part of the Husein-McMahon wartime correspondence which Saudi sources had unearthed. The letter, from the High Commissioner of Egypt to the Sherif of Mecca, dated 14 July 1915, read:

> England to acknowledge the independence of the Arab countries bounded on the ... east by the borders with Persia up to the Gulf of Basra, on the south by the Indian Ocean, with the exception of the position of Aden to remain as it is.[125]

Fuad Hamza had not produced the document out of concern for Palestine. It was to be a further year before Saudi Arabia took more than a passing interest in events in the mandate. Ibn Saud was more interested in the promise to recognise Arab independence, particularly in the Trucial sheikhdoms. If they were independent then he could deal with them as he pleased.

The arrangements for the ring fence, although not yet revealed to the Saudi Government, would emphasise Britain's sovereignty over the Gulf states. Ryan, in refusing Fuad Hamza's demands that the Trucial sheikhs attend future frontier negotiations,[126] once again let it be known that Britain's interpretation of her rights in the Gulf did not accord with the basic facts. He noted:

> I am indeed greatly alarmed by the application of the word 'sovereignty' to our position in regard to the Trucial states and Qatar. Even for international purposes King George's position in regard to those states cannot be precisely the same as his position in regard to UK, either as regards his rights or his responsibilities. Any assertion by us that we had sovereignty over the Trucial sheikhdoms and Qatar would cause him to throw a thousand fits.[127]

Ryan knew that the Gulf sheikhs were reassured only to the extent that Britain was prepared to protect them from Ibn Saud. Ryan noted: 'To put it bluntly the sheikhs have no reason for unqualified confidence in the protection of HMG against Bin Saud'.[128] Ryan referred to the speech of Lord Curzon who toured the Gulf in 1903 as Viceroy of India. Curzon had spoken of Britain's respect for the independence of the sheikhdoms and Britain's determination to uphold it, adding the famous phrase, 'We shall not wipe out the most unselfish page in history'.[129] Ryan added a postscript of his own to Curzon's words: 'HMG have tended increasingly to add to the page the somewhat selfish gloss that they are not committed to protect the sheikhs from aggression on the land side'.[130] To Ryan it was only natural for the Gulf rulers to reinsure with Ibn Saud. This tendency was likely to increase. Some years previously the Sheikh of Ras al Khaimah had already declared that in certain contingencies he would place himself under the protection of Ibn Saud rather than the British Government.[131]

The substance of Ryan's remarks since the beginning of the dispute suggested that he considered the British position dishonourable on two counts. Not only was Britain responsible for an impractical, untenable and illegal frontier separating Saudi Arabia from vast tracts of territory to the east; she was also maintaining a policy which ostensibly underwrote the 'independence' of the Trucial states, although it was primarily with oil that she was concerned.

(iv) *Ibn Saud's 'Red Line'*   The dispute gathered impetus from the spring of 1935. On 3 April Ryan was handed Saudi Arabia's precise territorial demands, calculated, it was claimed, on the recognised *diras* of the tribes allegedly recognising Saudi suzerainty.[132] They were more extensive than anything that Britain anticipated. In the north Ibn Saud laid claim to the southern part of Qatar, giving him access to the Gulf to the east of the sheikhdom. This would cut Qatar off from Abu Dhabi, leaving Qatar totally dependent on Saudi Arabia. In the east and south large areas were demanded up to Meridian 56°, which would leave Ibn Saud within striking distance not only of the Gulf, but also the Indian Ocean. For convenience the proposed Saudi frontier became known as the 'red line',[133] to distinguish it from Britain's step-by-step concessions known respectively as the green, yellow and brown lines.[134] The red line can be seen as the final acceptance by Ibn Saud of western territorial frontiers defining his Kingdom.

Within a week of receiving the red line frontier, Ryan delivered the green line as the first stage of compromise.[135] It was rejected outright. The sub-committee convened again to discuss alternative sources of strategy. The India Office was not prepared to accept Saudi Arabia's eastern frontier looping round to reach 56°. If pressed, it was prepared to accept the eastern Saudi frontier touching a point at 53°, but that would represent a final offer and was not to be put forward immediately.[136] This, in itself, showed some modification of the India Office position, but to avoid possible accusations of tampering with independent states it hoped that the Sheikhs of Qatar and Abu Dhabi would be formally associated with the negotiations at some stage.[137]

The Admiralty disliked the very idea of giving away something to Ibn Saud for no return, now that the frontier question was no longer going to form part of a *quid pro quo*. Ibn Saud could not force his territorial claims east of the blue line. He could not take advantage of the League of Nations; nor, the Admiralty stressed, could he demonstrate his actual sovereignty in eastern Arabia by other means.[138]

The Foreign Office and the War Office had to take a wider purview than did the Admiralty. The War Office urged that the maximum concessions be made to Ibn Saud, even being willing to accept an eastern frontier up to his claim of 56°. Such was the perceived need to keep the Saudi frontier away from potential oilfields in Qatar that Britain could afford to be generous with barren desert in the interior, where there were neither commitments to British protégés, nor strategic considerations at stake.[139] The Foreign Office concurred, particularly in the light of Britain's fragile legal position, the rising importance of the oil question, and the fact that Ibn Saud, sooner or later, was bound to move eastwards. Against this, there were dangers in giving territory to Ibn Saud over which he exercised, as yet, little control, particularly in the event of his death and the power scramble that might ensue. Rendel, unconvinced by the step-by-step approach of the India Office, proposed, in the last resort, an eastern frontier reaching at its furthermost point 54°.[140] Even that was far beyond the previous maximum concession agreed upon: the brown line along Meridian 52°.

The resignation of the sub-committee to making still greater concessions, rather than have Ibn Saud insist on international arbitration, marked the end of Rendel's desert zone and ring fence idea before it was even put to Ibn Saud. By pushing the acceptable eastern frontier of Saudi Arabia further and further east, the proposed area to be enclosed by the ring fence, which was to be appended to the eastern side of the frontier, got progressively smaller until it would have covered no more than one quarter of the area originally planned. The sub-committee agreed to abandon the desert zone concept and, in the interim, concede an eastern Saudi frontier along Meridian 53° while firmly denying Ibn Saud access to the Gulf east of Qatar.[141]

Fuad Hamza was due to arrive in London for further conversations in June 1935. In the intervening weeks both the British and Saudi Governments busily advanced their own interests. Britain made an unprecedented change in her commitment to a Gulf sheikh. The development of air power now enabled easier intervention inland. In May 1935, after lengthy preliminaries, the Political Resident informed the Sheikh of Qatar that he would henceforth be guaranteed British aerial protection against serious and unprovoked incursions. In return, several things were demanded, the most important of which was that the Sheikh grant an oil concession within his territory to APOC, which might then pass on to Iraq Petroleum.[142] This would forestall Holmes and American oil interests. Qatar was too near the strategically vital Bahrain, where a naval base was nearing completion, to risk foreign ventures.[143] The Sheikh accepted these 'terms' within a week.

To give political backing to this move the Foreign Office decided to discuss Saudi Arabia's eastern and southern frontiers, from Qatar round to the Aden Protectorate, as a single comprehensive unit.[144] This was to prevent meddling with the frontiers piecemeal, according to Saudi preference, and avert concentration on Qatar's frontiers.[145] This new defensive commitment to Qatar did not mark a general shift in British policy in the Gulf. It was an *ad hoc* measure taken to secure promising oil interests. When Ibn Saud heard of the arrangement he remonstrated with the Sheikh for having granted an oil concession without awaiting a settlement of the boundary question. Ibn Saud warned that if the concessionaires commenced work before the frontier was settled he would be compelled to protest and obstruct the operations.[146] This was to lead, by the autumn, to a secondary quarrel breaking out between the British Government and Ibn Saud for his having addressed the Sheikh of Qatar directly on a matter concerning the Sheikh's foreign affairs.[147]

While Britain was making private arrangements to secure her oil interests in Qatar, Ibn Saud, for his part, was trying to entice the British Government towards further compromise. A formula for prolonging the Treaty of Jedda was proposed. In May Saudi Arabia quite unexpectedly paid 10 per cent of the debt owed for arms supplied in 1929, as well as her share of the expenses for the 1930 arbitration tribunal that had adjudicated Saudi-Transjordanian raids.[148] The heir to the Saudi throne, the Emir Saud, also embarked on a three month tour of Europe and arrived in Britain in July 1935.

These palliatives did not achieve their aim. Further talks in London, once again involving both Ryan and Fuad Hamza, took place in June and July 1935 but brought the dispute no nearer to a solution, despite Rendel's reassurances (made with a veiled reference to his ill-fated scheme for a desert zone) that:

There was no question of attempting to establish a sharply defined frontier in the ordinary European sense with frontier posts and a close frontier patrol. It was, however, necessary to set some definite limit beyond which territorial sovereignty could not be exercised, even if such territorial sovereignty were not, in fact, exercised up to that limit. This would not prevent the tribes wandering freely from one territory to another, and no doubt suitable arrangements could eventually be made regarding their taxation.[149]

Not even further British concessions in the shape of the brown line proved to be a basis for agreement.[150] Fuad Hamza reminded the Foreign Office that Arab national sentiment would not permit Ibn Saud to surrender territory to which he had an established claim.[151]

By the time the Middle East Sub-Committee convened on 24 September 1935, a sense of satisfaction could be detected even though Ibn Saud had continued to reject all Britain's attempts at compromise. As the dispute had, by this time, stretched over a year and a half with no sign of a break-through, the stalemate began to have certain attractions to some departments, particularly now that an oil concession in Qatar had been secured. The force of Ibn Saud's earlier aversion to the blue line had gradually subsided. No doubt, as Ryan remarked, Ibn Saud could not escape the fact that mounting tension in the Red Sea involving Italy and Abyssinia would not permit a really serious clash with Britain.[152]

Shuckburgh, chairing the sub-committee, wondered whether the question was any longer urgent enough to warrant proceeding.[153] Over the Aqaba and Maan dispute, for example, the two sides had for practical purposes simply agreed to differ. The Colonial Office and the India Office were the strongest proponents of a new policy of constructive deadlock. The India Office maintained its opposition to the concept of fixed frontiers in south-east Arabia, which would make the sheikhdoms and Saudi Arabia coterminous, for that would simply transfer any territorial vacuum from the eastern to the western (Saudi) side of the new frontier.[154]

The Foreign Office preferred that Britain press on for a satisfactory solution. Ryan still feared for the future consequences of Anglo-Saudi relations if this injury to Ibn Saud's prestige was not healed.[155] But there were other, external factors by this time nudging the Foreign Office into further endeavours. There were fears that the American oil company would extend its operations south of Qatar, thereby presenting Britain with an embarrassing *fait accompli*. In the circumstances, the Foreign Office still felt that it was better to fix a boundary, no matter how disadvantageous from a British point of view, rather than leave the territorial situation fluid.[156] Furthermore, Britain was facing a situation of great delicacy in the Red Sea as Mussolini's pressures on Abyssinia intensified. Outright war was a matter of days away. The Italian Government was making strenuous efforts to court favour with Saudi Arabia. Rendel, unlike Ryan, feared that an intransigent

British attitude over an issue upon which Ibn Saud felt so strongly might drive him to seek political support from Italy.[157]

Rendel went so far as to admit that the tactics of the British Government, for which he had been largely instrumental, had been misguided. Britain's policy of artificial, arbitrary frontiers of dubious rationale could no longer be adequately defended.[158] Claims had, for example, been made for several villages on behalf of the Sheikh of Abu Dhabi, only for it to be subsequently conceded that the villages acknowledged Ibn Saud.[159] The sub-committee agreed to present one more frontier to Ibn Saud. Leaving behind the frontier devices of the previous fifteen years, such as neutral zones, tribal zones, and desert zones, on account of their impracticability, it was proposed to bisect empty desert with a new frontier, so that the *de facto* sovereignty of neither side extended up to it.[160] Rather than have a vacuum on one side of the frontier it was thought preferable to move it eastwards to create vacuums on both sides.

(v) *The 'Riyadh Line' and Deadlock*   Ibn Saud had invited the British Minister to travel, on his return to Arabia from London, to Riyadh. This reflected Ibn Saud's new philosophy of gradually opening up his Kingdom to western influences, and also indicated his continuing concern for the eastern frontier situation. This was the first visit to the Saudi capital of a senior British diplomat. Sir Samuel Hoare, the Foreign Secretary, instructed Ryan to emphasise Britain's desire to meet Ibn Saud's demands.[161] At Riyadh, on 25 November 1935, Ryan offered what was explicitly Britain's final offer, and which conveniently became known as the 'Riyadh Line'.[162] The greater part of Ibn Saud's territorial demands in the east were conceded. The blue line had run near to the 50th Meridian; Ibn Saud had claimed up to the 56th; the Riyadh line granted him up to the 55th at its furthest point.[163]

The Riyadh line was immediately rejected. The critical disagreement centred on the area around the base of Qatar. Ibn Saud demanded the upland region at the south-west of the Qatar peninsula, known as Jabal Nakhsh, presumably for its oil potentialities, and also the coastal inlet to the south-east, known as Khor el Odeid, which would give Saudi Arabia access to the Gulf east of Qatar, thus breaking the continuous chain of British Gulf dependencies and pressurising them all.[164] Ryan protested that Khor el Odeid formed an integral part of the sheikhdom of Abu Dhabi, even though the inlet lay over two hundred miles westwards along the coast. Despite the enticement of awarding Ibn Saud the GCB (Grand Cross of the Bath) to supersede his earlier KCIE from the Indian Empire, Ibn Saud flatly refused to consider the Riyadh line.[165]

Ryan, faced with yet another rejection, expressed his own doubts about Ibn Saud's desire for a settlement, and added his voice to those advocating stalemate.[166] Account also had to be taken of international developments elsewhere. The Italian attack on Abyssinia, so shortly after the Saudi-

Yemeni war, served to concentrate Ibn Saud's attention upon the other side of his Kingdom. The evolving troubles in Palestine led to him taking a concerted interest in Arab affairs. In November 1935 the long drawn out dispute between Saudi Arabia and Bahrain over transit dues was settled.[167] This removed one potential source of friction with Saudi Arabia, without Britain having to contemplate further territorial concessions as a bargaining counter on Bahrain's behalf. Moreover, at the end of 1935 and early in 1936, Petroleum Concessions (an offshoot of Iraq Petroleum) won new options the length of the Trucial coast, and Holmes was successfully approached for his services as a representative of the company.[168] The reluctance of the sheikhs to grant these oil rights, however, led to British aerial and naval displays off the coast and the 'impeding' of pearling dhows.[169]

The general tenor of Anglo-Saudi relations was not outwardly affected by failure to find a solution to the frontier question.[170] In October 1936 the renegotiation of the Treaty of Jedda was completed to the satisfaction of both parties. The arrival, in September, of Sir Reader Bullard to succeed Ryan after his six year tenure also smoothed the passage of relations.[171] Bullard's career had followed the same path as Ryan's, via the Levant Consular Service, both men stepping from Consul-General at Rabat to Minister in Jedda. Bullard spoke Arabic. His more scholarly approach was in marked contrast to the formality and protocol insisted upon by his predecessor (Bullard's father, incidentally, had been a dock labourer[172]). The new Minister already had much first-hand experience of the Arab world, and Arabia in particular. He had served as Governor of Baghdad in 1920 before moving to the Middle East Department of the Colonial Office. He had been British Agent and Consul in Jedda from 1923-25. Writing in 1957 even such a severe critic of Britain as Philby could describe Bullard as by far the best British diplomatic representative ever sent to Ibn Saud.[173]

Also at the end of 1936 an incident took place which further underlined Britain's ambivalent oil policy towards Arabia. Petroleum Concessions indicated to the Foreign Office that the Rub al Khali looked a promising source of oil. The company wished to obtain from Ibn Saud a concession covering all the territory not already included in the American concession, within whatever frontiers could be agreed upon.[174]

If oil had been the foremost British consideration it might have been supposed that support would be given to Petroleum Concessions. After all, a private arrangement might have been made with Ibn Saud to settle his eastern frontier generously, provided that he awarded an oil concession in his 'new' territory to that company. Instead, the Foreign Office discouraged the whole idea, pointing out that any application for a concession would give Ibn Saud an exaggerated idea of the economic value of the area in dispute and make him even more intransigent.[175] The Foreign Office urged delay to await frontier developments. Similarly, the following year, the Foreign Office put pressure on Iraq Petroleum to surrender part of the Qatar oil concession, including Jabal Nakhsh, to Ibn Saud and the American company.[176] Iraq Petroleum refused.

By 1937 the European drift towards war, and the realisation of the magnitude of the problems in Palestine, lent a completely new perspective to Anglo-Saudi relations. Over Palestine, the attitude taken by the independent Arab states was felt to be crucial to Britain, and Ibn Saud was outwardly showing a surprisingly moderate and constructive attitude.[177] The outstanding difficulty with the frontier was, by this time, largely concentrated on the base of the Qatar peninsula. Of the areas claimed by Ibn Saud, Jabal Nakhsh had already been allocated as part of the oil concession in Qatar, while Khor el Odeid had for over sixty years been recognised as under the sovereignty of the Sheikh of Abu Dhabi.[178] At the time, Uqair was the principal Saudi port. The Saudi Government claimed to want to construct a harbour at Khor el Odeid, although it was ill-suited for the purpose, being too shallow and covered in reefs.[179] Against this, the inlet provided the only land passage from Abu Dhabi to Qatar, along a well-established caravan route.

In the international circumstances prevailing, the War Office considered that Ibn Saud's frontiers no longer constituted a local problem but an imperial one.[180] As the strategic importance of the Middle East intensified, the War Office felt that Ibn Saud's co-operation was vital, and Britain should stop quibbling over minor issues: 'Bin Saud's friendship during the next ten years will be of much more importance to us than a few hundred miles of desert, or even oil bearing areas'.[181] This view was shared by the Air Ministry, having revised its aerial strategy since 1934, and the Foreign Office, which urged that Britain 'take [her] courage in both hands and offer as much as [she] can to Bin Saud'.[182]

The India Office stood alone against the turning tide of governmental opinion. Imperial interests, it was counter-claimed, affected the Gulf states too. Any further concessions to Ibn Saud would increase his prestige in the Gulf and draw the neighbouring sheikhs into his orbit.[183] The India Office wanted safeguards introduced into the newly revised Treaty of Jedda, such as had appeared in the 1915 treaty. Giving way, it was felt, would not offset the reaction to the recommendations for the partition of Palestine, shortly to be published, to which Ibn Saud was likely to be bitterly opposed.[184] The India Office felt appeasement to be objectionable in principle and unavailing in practice.[185] Any advantages accruing over Palestine would be temporary: the damage done to the Gulf in effecting such concessions was likely to be permanent.

In February 1937 Rendel and his wife departed on a formal invitation to Saudi Arabia which had been extended back in the autumn of 1935. Although his trip took in Iraq, Iran, and some of the Gulf states, its culmination was an east-west crossing of Saudi Arabia. Rendel's wife was the first European woman to cross Arabia openly as a Christian.[186] In Jedda, in March, Rendel and Bullard had several meetings with Ibn Saud and Sheikh

Hafiz Wabha, during which the discussions ranged from Italy, to Palestine, to Saudi Arabia's frontiers – on which no further progress was made.

Rendel did, however, give voice privately to yet another shift in British tactics. Rather than continue to deal with the frontier question as a whole, it was decided to seek progress by looking at the various sectors of the frontier individually.[187] This might distract Ibn Saud's attention from the base of Qatar, upon which the sub-committee was still holding firm. Bullard was, in any case, aware that a paper frontier would not restrain Ibn Saud if he was determined to extend his dominions, and it was not advisable to press Ibn Saud into agreements which Britain did not, in Bullard's opinion, really need.[188] Only if oil happened to be discovered in Qatar, but not in Hasa, was there any need to fear Ibn Saud's response. Bullard suggested offering Ibn Saud a royalty on any oil found under Qatar on the pretext that the oil-bearing strata ran partly under Saudi Arabian territory.[189] A similar scheme had been tried unsuccessfully in Iraq in the 1920s to help buy off Turkish intransigence over Mosul.[190] Although Rendel lent his support, Ibn Saud was unlikely to accept an offer of that kind because to do so would be tantamount to admitting that his main interest was oil.[191] In any case, the suggestion was blocked by the India Office.

With the problems in Palestine looming large Ibn Saud had found an ample stage upon which to declare himself champion of the Arab cause. He was not likely to accept any agreement that could be interpreted as signing away Arab soil to a foreign power and betraying that cause.[192] At the same time, oil was assuming a strategic significance that it had lacked in previous years. In case of war there might be difficulties with the supply of oil from Iraq and Iran, which necessarily concentrated British attention on alternative supplies from the southern end of the Gulf.

A search for possible sources of further territorial compromise alighted on the hitherto less contentious violet line that separated Saudi Arabia from the Aden Protectorate and the rest of southern Arabia. Insufficient sacrifices were agreed upon even to be worth tempting Ibn Saud.[193] Britain was, at the time, engaged in 'pacifying' the interior of the Hadramaut, and it was not considered expedient to bring further complications to the area. Moreover, the Sultan of Muscat, as feared, was showing great reluctance to fix his western frontier which had hitherto been left indeterminate to the fates of fortune. Talk of oil made him even more suspicious,[194] although he granted oil rights to Petroleum Concessions later in 1937. All this suggests further confirmation of the complex position held by oil in British policy towards eastern Arabia. Oil concessions that did not directly provoke Ibn Saud were welcomed. Those in or around Qatar, in the area claimed by the Saudi King, were less enticing – at least to the Foreign Office. The need for good Anglo-Saudi relations overrode the need for fresh oil concessions in disputed regions.

By the end of 1937 the situation was slipping away from the British Government. The Peel Report on Palestine had alienated the Arab world.

Reports suggested that Saudi agents were once again trying to establish control in the Buraimi area[195] which, although lying just inside the 56th meridian, was well north of Ibn Saud's territorial demands made in 1935. Increasing oil speculation had also led to American geological activity east of the Riyadh line, but west of the red line, in disputed territory. The sub-committee reluctantly admitted that there was little difference between what Britain was now prepared to concede and what Ibn Saud had demanded in his red line.[196] Shuckburgh intimated that if Ibn Saud was going to react badly over the Peel Report then it might be in British interests to keep him in financial difficulties by not handing over possible oil-bearing territories. Better, argued Shuckburgh, that Britain was threatened by a disunited and impoverished country than by one whose resources had just been augmented by courtesy of the British Government.[197]

Rendel and Bullard disagreed. Ibn Saud was, they reasoned, less likely to turn against Britain if his Kingdom had a measure of prosperity and economic stability.[198] For this reason the Foreign Office felt that if American oil personnel were exploring in disputed areas Britain should not intervene. This wholehearted appeasement of Ibn Saud will be examined in the following chapter. The Foreign Office view was modified by the sub-committee, which agreed, however, to Saudi Arabia being informed that Britain was prepared to reopen negotiations. In the meantime the hope was expressed that oil operations would be restricted to undisputed territory. A joint Anglo-Saudi topographical mission was proposed, to clear up uncertainties over the precise position of certain physical features in the disputed region.[199] Ibn Saud agreed to restrain American prospecting in disputed areas – if British-backed companies would do likewise. He declined, however, the offer of a topographical survey, preferring a broadly acceptable frontier to precede such a mission.[200]

In February 1938, following Cabinet instructions to secure Ibn Saud's goodwill,[201] Rendel successfully had the Khor el Odeid question removed from inter-departmental consultation and endeavoured to persuade the Cabinet to cede the inlet to Ibn Saud.[202] What Rendel was, in fact, proposing was the deliberate breach of Britain's chain of Gulf dependencies. He pointed out that the Sheikh of Abu Dhabi enjoyed no revenue from Khor el Odeid, nor did he exercise any authority there, let alone have any geographical basis for such authority.[203] The figure of £25,000 was mooted as compensation to the Sheikh for the cession of the inlet. Rather than wait for a Saudi *fait accompli*, Rendel insisted that any protection of Abu Dhabi be exercised on Britain's terms, not the Sheikh's.[204]

Rendel appears to have believed that Ibn Saud's goodwill could be secured by offering him an outlet to the Gulf east of Qatar, enabling Saudi trade to avoid the difficult waters of the Gulf of Bahrain, which had to be negotiated when using the port of Uqair.[205] All this was, of course, rationalisation. The Foreign Office faced international crises in Europe and Palestine, and had little option but to seek friends where she could, no matter what obligations had to be sacrificed in the process. It was genuinely regretted that Khor el Odeid had not been ceded in 1935, at a time when the total frontier position might have been acceptable to Ibn Saud.[206]

As will be seen, Rendel feared that, because of Palestine, Saudi Arabia might, in the event of a European war, ally herself with Britain's enemies.[207] Ibn Saud had recently shown considerable concern about the security of his Kingdom in the event of a war breaking out in Europe. Rendel drew parallels with the Great War when, had the dangers of Turkey and Bulgaria aligning themselves with Germany been fully appreciated, preventative action might have been taken and the course of history perhaps changed.[208] British policy, Rendel urged, should consider how to forestall history repeating itself with regard to Saudi Arabia, namely by a generous settlement of the eastern frontier question. He ought to have carried his analogy further. In 1913 Britain approached the Anglo-Turkish Conventions with the similar aim of being not ungenerous to the Porte as regards territorial issues.[209] That 'generosity', however, had *not* countered Turkish moves towards Germany.

It is no accident that Foreign Office talk in the post-Eden era (the Foreign Secretary resigned in February 1938) was reminiscent of that towards Hitler; Ibn Saud having no more territorial demands in eastern Arabia, and so forth. Neither was it considered that putting pressure on the Sheikh of Abu Dhabi would reflect badly on Britain's image in the Arab world, and make Ibn Saud even more susceptible to accusations of being a British stooge.

Neither the War Office nor the service departments opposed ceding Khor el Odeid to Ibn Saud. Petroleum Concessions had been granted a prospecting licence by the Sheikh of Abu Dhabi, and that added a further reason for established frontiers in eastern Arabia. As Saudi Arabia already had ample access to the Gulf, there was no overriding strategic objection to a breach in the chain of British Gulf protégés.[210] The War Office insisted that Ibn Saud and the Sheikh of Abu Dhabi be seen in their proper perspectives.[211] With the exception of Jabal Nakhsh, which because of its inclusion with the Qatar oil concession zone was not considerable negotiable, the War Office saw no insurmountable objection to Ibn Saud having all that he claimed. Reviewing the progress of the sub-committee on the question since 1934, the War Office confessed that 'the decisions of this committee over the past few years in which we had gradually yielded point after point to Bin Saud had been a "dog in a manger" policy not worthy of the British Empire'.[212] Only the Secretary of State for India (Lord Zetland) and the Viceroy balked at the cession of Khor el Odeid to Saudi Arabia. The admittedly tenuous link between the Sheikh of Abu Dhabi and Khor el Odeid was no reason to hand it over to Saudi Arabia, 'any more than we could give Australia to Japan'.[213]

The last occasion on which Saudi Arabia's eastern frontiers were discussed before the outbreak of war was between Bullard and Fuad Hamza in

Jedda in March 1938,[214] just as oil was being discovered in large quantities in Hasa. But the time for diplomatic initiatives such as arbitration had passed. By 1939 hostility to Britain in Iraq; the widespread belief in Arab circles that Britain was pursuing a forward policy in the Gulf and southern Arabia; and the flow of oil from Saudi Arabia – not to mention a world war, combined to postpone any further attempts to fix Saudi Arabia's eastern frontiers. Thereupon the whole matter lapsed for a decade until, in 1949, it was resurrected by Ibn Saud in entirely new circumstances.

Summary and Conclusions

The handling of the frontier dispute in south-east Arabia illustrated a new maturity in Anglo-Saudi relations. The hazards to effective communication, whether physical or administrative, which have featured so prominently in previous chapters, did not significantly impede the management of the dispute. There were ample opportunities for face-to-face exposition of respective views, notably in Ibn Saud's opening up his Kingdom for the advantages of diplomatic intercourse as well as for mineral concessions. The nature of the problem further aided its management. The disagreement, while intense, did not take on an urgent quality in the 1930s. Indeed, there is something faintly comic about such British concern over scattered oases and empty desert. There were no third parties actively intruding into the dispute, either in the form of other Arab states or western powers,[215] although a basically insignificant frontier problem was coloured by the international background against which it was set. Furthermore, from the British side, the machinery established through the Middle Eastern (Official) Sub-Committee of the Committee of Imperial Defence in 1930 enabled departmental differences to be expressed and decisions reached more speedily than hitherto.

The policies of the various departments represented on the sub-committee invite comment. The Admiralty consistently took the view that the only genuine British interest in south-east Arabia was oil. Providing that oil supplies were secure, it mattered little whether Ibn Saud punctured the ring of Gulf sheikhdoms or not.

The stance of the Air Ministry mellowed over the years. Between 1934 and 1939 the Air Ministry offered contradictory assessments of Britain's requirements in south-east Arabia. In 1934 its attitude resumed where it had left off in Iraq in 1930, hostile to Ibn Saud, and with an overriding need to cater for the technical limitations of aircraft operating in arduous conditions. By 1939, however, the Air Ministry saw no strategic objections to ceding Khor el Odeid to Ibn Saud. The reason for this shift lay not with a reappraisal of general British policy but with the rapid development of aerial technology. By 1939 aircraft facilities extended along the Gulf where they had been absent earlier in the decade. There was, then, no longer any need to worry about creating neutral zones to keep Ibn Saud away from Qatar.[216]

The position of the India Office was somewhat analogous to that of the Colonial Office during the *Ikhwan* rebellion. Both departments were primarily involved in safeguarding Arab states from the threat of Saudi incursions. Unfortunately for the India Office, the Trucial sheikhdoms did not constitute as great an imperial issue as did the mandates. Nor were the sheikhdoms directly threatened by Saudi predations. The issues – oil, protection of the Gulf states, prestige, and appeasement of Ibn Saud – were all poorly defined in comparison with the threat presented by the *Ikhwan* rebellion. Consequently, the India Office by the late 1930s found itself largely isolated from the mainstream of governmental opinion.

It will be recalled that in the 1920s the then Political Resident, Prideaux, had been aware of Saudi activity in the Buraimi region, and was philosophical about the eventual absorption of the area into Ibn Saud's dominions. At the time of Prideaux's foreboding, however, he was speaking to deaf ears. Britain was not going to initiate frontier negotiations in sparsely inhabited deserts that appeared to be devoid of mineral temptation. From 1933 the arrival of the oil factor brought a swift reassessment of the frontier situation. The India Office became intractably opposed to any fixed frontiers, concentrating on the political and strategic vulnerability of the Gulf states, while becoming more and more isolated as other departments forsook the strategic question in favour of the political objective of appeasing Ibn Saud.

The Foreign Office's concerns covered political, strategic and oil factors. This involved some rather extreme shifts of policy as the political environment changed during the 1930s. The Foreign Office in 1934 was already committed to a legalistic interpretation of Saudi Arabia's eastern frontier. It is natural for the department of state dealing with foreign affairs to lay stress on formal treaties and their ramifications. Yet by 1939 the Foreign Office was even urging the cession of Khor el Odeid to Saudi Arabia. Unlike the India Office, the Foreign Office had to keep both eyes on the world as a whole. That world in 1939 was very different from that perceived in 1934. Palestine, Italian enterprise in the Red Sea, and the deteriorating situation in Europe all served to make the need for an unembittered Ibn Saud paramount. Even questions concerning oil and the removal of potential threats to the Gulf sheikhs had to take second place behind winning Ibn Saud's acquiescence in British policies elsewhere.

A prominent feature of the dispute was the array of British tactics and devices used to try and reach a settlement as expediency demanded.[217] Rendel's short-lived 'ring fence' would have provided the student of international relations with an unprecedented solution to a territorial dispute. Even so, it is possible to detect traces of inertia; the habitual British reluctance to meddle with Arabian frontiers, and the vague hope that the problem would go away of its own accord. For his part, Ibn Saud's motives were quite straightforward, being an amalgam of expansionist aims, coupled with a not unnatural urge to secure possible oil-producing areas to ease the financial strain on his country. Both these factors were harnessed to an opportunistic temperament. Small wonder that Ibn Saud showed little inclination to accept ever greater British concessions when each rejection brought still greater ones.

The south-east Arabian frontier dispute cannot be fully understood without putting it in the context of other Anglo-Saudi territorial problems, and Britain's wider outlook on the Middle East and the world during the course of the dispute. This issue provided a classic instance of British *ad hoc* policy towards Ibn Saud. Unlike Aqaba and Maan, for example, the British Government soon demonstrated that it saw very little that was absolutely vital in south-east Arabia. By 1939 almost every one of Ibn Saud's earlier demands could have been met. As had happened over Aqaba and Maan, the British Government acknowledged its legal position to be shaky. In neither instance would it have been confident about going before an international tribunal. Over the one dispute (Aqaba and Maan) Britain was not prepared to yield: over the other she was. There were several reasons for this. Aqaba and Maan, in 1925, was an all or nothing affair without opportunity for territorial compromise. South-east Arabia was a vast, poorly populated tract where proposed frontiers drawn at various co-ordinates could not seriously affect Britain's strategic position. The sheikhdoms themselves were interested only in pearling and the Gulf; not in the desert behind them.

In 1925 Britain could deal freely with the Middle East, untroubled either by European rivalry or hostile actors on the Arab stage. Oil played no part in the Aqaba-Maan dispute, yet on strategic grounds the area was considered indispensable for British and Transjordanian interests. Nothing in south-east Arabia was invested with such importance, except the political goal of maintaining good relations with Ibn Saud. Almost every department of state, with the exception of the India Office, queried how Britain had got into the problem in the first place, and this chapter has quoted several of the self-recriminations over Britain's early handling of the dispute. Nor could the British Government complain of lack of information, or of not being forewarned. Prideaux's warnings of 1926, and Ryan's gravely worded memoranda of 1934 fully revealed the extent of the difficulties ahead for Britain – even if they were not to be fully realised until the 1950s.

The dispute further reveals the ambivalence of Britain's attitude towards Arabian oil. Oil was, generally, of significance to certain government departments at certain times. Oil questions were naturally more prominent in 1939 than in 1934. More and more Arabian concessions were sought and won. But this increased emphasis was, in its turn, offset by the greater political need to appease Ibn Saud. Consequently, oil was never a determining factor in British policy towards Saudi Arabia, even though it had been largely oil questions that had sparked off, and sustained, the frontier dispute. British policy towards Ibn Saud, while conscious of oil, was never dictated by oil.[218] Britain was acutely conscious of the need to protect and expand oil operations within Gulf territories for which she was responsible. Saudi Arabia's oil, in contrast, offered little temptation. Britain had less control over oil supplies from independent states than from dependent ones. The difficulty was presented by there being no agreed frontier separating one from the other.

Similar ambivalence also characterised Britain's commitment to the Gulf sheikhs. The historic obligation to protect them led to confusion as to how that could best be achieved, and how to reconcile that undertaking with the desire to appease Ibn Saud.

The British decision to try to hold Saudi Arabia to the blue line was both short-sighted and untenable. It created an atmosphere that was never entirely erased, and which contributed greatly to the souring of Anglo-Saudi relations in later years.[219] The blue line in 1934 was an anachronism, a reminder of imperialistic thinking prior to the First World War when large empires could attempt to carve up territory over which they had no declared jurisdiction or even explicit interest. It was also an unrealistic frontier by 1934, it being openly accepted that the true limits of Saudi sovereignty traversed it. Nonetheless, it should be added that Britain resurrected the blue line less out of imperialistic hankerings, such as the need for oil or territory, than from complacency and short-sightedness. The legal advisers only turned their minds to the blue line after it had been conveyed to Ibn Saud, not before. From then on Britain embarked upon a policy of gradual but considered retreat towards a solution more appropriate, both to the existing territorial and tribal situation in south-east Arabia, and to the conduct of relations between two independent states.

REFERENCES FOR CHAPTER NINE

1. Indeed, it was to become the most acute wrangle in the entire history of Anglo-Saudi relations, escalating in the early 1950s until relations were completely besmirched by what became known as the 'Buraimi' dispute. When, in the autumn of 1956, the British invasion of Suez took place, it proved to be the final provocation, and Saudi Arabia broke off diplomatic relations with Britain. They were not resumed until 1963.

   As a result of the international attention given to the dispute in the 1950s, it became the subject of many scholarly works, including a full-length account by J B Kelly, *Eastern Arabian Frontiers*. The relevant government documents were not available to Kelly, however, and he was obliged to draw heavily, as he admits (p. 24), on the British Memorial that was prepared and submitted to an arbitration tribunal that convened in 1955. The Memorials submitted by both the British and Saudi Governments contained, as one might expect, selected documents seeking to further the position of the respective governments, not to assist impartial scholarship. The British position, it will be shown in the light of the now-available documents, was not as strong nor, which is more important, was it seen from within to be as strong as Kelly has implied from the British Memorial.

   Kelly, of course, was more concerned by the more alarming events that characterised the post-Second World War phase of the dispute. Buraimi, for example, the oasis and cluster of villages which gave its name to the affair, had no specific significance in the 1930s and lay well outside any area to which Ibn Saud laid formal claim before 1949. Nonetheless, the developments of the mid-1930s form a major part of the case of both protagonists. Britain's negotiations with Saudi Arabia from 1934 contain many of the ingredients of the post-war dispute, and it is to these earlier developments that the historian of British policy must turn.

2. The frontier dispute examined here was, moreover, of a fundamentally different kind from that in northern Arabia. The *Ikhwan* rebellion was based on what political geographers would call a 'positional' dispute, arising over the actual location of the frontier or its interpretation. The dispute in south-east Arabia was a reflection of one party finding an attractive quality (oil) in the region of an undefined frontier (Prescott, p. 109). A further distinction can be drawn between territorial claims as a general instrument of policy (this being a permanent feature of Ibn Saud's policy) and the specific goal of strengthening the state by acquiring the 'attractive quality' in the area to be annexed (Prescott, p. 115). This feature is peculiar to Ibn Saud's campaign in south-east Arabia.

3. Much of the detail and background of the dispute concerns numerous tribes and place names which are exhaustively explored by Kelly. This chapter need not concern itself with such matters. Its only concern is to examine the attitudes and decision-making processes of the British Government in the handling of a dispute with Ibn Saud. Only when obscure place names affect the perceptions and arguments of the British government will reference be made to them.

4. Wakely (IO) to FO, 10 August 1926, FO E/4708/180/91: 371/11438.

5. Hurewitz, p. 414.

6. M Morsy-Abdullah, 'Britain and the Trucial States 1892-1939' (Unpublished Ph.D.), p. 36.

7. See P Sassoon, 'Air Power in the Middle East', *Journal of the Royal Central Asian Society*, 20 (1933), pp. 396-9.

8. In G W Bentley, 'The Development of the Air Route in the Persian Gulf', *Journal of the Royal Central Asian Society*, 20 (1933), p. 187.

9. Trenchard to Persian Gulf Sub-Committee, 24 October 1928, CAB 16/93.

10. Morsy-Abdullah, p. 59. In that same year an aerial base was established at Ras al Khaimah.

11. See Marlowe, *The Persian Gulf...*, p. 249. The route was designed to be kept close to coastlines in order to avoid tribal attacks and be able to call upon naval defence. Flying boats were also to be used on the imperial route; firstly, to avoid the political and military difficulties attending emergency landings among hostile tribes; secondly, to pre-empt French and Dutch requests for landing facilities in the Gulf (H Burchall, 'The Political Aspect of Commercial Air Routes', *Journal of the Royal Central Asian Society*, 20 (1933), pp. 82-4). Early in 1934 the Sheikh of Dubai offered refuelling facilities and an anchorage to the RAF and Imperial Airways.

12. Annual Report 1930.

13. Ryan suggested offering Ibn Saud £50 *per annum* for each air strip (Ryan to FO, No 55, 25 January 1932, FO E/682/507/25: 371/16022). Later this was raised to £1,000 *per annum* for all the air strips, although Ibn Saud demanded £5,000 gold *per annum* for each, plus the cost of officials, soldiers and construction (see FO E/78/78/25; FO E/3966/78/25: 371/16871).

14. Marlowe, op. cit., p. 249.

15. ibid., p. 250.

16. See Rendel, p. 82.

17. Prideaux to Amery, 9 June 1926, CO/20073/26. In 1922, during the Kuwait-Nejd frontier negotiations, Ibn Saud attempted to get the territory included in a possible oil concession to cover Qatar. He failed to do so only through the intervention of Sir Percy Cox.

18. ibid. It was not known to what extent Ibn Saud was authorising Ibn Jiluwi's *zakat*-collecting (see Morsy-Abdullah, pp. 202ff).

19. See *UK Memorial: Arbitration concerning Buraimi and the Common Frontier between Abu Dhabi and Saudi Arabia – Vol I*, pp. 34, 45 (hereafter: *UK Memorial*).

20. Prideaux to Amery, op. cit.; Prideaux to CO, 1 May 1926, CO/10743/26.

21. ibid.

22. Wakely (IO) to FO, 10 August 1926, FO E/4708/180/91: 371/11438.

23. See CO/10743/26. Kelly has suggested that it was acknowledged that Britain had implicit responsibility for defence of the sheikhdoms against external aggression, even though this was unsanctioned by treaty (*Arabia ...*, pp. 52-3). In fact Britain had neither the means

nor the wish to protect the sheikhdoms from the vicissitudes of Arabian politics. Hence the specific pledge to protect the rulers from attack by sea. The lack of agreed land frontiers suited British policy. Without frontiers there could be no violation of them. The lack of recognised frontiers consciously allowed for conflict between the Gulf rulers. Provided the security of the Gulf was maintained, rulers could attack each other with impunity (Alexander Melamid, 'The Political Geography of Trucial Oman and Qatar', *Geographical Review,* 43 (1953), p. 197). Against this Kelly maintains that there was almost a historical compulsion upon the British Government to uphold the integrity of the Gulf states against pretenders to their sovereignty, be they Persians, Turks, Egyptians or Saudis (*Eastern Arabian Frontiers,* p. 23). It should be remembered that the Saudis were geographical neighbours of the Gulf sheikhdoms and could not, unlike the other mentioned threats, pose a similar threat to British interests. Moreover, between 1915-27 Ibn Saud had been bound by treaty to respect Britain's special position in the Gulf, and since 1927 was pledged to maintain friendly relations with the sheikhdoms. Britain acknowledged no grounds, at least in the 1930s, upon which Ibn Saud could be accused of violating that particular clause of his 1927 treaty. Again, certain tribes in south-east Arabia had expressed allegiance to Al Saud on and off for over a century. This was not the case with the Egyptians, Turks or Persians.

24. Osborne (FO) minute, 20 August 1926, FO E/4858/633/91: 371/11444.
25. The 1913 Convention was intended to settle British and Ottoman spheres of influence in Arabia. The 1914 Convention finally confirmed the 1903-5 settlement of the Yemeni-Aden Protectorate frontier. The 1913 Convention was not ratified: the 1914 Convention was. Article Three of the 1914 Convention referred to, and incorporated, the blue line of Article Eleven of the 1913 Convention.
26. Wakely to FO, op. cit.
27. Osborne minute, 13 August 1926, FO E/4708/180/91: 371/11438.
28. See Foreign Secretary to Viceroy, 21 August 1926, L/P&S/11/924.
29. Rendel minute, 5 September 1934, FO E/5064/2429/25: 371/17940.
30. Haworth reports, 30 April 1927; 9 May 1927, L/P&S/10/1271.
31. Viceroy to SSI, 17 October 1928, L/P&S/10/1273.
32. See CAB 16/94.
33. *Umm al Qura,* 18 December 1931, in Ryan to FO, No 312, 23 July 1932, FO E/4175/946/25: 371/16023.
34. *Umm al Qura,* 19 February 1932, in Hope Gill to FO, No 109, 27 February 1932, FO E/1343/946/25: 371/16023.
35. Hope Gill, ibid.
36. Rendel minute, 22 August 1932, FO E/4175/946/25: 371/16023.
37. Annual Report 1933. The terms of the 1916 Anglo-Qatar treaty were vague as to British commitments. Under Article Ten, Britain promised to protect the sheikh from all aggression by sea. Article Eleven promised Britain's 'good offices' should the sheikh or his subjects be attacked by land, within the frontiers of Qatar.
38. APOC had obtained a two-year exploration licence from the Sheikh of Qatar in September 1932, shortly after SOCAL secured the Bahrain concession. Although Qatar was within the Red Line, Iraq Petroleum allowed APOC to operate as its nominee (Shwadran, p. 431).
39. *UK Memorial, Vol II,* p. 138.
40. See FO E/2481/279/91: 371/17813ff.
41. ME(O), 29th meeting, 23 February 1934, CAB 51/3.
42. Laithwaite memorandum, 'The Southern Boundary of Qatar and the Connected Problems', 26 January 1934, L/P&S/12/2136. From the point of view of oil concessions, there was an advantage in extending Qatar's southern frontier as far as possible. From the point of view of any landward defence for Qatar it was preferable that Qatar's frontier not be coterminous with that of Saudi Arabia, to avoid possible frontier disputes.
43. Ryan to FO, 14 February 1934, CAB 51/7.
44. Fowle to IO, 28 February 1934, CAB 51/7.
45. Morsy-Abdullah, p. 210.
46. See Rendel minute, 9 July 1934, FO E/4393/2429/25: 371/17939.
47. Ryan to FO, No 64, 18 April 1934, FO E/2429/2429/25: 371/17939.
48. See Chapter Six, page 154. There was a problem over the timing of any message to Ibn

Saud. If he was informed of the blue line while the war was going well against the Yemen it was feared that, having received no assistance from Britain, he would be encouraged to defy the decision. If, on the other hand, his Yemeni campaign was going badly, he might interpret Britain's statement as designed to take advantage of his difficulties by a new British 'forward policy' in the Gulf (Ryan to FO, op. cit.).

49. Ryan to Fuad Hamza, No 65, 28 April 1934, FO E/3167/279/91: 371/17813ff. The United States Embassy was provided with copies of the Anglo-Turkish Conventions on 24 April 1934 (Rendel to Millard (US Embassy), 24 April 1934, FO E/2481/279/91: 371/17813ff). There is no indication that the United States objected, at that time, to the blue line.

50. Kelly states that this was the first official intimation that Britain had had that Ibn Saud did not regard the blue line as his eastern frontier (*Eastern Arabian Frontiers*, p. 123). Britain's reluctance to pass on the blue line does not support this view. In any case, if Ibn Saud did not know about the blue line, he could not refute it. Kelly asserts: 'There is little doubt ... that both Ibn Saud and Cox ... understood it [the eastern frontier of Nejd] to be the blue line' (p. 113). 'The blue line was mentioned in the negotiations at Uqair in 1922 without drawing from him [Ibn Saud] any sign that he did not regard it as his eastern boundary' (pp. 114, 122). The Foreign Office was later to admit that between 1913 and 1934 Ibn Saud was not informed of the blue line. The Anglo-Turkish Conventions were never published by Britain either in the official *British Treaty Series* or the *British and Foreign State Papers* (Husain M Al Baharna, *The Legal Status of the Arabian Gulf States*, p. 232). According to Philby, 'The British Government put away these instruments which were all open to inspection until such time as it might suit their interests to produce them' (Philby, 'Arabia To-day', *International Affairs*, 14 (1935), p. 630).

On this matter some comparison with Aqaba is applicable. As with the blue line, Britain knew, long before Husein and Ibn Saud were informed, that Aqaba would not remain a part of the Hejaz (see page 44). Britain, it seemed, did not want to court trouble with Arabian monarchs by precipitately informing them of the limits of their kingdoms.

51. Fuad Hamza to Ryan, 20 June 1934, FO E/4451/279/91: 371/17813ff.

52. ibid. Two further arguments were also put forward, but neither of them was capable of substantiation. Ibn Saud claimed that the British Political Resident in the mid-1860s, Colonel Lewis Pelly, had recognised Saudi hegemony in south-east Arabia; and secondly, that the Saudis had supposedly patched up a quarrel between Qatar's rulers in the past (Ryan memorandum, 3 July 1934, FO E/5063/2429/25: 371/17940).

53. Ryan to FO, No 135, 8 May 1934, FO E/3551/2429/25: 371/17939; Fuad Hamza to Ryan, 13 May 1934, FO E/3651/279/91: 371/17813ff.

54. Ryan to Fuad Hamza, 15 June 1934, FO E/4341/279/91; FO E/3651/279/91: 371/17813ff.

55. Annual Report 1934. The climate at Taif was the least harsh of anywhere in Saudi Arabia. Accordingly, Ibn Saud spent much of the hot summer months in Mecca and Taif, returning to Riyadh for the autumn and winter.

56. Ryan to FO, No 166, 15 July 1934, FO E/4550/2429/25: 371/17940.

57. Ryan memorandum, 30 July 1934, FO E/5064/2429/25: 371/17940.

58. ibid. This does not accord with Kelly's judgment. Although speaking of the dispute in the 1950s, Kelly insists that British policy was not motivated primarily by considerations of oil, but by a natural reaffirmation of the nineteenth century Gulf policy of protecting the sheikhdoms (Kelly, 'The Buraimi Oasis Dispute', *International Affairs*, 32 (July 1956), pp. 319-20).

59. Ryan memorandum, 23 February 1932, FO E/1010/640/25: 371/16022.

60. See Ryan memorandum, 3 July 1934, FO E/5063/2429/25: 371/17940.

61. ibid. The revival of Turkish nationalism under Kemal Ataturk was seen as a persistent threat to the independence of the former Ottoman Arab provinces.

62. Ryan to FO, Jedda Situation Report for June 1934, 3 July 1934, FO E/4627/715/25: 371/17935.

63. Ryan memorandum, 3 July 1934, op. cit.

64. FO minute, 9 August 1934, ibid.

65. See Rendel minute, 5 September 1934, FO E/5064/2429/25: 371/17940.

66. See page 104.

67. Rendel minute, op. cit.

68. Ryan memorandum, 30 July 1934, FO E/5064/2429/25: 371/17940.
69. ibid.
70. Ryan to FO, 30 July 1934, CAB 51/7.
71. It is not the intention here to reproduce the volumes of legal argument that have appeared relating to the dispute. This section will offer a brief summary of those arguments and demonstrate that, contrary to most published accounts, the British Government privately admitted the shortcomings of its legal position.
72. See Herbert Liebesny, 'International Relations of Arabia: The Dependent Areas', *Middle East Journal,* 1 (1947), p. 160; J B Kelly, 'Sovereignty and Jurisdiction in Eastern Arabia', *International Affairs,* 34 (January 1958), pp. 16-24. In the 1950s the issue seemed to turn on whether Saudi Arabia could claim sovereignty and undisturbed possession. In the 1930s Britain examined whether she, herself, had such advantages.
73. This can be contrasted with Kelly's thesis which not only laid great emphasis on the legal aspects of the dispute, but also insisted that it was Saudi Arabia who stood in violation of them.
74. The validity of this Convention has never been settled to the satisfaction of both parties. Article Three of the 1914 Convention provided for the adoption of Article Eleven (which concerned the blue line) of the unratified 1913 Convention. In other words, validity was, according to the British position, given to a single Article of a draft convention which itself was never ratified, and so never had any legal force. This raises the legal issue of whether a treaty can be ratified in part, and whether the blue line could be proved valid when the instrument from which it was basically derived was never ratified (Al Baharna, pp. 227-8).
75. Beckett (FO legal adviser) minute, 29 August 1934, FO E/5064/2429/25: 371/17940. The Saudi Government have steadfastly denied any treaty with the Turks which accepted Ottoman suzereignty in 1914 (Al Baharna, pp. 233-4). The treaty was discovered by the Indian Expeditionary Force in the Basra archives.

   Although Britain tried to insist that Ibn Saud was an Ottoman subject, he acted independently when taking up arms against Ibn Rashid. Moreover, as a rule, successor states are not bound by the treaties of their predecessors, although there are exceptions, such as if the treaties relate to strictly local matters (Al Baharna, pp. 228-31).
76. Beckett minute, op. cit.
77. ibid.
78. ibid.
79. Rendel, ME(O), 42nd meeting, 24 September 1935, CAB 51/3.
80. Beckett minute, 29 August 1934, FO E/5064/2429/25: 371/17940.
81. ibid.
82. ibid.
83. Ryan minute, 12 September 1934, CAB 51/7.
84. Beckett minute, 29 August 1934, FO E/5064/2429/25: 371/17940.
85. Fitzmaurice (FO legal adviser) minute, 5 September 1934, ibid.
86. Beckett report, ME(O), 33rd meeting, 13 September 1934, CAB 51/3. The India Office, in contrast, clung to the view that the blue line had legal validity because Ibn Saud had accepted a Turkish title; he was bound as a successor to the Turks; and he was guilty of 'blackmail' in eastern Arabia (Morsy-Abdullah, p. 213).
87. Fitzmaurice minute, op. cit.
88. ibid. Kelly rightly asserts that the blue line frontier in 1914 roughly corresponded with the limits of Ibn Saud's *de facto* sovereignty at the time (*Eastern Arabian Frontiers,* pp. 111-2). Ibn Saud had described his ancestral territories as Nejd, Hasa and Qatif, all of which lay to the west of the blue line. Kelly takes this to bind Ibn Saud to those limits. Not only did the Foreign Office take a different view, but it can barely be wondered at that Ibn Saud should restrict his claims in 1915 within manageable limits. As he was only precariously holding Hasa, and was seeking outside support for his position, he was hardly likely at the time to have made far-reaching ancestral demands in south-east Arabia, which might have lost him the support of the British Government. It must also be remembered that Britain gave large areas of the Kuwaiti hinterland to Ibn Saud in 1922 without expressing concern for the future of the sheikhdom. Cox, himself, said that Ibn Saud thought himself justified, in principle, in regaining any territory that his forefathers held a century previously, even as a sphere of influence (Kelly, p. 119).

89. FO to Ryan, 9 July 1934, FO E/4393/2429/25: 371/17940.
90. Rendel minute, 9 September 1934, FO E/5064/2429/25: 371/17940.
91. A detailed secret memorandum prepared by the Foreign Office in April 1936, considering Britain's overseas commitments, placed British interests in the Gulf below those in the peninsula (i.e. Ibn Saud) and the Hashemite states (DBFP Series IA, Vol 1, pp. 846-81).
92. Annual Report 1934.
93. Rendel minute, 5 September 1934, FO E/5064/2429/25: 371/17940.
94. Rendel minute, 6 September 1934, ibid.
95. Vansittart minute, 9 September 1934, ibid.
96. ME(O), 33rd meeting, 13 September 1934, CAB 51/3.
97. Fowle, ibid.
98. Air Ministry, ibid. Aerial manoeuvres could not be confined within small territories such as Qatar.
99. ibid.
100. Rendel, ibid.
101. Conclusions, ibid.
102. Fuad Hamza conversation FO, 20 September 1934, FO E/5908/2429/25: 371/17940.
103. Rendel to Fuad Hamza, ibid. It appeared that although Fuad Hamza had come to discuss several outstanding issues, he had not come with definite instructions.
104. Annual Report 1934; Morsy-Abdullah, p. 215.
105. Rendel, ME(O), 37th meeting, 8 November 1934, CAB 51/3.
106. See ME(O), 37th meeting, ibid.
107. Hereafter: 'Historical Memorandum...,' 26 September 1934, CAB 51/7. Britain's whole position in India in the 1920s and '30s was under increasing pressure, as nationalist activity increased and the authorities had to contend with the rising star of Gandhi.
108. Kelly, *Eastern Arabian Frontiers*, pp. 120-1. Fowle also described *zakat* payments as 'danegeld pure and simple' (Fowle to SSI, 30 March 1934, CAB 51/3.)
109. Laithwaite (IO) minute on 'Historical Memorandum...,' 1 September 1934, CAB 51/7.
110. ibid.
111. Fowle minute, 21 September 1934, CAB 51/8.
112. ibid. Any attempt to draw boundaries, Fowle suspected, would lead to an inevitable rush of complaints and a deterioration of relations with Saudi Arabia.
113. WO, ME(O), 37th meeting, op. cit.
114. ibid. Britain prevented tribes from the area between the North-West provincial boundary of India and the international boundary from launching attacks into India, and protected them, in return, from Afghan incursions. Afghanistan's northern boundary with Russia formed the outer defence line of the British-Indian Empire. This was really, therefore, a threefold line (Eric Fisher, 'On Boundaries', *World Politics*, 1 (1948-49), p. 220).
115. Rendel memorandum, 15 November 1934, FO E/6928/2429/25: 371/17940; Beckett minute, 23 January 1935, FO E/394/318/25: 371/19007. For precise geographical coordinates of the desert zone, see Morsy-Abdullah, Appendix – Map 4.
116. See ME(O), 37th meeting, op. cit..
117. Rendel to Ryan, 24 & 31 January 1935, FO E/394/318/25: 371/19007.
118. Beckett minute, 25 January 1935, ibid.
119. See Rendel to Ryan, 25 January 1935, ibid.; IO, ME(O), 37th meeting, op. cit.
120. ibid.
121. Admiralty, ME(O), 37th meeting, op. cit.
122. Conclusions, ibid.
123. See Annual Report 1935.
124. See Morsy-Abdullah, p. 218.
125. In Ryan to Eden, No 7, 22 January 1935, FO E/496/318/25: 371/19007.
126. Morsy-Abdullah, p. 219.
127. Ryan to Rendel, 26 February 1935, FO E/1652/318/25: 371/19008.
128. Annual Report 1935.
129. ibid.
130. ibid.
131. ibid.
132. Fuad Hamza to Ryan, 3 April 1935, FO E/2700/77/91: 371/18905ff.

133. Saudi Arabia's 'red line' should not be confused with the Red Line operated by the Iraq Petroleum Company. The two lines are quite unrelated.
134. Rendel to Laithwaite, 8 April 1935, FO E/2237/77/91: 371/18905ff; Ryan was, incidentally, colourblind (Rendel, p. 83).
135. ibid.
136. IO, ME(O), 40th meeting, 15 April 1935, CAB 51/3.
137. ibid.
138. Admiralty, ibid.
139. WO, ibid.
140. Rendel, ibid.
141. Conclusions, ibid.
142. Annual Report 1935. The India Office refused to permit American companies negotiating concessions in Qatar or the Trucial states. Elsewhere in the Gulf, in Bahrain and Kuwait for example, which Kelly terms the 'Upper Gulf', containing the more wealthy and sophisticated sheikhdoms (J. B. Kelly, 'The Legal and Historical Basis of the British Position in the Persian Gulf', *St Antony's Papers: Middle Eastern Affairs – 1*, p. 120), the Government of India grudgingly admitted that it was no longer its policy to exclude foreign traders and concessionaires, provided political interests were safeguarded (Report of Political Dept. of British India, *British Interests in the Persian Gulf*, 25 June 1935, L/P&S/18B/450).
    In the event, the Iraq Petroleum Company authorised APOC to operate the Qatar concession which, in 1937, passed to the Petroleum Development (Qatar) Co. (Shwadran, *The Middle East, Oil and the Great Powers*, p. 431).
143. The India Office also started putting restrictions on American medical activities in the sheikhdoms (Morsy-Abdullah, p. 74).
144. See FO E/2705/77/91: 371/18905ff. On the question of oil concessions in Qatar and the Trucial sheikhdoms, see Morsy-Abdullah, pp. 69-82.
145. Rendel minute, 6 June 1935, FO E/2704/318/25: 371/19008.
146. Annual Report 1935.
147. Ibn Saud maintained that, if relations with the Sheikh of Qatar were to be friendly and peaceful, as the Treaty of Jedda stipulated, then it predicated the existence of some form of relations. Britain, it seemed, was forbidding the existence of any relations at all. For a detailed discussion on this particular Anglo-Saudi quarrel, see Al Baharna, pp. 75-6.
148. Annual Report 1935.
149. Rendel note of 1st meeting with Fuad Hamza, 24 June 1935, FO E/3944/77/91: 371/18905ff.
150. 2nd meeting, 25 June 1935, FO E/3946/77/91: 371/18905ff.
151. 3rd meeting, 2 July 1935, FO E/4126/77/91: 371/18905ff.
152. Annual Report 1935.
153. Shuckburgh, ME(O), 42nd meeting, 24 September 1935, CAB 51/3.
154. IO, ibid.
155. Ryan, ibid.
156. Rendel, ibid.
157. ibid.
158. ibid.; See Hoare to Ryan, No 309, 23 October 1935, L/P&S/12/2/2135.
159. Rendel, ME(O), 42nd meeting, op. cit.
160. ibid.
161. Hoare to Ryan, op. cit.
162. Ryan to Hoare, No 351, 30 December 1935, FO E/7574/77/91: 371/18905ff.
163. Hoare to Ryan, op. cit. See Morsy-Abdullah for details of the Riyadh line, pp. 227ff.
164. Annual Report, op. cit.
165. ibid.
166. Ryan to Hoare, op. cit.
167. Annual Report 1936.
168. Morsy-Abdullah, pp. 74-5. Petroleum Concessions was based in Bahrain in 1935, and set up an affiliate, Petroleum Development (Trucial Coast).
169. Morsy-Abdullah, p. 80.
170. Annual Report 1936.
171. Ryan had been obliged to remain in Jedda beyond the customary five-year term because,

for a time, no other ministerial post could be found for him. He became Minister in Albania.

172. D. C. Watt, *Personalities and Policies: Studies in the Formulation of British Foreign Policy in the Twentieth Century*, p. 41.

173. Philby, *Forty Years* ..., p. 74.

174. Annual Report 1936. For a discussion of oil and the frontier problems of the Trucial Coast, see Morsy-Abdullah, pp. 344ff.

175. Annual Report 1936.

176. Kelly, *Arabia* ..., p. 66. It appears that on this issue the Foreign Office was acting on its own initiative. Its policy of ceding Jabal Nakhsh did not have the endorsement of the Middle East (Official) Sub-Committee.

177. See Chapter Ten.

178. Rendel, ME(O), 49th meeting, 1 February 1937, CAB 51/3. Britain had first recognised Abu Dhabi's rights over Khor el Odeid in 1878. During the following decade Britain had to forestall several claims from Qatar for the inlet (Al Baharna, p. 261). In 1906 Cox had assured the Sheikh of Abu Dhabi that Britain would prevent the occupation of Khor el Odeid by anyone else (see FO E/2314/246/25: 371/23269).

179. Bullard to Halifax, Annual Report for 1937, 26 March 1938, FO E/2338/2338/25: 371/21908) (hereafter: Annual Report 1937).

180. WO, ME(O), 49th meeting, op. cit.

181. ibid.

182. Rendel, ibid.

183. IO, ibid.

184. ibid.

185. Kelly, *Arabia* ..., p. 67.

186. Rendel, pp. 97-8. For a full account of Rendel's Middle Eastern tour, see FO E/2312/2312/65: 371/20786. Before crossing Saudi Arabia, Rendel examined the disputed territory by air with Fowle.

187. See FO E/2124/258/91: 371/20776-7.

188. Bullard to Eden, No 47, 27 March 1937, ibid.; Annual Report 1937.

189. Bullard to Eden, ibid.

190. Annual Report 1937.

191. ibid.

192. Rendel, ME(O), 52nd meeting, 29 June 1937, CAB 51/4.

193. Annual Report 1937.

194. ibid.

195. ibid.

196. Rendel, ME(O), 53rd meeting, 8 November 1937, CAB 51/4.

197. Shuckburgh, ibid. Ibn Saud was still in serious financial difficulties. Even by 1937 the number of overseas pilgrims had only risen to around 50,000. (Annual Report 1937). Bullard considered that it was partly CASOC's failure, so far, to find oil that was leading to Ibn Saud taking a harder line on the frontier question.

198. Rendel and Bullard, ME(O), op. cit.

199. Bullard to Faisal, 4 December 1937, FO E/7572/258/91: 371/20776-7.

200. Faisal to Bullard, 19 December 1937, FO E/439/150/91: 371/20775.

201. See CAB 51/10.

202. Kelly, op. cit., pp. 66-7.

203. Rendel, ME(O), 56th meeting, 8 February 1938, CAB 51/4.

204. Kelly, op. cit., pp. 66-7.

205. Rendel, op. cit.

206. ibid.

207. ibid. See Chapter Ten.

208. ibid.

209. ibid. See pages 15-16.

210. Philips (Admiralty), ME(O), 56th meeting, op. cit.

211. Osborne (WO), ibid.

212. ibid. The Air Ministry, too, swung behind the demands for generous concessions. As the question of Khor el Odeid did not affect air communications, the Air Ministry considered its cession a political, not a strategic matter.

213. Gibson (IO), ibid. Shuckburgh, too, reminded the sub-committee of the problems associated with taking territory from one Arab state, which happened to be weak, and giving it to another which was strong (Shuckburgh, ibid.). This was what had happened in 1922 with regard to the Kuwait and Nejd frontiers.

214. Baggally (FO) memorandum, 22 March 1939, FO E/2314/246/25: 371/23269.

215. The United States Government was not yet active in support of American oil companies.

216. By 1935 the RAF network from the Mediterranean eastwards comprised the following Commands: the Mediterranean Command (Malta); the Middle East Command (Egypt, Palestine and Transjordan); the Iraq Command; the Aden Command; the India Command; and the Far East Command (Main, p. 43).

217. There is, of course, no such thing as a 'good' boundary. It is good only if it is not in dispute (Prescott, p. 23). A frontier could not have been drawn anywhere in south-east Arabia without being disputed by at least one party.

218. Monroe offers a similar conclusion, *Britain's Moment* ..., p. 104.

219. A brief account of the Buraimi dispute in the 1950s appears in the Epilogue.

CHAPTER TEN

The Arab World 1936-1939: Pan-Arabism and Palestine

The lapsing of Ibn Saud's interest in the League of Nations, brought about in part because of the failure of the League to quell Italian aggression against Abyssinia, was to lead to a major, if temporary re-orientation in Saudi Arabia's foreign policy in the late 1930s. Britain, too, in the face of deteriorating situations in Europe and Palestine, found herself viewing Anglo-Saudi relations increasingly in the context of global politics. The issues which affected those relations between 1936-39 were broadly of two kinds. From Europe came the escalating Italian interest in the Red Sea and the new German political thrust into regions hitherto outside German experience, including the Arabian peninsula. These European factors will be the subject of the following chapter. For the moment, attention is concentrated upon the Arab world, where violent developments in the administration of Palestine were coupled with detectable advances in Arab national consciousness. Accordingly, the international climate in the years 1936-39 meant that British policy towards Saudi Arabia was dictated less by the activities of Ibn Saud than by developments elsewhere which impinged upon his Kingdom.[1] It will be suggested that the years prior to the Second World War marked a radical shift in the substance of Anglo-Saudi relations. Partly because events elsewhere demanded British attention, London failed to perceive a change in direction in Saudi foreign policy designed to free the heartland of Islam from its vulnerability to British pressure. It will be proposed that it was not so much the granting of the Saudi oil concession to an American company in 1933 that marked Ibn Saud's determination to seek a counterweight to Britain, but various international developments, notably in Palestine, in 1936-37.

Failure to secure a satisfactory guarantee from either Britain or Italy by the mid-1930s, together with his disillusionment with the League of Nations, prompted Ibn Saud to search for a new policy that would increase the security of his Kingdom. One such consideration was pan-Arabism, for which 1936 proved to be a momentous year in the foreign policy of Saudi Arabia. Ibn Saud's foreign policy had previously centred around a few specific objectives, such as ridding his Kingdom of its backward image.[2] The constant need for revenue was always prominent, as was the need to thwart

Italian penetration of the Red Sea.[3] Furthermore, Ibn Saud had sought to protect his position by preventing excessive outside influences from penetrating Arabia and by safeguarding the responsibilities entrusted to Saudi Arabia as custodian of the Islamic Holy Places.[4] As Saudi Arabia was a new state, frontier problems were always going to be a dominant feature of her foreign relations, the more so with the emerging importance of Middle Eastern oil. In his inter-Arab dealings, Ibn Saud feared an unfavourable combination of Arab states directed against him, particularly any combination led by the Hashemites.[5] Opportunistically, Ibn Saud sought territorial expansion in the name of Al Saud and/or Wahhabism, mindful of the need to avoid protracted quarrels with Britain. The need for her political goodwill still dominated Ibn Saud's foreign policy up to 1936.

The Development of Arab National Consciousness

By 1936 Britain could not ignore perceptible advances in Arab national consciousness. This phenomenon is itself so complex in its roots and manifestations as to require some elaboration. Arab nationalism, pan-Arabism, and pan-Islamism were different forms of the fundamental drive among the Arab peoples for political emancipation. The emergence of nationalist consciousness in the Arab world can be seen to stem from several sources, periods and places. From one standpoint, the Napoleonic invasion of Egypt in 1798 heralded the beginning of Arab nationalism, by exposing the Arab provinces of the Ottoman Empire to European military, cultural, economic and political influences.[6] In Marlowe's words, it was:

> the impact of these influences on a culturally dormant, politically stagnant, and economically sterile society which set in train those diverse spiritual, intellectual, social and political ferments which go to make up Arab nationalism as we know it today.[7]

This process led directly to an Egyptian attempt to wrest an Arabian empire from the Turks in the 1830s; an endeavour which sought to 'Arabise' the Arab world.

Egypt, however, has never been ideally suited to speak for the Arabs as a whole. Her unique dependence on the Nile encouraged little trade with her Arab neighbours. She already had four thousand years of nationhood of her own, despite her subjugation by the Turks, and later the British. Consequently, Egyptians had no need to appeal to a common 'Arabism' when they already possessed 'Egyptianism'.[8]

A later and more direct spur to Arab nationalist activity came from the Turks. In the last thirty years of the nineteenth century the Turks became increasingly unpopular as Sultan Abd al Hamid II, as part of a Turkish resurgence, attempted to impose Ottoman domination on the remoter parts of the Empire. By the first decade of the twentieth century, intellectual and military groupings in the Mediterranean centres of Arab population –

Damascus, Beirut, Haifa and Jerusalem – were establishing secret societies and political programmes. A proclamation by the Arab National Committee in 1905 declared:

> The Turks dominate the Arabs only by dividing them on insignificant questions of ceremonial and religion, but the Arabs have recovered consciousness of their national, historical and racial unity, and desire to detach themselves from the worm-eaten tree of Othman, and to unite as an independent state. This new Arabia will extend as far as its natural frontiers, from the valleys of the Tigris and Euphrates to the Straits of Suez, from the Mediterranean Sea to Oman.[9]

These first roots of Arab nationalism were nourished by the activities of the 'Young Turks', who overthrew Abd al Hamid II in July 1908. The Young Turk revolution imposed itself heavily upon Arab lands, bringing with it a centralising momentum towards Constantinople and a conscious imitation of European institutions. The Young Turks sought to unite the Empire with all its races and religions: the Arab provinces would be exposed to Turkish customs, and the Arabic language suppressed in schools.[10]

It was in the urban centres, with their exposure to western influences and relatively advanced civic organisations, that the idea of an Arab renaissance and Arab nationalism first emerged, partly as a reaction to European ideas, and partly as a response to the pressure of Turkish nationalism. There was, in addition, a completely separate strand of Arab identity emerging from central Arabia. Wahhabism itself was one of the precursors of Arab nationalism in that it sought to create from the chaos of Arabia a state organisation held together by the ties of brotherhood and religion. This was a totally different phenomenon from that which began to flourish among the intellectuals of Damascus and other cities in the early twentieth century. The social and economic composition of central Arabia, and its isolation from European and Ottoman influences, had little in common with the nationalist sentiment of the Mediterranean Arabs.[11]

Nonetheless, the mutual obligations introduced in central Arabia among tribal members and with client tribes effectively became a form of nationalism.[12] Traditionally, the concept of 'nation' in central Arabia was synonymous with that of the Islamic community.[13] Only with the coming of the mandates, and the imposition of frontiers to delineate the Saudi state, was the western idea of nationalism and nation-state imported to central Arabia. The Saudi state had its frontiers shaped by Britain no less comprehensively than the other, dependent, Arab territories.

All these different facets of Arab nationalism were given impetus by the First World War, which brought Arabia to the centre of interest in world politics. Western notions of national self-determination and the liberation of small nations were exposed to the Arab world and emerged in a new form of Arab nationalism through the romantic and dynastic ingredients of Sherif Husein. Britain proclaimed her assistance in bringing Arab nationalism to fruition, assuming that by emphasising the 'nation', Arab nationalism would be opposed to the religious emphasis of Turkish pan-Islamism. Husein attempted to unite the urban and bedouin Arabs and, later, to revive the ancient glory of the Arabian Caliphate. Paradoxically, most of the Arab military involvement in the War occurred in the Arabian peninsula where nationalist consciousness was least advanced.[14]

Sherifian nationalism collapsed under the European power politics that followed the War and the Saudi conquest of the Hejaz in the mid-1920s. Britain, having given Arab nationalism its greatest boost from 1915, continued to do so in the 1920s and '30s as an unwitting target of the Arab cause. Having urged the Arabs to rid themselves of the Turks, the Arab grievances were then directed at Britain and France, who were seen as oppressors in the Levant and Mesopotamia no less than the Turks beforehand. The European powers did not have the saving grace of being Moslems, and, in the case of Britain, were simultaneously engaged in furthering Jewish nationalism on Arab soil. In consequence, much of the driving force of Arab nationalism in the inter-war years was largely a reaction to European political pressure.[15]

This applied less to Ibn Saud than to other Arab rulers. He brought his own particular interpretation of nationalism to the Arab world. Although Wahhabism also sought to repudiate and exclude European influences, the manipulation of the *Ikhwan* was a deliberate attempt at seeking the settlement of tribes and the basis of orderly government. Ibn Saud aimed at a spiritual rebirth, the reformation of every aspect of Arabian life, the awakening consciousness of Arab unity, the stamping out of tribal feuds and the uniting of the bedouin. Wahhabism stepped back into the heritage of Mohammad with the aim of unity based on monotheistic puritanism.

The division of the Ottoman territories into *vilayets* prior to 1914 was replaced, by 1922, by complete independence in some cases and virtual subjugation to European powers in others. This diversity brought with it a corresponding variation in the aims and tactics of nationalist activity.[16] Ibn Saud, not least because of his relationship with Mecca, could not easily distinguish pan-Arabism from pan-Islamism.[17] The 1926 pan-Islamic Conference saw him appealing to the Islamic, not just the Arab, world. It was religion that held the key to Ibn Saud's personal and dynastic ambitions. Aqaba, for example, was demanded as part of the Islamic Holy Land. The legal system of the Hejaz was based on the *Sharia*, that is, Koranic, not tribal, law. He shared with the other Arab rulers a common language, but not a common history, culture, interpretation of Islam, or forced subservience to European powers. Besides, pan-Islamism offered greater political opportunities for Ibn Saud than pan-Arabism.

Opinion is contradictory over Ibn Saud's commitment to a wider Arab cause, as opposed to his personal and dynastic ambitions. One authority cites Ibn Saud as proclaiming the principles of pan-Arabism and his willingness to accept the leadership of the Arab world as far back as 1923.[18]

in the grip of Wahhabi fanaticism. Religion, having served its purpose, was, by the mid-1930s, constrained within the practical demands of statehood. Moreover, strong efforts were made by Palestinians during the 1935 Pilgrimage to win sympathy in the Hejaz. This was thought to be displeasing to Ibn Saud, whose overriding interest lay in forbidding the Pilgrimage to be exploited for political purposes.[36]

The Re-orientation of Saudi Foreign Policy – 1936

By 1936 Ibn Saud had to take into consideration the Italian invasion of Abyssinia and the inability or unwillingness of Britain and the League to prevent it. The Arab world had witnessed, for the first time, a successful challenge to British supremacy in the Red Sea area. If Britain would not intervene to protect Abyssinia against Italy, she was equally unlikely to protect Saudi Arabia. Perhaps Ibn Saud shared the conviction held in many Arab circles that war in Europe, involving at least Britain and Italy, was inevitable and that the time was appropriate for further realisation of Arab national aspirations.[37] In any case, 1936 was a critical year as Ibn Saud took his first steps away from his perceived futile dependence on Britain for the security of his Kingdom towards building up relations with other Arab states.

At the end of 1935 Ibn Saud settled the dispute with the Sheikh of Bahrain over the transit dues imposed on trade passing through the archipelago to Nejd,[38] only to find the Sheikh calling for an economic and political union of the Gulf states directed, in part, against Ibn Saud.[39] In January 1936 Ibn Saud paid a state visit to Kuwait and paved the way for an end to the protracted trade blockade which was aimed at keeping Saudi tribes away from Kuwaiti influence; strangling the trade of his neighbour; and increasing the development and prosperity of his own Gulf ports.[40] Ibn Saud's visit, and the subsequent easing of tension between Saudi Arabia and Kuwait, demonstrated that, by 1936, the economy of the sheikhdom could not flourish on British naval protection alone without also enjoying Saudi goodwill.[41] This implied, at the very least, a partial *de facto* transfer of the political control over Kuwait from British to Saudi hands.[42]

More significantly, in April, the signing was announced of a Treaty of Arab Brotherhood and Alliance between Saudi Arabia and Iraq. The treaty was modelled on that between Saudi Arabia and the Yemen two years previously, containing similar provisions for the peaceful settlement of disputes and co-operation in resisting aggression.[43] The passage of the Saudi-Iraqi treaty was keenly followed by the British Government which, nonetheless, seemed reluctant to grasp the full implications of Ibn Saud's change of direction. In earlier years, when Ibn Saud and Feisal were at loggerheads, and when the *Ikhwan* raids were threatening the stability of northern Arabia, Britain was only too keen to promote cordial relations between the two rulers. The evolving maturity of both Iraq and Saudi Arabia in the following years, however, meant that Britain viewed any further rapprochement with some ambivalence. Strong independent Arab states which had no cause to curry favour with European rivals were welcomed by Britain. But as long as other parts of the Arab world, particularly Palestine and the Gulf sheikhdoms, were in such exposed positions with regard to their relations with Britain, there were strong arguments for not encouraging the development of pan-Arab moves. Accordingly, Britain was not going to sanction the Saudi-Iraqi treaty in its unabridged version. Article Six of the original draft treaty stated:

> The High Contracting Parties undertake to co-ordinate their objectives in regard to the peoples of neighbouring Arab countries and to exert peaceful efforts to help those peoples towards realisation of their aspirations for independence.[44]

The British Government interpreted this clause as providing for future interference in the affairs of Syria and Palestine.[45] Article Seven was aimed at similar possible intervention in the affairs of the Gulf sheikhdoms. The Jedda Legation was convinced that the initiative behind these two Articles had come from Saudi Arabia, and that the twin threats of Italy in the Red Sea and a permanent suspicion of Turkey's aims in the Arab world were primarily responsible.[46]

The Iraq Government, which could make no pledges that would conflict either with its own treaty with Britain or its obligations to the League, consulted the British Government throughout the treaty negotiations. For Iraq, the treaty was seen as little more than a gesture of sympathy between two Arab states, the greater share of the practical benefits accruing to Saudi Arabia. Without being seen to oppose the strengthening of friendly relations between Iraq and Saudi Arabia, the British Government discreetly put pressure on Iraq to drop the two Articles relating to interference in other Arab states.[47] Consequently, the final treaty ceased to be the pan-Arab document originally aimed at. Iraq, in any case, was to have troubles of her own. Before the end of the year she witnessed her first military coup, the first of its kind anywhere in the Arab world.

No sooner had this major breakthrough in Saudi Arabia's foreign policy been achieved than it was followed by a Saudi treaty with Egypt, leading to the establishment of diplomatic relations with Cairo. Saudi-Egyptian relations had been particularly strained for a decade as a result of a shooting incident involving Egyptian pilgrims during the 1926 Pilgrimage.[48] In the intervening years there had been no official relations between Egypt and Ibn Saud's Kingdom, due largely to the personal antipathy between Ibn Saud and King Fuad, and the latter's occasional designs on the Caliphate and the Hejaz.[49]

Egypt's own outlook on the world had changed with the Italian invasion of Abyssinia. Negotiations for the long sought-after treaty with Britain that would grant Egypt complete independence were then resumed in a mutual atmosphere of greater flexibility and determination to succeed. An Anglo-Egyptian Treaty of Preferential Alliance was signed in August 1936, just three months after the Saudi-Egyptian treaty had linked all four independent Arab states (Saudi Arabia, Egypt, Iraq and the Yemen) by treaty. Clearly Ibn Saud's policy was motivated less by pan-Arab sentiment than by political pragmatism: the desire for Saudi Arabia's security in the face of mounting disenchantment with Britain.

Before the year was out an exchange of notes between the British and Saudi Governments modified and prolonged the 1927 Treaty of Jedda. The principal changes were to the advantage of Saudi Arabia,[50] and were consummated by the arrival of the second British Minister to Jedda, Sir Reader Bullard. In 1937 the Yemen adhered to the Saudi-Iraqi treaty.[51] Transjordan, however, resisted closer ties with Saudi Arabia, largely because of the continuing frontier disputes.[52]

The Effect of Palestine on Anglo-Saudi Relations

Developments in the Palestine mandate from 1936 confronted Britain with the apparent insolubility of the problem inherited with the Balfour Declaration back in 1917. The 1936 disturbances, and the Peel Report that followed, constituted not only a turning point in Anglo-Saudi relations, but also in British policy towards the Arab world as a whole. It is important to see these developments alongside Ibn Saud's gradual embracement of pan-Arabism.

Palestine was of considerable importance to Britain: it provided a naval base in the eastern Mediterranean at Haifa; its proximity to the Suez Canal invested it with strategic significance; and its control by Britain prevented the French from holding the entire Levant coast. By 1936 the development of air routes and oil pipelines added to Palestine's strategic importance. There was, in addition, the perceived humanitarian and religious justification for a Jewish national home in Palestine, as well as the wider significance of an area that was central to the world's three great monotheistic religions.

The strike and disorders which swept through Palestine from April 1936 had as their ostensible cause the abandonment of plans for a Legislative Council with an inbuilt Arab majority.[53] The Jews refused to co-operate with the proposals and the House of Commons backed their refusal. With the imminent signing of the Anglo-Egyptian treaty, and an announcement that France was prepared to negotiate treaties with Syria and Lebanon, the Palestinians were the only Arabs east of Libya who had not attained, or were expected to attain, a limited national freedom.[54] These factors, coupled with increasing Jewish immigration and the trade disruption that accompanied the Italo-Abyssinian war, contributed to the Arab rebellion.[55] It appeared that Britain was incapable of controlling a country even as small as Palestine.

Prior to the 1936 disturbances Ibn Saud had paid little attention to events in Palestine, although, as has been seen, he was already instigating closer relations with his neighbours. To him, it has been suggested, the Europeanised Arabs of Palestine were mere agriculturalists, forsaking their Arab tribal ancestry.[56] As they were not Wahhabis, they were neither true Arabs nor true Moslems. Ibn Saud had been noticeably unwilling to allow himself to be used by either Palestinian or Syrian agitators,[57] although the Grand Mufti of Jerusalem had complained to Ibn Saud about Britain's Zionist policy, which was depicted as being calculated to destroy the Arab nation. Ibn Saud was exhorted to 'save the sacred land of Palestine'.[58] His cool response owed something to geography. The loss of Aqaba-Maan had deprived Saudi Arabia of a common frontier with Palestine. Saudi Arabia was not directly threatened by a Jewish spillover.

Fears of possible Saudi influence in Palestine affected the Foreign and Colonial Offices in different ways. Although the Colonial Office was formally responsible for Palestine, the Foreign Office was also involved with the League of Nations and the independent Arab world, and was traditionally somewhat detached from Zionism, preferring to put its trust in the region in the forces of Arab nationalism.[59] The 1936 disturbances and their aftermath thrust the Foreign Office deeper into the management of Anglo-Arab relations. Under the 1933 Saudi-Transjordanian treaty Saudi Arabia was entitled to appoint a Consul at Amman.[60] In March 1936 the Saudi Government, in line with its embryonic interest in pan-Arabism, proposed the establishment of a Saudi Arabian consulate in Palestine to cater for Saudi interests in Palestine and Transjordan. Sir Arthur Wauchope, the High Commissioner, concurred,[61] but when the riots commenced shortly afterwards the Colonial Office expressed strong objections to the idea. With the whole Arab question looming large it was feared that a Saudi consular officer in Palestine might become a focus for Palestinian Arab nationalism.[62] The Foreign Office, even at the outbreak of the disorders, did not want to snub Ibn Saud when the need for Arab goodwill was felt to be imperative.[63] The proposal was deferred.

Following the outbreak of disturbances the Saudi Government made a series of approaches to Britain. The Mufti hoped to rouse as many Arab states as possible. At the end of April Sheikh Yusuf Yasin approached Ryan for 'advice' on how Ibn Saud could avoid interference without damage to his prestige.[64] Ryan's 'advice' was blunt and emphatic. The Saudi King would neither promote his friendship with Britain, nor enhance his prestige in the Arab world at large if he concerned himself with a purely British problem in Palestine.[65]

Rebuffed from one quarter Ibn Saud approached the Foreign Office in London directly. Sheikh Hafiz Wahba explained to Oliphant how Ibn Saud was being upbraided as a coward for taking no public stand on the matter of Palestine.[66] As had happened during the *Ikhwan* rebellion, the Foreign Office was sensitive to Ibn Saud's dilemma. Arab and British demands on him were in collision. Rendel acknowledged that the recent increase in Jewish immigration into the mandate, as a result of Nazi policies, was bound to cause difficulties for Ibn Saud and all Arab rulers.[67] Ibn Saud could not publicly declare his sympathies with the Palestinian Arabs without antagonising Britain, whose support he still needed, if possible, in the Red Sea.[68]

The beleaguered Colonial Office, faced with a deteriorating situation, clutched at anything, even Saudi assistance. If Ibn Saud could use his influence to end the violence, then, the Colonial Office admitted, he could be doing a considerable service to the British Government.[69] Further Saudi representations were made in the second half of June, during which it appeared that the initial diffident request for 'advice' had transformed into a fully matured theory of diplomatic intervention. Wahba suggested Saudi Arabia joining with Iraq and the Yemen and making joint representations to the Palestinians to cease the disturbances in their own interests.[70] There is no indication that the British Government paused to consider Saudi motivation beyond face value explanations. The Colonial Secretary, Ormsby-Gore, enthusiastically welcomed the Saudi proposals.[71] Wahba was informed that the British Government gladly accepted Ibn Saud's offer of joint mediation.[72]

This decision has been interpreted by some scholars as one of the most fateful ever taken in the Middle East.[73] From the moment that Britain allowed other Arab states to mediate in Palestine it became a pan-Arab cause. The scope of the Saudi initiative continued to expand. Wahba suggested that Egypt and Transjordan be roped in to the joint appeal, and suggested a *quid pro quo*: a general amnesty and the stopping of Jewish immigration to precede a cessation of the disturbances.[74] Were it not for the fact that assistance had already been welcomed, the British Government would have had second thoughts about the whole business.

It was quite understandable for both Saudi Arabia and Iraq to wish to become associated with the Palestine problem, both to further Moslem solidarity and to increase their standing in the Arab world. Eden, the Foreign Secretary, recognised that the problem went far deeper than simply Palestine. If Saudi Arabia and Iraq were alienated it would threaten imperial communications and possibly shake British prestige throughout the Moslem world.[75] Furthermore, Iraq might have resented the Saudi initiative, and the need for inter-Arab consultation could have led to excessive procrastination. Would the Arab states presume that Ibn Saud was staking his leadership of the Arab world, and if so, how would they react? The Cabinet agreed to the principle of Arab mediation, but rejected the Saudi preconditions, especially the suspension of immigration.[76] To yield on this point would have weakened British prestige and possibly encouraged further Arab preconditions. The only assurance given to Saudi Arabia was the Colonial Office concession that the Arab grievances which had given rise to the disturbances would be thoroughly examined in a Royal Commission – once normality returned.[77]

The general reaction of the Foreign Office was one of pleasant, if uncritical, surprise at what appeared to be Saudi Arabia's desire to assist Britain. The nature of the rebellion – a peasant uprising and strike which was only later approved and co-ordinated by the Arab Higher Committee – may have frightened all the conservative Arab rulers in neighbouring states.[78] With regard to pan-Arabism, Ibn Saud's initiative over Palestine and his energetic signing of treaties with other Arab leaders vindicates Ryan's assessment that Saudi foreign policy was evolving:

> not in the direction of promoting the creation of a single united Arabia under one head, but of consolidating the mutual relations of the principal independent Arab states already in existence and making this serve the realisation of national aspirations in other Arab areas.[79]

On the question of extending the initiative to Transjordan and Egypt, further pan-Arab issues emerged for consideration. Although Abdullah would not have welcomed the assumption of Saudi primacy, permission was given for Transjordan's participation in a joint Arab appeal. Egypt was excluded. Not only were negotiations for the Anglo-Egyptian treaty in their final stages, but Sir Miles Lampson, High Commissioner in Cairo, wanted to keep Egypt out of all Palestinian and Arab affairs if possible.[80]

From July to October 1936 the situation seemed to be slipping from British control. Britain had agreed, in principle, to Arab interference in the political affairs of a state for whom she exercised responsibility. Whether or not Ibn Saud did use his influence with Palestinian Arabs, no abatement of the disturbances ensued.[81] Moreover, the Iraqi Government, spurred by the Saudi representations, began to take initiatives of its own, which were equally short-sightedly accepted by the Colonial Office. The Iraqi Foreign Minister, Nuri al Said, travelled to Palestine to mediate directly, thereby irritating Ibn Saud who doubtless feared that Iraq would take the credit for any settlement.[82] He attempted to emulate the Iraqi tactic by sending Fuad Hamza to Palestine, but the British Government vetoed the mission on the grounds that, like the Iraqi visit, it might arouse false hopes among the Arab population.[83]

The position was not eased by a three month absence from Jedda of a British Minister. Ryan had departed in June for his new post in Albania. His successor, Bullard, did not arrive till September, leaving the Legation in the hands of junior personnel at a particularly sensitive time. Disagreement surfaced within the British Government on how to expedite the Arab appeal. The Foreign Office began to see advantages in promising the cessation of Jewish immigration as a reward for ending the violence.[84] The Cabinet refused.[85] The Foreign Office proposals offered hostages to fortune. The only way to minimise the adverse consequences of Ibn Saud's hastily accepted mediation was to insist that it be unconditional.

From late September the British, Saudi and Iraqi Governments became involved in detailed negotiations concerning the exact text of the Arab appeal.[86] This, in effect, made Britain a party to it. Although she had neither proposed the appeal nor been involved in its early formulation, the final wording had the British stamp of approval. War Office pressure for a declaration of martial law, just as the appeal was about to be made, was headed off by energetic intervention from Rendel.[87] The War Office's aim was to demonstrate that it was not the Arab appeal, but British military action that would achieve the restoration of peace. On 10 October 1936 the Governments of Saudi Arabia, Iraq, Transjordan and the Yemen issued identical and simultaneous statements. Britain, having approved the wording, disassociated herself from the document. The appeal read:

> To our sons the Arabs of Palestine. We have been much distressed by the present situation in Palestine, and, in agreement with our brother Kings and the Amir, we appeal to you to restore tranquillity in order to prevent further bloodshed, relying on the good intentions of the British Government and their declared desire to see that justice is done. Be assured that we shall continue our endeavours to help you.[88]

The last sentence was included after the British Government agreed that any representations made by the Arab rulers should pass through ordinary diplomatic channels.[89] The Arab Higher Committee, which had insisted upon such an appeal, seized upon the opportunity to call off the strike. A month later the Peel Commission commenced its investigations into the causes of the disturbances. It very quickly became apparent that the manner in which peace had been restored was 'a blunder of some magnitude'.[90] The fact that no outward concessions had been made was interpreted in some quarters as a victory for Zionism. In effect, however, through the Arabs retaining their organisation, their arms, and their funds intact, and not having to give a pledge of future good faith, the situation resembled an armistice.[91] Duff Cooper, the Secretary of State for War, conceded that the Arabs had emerged with considerable prestige.[92] Saudi Arabia and other neighbouring states had been given an opening for a more active role in Palestine. As pressure mounted for Britain to respond with concessions of her own, largely at Saudi instigation, misgivings were expressed in several governmental departments about the wisdom of the 'mediation' policy.[93]

The British Government was not displeased with Ibn Saud's general attitude. Apart from his contribution to the appeal, he had kept a tight control on the internal expression of discontent in his Kingdom.[94] Besides, Hejazis seemed to be indifferent to the plight of Palestinians, being more concerned for the Moslems of India and the Dutch East Indies, which provided the bulk of the Pilgrimage.[95] The Mecca press had conspicuously avoided mention of the troubles, except to call for subscriptions for Palestinian victims of the disturbances.[96] For this assistance Eden instructed Bullard to convey his personal thanks to Ibn Saud.[97] Even when the strike was called off, and the Mecca press was permitted to demonstrate some sympathy towards the Arabs of Palestine, these articles were fewer in number and milder in content than those appearing in other Arab countries.[98] This was the minimum defiance that Ibn Saud felt it incumbent on him to show in order not to arouse the ire of the Arab world.

Various factors contributed to what, in Kedourie's words, made the British Government 'the prisoner of its policy'.[99] Within weeks of the appeal Iraq experienced a military coup, and, eager to shore up its position, her Government thenceforth took an intemperate policy on developments in Palestine. The Foreign Office was disinclined to moderate Iraqi stridency for fear of inducing yet more extremes of pan-Arabism.[100] The Permanent Mandates Commission in Geneva rebuked Britain for allowing foreign interference in the affairs of a mandated territory administered on behalf of the League.[101] Eden was, furthermore, young, and newly appointed as Foreign Secretary. Despite his grounding in Oriental affairs he rarely took issue with his Foreign Office officials on Middle Eastern policy.[102] It became apparent that, not only was the Foreign Office successfully asserting itself in the formulation of Middle Eastern policy, but its Eastern Department, and Rendel in particular, was beginning to exercise decisive influence in that policy and the promotion of Arab goodwill. Part of the reason for Foreign Office insistence on exercising its weight over Palestine lay with strategic considerations. The Italian victory in Abyssinia the previous spring had given a profound shock to British strategic thinking. Italy had successfully defied the British Mediterranean fleet and British troops and air forces in Egypt. This was to lead to a strategic re-calculation that took shape from the end of 1937 and which will be examined later.

To Rendel, the significance of the troubles in Palestine lay, not with the stability of the mandate, but with the reaction of the Arab and Moslem world at large threatening British interests throughout the Middle East.[103] The Palestine problem was seen as central to the affairs of the whole area and involved the entire Arab world. Rendel feared for the openings provided for Italian intervention throughout the region should the Palestine question go unresolved. Vansittart and Eden, his superiors, agreed.[104] Shortly after the appeal Rendel argued for a large scale amnesty as a reward for the Arab Kings, and urged a fixed ratio of Jews to Arabs in Palestine and the establishment of autonomous Jewish and Arab cantons as the only possible solution.[105] His visit to Saudi Arabia, early in 1937, reinforced his pessimism. Three years previously Ryan had solemnly warned that the territorial dispute in south-east Arabia would be the one issue upon which the future health of Anglo-Saudi relations hinged.[106] After meeting Ibn Saud, Rendel preferred to believe that Palestine was the key: 'the course of our future relations with King Bin Saud will depend almost entirely on the nature of the report of the Royal Commission and of the decisions which HMG take thereon'.[107] Equally significant, Rendel linked his fear for Anglo-Saudi relations with a personal interpretation of pan-Arabism:

> The Arabs outside Palestine have a quite special connexion with the Arabs in Palestine itself. The Arabs are a single race, occupying a vast

area not naturally divided into clearly distinct territories and which has frequently in the past been under single rule. They have a very strong racial and cultural unity, and I think it would be unreasonable to expect the individual branches of the Arab race to be indifferent to the future of those of their fellow Arabs under foreign administration.[108]

Rendel was persuaded that Ibn Saud was genuinely anxious to co-operate with Britain, even though the Arab world was apparently looking to him to defend the Arabs of Palestine. Rendel feared that, unless Britain modified her Palestine policy, Saudi Arabia would become a virtual British enemy, producing a domino effect throughout Arabia.[109] It is possible to endorse Kedourie's view that 'Rendel betrayed a gullibility ... as remarkable as it was dangerous'.[110] Saudi Arabia was a weak, vulnerable state. The protestations of her King about his responsibilities to the Arab world were little more than self-interest; and the supposed attraction of the Italians pure expediency.

It is possible that Ibn Saud was using the Palestine question and the threat of resorting to Italy not only to increase his prestige in the Arab world, but also to act as a bargaining lever to win satisfaction of his territorial claims in south-east Arabia, which had reached stalemate. Rendel would have made satisfaction of these claims a *quid pro quo*, in return for a favourable Saudi policy towards Palestine and Italy. The Saudi Government had, however, already ruled out this type of package deal solution some years previously.[111] Instead, Rendel urged the unconditional cession of much of the area being claimed as a reward for Ibn Saud's previous attitude over Palestine, and as an enticement for his future goodwill.[112] Rendel did not take the view that Ibn Saud would be more amenable to co-operation if he still had territorial grievances outstanding. Indeed, shortly after Rendel's departure from Saudi Arabia Ibn Saud made a further concession over the Kuwait trade blockade issue.[113]

The Impact of the Peel Commission Report – June 1937

In February 1937, while the Peel Commission was still investigating, and in an atmosphere which Ibn Saud described as heavy with Britain's enemies at work in the Arab world,[114] he proposed his own four-point solution to the Palestinian impasse: first, a complete amnesty; second, the total suspension of Jewish immigration, and if and when it was reintroduced, only on a strict percentage basis; third, legislation to protect Palestinian landowners; fourth, a constitutional government for Palestine, incorporating proportional representation, with guarantees to protect minorities, the Holy Places, justice, and British interests.[115] Ibn Saud suggested that Britain's twenty-year old promise to provide a Jewish national homeland had already been fulfilled in view of the large numbers of Jews who had already emigrated. The Saudi proposals were, in essence, not dissimilar to those being put forward by the Arab world as a whole. Ibn Saud's requests, and his success in urging the Arab Higher Committee to co-operate with the Royal Commission, were partly instrumental in Britain agreeing to the release of certain political internees.[116]

During 1936 and 1937 the Transjordan Desert Patrol reported that the tribes in northern Saudi Arabia were taking a strong interest in developments in Palestine, 'although their interest could be political, religious, racial, or the smell of loot'.[117] In case of further disorders in Palestine, the Transjordanian authorities, in March 1937, devised a scheme that would restrict the smuggling of arms and men from Iraq to Palestine via the emirate. Wauchope wanted the scheme extended to include traffic passing through northern Saudi Arabia into Transjordan.[118] He hoped that Ibn Saud would assist in the scheme. The Foreign Office resisted any approach to the Saudi Government, feeling that it questioned Ibn Saud's good faith and his intention to remain a good neighbour.[119] Britain was in no position to take Ibn Saud's continued co-operation for granted in view of the likely recommendations of the Peel Report.

The Peel Commission published its findings on 22 June 1937, although Bullard travelled to Riyadh to reveal the contents to Ibn Saud before they were made public.[120] This report constituted the principal watershed in Anglo-Saudi relations in the inter-war years. Its main provisions were for the mandate to be terminated, and for Palestine to be partitioned into a Jewish and an Arab state, the latter to be appended to Transjordan.[121] A White Paper adopted the Peel Report as official British policy. Criticism of the recommendations was intense and widespread within Parliament, the League, Palestine, and the Arab world at large.[122] Iraq, in particular, made violent protests, which contrasted with the comparative silence from Saudi Arabia.[123] Zionist reaction was ambivalent, welcoming the prospect of statehood, but hostile to the idea of a 'second' partition of the Jewish homeland (Transjordan having already been excluded from Balfour's original concept).[124]

Rendel anticipated a violent reaction from Ibn Saud to the Peel recommendations,[125] a prognostication reinforced by Wahba's 'extreme depression' and later hint of resignation.[126] In fact, Ibn Saud's initial response was muted.[127] It was only when virulent Iraqi reactions provoked no British public protest that Saudi sources began to express their own disapproval.[128] Ibn Saud's personal position was compromised by having urged the Palestinians to call off the strike and co-operate with the Royal Commission, only to be rewarded by the alienation of Arab territory. It was soon apparent that Ibn Saud was less concerned with the Arabs of Palestine than with the ambitions of Abdullah, who was actively intriguing with the Palestinian Arabs and who, with the support of Iraq, made no secret of hoping to absorb Palestine into a Greater Jordan.[129] Abdullah, therefore, alone among Arab rulers, welcomed partition, and was chastised by the Arab world.[130]

Ibn Saud's own interests, as he explained to Bullard, were threatened by the prospective renunciation of the British mandate over Transjordan.[131] It had always suited him to have his principal rivals conspicuously under British control. Abdullah's independence, if coupled with a British subsidy of some £2 million, would weaken Saudi Arabia's security.[132] Ibn Saud explained to Bullard that it was only the British mandate which kept Abdullah's intrigues in check.[133] He preferred that the whole territory remain under mandatory control, and that Abdullah be prevented from becoming King of an Arab Palestine.[134]

Although Ibn Saud was primarily concerned for the future of Trans-jordan, the Arab world's condemnation of partition soon enlisted his support. He later made clear to Bullard that he could not allow himself to be regarded as a traitor to the Arab cause.[135] His religious position with regard to Mecca, never mind his temporal position, could not ignore Jewish state-hood on Moslem soil. Ibn Saud was, he claimed, not his own master. The creation of a separate Jewish state would be a perpetual irritant in the Middle East and a source of international danger. If Britain persisted with her partition policy, she would bring about her own downfall in the Middle East, and possibly with it his own.[136] Rumours further underlined Ibn Saud's unease. He had heard that Britain was prepared to cease Jewish immigration forthwith, and then hand Palestine over to the Iraqi Government which in turn would throw Palestine open to unrestricted Jewish immigration. He was reassured by Bullard of the rumour's lack of foundation.[137]

As for wider Saudi reaction to the Peel Report, the Jedda Legation could only speculate. Ibn Saud's largely Syrian entourage was known to be hostile, and a central committee for the defence of Palestine was formed in Mecca.[138] Several of Britain's enemies were rubbing their hands. Italy strove to portray herself as the friend of all Arabs. Rendel and Oliphant frequently minuted about their fears that Britain's Palestine policy was driving Ibn Saud into the arms of the Italians.[139] Following the invasion of Abyssinia, virulent Italian propaganda was broadcast to the Middle East, taking full advantage of Britain's difficulties in Palestine. Turkish agents were at work in the Hejaz and in Palestine, proclaiming that the Arab Revolt during the First World War had led to Arab subjugation by Christians and Jews.[140]

Ibn Saud, whatever his feelings about partition, had no interest in letting unrest spread to his Kingdom. Arab nationalist groups hoped to convene a conference on Palestine in Mecca, but Ibn Saud refused to allow the city to be used for political purposes.[141] In Nejd the situation was even more difficult to gauge. The advent of motor traffic and the wireless had familiarised Nejdi tribesmen with the situation in Palestine. Talk was rife of the Nejdi *ulema* demanding a holy war against Palestine, with Ibn Saud to spearhead it.[142] The Wahhabis of Nejd, it was claimed, objected to the creation of a Jewish state on religious grounds.[143]

Furthermore, by October, evidence emerged of Saudi troop activity in the vicinity of the Transjordanian frontier, and arms smuggling was rumoured to be taking place in the Gulf of Aqaba.[144] As had happened ten years previously with the *Ikhwan* raids against Iraq, the British Government was fiercely divided on the question of Ibn Saud's complicity. The Colonial Office insisted that the accusation be investigated.[145] Rendel refused, considering that it was quite natural for Ibn Saud to take precautions against Abdullah's machinations.[146] Tribal intelligence from Kuwait suggested that Ibn Saud was succeeding in calming the anger of his northern tribes.[147]

H.R.P. Dickson, recently retired as Political Agent in Kuwait, paid a semi-official visit to Ibn Saud at Riyadh in October 1937.[148] He found Ibn Saud animated against the Jews, failing to understand why Christian Britain should support them, and urging Britain to retain the mandate. Ibn Saud warned that Britain was putting him in the same dilemma as during the *Ikhwan* rebellion, being faced with maintaining his position in his Kingdom and in the Arab world, or else breaking with Britain. Nonetheless, Dickson and Trott (the *Chargé d'Affaires* in Jedda) independently arrived at the conclusion, unlike Rendel, that Ibn Saud was not in any real danger of being forced by internal pressure to intervene in Palestine.[149] Even so, Dickson added his voice to those suggesting that Ibn Saud be rewarded for his constructive moderation by territorial concessions in south-east Arabia.[150] Rendel had found a partial ally, and an unexpected one considering that Dickson had previously been noted by the Foreign Office for his anti-Saudi opinions.[151]

Amid all this confusion – Italian propaganda, Ibn Saud's complicity, his real feelings towards the Jews and to Abdullah, his threatened flirtation with Italy, and his supposedly precarious position in his own Kingdom – the 'Rendelian' doctrine of the centrality of Palestine in Arab affairs, and Rendel's philosophy of appeasing Ibn Saud reached full bloom. Rendel, and the Foreign Office in general, worried that the Arab world would rebel against partition, and spoke of the Middle East as 'one organic whole' which would react against whatever happened in one of its constituent parts.[152] It was feared that Ibn Saud might permit the Italians to make use of the Arabian littoral. When Rendel and Bullard had an audience with Ibn Saud in March 1937 they wore local dress, an act of deference apparently employed by British diplomatic representatives nowhere else in the world.[153] Kedourie describes how:

> Ibn Saud came to be held in great awe in British official circles, his views accorded great respect, and his position in the Arab world believed to be very strong, even paramount.[154]

Such was Rendel's fear that Ibn Saud's survival depended on Saudi 'public opinion'[155] that the Foreign Office would have condoned a public anti-British outburst from him, if that would enhance his authority.[156] Private reassurances reached Ibn Saud that the British Government was not necessarily committed to partition,[157] although it is not apparent that Ibn Saud's driving motivation – fear of Hashemite aggrandisement – was fully appreciated. Bullard largely shared Rendel's general interpretation of Ibn

Saud's position. Kedourie describes his despatches as becoming almost hushed, reverential, devout – Bullard seeming to take for granted Ibn Saud's right to direct British policy.[158]

To British embarrassment, Ibn Saud, as soon as he had digested the Peel recommendations, intimated that, should the Transjordan mandate be terminated, he would reopen the Aqaba-Maan question, and would claim a formal desert corridor from Saudi Arabia into Syria so that Saudi tribes could migrate at will without hindrance.[159] The Peel Report attempted to reserve the strategic position of Aqaba by advocating Jewish use of a port in the Gulf of Aqaba. Ibn Saud's threat had serious ramifications. The British Government had, in the past, fastened on to the disputed area of Aqaba-Maan as one objection to Saudi membership of the League of Nations.[160] Ibn Saud was now threatening to do likewise for the proposed new Arab state.[161] League membership stipulated the prerequisite of well-defined and established frontiers – for the new state as much as for Saudi Arabia. The Foreign Office persuaded the Cabinet of the desirability of a range of measures designed to secure Ibn Saud's goodwill over Palestine. These included a Royal state visit to Saudi Arabia by Lord Athlone and Princess Alice (which took place in the spring of 1938), and reopening the question of possible financial assistance.[162]

Even more remarkable, in the light of issues previously examined in this study, were the territorial concessions contemplated by Rendel. He privately proposed the cession of Jabal Nakhsh in south-west Qatar to Saudi Arabia. Jabal Nakhsh was within the area covered by the APOC oil concession, and was the one contested area which the Middle East Sub-Committee had previously refused to contemplate handing to Ibn Saud.[163] There is, however, no indication that Rendel's proposal ever went before the sub-committee.

More noteworthy still, Bullard and the Foreign Office considered ceding Aqaba. In view of the importance that had been attached to the retention of Aqaba by Transjordan since 1925, this about-turn constitutes one of the most dramatic illustrations of Ibn Saud's standing in Foreign Office eyes by the late 1930s. Bullard suggested the transfer of the sovereignty of Aqaba, while drawing a new frontier a short distance to the west which would keep Saudi Arabia from marching with Palestine. A fresh port could be constructed across any new Palestine-Transjordan frontier which would, in any case, be a more suitable area in the Gulf of Aqaba for port facilities.[164] The Admiralty did not obstruct the Foreign Office proposal. Aqaba was still undeveloped, and in view of the growth of air transport fewer local strategic interests were affected. Despite this, possession of Aqaba would have given Saudi Arabia a stranglehold over any new Arab state incorporating Transjordan.[165] The idea of giving Aqaba to Ibn Saud went before the combined Chiefs of Staff before being rejected on wider strategic grounds, bearing in mind the enhanced Italian position in the Red Sea.[166]

The effects of Italy's successful Abyssinian campaign left their mark on

Britain's Palestine policy. By October 1937 Eden and the Chiefs of Staff feared imminent Italian aggression, somewhere or other, to distract from Italy's weakening economy, before Britain's rearmament was complete.[167] More crucially, Japan's invasion of China spelled the end of the existing policy of including defence of the Mediterranean within Britain's global strategy.[168] France would henceforth have to protect allied interests in the western Mediterranean and deter Italy in the event of British naval forces having to be mobilised in the Far East.[169]

The effect of this strategic re-think was to leave the Middle East 'self-sufficient' in case of future war.[170] As only minimal forces were available for policing the Middle East, greater emphasis was placed on good relations with Arab states. In this strategic context, the pan-Arab repercussions of the disturbances in Palestine had their unwelcome side-effects on the Foreign Office and the Chiefs of Staff. Apart from the risks of an out-and-out local conflagration, there was the hazard of having British troops tied up in the mandate when they could be needed to defend the Suez Canal in time of war. Furthermore, should Italy take advantage of her new strength at the southern end of the Red Sea to block the passage to the Canal, then Indian reinforcements would have to be despatched overland, through troubled Palestine.[171]

Early in 1938, against the background of the new 'self-sufficiency' policy, the Middle East (Official) Sub-Committee was charged with devising measures to gain the goodwill of Arab rulers.[172] Ibn Saud was a prominent target for these measures. In other words, there were strong strategic arguments, never mind the situation in Palestine, for appeasing Ibn Saud. Not least among Foreign Office considerations over partition was the fear of Saudi activity around Aqaba and Maan. The Chiefs of Staff calculated that the re-introduction of subsidies was the best way of buying off Ibn Saud.[173] As it turned out, faced with the opposition to partition expressed by the Foreign Office and the service departments, even the Colonial Office eventually turned against the scheme.[174]

Further disturbances in the wake of the Peel Report brought the mandate to the brink of civil war. By early 1938 firm evidence came to light that Ibn Saud was actively supporting the Mufti by smuggling arms and ammunition into Palestine.[175] In view of the German annexation of Austria and a fresh agreement reached between Britain and Italy over the Mediterranean and the Middle East,[176] both of which were widely interpreted as British diplomatic defeats, Rendel and Bullard remained staunch apologists for Ibn Saud.[177] The deteriorating situation in Palestine and the concerted hostility of almost the entire Arab world led to the despatch of another Royal Commission – the Woodhead Commission – which reported in October 1938 and abandoned the previous commitment to partition.[178] By then, Rendel no longer had a considerable impact on Britain's Middle Eastern policy. He had left London in May 1938 to become British Minister in Bulgaria.[179] The previous December he had successfully impressed upon the Cabinet the

need to reconsider partition,[180] but even afterwards continued to urge territorial concessions to Ibn Saud in an effort to win his goodwill.[181]

Signs of Arab-Axis collaboration were materialising at pan-Arab conferences held in 1937 and 1938.[182] Britain was expressly warned that
her seemingly pro-Zionist policies would lead the Arabs to turn to her
enemies.[183] Consequently, however unwittingly, Germany was a prime
mover in Britain's reassessment of partition.[184] The new Colonial Secretary,
Malcolm MacDonald, endorsed Rendel's doctrine: the abandonment of
partition, the limitation on Jewish immigration, and the full involvement
of the Arab states in the affairs of Palestine.[185] The British Government
acknowledged that the key to reconciliation between British imperialism
and Arab nationalism lay with Palestine.[186] A conference was summoned in
London early in 1939 of Arab leaders and Zionist representatives.[187] Prime
Minister Neville Chamberlain approved: 'Palestine has now become a pan-
Arab question and the Arab princes would be more likely to form a united
front if they were omitted from the conference than if they were invited to
attend'.[188] Included in the Saudi delegation was the pan-Arab Fuad Bey
Hamza, widely believed to be in Italian pay, whom Britain reluctantly
welcomed only at Ibn Saud's insistence.[189]

Behind the scenes, the Middle East (Official) Sub-Committee, building
on the Chiefs of Staff proposals, recommended a fresh policy of subsidies to
Arab leaders including £200,000 *per annum* to Ibn Saud.[190] A further
£25,000 was to be provided to Bullard to 'influence' Saudi officials, and
another £4,000 was destined for the Political Resident in the Gulf to reward
the sheikhs for 'intelligence'.[191]

The London Conference made no headway and was wound up on 17
March, the same day that the German armies invaded Czechoslovakia.[192]
Desperate for Arab support as Europe slid towards war, a British White
Paper formally rejected partition.[193] A Palestinian state, on the Iraq model,
was to be established within ten years, with limited Jewish immigration
which eventually would be subject to Arab acquiescence.[194] Zionist reaction
was one of outrage and betrayal. Although the Arab High Committee also
rejected the White Paper, it probably went some way towards reassuring Ibn
Saud, whose hope and prediction that Palestine would not become a Jewish
state appeared, for the time being, vindicated.[195]

Britain, Saudi Arabia and Pan-Arabism

Before attention turns to the further shift in Ibn Saud's foreign policy, and
his overtures to the Axis powers as a response to the Peel Report, it is
pertinent to consider concurrent British activities elsewhere in Arabia, and
the confused position the British Government adopted *vis à vis* pan-
Arabism. From 1937 Ibn Saud had cause for concern at British policy, not
only in Palestine, but throughout Arabia. In Iraq, a combination of military
chauvinism and anti-Zionism provoked tension, particularly in urban areas.

By 1939 few of the conditions prevailed for effective implementation of the 1930 treaty with Britain. Iraq, in addition, had overt designs on Kuwait, which prompted the Emir Faisal to ask the Foreign Office if Britain was prepared to allow Iraq to 'swallow up' the sheikhdom.[196]

The Gulf sheikhdoms were beginning to be affected by the western concept of 'nationalism'. Their rising generations were increasingly resentful that their rulers ignored the momentum of Arab nationalism for the sake of British convenience, and that the oil revenues were lining their rulers' pockets and not being used for the benefit of the people.[197] Pan-Arab speculation on a possible union of Gulf states intensified in the late 1930s. King Ghazi of Iraq instigated in 1936 an 'Association of Arabs of the Gulf' aimed at disseminating propaganda in the Gulf in favour of union with Iraq.[198] Kuwait was smitten with unrest from 1938, partly inflamed by Iraq, over the lack of consultation between the Sheikh and the population. Britain rejected calls for the union of Iraq and Kuwait.[199] Strikes broke out, and ill-feeling between the Sheikh and the Political Agent, Gerald de Gaury, resulted in short-lived consultative bodies, which the Sheikh rejected, only to find himself saddled with an Executive Council instead.[200]

The formation of a similar executive ruling council in Dubai unsettled Ibn Saud, who feared that such developments were British-inspired to impair the independence of the Gulf sheikhs.[201] Although Ibn Saud held the sheikhs in contempt, he did not want their powers curtailed in case reforming elements permeated his Kingdom.[202] Britain had, at the same time, benefited from a spate of oil concessions in the Gulf sheikhdoms, and the establishment of air bases in Sharjah and Dubai. Consequently, Britain sought strong local government to protect these interests. At one stage she sent a sloop to stand off Dubai.[203] Naturally, anything that resembled an extension of British control in the Gulf was resented by Ibn Saud. One of his reactions was to prohibit (until war broke out) the establishment of a British company, Gray Mackenzie and Co., at his new port of Ras Tanura on the Gulf.[204]

It was in southern and western Arabia that Ibn Saud had greatest cause for concern at British manoeuvrings. Shortly after the publication of the Peel Report Eden told the House of Commons:

> It has always been, and it is today, a major British interest that no great power should establish itself on the eastern shore of the Red Sea. I need hardly add that this applies to ourselves no less than to others.[205]

This statement must be treated with some caution, as one of the principal outcomes of partition would be that Britain would maintain her strategic position at the northern end of the Red Sea by retaining control over Aqaba. Furthermore, the improvement in Anglo-Yemeni relations that followed the treaty of 1934, coupled with the negative incentive of Italy's conquest of Abyssinia, encouraged Britain to pay greater attention to the Aden Protectorate,[206] which served as a buffer against Yemeni or any other threat to Aden. Britain's national interests and world commitments necessitated surer control of the Aden hinterland. In the worsening international climate Britain was not lightly going to relinquish her strategic grip on the Red Sea area, irrespective of Eden's disclaimer.

From 1937 Britain embarked upon several measures designed to safeguard her position in Aden and its environs. The withdrawal of ground forces from the Aden Protectorate, and their replacement by air power, left the problem of the internal defence of the Protectorate. The British Government was no longer willing to share control of an imperial base with India.[207] Aden itself was drawn more tightly to Britain by being removed from Indian responsibility and becoming a Crown Colony administered from London. The Protectorate, which had suffered periodic famines, as well as lawlessness, was incorporated into the Colony for administrative purposes.[208] Italy countered by renewing her treaty with the Yemen.

Britain's so-called 'protection' of, and 'jurisdiction' over, the Protectorate was accepted to be a pretence, unless she could create some internal order among the blood-feuds of the numerous tribal groupings. It was feared that if the British presence was not increased, and extended to include the Hadramaut to the east, then the tribes therein would fall into the orbit of Italy, the Yemen or Saudi Arabia.[209] Talk of oil must not be discounted either.[210] Not only had Ibn Saud's interest in southern Arabia been whetted by the long-standing dispute over the 'blue and violet lines', but the Saudi-Yemeni frontier settlement, which followed the 1934 war, extended Saudi sovereignty to large areas of the Hadramaut.[211] Britain therefore faced yet another potential frontier dispute with Ibn Saud.

Accordingly, in March 1937 the area subsumed within the Protectorate was extended to include the Hadramaut, as far east as Oman. The new area under protection became known as the Eastern Protectorate, to distinguish it from the original, or Western Protectorate. In effect, the whole of southern Arabia came under the control of the Governor of Aden. This greatly increased the official area of the Aden Protectorate.[212] The practical, as opposed to political, dimension of this policy was the appointment of political officers to the Protectorate, and the attempt to impose truces on the tribes. In April, Sir Bernard Reilly, long-serving head of the British establishment in Aden, became Governor and Commander-in-Chief of the Hadramaut.[213] Harold Ingrams, an officer on the Aden Protectorate staff, was posted to Makulla as Resident, having master-minded the signing of peace treaties with feuding chieftains under the pressure of British bombs.[214] Within a matter of weeks over a thousand treaties had been signed in the Hadramaut.[215]

Needless to say, these developments, alongside Britain's endeavours in Palestine, put Saudi Arabia on a collision course with Britain. To Philby, and to Ibn Saud, they constituted a British 'forward policy': the implementation of greater British control over Arabia. Rendel, so conscious of the need to appease Ibn Saud on the one hand, yet counter the Italians on the other, satisfied neither objective when he noted that Britain, in her activities in southern Arabia, was simply reserving for herself complete freedom of action within her sphere of influence.[216]

In retrospect, it is apparent that Arab unity, to the quest for which the British Government would lend its unqualified support from 1941,[217] was poorly conceived before the impetus of war. In 1915 the Arabs had a clear spokesman for their cause in Husein, whereas by 1939 there was not even a pretence of Arab solidarity; King Farouk in Egypt, Nuri al Said in Iraq, the Grand Mufti of Jerusalem and King Ibn Saud were all vying for the right to be regarded as the indisputable voice of the Arabs.[218] Self-interest had yet to be brushed aside for grander notions. Egypt was intoxicated with independence; Iraq was beset with turbulence; and Syria strove to find a peace treaty with France.[219] One scholar cites the participation of all the Arab governments in the Palestine Conference in London early in 1939 as constituting the first formal realisation of a genuine community of Arab states.[220]

The position of Ibn Saud in the pan-Arab movement is equally confused. Certainly, from around 1936, there was unprecedented Saudi contact with the other Arab states. From one perspective, the Saudi initiative on Palestine suggested that the rise of Saudi power was closely linked to Arab solidarity; Ibn Saud endeavouring to bring the ex-Ottoman provinces of the Arab world closer together.[221] Ibn Saud, in this venture, was succeeding where Husein, two decades previously, had failed, although he had none of the Sherifian advantages – custodianship of the Holy Places, the Hashemite heritage, British gold, or ready-made Kingdoms.[222]

From another perspective the Palestine factor served to undercut any Saudi drive towards pan-Arabism.[223] Ibn Saud's inability to openly court British hostility restricted his opportunity to co-ordinate pan-Arab activity. He was, furthermore, probably ill-disposed to indulge in pan-Arab politics that were inspired by Palestinians – Arabs regarded as of lesser stature than himself.[224] As has been seen, he was determined not to open up his Kingdom for the benefit of pan-Arab conferences. Neither did he send a delegate to the Arab Conference on Palestine at Bludan, in Syria, in 1937. It was one thing for Ibn Saud to outwardly support Moslem solidarity movements; it was quite another to encourage the popular xenophobia, intellectual agnosticism, and the reformist ideals which could permeate his Kingdom.

In addition, Ibn Saud was particularly anxious about the pan-Arab aspirations of Abdullah, who dreamt of a Greater Syria, eventually embracing Iraq, Syria, Lebanon, Palestine and Transjordan under Hashemite rule.[225] To counter this threat, Ibn Saud, it has been claimed, forged links with Syrian nationalist elements.[226] This reflects the extent of Ibn Saud's dilemma – realising that British policies in Palestine were putting pressure on his own position in the Arab world, while being even more afraid that if Britain relinquished her mandate for Palestine the way would be open for Abdullah to promote his schemes for a Greater Syria, the fruition of which would reduce the status of Al Saud to desert chieftains.[227] Saudi pan-Arabism, in other words, was linked firmly with political opportunism and expediency. For the time being, Ibn Saud and the other conservative Arab rulers had won the day. Those regimes outwardly co-operating with Britain over Palestine could point to the success of their moderation in bringing about the 1939 White Paper which shelved partition.

Equally complex was Britain's own attitude towards pan-Arabism before the Second World War. On the negative side Britain had much to lose from a flourishing pan-Arab movement. The installation of Hashemites across the Arab world in the early 1920s was itself a policy of pan-Arabism; to its critics, one of supporting Arab reaction. Yet by the late 1930s the Hejaz had fallen to Ibn Saud, Iraq was plagued by anti-British fervour, and Abdullah was conspiring to expand his territory. Nor could pan-Arabism be actively promoted by Britain without antagonising the French and the Zionists who, for their own reasons, did not wish to cultivate Arab interests in such a way.[228]

There again, pan-Arabism only seemed to flourish as a subversive movement. It seemed to thrive under oppression and wither in liberty.[229] Each Arab state jealously guarded its frontiers, its resources, its independence. One Middle East official argued that visions of a 'United States of Arabia or any Islamic confederation brought about by culture, religion and peaceful persuasion ... will tend to become an abstraction suitable for the entertainment of philosophers'.[230] Moreover, who would lead a British-inspired pan-Arab movement? Religion and political stature suggested Ibn Saud. Cultural heritage suggested Egypt, despite her poorly developed identity with the 'Arab' world. Britain's own vested interests remained, above all, in the Hashemites. This triangular struggle was to impede the development of pan-Arabism for many years.

British interest in pan-Arabism depended ideally upon there being no major disruptions in Anglo-Arab relations. British policy in Palestine proved to be totally opposite to the concept of a united Arab people. It was Britain's presence in the Middle East, and in particular her policies in Palestine, that was stirring up pan-Arab sentiment and enabling it to take root. The acceptance of Arab mediation in 1936 was one of the greatest boosts to pan-Arabism. It was not sound policy to lend assistance to a movement with anti-British inspirations, even though the Foreign Office, as has been seen, thought that to do so would best counter anti-British sentiment. Much of British officialdom was adamantly opposed to Britain associating herself with such movements. Lampson felt that Arabs could not be trusted.[231] Even Rendel, perhaps the leading British figure in the pan-Arab issue, was anxious to avoid encouraging anything in the way of a joint Arab policy on the Palestine question.[232] Moreover, the British Government fully appreciated that, in the event of another world war, the legacy of the Husein-McMahon 'promises' would prevent the Arab world believing future British pledges concerning Arab national aspirations.

In spite of all this, if it was not for the situation in Palestine and the vulnerability of the Gulf states, the aims of pan-Arabism would not have been inimical to British interests,[233] which could be enhanced by a strong, stable Saudi Arabia within a federation of Arab states. In such circumstances it would have been more difficult for any other European power to gain a foothold in the Arab world. Rendel argued forcefully that the Arabs:

> have produced, and are still producing, great leaders, and are capable of a patriotism which it may be unwise to ignore and difficult to suppress. There is a growing number of Arab nationalist leaders in Syria, Egypt and Iraq, and the example and prestige of Saudi Arabia, the Guardian State of the Holy Places of Islam, may yet prove a formidable force.[234]

Foreign Office encouragement of pan-Arabism, part conscious, part unconscious, has been illustrated in previous sections of this chapter. Other government departments were not so enthusiastic. Ever since 1936 rumours had abounded that the French Government was considering the independence of her Levant mandate and was intending to install a monarchy in Syria.[235] Ibn Saud would have viewed the Syrian throne going to Abdullah, or any other Hashemite prince, as a hostile act and a threat to his independence.[236] Although the French Government had not raised the question with London, the Foreign Office by 1939 preferred that the Syrian throne go to the strongest dynasty, the House of Saud, and saw the Emir Faisal as the ideal candidate.[237] The Colonial Office was equally anxious not to further the aspirations of Abdullah, but neither was it enthusiastic about endorsing a Saudi candidate, who would be antipathetic to Abdullah and the Iraq royal family.[238] Neither department wanted to provoke Ibn Saud by having a Hashemite on the Syrian throne. Ibn Saud might, in any case, have refused to have one of his sons installed as King of Syria, except in circumstances of absolute independence, which the French Government was not likely to entertain.[239] War interrupted this latest aspect of pan-Arabism before proposals for a Syrian throne matured.

Similarly, Neville Chamberlain was non-committal when telling the Emir Faisal in March 1939 that 'should the Arab countries at some future time desire union or some form of federation, Great Britain would consider this to be a question for negotiation and decision among the Arab states themselves'.[240] The India Office feared the prospect of the Trucial states joining an Arab federation, and hoped for some kind of precaution to prevent such an eventuality.[241] To the Foreign Office, by contrast, closer Arab union seemed to be a natural development, and it was therefore better for Britain to condone and, if possible, direct such moves rather than impede them.[242]

In summary, Britain had to consider how best to secure her position in the Middle East against both external and internal threats. Palestine threatened the advantages of pan-Arabism. Moreover, whereas the goals of Arab nationalism were shared by all Arabs, those of pan-Arabism were not, for they implied a partial or total surrender of newly won independence. Britain was, in effect, in a cleft stick. She could not openly support the aspirations of pan-Arabism: first, because everything she did was treated with suspicion by the Arab world, and such support would therefore have been counter-productive; second, because she could only support pan-Arabism by favouring the hegemony of one regime against the others. But nor could she actively retard pan-Arabism without being seen as a reactionary force, anxious to maintain her position in the Arab world at all costs. British ambivalence towards pan-Arabism was no less opportunistic than that of Ibn Saud.

Summary and Conclusions

Palestine added a new ingredient to pan-Arabism. Previous outbreaks of violence in the mandate, notably those in 1929 and 1933, had aroused no great interest among other Arab states.[243] Even before the disturbances of 1936 Ibn Saud had been moving towards closer relations with his neighbours, a product of Italian success in the Red Sea and British impotence. The momentum of this policy was partially responsible for the Saudi bid at mediation over Palestine; a bid given unexpected and concrete encouragement by the British Government. The Peel Report provided the final spur to the new direction of Saudi foreign policy.

Under Foreign Office instigation Palestine was portrayed as the focal point of Anglo-Arab relations. British relations with the Arab world were made to hinge upon the rejection of partition, for its implementation, the Foreign Office considered, would mean the total and perhaps permanent alienation of the Arabs. What was, from another point of view, simply a European demographic problem, became the crux of Anglo-Saudi and Anglo-Arab relations. The Foreign Office believed that the best way to secure Arab friendship and confidence, to maintain the faith of Indian Moslems, and safeguard imperial communications, oil supplies and British prestige, was to prevent the partition of Palestine.[244] This view, which became the predominant British view of the Middle East, implied a tentative accommodation with the emergent nationalist and pan-Arab trends, from the Wafd Party in Cairo to Ibn Saud in Riyadh. Although Rendel and the Foreign Office saw Saudi Arabia as the state around which it would be logical and politically prudent to build Arab unity, Britain's foremost commitments remained to the Hashemites.

In the event, permitting Arab states to influence British policy in Palestine greatly weakened British authority and prestige throughout the Arab world. In the case of Saudi Arabia it invited appeasement of a far-reaching order. In 1926, for example, Britain had fought shy of extending an official invitation to the Emir Faisal to visit Britain. By 1938 she was sending royal British visitors on a state visit to Riyadh. Of even greater import were the territiorial concessions contemplated by the Foreign Office. Both Aqaba and Jabal

Nakhsh had previously been considered of critical strategic or mineral importance to Britain.

It has been claimed that, over Palestine, Ibn Saud made no anti-British move in Arabia.[245] This, as will be explored in the following chapter, needs qualification. Ibn Saud had consistently followed two lines of policy over developments in Palestine: first, the avoidance of an outright breach with the British Government, in case his own immediate interests in the Red Sea were threatened; second, to use his influence where possible as a means of furthering his own position. He must, however, have felt aggrieved that, at a time when Palestine provided the touchstone of Arab statesmanship, his ultimate dependence on Britain obliged him to adopt a low-key policy.

The Italian invasion of Abyssinia had provided the initial push for Ibn Saud to seek alternative guarantees for his security instead of relying on Britain or the League of Nations. With the publication of the Peel Report this policy entered a further stage. Britain's policy was threatening her own, and his, position in the Middle East. Ultimately, as the next chapter will illustrate, a bold new initiative was seen as necessary to find a European replacement to counteract British folly. Largely unbeknown to the British Government, at some stage during the latter half of 1937, Ibn Saud appears to have become determined to free his Kingdom from its dependence on, and vulnerability to, Britain. Whether the spur came from his pan-Arab advisers or from himself is unclear, but Ibn Saud needed the support of another power. That power could not be Italy because of her own acquisitiveness in the Red Sea. Another state had to be approached which could act as a balance between Britain and Italy. She had to be untainted by imperialistic enterprise in the Middle East, while sharing the Arabs' animosity towards the Jews and the British. Germany fitted the bill.

REFERENCES FOR CHAPTER TEN

1. A crude indicator of this trend is the number of Foreign Office files of correspondence for Saudi Arabia. The figures are as follows: 1934 – 26 files; 1935 – 22; 1936 – 11; 1937 – 7; 1938 – 8; 1939 – 10. The figures, while revealing, are distorted by the arbitrary filing system adopted. Anglo-Saudi correspondence on Palestine, for example, was filed under 'Palestine'.
2. D.C. Watt, 'The Foreign Policy of Ibn Saud 1936-1939', *Royal Central Asian Journal*, 1963, p.39.
3. ibid.
4. Sheikh Rustum Ali, *Saudi Arabia and Oil Diplomacy*, p.viii.
5. Lipsky, p.138.
6. Marlowe, *Arab Nationalism* ..., p.7.
7. ibid.
8. ibid., p.10.
9. Hans Kohn, *A History of Nationalism in the East*, p.278.
10. ibid., pp.222, 275.

11. Whatever the proselytising characteristics of Wahhabism, the desire for a religiously inspired conquest of the Arab world under a ruling family is distinct from a recognition of the fundamental one-ness of the Arab people. Religious plunder and dynastic expansion cannot be confused with the intellectual construction of Arab nationhood.

12. Helms, pp. 53-4.

13. ibid., p. 225.

14. M.S. Elmandjra, 'The League of Arab States 1945-1955' (unpublished Ph.D.), p. 91.

15. Marlowe, op. cit., p. 1.

16. Antonius, p. 325.

17. At this point it is necessary to say something about Arab nationalism, pan-Arabism and pan-Islamism. Arab nationalism prior to 1914 has been seen as a doctrine of pan-Islamism, demanding the primacy of the Arabs within Islam (Elie Kedourie, *Islam and the Modern World*, p. 75. Hereafter: *Islam* ...). But the coming of statehood in the early 1920s emphasised their contradictions. One is concerned with the sanctity of territorial boundaries, the other with spanning them. Whereas nationalism seeks the supremacy of the state, pan-Arabism seeks the redundancy of the individual state. The common consciousness of Arabness could not flourish alongside impermeable state boundaries.

From around 1921 the vague concept of Arab nationalism was interrupted as the Arabs found themselves citizens of new geopolitical entities. Foreign intervention had stimulated the complete social, political, economic and 'national' realignment of the Arab world. This required a lengthy psychological adaptation of the Arabs' perceived racial and secular identity. The progress towards the independence of the new states could only be maintained against encroachment from neighbouring states. Was a citizen of Baghdad foremost an Iraqi or an Arab?

The ideals of pan-Arabism were assailed by practical considerations. How could pan-Arabism embrace the Christian Arabs? Iraq, then as now, had no desire to share her oil revenues with Syria. There is little obvious similarity between the Egyptian *fellah*, the Aden merchant, the Gulf pearl diver, the Iraqi marsh-dweller, the Lebanese Christian and the Arabian bedouin (RIIA, *British Interests* ..., p. 53) – except their language, and that has been described as the least suitable on earth for orderly and rational politics (F. S. Northedge, *Descent from Power: British Foreign Policy 1945-1973*, p. 99). Nonetheless, Kedourie has suggested that the Arab leaders thrown up by the War were pan-Arab by nature. Pan-Arabism was seen in terms of European principles, making language and nationality synonymous. Instead of the glories of an Arabian Caliphate, the Arabs found themselves laden with mandates, which not only prevented independence, but which dismembered the Arab nation (Elie Kedourie, 'Panarabism and British Policy', *Political Quarterly*, 28 (1957), pp. 137-8. Hereafter: Panarabism ...).

Pan-Islamism is a wider force than pan-Arabism. Not all Moslems are Arabs. In view of the Ottoman Empire's appeals to pan-Islamism during the First World War, it has often been considered as a contradiction of pan-Arabism. The obstacles to pan-Islamism lie in reconciling, for example, the Turks, Persians and Arabs – and, more particularly, different strands of Islam: Sunni, Shia, Wahhabi and Druze. These obstacles were not unwelcome to Britain (See FO E/3039/381/65: 371/19980) – pan-Islamism being potentially a considerable weapon against the British, French and Jews in the Middle East. The abolition of the Caliphate increased friction between Turks and Arabs, and impeded further unification of Moslems. As the only transnational Moslem institution, the Caliphate was seen as essential to Islamic unity. Nevertheless, the Arab world is, as Kedourie puts it, the 'cradle' of Islam, and both pan-Islamism and pan-Arabism sought the expulsion of the infidel (Kedourie, Panarabism ..., pp. 142-3). For a further discussion of the religious-political linkage see B. Tibi, *Arab Nationalism: A Critical Enquiry*.

18. Rihani, p. 236.

19. Major N. Bray to FO, 3 September 1929, FO E/4528/4528/91: 371/13741.

20. Bray memorandum, 18 October 1929, FO E/5405/4528/91: 371/13741. See also page 17.

21. ibid.

22. ibid.

23. Ryan to Rendel, 24 September 1930, FO E/5157/89/91: 371/14459.

24. G.A. Algosaibi, 'The 1962 Revolution in the Yemen and its Impact on the Foreign

Policies of the U.A.R. and Saudi Arabia' (unpublished Ph.D.), p. 262.

25. Abbas Kelidar, 'The Arabian Peninsula in Arab and Power Politics', in Derek Hopwood (Ed), *The Arabian Peninsula: Society and Politics*, p. 146.
26. Algosaibi, p. 273.
27. ibid.
28. Marlowe, op. cit., p. 29.
29. Marlowe, *The Persian Gulf* ..., p. 112.
30. Annual Report 1934.
31. ibid.
32. ibid.
33. Annual Report 1935.
34. *Umm al Qura*, 22 March 1935, ibid.
35. Annual Report 1935.
36. ibid.
37. ibid.
38. Annual Report 1936.
39. Watt, op. cit., p. 154.
40. Freeth and Winstone, p. 89. Britain insisted on the removal of the Kuwait blockade as part of the treaty renewal of October 1936 (Kelly, *Arabia*, ..., p. 236).
41. RIIA, *Political and Strategic Interests* ..., p. 176.
42. See *Survey ... 1936*, p. 788.
43. RIIA, op. cit., p. 174.
44. Annual Report 1936.
45. ibid.
46. ibid.
47. ibid.
48. *Survey ... 1936*, p. 790.
49. King Fuad died shortly before the signing of the Saudi-Egyptian treaty, although negotiations had begun before his death (Annual Report 1936).
50. See Chapter Three, pages 71-2.
51. Annual Report 1937.
52. Watt, op. cit., p. 153. Also in 1937, the fear of Italian penetration into the Middle East was partially responsible for a pan-Islamic pact between Iraq, Iran, Turkey and Afghanistan – the Saadabad Pact.
53. R. John and S. Hadawi, *The Palestine Diary – Vol I, 1914-1945*, pp. 254-7.
54. ibid.; RIIA, *Political and Strategic Interests* ..., p. 180.
55. Christopher Sykes, *Crossroads to Israel*, pp. 182-3.
56. Gerald de Gaury, *Faisal: King of Saudi Arabia*, p. 61.
57. Ward (FO) minute, 30 April 1935, FO E/2622/2621/25: 371/19019.
58. Annual Report 1936.
59. Beloff, p. 264.
60. Annual Report 1937.
61. Wauchope to Ryan, 21 March 1936, FO E/2406/608/25: 371/20063; CO/79126/36: 732/75.
62. CO to FO, 29 April 1936, CO/79126/36: 732/75, Brenan (FO) minute, 4 May 1936, FO E/2406/608/25: 371/20063.
63. FO minute, 16 May 1936, FO E/2423/608/25: 371/20063.
64. Ryan to FO, No 58, 30 April 1936, ibid. Kedourie, 'Great Britain and Palestine: The Turning Point', in *Islam* ..., p. 96 (hereafter: ... The Turning Point).
65. ibid. Kedourie, ibid., p. 97.
66. Wahba conversation Oliphant, 16 June 1936, FO E/3597/608/25: 371/20063.
67. Rendel minute, 1 May 1936, FO E/2423/608/25: 371/20063.
68. ibid.
69. Parkinson (CO) to Oliphant, 17 June 1936, FO E/3597/608/25: 371/20063.
70. Wahba conversation Oliphant, 23 June 1936, FO E/3783/94/31: 371/20021.
71. See FO memorandum, 27 June 1936, FO E/3982/94/31: 20021; Kedourie, op. cit., pp. 98-9.
72. Oliphant conversation Wahba, 3 July 1936, FO E/4109/94/31: 371/20021.
73. See Kedourie, op. cit., pp. 96-102. The title of Kedourie's paper is 'Great Britain and

Palestine: The Turning Point'. Such is the prominence of Ibn Saud in Kedourie's argument that the paper could have been sub-titled 'The Impact of Palestine on Anglo-Saudi Relations'.

74. Annual Report 1936; Kedourie, op. cit., p. 99.
75. Eden memorandum, 20 June 1936, CAB 178(36).
76. CAB conclusions, 9 July 1936, CAB 51(36); 15 July 1936, CAB 52(36).
77. Oliphant conversation Wahba, 23 June 1936, FO E/3783/94/31: 371/20061; Annual Report 1936.
78. Monroe, *Britain's Moment* ..., p. 86.
79. Annual Report 1936.
80. Lampson to Vansittart, 8 July 1936, No 658, FO E/4257/94/31: 371/20021.
81. Kedourie, op. cit., p. 101.
82. Annual Report 1936.
83. ibid.
84. Kedourie, op. cit., p. 105.
85. ibid.
86. See FO E/6296/94/31: 371/20027.
87. Kedourie, op. cit., p. 109.
88. Annual Report 1936.
89. ibid.
90. Kedourie, op. cit., p. 110.
91. H.J. Simson, *British Rule and Rebellion*, pp. 289-90.
92. Kedourie, op. cit., p. 110.
93. See FO E/7297/94/31: 371/20029; CO/75528/93/36: 732/310-1.
94. Annual Report 1936.
95. Calvert (Jedda) to Eden, No 244, 31 August 1936, FO E/5474/94/31: 371/20023.
96. Annual Report 1936.
97. Eden to Bullard, 11 October 1936, FO E/6851/131/25: 371/20058-9.
98. Annual Report 1936.
99. Kedourie, ... The Turning Point, p. 112.
100. See FO E/4597/22/31: 371/20811.
101. Kedourie, op. cit.
102. ibid. Eden studied Oriental languages at university. See Clive Leatherdale, 'The British Press and the Suez Crisis 1956' (unpublished M.Sc.Econ.), pp. 12-19.
103. Kedourie, op. cit., pp. 113-4.
104. Rendel memorandum, 14 September; Vansittart minute, 15 September; and Eden minute, 16 September 1936, FO E/5815/3334/65: 371/19983.
105. Rendel minute, 14 January 1937, FO E/317/22/31: 371/20804; Kedourie, op. cit., p. 144.
106. See pages 227-8.
107. Rendel memorandum, 12 April 1937, in Kedourie, op. cit., p. 116.
108. Rendel to Downie (CO), 28 April 1937, ibid.
109. Kedourie, op. cit., p. 117.
110. ibid.
111. See page 233.
112. Rendel ME(O), 49th meeting, 1 February 1937, CAB 51/3.
113. Bullard to Ryan, 26 March 1937, Ryan Papers, Box 6, File 5, MEC.
114. Annual Report 1937.
115. ibid.
116. Annual Report 1936.
117. ibid.
118. Annual Report 1937; Kedourie, op. cit., pp. 119-20.
119. Annual Report 1937.
120. ibid.
121. ibid; Sykes, pp. 205-6.
122. Sykes, p. 214.
123. Watt, op. cit., p. 154.
124. Sykes, pp. 211, 215.
125. See FO E/3831/22/31: 371/20808.

126. See FO E/3854/22/31: 371/20808.
127. Kedourie, op. cit., p. 150.
128. ibid., pp. 152, 154.
129. Watt, op. cit., pp. 154-5.
130. Kedourie, ... The Turning Point, p. 121.
131. Annual Report 1937.
132. Watt, op. cit., p. 155; Kedourie, op. cit., p. 150.
133. Annual Report 1937.
134. Wahba conversation Rendel, 14 July 1937, FO E/4063/22/31: 371/20809; and see FO E/4458/22/31: 371/20810.
135. Annual Report 1937.
136. ibid.
137. ibid.
138. ibid.
139. See FO E/4167/22/31: 371/20809; FO E/7427/22/31: 371/20823.
140. Annual Report 1937.
141. ibid.
142. ibid.; Kedourie, op. cit., p. 121. A debate ensued within the British Government over how dependent Ibn Saud was on the support of the Nejd *ulema*, Rendel taking the view that Ibn Saud was exceptionally vulnerable, despite the virtual extinction of the *Ikhwan* who had sustained the *ulema*.
143. Wahba conversation Rendel, 20 July 1937, FO E/4167/22/31: 371/20809.
144. Annual Report 1937; Kedourie, op. cit., p. 120.
145. Kedourie, op. cit., p. 120.
146. See FO E/6320/22/31: 371/20818; CO/79180/37: 732/82.
147. Annual Report 1937.
148. FO E/7201/22/31: 371/20822.
149. ibid.; Trott to FO, No 152, 28 September 1937, FO E/6063/22/31: 371/20817.
150. FO E/7201/22/31: 371/20822.
151. See page 156.
152. Michael J. Cohen, 'British Strategy and the Palestine Question 1936-1939', *Journal of Contemporary History*, 7 (July–October 1972), p. 173.
153. Kedourie, *Islam* ..., pp. 67-8.
154. ibid., p. 68.
155. Rendel minute, 29 December 1937, FO E/7537/22/31: 371/20823.
156. Baggally (FO) minute, 18 August 1937, FO E/4881/27/31: 371/20812.
157. Kedourie, '... The Turning Point', p. 153.
158. ibid., pp. 122-3.
159. Trott to FO, 1 August 1937, FO E/4918/580/25: 371/20841; Wahba conversation Rendel, 14 July 1937, FO E/4063/22/31: 371/20809.
160. See pages 173, 178, 180.
161. Rendel minute, 16 July 1937, FO E/4034/22/31: 371/20808.
162. Rendel minute, 29 December 1937, FO E/7537/22/31: 371/20823.
163. See page 246.
164. Bullard to Rendel, 7 December 1937, FO E/7609/22/31: 371/20823; Oliphant minute, 7 August 1937, FO E/4458/22/31: 371/20810.
165. Adm to FO, 16 September 1937; Rendel minute, 21 September 1937, FO E/5466/22/31: 371/20814.
166. See FO E/7609/22/31: 371/20823.
167. CP 248, CAB 24/271; CAB 29/89, 20 October 1937.
168. Cohen, p. 162.
169. ibid., pp. 163-4.
170. ibid., p. 162.
171. ibid., p. 163.
172. ibid., pp. 163-4.
173. Chiefs of Staff Sub-Committee, 21 February 1938, in Cohen, ibid.
174. See Cohen, pp. 168, 182.
175. See Kedourie, op. cit., pp. 154-5.
176. See Chapter Eleven.

177. See Bullard to MacMichael (Jerusalem), 1 May 1938, FO E/3123/10/31: 371/21876; Bullard to FO, 6 June 1938, FO E/3791/10/31: 371/21823.
178. Sykes, pp. 222-9.
179. Rendel, p. 136.
180. Kedourie, op. cit., p. 166.
181. Rendel minute, 29 December 1937, FO E/7537/22/31: 371/20823.
182. Sykes, p. 230; R. Melka, 'Nazi Germany and the Palestine Question', *Middle Eastern Studies*, 5 (1969), p. 228.
183. John Marlowe, *The Seat of Pilate: An Account of the Palestine Mandate*, pp. 145-6, 151-2.
184. See Melka, p. 228.
185. Kedourie, op. cit., p. 167.
186. See Melka, p. 227.
187. Sykes, p. 230. The Arab delegations came from Palestine, Saudi Arabia, Egypt, Iraq, Transjordan and the Yemen.
188. Kedourie, p. 167.
189. Bullard to FO, Nos 9-10, 6 & 10 January 1939, FO E/177/177/25: 371/23268 & FO E/282/174/25: 371/23268; FO to Bullard, No 15, 15 January 1939, FO E/396/174/25; 371/23268.
190. ME(O), 24 January 1939, CAB 51/11.
191. ibid. It is not apparent from the documents whether these recommendations were put into action. As is made clear in the following chapter, the German Government had information that Fuad Hamza was in British – never mind Italian – pay.
192. Fisher, p. 443; Sykes, p. 233.
193. With the increasing importance of Arab oil, an Arab-Axis alliance was unthinkable to Britain. In Sykes' words: 'To have opened a major quarrel with the Arab states when Europe was moving towards war would have been an act of folly by Great Britain without precedent' (Sykes, p. 198).
194. Fisher, p. 443; Sykes, pp. 235-6.
195. Stonehewer-Bird to Halifax, No 62, FO E/2720/1194/25: 371/24589.
196. Faisal conversation Oliphant, 24 March 1939, FO E/2241/177/25: 371/23269.
197. *Survey ... 1936*, p. 792; Morsy-Abdullah, p. 158.
198. Kelly, *Arabia* ..., p. 276.
199. ibid.
200. Fowle (Political Resident) to IO, 23 January 1939, in FO E/246/246/25: 371/23269.
201. Bullard to Halifax, No 231, 13 December 1938, ibid.
202. ibid.
203. Fowle to IO, op. cit.; Morsy-Abdullah, p. 161. British relations with Dubai were conducted solely through the Sheikh, not through the *majlis*, which was behind the administrative and political reforms. For a detailed account of reforms in Dubai, see Morsy-Abdullah, pp. 152-66.
204. Bullard to Halifax, op. cit.
205. Eden to House of Commons, 19 July 1937, in RIIA, *Political and Strategic Interests* ..., p. 161.
206. Strictly speaking the Aden Protectorate was a mass of small protectorates. Eventually, some twenty-four states comprised the Aden Protectorate (King, p. 41).
207. Gavin, p. 256.
208. Wenner, p. 161. Aden had been administered from Bombay until 1932, and for the next five years from the Imperial Government at New Delhi.
209. Ingrams memorandum, 20 January 1937, FO 905/48.
210. Petroleum Concessions Ltd. was awarded an exploration licence for the whole of the Aden Protectorate.
211. Ingrams memorandum, op. cit.
212. Wenner states that the Aden Protectorate was extended from 9,000 to 42,000 square miles. (Wenner, pp. 162-3). Philby preferred the figure of 100,000 square miles 'annexed', as he put it, to the British Empire. (H. St J.B. Philby, 'British Bombs over Arabia', *World Review*, (January 1938), p. 25). King puts the maximum area of the Aden Protectorate as 112,000 square miles (King, p. 41).
213. Philby, op. cit., p. 25.
214. Bullard, *Britain* ..., p. 117; Watt, op. cit., p. 154.

215. Gavin, pp. 302-3.
216. Rendel memorandum, FO E/1563/880/91: 371/21826. At a time when the dominant note in Britain was anti-imperialist it is significant that Gavin cannot offer an adequate explanation of British expansion in the Aden interior in the 1930s (Gavin, pp. 276-7).
217. See Elmandjra, p. 149.
218. Klieman, p. 253.
219. See Monroe, *Britain's Moment* ..., p. 86.
220. Elmandjra, p. 141.
221. *Survey ...1936*, p. 783.
222. ibid.
223. Annual Report 1937.
224. ibid.
225. See Marlow, *Arab Nationalism* ..., p. 37.
226. ibid.
227. ibid.
228. See Monroe, op. cit., p. 83.
229. MacKereth (Damascus) memorandum, 15 May 1936, FO E/3039/381/85: 371/19980.
230. ibid.
231. Lampson to Oliphant, 24 April 1939, FO E/3416/3416/65: 371/23194.
232. Rendel conversation Wahba, 19 October 1936, FO E/6600/94/31: 371/20027.
233. See RIIA, op. cit., p. 176.
234. In Kedourie, op. cit., p. 162.
235. Bullard to Halifax, No 100, 18 June 1939, FO E/4769/177/25: 371/23269.
236. Trott to Halifax, No 122, 18 July 1939, FO E/5392/246/25: 371/23269.
237. Oliphant minute, 1 September 1939, ibid.
238. Baggally (FO) minute, 2 September 1939, ibid.
239. FO to Trott, 2 September 1939, ibid.
240. See FO E/2428/177/25: 371/23269.
241. IO to FO, 1 April 1939, ibid.
242. FO minute, 5 April 1939, ibid.
243. Marlowe, op. cit., p. 34.
244. See Kedourie, op. cit., p. 166.
245. ibid., p. 69.

CHAPTER ELEVEN

The Approach of World War Two: The Impact of Italy and Germany on Anglo-Saudi Relations

While Britain was being distracted after 1936 by the mounting unrest in Palestine, two European powers were taking advantage by making inroads into her jealously guarded pre-eminence in Arabia. The Red Sea policy of Mussolini's Italy has already been considered up to the Saudi-Yemeni war of 1934.[1] Thereafter, the Italian invasion of Abyssinia and consequent diplomatic initiatives in the Red Sea area served to underline the Italian menace to Saudi Arabia. Germany, too, from the end of 1937, increased her contacts with Ibn Saud.

The Mounting Italian Presence in the Red Sea: The Conquest of Abyssinia

British and Saudi fears of Italian expansion in the Red Sea did not cease with the Yemeni setback in the war of 1934. Ever since Ibn Saud became a Red Sea ruler in 1925 he had sought a British guarantee of intervention to offset Italian adventures in western Arabia. In the wake of his victory over the Imam, both Britain and Saudi Arabia, in their different ways, sought to smooth relations with Italy. In September 1934 a joint Anglo-Italian communiqué disclaimed aggression in the Red Sea.[2] European considerations, notably the need to safeguard Austrian independence,[3] precipitated the Stresa Agreement of April 1935 between Britain, Italy and France, designed to oppose any unilateral repudiation of treaties – for that might endanger the peace of Europe.[4] Significantly, the Agreement ignored Africa, where the first move of Italian aggression against Abyssinia was committed in December 1934, at Walwal.[5] This omission has been interpreted as British resignation to Italian empire-building in Africa — the price to be paid for her support in Europe.[6]

The full-scale Italian invasion of Abyssinia, in October 1935, shattered the general cordiality of Anglo-Italian relations, and subsequently dealt the death blow to the League of Nations.[7] The conflict evoked a split in British governmental opinion *vis à vis* Italy. Britain had no fundamental interests in Abyssinia, therefore its fate was largely immaterial. British military observers did not anticipate a quick or simple Italian victory, but either way, there was no question of confronting Italy with a show of British military force.[8] One British school of thought saw Germany as the principal threat to world peace, and everything else, including the appeasement of Mussolini, as subordinate.[9] Men like Churchill and Vansittart cared little about the fate of Abyssinia, but felt that the alliance of Italy with Germany might deal a fatal blow to European peace.[10] Accordingly, this view was not averse to Italy satisfying her territorial lust in Abyssinia. The Board of Trade and the Admiralty, too, were reluctant to prohibit Italian ships from using the ports of the League states, as such actions were seen to be provocative and could, in any case, only be achieved by force.[11]

An alternative standpoint was taken up by those younger men in the British Government with a less developed grievance against Germany. This school urged a correspondingly tough line against Italy, together with a greater commitment to the League. Anthony Eden, Minister for League Affairs, and, from December 1935, Foreign Secretary, typified this school.[12] While paying lip service to the terms of the Covenant and the need for firm action, almost every member of the Cabinet was reluctant to challenge Italy, being painfully aware that British forces were in no state to risk war.[13] The dilemmas in British policy led directly to the Hoare-Laval fiasco, the ineffectual sanctions policy of the League, and the unhindered Italian annexation of Abyssinia in May 1936.[14]

Saudi Arabia, likewise, feared the consequences of increased Italian activity in the Red Sea, although the later months of 1934, in the wake of the Treaty of Taif, had witnessed a brief Italo-Saudi rapprochement. Fuad Hamza had an audience with Mussolini in Rome, and was quoted in the Italian press as saying, 'The presence of Italy in the Red Sea is a guarantee for us of equilibrium and peace'.[15] Here was further confirmation of the Saudi policy of playing off the two European powers against each other. Early in 1935 the Italian Government offered, on nominal terms, to train Saudi youths in aviation techniques. The Emir Saud visited Italy, and the Italian Legation in Jedda was expanded.[16]

Following Italy's invasion of Abyssinia, Ibn Saud reverted to seeking British reassurances by offering 'unlimited professions of friendship'.[17] Fuad Hamza told Ryan that the Italian Government had offered £½ million in gold and arms in return for a few thousand camels to be shipped to Abyssinia.[18] Saudi Arabia feared that the Italo-Abyssinian war would close the Suez Canal and affect trade and pilgrim traffic in the Red Sea.[19] In the event, few camels were shipped for Italian use although, during the course of 1936, Saudi Arabia benefited from the gift of six Italian aeroplanes, together with Italian arms consignments and a flourishing trade between Hejazi merchants and Italian forces.[20]

Britain was anxious not to be seen to take a back seat in matters concerning the Red Sea.[21] She therefore attempted to reassure Ibn Saud by reversing her earlier decision not to communicate parts of the 1927 Rome

Agreement to the Saudi Government.[22] Although Saudi Arabia adopted an attitude of neutrality, Ibn Saud had to take account of the widespread hostility throughout the Arab world to the Italian invasion. Despite this, Fuad Hamza was widely believed to be hand-in-glove with Rome.[23] Both he and Yusuf Yasin were in close touch with nationalist elements in Palestine and Syria that had lent themselves to Italian propaganda.[24] Only there, remote from Italian colonial practices in her Libyan colony, was Italy at all popular[25] – at least, she could hardly be worse than Britain or France. Upon the announcement of Italy's annexation of Abyssinia, Ryan successfully persuaded the Saudi Government against hasty recognition.[26] Just before his final departure from Jedda, in June 1936, for the Legation in Albania, the British Minister offered a detailed personal assessment of the state of Anglo-Saudi relations in the wake of the Italo-Abyssinian war:

> Ibn Saud watches as best he can events in Europe, but he has little true comprehension of them, much less of such concepts as that of collective security upheld by moral force. He has little real interest in Abyssinia and has seen in the recent conflict not so much a war between Italy and an African power, as a struggle between Italy and Britain. He sees in the result a sweeping victory for Italian force in their struggle. Obsessed for many years with Italy he fears that they will turn on the Arabian peninsula. As a Moslem ruler still engaged in consolidating his position in Arabia, and jealous of his newly won independence, he has no genuine love for Britain, a power which blocks his way in various directions, but he has much less to fear from British policy on this side than he thinks he has from Italy. The only fortunate feature of this is that Ibn Saud probably believes that it was not so much the ability as the will to save Abyssinia that was wanting in the attitude of H.M.G. as conceived in his simple mind. He probably still believes that a breach with them would be fatal to him, and hopes against hope that they will see him through in the event of a breach between him and any other European power. He dare not go against Britain. He dare not offend Italy. 'Neutrality' is more than ever his slogan because, as I have said, he has seen not a war in Africa, but a conflict, not yet ended, between Britain and Italy. He does not yet know what its effects in Arabia may be, and it is with reference to this struggle that he clings to the slogan.[27]

During the three month gap between the departure of the old, and the arrival of the new, British Minister in Jedda, the Legation was preoccupied with more than just Ibn Saud's response to the disturbances in Palestine. Calvert passed on disturbing rumours reaching the Legation concerning Ibn Saud's reaction to the annexation of Abyssinia. The Italian success had thrust Italy into the Islamic world almost on a par with Britain, an achievement reinforced by her 'assistance' in Palestine. Britain was no longer, it appeared, the sole dominant power in the Mediterranean and the Middle

East. With the Italian victory and the decline in British prestige, both in Palestine and in the Red Sea, the Arabs, so the rumours went, no longer needed to fear the British 'bugbear', but could, and should, turn to Italy.[28]

The post-Abyssinian years saw Britain wrestling ever more intently with the Italian problem: should she appease Mussolini, in view of the pressing dangers in Europe, or take a hard line, knowing that Italy was weaker than Germany or Japan?[29] The Montreux Convention regarding the Turkish Straits, in July 1936, convened without Italian participation; the Rome Government still smarting from the effects of the League's policy of sanctions.[30] In January 1937 the British and Italian Governments jointly declared their intention to prevent friction in the eastern Mediterranean and the Red Sea.[31] When Rendel visited Ibn Saud, in March 1937, he suggested that Mussolini would be unlikely to embark upon any policy, whether in the Middle East or elsewhere, which would bring him into conflict with Britain, particularly in view of her rearmament. Rendel explained that Saudi Arabia's security lay in the knowledge that any threat to her constituted a threat to Britain, and these common interests provided a stronger bond between the two countries than could the defensive treaty which Ibn Saud was seeking.[32]

Whereas British policy towards Saudi Arabia was based on the need for a strong and totally independent Saudi state, the key to Italian interest lay elsewhere, primarily in Europe, but also in the Mediterranean and Africa. The British Government was not in a position to enter into any formal commitment to Saudi Arabia because Anglo-Italian relations depended, in the main, on central European politics. Nevertheless, Britain, as Europe began the downhill slide towards war, acknowledged the need to secure the goodwill of the world's non-aligned states. The Chiefs of Staff had to relate British policy to British strength. In December 1937, they warned:

> We cannot foresee the time when our defence forces will be strong enough to safeguard our trade, territory and vital interests against Germany, Italy and Japan at the same time. ... We cannot exaggerate the importance from the point of view of Imperial defence of any political or international action which could be taken to reduce the numbers of our potential enemies and to gain the support of potential allies.[33]

Palestine, of course, cut right across this recommendation. With regard to Saudi Arabia, appeasement was being extended as a result of both the policies in Palestine and the perspective of imperial defence. This manifested itself in such ways as reconsidering British policy over the Hejaz Railway. The line as far south as Maan had been reconstructed, but the part that ran through the Hejaz, and which had been most severely damaged by Lawrence in the First World War, had not, owing to lack of finance. Ibn Saud insisted that the line be treated as an indivisible entity, a Moslem possession to be maintained by funds from Syria, Palestine and Transjordan. The

Railway had been built by public subscription throughout the Moslem world.[34] Britain and France, in contrast, held each segment of the line to be the responsibility of the state through which it passed.[35]

By the late 1930s, however, political considerations, namely the need to win Ibn Saud's goodwill in a deteriorating world, caused a re-think in British attitudes. In December 1937 the Cabinet agreed, in principle, to the possibility of financial assistance being extended to restoring the Hejaz section of the Railway.[36] Bullard, when consulted, had initially dampened the idea as being of no lasting benefit to Saudi Arabia, but by 1939, as Europe veered towards the brink of war, he began to have a change of heart. Some gesture, he felt, was appropriate to demonstrate Britain's appreciation for Ibn Saud's co-operation and moderation towards Palestine.[37] The outbreak of war interrupted further discussions on the future of the Hejaz Railway.

The Anglo-Italian Agreement of April 1938

The Mediterranean repercussions of the Spanish Civil War and the creation of the Rome-Berlin Axis stirred increasing anxiety in Britain about her position in the eastern Mediterranean and the Middle East. Anti-British radio propaganda from Bari began in 1935 and had an inflammatory effect on developments in Palestine, providing an added sore to Anglo-Italian relations.[38] Yet even after his success in Abyssinia Mussolini was still reluctant to break completely with Britain. Despite renewing her treaty with the Yemen in 1937, Italy endeavoured in the spring of 1938 to reduce friction in Anglo-Italian relations, particularly in the Red Sea and southwest Arabia.[39] Since Italy's acquisition of Abyssinia three-quarters of her colonial interests lay beyond the Suez Canal.[40] From the Italian perspective, Britain's policy in Palestine, the Gulf, and southern Arabia was seen as promoting, at the very least, exclusive influence throughout Arabia at the expense of Italy's few footholds in the Red Sea.[41] Italy complained that British extension of the boundaries of the Aden Protectorate breached the 1927 Rome Agreement; constituted a British 'forward policy'; and disturbed the *status quo* in southern Arabia.[42]

Anglo-Italian talks in Rome lasted from February to April 1938. In the meantime, there had been a major casualty within the British Government. In February, Eden resigned over Chamberlain's insistence on appeasing Italy.[43] In Rome, Rendel presented the British view on the Middle East and the Red Sea, agreement over which he later described as the most difficult part of the whole negotiations.[44] In reaching a settlement Italy was hoping to prise Britain away from France, while Britain endeavoured to reduce Italian dependence on Germany, as well as ease her anxiety about the security of the Red Sea route.[45] Palestine was conveniently overlooked. The resultant document mentioned Saudi Arabia and the Yemen by name, pledging both signatories not to seek a privileged political position in either state, and to prevent other countries from doing so. The *status quo* on the islands of the Red Sea was to be maintained. Britain and Italy agreed to recognise and respect each other's sphere of influence in the Red Sea region, and the anti-British propaganda from Bari was suspended.[46]

The Anglo-Italian Agreement did little to ease Britain's position either in the Middle East or in the world at large. The document implicitly accepted the idea that Italy had equal rights and interests in the region, and aroused much opposition in the House of Commons for being too conciliatory to Italy.[47] It was negotiated too late to have any lasting effect on European politics, for even while the negotiations were proceeding, German forces were occupying Austria. Moreover, the outcome served to unsettle Ibn Saud who depended upon Anglo-Italian tension. He interpreted the Agreement, with its insistence that neither Britain nor Italy would acquire a privileged political position in his Kingdom, as a personal affront, as if a joint Anglo-Italian protectorate had been placed over Saudi Arabia.[48] He refused to acknowledge the Agreement, and his anxiety over its provisions carried on well into 1939. So long as the two powers had reason to mistrust each other, each would covet Ibn Saud's support. Whereas outright hostility between Britain and Italy ran the risk of embroiling Saudi Arabia, or else threatening the trade lanes through the Red Sea, Anglo-Italian harmony carried the implication that the two powers could dispose of the Red Sea area as a virtual condominium.

Rendel, somewhat naïvely, considered that Ibn Saud was not compromised by the Agreement.[49] Rendel had been in close touch with Wahba throughout the negotiations, and viewed the relevant sections of the Agreement as designed to ensure the maintenance of the independent states of the Red Sea.[50] The Agreement was seen as little more than a confirmation and strengthening of the principles encapsulated in the 1927 Rome Agreement. Saudi Arabia was reassured that she could conduct relations with any other state just as freely as before.[51] Besides, no other power was bound to the document or was asked to recognise it – the Agreement being between Britain and Italy alone. Others in the Eastern Department were prepared to be a little more realistic. Eyres noted that the Saudi Government felt its independence to be limited and admitted, 'There is some truth in this'.[52] When two independent states go out of their way to recognise the independence of another, it carries the suggestion of the opposite.

The Anglo-Italian Agreement had certain other ramifications. Italy announced her intention to adhere to the London Naval Treaty of 1936, and became a party to the 1936 Montreux Straits Convention.[53] The Soviet Union, moreover, was encouraged to close its Legations in both Saudi Arabia and the Yemen. Historically, Russia has always regarded the Middle East as an obstruction to her hopes of expansion to, and communication with, the Indian Ocean. From 1925 the Saudi state had become the spiritual home of many Soviet Moslems.[54] For much of the inter-war period the Bolshevik regime paid little attention to the Arabs, except in the cause of embarrassing Britain. The Soviet Union had been the first state to recognise the Saudi conquest of the Hejaz. The Comintern had applauded Ibn Saud's victory, seeing in him the leader of a nascent, anti-British, nationalist movement.[55] These sentiments had cooled when Ibn Saud sought a treaty with Britain, and when the Soviet Union failed to win a trade agreement with him in 1928. From that time, Soviet attention turned increasingly to the Yemen, which was more backward than the Hejaz and possessed, in the Imam, a ruler more anti-British than Ibn Saud appeared to be. In November 1928 the Soviet Union had signed a Treaty of Friendship and Commerce with the Yemen. Nonetheless, the Soviet Union was the first state to establish full diplomatic relations with Hejaz-Nejd, in 1929, and to be represented in Jedda by a Moslem Minister, Kerim Hakimov.

By the late 1930s circumstances combined to cause the Soviet Government to re-think its position in the Red Sea. The growth of pan-Islamism enticed Moslem loyalties from within the Soviet Union. Pan-Arabism, too, although ostensibly directed against the West had wide-ranging religious and racial overtones.[56] The onslaught of the Soviet purges, together with years of unprofitable trading relations with Saudi Arabia and the Yemen, the need for British co-operation in Europe against Germany and Italy, and the local effects of the Anglo-Italian Agreement, combined to prompt the Soviet Union into withdrawing all her diplomatic and financial personnel from the Middle East.[57]

The Arabs in general were little impressed by the supposed threat of communism before the Second World War. No Arab ruler had any direct experience of it. To the Arabs, the threat of communism was viewed as a deliberate distraction by the West against the real enemy, European imperialism.[58] In any case, Ibn Saud would have had little affection for the Godless proximity of the Soviet Union, which was actively preventing Soviet Moslems from making the Pilgrimage.[59] The Soviet Union was also, in the late 1930s, forging closer ties with Turkey.[60]

The British Government had never been unduly alarmed at Soviet attempts to penetrate Arabia during this period. The Soviet Union had neither the means of penetration, nor the willing ally in Ibn Saud to assist it.[61] With Moslem pilgrims arriving annually from all over the world, including the Soviet Union, the Hejaz was a natural focal point for anti-European agitation. Yet not even reports that the Soviet Union had approached Ibn Saud about joining a proposed pact which would include the Soviet Union, Turkey, Persia and Afghanistan, to be directed at Britain, generated undue concern in the Foreign Office.[62] This attitude appeared vindicated as Soviet interest in Ibn Saud declined during the 1920s and '30s.

Italy's invasion of Albania in April 1938, the same month as the Anglo-Italian Agreement was signed, finally disposed of Mussolini's pretensions to be the protector of Islam. In March 1939 the Saudi Government unearthed part of the recently published Husein-McMahon correspondence, pointing out the worthlessness of British guarantees.[63] This did not discourage Ibn

Saud from approaching Neville Chamberlain directly on the question of an Anglo-Saudi treaty of alliance.[64] The Admiralty calculated that Saudi Arabia was immune to Italian attack. Italy would not benefit by occupying the Hejaz from which to attack British communications. Supplies for her own forces would then have to be transported by sea from Eritrea, with all the attendant risks.[65] Italy's existing bases in Eritrea were strategically more favourable for threatening the Red Sea passage than fresh ones in Arabia would have been. Nor was there a realistic threat of any European power wantonly attacking Saudi Arabia. Italy was unlikely to want to add Saudi Arabia to her list of enemies, particularly when she could occupy the Yemen and the Red Sea islands to secure her interests.[66] But if such an eventuality did arise Britain would want to retrieve the situation, so that assistance would then automatically be granted to Saudi Arabia.[67] As with previous Saudi enquiries, Britain would not contemplate formal alliance commitments.

Saudi Arabia's Courtship of Germany

From 1937 British policy towards Saudi Arabia has to be put into the perspective of an impending global war. The other external factors intruding into Anglo-Saudi relations, predominantly Italy and Palestine, paled alongside the threat of war with Germany. From Ibn Saud's point of view, relations with Britain were at an all-time low. When the number of Saudi grievances are taken into account, British illusions of Saudi 'friendship and goodwill' become quite extraordinary. Beginning with the Italian invasion of Abyssinia, Saudi Arabia's security was threatened from all directions. With that conflict Britain had revealed her inability or unwillingness to protect Saudi Arabia's western flank. To the north Ibn Saud was threatened by a combination of Britain's policy in Palestine, the grandiose ambitions of Abdullah, and some of the more revolutionary ingredients of pan-Arabism – themselves partially inspired by the British. In the Gulf and southeast Arabia Britain was lending herself to popular reform, gaining oil concessions and strategic aerial bases, and taking an intransigent attitude over Saudi Arabia's frontiers. In southern Arabia British bombs were, in part, designed to pre-empt Saudi expansion into the Hadramaut, and the whole process climaxed where it had begun – in the Red Sea – with Britain and Italy jointly declaring a condominium over western Arabia. These issues may not have been seen from Britain as either very grave, or even directed at Saudi Arabia, but from the Saudi perspective they amounted to a desperate need to find an alternative source of support, especially now that, due to Palestine, no salvation could be found through pan-Arab initiatives.

Ibn Saud's need to reduce his dependence on Britain provided him with the perfect opportunity to play off the European powers.[68] Watt describes him as 'clearly adept at being all things to all men'. To Britain, Ibn Saud used the language of friendship, loyalty and ideological affinity; to Italy, and from

1937 to Germany, Ibn Saud spoke of the threatening and alien hand of Britain.[69]

Just as the Peel Report presented Ibn Saud with the final spur to reconsider his foreign policy, so it also invited Germany to take a closer look at Arab affairs. Prior to mid-1937 the Nazi Government had taken little interest in Palestine, except from domestic considerations, namely the encouragement of Jewish emigration.[70] The consequences of partition and the formation of a Jewish state posed a considerable hindrance to German interests, which were best served by keeping world Jewry dispersed, not giving them international respectability by the creation of their own Germanophobe state.[71] The Peel recommendations made the Jews, for the first time, an issue in German foreign policy as opposed to domestic policy.[72] Paradoxically for Berlin, the despatching of Jews to Palestine threatened to increase German-Arab tension. A Jewish state was, in effect, being built in Palestine as a result of Jewish immigration, with German capital and skills acquired in Germany.[73] Nonetheless, the spectre of an anti-German Jewish state does not appear to have counted for much in German foreign policy.[74] The Foreign Minister, Von Neurath, accepted partition, seeking only the security of German settlers in the proposed Jewish area.[75]

Saudi overtures to the Third Reich commenced in the summer of 1937, following publication of the Peel Report, through the search for arms supplies.[76] Britain had always been an unsatisfactory supplier of arms to Ibn Saud, both in kind and in quantity.[77] In the past, War Office and Treasury restrictions had limited Ibn Saud to small quantities of obsolescent weaponry.[78] In November 1937 Ibn Saud's personal secretary Yusuf Yasin journeyed to Baghdad to ask the German Minister in Iraq, Dr Fritz Grobba (the only German diplomat of any standing accredited to an Arab capital), for arms and aid for Palestine.[79] Credit facilities were requested. Yusuf Yasin also extended an invitation for German diplomatic representation in Jedda.[80]

The German Government rejected all Arab demands for a public statement on Palestine and insisted on strict secrecy on any German-Arab developments, as did Ibn Saud.[81] This was possibly due to German unwillingness at that stage to confront either Britain or France in the Middle East, and also because of a low assessment of the potentialities of Arab nationalism, bearing in mind the Arabs' ultimate dependence on Britain and her determination to pursue her interests in Palestine.[82] There was always the risk that rising Arab fervour could be channelled indiscriminately towards all European powers, including Germany. Jewish intelligence in Palestine was already very able.[83] Besides, Hitler had to contend with the embarrassment of having placed the Arabs low down on his race ladder in Mein Kampf.[84]

Undoubtedly the main reason for German restraint lay with Anglo-German relations. Berlin knew that Britain regarded the Middle East as a vital area, and still hoped to reach an accord with London which would give Hitler a free hand in central and eastern Europe.[85] This co-operation would be less forthcoming if Anglo-German tension increased as a result of German assistance to Arab nationalism. There was, moreover, the position of Italy to be taken into consideration. Italy was already entangled with Britain in the region. Italy, more than Germany, opposed partition because the earmarked Jewish state would, in effect, become a British stronghold in the eastern Mediterranean.[86]

Germany's stance on Palestine and the Arab world shifted as international tension mounted. In the summer of 1938 Fuad Hamza made arms-hunting trips to both Rome and Berlin. The Italian and German Governments were assured of Ibn Saud's need for assistance to free his Kingdom from British pressure, and to fortify his tribesmen against British subversion.[87] Fuad Hamza warned that political and economic circumstances might compel Ibn Saud actively to co-operate with Britain.[88] Although the Italian Government reacted favourably to the arms request, the response from Berlin was somewhat restrained. Inter-departmental wrangles with the German Government did not expedite matters, and the shortage of foreign currency in the Reich led to a reluctance to supply arms on credit.[89] Although Germany was well aware of the benefits of prising Saudi Arabia away from Britain, tension in Europe had not yet reached the level required for Germany to part with much needed capital.

Nonetheless, by the time of the Munich talks in September 1938 Germany was engaged in financing Arab rebels and preparing arms shipments to Palestine via Iraq and Saudi Arabia.[90] Consequently, when partition was averted through the Woodhead Commission in the same month, this provided an unexpected setback to Germany's developing understanding with the Arabs. The annexation of the Sudetenland then produced further Arab fears of German intent. The threat of a European war had a noticeably greater impact upon Hejazis than did the fate of their Arab brothers in Palestine. Chamberlain's ill-fated trip to Munich brought British prestige in the Middle East to its nadir.[91] In the Hejaz, however, the British Prime Minister's apparent avoidance of war and the threat to the Pilgrimage brought demonstrations of relief. In the bazaars of Jedda the cry went up of 'Yahya Jimberlin' – long live Chamberlain.[92]

It took the personal energetic intervention of Grobba himself to encourage even stronger German approaches to Ibn Saud and to exploit their common grievances against international Jewry. But Berlin remained suspicious that Ibn Saud was not unaware of the advantages to be had from playing off the European powers.[93] Only in September 1938, as the Sudetenland was being annexed, was it agreed to establish diplomatic relations with Saudi Arabia to enable Grobba to withdraw from Iraq to a neutral country if the need arose.[94]

The first weeks of 1939 marked a visible turning point in German attitudes. The German Government was swift to take advantage of the

London Conference on Palestine by trying to exploit its likely failure. In February Grobba presented his credentials to Ibn Saud as the first German Minister to Saudi Arabia. Grobba continued to hold his position in Baghdad, where he was normally resident. There was no permanent German diplomatic representation in Jedda.[95]

Although Ibn Saud conveyed to the British Government his distaste at having German officials temporarily on his soil, there is every reason to think that he was pleased at the establishment of formal diplomatic relations with Germany[96] – the first foreign power without an appreciable Moslem population to establish diplomatic relations with Saudi Arabia. Ibn Saud had demonstrated his sympathy with Germany's 'Jewish problem'. Behind his reassurances that Britain was still his only true friend against the 'ravening wolves' of Italy, Germany and Turkey,[97] dissatisfaction with Britain had probably reached its peak. Despite the alarming strategic implications of a possible future secure German diplomatic base behind British lines, Bullard disarmingly suggested that the main purpose of the establishment of diplomatic relations was to further the ends of good relations and commerce.[98] Whatever the reason, Germany had every incentive to see Saudi Arabia as secure as possible in order to maintain her independence and resistance to Britain. The Foreign Office was confident that Saudi Arabia would not open up a legation in Germany, and was reassured that the only countries hosting Saudi Legations were allied countries – Britain, France, Egypt and Iraq.[99] Nonetheless, in D.C. Watt's words, the establishment of diplomatic relations with Germany enabled Ibn Saud to be free from the 'Anglo-Italian nutcrackers'.[100]

Grobba took full advantage of his audiences with Ibn Saud to air the full range of Saudi grievances. Although Germany was asked to restrain Italian activity in the Yemen, Berlin was hampered by having already agreed to her Axis partner's Red Sea sphere of influence.[101] Ibn Saud directed his main tirade against Britain. It is interesting that Grobba began to be persuaded by Ibn Saud's 'goodwill' and 'sincerity' no less than certain British officials in the past. Ibn Saud urged closer political and economic co-operation with Germany, preferably through a treaty.[102] Grobba was not persuaded by the general impression that Ibn Saud was a friend and pliable tool of the British:

> He [Ibn Saud] feels himself to be encircled and oppressed by England and has the desire to free himself from this encirclement if possible. Out of prudence he assumes a friendly attitude towards the British, but in the depths of his heart he hates them and complies with their desires only reluctantly.[103]

Ibn Saud denounced British assurances as lies.[104] Britain's policy was seen as directed solely towards firmly establishing her rule over the Arab territories and bringing them under her subjugation. Britain even wanted to penetrate Saudi Arabia and deprive her of her independence. Ibn Saud sought to free himself from Britain's odious influence in as unostentatious a way as possible, by seeking support to create a stronger international position for himself. Ibn Saud, apparently, had great respect for the Führer. In view of their joint antipathy to the Jews, and Germany's lack of political ambition in the Arab world, Ibn Saud promised benevolent neutrality, 'if not more', in the event of war. Italy had, Grobba was reminded, received similar 'benefits' during her Abyssinian campaign, despite supposed British pressure to impose sanctions.[105]

Grobba put forward a comprehensive range of arguments to his Government why advantage should be taken of Ibn Saud's offer of benevolent neutrality. Arms, as a sign of goodwill, was the crux. If Germany did not provide them Italy would, and the opportunity would be lost. Economically, there was the temptation of Saudi Arabia's revenues from oil, and possibly gold reserves, which could enable her to become a future market for German goods. Politically and religiously there was the great influence that Ibn Saud exerted throughout the Islamic world, even though he was not Caliph. His attitude in a future European war was crucial to Germany, thought Grobba. The German Minister expected, wrongly as it turned out, that Britain would pay a considerable price for Ibn Saud's active participation on her side, an eventuality that had to be forestalled.[106]

Strategically, there were advantages to Germany in establishing a good relationship with Ibn Saud in view of the British imperial routes which passed on all sides of his Kingdom.[107] This was true irrespective of the fact that the Arab world lay beyond the likely theatres of an impending European war. Arab neutrality would be beneficial, not only from the point of view of German prestige, but also for providing bases for possible espionage and diversionary activity in the enemy's rear.[108] Existing German diplomatic or consular posts in Baghdad, Cairo, Jerusalem and Beirut were unlikely to withstand British pressure in the event of war. German officials there would either be interned or expelled.[109] As the Yemen was firmly within Italy's sphere of influence this left only Saudi Arabia to interest Berlin. Saudi Arabia was free of alliance commitments to Britain, and there were no British military bases stationed there. Ibn Saud could hardly outwardly oppose Britain, whose fleets patrolled the Red Sea and the Gulf, and who possessed air bases in Egypt, Iraq and Aden. Because of the religious sensitivity of the Holy Places Ibn Saud was, calculated Grobba, bound to prefer a policy of neutrality if at all possible.

Grobba added his own personal guarantee that Ibn Saud would not only pay for the arms, but would also settle small existing debts to Germany.[110] In a manner reminiscent of British despatches Grobba added: 'His frank statements to us are a sign of his absolute confidence in us. ... His whole personality is a guarantee that he will keep his word to us, even if it is only given orally'.[111] To give effect to his new-found opportunities with Germany Ibn Saud dismissed an Italian air-training mission from the Hejaz, and entered into discussions with a view to obtaining German rifles, ammunition, anti-aircraft guns, armoured cars and a cartridge factory – all to be paid for with £½ million in credit.[112] Clearly there was more to Ibn Saud's reasoning than just the mere possession of arms, which were available from Italy. As late as August 1939 Saudi Arabia concluded an arms agreement with Italy.[113] Arms negotiations with Germany both restrained Italy, for whom affairs in the Yemen left an ineradicable suspicion, and acted as a counterpoise to Britain.[114]

Despite Grobba's personal endorsement of Ibn Saud's claims, his Government continued to move cautiously. In April Grobba was informed that there was no change in Germany's Arabian policy because Ibn Saud's real outlook was still uncertain. Germany had no interest in a German-Saudi treaty of friendship, and arms deliveries were 'out of the question'.[115] Ibn Saud's reluctance to criticise Britain over her Palestine policy had led to accusations of his servility from some Arab circles. The German Government did not wish to become involved in internal Arab rivalries, nor to raise Italian suspicions. It took a passionate reply from Grobba to effect an about-turn in German policy. Grobba stressed Ibn Saud's hatred of Britain. The King, apparently, had his own doubts about Fuad Hamza, who was 'reliably' known to be a British agent.[116] Grobba pleaded: 'I think that in Saudi Arabia a unique opportunity presents itself for us', and emphasised the need for one German diplomat to be in a position to withdraw to neutral Jedda, if necessary, if that could arranged.[117] Even Germany's ally Japan had come to realise Saudi Arabia's potential and sent her Minister in Cairo to negotiate a treaty of trade and friendship at Riyadh.[118]

By this time developments in Europe were accelerating rapidly. Germany had absorbed the truncated Czech state and Italy had invaded Albania. A German Foreign Office official minuted on Grobba's despatch, 'I have allowed myself to become convinced by this letter'.[119] It was appreciated that German opportunities in all the other Arab states were receding as Britain tightened her grip and Arab nationalist movements, as in Palestine, were temporarily appeased.[120] One of Ibn Saud's envoys, a notoriously pro-German Tripolitanian, Khalid al Qarqani, met Hitler and the German Foreign Minister, Ribbentrop, at Obersaltzberg in June 1939.[121] An arms agreement was successfully concluded the following month.[122] Four thousand rifles were included as a gift.[123] In view of growing Italian unpopularity in the Red Sea, the risk of treading on Italian toes was minimised when Silitti, the Italian Minister at Jedda, welcomed German co-operation in Saudi Arabia.[124]

British officials in the Middle East were more agitated by these developments than was the Foreign Office. Lampson felt that the whole Arab world, never mind Saudi Arabia, was drifting towards the Axis.[125] British and French policies in Palestine and Syria were bound, Lampson argued, to lead the Arabs sooner or later to seek their salvation elsewhere. The Arabs must have felt that they were being driven into the Mediterranean as uncompromisingly as in the days of the Crusades. Lampson feared that British policy in the Hadramaut, Oman, and the Gulf would lead to a

German 'Lawrence' to stir up the Arabs against Anglo-French-Turkish domination.[126] 'With our natural distaste for general ideas we have no comprehensive view at all of the situation in the Arab world. We have taken on much more than we can manage in those parts.'[127] The Colonial Office was inclined to agree. It proposed a 'Department of Arabian Affairs' – naturally under Colonial Office supervision.[128]

The Foreign Office reacted philosophically to this indictment. It doubted whether, in 1939 any more than in 1919, it was possible to have a 'comprehensive' view of the Arab world. Watertight departments had their disadvantages, and which officials would want to spend their working lives in Arabia?[129] The Arab countries had to be dealt with as efficiently as possible. 'When we cannot please one without displeasing another we must weigh our major against our minor interests.'[130]

The extent of British knowledge of Ibn Saud's courtship of Germany is difficult to ascertain. Britain was aware of Saudi arms-hunting trips to Europe, not only from her own sources, but also because Ibn Saud was careful to keep her informed of his international dealings, if not the motives behind them. It was fully appreciated by the British Government that Ibn Saud might turn to Germany, particularly over the issue of his disputed eastern frontiers.[131] Knowledge of Saudi Arabia's proposed arms deals with Britain's enemies was not necessarily viewed with alarm. It was considered quite natural for Ibn Saud to seek to obtain arms from Germany which Britain could not, or would not, supply – especially if Germany was offering favourable credits.[132]

The Issue of Saudi Arabia's 'Neutrality'

It was not so much the question of German arms per se, as the political price that Saudi Arabia was expecting to pay, that perturbed the British Government. In return for German armaments Saudi Arabia was to agree to a declaration of neutrality in the event of war in Europe.[133] Germany was not going to put arms into the hands of a possible future enemy, any more than was Britain. The question was, would Saudi Arabia's neutrality suit British as well as German interests? By August 1939 British minds turned increasingly to consider the problem.

Ibn Saud repeatedly approached the British Government on the question of his neutrality. It was assumed that his basic grievance was the arms issue.[134] It was not perceived that his policy was to play off Britain and Germany and enjoy any benefits which accrued. It was to Ibn Saud's advantage to procrastinate with Germany, to increase the chance of drawing her influence into the Middle East. He reassured Britain that his protracted negotiations with Germany were tactical, while simultaneously informing Berlin that his caution was due to his delicate position with Britain.[135]

Saudi Arabia possessed no armed services to speak of, which could be of assistance to the allies.[136] Nor, even with her recent oil discoveries, did she produce any commodity of which Britain was in need, and which could not be supplied without indulging in unneutral conduct.[137] As things stood, Ibn Saud's favourable disposition towards Britain, which his private assurances seemed to indicate, was hoped to impress the Arab world. He could manifest his goodwill without any departure from technical neutrality.[138]

There were, in addition, fears that Ibn Saud would exact a heavy price for declaring for the allies. He could be expected to demand arms and finance before, during and after hostilities, on a larger scale than Britain could contemplate, and insist that Britain divert some of her armed forces to protect his Kingdom. Should the allies emerge victorious, Ibn Saud would want 'rewarding' for his contribution, perhaps by demanding territory from his neighbours. All in all, because Saudi Arabia could offer Britain so little and *vice versa*, it was considered to be in both countries' interests that she remain neutral.[139] Lord Halifax, the Foreign Secretary, concurred, preferring that Ibn Saud did not declare for the allies, but remain neutral.[140]

This debate took place within the wider strategic context of the Middle East's likely role in the war. With the vulnerability of Singapore and the Dominions of Australasia, Empire considerations extended way beyond India. By 1939, Indian interests in the Gulf were minimal, the centre of gravity having moved west, to the Arabian peninsula itself. In that year the strategic route from Britain through the Mediterranean to the Red Sea, to the Indian Ocean, and to Singapore, together with garrisons in Palestine, Egypt and the Sudan accounted for twenty-two battalions of British infantry (with thirteen extra battalions as reinforcements in Palestine).[141] One bomber squadron was stationed in Aden, five in Iraq in fulfilment of treaty obligations, while the number in Palestine and Transjordan varied according to the local situation.[142]

Nonetheless, in 1939 British strategists were contemplating whether to abandon the Mediterranean route in favour of the Cape route in time of war. Although Britain had secure land and air bases at the eastern end of the Mediterranean, she was vulnerable at its centre and at its western entrance. The increased range, speed and carrying power of modern aircraft, coupled with the virtues of the submarine in narrow waters, made it doubtful whether the Mediterranean could be held as a strategic and trade route – presupposing the hostility of Italy – in wartime. This school of thought, out of perceived necessity, advocated the abandonment of Malta, in spite of the demoralising effect on Britain's position in the Middle East and India of sacrificing the Mediterranean route.[143] Egypt and Palestine would be open to invasion, and Britain's standing in the whole Moslem world would collapse. Some 9–14 per cent of Britain's imports came through the Suez Canal, including oil from Iran, together with supplies of tin, rubber, jute, manganese ore, rice, tea and cotton. A further 11 per cent of raw materials and foodstuffs came from within the Mediterranean, as did the 4 per cent of Britain's oil imports which arrived from Iraq, through the Haifa pipeline.[144]

While this debate was proceeding, it was appreciated that a Saudi declaration of neutrality could have an adverse effect on other Arab states, particularly Iraq.[145] Should Baghdad undergo a political crisis then Britain might have to think again about the desirability of Saudi Arabia's neutrality. Saudi territory was unlikely to be of any use to British forces in war-time, unless developments in Iraq necessitated an alternative communications route from Kuwait to Haifa, by-passing Iraq through northern Saudi Arabia.[146] The War Office wanted to inspect a possible Saudi route to ascertain its financial viability, although it still had faith in the Anglo-Iraqi Treaty of Preferential Alliance of 1930, which permitted Britain to retain airbases in Iraq and make use of all Iraq's facilities for the transit of British armed forces.[147] The War Office was confident that the Iraq Government would fulfil its obligations under the treaty.[148] Nonetheless, an alternative route as a standby was considered desirable, and it was hoped that Ibn Saud would agree to its development without departing from his neutrality. Germany could be fobbed off with the explanation that the route was being developed for commercial, not military, purposes.[149] However, an alternative route had to be usable when the need arose, in which case Ibn Saud would have to become an ally, or else perform acts of so unneutral a character as to expose himself to the risk of being treated as a belligerent.

Various alternative courses of action presented themselves to the British Government vis à vis Saudi neutrality. If Saudi Arabia did sign a formal document with Germany it would presumably contain standard clauses to the effect that neither party would join with third powers in any activities prejudicial to the interests of the other party. This outcome could constitute a significant defeat for British diplomacy, and loss of prestige, if it was assumed by other Arab states that Ibn Saud was sympathetic to the Axis. One possible way of minimising these adverse effects would be for Ibn Saud to declare publicly that he had consulted the British Government before-hand – and that London had offered no objection against, or had even approved, his neutrality. Ibn Saud might then be persuaded into making similar undertakings with Britain in respect of unnamed enemies.[150]

It is difficult, with hindsight, to conceive of Ibn Saud partaking of such tortuous diplomacy, particularly with the knowledge that his seeking British advice was tactical, and not a true reflection of his thinking. There again, Saudi neutrality would in any case have been restricted by the terms of the Treaty of Arab Brotherhood and Alliance with Iraq (1936) and the Yemen (1937). As Iraq and Saudi Arabia were formal allies, a Saudi pledge of neutrality could not override the prior obligation to assist Iraq, should that country be attacked. Unfortunately, Saudi obligations under that treaty 'were of a somewhat indefinite character', and could not strictly be interpreted as an absolute obligation to resort to arms in the defence of a fellow signatory.[151]

In summary, while approving of Saudi Arabia's neutrality in the event of war, the British Government was concerned at the form that that neutrality could take in connection with the negotiations for German armaments. It was one thing privately to wish and advise Ibn Saud to remain neutral, but quite another to have him assure a prospective enemy of his neutrality. One possible benefit to Britain was that Germany might be obliged to furnish Ibn Saud with arms and credit, which she could ill afford, and which gave her nothing in return except Saudi Arabia's neutrality, to which Britain did not object in any case.[152] All that Britain ultimately cared about was that German arms were not paid for in sterling or in gold, but in blocked marks. Such was Saudi Arabia's past record on repayment of foreign debts that it was doubtful whether Germany would ever be reimbursed. Again, Germany could no more be convinced of Saudi sympathies than could Britain.[153] In the event, by the eve of war, £125,000 was earmarked as British political credits for Saudi Arabia, and the decision on the Nejd communications route was left for consideration among the service departments.[154]

The announcement of the German-Soviet Non-Aggression Pact towards the end of August 1939 transformed the outlooks of both Britain and Saudi Arabia. German reconciliation with the communist, atheistic Soviet regime confused Ibn Saud. Britain, too, made hasty recalculations. The loss of the Soviet Union from the allied side of the European equation made the position of all the world's non-aligned states that much more sensitive, and gave Britain an added reason for wishing to withhold any statement of Saudi neutrality under German terms.[155]

The German Government, aware of Saudi disenchantment, dropped its demands for a declaration of neutrality as a prerequisite for arms sales.[156] Ibn Saud, however, once war was declared at the beginning of September, withdrew from the transaction completely, pending developments in the hostilities.[157] Doubtless he appreciated that a British blockade would have intercepted any German arms, while completely souring his own relations with Britain.[158] No doubt, too, Ibn Saud calculated that, in the event of an allied victory, plenty of free German arms might come his way.[159]

The actual outbreak of war found Ibn Saud offering private sympathies to Britain, despite the continuing Anglophobia of most of his inner council.[160] His reassurances of benevolent neutrality, not having been engineered by Germany, coupled with a Saudi Royal Decree which forbad the dissemination of propaganda in Saudi Arabia, was felt from London to be the best outcome for Britain.[161] This view was not shared by British officialdom throughout much of the Middle East. The High Commissioner, and the Resident in Amman, for example, both urged a public indication by Ibn Saud of his goodwill towards the allies,[162] even though he had not signed a treaty of alliance with either Britain or France that called for such action. Britain could no more expect a public declaration of solidarity from neutral Saudi Arabia than she could from, say, Norway or Afghanistan, especially when she was unable to offer anything in return for that loyalty. If Britain could not meet the urgent military requirements of allied countries like Egypt and Iraq, then she could hardly supply arms to Saudi Arabia, particularly when Ibn Saud had just received a large arms consignment from Italy and was not in immediate risk of attack.[163]

Despite Iraq, Transjordan and Egypt being formal British allies, anti-British agitation in those countries made a propaganda-free Saudi neutrality no less helpful to the allied cause.[164] Ibn Saud, should he formally declare his support, only for the allies to lose the war, would be in a difficult position regarding his future with Germany. He would, in addition, be exposed to political and religious haranguing from German radio stations which were at the time exempting him from vilification. Indeed, a public declaration for the allies might tempt other Arab leaders, with anti-British sentiments, to demonstrate that they, unlike Ibn Saud, were not under British influence. Mischievous elements may have suggested that, for a second time, the Holy Places of the Hejaz were under a British wartime protectorate.[165]

Perhaps by September 1939 Ibn Saud's infatuation with Germany had passed, and he had come to the view, contrary to that of many of his advisers, that an allied victory best suited the interests of his Kingdom. With Saudi Arabia's dependence on the Pilgrimage, hers was a particular and fundamental dislike of foreign wars, which could threaten the sealanes and the overland routes to the Hejaz. Ibn Saud would have balanced German words against the ease and ruthlessness with which British military force could be deployed against him, to cut off his Kingdom from the outside world.[166] He would have appreciated that, with Britain's concern for free access to the East, she was the power most likely to see him safely through the war.[167] Ibn Saud permitted a British representative, Captain Gerald de Gaury, the Political Agent in Kuwait, to reside in Riyadh as an exceptional measure designed to ease communications between the British and Saudi Governments.[168] Such an act would have been unthinkable only a few years previously. The Government of India, from whom de Gaury was seconded, doubted whether he was of sufficient calibre to act as special envoy to 'one of the most outstanding personalities of our time'.[169] The Foreign Office considered this implicit analogy with 1917 to be ill-founded. De Gaury was to be a representative of the Jedda Legation: Ibn Saud was no longer the minor potentate in need of a 'special envoy'.[170]

One other factor needs to be introduced to account for Ibn Saud's retreat from his brief flirtation with Germany. He had been, for the previous year or so, in receipt of oil royalties. Ibn Saud found that he was easily able to play on the fears of the American oil companies.[171] Largely as a consequence of this, the United States established formal diplomatic relations with Saudi Arabia. Judge Bert Fish, American Minister in Egypt, was also accredited, in June 1939, to Saudi Arabia,[172] although he was not to present his credentials to Ibn Saud until 1940. Through diplomatic relations with the United States Ibn Saud had found his counter-balance to Britain. America was both more powerful and less suspect than Germany.

By December 1939 Bullard still calculated that Ibn Saud's private reassurances of benevolent neutrality were genuine, despite rumours of Saudi troop movements aimed at seizing Kuwait while British attention was distracted. Should the allies lose the war, however, then Bullard anticipated that Ibn Saud would attempt to annex the Gulf states in order to pre-empt similar moves by Iraq or Iran.[173]

Summary and Conclusions

British policy towards Ibn Saud from 1936, as previously illustrated over Palestine, was concerned with events in a wider theatre, there being little in the way of Anglo-Saudi relations *per se* to warrant active British attention.

The Anglo-Italian Agreement of 1938 invites certain parallels with the 1913-14 Anglo-Turkish Conventions. Both documents revealed British collaboration with other powers at Ibn Saud's expense. Both invited tension in Anglo-Saudi relations through different interpretations of their purpose and contents. Both talked of spheres of influence, one in the east of Arabia (and still in contention in the late 1930s), the other in the west. Faced with what he saw as a British forward policy in southern and eastern Arabia in the late 1930s, and Italian consolidation in the Red Sea, it was understandable for Ibn Saud to fear Arabia being squeezed in the grip of alien powers. Moreover, both the Anglo-Turkish Conventions and the Anglo-Italian Agreement took place against a backdrop of approaching war, Britain negotiating in the context of trying to appease a potential enemy.

Yet Ibn Saud was mistaken in thinking that Britain was, with Italy, treating Arabia in the same cavalier fashion as she had with Turkey a quarter of a century previously. In 1913 Britain was an emerging power in the Middle East; in 1938 a declining, if still pre-eminent one. The Anglo-Italian Agreement was designed essentially to reduce tension between the two powers through a face-saving formula – as is evident in Britain's tacit acceptance of equal Italian interests in the Red Sea area – rather than as further confirmation of Britain's forward policy in Arabia. Britain's aim was to immunise the Middle East, including Saudi Arabia, from other European powers, not to dominate it as Ibn Saud feared. At the same time, Ibn Saud could not be seen to have Britain safeguard his independence. While wanting, and needing, her support (if possible by arms and through a defence treaty) he did not want Britain to be the arbiter of his fate, any more than he wanted Italy or Germany to be likewise.

The Anglo-Italian Agreement, moreover, involved the British Government in some rather dubious logic with regard to Anglo-Saudi relations. Britain was, with one hand, trying to appease Ibn Saud over Palestine, while, with the other, trying to appease Italy at Ibn Saud's expense. Rendel, the central figure in both episodes, appeared not to see the contradictions. For all his fawning over Ibn Saud, Rendel was correct when he noted, some twenty years later, that Ibn Saud would have been prepared to keep on good terms with Britain until he saw the Peel Report.[174] Palestine was the single issue that wrecked British relations with Ibn Saud and with the whole Arab world. Nonetheless, as noted in the previous chapter, Rendel, as a response to the troubles in Palestine, sought accommodation with Ibn Saud and with pan-Arabism, seeing in Ibn Saud the nascent leader of the Arab world. Yet within nine months of the Peel Report Rendel engineered an agreement with Italy which, whether or not it impaired Saudi independence, did nothing to enhance the status he had earlier bestowed upon Ibn Saud.

The Anglo-Italian Agreement, on top of the Peel Report, increased Ibn Saud's determination to free his Kingdom from its perceived vulnerability to both powers – a vulnerability which was enhanced by their apparent working in tandem. In this connection, the attractiveness of Germany, as an enemy of the Jews and Britain, while being the stronger partner in an alliance with Italy, had a logical appeal. So logical, in fact, that it is worthy of comment as to how the British Government failed to appreciate the possible realignment of Saudi foreign policy. Part of the explanation lay with the circumstances of 1939. British minds were on Europe, and, to a lesser extent, on Palestine. Whereas Ibn Saud was obsessed with the spectre of Britain, Saudi Arabia was only on the periphery of British attention. Besides, it was not so much the fact of Saudi Arabia's flirting with the Axis of which Britain was unaware, as the reasons behind it. The British Government never appreciated the extent of Ibn Saud's grievances.

Britain, as war approached, hoped to reduce the number of her potential enemies, although this involved certain contradictions, such as appeasing Ibn Saud over Palestine and then antagonising him by appeasing Italy. Positive efforts to win his goodwill were restricted, apart from reconsidering partition, to relatively inconsequential matters, such as the Hejaz Railway, which were not bound up with fundamental issues of British foreign policy. The areas of gravest concern to Ibn Saud from 1936-39, Palestine and Italy, lay within Britain's wider outlook, within which he had to be seen in perspective. Britain was not going to enter into an alliance with Saudi Arabia. If Saudi Arabia was to be defended it would be on Britain's terms, not Ibn Saud's. Besides, Britain had little to gain therefrom, in view of the political and military hazards of intervention in Saudi Arabia, namely accusations of Christian interference and the undesirability of physical involvement.

The coming of the German factor posed altogether different problems. The establishment of diplomatic relations with Germany was a success for Ibn Saud, albeit a short-lived one, offsetting the humiliation imposed by the Anglo-Italian Agreement. Ibn Saud's security was seen in terms of drawing in European counter-balances to Britain so that he could take from each, and give to none. In the final resort, however, the German-Soviet pact, followed by the outbreak of war, seems to have confronted Ibn Saud with the stark reality that his ultimate survival depended on Britain. It has been suggested that the activities of the Saudi Arabian Government from 1937 – the negotiations with Germany, the secret contributions to the Arabs of Palestine, and the deliberate diversion of arms to the mandate – would have been considered subversive by the British Government, had it known about them.[175] But the British Government *did* know. Britain was well aware of Ibn Saud's arms negotiations with Italy and Germany, and also of Saudi aid to Palestine. Rather than consider these activities as 'unfriendly', Rendel and Bullard, as has been seen, were quick to exonerate Ibn Saud. Pressure from the Arab world, it was believed, made such activities inevitable. In the circumstances, they were relieved to think that Saudi assistance to Palestine was comparatively insubstantial.

It is true that Ibn Saud seemed to be unique among Arab leaders in his awareness of the balance of power in the Middle East.[176] This was exemplified when, after war broke out, Ibn Saud quickly saw his future with the allies. At heart, the interests of Germany were not his own.

Ibn Saud's prominent standing in the Arab world is evidenced by Britain's concern over the conditions of his neutrality status in the impending war. Contrary to the view of one authority that Ibn Saud made no anti-British move in Arabia over Palestine,[177] it is argued here that for a brief period in the late 1930s, approximately coinciding with Bullard's tenure as British Minister (he departed in December 1939), Ibn Saud was intent on an anti-British policy. For the first time, his interests appeared to diverge from those of Britain. Only with the German-Soviet Pact and the outbreak of war did they converge once more.

REFERENCES FOR CHAPTER ELEVEN

1. See Chapter Six.
2. Northedge, *The Troubled Giant*, p. 493.
3. Reynolds, p. 102.
4. Northedge, p. 412.
5. ibid., pp. 407, 412; Rendel, p. 132.
6. Northedge, p. 412.
7. Rome saw the conflict as a private quarrel between Italy and Abyssinia, whereas London saw the whole enterprise as a challenge against the international order based on Geneva (Macartney and Cremona, p. 178).
8. Northedge, pp. 414-15.
9. Rendel, p. 134.
10. Northedge, p. 415.
11. Earl of Avon, *Facing the Dictators*, p. 279.
12. Northedge, pp. 416-18.
13. Viscount Norwich (Duff Cooper), *Old Men Forget*, pp. 193-4.
14. Northedge, pp. 420-5.
15. Annual Report 1934.
16. Annual Report 1935.
17. ibid.
18. ibid.
19. Calvert (Jedda) to FO, No 210, 11 November 1935, FO E/5678/5599/25: 371/19020.
20. Annual Report 1936; Watt, 'The Foreign Policy of Ibn Saud 1936-1939', p. 154.
21. Campbell (FO) minute, 28 August 1935, FO E/5599/5599/25: 371/19020.
22. Annual Report 1935. The British Government had considered, and rejected, the idea of

conveying the contents of the Rome Agreement to Ibn Saud in May 1934 (see page 155).
23. As will be seen, German sources considered Fuad Hamza to be a British agent.
24. Annual Report 1935.
25. Monroe, *Britain's Moment* ..., p. 84.
26. Annual Report 1936.
27. ibid.
28. Calvert to Rendel, 28 July 1937, FO 905/44.
29. Kennedy, 'Appeasement ...', *British Journal of International Studies*, p. 173. As the 1930s progressed the Cabinet and the Foreign Office never lost sight of the world-wide vulnerability of British interests. From 1934 it appeared that the most likely future adversary would be Germany, in which case, any major quarrel with a third power, such as Italy, was something to be avoided if possible (Medlicott, p. xviii). It was hoped that foreign crises in general could be postponed pending British rearmament.
30. Bullard, *Britain* ..., pp. 92-3.
31. ibid., p. 89; RIIA, *Political and Strategic Interests* ..., p. 137.
32. Annual Report 1937.
33. In H. Pelling, *Britain and the Second World War*, pp. 22-3.
34. Baker, p. 18.
35. FO memorandum, 27 January 1939, FO E/953/625/25: 371/23271.
36. ibid. A 1935 estimate put the cost of restoring the Hejaz section of the Railway at £190,000.
37. ibid.
38. Hurewitz, p. 522. For more on Italian propaganda see C. A. Macdonald, 'Radio Bari: Italian Wireless Propaganda in the Middle East and British Countermeasures 1934-1938', *Middle Eastern Studies*, 13 (1977), pp. 195-207.
39. Rendel, p. 132.
40. RIIA, op. cit., p. 124.
41. Rendel, p. 132.
42. Rendel memorandum, 23 February 1938, FO E/1327/880/91: 371/21826.
43. Northedge, pp. 483-4. Eden and Chamberlain disagreed on how to check Italian hostility. Eden wanted accelerated rearmament, tightened military alliances, the cultivation of Anglo-American relations, and an end to appeasement. Chamberlain wanted to continue the appeasement of Italy in an attempt to break up the Axis (Hurewitz, p. 523).
44. Rendel, p. 134. It was in the Levant and Arabia that Italy harboured the greatest resentment against Britain. She had not, for example, been informed of the Husein-McMahon negotiations, despite her interests in the Red Sea (Macartney and Cremona, p. 182).
45. Rendel memorandum, 23 February 1938, FO E/1327/880/91: 371/21826.
46. RIIA, op. cit., p. 179. The Agreement was intended to apply only after the withdrawal of the Italian forces from Spain. Chamberlain waived this restriction in November 1938 (Hurewitz, p. 523).
47. Seton-Williams, p. 202.
48. Watt, op. cit., p. 156.
49. Rendel to Bullard, 19 June 1957, Rendel Papers, MEC.
50. ibid.; FO E/954/61/91: 371/21830.
51. FO E/239/61/91: 371/21830.
52. Eyres (FO) minute, 13 December 1938, FO E/7810/880/91: 371/21830.
53. RIIA, *Political and Strategic Interests* ..., p. 137. The Convention abolished the international control of the Straits (the Dardanelles, the Sea of Marmara, and the Bosphorus) imposed at Lausanne. Turkish sovereignty over the Straits was reimposed, but freedom of peacetime commerce for all nations was guaranteed.
54. See S. G. Page, *The USSR and Arabia: the Development of Soviet Politics and Attitudes towards the Countries of the Arabian Peninsula.*, pp. 9-10.
55. ibid., p. 16.
56. Kelly, *Arabia* ..., p. 463.
57. Page, p. 17; Hurewitz, p. 417.
58. See RIIA, *British Interests* ..., p. 72.
59. Bullard to Halifax, No 150, 24 October 1939, FO E/7409/177/25: 371/23269.
60. ibid.

61. See FO E/2258/155/91: 371/11436. Ibn Saud's position over Mecca meant that he dare not forge close relations with the atheistic Soviet regime.
62. Clayton to Oliphant, 9 June 1927, FO E/2586/119/91: 371/12245.
63. Bullard to FO, 23 March 1939, FO E/2982/177/25: 371/23269.
64. Ibn Saud to Neville Chamberlain, 2 January 1939, FO E/1444/177/25: 371/23268.
65. Admiralty to FO, 25 April 1939, FO E/3041/177/25: 371/23269.
66. FO to Bullard, April 1939, FO E/2827/177/25: 371/23269.
67. ibid.
68. This view is also maintained by Watt, op. cit., p. 152.
69. ibid. Rendel, unconvincingly, tried to play down Ibn Saud's 'Machiavellianism'. To Rendel, while some playing off of natural enemies was understandable, Ibn Saud never thought seriously about using the Italians as a counter-weight to Britain (Rendel to Bullard, 19 June 1957, Rendel Papers, MEC).
70. Lukasz Hirszowicz, *The Third Reich and the Arab East,* pp. 29-30.
71. The position of Palestine bore comparison with the Vatican, which was seen as the base for political Catholicism.
72. By the end of the 1920s about 1,800 German Christians lived in Palestine. For an account of the delicate position of the German Palestine community in relation to the German Government, see H. D. Schmidt, 'The Nazi Party in Palestine and the Levant 1932-1939', *International Affairs,* 28 (1952), pp. 460-9.
73. Hirszowicz, p. 31. Other German sources were not so alarmist, minimising the adverse affects of Jewish emigration. Jews emigrating to Palestine were encouraged, for example, to deposit their assets in a special account in Germany, which would then be drawn upon to pay for German exports to Palestine. (Melka, p. 221). Moreover, the number of Jews emigrating to Palestine from Germany was considerably smaller than that from other European countries, notably Poland (Melka, p. 230).
74. Melka, p. 224.
75. DGFP Series D, Vol V, pp. 768-9.
76. Ibn Saud's personal physician was involved in these enquiries.
77. Bullard, *The Camels Must Go,* p. 212.
78. Rendel to Bullard, 19 June 1957, Rendel Papers, MEC. With the increase in Italian and German expansionism Britain's ability to supply Arab countries with modern arms declined.
79. Grobba to German Foreign Ministry, 9 November 1937, DGFP, Series D, Vol V, No 574, pp. 769-71. Following the publication of the Peel Report, Grobba received several Arab delegations (Hirszowicz, p. 34-5).
80. Watt, op. cit., p. 156.
81. Hirszowicz, p. 36.
82. ibid., pp. 36-7.
83. Schmidt, p. 467.
84. Hirszowicz, pp. 45-6.
85. Germany was not yet sending out anti-British propaganda broadcasts.
86. Hirszowicz, p. 41.
87. Watt, op. cit., p. 156.
88. German memorandum: Von Hentig (Head of Political Division VII), 27 August 1938, DGFP, Series D, Vol V, No 582, p. 789.
89. Watt, op. cit., p. 156.
90. Hirszowicz, p. 43. For a discussion of the extent of this aid, see Melka, p. 225.
91. See Fisher, p. 442.
92. Trott to FO, 3 October 1938, FO E/6069/738/25: 371/21905.
93. Hirszowicz, p. 49. Berlin feared the unreliability of the Arabs and that German arms might be turned against Germany.
94. ibid.
95. Bullard to FO, Jedda Report for February 1939, FO E/588/588/25: 371/23271.
96. Watt, op. cit., p. 156.
97. ibid.
98. See Stonehewer-Bird to Halifax, No 62, FO E/2720/1194/25: 371/24589.
99. Bullard to Halifax, Political Situation for 1939, 19 September 1939, FO E/7107/549/25: 371/23271.

100. Watt, op. cit., p. 158.
101. ibid, p. 155. There are, nonetheless, indications of considerable German-Italian rivalry in the Middle East.
102. Grobba to German Foreign Ministry, 18 February 1939, DGFP, Series D, Vol V, No 589, pp. 800-2. Ibn Saud also urged German diplomatic support for his territorial claims against Britain.
103. ibid, p. 800.
104. ibid, p. 808.
105. ibid, pp. 801, 808-9. It is unclear what benefits Italy received from Ibn Saud, or whether Britain did put pressure on him to impose sanctions. See page 182.
106. ibid., pp. 803-6.
107. ibid., p. 803.
108. Hirszowicz, p. 47.
109. Grobba, op. cit., p. 803.
110. ibid., p. 805. These debts dated back several years to when the pre-Nazi Government had an Honorary Consul in Jedda.
111. ibid., p. 806.
112. Trott to FO, 9 August 1939, FO E/5867/735/25: 371/23272.
113. Trott to FO, 16 August 1939, FO E/6267/735/25: 371/23272.
114. Watt, op. cit., p. 158.
115. Woermann, Under-State Secretary, to Grobba, 18 April 1939, DGFP, Series D, Vol V, No 592, pp. 813-14.
116. Grobba to Woermann, 2 May 1939, DGFP, Series D, Vol VI, No 313, pp. 403-4. It was believed that Fuad Hamza had not passed on German funds to Palestine, and that he was engaged in a long-standing quarrel with Yusuf Yasin.
117. ibid, pp. 405-7.
118. ibid., p. 406.
119. ibid., Woermann note, 5 May 1939.
120. Von Hentig memorandum, 22 May 1939, DGFP, Series D, Vol VI, No 422, pp. 555-6.
121. ibid.; Watt, op. cit., pp. 153-8.
122. Watt, op. cit., p. 158. The intention was that the deal remain secret, but such a visit at that time could hardly go unnoticed. Details of Qarqani's visit were published by Reuters; from Bari; and even by the German press (Hirszowicz, p. 59).
123. Hirszowicz, pp. 58-9.
124. Von Hentig memorandum, op. cit., pp. 555-6.
125. Lampson (Cairo) to Oliphant, 26 June 1939, FO E/4815/735/25; 371/23272.
126. ibid.
127. ibid.
128. See CO/78365/38: 725/61.
129. Eyres (FO) minute, 6 January 1939, FO E/61/61/91: 371/21830.
130. Baggally (FO) minute, 8 July 1939, FO E/4815/735/25: 371/23272.
131. Bullard to Halifax, No 231, 13 December 1939, FO E/246/246/25: 371/23269.
132. Bullard to Halifax, No 140, 19 September 1939, FO E/7017/549/25: 371/23271.
133. Trott to FO, 16 August 1939, FO E/6267/735/25: 371/23272; Watt, op. cit., p. 157.
134. Eyres (FO) minute, 14 August 1939, FO E/5676/735/25: 371/23272.
135. See Al Qarqani report to Ibn Saud, 20 July 1939, enclosed in Trott to FO, 9 August 1939, FO E/5867/735/25: 371/23272; Watt, op. cit., p. 158.
136. In 1939 Ibn Saud had a standing uniformed army of some 2,500 men, trained by ex-Turkish officers (Ibrahim al Rashid, *Saudi Arabia Enters the Moslem World: Secret US Documents on the Emergence of the Kingdom of Saudi Arabia as a World power 1936-1949, Vol I*, p. 42).
137. FO circular to Adm, WO, and AM, 22 August 1939, FO E/5763/735/25: 371/23272.
138. ibid.
139. ibid.
140. ibid.
141. RIIA, *Political and Strategic Interests ...*, p. 281.
142. ibid., p. 289.
143. ibid., pp. 127-8.
144. ibid., pp. 128-30.

145. See Eyres minute, 14 August 1939, FO E/5676/735/25: 371/23272.
146. FO circular, op. cit.
147. See Hurewitz, pp. 421-4.
148. FO circular, op. cit.
149. ibid.
150. ibid.
151. ibid.
152. ibid.
153. See Bullard to Halifax, No 140, Political Situation for 1939, 19 September 1939, FO E/7017/549/25: 371/23271.
154. FO circular, op. cit.
155. FO to Trott, 23 August 1939, FO E/5931/735/25: 371/23272.
156. Bullard to Halifax, No 150, 24 October 1939, FO E/7409/177/25: 371/23269. The German documents do not cover this period. The information came from the Saudi Government to the British Legation.
157. See Trott to FO, No 132, 12 October 1939, FO E/6913/735/25: 371/23272.
158. Watt, op. cit., p. 158. Britain's domination of the Red Sea and the Gulf gave her control of all Saudi Arabia's essential imports.
159. Trott to FO, op. cit.
160. Stonehewer-Bird to Halifax, No 62, FO E/2720/1194/25: 371/24589; Watt, op. cit., p. 159.
161. Stonehewer-Bird to Halifax, ibid.
162. MacMichael (Amman) to MacDonald, 23 October 1939, in FO E/7721/246/25: 371/23269.
163. WO to FO, 24 November 1939, FO E/7722/394/25: 371/23271.
164. Bullard to FO, Jedda Report for November 1939, 371/23271.
165. ibid.
166. Watt, op. cit., pp. 158-60.
167. See Bullard, *The Camels Must Go,* p. 213.
168. Bullard to Halifax, No 150, op. cit.
169. In Trott to FO, 13 September 1939, FO E/6475/6278/25: 371/23275.
170. FO minute, ibid.
171. Watt, op. cit., p. 159.
172. Stonehewer-Bird to Halifax, No 62, op. cit.
173. Bullard to Halifax, No 170, 2 December 1939, FO E/8086/253/25: 371/23269. For a discussion of Iranian claims in the Gulf, see Morsy-Abdullah, pp. 239-327.
174. Rendel to Bullard, 19 June 1957, Rendel Papers, MEC.
175. Watt, op. cit., p. 159.
176. ibid., p. 160.
177. Kedourie, *Islam ...,* p. 69. See page 286.

CHAPTER TWELVE

Britain and Saudi Arabia 1925-1939: the Imperial Oasis

Kedourie has remarked that 'the policy of one country towards another is, at best, a poor, makeshift thing ... and must be grounded upon ignorance, irrelevance, and misunderstanding'.[1] The tone of this remark could almost have been penned with Britain and Saudi Arabia in mind. Seldom can Britain have exercised full diplomatic relations with a king and country about which she knew so little.

Throughout the inter-war years the degree of personal contact between Britain and Saudi Arabia was minimal.[2] In 1925 the number of westerners resident in Jedda was no more than a dozen. Fourteen years later the number had not risen above sixty, although some three hundred Americans were, by then, to be found in Hasa. These figures in themselves reveal some of the difficulties encountered in the framing of British policy towards Saudi Arabia. The other Middle Eastern states, such as Egypt, the mandates, and the Gulf network, entertained a panoply of British officialdom with decades, sometimes centuries, of British involvement. Some played host, at one time or another, to an active British military presence. Native levies and a British naval squadron guarded the Gulf. RAF planes and armoured cars, and/or ground forces, were based elsewhere.

In contrast, British dealings with Saudi Arabia were exercised against a backdrop of almost unrelieved ignorance. Arabia remained a remote and isolated land from which the British Government could glean little accurate information. Normal governmental 'intelligence' could not function. There was no reliable press. Travel was prohibited. Communications of all kinds were slow and inefficient. There were no private or commercial links of any note. Governmental servants familiar with Jedda or the Gulf could offer little insight into the life or politics of the interior.

In passing, it is as well to be reminded that it was largely due to the remoteness and inaccessibility of Saudi Arabia that Ibn Saud had become the first Arab potentate to win recognition of his complete internal and external sovereignty by the British Government. The acknowledgement of Ibn Saud's independence was not a reflection of the especial status or attributes seen in man or territory, but the complete lack of any desire or need on Britain's part to derive advantage from him or his dominions. Arabia at that time seemed completely immune from the theatre of great power rivalry.

In view of the paucity of information possessed by policy-makers in London, the role of the British Legation in Jedda took on an even greater significance in the shaping of British policy than did comparable diplomatic missions in other countries. Before Ryan arrived recourse had to be taken to the personal emissary to expedite British policy, invariably Sir Gilbert Clayton. Ryan's immediate successors, significantly, all had previous mission experience in Jedda.

The role of the British Minister was further emphasised by Ibn Saud's preference for Jedda, rather than his own Legation in London, as the main channel for the two-way flow of communication. The general unfamiliarity of Nejdis with the outside world was reflected in Ibn Saud's enforced choice of outsiders (non-Wahhabis) to fill most of his important government posts, most of whom were more Anglophobic than he. The King rarely visited Jedda personally, leaving the British Legation to operate for most of the time through the Deputy Foreign Minister, the Lebanese Fuad Bey Hamza, who could not, in any case, take major decisions without reference to Ibn Saud.

In this context, it cannot be wondered at that British policy towards Ibn Saud was, of necessity, a low-key affair. Circumstances, both political and physical, did not allow intense diplomatic activity. Consequently, the British penchant for a reactive foreign policy, to avoid fixed principles and operate with a flexibility of response according to prevailing conditions,[3] was given concrete encouragement in the case of Saudi Arabia.

The clarity of British policy was further blurred by the complete dichotomy between European and Arab perspectives on political and social traditions, and by the contrast between the seeming unimportance of Saudi Arabia and the stature of her King. Saudi Arabia was an uninviting and under-developed state. She appeared to have no worthwhile resources. Apart from the main cities of the Hejaz, she lacked any kind of infrastructure or refinements associated with modern statehood. Her subjects were few in number, scattered, and many of them bedouin. The total Saudi income in 1932 amounted to only around £600,000 gold *per annum*.[4] In fact, there was nothing at all about Saudi Arabia to warrant any British diplomatic relations, except for the religious significance of Mecca, and the one unifying factor of almost the whole peninsula – the King – who wielded political and religious influence out of all proportion to the resources of his Kingdom.

Arabia was among the most primitive of Arab lands: Ibn Saud the most prominent and influential of Arab rulers. As if unable to grasp the contrast, departmental minutes veered capriciously, ranging from likening Ibn Saud to a semi-civilised savage, to being almost awestruck at his astuteness and acumen. In part, the British Government was a victim of the aura of romance and mystery within which Arabia basked until the growth of oil operations killed off the bedouin lifestyle and exposed the peninsula to the familiarity that could breed contempt. Prior to 1939 Philby was perhaps the only genuine authority on Arabia, himself immersed in idolatry of Ibn Saud. It is important to stress that even by the late 1930s Saudi Arabia was viewed by many as nothing more than a large group of tribes temporarily under the control of one man. The renowned explorer Bertram Thomas, who crossed the Rub al Khali in 1931, six years later spoke of Arabia not being a political entity, but a fragmented, tribal society.[5]

From one point of view, Ibn Saud appeared a genuine candidate for the Great Man school of history. From exile at the turn of the century he had come to a position of dominance in the Arab world and had welded all his dominions into a state which bore his name. Very rarely in recent history has the name of a state embraced that of its founder. Ibn Saud's were achievements of a formidable nature. He withstood a threefold threat to his regime: through European intervention, hostility from some of his Arab neighbours, and from the internal dissension of the *Ikhwan*. Western admirers of Ibn Saud were not restricted to sycophants like Philby. This book has paid testimony to the tributes of some who met Ibn Saud. One of Bullard's final despatches in 1939 noted: 'I do not think that the possession of a certain greatness of mind can be denied to him. ... On the whole he has shown himself a great ruler'.[6] This attitude was not always well received by other British officials in the Arab world, who preferred to see a little less deference coming from London and Jedda, and a little more realism. Glubb, for example, was quite explicit in 1931: 'He [Ibn Saud] is a primitive, twopenny-halfpenny monarch, clinging precariously to a shaky thronelet'.[7]

There again, circumstances had combined to provide Ibn Saud with opportunities for aggrandisement denied to other Arab rulers at other times. His rise to power coincided with the decline of the Turks. He was able to avail himself of western technology which had been made possible by the opening up of the Suez Canal. Thanks to the British subsidy and later military assistance (in 1929-30), he was better able to buy the allegiance of intransigent tribes and extend his influence. The *Ikhwan* gave Ibn Saud a fighting machine, serving as both a police force and an army, unprecedented in the history of Arabia. Courtship by outside powers sanctioned his rule to the world at large.[8] One ingredient alone remained to be exploited by the succeeding generation in Saudi Arabia: oil.

The confused British perceptions of Ibn Saud have to be seen in the context of Britain's interests in the Middle East. Those interests were primarily strategic. Britain sought unmolested movement through the Arabian corridor of ships, planes, troops and merchandise. Those movements required stability in Arabia, which Ibn Saud in the main provided. There were no questions of a moral nature at stake. It did not matter whether Ibn Saud was a good or just King, nor that he was particularly favourably disposed towards Britain. All that mattered was that he was strong enough to keep order; to safeguard the Pilgrimage; and to prevent his tribes from causing trouble within neighbouring British-backed states.

What is noteworthy is the array of ambiguities, contradictions and misperceptions involved in Britain seeking the stability of Saudi rule in Arabia. Seldom can a state have posed so many threats to its neighbours, which were vital British interests, as could Saudi Arabia. The doctrine of Wahhabism and the dynastic ambitions of Al Saud were explicit threats to the Gulf and to the mandates. Communications and technology had rapidly advanced so that central Arabia was no longer immune from assault from the British bases which circumvented Ibn Saud's Kingdom. The military option against Saudi Arabia (were relations ever to have deteriorated to the extent that it was considered) was prohibited because of her religious significance. Any attack on Saudi Arabia, the spiritual home of Islam, by a non-Moslem power would have led to the alienation of the entire Moslem world. This was something that Britain, with her own Moslem empire, could never contemplate. The short-lived and ill-publicised RAF sorties from the mandates on *Ikhwan* raiders constituted the maximum possible physical leverage against the Saudi state – and Nejd, at the time, was not yet formally joined to the sacred Hejaz.

The desire for stability in Arabia, coupled with the intrinsic threat to the mandates, meant that Britain was continually obliged to trade off her interests. The stronger the Saudi state became, with Ibn Saud successfully imposing internal order and stability, the greater the threat to the mandates could have become. Provided that stability in Arabia was maintained, Britain dealt with the concomitant threats to the Hashemite regimes and the Gulf sheikhdoms on their merits: by negotiation, by appeasement, or, in the case of the *Ikhwan* rebellion, by limited force.

Ibn Saud could doubtless have annexed the Gulf sheikhdoms at will, a fact fully appreciated by the British Government, which was painfully aware of its own inability to resist such moves. Only in 1925, when Aqaba and Maan were annexed for Transjordan (itself an act of religious provocation as the said towns were claimed for the Moslem Holy Land) did Britain actively intervene to limit Saudi expansionism in the years covered by this study. Thereafter, diplomatic methods were favoured, although the Hadda and Bahra Agreements of the same year marked the last successful attempts to limit Ibn Saud's territorial ambitions by diplomatic means. Even the word 'successful' is used with some caution in the light of the later Iraq-Nejd frontier conflagration, which was to some extent inflamed by the wording and provisions of the Bahra Agreement.

British disagreement on the most suitable policy towards Ibn Saud peaked around 1931, during the Transjordan-Nejd frontier disturbances. The position customarily adopted from London, particularly as Foreign Office influence in handling policy towards Ibn Saud increased, is best described as appeasement.[9] As Britain's military forces stationed in the Middle East were intended as a strategic reserve, available for instant movement in any direction, not as a static garrison, then it was natural that Britain should seek to retain her influence where possible by consent, not force.[10] British policy was, therefore, to appease Ibn Saud to the extent that it was compatible with ultimate strategic control.[11] Nowhere was this policy better illustrated than over the south-east Arabian frontier dispute where, over the course of several years, Britain sought a settlement by gradually extending the territory she was prepared to cede to Saudi sovereignty. Nor could strategic questions always be distinguished from political ones. As demonstrated over Aqaba-Maan and the blue line, what was considered strategically vital one moment, was expendable the next.

Appeasement has its own logic, particularly for a declining power, already overstretched, and reluctant to engage in overseas hostilities. In the late 1920s and early '30s, however, a certain school of Arabists, to which Glubb belonged, castigated the appeasement approach in favour of upholding British prestige. Glubb went so far as to suggest that the single most important reason for the continuing desert friction between the Wahhabis and their neighbours was that Britain's prestige in the Arabian deserts was so low.[12] Concessions and appeasement, to this school of thought, were regarded by a predatory race such as the Arabs as a sign of weakness. A policy of firmness, by contrast, was greeted with instant respect, particularly in the case of Ibn Saud who, through impending bankruptcy, the risk of tribal revolt, and dynastic enemies along his frontiers, could not have survived if Britain turned resolutely against him. Glubb's preferred policy would have been on the following lines:

> There is no use imagining that we are dealing with a civilised government, apprehensive of public opinion, or restrained by moral considerations. We are dealing with a greedy, savage, and predatory people who regard war and rapine as the natural occupation of man ..., who have learnt sufficient from us to know that we can be put off by specious talk of friendship while they simultaneously rob, abuse, insult, and despise us, and who will stop at no treachery ..., the same as the tribesmen of the North-West Frontier of India. With them we have realised that, at regular intervals, a punitive expedition is necessary to keep them in order and restore our prestige ... but Bin Saud, for some inexplicable reason, we insist on treating like the USA.[13]

It must not be overlooked that Ryan, at about the same time, though for different reasons, was equally disillusioned at the line of policy being laid down from afar, and came close to resigning his post in protest. Ryan, though working on the other side of the Saudi-Hashemite divide from Glubb, shared a certain sympathy with the latter's sentiments, and felt himself quite out of touch with London. Interestingly, from his perspective, rather than likening the treatment of Ibn Saud with the United States, Ryan associated it with the other extreme, Ibn Saud being dealt with as a minor

desert chieftain. This perfectly illustrates the ambivalence with which Ibn
Saud was perceived:

> I am, perhaps, inclined to pessimism regarding our future position in
> the East generally, and to some extent agree with those who think that
> the only thing that semi-civilised people understand is force. ... We
> can't expect to have it both ways with Bin Saud, i.e., we can't give him
> the position of an international equal and treat him at the same time
> like the Sheikh of Ras al Khaima. ... We have all to face the certainty
> that prestige can't be maintained *vis à vis* of independent Eastern
> states by our out of date methods, and our prestige will have to assume
> a new character, not the old prestige based on our superiority in
> civilisation. ... This is not an inter-departmental matter, it is a question
> of historical evolution and the effect therein of policy. ... As regards
> Bin Saud, I am all for a friendly policy up to the point at which he
> becomes finally impossible to deal with. I think it is even betting
> whether he goes to pieces or becomes a menace to us in the next few
> years. Meanwhile, I try, perhaps not very successfully, to contribute to
> the success of a friendly policy without letting him have it all his own
> way.[14]

The general thrust of these criticisms suggests another dimension in which
to see the framing of British policy. There was more than just departmental interests, pulling in different directions and denying the cohesiveness
necessary to construct a more uniform approach to Ibn Saud. There was also
a psychological dimension, which saw the policy debate not as one between
the equally remote departments in London, but between, on the one hand,
British officials on the spot, more or less familiar with the Arab world and
the Arab mentality, and, on the other, the whole bureaucratic apparatus in
London dependent on the information of its officials.[15] British Orientalists
spanned a wide spectrum. Partisan considerations were present. Ryan may
have taken a different view from Glubb, but his approach was also very
different from that of his successor, Bullard. British officials in the Gulf were
often anti-Saudi and patronising to the Arabs in general, although some
established a tradition of learned Arabists. Lorimer's *Gazetteer of the
Persian Gulf*, for example, completed in 1915, became the indispensable
source book on tribal life in eastern Arabia for half a century.[16]

Klieman's summary of British policy in the Middle East in the inter-war
years holds true for Saudi Arabia:

> Britain's inter-war policy towards the Middle East, with its recourse to
> balances and compromises, reflected the primary emphasis in London
> upon immediate advantage and short-term interests. By localising
> and reflecting regional discontent, by appeasing Arab nationalism
> only when compelled to do so under pressure, and by supporting
> conservative leaders and classes, the British succeeded in fostering an

impression of order and calm throughout the Arab world in the period 1922-39 only to delude themselves.[17]

These 'delusions' were particularly apparent over Saudi Arabia. Misperceptions on both sides coloured Anglo-Saudi relations. The driving forces of the foreign policies of both Britain and Ibn Saud pointed to a fundamental clash of interests. To Britain, it was the stability of the Middle East as a whole, not just Saudi Arabia, that was important. Centuries of experience with Orientals had taught Britain the virtues and economies associated with indirect rule and the indiscriminate use of treaties and subsidies. This policy was undimmed by the 1930s. The Middle East was kept quiescent by signing treaties with every potentate of any standing. A corollary of this policy was that natural enemies found themselves linked to Britain by treaties. Saudi Arabia, Egypt, the Yemen, Transjordan, Iraq, the Gulf network and the Chiefs of the Aden Protectorate, all had treaties with Britain by the 1930s.

This policy, while intended to serve British interests, was not well suited to Arab psychology. An ancient Arab proverb declares:

The enemy of my friend is my enemy.
The enemy of my enemy is my friend.[18]

... which, by extension, with Arabia harbouring so many animosities and with Ibn Saud's neighbours benefiting from British protection, meant that to him Britain was an enemy. Each of his rivals in the Arab world seemed to be enjoying greater British favours than he. Arms and financial aid, it seemed, were offered to all but him. Egypt and the mandates were direct beneficiaries of the British Treasury, and even in the Gulf British policy appeared to be directed towards making Saudi Arabia commercially dependent on Kuwait and Bahrain. Ibn Saud, despite all his proclaimed past assistance to Britain (such as aiding her in the First World War, prohibiting raiding across frontiers, taking her advice on foreign policy matters, etc.), was largely excluded from British assistance. By far the greatest beneficiaries of British benevolence were, from Ibn Saud's position, the Hashemites, who, ever since 1915, had been recipients of British gold, and been elevated by Britain into artificial significance in the Arab world. They had even been provided with ready-made kingdoms; a fact worsened by their being situated on supposedly Saudi soil, stretching from Aqaba across to the Gulf, and northwards into Saudi ancestral domains. The Hejaz, Transjordan and Iraq, as the map of the Middle East reveals, enclosed Nejd in a wedge-shaped vice.

It is hardly surprising that Ibn Saud, as ignorant of British ways as they were of his, interpreted these acts as deliberately conspired against him. Consequently, his attitudes towards the British, never sympathetic because they were not of his race or his religion, reached depths of resentment and suspicion that were rarely perceived in London. To give but one example, when emergency landing strips for Imperial Airways were sought by Britain in Hasa, it was never appreciated that such intrusions were anathema both to

Ibn Saud and the Nejdi *ulema*. 'May God protect us from her evil', Ibn Saud is reported as saying in Kuwait.[19]

With all Britain's wealth of experience of Oriental peoples, the failure to see Ibn Saud's blandishments (his assertion that Britain would always be his first friend, and his generally telling her what she wanted to hear) for what they were, is worthy of some surprise. Two separate British Ministers in the Annual Reports of 1943 and 1945 expressly proclaimed how Ibn Saud was *not* doing what any normal Arab would do, and was *not* playing Britain off against the United States.[20] Rendel, one of the major figures in British policy-making towards Saudi Arabia, remarked, after meeting Ibn Saud in 1937: 'It is perilous to attribute complete sincerity to anyone where international politics are concerned ... but ... I would say that I have seldom met anyone who gave me so strong an impression of sincerity and directness'.[21]

Uncertainty over Ibn Saud's underlying attitudes towards Britain came to prominence during the *Ikhwan* rebellion (when his own part in the activities of his warring tribesmen was never satisfactorily ascertained) and reopened during the Palestine disturbances from 1936. Rendel's above remark can be compared with that of Ryan, offered in 1930: 'Bin Saud is fundamentally pan-Arab and anti-European, and he chafes a good deal now that he is up against us at so many points. He will catch us out all he can, especially when anti-Hashemite feelings come into play'.[22]

Such contrasting perceptions of Ibn Saud did little to make the formulation of British policy any easier. A further complicating factor was that British policy towards Saudi Arabia had to be considered alongside that towards the Hashemites. At root, Britain was supporting two rival dynasties. North of a line linking Aqaba with Kuwait, running approximately along the 30th parallel, Britain had staked her strategic interests in two Hashemite states. Below that line natural forces had thrust up Ibn Saud, to whose rule Britain eventually became equally committed. Such a policy was as potentially dangerous to Britain as it was incomprehensible to the Arabs. Britain's favoured policy in any sensitive area of the globe amenable to British pressure was either *divide et impera*, backed up by treaties and subsidies, or else the selection of one prominent chief or family who was offered undivided support. This latter policy had earlier been pursued in Arabia, by singling out the Hashemites as Britain's principal protégés. But from 1925 Britain found herself encouraging the growth of two dynasties, mutually hostile. Ibn Saud often revealed his complete unwillingness or inability to appreciate that Britain did not ultimately control the policies of the Hashemites, preferring to regard them as British-dependent, in contrast to his own complete sovereignty. Without their British military guarantee Ibn Saud reckoned the Hashemite states to be unviable.

At this point, some explanation must be offered as to why Britain should have supported two rival dynasties in Arabia – three, if one includes the Imam. Her commitment to the Hashemites stemmed from several factors. There was the perceived obligation owed to the Sherifs for their part in the war against the Turks. Feisal and Abdullah, since their installation in the mandates, had been considered reasonably well-disposed towards Britain, from gratitude if nothing else. There was no satisfactory alternative to Hashemite rule in Iraq and Transjordan. On the other hand, there was the problem of sustaining a truncated 'Sherifian solution' to the Middle East after the loss of the Hejaz, with an expansionist Saudi regime in its place.

Britain's motives for supporting Ibn Saud were of a different order. Power politics had been allowed to take its normal course in Arabia, resulting in Ibn Saud's rapid emergence to a position of unchallenged supremacy, at which point power politics was compelled to co-exist with Britain's strategic concern for his relations with his neighbours. It was Ibn Saud's achievements, rather than his heritage, that Britain could not neglect. Britain was concerned only that Arabia be under ordered government, through whatever source, over which Britain could exercise some influence through normal diplomatic channels. It was only through ordered government that the safety of the world's Moslem pilgrims – many of whom were British subjects or under British protection – could be ensured. This was particularly significant in the case of India, whose Moslems came to look upon Ibn Saud as holding a position in the Moslem world analogous to that formally held by the Sultan of Turkey. Stability among the Gulf sheikhdoms was also considered to stem from good relations with Ibn Saud. In other words, colonial interests of one form or another impinged on British relations with Saudi Arabia. The fact that Ibn Saud was, of necessity, dealt with through Colonial Office considerations, and that Britain was an infidel power, engineered a situation made for misunderstanding.

Notwithstanding the contrasting nature of Britain's commitments to the Hashemites and to Ibn Saud, at no time between 1925 and 1939 did any question arise in London of choosing between the two dynasties, or subordinating the interests of one to the other. The importance of the strategic corridor from Amman to Basra, and of Iraqi oil, meant that Britain had tied her flag to the Hashemites. The need to support Ibn Saud at the same time posed the dilemma. Fortunately for Britain, Saudi-Hashemite tension was less evident in 1939 than in 1925. This was initially due to Britain's policy of reconciliation, but later the product of local factors: the death of Feisal, the emerging statehood of both Saudi Arabia and Iraq, and the first indications of pan-Arab sentiment.

The mutual misperceptions of the British and Saudi Governments were not without their favourable side-effects. Not only did the British Government fail to attribute Ibn Saud's 'friendship' to a *realpolitik* rooted in fear and suspicion, but Ibn Saud equally failed to appreciate the positive aspects of British policy towards his regime. He underestimated that the continuing stability of his rule was a valuable asset to the British Government. Had he known that, whatever the degree of Britain's commitment to the Hashemites to the north, it was not her intention to favour them at his expense in Arabia, he might have embarked upon a more ambitious and aggressive policy of expansion. Ibn Saud's obsession with the Hashemites acted as a cloak through which he could never accurately ascertain British policy as being equally committed to both dynasties in their respective domains.

For its part, the British Government consciously underplayed its hand. It was never admitted to Ibn Saud that he was a bastion in its scheme of things in the Middle East. He was reassured only when necessary that Britain was not likely to stand aside in the event of his Kingdom being threatened by an outside power. Britain was not, however, prepared to enter into any defensive alliance with Saudi Arabia, as she had done with other Arab states. To have done so would have been counter-productive. Apart from possibly dragging a Christian power into a war not of its choosing, between two or more Moslem states all linked to Britain by treaty, a defensive alliance might have reduced Ibn Saud's caution in his external affairs. Backed by a British treaty he might have been spurred to a more aggressive posture towards his Arab neighbours, confident that any reverses he might suffer would evoke British intervention.

At this point, something of a paradox emerges. Rather than seeing Anglo-Saudi relations as a persistent struggle, with Ibn Saud seeking to enlarge his Kingdom to the north, east and south, and Britain restraining him, the picture that emerges instead is of Britain and Saudi Arabia enjoying, at least until 1936, a broad harmony of interests. All that Britain wanted from Arabia was stability, which Ibn Saud had shown that he could provide. In consequence, British policy was based on maintaining a strong, well-governed, and wholly independent Saudi state, harbouring few grievances against Britain.

Ibn Saud may have been hostile to all western influences. He could not, however, out of political prudence, but co-operate with Britain. Ibn Saud seemed to have an intuitive grasp that politics was the art of the possible, that ends had to be related to means, and that the best had to be made of what could not be changed. As a result, he was careful to keep his expansionist designs within the framework of British hegemony in the Middle East – as long as that hegemony lasted. There was no suggestion of 'friendship' with Britain. She hemmed him within frontiers almost all of which were of her choosing. Yet Ibn Saud was vulnerable. But for Britain, there was the real risk that the Italians and the Hashemites would advance their interests in Arabia against his own. Britain at least was the devil he knew, and to a king who knew so little of the outside world, that was no small virtue.

Whatever Britain's other shortcomings, she had not impeded the flowering of his rule, from the time of his exile in Kuwait at the turn of the century, to his becoming King of Saudi Arabia. Within certain territorial limits he could do as he liked, though Ibn Saud may not have realised this. Although Ibn Saud's Kingdom was excluded from Britain's formal defensive umbrella over the Middle East, its shadow fell over Saudi Arabia. Such was Britain's concern that nothing threaten the stability of the Middle East, Ibn Saud would have benefited from that axiom no less than Abdullah or Feisal. Final confirmation of the ultimate sharing of interests was provided in the autumn of 1939, when Ibn Saud withdrew from negotiations with the German Government in the knowledge that Britain's preoccupation with Middle Eastern security and the safety of Islam's Holy Places was his surest guarantee of all. Ibn Saud had to acknowledge, however reluctantly, that British goodwill was a necessary condition of his ultimate survival.

Britain and Saudi Arabia, up to 1936, operated within an undeclared *modus vivendi*. A British collapse in the Middle East would have exposed Saudi Arabia to predations of every kind, European and Hashemite, the known and the unknown. At the same time, without Ibn Saud's potential enemies, he would have had less need of the British protective shield from which he benefited without the sacrifice of his independence. He could only play off the European powers when they were there to be played off. Yet, as a rule, the sources of conflict between Britain and Saudi Arabia were subsumed within their wider harmony of interests.

This *modus vivendi* was not a constant factor. The international positions of both countries stood in sharp relief between 1925 and 1939. Put simply, Britain was a declining power while Saudi Arabia was an emerging one. Britain was no longer the clear leader of the world's maritime nations, her share in world shipping falling from 41.6 per cent in 1914 to 26.7 per cent in 1937.[23] In 1925 Britain had been in unchallenged control throughout the Arab world – apart from the Levant coast which was under the French, and the Yemen. No European rivals threatened her position. By 1939 the picture was very different. Iraq and Egypt had won their independence and fostered elements hostile to Britain. The Yemen had signed treaties with Italy and the Soviet Union. Britain was resorting to bombs in the Hadramaut, and the Gulf sheikhdoms were becoming excited at the promise of popular reforms. The United States was in the first stages of building an oil empire in eastern Saudi Arabia. Britain had signed agreements with Italy in 1927 and 1938, the latter virtually conceding Roman rights in the Red Sea area on a par with Britain's, and German diplomacy appeared to be having disquieting success.

Most important of all, British policy in Palestine from 1936, together with these other factors, convinced Ibn Saud that Britain was no longer the guarantor of his survival, but the guarantor of his fate. Only with the outbreak of war did Ibn Saud revert to his earlier dependence on Britain. In 1915 the Arab world had looked to Britain as its redeemer against the Turks. By 1939 British prestige had sunk to the extent that several Arab leaders, not just Ibn Saud, had turned to Germany for their salvation. Yet these setbacks to Britain's composure did not undermine her strategic control over the Middle East. The Iraqi oilfields, the Transjordan-Gulf air route, the reserve base near the Suez Canal, and the sea route to the East were not seriously threatened.[24]

Saudi Arabia had gone from strength to strength politically, if not economically. Since 1925 Ibn Saud's religious significance had adapted from personifying the excesses of Wahhabism to symbolising the international Islamic community. By the late 1930s the *Ikhwan* had been disbanded, and Ibn Saud enjoyed treaties with his principal neighbours. Nonetheless, in terms of Ibn Saud's reducing his political isolation and ultimate dependence on Britain, there had been but slight progress. The joining of the Arab League and the United Nations, and the benefits of the economic miracle that would transform his Kingdom, all lay in the future. The 1930s witnessed no more than a tentative flirting with the League of Nations and gestures at pan-Arabism. Even in the face of Britain's gradual retrenchment and the emergence of political and economic rivals in the Middle East, by September 1939 Ibn Saud appreciated that his dependence on Britain was as strong as ever.

This book has identified certain specific areas for concentrated attention. The first of these was the problem of the mechanics of British policy formation. The unwieldy apparatus in existence when Ibn Saud was crowned King of the Hejaz, whereby Arabia was split into an ill-conceived jigsaw of Colonial Office, Foreign Office and India Office responsibility, had been replaced by the 1930s with a more rational arrangement, more in tune with the political realities in Arabia. The role of the Colonial Office over the whole Arab world dwindled, with the everyday management of relations with Saudi Arabia, by the 1930s, more or less in the hands of the Foreign Office. This development was enhanced by two factors: first, the increasing international interest in Saudi Arabia in the 1930s; and second, the reduction in Saudi-Hashemite tension from 1930 which had earlier thrust the Colonial Office into the forefront of Anglo-Saudi relations.

With a newly formed, expansionist-orientated state sharing frontiers with a host of territories linked to Britain, it was naturally in her interests to have Saudi Arabia's land frontiers defined and respected in the western tradition. Western concepts of geographical 'frontier' and 'nation-state' created major changes in Arab political behaviour.[25] Territorial problems constituted the bulk of Anglo-Saudi relations. Saudi Arabia has over 1,400 miles of land frontiers, excluding southern and eastern Arabia where the frontiers have never been settled.[26] There were disputes and/or hostilities in every corner of the Saudi state in the inter-war years. Two of those disputes, the *Ikhwan* rebellion and the Saudi-Yemeni war, were settled by force. Two others, Aqaba-Maan and the blue line, drifted unresolved beyond the Second World War.

It is significant that the British positions in both these latter disputes, occurring at the beginning and end of this study, were seen to have shaky legal foundations. This, as much as anything, contributed to the loosely formulated Monroe Doctrine over Arabia. Britain preferred to keep rival states and meddling institutions, like the League of Nations, away from Saudi Arabia, enabling Britain to exercise what influence she could with Ibn Saud, and maintain her position through bilateral diplomacy. The blue line was an anachronism, a blatant harkback to an imperial settlement in an imperial age. In very different circumstances Britain was prepared to turn that dispute over to international jurisdiction in the 1950s. There is every indication that she would have been most reluctant to do so in the 1930s. As it was, Aqaba-Maan and the blue line constituted two of the most protracted desiderata to disturb Anglo-Saudi relations.

It remained a bulwark of British policy to prevent the intrusion of a potentially hostile great power in the Middle East. With regard to Arabia, a tacit distinction was made between political and economic penetration. Italy's political ambitions were kept at bay by formalising Britain's own non-intervention in the peninsula through the Anglo-Italian Agreements of 1927 and 1938. American oil speculation in Saudi Arabia went unchallenged by the British Government, partly because oil questions were considered primarily the sphere of private enterprise, save in time of shortage or national emergency; partly because isolationist America did not present an image of imperial rivalry in the Middle East; partly because Britain retained overall control over most of the oil-producing territories in the Gulf region; and partly because, in the *laissez-faire* ethos of the time, economic stimulus and competition was welcomed rather than shunned. Italian oil interests, by contrast, because they represented a political, not just an economic, threat drew a less casual response from the British Government.

On a practical note, Britain doubted the oil-bearing capacity of the Arabian mainland, and fully expected the American company to realise its error and withdraw from Hasa sooner or later. Oil was felt to be important only by certain government departments at certain times. British governmental concern for Arab oil was restricted to British-dependent territories: Iraq and the Gulf. Saudi Arabia lay outside this interest. The economic, as opposed to the territorial, aspect of oil concessions in Saudi Arabia can be put down as a 'red herring' as regards British policy in the 1930s.

The concept of 'sphere of influence' has ambivalent application as regards British policy towards Saudi Arabia. The claim that Ibn Saud was amenable to British pressure can only be sustained with considerable qualification in the light of the evidence adduced herein. Imperialism, in its classic nineteenth-century sense, was almost extinct by the 1930s, as illustrated by the improvised imperial methods imposed on the mandated territories.[27] Nevertheless, with the disappearance of the old autocratic military empires during the First World War, Britain was that much more exposed to the taunts of imperialism.[28]

The lure of economic gain and exclusion of foreign commercial competition was largely absent from British policy. The easy success of American oil ventures testifies to that conclusion. Neither was Saudi Arabia suitable for investment, or exploited for cheap labour or as a potential market for British goods. In 1939 Saudi Arabia took only about £100,000 worth of British exports.[29] No subsidies were paid to Saudi Arabia in the years covered by this study.

Strategically, no British forces were ever stationed on Saudi soil, nor were there any serious attempts to win military or naval facilities there. No military or diplomatic careers were likely to be advanced by Arabian adventures. Politically, there was no reward in treating Ibn Saud as anything other than as a fully independent monarch. The British Minister held no advantages, either official or unofficial, over those of other powers represented in Jedda. The inaccessibility of the Arabian interior and the religious intensity of Wahhabism did not entice the kind of missionary activity which so often elsewhere paved the way for later governmental interest. There were no British 'settlers' to protect. There was no interest in cultural or ideological penetration of Saudi Arabia. Britain did not tacitly reserve for herself the right to oust the Saudi ruler, as she was later to do with certain Gulf rulers.

Any imputation that in the 1930s the King of Saudi Arabia was sub-servient to British pressure[30] can hardly be sustained. On most of the issues examined in these pages Britain treated Ibn Saud with full regard to inter-national protocol. His foreign relations were not constrained, nor was he restricted in the disposal of mineral resources. Britain was quite unable to put pressure of any kind on Ibn Saud, be it through economic dependence, military superiority or subversion, appropriate to her massive presence in the Middle East. The unique position of Mecca and Medina immuned Saudi Arabia from external attack by non-Moslem sources. On the contrary, such was Britain's determination to avoid accusations of retaining undue influence with Ibn Saud – largely to appease Islamic sentiment – and so jealously guarded was his independence, that Glubb and others accused the British Government of treating Ibn Saud as too 'independent' for Britain's own good. As a general rule, Ibn Saud rejected anything in the way of British attempts to compromise his independence. Accordingly, Britain did not risk such rejection. From the perspective of British policy-makers at the time, Saudi Arabia enjoyed complete independence.

This is not to say that traces of an imperialistic frame of mind cannot be detected in British policy. Britain was still an imperial power, and old habits could not lightly be dispensed with. Saudi Arabia affected imperial con-siderations in all directions. It is for this reason that overall policy control rested with the Colonial Office for several years after British recognition of Ibn Saud's independence. Saudi Arabian territory may not have constituted any of the lanes of Empire, but those lanes passed all around the Kingdom. Consequently, while not directly an imperial factor, Saudi Arabia was viewed in terms of imperial issues, and approached in terms of imperial defence. Every one of Saudi Arabia's land frontiers, with the exception of the Yemen, was laid down by Britain. If one takes Fieldhouse's definition that, in its most general sense, imperialism refers to the tendency of one state to control another, by whatever means and for whatever purposes,[31] then Britain's imposition of Saudi Arabia's frontiers, for the explicit purpose of strengthening her own interests in the mandates, the Gulf and southern

Arabia, offers the clearest example of her underlying dominance over Ibn Saud's external affairs.

In addition, there was the unsuccessful attempt by the Foreign Office to exert Capitulatory rights over Ibn Saud's Kingdom, and the India Office's seeking of religious privileges for pilgrims. Other examples, such as the supremacy of the British text of the Treaty of Jedda, the British right to manumit slaves who found their way into British diplomatic sanctuary, and Ibn Saud's formal obligation to maintain friendly relations with the Gulf sheikhdoms, did purport to put restraints on Ibn Saud's complete and absolute independence. Comparable privileges, where applicable, were denied to other states seeking treaties with Ibn Saud, and indeed, the restrictions on language and slavery were excluded from the revised Treaty of Jedda in 1936.

The manner of Britain's handling of the Aqaba-Mann and the blue line disputes is particularly illuminating. Britain's preference that they should not go before international arbitration, and her reluctance to encourage Saudi membership of the League of Nations, which could have provided machinery for such arbitration, reaffirms Britain's preference for excluding all possible intrusion into Anglo-Saudi relations. Britain, as had been her preference for centuries, did not wish to exploit Arabia, but only to discourage its links with the outside world. That, it was felt, was the simplest means of retaining the peninsula within Britain's strategic sphere of influence. As late as 1938, when Ibn Saud's international standing had never been greater, Britain's imperial fears led to an agreement with Italy, the tone of which, rather than its content, evoked images of imperial power-sharing and spheres of influence reminiscent of the 1913 Anglo-Turkish Convention. In both instances a world war rendered the documents anachronistic.

Attempted definitions of 'sphere of influence' are of little assistance in explaining Britain's relationship with Saudi Arabia.[32] The positive incentives involved in establishing a sphere of influence, whether to pave the way for military intervention (naval demonstrations or punitive expeditions); economic advantages (tariff agreements or control of banking facilities); or political influence (pre-eminence of diplomatic/consular staff or control of succession) are inappropriate to describe British policy towards Saudi Arabia. Britain's was a much looser, informal, 'negative' concept, aimed simply at discouraging third parties from gaining political influence with Ibn Saud.[33] Even this approach had to be modified to fit changing circumstances. The 1938 Agreement with Italy, for instance, was a defensive arrangement; Britain giving away more than she received in terms of asserting her special position in Arabia.

British policy towards Saudi Arabia did not affect Britain's fundamental standing in the world, either by involving questions of national security or national prestige, or by touching on values and symbols important to society as a whole.[34] Only occasionally did Anglo-Saudi relations involve the Prime Minister of the day and senior members of the Cabinet. There was little public awareness in Britain about Saudi Arabia up to 1939. Little has been said about the role of central government or senior statesmen in policy formation with regard to Ibn Saud. British policy was essentially a departmental affair, rarely warranting interference from the Cabinet or provoking Questions in the House of Commons. In that sense, individuals continued to be prominent in the manufacture of British policy. The tradition of Shakespear and Cox was continued by Clayton, Ryan, Bullard and Rendel.

On the other hand, while British policy rarely took on either urgency or drama, certain aspects of Saudi Arabia's geo-political position combined, at times, to elevate that state into greater prominence. Saudi Arabia's strategic position between the two routes to the East, was a constant factor in British policy. So was her religious significance for the entire Moslem world, and her geographical location at the nucleus of Britain's Middle Eastern concerns. Nor must it be overlooked that, in fact if not in name, Britain was at war with Nejd in 1928, inviting intervention at the highest levels of the British Government. Similarly, on political grounds, Ibn Saud's own personal standing, considerable as it was in 1925, flourished to the extent that by 1939 he constituted the unchallenged leading Arab and Moslem figure with all the influence over the rest of the Islamic world that his stature implied. Consequently, British policy in the Middle East, while not always centred on Saudi Arabia, always had to take account of that country and its King. As the 1920s and '30s progressed, Ibn Saud became increasingly linked with higher issues of international diplomacy – a process reinforced by a shrinking world due to improved technology and communications.

Inasmuch as Britain sought the stability of Arabia, and was happy to entrust the task of maintaining it to Ibn Saud, British policy was successful. Saudi Arabia was more stable in 1939 than she had ever been, a somewhat painful reminder to Britain, whose direct intervention in the affairs of other Arab states had produced varying degrees of political unrest or civil disorder. Ibn Saud was, moreover, after a two–three year period of reorientation in his foreign policy, still persuaded that his destiny stood or fell with that of Britain.

In conclusion, it is possible to endorse the verdict of the Royal Institute of International Affairs given in 1939: 'Because of its geographical position, its leadership of the Arab world, and its military strength, friendship with Saudi Arabia is a *vital* British interest'.[35] (author's italics)

REFERENCES FOR CHAPTER TWELVE

1. Kedourie, *England* ..., p. 9.
2. Rather than confuse the reader by switching references between Hejaz-Nejd and Saudi Arabia, the name Saudi Arabia will be used throughout to refer to Ibn Saud's Kingdom between 1925 and 1939.
3. Vital has suggested that British foreign policy follows: 'The adoption of the line of least intellectual resistance. ... The basis of the defensive posture is keeping open as many options as possible. ... Such a posture naturally militates against clarity of position and commitment, and encourages attempts to conciliate, to play for safety, and to prefer the familiar and the controllable. ... It [British foreign policy] is geared, essentially, to the handling of problems as they arise, rather than to the definition of goals and objectives in terms of which such problems as arise are to be dealt with. In this sense it may be regarded as passive in total approach, and predicated, implicity at any rate, on a preference for the static, the secure, and the comfortable' (David Vital, *The Making of British Foreign Policy*, p. 109-10).
4. George Kirk, *The Middle East in the War: Survey of International Affairs – Vol II, 1939-1945*, p. 354. This constituted a drop of over 50% in two years. Saudi exports consisted, in the main, of hides, skins and pearls. Her chief imports at this time were foods and textiles (US memorandum, Dept. of State – Division of Near Eastern Affairs, 27 January 1931, Rashid, Vol III, pp. 110-11).
5. Bertram Thomas, *The Arabs*, pp. 238, 250.
6. Bullard to Halifax, 2 December 1939, FO E/8086/253/25: 371/23269.
7. Glubb to Officer Commander Arab Legion, in CO to FO, 15 December, 1931, CO/89421/31: 831/13.
8. See Helms, p. 25.
9. 'Appeasement' has become one of those terms which, due to overuse, has attracted an abundance of literature. Too often it has degenerated into an expression of political abuse. Here, following Medlicott's example, it is used simply as it was meant at the time – as the search for peace (Medlicott, p. xix).
10. Marlowe, *Arab Nationalism* ..., pp. 25-6.
11. ibid.
12. Glubb to Officer Commanding Arab Legion, op. cit.
13. ibid.
14. Ryan to Rendel, 13 April 1931, FO E/2237/2237/25: 371/15299.
15. Despite the merger of the Foreign Office and the Diplomatic Service in 1919, hoping to provide men in London with first-hand experience abroad, there was, during the inter-war years, an increase in departmental staff who never served abroad. Rendel was the first Foreign Office official to visit Saudi Arabia, in 1937. It is also natural for political servants at home to seek to impose pre-conceived notions on foreign affairs upon agents in the field, and to place the greatest confidence in those whose reports confirmed their own views (G. A. Craig, 'The Professional Diplomat ...', in Craig and Gilbert, p. 150).
16. J. G. Lorimer, *Gazetteer of the Persian Gulf, Oman and Central Arabia*, 6 vols. It was republished in 1970.
17. Klieman, p. 252.
18. Kiernan, frontispiece.
19. Ibn Saud to Sheikh of Kuwait, 1 June 1933, in FO E/3126/3126/25: 371/17941.
20. See Jordan to Eden, Annual Report for 1943, FO E/1293/1293/25: 371/40283; Grafftey-Smith to Bevin, Annual Report for 1945, FO E/2249/2249/25: 371/52823.
21. Rendel memorandum, 23 April 1937, FO E/2312/2312/65: 371/20786.
22. Ryan to Rendel, 24 September 1930, FO E/5157/89/91: 371/14459.
23. RIIA, *Political and Strategic Interests* ..., p. 124. Britian had surrendered her naval paramountcy in 1922. The Washington Naval Agreements even specified what type of ships each fleet could possess (Morris, *Farewell the Trumpets*, p. 217.)

24. The Middle East, from 1939, played the role that imperial planners had envisaged. It formed an effective barrier, preventing German forces from linking up with the Japanese (Beloff, p. 255).
25. See Helms, p. 272.
26. There are reports that the eastern frontier question was disposed of in 1977. The lengths of Saudi Arabia's land frontiers are as follows: Iraq – 444 miles; Palestine and Transjordan – 460 miles; Kuwait – 165 miles; the Neutral Zones – 124 miles; the Yemen – 233 miles (S. W. Boggs, *International Boundaries: A Study of Boundary Function and Politics*, pp. 210-12).
27. There were only sporadic attempts at overseas territorial expansion in the classic mould after 1918, such as the Italian invasion of Abyssinia and the Japanese advance into Manchuria.
28. See Beloff, p. 347.
29. Kirk, op. cit., p. 354.
30. See, for example, Fisher, p. 441.
31. D. K. Fieldhouse, *Colonialism 1870-1945*, p. 1.
32. What exactly constitutes a 'sphere of influence' is difficult to establish. It has been proposed that the international value of the concept lies in its resistance to firm definition (G. W. Rutherford, 'Spheres of Influence', *American Journal of International Law*, 20 (1926), p. 300). See also M. F. Lindley, *The Acquisition and Government of Backward Territory in International Law*, p. 207.
    A sphere of influence has been described as the reserving of a territory from the political interference of another state (see Prescott, pp. 47-8; T. H. Holdich, *Political Frontiers and Boundary Making*, p. 96). For example, this happened when Britain staked her pre-eminent position in southern and eastern Arabia against the Turks in the Anglo-Turkish Convention of 1913. Furthermore, a European power might have no responsibilities, but still exercise a preferential or exclusive right to develop an area economically or control it politically (see Walter C. Langsam, *In Quest of Empire*, p. 56). Porter suggests that spheres of influence were areas within which it was agreed that the respective tenants could turn into colonies if they wanted, with other powers not intervening. Similarly, spheres of influence were often designed to forestall quarrels over territory that imperial powers did not feel was worth quarrelling over (Bernard Porter, *The Lion's Share*, pp. 108, 114).
33. For a discussion on 'positive' and 'negative' features of spheres of influence, see Rutherford, pp. 300ff.
34. The analysis is Wallace's, see Wallace, pp. 12-13.
35. RIIA, *Political and Strategic Interests* ..., p. 181.

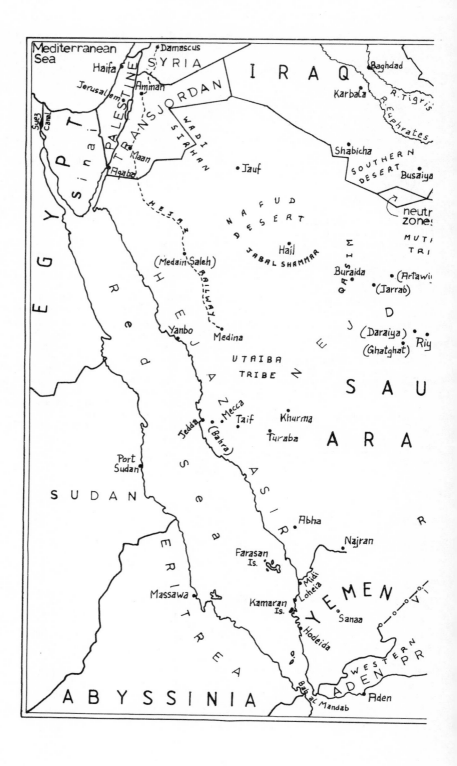

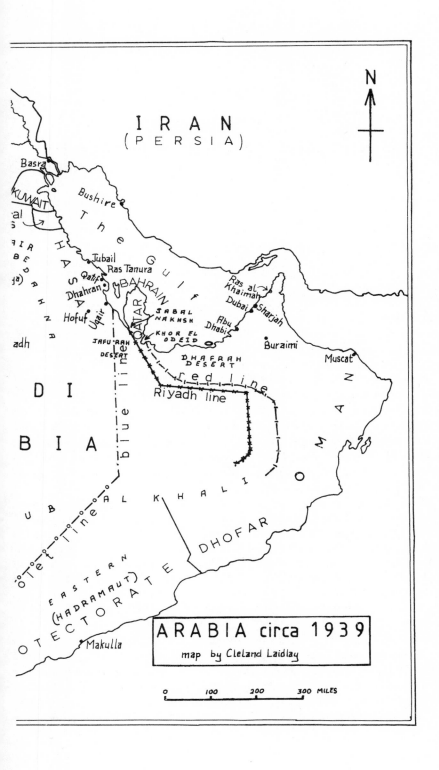

ARABIA circa 1939

map by Cleland Laidlay

British Policy Towards Saudi Arabia from 1939

Britain and Saudi Arabia 1939-1945

It was during the course of the Second World War that Saudi Arabia was finally wrested out of the British sphere of influence and into that of the United States. Both Britain and America were drawn to Arabia, but for different purposes. Britain, as in 1914, had her priorities dictated by the short-term need to win the war. The goodwill of the entire Moslem world, which had induced the commitment to Husein from 1915, could best be achieved by gaining the support of the ruler of Mecca – Ibn Saud.

The Second World War temporarily put an end to American oil operations in Hasa, as world oil markets were disrupted and US tankers could no longer be spared for the hazardous journey to the Gulf.[1] Isolated Italian bombing of Bahrain and the Dhahran oilfields in Hasa, in December 1940, demonstrated the vulnerability of the Gulf to enemy attacks.[2] On the other side of the Kingdom the Hejaz had seen a mild financial panic upon the outbreak of war,[3] and the general international situation caused the collapse of the Pilgrimage in the spring of 1941.[4]

Consequently, in order to combat the pro-Axis sympathies of other Moslem states, Britain sought to generate goodwill by keeping the Moslem Holy Land from starvation and bankruptcy. Supplies of food arrived from Egypt and India.[5] More significantly, Britain re-introduced her World War One policy of subsidies. In 1940 Saudi Arabia received a British subsidy of £100,000. From March 1941, when the United States Lend-Lease Act was passed, this amount was raised substantially. Almost £1 million was donated by Britain to Saudi Arabia in 1941, and by 1942 the figure was around £3 million.[6]

The war, moreover, provided the spur by which Britain generated political proposals aimed at the Arab world, much as had happened from 1915. Once again Britain was obliged to shore up the Arabs against defection to another power, and once again ideas aimed at furthering the Arabs' national identity were put forward. Rather than be seen to be indifferent to, or even hindering, Arab aspirations for some kind of federation, Anthony Eden, the

Foreign Secretary, announced, in May 1941, his active encouragement of Arab unity.[7] If nothing else, the creation of a League of Arab states would distract attention from Palestine and from the rivalry with France in the Levant. For the first time, a Ministry of State for the Middle East, under Oliver Lyttleton, was established, and a comprehensive Middle Eastern Supply Centre set up to treat the area as a single political and economic unit.[8] Britain also stabilised the Treaty of Jedda through a further exchange of notes with Saudi Arabia in October 1943 which automatically prolonged the treaty.

Yet, even with a new British policy of seeking to actively assist Arab unity, there was some ambivalence as to whether Britain saw Saudi Arabia as part of that unity. While it was natural for Britain to want an Arab federation to be as inclusive as possible, she may have preferred such a concept to include only those states handgroomed by Britain and tied to her by treaties of alliance, not neutral countries like Saudi Arabia.[9] Despite his treaties with Iraq and Egypt, Ibn Saud continued to hold those states in deep suspicion. There could have been a conflict of interest within an Arab federation when some Arab states were British allies and others were not. Nor was it clear whether Ibn Saud would want to become part of an Arab federation at British connivance or instigation. He may have feared a British plot to return to the earlier policy of Hashemite domination of the Arab world, and anticipated resuscitation of Egypt's historic claims to the Caliphate.

In the event, Ibn Saud was both cautious and suspicious of the planned Arab League, reluctant to entertain any notions of relinquishing total sovereignty.[10] The League, which Saudi Arabia joined as a founder member in March 1945, served merely, at least initially, to institutionalise Arab rivalry rather than dissipate it.[11] Only with regard to hostility to British policy in Palestine could the members of the Arab League agree among themselves.

Following the outbreak of war, Ibn Saud accompanied his declared neutrality with informal expressions of commitment to the allies. The presence of de Gaury, as a representative of the Jedda Legation stationed in Riyadh, was designed as a temporary measure, but when the war ceased to be the short, sharp conflict it was expected to be, the facility for British representation was extended. Grobba, the German Minister in Baghdad, was duly handed his passport by the Iraq Government, but was refused permission by Ibn Saud to set up residence in Jedda.[12] Shortly after the Italian entry into the war, the British Minister successfully requested that Ibn Saud ask Rome to withdraw its Legation, which it did in February 1942, whereupon neither Axis power was represented in Saudi Arabia.[13]

In fact, there were notable changes in Jedda's diplomatic personnel during the course of the Second World War. Britain sent a series of Ministers, each of whom was familiar with Arabia from earlier days, following in the Bullard tradition. Throughout the 1930s Saudi Arabia had only seen two British Ministers, Ryan and Bullard. The latter was succeeded by Hugh

Stonehewer-Bird, British Agent and Consul in Jedda in the late 1920s. His successor, from 1942 until January 1945, was Stanley Jordan, Acting British Agent and Consul in Jedda at the time of Ibn Saud's final conquest of the Hejaz. Jordan was, in turn, replaced by Laurence Grafftey-Smith, whose previous experience of Jedda had been during the last years of Husein's reign. On Saudi Arabia's part, Fuad Bey Hamza, the Lebanese Druze, was posted, appropriately, as the first Saudi Minister to France, in November 1939.

In view of Ibn Saud's ability of being all things to all men, and his proven agility in playing off Britain, Italy and Germany in the late 1930s, the historian is wise to treat with some caution his repeated protestations of loyalty to the allies during the war. In the Hejaz there was some enthusiasm at Britain's and France's early reversals, doubtless because of their policies in Palestine and Syria. If Ibn Saud did want an allied victory, then it would have had more to do with questions of hard finance than with any less tangible sentiments. His oil concessions were, after all, tied up in western hands, and the sooner an allied victory came, the sooner his revenues would start to flow again.

Moreover, by 1943, after the German setbacks at Stalingrad and Alamein, and the entry of the United States into the war, Ibn Saud had every reason to be confident of eventual victory. Even while the situation in Egypt was still critical Ibn Saud allowed Middle East Command to take over, without payment, 75 cars and lorries for which he had paid. This act prompted the comment from Jedda that 'Britain, in all her long history, can seldom have had such loyal support from a foreign power, either in adversity or success'.[14]

There is another side to Ibn Saud's supposed wartime confidence in Britain. After Eden's endorsement of an Arab federation, Ibn Saud is reported to have said, 'The English keep enjoining the Arabs to be united. I wonder what is behind all this'.[15] De Gaury reported that behind Ibn Saud's refusal to entertain German representation on Saudi soil from 1940 lay the less than friendly rider that Ibn Saud would permit no German Legation to be opened in Jedda until and unless the Germans occupied Suez, whereupon British supplies to Saudi Arabia would be cut off.[16] The suggestion is that Ibn Saud was watching the way the political and military wind was blowing, and that talk of his 'loyalty' to Britain was no less fanciful after 1939 than before.[17]

The United States, unlike Britain, became involved in Saudi Arabia less out of the short-term aims of winning the war, than with long-term aims with regard to the future. The passing of the Lend-Lease Act provided the spur to American involvement. At first, this involvement was confined to CASOC, who urged that the facility be extended to Saudi Arabia[18], even though that state at the time housed no diplomatic or consular representative of the United States. Furthermore, Saudi Arabia was not an ally, and did not meet the Act's requirements for democratic government. Roosevelt, for the time being, was content to allow British influence to predominate in Saudi

Arabia, and did little to meet CASOC's later allegations that Britain was supplying Saudi Arabia with American Lend-Lease and taking the credit for doing so.[19]

It was not until February 1943, as the importance of post-war Saudi oil began to be realised, with the fear that Britain was gradually excluding American influence from Saudi Arabia, that Roosevelt decreed Saudi Arabia to be eligible for Lend-Lease.[20] It is that year, not 1933 when SOCAL won the Hasa concession, which marks the beginning of American political interest in Saudi Arabia, and the substitution of her predominance in Saudi affairs at the expense of that of Britain. A US Legation had been opened in 1942, and before the end of the war a US Consulate had even been estabished in Dhahran to cater for the interests of the oil-company workers.

Between 1943 and 1945 Anglo-American relations were strained by the struggle for supremacy in Saudi Arabia and for her oil reserves, culminating in January 1945 with the State Department successfully demanding the removal of the then British Minister, Jordan, for supposedly unfairly hindering American interests in Saudi Arabia.[21] It was a struggle that Britain, dependent on American military support in Europe during the war and after, was in no position to win. In 1944 an ostensible understanding was reached in London and Washington that, while British political interests predominated in Saudi Arabia, for America economic interests were paramount. It was agreed that Britain should head a future military mission to Saudi Arabia and the United States should head a future financial mission.[22] From 1944 the subsidy to Saudi Arabia would be a joint one, shared equally between Britain and the United States.[23]

On a personal level, too, American diplomacy towards Saudi Arabia intensified. The Emirs Faisal and Khalid went to Washington in September 1943, where they met Roosevelt and Cordell Hull before going on to London.[24] Then, in February 1945, Ibn Saud himself met Roosevelt and Churchill, separately, in Cairo, upon their return from the Yalta Conference.[25] The following month Ibn Saud agreed to the formality of declaring war on Germany and Japan, with the proviso that the Holy Cities, Mecca and Medina, be kept neutral, thereby paving the way for Saudi Arabia to be admitted as a founder member of the United Nations.[26] By joining the Arab League and the United Nations in the space of a few weeks, early in 1945, Ibn Saud brought about a dramatic end to his country's previous isolation. As had happened during the First World War, Ibn Saud kept his dominions out of the fighting altogether.

Despite Ibn Saud's resentment at American policy over Palestine, by the end of the war the United States had succeeded in completely ousting Britain from her previous pre-eminence in the affairs of Saudi Arabia. ARAMCO, as the American oil company became known in 1944, recommenced its operations with renewed vigour from that year, when Italy was out of the war and Germany in retreat. In 1946 a pipeline was constructed from Hasa to the Mediterranean. Britain's supply programme to Saudi

Arabia in 1945 amounted to only £1¼ million, half of her 1944 contribution to the Anglo-American joint subsidy. In 1946 Britain was obliged to withdraw her contribution entirely. The British Government was well aware that these measures would have been received badly in Saudi Arabia, and that its reduced contribution would have advertised an apparent difference of opinion with the United States over the extent of Saudi needs.[27] The timing of the reduction was also awkward, for it coincided with the end of the war in Europe, thereby creating the inevitable impression that Britain's earlier assistance had been measured by British, not Saudi, needs. Nonetheless, the total non-recoverable British financial assistance to Saudi Arabia during the war amounted to several times that of the United States.[28] The morale of the British Legation in Jedda at this time had, perhaps, never been lower. Grafftey-Smith reported that:

> To one who ... last knew this territory in the days of Husein, the recent US invasion of the Arabian political and economic scene is a remarkable and somewhat disturbing phenomenon. It may be stimulating that British initiative and enterprise should be vigorously challenged in the heart of Islam where British influence has been for so long predominant, but it is painful, to say the least, that this challenge should, for reasons both of higher policy and temporal material necessity, provoke no active response either from HMG or British industry and commerce. The role of HM Minister in a territory which appears to have been abandoned to US economic penetration is an ungrateful one.[29]

Britain and Saudi Arabia since 1945

The coming of the post-war era saw Britain's position in the Middle East complicated by a number of factors. The disappearance of Italy and Germany from the region, the Soviet withdrawal from northern Iran, France's collapse, and the seeming reluctance of the United States to take on any further formal responsibilities in an area on the opposite side of the globe, left the whole Middle East, for outward appearances, as much within Britain's grasp as when she entered the war. The sole exception was Saudi Arabia, where American oil interests had pushed Britain's earlier influence aside. But, as Saudi Arabia had never enjoyed an exclusively intimate relationship with Britain, as in the case of, say, Egypt or Iraq, the loss was not of great strategic significance. Saudi Arabia was still under allied, if not British influence. Britain's own weakness gave her continued predominance elsewhere in the region a somewhat hollow glow. Moreover, the withdrawal from India in 1947 meant that the *raison d'être* behind the whole British apparatus for defending the strategic routes through the Middle East was withdrawn at the same time.

In the meantime, Saudi Arabia's relations with the West, both with Britain and the United States, were strained by events in Palestine. The arrival of a British Labour Government with expressed sympathies for

Zionism (having, when in Opposition, opposed the 1939 White Paper) did not ease Ibn Saud's fear for the future of the mandate.[30] As for the United States, her success in Saudi Arabia was achieved in the face of her support of Zionist aims in Palestine. Paradoxically, the American Government was simultaneously supporting the aspirations of a Jewish state, while pouring in funds to an Arab king pledged to give moral and material help to the Palestinian Arabs. At Cairo, Roosevelt had undertaken to consult Ibn Saud before taking any initiatives on Palestine, though the promise did not survive the President's death two months later. When the state of Israel came into existence in 1948, Saudi Arabia took no part in the fighting,[31] nor was there any attempt to use her oil to influence the outcome. Indeed, there is every reason to suppose that, despite Saudi Arabia's adherence to the Arab League, she was more concerned with her oil revenues and the fear of the Hashemites – now that Abdullah was King of an enlarged Jordan – than with the future of Palestine.[32]

The arrival of the 1950s brought even greater tension to the Arab world. International politics in general had to be seen in the context of the onset of the Cold War. In addition, the three contenders for the leadership of the Arabs – Egypt, Saudi Arabia and the Hashemites – each witnessed devastating changes. In 1951 King Abdullah was assassinated. The following year saw the Egyptian revolution, the overthrow of King Farouk, and the eventual rise to power of Nasser. Saudi Arabia, already transformed by her new-found oil wealth, suffered the further traumas that followed the death of her founder, Ibn Saud, in November 1953. He was succeeded by his eldest son Saud, the official heir apparent for twenty years. A newly-formed Saudi Council of Ministers attempted to delegate responsibility away from the throne. The Emir Faisal was given the posts of both Prime Minister and Foreign Minister, though in effect the King's powers remained undiluted.

The western response in the Middle East to the Cold War was to inspire blocks of states (for example, in the 'northern tier' and Baghdad Pact concepts) to form a barrier against the underbelly of the Soviet Union. These pacts would, as a side-effect, partially offset the strength of Nasser's virulently anti-western type of pan-Arabism. These schemes, by seeking to strengthen the northern, Hashemite states, gave common cause to an unlikely Saudi-Egyptian rapprochement as a prop to Arab solidarity free from dependence on the West. This process reached a peak in the mid-1950s. In October 1953 a strike of Saudi employees hit ARAMCO operations. Saudi Arabia embarked upon a whole series of treaties with other Arab states aimed at enhancing Arab solidarity against the dual threat of the West and the Hashemites. Even Philby fell foul of the new Saudi King, and was obliged to leave the country for a period.

Such was the backdrop to the Buraimi crisis. The dispute over Saudi Arabia's south-eastern frontiers, which had first emerged in the 1930s, resurfaced with far greater acrimony from 1949. In that year ARAMCO staff, along with Saudi guards, began to survey areas beyond the modified

Riyadh line, which had been laid down by Britain in 1937 as marking her view of Saudi Arabia's eastern frontier.[33] After complaints from the Sheikh of Abu Dhabi about encroachment within his territory, Saudi Arabia put forward a territorial claim which extended right up to the Buraimi oasis on the Abu Dhabi-Muscat frontier.[34] Her previous formal claim, the 1935 red line, had extended nowhere near Buraimi.

Perhaps this claim was prompted by developments in Palestine and Transjordan. A more likely explanation lay with the perceived effects of Britain having withdrawn from India in 1947. The Gulf sheikhdoms, it was thought, no longer held the same significance in British strategic policy. Indeed, relations with those sheikhdoms were eventually transferred to the Foreign Office.[35] But, if Britain's interest in Arabia had less of a strategic justification from 1947, then there arose an equally powerful replacement – oil. The end of the Empire in India coincided with the emergence of the modern oil era. Britain substituted one rationale for her presence in the Middle East for another. As a consequence, British interest in Arabia switched from the largely maritime to the territorial. Saudi Arabia, too, found an additional, material incentive for her traditional territorial expansion. Given the added ingredients of Britain's continuing defence commitments to the Gulf sheikhdoms, together with a vast, virtually uninhabited, possibly oil-producing land-mass in south-eastern Arabia, then the situation was ripe for a protracted and bitter quarrel. The problem was made worse by questions of prestige; Britain digging in to try to halt a continuing series of reversals in the Middle East.

During 1947-48 Petroleum Concessions Ltd had been exploring for oil deposits around Buraimi.[36] None had been found, but Buraimi had begun to take on symbolic significance. Although of no great consequence in itself, whoever controlled the Buraimi oasis would control much of the vast hinterland of south-east Arabia. The dispute continued until the mid-1950s, witnessing a series of short-lived agreements interspersed with physical attempts to seize the oasis both by Saudi forces and British-officered Levies from Trucial Oman. At the height of the dispute Ibn Saud died, a disorientated and confused old man, distressed by the material changes that had swept his Kingdom in his last years. It is a matter of some debate whether Ibn Saud in his prime would have led his country into such a quarrel with Britain. The British press did not dwell on such matters, as the eulogies that followed his death testified.[37]

Arbitration in 1955, for which the British and Saudi Memorials were prepared in evidence, was no more successful than previous attempts to end the dispute. Sir Reader Bullard, head of the British delegation, accused his opposite number, Sheikh Yusuf Yasin, of manipulation of witnesses, and resigned. Shortly thereafter, the Belgian President and the Cuban member of the tribunal also resigned, whereupon the tribunal disintegrated.[38] This was followed by a further Saudi military pact with Egypt, and Britain sending in Trucial Oman Levies to occupy the Buraimi oasis. Unlike the reaction to the Suez invasion a year later, the occupation of Buraimi met with the full support in Parliament of the Labour Opposition.[39] The whole dispute, as a side-effect, did little for Anglo-American relations. United States lawyers, under obvious pressure from American oil interests, presented the Saudi case for the tribunal, and Washington expressed fears that British activities in Saudi Arabia were prejudicial to the standing of the western world in the Middle East and the need to combat Nasserism.[40]

Saudi Arabia threatened to break off diplomatic relations with Britain and turn for support to the Soviet Union who had, in October 1955, signed a further treaty with the Yemen. Instead, Saudi Arabia submitted the whole dispute to the United Nations. The nadir of Anglo-Saudi relations was reached in the autumn of 1956. The British invasion of Suez, coming on top of the Baghdad Pact and the Buraimi crisis, provided the opportunity for Saudi Arabia to demonstrate her solidarity with Egypt and her opposition to Britain. Diplomatic relations with Britain were severed.

1956 proved to be, in its way, another watershed for both Britain and Saudi Arabia – as well as for American policy in the Middle East. For Britain, the fiasco of Suez marked the beginning of the end for her position in the Middle East. If she could no longer keep the Canal open, either by diplomacy or force, how could she cope with the Arab world beyond? Following the Iraqi coup in 1958, which brought about the end of the Hashemite dynasty in that country, Britain embarked upon a series of withdrawals from the Middle East. She granted Kuwait her independence in 1961, left Aden in 1968, and finally withdrew from the Trucial states, where her Arab involvement had first begun, in 1971.

For Saudi Arabia the infatuation with Egypt passed soon after the Suez war. The closure of the Canal harmed Saudi oil interests, and Nasser's brand of nationalism began to suggest to Saudi Arabia that he was seeking personal domination of the Arab world. By 1957 the relative conservatism of the Hashemite Kingdoms offered greater attractions to Saudi Arabia,[41] and the composition of the 'Arab triangle' took on yet another complexion. In that same year, the United States stepped in to the political responsibilities being abdicated by Britain. The Eisenhower Doctrine pledged American support for Middle Eastern states to combat communism. King Saud was invited to Washington, and a period of closer Saudi relations with the United States ensued.[42]

The 1950s was an era of wanton profligacy in Saudi Arabia. Mismanagement of oil revenues, together with the political turbulence shaking the Middle East, finally brought about King Saud's formal delegation of responsibilities to Faisal in 1958, a process culminating after a brief return to the royal prerogative with Saud's abdication in 1964, and Faisal being crowned King. By that time Saudi Arabia had passed through a further crisis. A revolt in the Yemen in 1962, supported by Nasser, saw Saudi Arabia striving once more for stability in the Arabian peninsula. Diplomatic relations with Britain were restored, and the Buraimi dispute handed over to the Secretary General of the United Nations acting in a personal capacity.[43] By the mid-1960s, Saudi Arabia's fear of Egypt, and the threat of untoward political developments along the southern and eastern littorals of Arabia, coupled with Britain's inevitable withdrawal from the Gulf, brought about what one scholar described as a virtual Anglo-Saudi alliance.[44]

REFERENCES FOR EPILOGUE

1. Howarth, p. 184.
2. Walt, pp. 144-5.
3. Stonehewer-Bird to Halifax, No 62, Political Review for 1939, FO E/2740/1194/25: 371/24589.
4. Stonehewer-Bird to FO, Annual Report for 1941, 30 June 1942, FO E/4326/4326/25: 371/31460.
5. Howarth, p. 186.
6. Marlowe, *The Persian Gulf* ..., p. 132.
7. Elmandjra, p. 149.
8. ibid.
9. ibid., pp 157-62.
10. S.G. Zamzami, 'The Origins and Evolution of the Arab League in its Struggle for Arab Unity and Independence' (unpublished M. Phil), p. 53.
11. Abbas Kelidar, 'The Arabian Peninsula in Arab and Power Politics', in Hopwood (Ed.), p. 146.
12. Saudi Arabia did not actually break off diplomatic relations with Germany.
13. Wakely (Jedda) to FO, Annual Report for 1942, 27 January 1943, FO E/1102/1102/25: 371/35155.
14. ibid.
15. Zamzami, p. 59.
16. De Gaury, *Faisal* ..., p. 65.
17. This is an area of significant research for future historians. The British Government have restricted many of the documents relating to Saudi Arabia in the Second World War from being released under the 30-year rule.
18. Walt, pp. 157-65.
19. ibid., pp. 173, 207, 209.
20. ibid., p. 218.
21. Kirk, p. 363.
22. ibid., p. 362.
23. Jordan to Eden, Annual Report for 1944, 27 January 1945, FO E/952/952/25: 371/45546.
24. De Gaury, pp. 68-9.
25. Philby, *Arabian Jubilee*, p. 244.
26. Annual Report 1945.
27. ibid.
28. Walt, p. 229.
29. Annual Report 1945.
30. ibid.
31. Philby, *Forty Years* ..., p. 50.
32. Lipsky, p. 144.
33. Hawley, p. 188. Small concessions had been made on top of the Riyadh line.
34. Kelly, *Eastern Arabian Frontiers*, p. 140.

35. Hawley, p. 168. There was no longer a Government of India or India Office, with long-standing familiarity with the Gulf, to protect the interests of the sheikhdoms.
36. Kelly, op. cit., p. 139.
37. See, for example, *The Times*, 10 November 1953.
38. Hawley, p. 190; Kelly, op. cit., p. 203.
39. See *New York Herald Tribune*, 27 October 1953.
40. Kelly, op. cit., p. 266.
41. Lipsky, p. 142.
42. Charles Cremeans, *The Arabs and the World: Nasser's Arab Nationalist Policy*, p. 109.
43. Kelly, op. cit., p. 268.
44. Peter Mangold, 'The Role of Force in British Policy Towards the Middle East 1957-1966', (unpublished Ph. D.), pp. 72, 166, 175.

Sources and Bibliography

PRIMARY SOURCES

PUBLIC RECORDS OFFICE

Foreign Office

Political (Eastern)	Series 371
	/65 General
	/91 Arabia
	/31 Palestine
	/25 Hejaz-Nejd (1931-33)
	/25 Saudi Arabia (from 1934)
Confidential Prints	Series 406 Eastern Affairs
Embassy and Consular Archives	Series 905 1-70
	Saudi Arabia (from 1934)
Jedda Agency Papers	Series 686 1914-25

Colonial Office

Aden	Series 725
Arabia	Series 727 until 1926
Iraq	Series 730
Middle Eastern	Series 732
Palestine	Series 733
Transjordan	Series 831

Cabinet

CID minutes and meetings	CAB 2	1-9
CID Colonial and Overseas Defence Committee remarks ...		
	CAB 9	
		/20 1929-33
		/21 1933-39
CID Sub-Committees	CAB 16	
		/93 Persian Gulf meetings
		/94 Memoranda
		/95 Political Control: Persian Gulf Sub-Committee.
Cabinet Minutes	CAB 23	

Cabinet Memoranda CAB 24

/174
/193
/195
/196

CID Middle East Questions CAB 51

/1 Ministerial Sub-
Committee
/2-11 Official Sub-Committee

INDIA OFFICE LIBRARY

L/P&S Political and Secret Dept. Records
/10 Subject Files 1902-31
/12 External Collections 1931-49
/18B Memoranda (Arabia and Persian Gulf)
/20 Library

PRIVATE PAPERS COLLECTION, MIDDLE EAST CENTRE, ST. ANTONY'S COLLEGE, OXFORD

Sir Reader Bullard (letters to Ryan, in Ryan's private papers)

Sir Gilbert Clayton (Diary of Mission to Ibn Saud 1925-26; Proposed Green Book on Iraq-Nejd Frontier Negotiations 1928)

H.R.P. Dickson

H. St. J.B. Philby

Sir George Rendel

Sir Andrew Ryan

PRIVATE PAPERS COLLECTION, SUDAN ARCHIVE, UNIVERSITY OF DURHAM

Sir Gilbert Clayton

GOVERNMENT AND OFFICIAL PUBLICATIONS

Admiralty: Naval Intelligence Division, *Iraq and the Persian Gulf,*
Geographical Handbook Series,
1944, Oxford

Admiralty: Naval Intelligence Division, *Western Arabia and the Red Sea,*
Geographical Handbook Series,
1946, Oxford

Documents on British Foreign Policy

Documents on German Foreign Policy

Foreign Relations of the United States

GB Foreign Office, Central Office of Information, *UK Memorial: Arbitration on Buraimi and the Abu Dhabi–Saudi Arabia Frontier,* 1955, HMSO

SECONDARY SOURCES

THESES

Adelson, R.D., 'Mark Sykes and the Formation of British Policy Towards the Middle East, 1915-1919,' B. Litt., Oxford, 1970

Algosaibi, G.A., 'The 1962 Revolution in Yemen and its Impact on the Foreign Policies of the U.A.R. and Saudi Arabia', Ph.D., U.C.L., 1971

Badrud-Din, A.A., 'The Arab League in Palestine, 1944-1949', B. Litt., Oxford, 1960

Davis, C., 'British Oil Policy in the Middle East, 1919-1932', Ph.D., Edinburgh, 1975

Elmandjra, M.S., 'The League of Arab States, 1945-1955', Ph.D., L.S.E., 1958

Enayet, H., 'The Impact of the West on Arab Nationalism, 1952-1958', Ph.D., L.S.E., 1962

Foley, Elizabeth, 'Britain and the Persian Gulf, 1947-1972', M.Sc.Econ., U.C.W., Aberystwyth, 1973

Gomma, A.M.H., 'The Foundation of the League of Arab States: British Wartime Diplomacy and Inter-Arab Politics, 1941-1945', D.Phil., Oxford, 1973

Al Jazairi, M., 'Saudi Arabia: A Diplomatic History, 1924-1964', Ph.D., Utah, 1970

Kent, M.R., 'British Government Interest in Middle Eastern Oil Concessions, 1900-1925', Ph.D., L.S.E., 1969

Al Khatrash, F.A., 'British Political Relations with Kuwait, 1890-1921', M.A., Durham, 1971

Leatherdale, C.A., 'The British Press and the Suez Crisis 1956', M.Sc.Econ., U.C.W., Aberystwyth, 1976

Leatherdale, C.A., 'British Policy Towards Saudi Arabia 1925-1939', Ph.D., Aberdeen, 1981

Mangold, P., 'The Role of Force in British Policy Towards the Middle East, 1957-1966', Ph.D., L.S.E., 1973

Morsy-Abdullah, M., 'Britain and the Trucial States, 1892-1939', Ph.D., Cambridge, 1975

Niama, Khadim, 'The Arab States in the United Nations, 1945-1955', M.A., U.C.W., Aberystwyth, 1966

Niama, Khadim, 'Anglo-Iraqi Relations During the Mandate', Ph.D., U.C.W., Aberystwyth, 1974

Peck, Malcolm, 'American Foreign Policy towards Saudi Arabia', Ph.D., Tufts, 1970

Al Shibly, G.T.A., 'Iraqi-British Relations with Special Reference to Inter-Arab Politics, 1948-1958', M. Litt., Aberdeen, 1973

Silverfarb, Daniel, 'British Relations with Ibn Saud of Nejd, 1914-1919', Ph.D., Wisconsin, 1972

Troeller, Gary, 'British Policy Towards Ibn Saud, 1910-1926', Ph.D., Cambridge, 1972

Walt, J., 'Saudi Arabia and the Americans, 1928-1951', Ph.D., Northwestern, 1960

Zamzami, S.G., 'The Origins and Evolution of the Arab League in its Struggle for Arab Unity and Independence', M.Phil., Reading, 1974

BOOKS (Place of publication given only if not London)

Abidi, A.H.H., *Jordan: A Political Study 1948-1957*, Asia Publishing House, 1965

Ali, Sheikh Rustum, *Saudi Arabia and Oil Diplomacy*, Praeger: New York, 1976

Allen, H.C., *Great Britain and the United States*, Odhams, 1954

Almana, Mohammed, *Arabia Unified: A Portrait of Ibn Saud*, Hutchinson Benham, 1980

Amery, Leopold S., *My Political Life – Vol II, War and Peace*, Hutchinson, 1953

Amin, Abdul Amir, *British Interests in the Persian Gulf*, Brill: Leiden, 1967

Anderson, M.S., *The Eastern Question 1774-1923*, Macmillan, 1974

Antonius, George, *The Arab Awakening*, Hamish Hamilton, 1938

Avon, Earl of, *Facing the Dictators*, Cassell, 1962

Badeau, John S., *The American Approach to the Arab World*, Harper & Row: New York, 1968

Al Baharna, Husain M., *The Legal Status of the Arabian Gulf States*, Manchester University Press: Manchester, 1968

Baker, Randall, *King Husain and the Kingdom of Hejaz*, Oleander Press: Cambridge, 1980

Barber, James, *Imperial Frontier: A Study of Relations between the British and the Pastoral Tribes of North-East Uganda*, East Africa Publishing House: Nairobi, 1968

Bartlett, C.J., *The Long Retreat: A Short History of British Defence Policy 1945-1970*, Macmillan, 1971

Belgrave, Sir C., *Personal Column*, Hutchinson, 1960

Beloff, Max, *Imperial Sunset – Vol I, Britain's Liberal Empire 1897-1921*, Methuen, 1969

Besson, Yves, *La Fondation du Royaume d'Arabia Saoudite*, Editions des Trois Continents: Lausanne, 1980

Boggs, S.W., *International Boundaries: A Study of Boundary Function and Politics*, AMC Press: New York, 1966

Bray, N.N.E., *Shifting Sands*, Unicorn Press, 1934

Brown, E. Hoagland, *The Saudi Arabia-Kuwait Neutral Zone*, Middle East Research & Publishing Centre: Beirut, 1963

Bullard, Sir Reader, *Britain and the Middle East, from Earliest Times to 1950*, Hutchinson, 1952

Bullard, Sir Reader, *The Camels Must Go*, Faber, 1961

Burgoyne, Elizabeth, *Gertrude Bell: From her Personal Papers 1914-1926, 2 Vols*, Benn, 1961

Busch, Briton C., *Britain and the Persian Gulf 1894-1914*, University of California Press: Berkeley, 1967

Busch, Briton C., *Britain, India and the Arabs*, University of California Press: Berkeley, 1971

Cassels, Alan, *Mussolini's Early Diplomacy*, Princeton University Press: New Jersey, 1970

Cecil, Viscount, *A Great Experiment*, Cape, 1941

Cheney, Michael S., *Big Oilman from Arabia*, Heinemann, 1958

Churchill, Winston, *The Gathering Storm*, Cassell, 1967

Churchill, Winston, *The World Crisis (the Aftermath)*, Thornton Butterworth, 1929

Clements, Frank A., *Saudi Arabia (A Bibliography)*, Clio Press: Oxford, 1979

Collins, Robert O. (Ed.), *An Arabian Diary: Sir Gilbert Clayton*, University of California Press: Berkeley, 1969

Cooper, Duff, *Old Men Forget*, Hart Davis, 1953
Craig, G.A. and Gilbert, F. (Eds.), *The Diplomats 1919-1939*, Princeton University Press, 1953
Coen, Terence Creagh, *The Indian Political Service*, Chatto & Windus, 1971
Cremeans, Charles D., *The Arabs and the World: Nasser's Arab Nationalist Policy*, Praeger, 1963
Cross, Colin, *The Fall of the British Empire*, Paladin, 1970
Curzon, Lord, *Frontiers*, Romanes Lectures: OUP, 1907
Darby, Philip, *British Defence Policy East of Suez 1947-1968*, OUP, 1973
Darwin, J., *Britain, Egypt and the Middle East 1918-1922*, Macmillan, 1981
Davies, C.C., *The Problem of the North-West Frontier 1890-1908*, OUP, 1939
DeNovo, John, *American Interests and Policies in the Middle East 1900-1939*, University of Minnesota Press: Minneapolis, 1963
Dickson, H.R.P., *The Arabs of the Desert*, G. Allen & Unwin, 1949
Dickson, H.R.P., *Kuwait and Her Neighbours*, G. Allen & Unwin, 1956
Dockrill, Michael L. and Gould, J. Douglas, *Peace Without Promises: Britain in the Peace Conferences 1919-1923*, Batsford Academic, 1981
Doughty, Charles, *Travels in Arabia Deserta*, Cape, 1964
Eddy, William A., *Franklin D. Roosevelt meets Ibn Saud*, American Friends of the Middle East, 1954
Feis, Herbert, *Petroleum and American Foreign Policy*, Stanford: California, 1944
Fieldhouse, D.K., *Colonialism 1870-1945*, Weidenfeld & Nicolson, 1981
Finnie, David, *Desert Enterprise: The Middle East Oil Industry and its Local Environment*, Harvard University Press: Cambridge, Mass., 1958
Fisher, Sidney N., *The Middle East: A History*, Routledge & Kegan Paul, 1969
Fitzsimons, M.A., *Empire by Treaty: Britain and the Middle East in the Twentieth Century*, Benn, 1965
Freeth, Zahra and Winstone, Victor, *Kuwait: Prospect and Reality*, G. Allen & Unwin, 1972
Frischwasser-Ra'anan, H.F., *Frontiers of a Nation: A Re-evaluation of the Forces which Created the Palestine Mandate and Determined its Territorial Shape*, Batchworth, 1955
de Gaury, Gerald, *Arabia Phoenix*, Harrap, 1946
de Gaury, Gerald, *Faisal: King of Saudi Arabia*, Arthur Barker, 1966
Gavin, R.J., *Aden Under British Rule 1839-1967*, Hurst & Co., 1975
Gibbs, N.H., *Grand Strategy, Vol I*, HMSO, 1976
Glubb, John Bagot, *Arabian Adventures: Ten Years of Loyal Service*, Cassell, 1978
Glubb, John Bagot, *Britain and the Arabs*, Hodder & Stoughton, 1959
Glubb, John Bagot, *The Story of the Arab Legion*, Hodder & Stoughton, 1959
Glubb, John Bagot, *War in the Desert*, Hodder & Stoughton, 1960
Grafftey-Smith, Lawrence, *Bright Levant*, Murray, 1970
Graves, Philip, *The Life of Sir Percy Cox*, Hutchinson, 1941
Graves, Philip (Ed), *Memoirs of King Abdullah of Transjordan*, Cape, 1950
Habib, John S., *Ibn Saud's Warriors of Islam: The Ikhwan of Najd and their Role in the Creation of the Saudi Kingdom 1910-1930*, Brill: Leiden, 1978
Hamilton, Mary Agnes, *Arthur Henderson: A Biography*, Heinemann, 1938
Hamilton, Mary Agnes, *Sidney and Beatrice Webb*, Sampson Low, 1933
Hartshorn, J.E., *Oil Companies and Governments: An Account of the International Oil Industry in its Political Environment*, Faber & Faber, 1967
Hawley, Donald, *The Trucial States*, G. Allen & Unwin, 1970
Helms, Christine Moss, *The Cohesion of Saudi Arabia: Evolution of Political Identity*, Croom Helm, 1981
Hickinbotham, Tom, *Aden*, Constable, 1958

Higham, Robin, *Britain's Imperial Air Routes 1918-1939*, G.T. Foulis & Co., 1960

Hirszowicz, Lukasz, *The Third Reich and the Arab East*, Routledge & Kegan Paul, 1966

Hogarth, D.G., *Arabia*, Hutchinson, 1922

Holden, David, *Farewell to Arabia*, Faber, 1966

Holden, David and Johns, Richard, *The House of Saud*, Pan, 1982

Holdich, T.H., *Political Frontiers and Boundary Making*, Macmillan, 1916

Hopwood, Derek (Ed), *The Arabian Peninsula: Society and Politics*, G. Allen & Unwin, 1972

Hoskins, Halford, *Middle East Oil in United States Foreign Policy*, Public Affairs Bulletin 89: Washington, 1950

Hourani, Albert, *Arabic Thought in the Liberal Age 1798-1939*, OUP, 1962

Howarth, David, *The Desert King: The Life of Ibn Saud*, Quartet, 1980

Hull, Cordell, *Memoirs II*, Hodder & Stoughton, 1948

Hurewitz, J.C., *The Middle East and North Africa in World Politics: A Documentary Record – Vol II, 1914-1945*, Yale University Press, 1979

Ingrams, Harold, *Arabia and the Isles*, Murray, 1966

Ingrams, Harold, *The Yemen: Imams, Rulers and Revolutions*, Murray, 1963

Jeffries, Sir Charles, *The Colonial Office*, G. Allen & Unwin, 1956

John, R. and Hadawi, S., *The Palestine Diary – Vol I, 1914-1945*, New World Press: New York, 1972

Johnson, Franklyn A., *Defence by Committee: The British Committee of Imperial Defence 1885-1959*, OUP, 1960

Jones, Roy E., *The Changing Structure of British Foreign Policy*, Longmans, 1974

Jones, S.B., *Boundary-Making: A Handbook for Statesmen*, Columbia University Press: New York, 1945

Kedourie, Elie, *The Chatham House Version and Other Middle Eastern Studies*, Weidenfeld & Nicholson, 1970

Kedourie, Elie, *England and the Middle East: The Destruction of the Ottoman Empire 1914-1921*, Harvester Press, 1978

Kedourie, Elie, *Islam and the Modern World*, Mansell, 1980

Kelly, J.B., *Arabia, the Gulf and the West*, Weidenfeld & Nicolson, 1980

Kelly, J.B., *Britain and the Persian Gulf 1795-1880*, Clarendon Press: Oxford, 1968

Kelly, J.B., *Eastern Arabian Frontiers*, Faber & Faber, 1964

Kiernan, Thomas, *The Arabs*, Abacus Sphere, 1975

King, Gillian, *Imperial Outpost – Aden: Its Place in British Strategic Policy*, OUP, 1964

Kirk, George, *The Middle East in the War: Survey of International Affairs, Vol II, 1939-1945*, OUP, 1954

Klieman, Aaron S., *Foundations of British Policy in the Arab World: The Cairo Conference of 1921*, John Hopkins, 1970

Kohn, Hans, *A History of Nationalism in the East*, Routledge, 1929

Kumar, Ravinder, *India and the Persian Gulf Region 1858-1907*, Asia Publishing House, 1965

Lacey, Robert, *The Kingdom*, Hutchinson, 1981

Lackner, Helen, *A House Built on Sand: A Political Economy of Saudi Arabia*, Ithaca Press, 1978

Lamb, Alastair, *Asian Frontiers: Studies in a Continuing Problem*, Pall Mall, 1968

Langsam, Walter C., *In Quest of Empire*, Foreign Policy Report of Foreign Policy Association: New York, 1939

Laqueur, W.Z., *Communism and Nationalism in the Middle East*, Routledge & Kegan Paul, 1956

Laqueur, W.Z., *The Soviet Union and the Middle East,* Routledge & Kegan Paul, 1959

Lawrence, T.E., *Seven Pillars of Wisdom,* Cape, 1935

Lebkicher, Rentz & Steineke, *The Arabia of Ibn Saud,* R.F. Moore: New York, 1952

Lipsky, George A., *Saudi Arabia: Its People, Its Society, Its Culture,* Human Relations Affairs Press: New Haven, 1959

Long, David, *Saudi Arabia,* Washington Papers 39; Sage Publications: Beverly Hills, 1976

Longrigg, S.H., *Iraq: 1900-1950,* OUP, 1953

Longrigg, S.H., *Oil in the Middle East: its Discovery and Development,* OUP, 1968

Lorimer, J.G., *Gazetteer of the Persian Gulf, Oman and Central Arabia – 6 Vols,* republished by Cregg International, Westmead, 1970

Lowe, C.J. and Marzari, F., *Italian Foreign Policy 1870-1940,* Routledge & Kegan Paul, 1975

Macartney, Maxwell H.H., and Cremona, Paul, *Italy's Foreign and Colonial Policy 1914-1937,* OUP, 1938

Macro, Eric, *Yemen and the Western World since 1571,* Praeger: New York, 1968

Main, Ernest, *Iraq: From Mandate to Independence,* G. Allen & Unwin, 1935

Marlowe, John, *Arab Nationalism and British Imperialism,* Cresset Press, 1961

Marlowe, John, *The Persian Gulf in the Twentieth Century,* Cresset Press, 1962

Marlowe, John, *The Seat of Pilate: An Account of the Palestine Mandate,* Cresset Press, 1959

Marston, Thomas, *Britain's Imperial Role in the Red Sea Area 1800-1878,* Shoestring, 1961

Medlicott, W.N., *British Foreign Policy Since Versailles 1919-1963,* Methuen, 1968

Meinertzhagen, R.M., *Middle East Diary 1917-1956,* Cresset Press, 1959

Mejcher, Helmut, *Imperial Quest for Oil: Iraq 1910-1928,* St Antony's Middle Eastern Monographs: Oxford, 1976

Meulen, D. Van der, *The Wells of Ibn Saud,* Murray, 1957

Mikesell, R.F. and Chenery, H.B., *Arabian Oil: America's Stake in the Middle East,* North Carolina University, 1949

Mohr, Anton, *The Oil War,* Harcourt & Brace, 1926

Monroe, Elizabeth, *Britain's Moment in the Middle East: 1914-1956,* Chatto & Windus, 1963

Monroe, Elizabeth, *Philby of Arabia,* Faber & Faber, 1973

Morris, James, *Farewell the Trumpets: An Imperial Retreat,* Faber & Faber, 1978

Morris, James, *The Hashemite Kings,* Faber & Faber, 1959

Musil, Alois, *Northern Negd,* American Geographical Society, New York, 1928

Nash, Gerald D., *United States Oil Policy 1890-1964,* University of Pittsburgh, 1968

Niblock, T. (Ed), *State, Society and Economy in Saudi Arabia,* Croom Helm, 1982

Northedge, F.S., *Descent from Power: British Foreign Policy 1945-1973,* G. Allen & Unwin, 1974

Northedge, F.S., *The Troubled Giant: Britain Among the Great Powers,* Bell, 1966

Orde, Anne, *Great Britain and International Security 1920-1926,* Royal Historical Society, 1978

Page, S.G., *The USSR and Arabia: The Development of Soviet Policies and Attitudes Toward the Countries of the Arabian Peninsula,* Central Asian Research Centre, 1971

Parkinson, Sir Cosmo, *The Colonial Office from Within,* Faber, 1947

Peake, F.G., *History and Tribes of Jordan,* University of Miami Press, 1958

Pelling, H., *Britain and the Second World War,* Collins: Glasgow, 1972

Petrie, Sir Charles, *The Chamberlain Tradition,* Lovat Dickson, 1938

Petrie, Sir Charles, *The Life and Letters of the Rt. Hon. Austen Chamberlain, Vol II*, Cassell Press, 1940

Philby, H. St. J. B., *Arabia*, Benn, 1930

Philby, H. St. J. B., *Arabia of the Wahhabis*, Frank Cass, 1977

Philby, H. St. J. B., *Arabian Days*, Robert Hale, 1948

Philby, H. St. J. B., *Arabian Jubilee*, Robert Hale, 1952

Philby, H. St. J. B., *Arabian Oil Ventures*, Middle East Institute: Washington, 1964

Philby, H. St. J. B., *Forty Years in the Wilderness*, Robert Hale, 1957

Philby, H. St. J. B., *Saudi Arabia*, Benn, 1955

Porter, Bernard, *The Lion's Share*, Longmans, 1975

Prescott, J. R. V., *The Geography of Frontiers and Boundaries*, Hutchinson, 1965

Al Rashid, Ibrahim, *Documents on the History of Saudi Arabia, 3 Vols*, Documentary Publications: Salisbury, North Carolina, 1976

Al Rashid, Ibrahim, *Saudi Arabia Enters the Modern World: Secret US Documents on the Emergence of the Kingdom of Saudi Arabia as a World Power 1936-1949, 2 Vols*, Documentary Publications: Salisbury, North Carolina, 1980

Rendel, Sir George, *The Sword and the Olive*, Murray, 1957

Reynolds, P. A., *British Foreign Policy in the Inter-War Years*, Longmans, 1954

Rihani, Ameen, *Ibn Saoud of Arabia: His Land and His People*, Constable, 1938

Robertson, Esmonde M., *Mussolini as Empire Builder*, Macmillan, 1977

Robinson, Kenneth, *The Dilemmas of Trusteeship: Aspects of British Colonial Policy Between the Wars*, OUP, 1965

Roskill, Stephen, *Hankey: Man of Secrets – Vol II, 1919-1931*, Collins, 1972

Royal Institute of International Affairs, *British Interests in the Mediterranean and the Middle East*, OUP, 1958

Royal Institute of International Affairs, *The Middle East in the War Years*, OUP, 1948

Royal Institute of International Affairs, *Political and Strategic Interests of the United Kingdom*, OUP, 1939

Rubin, Barry, *The Great Powers in the Middle East 1941-1947*, Frank Cass, 1981

Russett, Bruce M., *Community and Contention: Britain and America in the Twentieth Century*, MIT Press: Pittsburgh, Mass., 1963

Ryan, Sir Andrew, *The Last of the Dragomans*, Geoffrey Bles, 1951

Sanger, R. H., *The Arabian Peninsula*, Cornell University, Ithaca, 1954

Searight, Sarah, *The British in the Middle East*, Weidenfeld & Nicolson, 1969

Seton-Williams, M. V., *Britain and the Arab States: A Survey of Anglo-Arab Relations 1920-1948*, Luzac, 1948

Sheean, Vincent, *Faisal: The King and his Kingdom*, University Press of Arabia, 1975

Shwadran, Benjamin, *Jordan: A State of Tension*, Council For Middle Eastern Affairs Press, 1959

Shwadran, Benjamin, *The Middle East, Oil and the Great Powers*, John Wiley: New York, 1973

Sluglett, Peter, *Britain and Iraq 1914-1932*, Ithaca Press, 1976

Snyder, Louis L. (Ed), *The Imperialism Reader: Documents and Readings on Modern Expansionism*, Kenniyat Press: New York, 1962

Steiner, Z., *The Foreign Office and Foreign Policy 1894-1914*, Cambridge University, 1969

Stevens, John H., *A Bibliography of Saudi Arabia*, Occasional Paper Series 3: Durham, 1973

Stocking, George W., *Middle Eastern Oil*, Allen Lane: Penguin Press, 1970

Storrs, Ronald, *Orientations*, Nicholson & Watson, 1945

Strang, Lord, *The Foreign Office*, G. Allen & Unwin, 1955

Sykes, Christopher, *Crossroads to Israel*, Collins, 1965
Thesiger, Wilfred, *Arabian Sands*, Longmore Green & Co., 1960
Thomson, David, *England in the Twentieth Century*, Pelican, 1965
Thornton, A.P., *The Imperial Idea and its Enemies*, Macmillan, 1959
Thomas, Bertram, *The Arabs*, Thornton Butterworth, 1937
Tibi, B., *Arab Nationalism: A Critical Enquiry*, Macmillan, 1981
Toynbee, Arnold, *Survey of International Affairs, 1925, Vol I*, OUP, 1927
Toynbee, Arnold, *Survey of International Affairs, 1928*, OUP, 1929
Toynbee, Arnold, *Survey of International Affairs, 1930*, OUP, 1931
Toynbee, Arnold, *Survey of International Affairs, 1934*, OUP, 1935
Toynbee, Arnold, *Survey of International Affairs, 1936*, OUP, 1937
Troeller, Gary, *The Birth of Saudi Arabia: Britain and the Rise of the House of Saud*, Frank Cass, 1976
Tugendhat, Christopher, *Oil: The Biggest Business*, Eyre & Spottiswoode, 1968
Twitchell, Karl S., *Saudi Arabia*, Princeton: New Jersey, 1958
Vital, David, *The Making of British Foreign Policy*, G. Allen & Unwin, 1968
Wahba, Sheikh Hafiz, *Arabian Days*, Arthur Barker, 1964
Wallace, William, *The Foreign Policy Process in Britain*, Royal Institute of International Affairs, G. Allen & Unwin, 1976
Walpole, Norman C. (et al), *Area Handbook for Saudi Arabia*, American University Press, 1971
Walters, F.P., *A History of the League of Nations, 2 Vols*, OUP, 1952
Waterfield, Gordon, *Professional Diplomat: Sir Percy Loraine*, Murray, 1973
Watt, D.C., *Personalities and Policies: Studies in the Formulation of British Foreign Policy in the Twentieth Century*, Longmans, 1965
Wenner, M.V., *Modern Yemen, 1918-1966*, John Hopkins: Baltimore, 1967
Williams, Ann, *Britain and France in the Middle East and North Africa 1914-1967*, Macmillan, 1968
Williams, Kenneth, *Ibn Saud: Puritan King of Arabia*, Cape, 1933
Wilson, Arnold T., *Loyalties: Mesopotamia 1914-1917, Vol II*, OUP, 1931
Wilson, Arnold T., *The Persian Gulf*, G. Allen & Unwin, 1954
Winder, R. Bayly, *Saudi Arabia in the Nineteenth Century*, Macmillan, 1965
Winstone, H.V.F., *Captain Shakespear*, Cape, 1976
Winstone, H.V.F., *Gertrude Bell*, Cape, 1978
Woodcock, George, *Who Killed the British Empire?* Cape, 1974
Zahlan, R.S., *The Creation of Qatar*, Croom Helm, 1979
Zahlan, R.S., *The Origins of the United Arab Emirates: A Political and Social History of the Trucial States*, Macmillan, 1978
Zeine, Zeine N., *The Emergence of Arab Nationalism*, Caravan: New York, 1973
Zimmern, Alfred, *The League of Nations and the Rule of Law 1918-1935*, Macmillan, 1936

ARTICLES

Anon., 'The Future of Arabia', *Near East & India* XXX 806, October 1926
Anon., 'Great Britain and King Ibn Saud', *Near East & India* XXXI 829-30, April 1927
Anon., 'Hostilities in the Hejaz', *Near East & India* XXVIII 539, November 1925
Anon., 'The Idrisi of Asir', *Near East & India* XXX 796, August 1926
Anon., 'Iraq and Nejd', *Near East & India* XXXIX 1029, February 1931
Anon., 'Iraq and a United Arabia', *Near East & India* XXXIX 1037, April 1931
Anon., 'Italy and Arabia', *Near East & India* XXXII 842, July 1927
Anon., 'Peace and Arabia', *Near East & India* XXXVII 975, January 1930
Anon., 'Rapprochement in Arabia', *Near East & India* XXXVII 981, March 1930
Anon., 'Suspicion in Arabia', *Near East & India* XXXI 832, April 1927
Anon., 'The Wahhabis and the Hejaz', *Near East & India* XXXII 858, October 1927
Anon., 'War Alarms in Arabia', *Near East & India* XXXI 820, February 1927
Barbour, N. 'Britain and the Rise of Arab Nationalism', *The Fortnightly,* July 1951
Bentley, G. W., 'The Development of the Air Route in the Persian Gulf', *Journal of the Royal Central Asian Society* 20, 1933
Buchan, Alistair, 'Britain and the Indian Ocean', *International Affairs,* April 1966
Bullard, Sir Reader, 'Portrait of Ibn Saud', *The Listener,* 4 February 1954
Burchall, H., 'The Air Route to India', *Journal of the Royal Central Asian Society* 14, 1927
Burchall, H., 'The Political Aspect of Commercial Air Routes', *Journal of the Royal Central Asian Society* 20, 1933
Byrd, Peter, 'Regional and Functional Specialism in the British Consular Service', *Journal of Contemporary History* 7, January-April 1972
Carruthers, D., 'Captain Shakespear's Journey to East Arabia', *Geographical Journal,* 1922
Clayton, Sir Gilbert, 'Arabia and the Arabs', *Journal of the Royal Institute of International Affairs,* January 1929
Cohen, M.J., 'British Strategy and the Palestine Question 1936-1939', *Journal of Contemporary History* 7, July-October 1972
Craig, Gordon A., 'The British Foreign Office from Grey to Chamberlain', Craig and Gilbert (Eds) *The Diplomats 1919-1939,* 1953
Craig, Gordon A., 'The Professional Diplomat and his Problems 1919-1939', *World Politics* 4, 1952
Crane, Charles R., 'Visit to the Red Sea Littoral and the Yaman', *Journal of the Royal Central Asian Society* 15, 1928
Dame, Louis P., 'From Bahrain to Taif: A Missionary Journey across Arabia', *Moslem World* 28, 1933
Davison, Roderic H., 'Where is the Middle East?', *Foreign Affairs* 38, July 1960
Fieldhouse, D.K., 'Imperialism', *Economic History Review* 2nd series XIV
Fisher, Eric, 'On Boundaries', *World Politics* 1, 1948-49
Hamza, Fuad, 'Najran', *Journal of the Royal Central Asian Society* 22, 1935
Hay, Rupert, 'The Persian Gulf States and their Boundary Problems', *The Geographical Journal* CXX, December 1954
Hogarth, D.C., 'Wahhabis and British Interests', *Journal of the British Institute of International Affairs* 20, September 1925
Hoskins, Halford, 'Background of the British Position in Arabia', *Middle East Journal* 1, April 1947

Hourani, Albert, 'The Present State of Islamic and Middle Eastern Historiography', Elie Kedourie, *Europe and the Middle East,* 1980

Hughes, H. Stuart, 'The Early Diplomacy of Italian Fascism 1922-1932', Craig and Gilbert (Eds), *The Diplomats 1919-1939,* 1953

Kedourie, Elie, 'Great Britain and Palestine: The Turning Point', Elie Kedourie, *Islam and the Modern World,* 1980

Kedourie, Elie, 'Panarabism and British Policy', *Political Quarterly* 28, 1957

Kelidar, Abbas, 'The Arabian Peninsula in Arab and Power Politics', Hopwood (Ed), *The Arabian Peninsula,* 1972

Kelly, J. B., 'The Buraimi Oasis Dispute', *International Affairs* 32, July 1956

Kelly, J. B., 'The Legal and Historical Basis of the British Position in the Persian Gulf', *St. Antony's Papers No 4: Middle Eastern Affairs – 1,* Chatto & Windus, 1958

Kelly, J. B., 'Sovereignty and Jurisdiction in Eastern Arabia, *International Affairs* 34, January 1958

Kennedy, Paul M., 'Appeasement and British Defence Policy in the Inter-War Years', *British Journal of International Studies* 4, 1978

Kennedy, Paul M., 'The Tradition of Appeasement in British Foreign Policy 1865-1939', *British Journal of International Studies* 2, 1976

Kirk, George, 'The Arab Awakening Reconsidered', *Middle Eastern Affairs* 13, June-July 1962

Kirk, George, 'Ibn Saud Builds an Empire', *Current History,* December 1934

Knorr, Klaus, 'Theories of Imperialism', *World Politics,* 4, 1952

Kohn, Hans, 'The Unification of Arabia', *Foreign Affairs* 13, October 1934

'L', 'Downing Street and Arab Potentates', *Foreign Affairs* 5, 1927

Lapidus, Ira M., 'The Separation of State and Religion in the Development of Early Islamic Society', *International Journal of Middle Eastern Studies* 12, 1975

Lewis, C. C., 'Ibn Saud and the Future of Arabia', *International Affairs* 12, July 1933

Liebesny, Herbert, 'International Relations of Arabia: the Dependent Areas', *International Affairs* 34, January 1958

Macdonald, C. A., 'Radio Bari: Italian Wireless Propaganda in the Middle East and British Counter-measures 1934-38', *Middle Eastern Studies* 13, 1977

Macdonald, D. B., 'The Caliphate', *Moslem World* 7, 1917

Macdonald, Norman W., Arabia: The British Connection II', *Contemporary Review* 236, February 1980

Margoliouth, D. S., 'The Latest Developments of the Caliphate Question', *Moslem World* 14, 1924

Melamid, Alexander, 'The Buraimi Oasis Dispute', *Middle Eastern Affairs* 7, February 1956

Melamid, Alexander, 'Oil and the Evolution of Boundaries in Eastern Arabia', *Geographical Review* 44, 1954

Melamid, Alexander, 'Political Geography of Trucial Oman and Qatar', *Geographical Review* 43, 1953

Melka, R., 'Nazi Germany and the Palestine Question', *Middle Eastern Studies* 5, 1969

Metta, Vasuedo B., 'Ibn Saud, Aspirant for Leadership of the Moslem World', *Current History* 24, April 1926

Musil, Alois, 'Religion and Politics in Arabia', *Foreign Affairs:* New York, July 1928

Nightingale, R., 'Personnel of the British Foreign Office and Diplomatic Service', *Fabian Tract* 232, 1930

Pearcy, G. Etzel, 'The Middle East: An Indefinable Region', *Department of State Bulletin,* March 1959

Peursem, G. Van der, 'Guests of Ibn Saud', *Moslem World* 26, April 1936

Philby, H.St.J.B., 'Arabia To-day', *International Affairs* 14, September-October 1935

Philby, H.St.J.B., 'Britain and Arabia', *Nineteenth Century & After* 117, 1935

Philby, H.St.J.B., 'British Bombs over Arabia', *World Review,* January 1938

Philby, H.St.J.B., 'Pax Wahhabica', *The English Review,* March 1933

Philby, H.St.J.B., 'Trouble in Arabia: Iraq and Nejd Frontier', *Contemporary Review,* June 1928

Porath, Yeyoshua, 'The Palestinians and the Negotiations for the British-Hejazi Treaty 1920-1925', *Asian and African Studies* 8, 1972

Rappard, W.E., 'The Practical Working of the Mandates System', *Journal of British Institute of International Affairs,* September 1925

Rentz, George, 'The Iraq-Nejd Frontier', *Journal of the Royal Central Asian Society* 17, 1930

Rentz, George, 'Wahhabism and Saudi Arabia', Hopwood (Ed), *The Arabian Peninsula,* 1972

Rosenfeld, Henry, 'The Social Composition of the Military in the Process of State Formation in the Arabian Desert — Part 1'
'The Military Force used to Achieve and Maintain Power and the Meaning of its Social Composition: Slaves, Mercenaries and Townsmen — Part 2', *Journal of the Royal Anthropological Institute* 95, 1965

Rutherford, Geddes W., 'Spheres of Influence: An Aspect of Semi-Suzerainty', *American Journal of International Law* 20, 1926

Sassoon, P., 'Air Power in the Middle East', *Journal of the Royal Central Asian Society* 20, 1933

Schmidt, H.D., 'The Nazi Party in Palestine and the Levant 1932-1939', *International Affairs* 28, October 1952

Sluglett, Peter, and Farouk-Sluglett, Marion, 'The Precarious Monarchy: Britain, Abd al-Aziz ibn Saud and the Establishment of the Kingdom of Hijaz, Najd and its Dependencies, 1925-1932', Niblock, *State, Society and Economy in Saudi Arabia,* 1982.

Smalley, W.F., 'Ibn Saud and the Wahhabis', *Moslem World* 22, 1932

Sweet, Louise E., 'Camel Raiding of North Arabian Bedouin: A Mechanism of Ecological Adaption', *American Anthropologist* 67, 1965

Tonietti, Alphonse, 'Arabia's New Warrior King', *Current History* 24, 1926

Watt, D.C., 'The Arabian Peninsula in British Strategy', *Military Review,* February 1961

Watt D.C., 'The Foreign Policy of Ibn Saud 1936-1939', *Journal of the Royal Central Asian Society,* April 1963

Webster, C.K., 'British Policy in the Near East', P.W. Ireland (Ed), *The Near East,* Chicago, 1942

Williams, Kenneth, 'Arabs on the Side of Democracy', *Great Britain and the East* LIII, September 1939

Winkler, H.R., 'Arthur Henderson', Craig and Gilbert (Eds), *The Diplomats 1919-1939,* 1953

Winkler, H.R., 'The Development of the League of Nations Idea in Great Britain 1914-1919', *Journal of Modern History,* June 1948

Winkler, H.R., 'The Emergence of a Labour Foreign Policy in Great Britain 1918-1929', *Journal of Modern History,* September 1956

APPENDIX 1

Chronology

1600	Royal Charter granted to East India Company
c. 1745	Mohammad Ibn Saud converted to Wahhabism
1798	Napoleon's drive into Egypt leads to British treaty with Sultan of Muscat
1811	Height of first Wahhabi Empire
1815	Congress of Vienna supports maintenance of Ottoman Empire
1818	Daraiya, the Saudi capital, destroyed by Egyptians
1839	India annexes Aden
1840	Final Egyptian withdrawal from Arabia
1853	Treaty of Peace in Perpetuity between Britain and the Gulf sheikhs
1865	Colonel Lewis Pelly, Political Resident in the Gulf, travels to Riyadh
1869	The Suez Canal opens
1882	Britain occupies Egypt
1899	British Treaty with Kuwait
1902	Ibn Saud captures Riyadh from Ibn Rashid
1908	The first oil in the Middle East found in Persia
	Young Turk Revolution
	Hejaz Railway reaches Medina
	Husein ibn Ali becomes Sherif of Mecca
1910	Captain Shakespear becomes the first Englishman to meet Ibn Saud
1913	British Government buys majority of Anglo-Persian Oil Company's shares
April 1913	Ibn Saud occupies Hasa
July 1913	The Anglo-Turkish Convention
May 1914	Ibn Saud signs treaty with the Turks
June 1914	A second Anglo-Turkish Convention, mentioning the 'blue line', ratified
November 1914	Britain and Turkey at war
January 1915	Shakespear killed
December 1915	The first Anglo-Saudi treaty signed
June 1916	Husein proclaims Arab Revolt
1917	Aqaba and Maan occupied during Arab Revolt
November 1917	Philby first meets Ibn Saud
autumn 1918	Saudi forces attempt to occupy Khurma and Turaba
1920	San Remo conference assigns the mandates
	Feisal dethroned in Syria
	Ibn Saud occupies mountainous areas of Asir

1921	Colonial Office takes overall responsibility for the Middle East
	The Cairo Conference imposes the Hashemites on the mandates
	Ibn Saud defeats Ibn Rashid and becomes Sultan of Nejd
	Feisal crowned King of Iraq
May 1922	Treaty of Mohammera settles tribal issues between Iraq and Nejd
December 1922	Uqair Protocol settles Iraq-Nejd frontier
1923	Major Frank Holmes secures the Hasa oil concession
May 1923	Abdullah proclaims independent Emirate of Transjordan
December 1923	(until April 1924) Kuwait Conference
March 1924	The Turks abolish the Caliphate. It is taken up by Husein
	The British subsidy to Ibn Saud expires
August 1924	Saudi forces invade the Hejaz
October 1924	Mecca falls to Ibn Saud. Husein abdicates and is succeeded by Ali
	Husein moves to Aqaba
May 1925	Ibn Saud threatens to move his forces on Aqaba
June 1925	Husein leaves Aqaba under British pressure
July 1925	Transjordan annexes Aqaba and Maan
November 1925	Clayton negotiates Hadda and Bahra Agreements with Ibn Saud
December 1925	King Ali surrenders to Ibn Saud
January 1926	Ibn Saud is crowned King of the Hejaz
February 1926	Britain recognises Ibn Saud as King of the Hejaz
June 1926	Britain lifts arms embargo over the Red Sea area
September 1926	Italy signs treaty with the Yemen
October 1926	Ibn Saud and the Idrisi of Asir sign Treaty of Mecca
March 1927	Britain and Italy sign the Rome Agreement
May 1927	Britain and Ibn Saud sign the Treaty of Jedda
October 1927	Oil found in Kirkuk, Iraq
November 1927	The *Ikhwan* massacre Iraqis at Busaiya police post
Jan-Feb 1928	Britain and Nejd engaged in frontier war
May 1928	Clayton's first visit to Ibn Saud to discuss frontier posts
August 1928	Clayton's second visit ends in failure
	Failure of Haifa Conference on the future of the Hejaz Railway
September 1928	Southern Desert Camel Corps formed in Transjordan under Glubb
November 1928	Ibn Saud declares war on the *Ikhwan*
	Soviet treaty with the Yemen
December 1928	SOCAL takes control of the Bahrain oil concession
March 1929	Ibn Saud defeats the *Ikhwan* at the battle of Sibila
June 1929	Ramsay MacDonald forms his second Labour Government
1930	Philby becomes a Moslem
	The Official Sub-Committee for Middle Eastern questions established
January 1930	The *Ikhwan* leaders surrender in Kuwait
February 1930	Ibn Saud and Feisal meet on board *HMS Lupin*
May 1930	Sir Andrew Ryan becomes first British Minister to the Hejaz
November 1930	Ibn Saud annexes Asir

1931	At the Hejaz National Conference Ibn Saud reaffirmms that mineral concessions will only go to Moslems
February 1931	Charles Crane visits Ibn Saud at Jedda
May 1931	The United States recognises Ibn Saud
August 1931	Ramsay MacDonald forms National Government
autumn 1931	Japan invades Manchuria
January 1932	Philby commences his crossing of the Rub al Khali
February 1932	Italy signs a treaty with Ibn Saud
April 1932	Ibn Saud adheres to the Kellogg Pact for the renunciation of war
May 1932	Oil found in Bahrain
	Ibn Rifada's revolt against Ibn Saud
July 1932	American oil interests approach Philby in London
September 1932	Ibn Saud changes the name of his dominions to Saudi Arabia
October 1932	The mandate over Iraq ends and she enters the League of Nations
	The Idrisi revolts against Ibn Saud
February 1933	SOCAL wins Philby's support for the Hasa oil concession
April 1933	Ibn Saud and Abdullah recognise each other's regimes
	British and Iranian Governments agree new terms for Anglo-Persian Oil Co.
May 1933	Ibn Saud grants Hasa concession to SOCAL
February 1934	Britain signs treaty with the Yemen
March-May 1934	Saudi-Yemeni war
April 1934	Ibn Saud is informed that Britain regards his south-eastern frontier as the 'blue line'
June 1934	Saudi-Yemeni Treaty of Taif, of Islamic Friendship and Brotherhood
July 1934	Ryan visits Taif. The first occasion British Minister goes beyond Jedda
September 1934	Fuad Hamza discusses Saudi Arabia's south-eastern frontier in London
	Anglo-Italian communiqué disclaims aggression in the Red Sea
April 1935	Ibn Saud proposes his 'red line' frontier
	Stresa front agreement
June-July 1935	Fuad Hamza has further talks with the Foreign Office in London
October 1935	Italy invades Abyssinia
November 1935	Ryan visits Riyadh and presents 'Riyadh line'
	Dispute with Ibn Saud over Bahrain customs dues settled
1936	Petroleum Concessions Ltd. wins the Hejaz oil concession
January 1936	Ibn Saud visits Kuwait
April 1936	Saudi Arabia and Iraq sign Treaty of Brotherhood and Alliance
	The Palestine strike begins
May 1936	Saudi Arabia and Egypt sign treaty
August 1936	Britain and Egypt sign treaty
September 1936	Bullard becomes British Minister in Jedda
October 1936	Britain and Saudi Arabia agree revised Treaty of Jedda
	Joint appeal made by Arab leaders to end the strike in Palestine

March 1937	George Rendel visits Saudi Arabia
June 1937	The Peel Commission publishes its report on Palestine
November 1937	Yusuf Yasin visits the German Minister in Baghdad
February 1938	Eden resigns as Foreign Secretary
March 1938	The Earl and Countess of Athlone visit Saudi Arabia
	Oil found in Hasa in commercial quantities
April 1938	Anglo-Italian Agreement signed
Jan-March 1939	Conference in London of Arab leaders on Palestine
January 1939	Dr Fritz Grobba travels to Jedda as German Minister
May 1939	Pipeline from Dhahran oilfield to port of Ras Tanura opens
June 1939	Saudi envoy meets Hitler
August 1939	German-Soviet Non-Aggression Pact
September 1939	World War Two begins

APPENDIX 2

Dramatis Personae

Abdullah ibn Husein	2nd son of Husein ibn Ali. Emir of Transjordan
Ali ibn Husein	1st son of Husein ibn Ali. King of the Hejaz – October 1924–December 1925
Mohammad Ali	Ottoman Viceroy of Egypt. Ordered invasion of Nejd
Leopold S. Amery	Colonial Secretary 1925-29
W.E. Beckett	Foreign Office legal adviser
Earl of Birkenhead	Secretary of State for India 1924-28
Colonel Hugh Biscoe	Political Resident in the Gulf 1929-31
William Bond	Acting British Agent/Consul Jedda 1929. Chargé d'Affaires 1929-30
Sir Reader Bullard	Governor of Baghdad 1920. British Agent/Consul Jedda 1923-25. British Minister Jedda 1936-39
Sir John Cadman	Chairman of Iraq Petroleum Company
A.S. Calvert	British Consul, 2nd Secretary, Chargé d'Affaires Jedda 1933-36
Sir Austen Chamberlain	Secretary of State for India 1915-17. Foreign Secretary 1925-29
Sir John Chancellor	High Commissioner of Palestine 1928-31
Winston Churchill	Colonial Secretary 1921-22
Sir Gilbert Clayton	Director of Intelligence Egypt 1914-17. Chief Political Officer Egyptian Expeditionary Forces 1917-19. Adviser to Egyptian Ministry of Interior 1919-22. Chief Secretary Government in Palestine 1922-25. Special Envoy to Ibn Saud 1925-28. High Commissioner of Iraq 1929
Sir Kinahan Cornwallis	Adviser to Iraq Ministry Interior 1921-35, as successor to Philby
Sir Percy Cox	Political Resident in the Gulf. Chief Political Officer Indian Expeditionary Force 1914-18. High Commissioner of Iraq 1920-23
Charles Crane	American philanthropist. Initiated American interest in Saudi oil
Lord Curzon	Viceroy of India 1899-1905. Foreign Secretary 1919-24
Faisal al Dawish	Prominent *Ikhwan* chief. Leading instigator of *Ikhwan* rebellion
H.R.P. Dickson	Political Agent in Bahrain c.1920. Political Agent in Kuwait 1929-36
Sir Henry Dobbs	High Commissioner of Iraq 1923-29
Sir Eric Drummond	British Ambassador in Rome 1933-39
Anthony Eden	Minister for League of Nations Affairs 1935. Foreign Secretary 1935-38
Faisal ibn Abd al Aziz	2nd son of Ibn Saud. Viceroy of the Hejaz. Saudi Foreign Minister

Feisal ibn Husein	3rd son of Husein ibn Ali. King of Iraq 1921-33
Judge Bert Fish	US Minister in Egypt and, from June 1939, Minister to Saudi Arabia
C.G. Fitzmaurice	Foreign Office legal adviser
Col. Trenchard Fowle	Political Resident in the Gulf 1932-1939
King Fuad	King of Egypt until 1936
Gerald de Gaury	Political Agent in Kuwait 1936-39. British representative to Ibn Saud from 1939
Ghazi ibn Feisal	King of Iraq 1933-39
Cecil Hope Gill	British Chargé d'Affaires Jedda 1930-33
John Bagot Glubb	British Military Intelligence Officer Iraq. Administrative Inspector for Iraq Government 1926-30. Transferred to Transjordan in 1930
Sir Ronald Graham	British Ambassador in Rome 1921-33
Dr Fritz Grobba	German Minister in Iraq from 1932, and to Saudi Arabia from 1939
Kerim Hakimov	Soviet Minister in Jedda
Lord Halifax	Foreign Secretary 1938-40
Fuad Bey Hamza	Syrian Druze member of Saudi Government. Deputy Foreign Minister
Colonel L. Haworth	Political Resident in the Gulf 1927-29
Arthur Henderson	Foreign Secretary 1929-31
Sir Samuel Hoare	Secretary of State for Air. Secretary of State for India. Foreign Secretary 1935
Major Frank Holmes	New Zealand entrepreneur with Eastern and General Syndicate
Sir Francis Humphrys	High Commissioner of Iraq from 1929
Lord Kitchener	British Minister Egypt 1911-14. Secretary of State for War 1914-16
Husein ibn Ali	Sherif of Mecca 1908-16. King of the Hejaz 1916-24
Herbert Jakins	Acting British Agent/Consul Jedda 1927-29
Abdullah ibn Jiluwi	Cousin of Ibn Saud. Governor of Hasa
Stanley R. Jordan	Acting British Agent/Consul Jedda 1925-26. British Minister Jedda 1943-45
J.G. Laithwaite	India Office, Political Department
Sir Miles Lampson	British High Commissioner of Egypt 1933-36, then British Ambassador
Lord Lloyd	High Commissioner of Egypt 1925-29
Stephen Longrigg	Representative of the Iraq Petroleum Company
Francis B. Loomis	Former American Under Secretary of State. Connected with SOCAL
Malcolm MacDonald	Colonial Secretary from 1938
Norman Mayers	Acting British Agent/Consul Jedda 1926-27
Sir Henry McMahon	First British High Commissioner of Egypt 1914-16
Lord Monteagle	Head of Eastern Department Foreign Office, late 1920s
Major More	Political Agent in Kuwait 1920-29
Sheikh Mubarak	Sheikh of Kuwait 1896-1915
Von Neurath	German Foreign Minister until January 1938
Sir Lancelot Oliphant	Head of Eastern Department Foreign Office, early and mid-1920s. Assistant Under Secretary of State Foreign Office 1928-36, and deputy Under Secretary from 1936
William Ormsby-Gore	Colonial Secretary 1936-38
Sir Cosmo Parkinson	Assistant Under Secretary of State Colonial Office 1931-

	37. Permanent Under Secretary from 1937
Colonel Lewis Pelly	British Resident in the Gulf. Travelled to Riyadh in 1865
H. St. J. B. Philby	Adviser to Iraq Ministry of Interior 1920-21. Chief British Representative in Transjordan. From 1926-60 explorer and scholar of Arabia
Lord Plumer	High Commissioner of Palestine 1925-28
Colonel Prideaux	Political Resident in the Gulf 1924-27
Khalid al Qarqani	Tripolitanian member of Ibn Saud's inner council
Al Rashid	Rival dynasty to the House of Saud. Supported by the Turks
Sir Bernard Reilly	Political Resident, and Chief Commissioner in Aden
George Rendel	Head of Eastern Department Foreign Office 1930-38
Von Ribbentrop	German Foreign Minister from January 1938
Sir Andrew Ryan	First British Minister in Jedda 1930-36
Sir Herbert Samuel	High Commissioner of Palestine 1920-25
Abd al Aziz ibn Saud	Founder of modern Saudi Arabia. Emir of Nejd 1902. Sultan of Nejd 1921. King of the Hejaz 1926. King of Saudi Arabia 1932
Mohammad ibn Saud	Nejdi emir. Converted to Wahhabism c. 1745
Captain W. Shakespear	British Political Agent in Kuwait. Killed in 1915
Sir John Shuckburgh	Assistant (later Deputy) Under Secretary of State Colonial Office. Head of Middle East Department
Sir John Simon	Foreign Secretary 1931-35
Sir Lee Stack	Governor-General of the Sudan and Sirdar of the Egyptian Army. Assassinated 1924
Hugh Stonehewer-Bird	British Agent / Consul Jedda 1927-30. British Minister in Jedda from 1945
Ronald Storrs	Arab Bureau. Military Governor and Civil Governor Jerusalem 1917-20
Abdullah Sulaiman	Nejdi member of Saudi Government. Minister of Finance
Sir Hugh Trenchard	Chief of the Air Staff
Alan Trott	Sometime British Chargé d'Affaires Jedda from 1937
Karl Twitchell	American mining engineer introduced by Crane to search for minerals in Saudi Arabia
Sir William Tyrrell	Permanent Under Secretary of State Foreign Office 1925-30
Sir Robert Vansittart	Permanent Under Secretary of State Foreign Office 1930-37
Sheikh Hafiz Wahba	Egyptian member of Saudi Government. First Saudi Minister in London
Mohammad ibn Wahhab	Moslem theologian giving his name to puritan doctrine
L. Wakely	India Office. Assistant (later Deputy) Under Secretary of State
Sir Arthur Wauchope	High Commissioner of Palestine 1931-38
Sidney Webb (Lord Passfield)	Colonial Secretary 1929-31
Imam Yahya	Imam (sometimes styled King) of the Yemen
Yusuf Yasin	Syrian member of Saudi Government. Political Secretary

APPENDIX 3

Treaties

1. Treaty of Peace in Perpetuity, 1853
2. Article 11, Anglo-Turkish Convention, July 1913
3. Article 3, Anglo-Turkish Convention, March 1914
4. Ottoman-Saudi Treaty, May 1914
5. Anglo-Idrisi Treaty, April 1915
6. Anglo-Saudi Treaty, December 1915
7. Anglo-Qatar Treaty, November 1916 (An example of Britain's Gulf treaties)
8. The Bahra Agreement, November 1925
9. The Hadda Agreement, November 1925
10. Treaty of Mecca (Ibn Saud and the Idrisi), October 1926
11. Anglo-Italian Rome Agreement, March 1927
12. Treaty of Jedda (Britain and Ibn Saud), May 1927
13. The Exchange of Notes on Aqaba and Maan, appended to the Treaty of Jedda
14. Anglo-Yemeni Treaty, February 1934
15. Anglo-Italian Agreement, April 1938

1. Treaty of Peace in Perpetuity, 1853

TREATY OF PEACE IN PERPETUITY AGREED UPON BY THE CHIEFS OF THE
ARABIAN COAST ON BEHALF OF THEMSELVES, THEIR HEIRS AND
SUCCESSORS UNDER THE MEDIATION OF THE RESIDENT IN THE
PERSIAN GULF, 1853.

We, whose seals are hereunto affixed, Sheikh Sultan bin Suggur, Chief of Rass-ool-Kheimah, Sheikh Saeed bin Tahnoon, Chief of Aboo Dhebbee, Sheikh Saeed bin Butye, Chief of Debay, Sheikh Hamid bin Rashed, Chief of Ejman, Sheikh Abdoola bin Rashed, Chief of Umm-ool-Keiweyn, having experienced for a series of years the benefits and advantages resulting from a maritime truce contracted amongst ourselves under the mediation of the Resident in the Persian Gulf and renewed from time to time up to the present period, and being fully impressed, therefore, with a sense of the evil consequence formerly arising, from the prosecution of our feuds at sea, whereby our subjects and dependents were prevented from carrying on the pearl fishery in security, and were exposed to interruption and molestation when passing on their lawful occasions, accordingly, we, as aforesaid have determined, for ourselves, our heirs and successors, to conclude together a lasting and inviolable peace from this time forth in perpetuity and do hereby agree to bind ourselves down to observe the following conditions:–

ARTICLE 1.

That from this date, *viz.,* 25th Rujjub 1269, 4th May 1853, and hereafter, there shall be a complete cessation of hostilities at sea between our respective subjects and dependants, and a perfect maritime truce shall endure between ourselves and between our successors, respectively, for evermore.

ARTICLE 2.

That in the event (which God forbid), of any of our subjects or dependants committing an act of aggression at sea upon the lives or property of those of any of the parties to this agreement, we will immediately punish the assailants and proceed to afford full redress upon the same being brought to our notice.

ARTICLE 3.

That in the event of an act of aggression being committed at sea by any of those who are subscribers with us to this engagement upon any of our subjects or dependants, we will not proceed immediately to retaliate, but will inform the British Resident or the Commodore at Bassidore, who will forthwith take the necessary steps for obtaining reparation for the injury inflicted, provided that its occurrence can be satisfactorily proved.

We further agree that the maintenance of the peace now concluded amongst us shall be watched over by the British Government, who will take steps to ensure at all times the due observance of the above Articles, and God of this is the best witness and guarantee.

Approved by the Governor-General in Council on 24th August 1853.

2. Article 11, Anglo-Turkish Convention, July 1913

The Ottoman *Sanjak* of Najd, the northern limit of which is indicated by the demarcation line defined in Article 7 of this Convention, ends in the south at the gulf facing the island of *al-Zakhnuniyah,* which belongs to the said *Sanjak.* A line beginning at the extreme end of that gulf will go directly south up to the *Rub al-Khali* and will separate the Najd from the peninsula of *al-Qatar.* The limits of the Najd are indicated by a blue line on the map annexed to the present Convention. The Ottoman Imperial Government having renounced all its claims to the peninsula of *al-Qatar,* it is understood by the two Governments that the peninsula will be governed as in the past by shaykh Jasmin bin Thani and his successors. The Government of Her Britannic Majesty declares that it will not allow the interference of the shaykh of Bahrein in the internal affairs of al-Qatar, his endangering the autonomy of that area or his annexing it.

3. Article 3, Anglo-Turkish Convention, March 1914

... The boundary of Ottoman territory shall follow a direct line which runs from Lakmat al-Shu'ub north-eastwards to the desert of Rub al-Khali at an angle of 45 degrees. This line shall join in the Rub al-Khali on parallel 20 degrees, the straight and direct line southwards which leaves the Gulf of al-Uqair at a point on the south coast, and which separates the Ottoman territory of the Sanjak of Najd from the territory of Qatar, in accordance with Article 11 of the Anglo-Ottoman Convention of the 29th July, 1913, relative to the Persian Gulf and the surrounding territories. The first of the two lines is shown in violet and the second in blue on the special map annexed hereto ...

4. Ottoman-Saudi Treaty, May 1914

TREATY BETWEEN IBN SAUD AND THE OTTOMAN GOVERNMENT,
MAY 15, 1914

Translation of Treaty between Ibn Saud and the Turks

Article 1. This Treaty is signed and executed between the Wali and Commandant of Basrah, Suleiman Shafik Pasha, who is specially empowered by Imperial Iradeh, and H.E. Abdul Aziz Pasha Al-Saood, Wali and Commandant of Najd: This Treaty is relied on by the Imperial Government and consists of 12 articles, explaining secret matters mentioned in the Imperial Firman dated .... with reference to the Vilayet of Najd. The text of this Treaty shall be secret, and relied upon.

Article 2. The Vilayet of Najd is to remain in charge of Abdul Aziz Pasha Al-Saood so long as he is alive, according to the Imperial Firman.
        After him it will go to his sons and grandsons by Imperial Firman, provided that he shall be loyal to the Imperial Government and to his forefathers, the previous Walis.

Article 3.   A Technical Military Official shall be appointed by the said Wali and Commandant [Ibn Saud] to live wherever he wishes: if he sees fit and necessary he may introduce Turkish officers for the fundamental technical training of Local Troops, and their number shall depend upon the choice and wishes of the said Wali and Commandant [Ibn Saud].

Article 4.   A Number of soldiers and gendarmerie, as deemed fit by the Wali and Commandant aforesaid, shall be stationed at seaports such as Katif, and Ojair, &c.

Article 5.   All the business of the Customs, Taxes, Ports and Light houses shall be exercised subject to the international rights of Governments, and shall be conducted according to the principles of the Turkish government under the direction of the said Wali and Commandant.

Article 6.   Till the sources of the revenues reach a degree sufficient to meet the requirements of the Vilayet and the local expenditure and military dispositions according to the present circumstances and normal conditions of Najd, the deficiency in the budget shall be met from the Customs, Posts, Telegraphs and Ports revenue; and if there is a surplus, it should be sent to the Porte with a report.

If the local revenue is sufficient to meet all expenses, the income of the Posts, Telegraphs and Customs shall be remitted to their respective Departments. Also as regards local incomes other than those mentioned above, if there is any surplus, 10 per cent of it shall be sent to the Government Treasury.

Article 7.   The Turkish flag shall be hoisted on all Government buildings and places of importance on the sea and on the land, and also on boats belonging to the Vilayet of 'Najd.

Article 8.   Correspondence shall be conducted with the Marine Department for the regular supply of arms and ammunition.

Article 9.   The said Wali and Commandant is not allowed to interfere with, or correspond about foreign affairs and international treaties, or to grant concessions to foreigners.

Article 10.   All the correspondence of the Wali and Commandant shall be direct with the Imperial Ministries of Interior and Marine, without intermediary.

Article 11.   Post Offices shall be established in the Vilayet of Najd, in order to facilitate communication; and arrangements shall be made to despatch posts to the necessary places in a fitting manner; Turkish stamps shall be affixed to all letters and packages.

Article 12.   If, God forbid, the Government should have to fight with a foreign power or if there should be any internal disturbance in any Vilayet and the Government asks the said Wali for a force to co-operate with its own forces it is incumbent on the Wali to prepare a sufficient force with provisions and ammunition, and to respond to the demand at once, according to his power and ability.

5. Anglo-Idrisi Treaty, April 1915

BRITISH TREATY WITH THE IDRISI SAIYID OF SABYA
30 April 1915

This Treaty of Friendship and Goodwill is signed by Major-General D. G. L. Shaw, the Political Resident, Aden, on behalf of the British Government, and by Sayed Mustafa bin Sayed Abdul Ali on the part of His Eminence Saiyid Muhammad bin Ali bin Muhammad bin Ahmed bin Idris, the Idrisi Saiyid and Amir of Sabia and its environments.

2. Its main objects are to war against the Turks and to consolidate a pact of friendship between the British Government and the Idrisi Saiyid, abovementioned and his Tribesmen.

3. The Idrisi Saiyid agrees to attack and to endeavour to drive the Turks from their stations in the Yemen and to the best of his power to harrass the Turkish troops in the direction of the Yemen, and to extend his territories at the expense of the Turks.

4. The Saiyid's prime objective will be against the Turks only, and he will abstain from any hostile or provocative action against Imam Yahya so long as the latter does not join hands with the Turks.

5. The British Government undertakes to safeguard the Idrisi Saiyid's territories from all attack on the seaboard from any enemy who may molest him; to guarantee his independence in his own domain and at the conclusion of the war to use every diplomatic means in its power to adjudicate between the rival claims of the Idrisi Saiyid and the Imam Yahya or any other rival.

6. The British Government has no desire to enlarge its borders in Western Arabia, but wishes solely to see the various Arab rulers living peacefully and amicably together each in his own sphere, and all in friendship with the British Government.

7. As a mark of its appreciation of the work to be performed by the Idrisi Saiyid, the British Government has aided him with both funds and munitions and will continue to assist him in the prosecution of the war so long as it lasts in accordance with the measures of the Idrisi's activities.

8. Finally, while maintaining a strict blockade on all Turkish ports in the Red Sea, the British Government has for some months past been giving the Idrisi Saiyid full and free scope to trade and traffic between his ports and Aden, and this concession the British Government in token of the friendship existing will continue uninterruptedly to maintain.

9. This Treaty will be held to be valid after its ratification by the Government of India.

6. Anglo-Saudi Treaty, December 1915

TREATY BETWEEN ABDUL AZIZ IBN SAUD AND THE GOVERNMENT OF THE UNITED KINGDOM, DECEMBER 26, 1915

Preamble

The High British Government on its own part, and Abdul Aziz bin Abdur Rahman bin Faisal Al-Saud, Ruler of Najd, El Hassa, Qatif and Jabail, and the towns and ports belonging to them, on behalf of himself, his heirs and successors, and tribesmen being desirous of confirming and strengthening the friendly relations which have for a long time existed between the two parties, and with a view to consolidating their respective interests – the British Government have named and appointed Lieutenant-Colonel Sir Percy Cox, K.C.S.I., K.C.I.E, British Resident in the Persian Gulf, as their Plenipotentiary, to conclude a treaty for this purpose with Abdul Aziz bin Abdur Rahman bin Faisal Al-Saud.

The said Lieutenant-Colonel Sir Percy Cox and Abdul Aziz bin Abdur Rahman bin Faisal Al-Saud, hereafter known as "Bin Saud" have agreed upon and concluded the following Articles:–

(I)

The British Government do acknowledge and admit that Najd, Al Hasa, Qatif and Jabail, and their dependencies and territories, which will be discussed and determined hereafter, and their ports on the shores of the Persian Gulf are the countries of Bin Saud and of his fathers before him, and do hereby recognise the said Bin Saud as the independent Ruler thereof and absolute Chief of their tribes, and after him his sons and descendants by inheritance; but the selection of the individual shall be in accordance with the nomination (i.e. by the living Ruler) of his successor; but with the proviso that he shall not be a person antagonistic to the British Government in any respect; such as, for example, in regard to the terms mentioned in this Treaty.

(II)

In the event of aggression by any Foreign Power on the territories of the countries of the said Bin Saud and his descendants, without reference to the British Government and without giving her an opportunity of communicating with Bin Saud and composing the matter, the British Government will aid Bin Saud to such extent and in such a manner as the British Government after consulting Bin Saud may consider most effective for protecting his interests and countries.

(III)

Bin Saud hereby agrees and promises to refrain from entering into any correspondence, agreement, or treaty, with any Foreign Nation or Power, and further to give immediate notice to the political authorities of the British Government of any attempt on the part of any other Power to interfere with the above territories.

(IV)

Bin Saud hereby undertakes that he will absolutely not cede, sell, mortgage, lease, or otherwise dispose of the above territories or any part of them, or grant concessions within those territories to any Foreign Power, or to the subjects of any Foreign Power, without the consent of the British Government.

And that he will follow her advice unreservedly provided that it be not damaging to his own interests.

(V)

Bin Saud hereby undertakes to keep open within his territories, the roads leading to the Holy Places and to protect pilgrims on their passage to and from the Holy Places.

(VI)

Bin Saud undertakes, as his fathers did before him, to refrain from all aggression on, or interference with the territories of Kuwait, Bahrain, and of the Shaikhs of Qatar and the Oman Coast, who are under the protection of the British Government, and who have treaty relations with the said Government; and the limits of their territories shall be hereafter determined.

(VII)

The British Government and Bin Saud agree to conclude a further detailed treaty in regard to matters concerning the two parties.

Dated 18th Safar 1334 corresponding to 26th December, 1915.

7. Anglo-Qatar Treaty, November 1916

BRITISH TREATY WITH THE SHAIKH OF QATAR
3 November 1916

I.   I, Shaikh Abdullah bin Jasim bin Thani, undertake that I will, as do the friendly Arab Shaikhs of Abu Dhabi, Dibai, Shargah, Ajman, Ras-ul-Khaima and Umm-al-Qawain, co-operate with the High British Government in the suppression of the slave trade and piracy and generally in the maintenance of the Maritime Peace. To this end, Lieutenant-Colonel Sir Percy Cox, Political Resident in the Persian Gulf, has favoured me with the Treaties and Engagements, entered into between the Shaikhs abovementioned and the High British Government, and I hereby declare that I will abide by the spirit and obligations of the aforesaid Treaties and Engagements.

II.   On the other hand, the British Government undertakes that I and my subjects and my and their vessels shall receive all the immunities, privileges and advantages that are conferred on the friendly Shaikhs, their subjects and their vessels. In token whereof, Sir Percy Cox has affixed his signature with the date thereof to each and every one of the aforesaid Treaties and Engagements in the copy granted to me and I have also affixed my signature and seal with the date thereof to each and every one of the aforesaid Treaties and Engagements, in two other printed copies of the same Treaties and Engagements, that it may not be hidden.

III.   And in particular, I, Shaikh Abdullah, have further published a proclamation forbidding the import and sale of arms into my territories and port of Qatar; and in consideration of the undertaking into which I now enter, the British Government on its part agrees to grant me facilities to purchase and import, from the Muscat Arms Warehouse or such other place as the British Government may approve, for my personal use, and for the arming of my dependents, such arms and ammunition as I may reasonably need and apply for in such fashion as may be arranged hereafter through the Political Agent, Bahrein. I undertake absolutely that arms and ammunition thus supplied to me shall under no circumstances be re-exported from my territories or sold to the public, but shall be reserved solely for supplying the needs of my tribesmen and dependents whom I have to arm for the maintenance of order in my territories and the protection of my Frontiers. In my opinion the amount of my yearly requirements will be up to five hundred weapons.

IV   I, Shaikh Abdullah, further undertake that I will not have relations nor correspond with, nor receive the agent of, any other Power without the consent of the High British Government; neither will I, without such consent, cede to any other Power or its subjects, land either on lease, sale, transfer, gift, or in any other way whatsoever.

I also declare that, without the consent of the High British Government, I will not grant pearl-fishery concessions, or any other monopolies, concessions, or cable landing rights, to anyone whomsoever.

VI.   The Customs dues on the goods of British merchants imported to Qatar shall not exceed those levied from my own subjects on their goods and shall in no case exceed five per cent, *ad valorem*. British goods shall be liable to the payment of no other dues or taxes of any other kind whatsoever, beyond that already specified.

VII.   I, Shaikh Abdullah, further, in particular, undertake to allow British subjects to reside in Qatar for trade and to protect their lives and property.

VIII.   I also undertake to receive, should the British Government deem it advisable, an Agent from the British Government who shall remain at Al Bidaa for the transaction of such business as the British Government may have with me and to watch over the interests of British traders residing at my ports or visiting them upon their lawful occasions.

IX.   Further, I undertake to allow the establishment of a British Post Office and a Telegraph installation anywhere in my territory whenever the British Government should hereafter desire them. I also undertake to protect them when established.

X.   On their part, the High British Government, in consideration of these Treaties and Engagements that I have entered into with them, undertake to protect me and my subjects and territory from all aggression by sea and to do their utmost to exact reparation for all injuries that I, or my subjects, may suffer when proceeding to sea upon our lawful occasions.

XI.   They also undertake to grant me good offices, should I or my subjects be assailed by land within the territories of Qatar. It is, however, thoroughly understood that this obligation rests upon the British Government only in the event of such aggression whether by land or sea, being unprovoked by any act or aggression on the part of myself or my subjects against others.

8. The Bahra Agreement, November 1925

THE BAHRA AGREEMENT

Signed at Bahra Camp on 1 November 1925 by Sir Gilbert Clayton and Abd Al Aziz ibn Saud

1. The State of Iraq and Nejd severally recognise that raiding by tribes settled in their territories into the territory of the other state is an aggression which necessitates the severe punishment of the perpetrators by the Government to which they are subject and that the chief of the tribe committing such aggression is to be held responsible.

2. (a) A special tribunal shall be set up, by agreement between the two Governments of Iraq and Nejd, which shall meet from time to time to enquire into the particulars of any aggression committed across the frontier between the two states, to assess the damages and losses and to fix the responsibility. This tribunal shall be composed of an equal number of representatives of the Governments of Iraq and Nejd, and its presidency shall be entrusted to an additional person, other than the aforesaid representatives, to be selected by the two Governments in agreement. The decisions of this tribunal shall be final and executory.
   (b) When the tribunal has fixed the responsibility, assessed the damages and losses resulting from the raid, and issued its decision in that respect, the Government to whom those found guilty are subject shall execute the aforesaid decision in accordance with tribal customs, and shall punish the guilty party in accordance with Article 1 of the present Agreement.

3. Tribes subject to one of the two Governments may not cross the frontier into the territory of the other Government except after obtaining a permit from their own Government and after the concurrence of the other government; it being stipulated, however, in accordance with the principle of the freedom of grazing, that neither government shall have the right to withhold such permit or concurrence if the migration of the tribe is due to grazing necessities.

4. The two Governments of Iraq and Nejd undertake to stand in the way, by all the means at their disposal other than expulsion and the use of force, of the emigration of any tribe or section of a tribe from one of the two countries into the other unless its emigration takes place with the knowledge and consent of its Government. The two Governments undertake to abstain from offering any present of whatsoever kind to refugees from the territories of the other government, and to look with disfavour on any of their subjects who may seek to entice tribes belonging to the other Government or to encourage them to emigrate from their country into the other country.

5. The Governments of Iraq and Nejd may not correspond with the Chiefs and Sheikhs of tribes subject to the other state on official or political matters.

6. The forces of Iraq and Nejd may not cross the common frontier in pursuit of offenders except with the consent of both Governments.

7. Sheikhs of tribes who hold an official position or who have flags showing that they are the leaders of armed forces may not display their flags in the territory of the other state.

8. In case one of the two Governments were to call upon tribes residing in the territory of the other state to furnish armed contingents, the said tribes will be

free to respond to the call of their Government on condition that they betake themselves with their families and belongings in complete tranquility.

9. In case a tribe were to emigrate from the territory of one of the two Governments into the territory of the other Government and were subsequently to commit raids into the territory in which it formerly resided, it will be open to the Government into whose territory this tribe has immigrated to take from it adequate guarantees on the understanding that, if a similar aggression were to be repeated by the tribe, those guarantees would be liable to confiscation, without prejudice to the punishment to be inflicted by the Government as provided in Article 1, and without prejudice to whatever impositions may be decreed by the tribunal specified in Article 2 of the present Agreement.

10. The Governments of Iraq and Nejd undertake to initiate friendly discussions with a view to concluding a special agreement in respect of the extradition of criminals in accordance with the usage prevailing among friendly states, within a period not exceeding one year from the date of the ratification of the present Agreement by the Government of Iraq.

11. The Arabic version is the official text to be referred to in the interpretation of the Articles of the present Agreement.

12. The present Agreement shall be known as 'The Bahra Agreement'.

9. The Hadda Agreement, November 1925

THE HADDA AGREEMENT

Signed at Bahra Camp on 2 November 1925 by Sir Gilbert Clayton and Abd Al Aziz ibn Saud

1. The Frontier between Nejd and Trans-Jordan starts in the northeast from the point of intersection of meridian 39°E and parallel 32°N, which marks the termination of the frontier between Nejd and Iraq, and proceeds in a straight line to the point of intersection of meridian 37°E and parallel 31°30'N, and thence along meridian 37°E to the point of its intersection with parallel 31°25'N. From this point, it proceeds in a straight line to the point of intersection of meridian 38°E and parallel 30°N, leaving all projecting edges of the Wadi Sirhan in Nejd territory; and thence proceeds along meridian 38°E to the point of its intersection with parallel 29°35'N. The map referred to in this Agreement is that known as the 'International' Asia Map, 1:1,000,000.

2. The Government of Nejd undertake not to establish any fortified post at Kaf or in its neighbourhood as a military centre; and should they at any time consider it necessary to take exceptional measures in the neighbourhood of the frontier with a view to the maintenance of order or for any other purpose, involving the concentration of armed forces, they engage to notify His Majesty's Government without delay. The Government of Nejd undertake to prevent by all the means at their disposal, any incursions by their forces into the territory of Trans-Jordan.

3. In order to avoid misunderstanding over incidents which may arise in the neighbourhood of the frontier, and to promote mutual confidence and full co-operation between His Majesty's Government and the Government of Nejd, the two parties agree to maintain constant communication between the Chief British Representative in Trans-Jordan or his delegate and the Governor of the Wadi Sirhan.

4. The Government of Nejd undertake to maintain all established rights that may be enjoyed in the Wadi Sirhan by tribes not under their jurisdiction, whether such rights appertain to grazing or to habitation, or to ownership, or the like; it being understood that those tribes, so long as they reside within Nejd territory, will be subject to such internal laws as do not infringe on those rights. The Government of Trans-Jordan undertake to extend identical treatment to Nejd subjects who may enjoy similar established rights in Trans-Jordan territory.

5. The Governments of Nejd and Trans-Jordan severally recognise that raiding by tribes settled in their territories into the territory of the other state is an aggression which necessitates the severe punishment of the perpetrators by the Government to which they are subject, and that the chief of the tribe committing such aggression is to be held responsible.

6. (a) A special tribunal shall be set up, by agreement between the two Governments of Nejd and Trans-Jordan, which shall meet from time to time to enquire into the particulars of any aggression committed across the frontier between the two states, to assess the damages and losses and to fix the responsibility. This tribunal shall be composed of an equal number of representatives of the Governments of Nejd and Trans-Jordan, and its presidency shall be entrusted to an additional person, other than the aforesaid representative, to be selected by the two Governments in agreement. The decision of this tribunal shall be final and executory.
(b) When the tribunal has fixed the responsibility, assessed the damages and losses resulting from the raid, and issued its decision in that respect, the Government to whom those found guilty are subject shall execute the aforesaid decision in accordance with tribal customs, and shall punish the guilty party in accordance with Article 5 of the present Agreement.

7. Tribes subject to one of the two Governments may not cross the frontier into the territory of the other Government except after obtaining a permit from their own Government and after the concurrence of the other government; it being stipulated however, in accordance with the principle of freedom of grazing, that neither Government shall have the right to withhold such permit or concurrence if the migration of the tribe is due to grazing necessities.

8. The two Governments of Nejd and Trans-Jordan undertake to stand in the way, by all means at their disposal other than expulsion and the use of force, of the emigration of any tribe or section of a tribe from one of the two countries into the other unless its emigration takes place with the knowledge and consent of its Government. The two Governments undertake to abstain from offering any present of whatsoever kind to refugees from the territories of the other Government, and to look with disfavour on any of their subjects who may seek to entice tribes belonging to the other Government or to encourage them to emigrate from their country into the other country.

9. The Governments of Nejd and Trans-Jordan may not correspond with the Chiefs and Sheikhs of tribes subject to the other state on official or political matters.

10. The forces of Nejd and Trans-Jordan may not cross the common frontier in the pursuit of offenders, except with the consent of both Governments.

11. Sheikhs of tribes who hold an official position or who have flags showing that they are the leaders of armed forces may not display their flags in the territory of the other state.

12. Free passage will be granted by the Governments of Nejd and Trans-Jordan to travellers and pilgrims, provided they conform to those regulations affecting travel and pilgrimage which may be in force in Nejd and Trans-Jordan. Each Government will inform the other of any regulation issued by it in this manner.

13. His Britannic Majesty's Government undertake to secure freedom of transit at all times to merchants who are subjects of Nejd for the prosection of their trade between Nejd and Syria in both directions: and to secure exemption from customs and other duty for all merchandise in transit which may cross the Mandated territory on its way from Nejd to Syria or from Syria to Nejd, on condition that such merchants and their caravans shall submit to whatever customs inspection may be necessary, and that they shall be in possession of a document from their Government certifying that they are *bona fide* merchants; and provided that trading caravans carrying merchandise will follow established routes, to be agreed upon hereafter, for their entry into and their exit from the Mandated territory; it being understood that the above restrictions will not apply to trading caravans whose trade is confined to camels and other animals, or to tribes migrating in accordance with the preceding Articles of the present Agreement. His Britannic Majesty's Government further undertake to secure such other facilities as may be possible to merchants who are subjects of Nejd and who may not cross the area under British Mandate.

14. This Agreement will remain in force for so long as His Britannic Majesty's Government are entrusted with the Mandate for Trans-Jordan.

15. The present Agreement has been drawn up in the two languages, English and Arabic, and each of the high contracting parties shall sign two English copies and two Arabic copies. Both texts shall have the same validity, but in case of divergence between the two in the interpretation of one or other of the Articles of the present Agreement, the English text shall prevail.

16. The present Agreement will be known as the Hadda Agreement.

10. Treaty of Mecca (Ibn Saud and the Idrisi), October 1926

PROTECTORATE (MECCA) AGREEMENT: ASIR AND HEJAZ,
NEJD AND DEPENDENCIES

21 October 1926

(Promulgated 7 January 1927)

Praise be to God alone!
Between the King of the Hejaz, Sultan of Nejd and its dependencies: and the Imam Sayyid al-Hassan ibn Ali al-Idrisi. Desiring a complete understanding and with a view to the preservation of the existence of the Arab countries, and to the strengthening of ties between the Princes of the Arab peninsula, the following

agreement has been reached between His Majesty the King of the Hejaz, Sultan of Nejd and its dependencies, Abdul-Aziz ibn Abdul-Rahman Al Faisal Al Saud and His Lordship the Imam of Asir, the Sayyid al-Hassan ibn Ali al-Idrisi:–

ART. 1. His Lordship the Imam Sayyid al-Hassan ibn Ali al-Idrisi acknowledges the ancient marches described in the treaty of the 10th Safar, 1339, made between the Sultan of Nejd and the Imam Sayyid Mohammad ibn Ali al-Idrisi, and which were at that date subject to the House of Idrisi, as being in virtue of this agreement under the suzerainty of His Majesty the King of Hejaz, Sultan of Nejd and its dependencies.

2. The Imam of Asir may not enter into political negotiations with any Government or grant any economic concession to any person except with the sanction of His Majesty the King of Hejaz, Sultan of Nejd and its dependencies.

3. The Imam of Asir may not declare war or make peace except with the sanction of His Majesty the King of the Hejaz, Sultan of Nejd and its dependencies.

4. The Imam of Asir may not cede any part of the territories of Asir described in Article 1.

5. The King of the Hejaz, Sultan of Nejd and its dependencies, recognises the rulership of the present Imam of Asir, during his lifetime, of the territories defined in Article 1, and thereafter (extends the same recognition) to whomsoever the House of Idrisi and the competent authorities of the Imamate may agree upon.

6. The King of the Hejaz, Sultan of Nejd and its dependencies, agrees that the internal administration of Asir, the supervision of its tribal affairs, appointments and dismissals, for example, pertain to the rights of the Imam of Asir, provided such administration is in harmony with Sharia law and justice according to the practice of both Governments.

7. The King of the Hejaz, Sultan of Nejd and its dependencies, undertakes to repel all internal and external aggression which may befall the territories of Asir as defined in Article 1 and this by agreement between the two contracting parties according to the circumstances and exigencies of interest.

8. Both parties agree to adhere to this agreement and to carry out its obligations.

9. This agreement will be effective after confirmation by the two high contracting parties.

10. This agreement has been drawn up in Arabic in two copies, of which one will be preserved by each of the two contracting parties.

11. This agreement will be known as "the Mecca Agreement".

11. Anglo-Italian Rome Agreement, March 1927

THE ANGLO-ITALIAN ROME AGREEMENT, 11 MARCH 1927

1. It is the common interest of the two Governments to pursue a policy of pacification in order to avoid, as far as possible, conflicts between various Arab chiefs.

2. Such influence as the two Governments may be in a position to exercise with Ibn Saud, the Imam, and the Idrisi shall be directed towards eliminating the causes of conflict in order to arrive, if possible, at pacific and friendly settlements between those chiefs.

3. While continuing to exert their influence in the cause of peace the two Governments should not intervene in any conflict which may break out between those chiefs.

4. The guiding principle in British policy in the Red Sea is the security of imperial communication with India and the East. For this purpose His Majesty's Government regard it as a vital imperial interest that no European power should establish itself on the Arabian shore of the Red Sea, more particularly on Kamaran or the Farasan Islands, and that neither Kamaran nor the Farasan Islands shall fall into the hands of an unfriendly Arab ruler.

It is in the interest of Italy, in view of her possessions on the western coast of the Red Sea, that no European power should establish itself on the Arabian shore of the Red Sea, more particularly on Kamaran or the Farasan Islands, and that neither Kamaran nor the Farasan Islands shall fall into the hands of an unfriendly Arab ruler.

5. There shall be economic and commercial freedom on the Arabian coast and islands of the Red Sea for citizens and subjects of the two countries and that the protection which such citizens and subjects may legitimately expect from their respective Governments shall not assume a political character or complexion.

6. The presence of British officials at Kamaran is solely for the purpose of securing the sanitary service of pilgrims to Mecca, but for administrative reasons His Majesty's Government cannot agree with the Italian request for participation of Italian doctors in the quarantine service. His Majesty's Government will reconsider the above point when the number of pilgrims originating in the Italian colonies or possessions increases to such an extent as to justify the presence of an Italian doctor.

7. That it is in the common interest of the two Governments to use their respective influence with the Arab chiefs in such a manner as to safeguard as far as may be possible the mutual interests of Italy and Great Britain, and that it is desirable that the two Governments should maintain close touch with each other in all questions affecting the Red Sea and southern Arabia in order to avoid misunderstanding between them or misapprehension on the part of the Arab chiefs in regard to the policies which the two Governments intend to follow in the above mentioned areas.

12. Treaty of Jedda (Britain and Ibn Saud), May 1927

TREATY (JEDDA): THE UNITED KINGDOM AND KING IBN SAUD OF THE HEJAZ
AND OF NEJD AND ITS DEPENDENCIES
20 May 1927
(ratifications exchanged, Jedda, 17 September 1927)

ART. 1   His Britannic Majesty recognises the complete and absolute independence of the dominions of his Majesty the King of the Hejaz and of Nejd and its Dependencies.

ART. 2   There shall be peace and friendship between His Britannic Majesty and his Majesty the King of the Hejaz and of Nejd and its Dependencies. Each of the high contracting parties undertakes to maintain good relations with the other and to endeavour by all the means at its disposal to prevent his territories being used as a base for unlawful activities directed against peace and tranquility in the territories of the other party.

ART. 3   His Majesty the King of the Hejaz and of Nejd and its Dependencies undertakes that the performance of the pilgrimage will be facilitated to British subjects and British-protected persons of the Moslem faith to the same extent as to other pilgrims, and announces that they will be safe as regards their property and their person during their stay in the Hejaz.

ART. 4   His Majesty the King of the Hejaz and of Nejd and its Dependencies undertakes that the property of the aforesaid pilgrims who may die within the territories of His Majesty and who have no lawful trustee in those territories shall be handed over to the British Agent in Jeddah or to such authority as he may appoint for the purpose, to be forwarded by him to the rightful heirs of the deceased pilgrims; provided that the property shall not be handed over to the British representative until the formalities of the competent tribunals have been complied with and the dues prescribed under Hejazi or Nejdi laws have been duly collected.

ART. 5   His Britannic Majesty recognises the national (Hejazi or Nejdi) status of all subjects of His Majesty the King of the Hejaz and of Nejd and its Dependencies who may at any time be within the territories of His Britannic Majesty or territories under the protection of His Britannic Majesty.

Similarly, His Majesty the King of the Hejaz and of Nejd and its Dependencies recognises the national (British) status of all subjects of His Britannic Majesty and of all persons enjoying the protection of His Britannic Majesty who may at any time be within the territories of His Majesty the King of the Hejaz and of Nejd and its Dependencies; it being understood that the principles of international law in force between independent Governments shall be respected.

ART. 6   His Majesty the King of the Hejaz and of Nejd and its Dependencies undertakes to maintain friendly and peaceful relations with the territories of Kuwait and Bahrain, and with the Sheikhs of Qatar and the Oman Coast, who are in special treaty relations with His Britannic Majesty's Government.

ART. 7   His Majesty the King of the Hejaz and of Nejd and its Dependencies undertakes to co-operate by all means at his disposal with His Britannic Majesty in the suppression of the slave trade.

ART. 8   The present treaty shall be ratified by each of the high contracting parties and the ratifications exchanged as soon as possible. It shall come into force on the day of the exchange of ratifications and shall be binding during seven years from that date. In case neither of the high contracting parties shall have given notice to the other six months before the expiration of the said period of seven years of his intention to terminate the treaty it shall remain in force and shall not be held to have terminated until the expiration of six months from the date on which either of the parties shall have given notice of the termination to the other party.

ART. 9   The treaty concluded between His Britannic Majesty and His Majesty the King of the Hejaz and of Nejd and its Dependencies (then Ruler of Nejd and its Dependencies) on the 26th December, 1915, shall cease to have effect as from the date on which the present treaty is ratified.

ART. 10   The present treaty has been drawn up in English and Arabic. Both texts shall be of equal validity; but in case of divergence in the interpretation of any part of the treaty the English text shall prevail.

ART. 11   The present treaty shall be known as the Treaty of Jeddah.

13. The Exchange of Notes on Aqaba and Maan, appended to the Treaty of Jedda

EXCHANGE OF NOTES ATTACHED TO 1927 TREATY OF JEDDA:
RE: AQABA AND MAAN

Sir Gilbert Clayton: His Majesty's Government regard the above mentioned frontier as being defined as follows:

> The frontier between the Hejaz and Transjordan starts from the inter-section of meridian 38°E and parallel 29°35'N which marks the termination of the frontier between Nejd and Transjordan, and proceeds in a straight line to a point on the Hejaz Railway two miles south of Mudawara. From this point it proceeds in a straight line to a point on the Gulf of Aqaba two miles south of the town of Maan.

Ibn Saud: ... we find it impossible, in the present circumstances, to effect a final settlement of this question. Nevertheless in view of our true desire to maintain cordial relations based on solid ties of friendship, we desire to express to your Excellency our willingness to maintain the status quo in the Maan-Aqaba district, and we promise not to interfere in its adminis-tration until favourable circumstances will permit a final settlement of this question.

14. Anglo-Yemeni Treaty, February 1934

TREATY OF FRIENDSHIP AND MUTUAL COOPERATION:
BRITAIN AND YEMEN

11 February 1934

ART. 1. His Majesty the King of Great Britain, Ireland and the British Dominions beyond the Seas, Emperor of India, acknowledges the complete and absolute independence of His Majesty the King of the Yemen, the Imam, and his kingdom in all affairs of whatsoever kind.

ART. 2. There shall always be peace and friendship between the high con-tracting parties, who undertake to maintain good relations with each other in every respect.

ART. 3. The settlement of the question of the southern frontier of the Yemen is deferred pending the conclusion, in whatever way may be agreed upon by both high contracting parties in a spirit of friendship and complete concord, free from any dispute or difference, of the negotiations which shall take place between them before the expiry of the period of the present treaty.

Pending the conclusion of the negotiations referred to in the preceding para-graph, the high contracting parties agree to maintain the situation existing in regard to the frontier on the date of the signature of this treaty, and both high contracting parties undertake that they will prevent, by all means at their disposal, any violation by their forces of the above-mentioned frontier, and any interference by their subjects, or from their side of that frontier, with the affairs of the people inhabiting the other side of the said frontier.

ART. 4. After the coming into force of the present treaty, the high contracting parties shall, by mutual agreement and concord enter into such agreements as shall be necessary for the regulation of commercial and economic affairs, based on the principles of general international practice.

ART. 5. (1) The subjects of each of the high contracting parties who wish to trade in the territories of the other shall be amenable to the local laws and decrees, and shall receive equal treatment to that enjoyed by the subjects of the most favoured Power.

(2) Similarly, the vessels of each of the high contracting parties and their cargoes shall receive, in the ports of the territories of the other, treatment equal to that accorded to the vessels and their cargoes of the most favoured Power, and the passengers in such vessels shall be treated in the ports of the territories of the other party in the same manner as those in the vessels of the most favoured Power therein.

(3) For the purposes of this article in relation to His Majesty the King of Great Britain, Ireland and the British Dominions beyond the Seas, Emperor of India:

(a) The word "territories" shall be deemed to mean the United Kingdom Great Britain and Northern Ireland, India and all His Majesty's Colonies, protectorates and all mandated territories in respect of which the mandate is exercised by His Majesty's Government in the United Kingdom.

(b) The word "subjects" shall be deemed to mean all subjects of His Majesty wherever domiciled, all the inhabitants of countries under His Majesty's protection, and, similarly, all companies incorporated in any of his Majesty's territories shall be deemed to be subjects of His Majesty.

(c) The word "vessels" shall be deemed to mean all merchant vessels registered in any part of the British Commonwealth of Nations.

ART. 6. This treaty shall be the basis of all subsequent agreements that may be concluded between the high contracting parties now and in the future for the purposes of friendship and amity. The high contracting parties undertake not to assist nor to connive at any action directed against the friendship and concord now sincerely existing between them.

ART. 7. The present treaty shall be ratified as soon as possible after signature, and the instruments of ratification shall be exchanged at Sana. It shall come into force on the date of the exchange of ratifications, and shall thereafter remain in force for a period of forty years.

15. Anglo-Italian Agreement, April 1938

AGREEMENT ON MUTUAL INTERESTS IN THE MEDITERRANEAN: THE UNITED KINGDOM AND ITALY

16 April 1938

ANNEX 3. ANGLO-ITALIAN AGREEMENT ON CERTAIN AREAS IN THE MIDDLE EAST

The Government of the United Kingdom of Great Britain and Northern Ireland and the Italian Government,

being desirous of ensuring that there shall be no conflict between their respective policies in regard to the areas in the Middle East referred to in the present agreement, being desirous, moreover, that the same friendly spirit which has attended the signing of to-day's Protocol, and of the documents annexed thereto, should also animate their relations in regard to those areas,

have agreed as follows:

ART. 1.　Neither Party will conclude any agreement or take any action which might in any way impair the independence or integrity of Saudi Arabia or of the Yemen.

ART. 2.　Neither Party will obtain or seek to obtain a privileged position of a political character in any territory which at present belongs to Saudi Arabia or to the Yemen or in any territory which either of those States may hereafter acquire.

ART. 3.　The two Parties recognise that, in addition to the obligations incumbent on each of them in virtue of Articles 1 and 2 hereof, it is in the common interest of both of them that no other Power should acquire or seek to acquire sovereignty or any privileged position of a political character in any territory which at present belongs to Saudi Arabia or to the Yemen or which either of those States may hereafter acquire, including any islands in the Red Sea belonging to either of those States, or in any other islands in the Red Sea to which Turkey renounced her rights by Article 16 of the Treaty of Peace signed at Lausanne on the 24th July, 1923. In particular they regard it as an essential interest of each of them that no other Power should acquire sovereignty or any privileged position on any part of the coast of the Red Sea which at present belongs to Saudi Arabia or to the Yemen or in any of the aforesaid islands.

ART. 4.　(1)　As regards those islands in the Red Sea to which Turkey renounced her rights by Article 16 of the Treaty of Peace signed at Lausanne on the 24th July, 1923, and which are not comprised in the territory of Saudi Arabia or of the Yemen, neither Party will, in or in regard to any such island:

(a)　establish its sovereignty, or

(b)　erect fortifications or defences.

(2)　It is agreed that neither Party will object to:

(a)　the presence of British officials at Kamaran for the purpose of securing the sanitary service of the pilgrimage to Mecca in accordance with the provisions of the Agreement concluded at Paris on the 19th June, 1926, between the Governments of Great Britain and Northern Ireland and of India on the one part, and the Government of the Netherlands, on the other part; it is also understood that the Italian Government may appoint an Italian Medical Officer to be stationed there on the same conditions as the Netherlands Medical Officer under the said Agreement;

(b)　the presence of Italian officials at Great Hanish, Little Hanish and Jebel Zukur for the purpose of protecting the fishermen who resort to those islands;

(c)　the presence at Abu Ail, Centre Peak and Jebel Teir of such persons as are required for the maintenance of the lights on those islands.

ART. 5.　(1)　The two Parties agree that it is in the common interest of both of them that there shall be peace between Saudi Arabia and the Yemen and within the territories of those States. But, while they will at all times exert their good offices in the cause of peace, they will not intervene in any conflict which, despite their good offices, may break out between or within those States.

(2)　The two Parties also recognise that it is in the common interest of both of them that no other Power should intervene in any such conflict.

ART. 6.　As regards the zone of Arabia lying to the east and south of the present boundaries of Saudi Arabia and of the Yemen or of any future boundaries which may be established by agreement between the Government of the United Kingdom, on the one hand, and the Governments of Saudi Arabia or of the Yemen, on the other:

(1)   The Government of the United Kingdom declare that in the territories of the Arab rulers under their protection within this zone:

(a)   no action shall be taken by the Government of the United Kingdom, which shall be such as to prejudice in any way the independence or integrity of Saudi Arabia or of the Yemen (which both Parties have undertaken to respect in Article 1 hereof), within any territory at present belonging to those States or within any additional territory which may be recognised by the Government of the United Kingdom as belonging to either of those States as a result of any agreement which may hereafter be concluded between the Government of the United Kingdom and the Government of either of them;

(b)   the Government of the United Kingdom will not undertake, or cause to be undertaken, any military preparations or works other than military preparations or works of a purely defensive character for the defence of the said territories or of the communications between different parts of the British Empire. Furthermore, the Government of the United Kingdom will not enrol the inhabitants of any of these territories, or cause them to be enrolled, in any military forces other than forces designed and suited solely for the preservation of order and for local defence;

(c)   while the Government of the United Kingdom reserve the liberty to take in these territories such steps as may be necessary for the preservation of order and the development of the country, they intend to maintain the autonomy of the Arab rulers under their protection.

(2)   The Italian Government declare that they will not seek to acquire any political influence in this zone.

ART. 7.   The Government of the United Kingdom declare that within the limits of the Aden Protectorate as defined in the Aden Protectorate Order, 1937, Italian citizens and subjects (including Italian companies) shall have liberty to come, with their ships and goods, to all places and ports and they shall have freedom of entry, travel and residence and the right to exercise there any description of business, profession, occupation or industry, so long as they satisfy and observe the conditions and regulations from time to time applicable in the Protectorate to the citizens and subjects and ships of any country not being a territory under the sovereignty, suzerainty, protection or mandate of His Majesty the King of Great Britain, Ireland and the British Dominions beyond the Seas, Emperor of India.

ART. 8.   (1)   Should either Party at any time give notice to the other that they consider that a change has taken place in the circumstances obtaining at the time of the entry into force of the present Agreement such as to necessitate a modification of the provisions of the Agreement, the two Parties will enter into negotiations with a view to the revision or amendment of any of the provisions of the Agreement.

(2)   At any time after the expiration of a period of ten years from the entry into force of this Agreement either party may notify the other of its intention to determine the Agreement. Any such notification shall take effect three months after the date on which it is made.

ANNEX 4.   DECLARATION ON PROPAGANDA

The two Governments welcome the opportunity afforded by the present occasion to place on record their agreement that any attempt by either of them to employ the methods of publicity or propaganda at its disposal in order to injure the interests of the other would be inconsistent with the good relations which it is the object of the present Agreement to establish and maintain between the two Governments and the peoples of their respective countries.

ANNEX 8.   DECLARATION ON THE SUEZ CANAL

The Government of the United Kingdom and the Italian Government hereby reaffirm their intention always to respect and abide by the provisions of the Convention signed at Constantinople on the 29th October, 1888, which guarantees at all times and for all Powers the free use of the Suez Canal.

INDEX